American Public Administration

American Public Administration

Public Service for the 21st Century

Robert A. Cropf

St. Louis University

PEARSON

Longman

New York   Boston   San Francisco
London   Toronto   Sydney   Tokyo   Singapore   Madrid
Mexico City   Munich   Paris   Cape Town   Hong Kong   Montreal

Editor-in-Chief: Eric Stano
Supplements Editor: Brian Belardi
Media Producer: Melissa Edwards
Executive Marketing Manager: Ann Stypuloski
Production Manager: Eric Jorgensen
Project Coordination, Text Design, and Electronic Page Makeup: Electronic Publishing Services Inc., NYC
Cover Design Manager: John Callahan
Cover Image: Courtesy of Veer, Inc.
Photo Researcher: Tobi Zausner
Senior Manufacturing Buyer: Roy L. Pickering, Jr.
Printer and Binder: Courier Corp.
Cover Printer: Coral Graphic Services, Inc.

For permission to use copyrighted material, grateful acknowledgment is made to the copyright holders acknowledged throughout this book, which are hereby made part of this copyright page.

Library of Congress Cataloging-in-Publication Data

Cropf, Robert A.
  American public administration: public service for the twenty-first century/Robert Cropf.
    p. cm.
  Includes bibliographical references and index.
  ISBN-13: 978-0-321-09691-3 (hardcover)
  ISBN-10: 0-321-09691-6 (hardcover)
  1. United States—Politics and government. 2. Public administration—United States. 3. Administrative agencies—United States—Management. 4. Executive departments—United States—Management.
5. Leadership—United States. I. Title.
  JK421.C76 2008
  351.73—dc22

2007025200

Please visit us at www.ablongman.com

ISBN-13: 978-0-321-09691-3
ISBN-10: 0-321-09691-6

1 2 3 4 5 6 7 8 9 10—CRW—10 09 08 07

Contents

Preface

American Public Administration: Public Service for the 21st Century

As we go forward into the twenty-first century, we face a time of both increased uncertainty and new directions in American public administration. The global war on terrorism, the information age, globalization, and the economic impacts of climate change are just a few of the forces having a significant impact on public service in the new century. As a result, it is both an exciting and a challenging time to be in the public service. In the current environment, effective public administration requires not just the traditional skills of the past, but new ones to support the roles of change catalyst, facilitator, negotiator, and community leader. Thus, an introductory textbook in public administration must not only introduce students to the concepts, theories, themes, and practices integral to understanding American public service but also must provide them with a sense of the tasks and challenges that will confront them in the public workforce today.

This book is mainly directed toward the following types of students:

- Upper-division undergraduate political science majors taking an introductory course in public administration.
- First-year students in an MPA or similar degree program taking the required introductory course in public administration.

However, other students who might find this book useful include the following:

- Graduate and undergraduate students who have never taken a public administration course before and may never take another one again (e.g., students in urban affairs, political science, criminal justice, and other programs).
- Advanced nontraditional students (adult learners) who are taking an introductory public administration course in the evening division of a community college.

The enormity of the field of public administration, encompassing as it does such diverse areas as political science, organizational theory, psychology, and economics, requires a textbook to focus on the essential topics, which means leaving aside some interesting but less important ones simply because there is not enough space. Even covering the essential aspects of the field can be an enormous undertaking. An additional challenge occurs when the students are unfamiliar with some fundamental concepts because they have not previously taken courses in American political processes and institutions, as is becoming the case as public administration and public affairs programs increasingly attract students from a wide variety of academic specializations as well as foreign countries. Thus, students may not come to the text with a general knowledge of the topic or related history.

Features of the Book

With the number of outstanding public administration textbooks currently on the market (itself a testament to the vitality of the field and the intense interest it generates), what does this one have to offer the student and instructor that the others do not? Despite the general excellence of many public administration textbooks, a number of important issues in public administration are either not being currently addressed or are being addressed inadequately. Or these topics are addressed in some books but not all of the topics are addressed in one book. To address this situation, this text includes discussion of the following:

- Public administration now occurs within a broader context. With the growth of the nonprofit sector, quasi-governmental entities, and the increasing importance of private firms in the delivery of public services, a text must now include coverage of those areas and can no longer concentrate solely on government operations. This is particularly true after September 11, 2001, and the increasing focus on terrorism and homeland security concerns. Throughout, the book uses examples from the war on terrorism and issues related to homeland security because they reflect the environment many public servants must be prepared to deal with, especially at the federal level.

- Over the past several decades, many state governments have taken the lead in areas such as welfare and healthcare. Furthermore, most public sector employees in the United States work for state or local government. In general, however, most American public administration textbooks tend to focus on the federal government and give very little attention to administration at the state and local levels. In light of this, the book devotes more attention to state and local government. One chapter addresses federalism and intergovernmental relations and their effects on public management. Throughout the book, many of the examples and illustrations are from the state and local government levels.

- Uncertain times demand exceptional leaders, and contemporary society imposes a new set of demands on public leadership. Leadership today involves as much facilitating and negotiating with community and other stakeholders as outright "leading." The public sector requires individuals who can form coalitions with private and nonprofit organizations and work with the community. Chapter 10, on leadership, discusses the characteristics of effective leadership in contemporary society. Chapter 6 on civil society and public administration links effective public management with citizen empowerment. Today's outstanding public leaders enable ordinary citizens to accomplish great things on their own with a minimum of government assistance.

- One of the most significant changes of the last two decades is the growing importance of nonprofits as the chief intermediaries between citizens and government. The growth of the nonprofit sector has been viewed by some individuals in the public sector—concerned with competition over service responsibilities and resource allocation—with a mixture of alarm and suspicion. Viewed from another perspective, however, nonprofits can have positive consequences for public organizations. This book discusses the role of nonprofits and public administration's response to the rise of nonprofits. For example, the role of nonprofit organizations in providing public services is discussed in Chapter 12, on privatization.

- Civil society has received considerable academic and media attention. Public servants can be a significant force promoting civic engagement through traditional and innovative means, including increased use of computers to broaden citizen access to information. The role of government as the major catalyst for building social and political capital and as facilitating the civil society is examined in Chapter 6. Many of the chapters include a section that focuses specifically on the link between civil society and issues raised in the chapter, as for example in Chapter 4, where a special feature examines civil society and governmental reform.

- The events of September 11, 2001, and the war on terrorism have contributed to a vigorous debate within the public administration community regarding ethics and moral decision-making. The traditional approach toward ethics is decidedly legalistic—focusing on codes and professional standards. The importance of these guidelines tend to overshadow the public servant in the role of a moral agent capable of making choices. Chapter 3 looks at internalizing ethical norms as a means of reducing the possibility of administrative evil, and the chapter stresses the need for a communitarian ethics in public service.

Further, this book is written in a style that is free of technical jargon but does not oversimplify the material for the reader. The relevance of public administration to contemporary society is underscored by frequent references to recent events and literature. Wherever possible, recent scholarship is included from the field's premier journals, such as *Public Administration Review, Administration and Society, Journal of Public Administration Research and Theory*, as well as other scholarly journals.

Important concepts appear in bold typeface and are defined in marginal notes within the chapter and in a glossary at the end of the book. Other important pedagogical features in the book are chapter introductions and chapter summaries, a list of key terms at the end of each chapter, and a list of relevant websites. Case studies and special vignettes highlight particular topics in most chapters. Tables, figures, and photographs contribute further to an understanding of the chapter topics. Charts and graphs in nearly every chapter present information in formats that are easy for readers to follow and comprehend.

This book addresses the need for a textbook that covers the traditional material in a comprehensive manner but also addresses the cutting-edge concerns of contemporary public administrators, and does so in a style that is "user friendly."

Organization of the Book

This book is organized into three major sections: (1) The political and social ecology of American public administration, (2) Organization theory and behavior, and (3) The core functions of public administration.

The first part of the book deals with the political-social ecology of American public administration and introduces the reader to the general subject of public administration. Important structural and contextual matters are discussed briefly but in-depth enough to give novices an understanding of the topics. Chapter 1 discusses the importance of studying the subject, defines public administration, and sets out the important differences between public and business administration. The chapter also deals with the power of public administration in current American society and introduces a theme returned to throughout the book: the important role public administrators can play in helping to empower ordinary citizens and strengthen civil society.

Chapter 2 develops the theme of public administration power by putting it within the context of a growing government sector and pointing out some important trends in the growth of government. The chapter also provides a brief overview of some of the major explanations for this growth and discusses the impact on civil society stemming from the growth of the administrative state. Chapter 3 considers the importance of ethics in public administration. Ethics, this chapter points out, is more than just professional codes and laws; it includes moral decision-making and ethical leadership. The question of whether these are skills that can be transmitted to public administrators is discussed in this chapter.

Chapter 4 outlines the political and governmental environment in which public administrators operate. The three branches of government are covered, as are the mechanisms that limit bureaucratic power in each branch. The chapter concludes with a section on reinventing government viewed as a point on the continuum of governmental reform. Chapter 5 examines the complex interplay of federalism, intergovernmental relations, and public administration. As state and local governments are called on to do more in the federal system, public administrators are being confronted with a complicated political environment characterized by fragmentation, decentralization of authority, and fiscal confusion. In this environment, political authority is frequently diffuse and management of programs is a difficult endeavor at best. Chapter 6 focuses on civil society and public administration. Civil society is defined and the role of interest groups examined. The chapter also addresses social capital, civic engagement, voluntary associations, the importance of civil society, and obstacles to the functioning of competent communities.

The second part of the book consists of three chapters that focus on organizational theory and behavior. Chapter 7 examines the evolution of organizational theory from the early days of classical organization theory to current postmodernism. Chapter 8 provides an overview of the dimensions of organization, including formalization, centralization, and complexity. It also focuses on the influence these organizational dimensions have on organizational power. Chapter 9 examines three significant issues that concern organizational theorists: motivation, decision-making, and organizational culture. The chapter discusses some of the most important recent theories of organizational change, including total quality management.

The third part of the book addresses some key functions of public administration. Chapter 10 deals with leadership and leadership issues in public organizations. The policy process is the focus of Chapter 11, which covers the stages of the policy process and models of policy-making. Chapter 12 discusses privatization, which is not typically thought of as a core function of public administration but is increasingly a fact of life for public administrators, regardless of the vagaries of which political party is in control. Chapter 13 describes the budgetary process and its central role within public administration. Chapter 14 deals with the important topic of human resource administration in public organizations. The evolution of public human resource systems, particularly the merit system, and key components of human resource administration are discussed. The chapter also examines labor–management relations in the public sector. Chapter 15, the final chapter, looks at managing information resources. This includes far more than management information systems as governments head more decisively in the direction of e-government and the virtual town hall.

Instructor Supplements

The publisher has prepared ancillary items that adopters of this book may find highly useful.

Instructor's Manual/Test Bank (Download only)

This resource includes chapter overviews, student learning objectives, key terms, and multiple-choice questions for each chapter of the text. Available exclusively on the Instructor's Resource Center (www.ablongman.com/IRC).

Computerized Test Bank (Download only)

This resource contains all of the test items found in the Instructor's Manual/ Test Bank. The software allows professors to edit existing questions and add their own items. Available exclusively on the Instructor's Resource Center (www. ablongman.com/IRC).

Acknowledgments

A work like this one is the result of the efforts and dedication of more than just the single author whose name is on the cover. Among the many who contributed their labor, ideas and insights special thanks must go to William "Scott" Krummenacher and Colonel George Reed whose contributions warrant their sharing author credits for chapters 10 and 11 respectively. I am grateful to Eric Stano, my editor at Pearson Longman, whose patient assistance over the years has been invaluable. My gratitude also goes to the several editorial assistants at Pearson

Longman who worked with me throughout the process, and the many colleagues who read the manuscript and offered their helpful comments and suggestions: Robert F. Abbey, Jr., *Troy University;* Shamima Ahmed, *Northern Kentucky University;* Emmanuel Amadi, *Mississippi Valley State University;* Joe Blankenau, *Wayne State College;* J. Michael Blitzer, *Catawba College;* John Bohte, *Oakland University;* Carol Sears Botsch, *University of South Carolina, Aiken;* Cynthia Bowling, *Auburn University;* Kathe Callahan, *Rutgers University;* Stephen Cupps, *Marshall University Graduate College;* Brian S. Davis, *Ohio University;* Karen Evans, *Indiana University Northwest;* Herbert Gooch, *California Lutheran University;* Thomas Greitens, *Northern Illinois University;* Jeffrey D. Greene, *University of Montana;* Barbara Headrick, *Minnesota State University–Moorhead;* Gary Johnson, *University of North Carolina–Charlotte;* Christine Ludowise, *Georgia Southern University;* Stephen Ma, *California State University–Los Angeles;* Art Morin, *Fort Hays State University;* Patrick Plumlee, *University of North Florida;* Diane-Michelle Prindeville, *New Mexico State University;* Chris Reddick, *University of Texas at San Antonio;* Lucy Rich, *University of Illinois at Urbana-Chapagne;* Pamela Rogers, *University of Wisconsin–La Crosse;* Brett Sharp, *University of Central Oklahoma;* Samuel Shelton, *Troy State University.* Lake Lloyd and her team at Electronic Publishing Services accomplished the tedious task of copyediting. Thanks must go to another large group of people, my graduate assistants who helped with the research. Finally, I owe the biggest debt of all to my family: Gail, Jeremy, and Hannah, who gently prodded me when I most needed it.

ROBERT A. CROPF

CHAPTER 1

Public Service in the Twenty-First Century

▪ SETTING THE STAGE

On September 11, 2001, two hijacked commercial jetliners slammed into the twin towers of the World Trade Center in New York City. Another one destroyed part of the Pentagon, while a fourth crashed in a Pennsylvania field after a struggle between the terrorists and some of the passengers, far away from its intended target of either the White House or the Capitol. Altogether these were the worst acts of terrorism ever committed in U.S. history. The first people arriving on the disaster scenes in New York, Virginia, and Pennsylvania were public servants—police officers, firefighters, and emergency service workers. Shortly after September 11, the following passage in a *New York Times* editorial singled out for praise the New York City firefighters who went into the collapsing towers to rescue office workers, but the same could apply equally well to the other public servants who risked their lives to come to the aid of their fellow citizens:

> Firefighters stand apart from the rest of us, simply by the fact that they are trained to run toward a blaze and not away from it. That impulse, which amounts to a special vocation, is their greatest tool in protecting their communities. On Tuesday that learned instinct drew many of them into the World Trade Center at a time when the burning fuel from two crashed jetliners was creating heat that could buckle steel. There were people in those buildings, and the firefighters went to get them.[1]

This editorial presents a positive image of public employees. Far more common, however, is the negative stereotype of the government bureaucrat found in this version of the classic "light bulb" joke:

> *Q: How many bureaucrats does it take to screw in a light bulb?*
> *A: Any number, but they always screw it up.[2]*

Other examples of this antibureaucratic bias can be found in books with titles such as *Great Government Goofs, Porkbarrel,* and the *Federal Subsidy Beast,* which tell readers what is wrong with government and government workers.[3] Talk radio personalities who regularly denounce government workers provide another example. Then there is the image of the federal official found on television and movies, which ranges from the inept and bumbling to the villainous conspirators of TV shows like *The X-Files* and *24.* The media, however, are not alone in bureaucrat bashing. Many recent politicians—including presidents

Police, firefighters and emergency medical workers, (such as those shown here) are "first responders" in a disaster such as 9/11 or Hurricane Katrina. SOURCE: Stockbyte/Getty Images

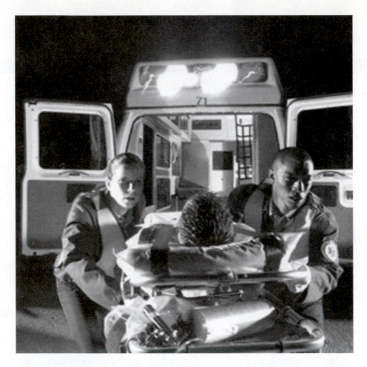

from Jimmy Carter to George W. Bush—have criticized "big government and bureaucracy." In 1992, for example, third-party candidate Ross Perot capitalized on widespread discontent with government by winning 19 percent of the votes in the presidential election, the most votes of any third-party candidate in history. In 1994, the Newt Gingrich–led Republicans recaptured the House of Representatives with a strongly antigovernment, antibureaucratic message as part of their "Contract with America." In his 1997 state of the union message, President Bill Clinton declared an end to the era of big government, shortly after he effectively put an end to the federal welfare program called Aid to Families with Dependent Children (AFDC).

These examples show how common it is for politicians to use criticism of government and bureaucrats to score points with voters to win elections. Indeed, public trust in government, as shown in Figure 1.1, has generally been low (beneath 50 percent) in the period

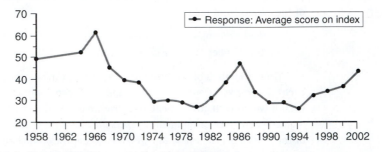

Figure 1.1   Trust in Government Index, 1958–2002

SOURCE: Adapted from the *Trust in Government Index, 1958–2000, National Election Studies.* (www.electionstudies.org)

Nonprofit organization An organization whose main purpose is to provide a service to the public, as opposed to making a profit; examples include the United Way, the Red Cross, and many hospitals and universities. See 501 (c) 3.

since the social upheaval of the 1960s. Thus, campaigning against government is generally a smart electoral strategy.

Unfortunately, it usually takes a disaster like 9/11 to make us recognize the government's vital role and the important contributions public employees make in society (for example, public trust in government enjoyed a resurgence after 9/11 as Figure 1.1 shows). Vignette 1.1 discusses the relationship between increased public support of government during a crisis. In most cases, however, as soon as the emergency conditions begin to fade, the public's support of government returns to pre-crisis levels.

Few public employees, of course, actually risk their lives when they go to work every day. However, many, if not most, probably share with the police officers, firefighters, and

VIGNETTE 1.1   Crisis and Public Attitudes Toward Government

Shortly after September 11, 2001, the *New York Times* asked several prominent scholars to discuss the event's effects on public support for the government. "Trauma and war bring out communal solidarity and remind people of why we have government," said Francis Fukuyama, a professor of international affairs at Johns Hopkins University. "But the fact that the numbers keep moving around shows that it can be quite ephemeral. Foreign policy crises and national security threats are generally times of state-building, but only if government is seen as being effective. If we screw up the military side of things and the anthrax problem, things could change a lot."

Pollsters are used to presidential approval ratings going up and down, sometimes dramatically within a short period, but trust in government has been a much less volatile index and one that social scientists consider a more useful barometer of the public's attitude toward government (see Figure 1.1). Trust in government went up during the 1991 Persian Gulf War, but by only about 7 percentage points in a *Washington Post*/ABC News poll, a fraction of the 22-point rise reported shortly after 9/11. "Part of it is rallying around the flag in a time of crisis," said Robert Putnam, a professor of political science at Harvard University who has written extensively about the decline of public trust in his book *Bowling Alone*, "but part of it reflects something deeper: the only people going up the stairs of the World Trade Center while everyone else was going down were government officials. The events made us all

realize the government does important work." He was quick to add: "This is a big jump, and if it should persist, it would change the whole political climate. But no one knows how the country would react to repeated terrorist attacks."

"All of a sudden you have Republicans sounding like liberals," said C. W. Brands, a historian at Texas A&M University and the author of *The Strange Death of American Liberalism*, which ascribed the decline of liberalism and of trust in government to the waning of the Cold War. "A crisis makes liberals out of everyone, in the sense of people seeing a positive role for government. My theory is that if this crisis persists, people will get used to the idea of looking to government to solve problems and it will spill over into other areas."

By 2003, major polls showed that public trust and confidence in governmental institutions had declined again. A *Newsweek* poll conducted in October 2003, for example, found that a majority of Americans (52 percent) trust the government to do what's right only some of the time. In September 2003, when the Gallup Poll asked citizens how much trust and confidence they have in general in men and women in political life who either hold or are running for public office, 54 percent said a fair amount and 36 percent said not very much. This figure represented a slight decline from 56 percent in the fair-amount category and a 5 percent increase in the not-very-much category from July 2000—before the events of 9/11!

emergency workers of 9/11 the belief that public service is a "special vocation." Indeed, idealism, the belief that public service is a noble profession, motivates many public employees. Thus, many people who are attracted to public service often experience a "call to duty," especially when they are young. This impulse to serve the greater good by working in government is perhaps best summed up by the stirring words from President John F. Kennedy's inaugural address: "Ask not what your country can do for you—ask what you can do for your country."

Civil society The domain of social life independent of government and private markets, consisting of voluntary and civic associations, necessary for the proper functioning of society.

Serving your country or community in the twenty-first century includes much more than working for a government agency, however. Today, public service encompasses careers in **nonprofit organizations** that also help improve society. Indeed, the idea that public service requires a broad vision that encompasses **civil society** as well as government is a central theme of this book.

CHAPTER PLAN

Although the importance of public administration should be obvious by now, in this chapter, we begin by discussing why public administration is a worthwhile subject of study. Clearly, an important step in arriving at an understanding of the subject involves definition of the term. Thus, we develop a definition of public administration drawing on the contributions of several authors in the field. The next section of the chapter explores a topic that has long occupied the attention of students of public administration: the similarities and differences between public and business administration. One major characteristic of public administration distinguishing it from business is the legitimate use of public power by the bureaucracy, which is an issue we explore next in this chapter. Finally, there is recognition on the part of many people that government cannot—indeed should not—attempt to do everything by itself. As catastrophes like Hurricane Katrina show, voluntary associations and business must share with government the responsibility for making our complex society work. Thus, in the last section, we elaborate on a theme that we will return to frequently throughout the book: the importance of civil society and the role that public administration can play in helping to strengthen the bonds between citizens and between citizens and their government.

Why Study Public Administration?

When disaster strikes, citizens depend on government to immediately restore order and provide assistance to the survivors. The harrowing scenes after Hurricane Katrina remind us of the need for government to respond quickly to alleviate human suffering and the tragic consequences of its failure to do so. In a world where natural and human-made disasters can occur at any time, U.S. citizens expect government to plan for crises (for example, the government had a plan to combat the bird flu in 2005) and believe government should be more proactive with regard to these events. In addition, we take for granted that government is there to pick up garbage, fix roads, supply clean water. and provide all of the other essential services that make modern civilization possible. From national defense to schools to healthcare, there is hardly an area of life where government does not have a vital role to play. This has led over time to an expansion in both the size and scope of government's influence.[4] The following excerpt is from a public administration textbook written forty years ago:

> The scale and importance of public administration in our society have increased sharply in recent years, and the line between public and private activities has become more tenuous. Perhaps the basic factor in this development has been the expanding role of the United States in world affairs. Not only have the Cold War and the emergence of Russia and China as strong contenders for world leadership in economic and military fields saddled our government with new responsibilities, but the balance of power within government has also shifted, with the military now enjoying unprecedented influence.[5]

Despite the passage of many years, the authors' observations, with only some slight modifications, could still accurately describe public administration's place in contemporary society. The U.S. role in world affairs is even larger now than at any other time in history as a result of the end of the Cold War and September 11. One immediate consequence of the end of the Cold War had been the declining influence of the U.S. military, which resulted in budget cutbacks throughout the 1990s. September 11 and the war on terrorism, however, have once more elevated the military and security issues to a central place in the attention of policymakers.

The central role government plays in guarding our safety is obviously an excellent reason for studying public administration. Another one is to develop a better understanding of the growing interdependence of businesses, nonprofit organizations, and government in order to become more informed citizens and better consumers of public services. Many examples abound of this interdependence among the sectors: a church group receives a large federal grant that will allow it to expand its after-school youth program; a minority construction firm receives a contract from a municipal government to build a garage; a university's medical school is granted permission from the federal government to conduct experiments on human beings, which may lead to a major scientific breakthrough; a private housing developer must comply with a municipality's building codes in order to construct affordable housing; a factory's emissions are limited by federal antipollution regulations, with local government monitoring to ensure compliance. This list could go on to cover many pages.

Nowhere is the federal government more central to the lives and activities of millions of citizens than in the national economy. At the national level, **monetary policy** and **fiscal policy** help determine the general economic conditions that affect both business and nonprofit organizations. For example, government purchases of goods and services from private and

Monetary policy The federal government's management of the economy by the manipulation of the money supply, interest rates, and credit; the Federal Reserve banking system is responsible for directing monetary policy.

Fiscal policy Using the budget (i.e., government expenditures and revenues) to manage the economy; the counterpart to monetary policy.

nonprofit organizations account for billions of dollars annually. The economic decisions and activities of these organizations help generate the revenues necessary for government to function. Furthermore, federal tax laws determine which organizations receive nonprofit status. Obtaining **501 (c) 3** status means that a nonprofit organization is exempt from paying federal income tax. On a more industry-wide level, government regulations directly affect the activities of firms, while state boards regulate entry into professions ranging from law to pharmacy. These are just a few examples that show the interdependence of government with all types of organizations.

Public service provides a wealth of challenging employment opportunities, and this provides another good reason for studying public administration. Altogether, government in the United States employs roughly 22 million people, approximately 4 million at the national level (including military personnel), and 18 million at the state and local levels, making it the single largest employer (see Table 1.1). By contrast, even the largest private firms employ only 1.5 million (see Table 1.2). Public service workers occupy a multitude of occupational and professional niches: "Bureaucrats operate bridges, investigate crimes, manage forests, program computers, arbitrate labor disputes, counsel teenagers, calculate cost-benefit ratios, operate sea-rescue cutters, run libraries, examine patent applications, inspect meat, negotiate contracts, and so on and so forth."[6]

Many, but not all, graduates of public administration programs work for government agencies. Large numbers end up working for nonprofit organizations, and increasingly, more private companies employ people trained in public administration.[7] As the scope and influence of public administration expands, a large number of talented people view it as an exciting career path. Individuals who enter a public administration program typically fall along a

501 (c) 3 The provision of the federal income tax code giving nonprofit organizations special tax-exempt status. See nonprofit organizations.

TABLE 1.1 Employment by Level of Government and Type (in thousands)

Year	Nonmilitary Federal Personnel	Uniformed Military Personnel	Total Federal Personnel	Total State and Local Personnel	All Units of Government
1962	2,515	2,840	5,354	6,459	11,903
1965	2,528	2,687	5,215	7,696	12,911
1970	2,982	3,104	6,085	9,822	15,907
1975	2,897	2,164	5,061	11,937	16,998
1980	2,876	2,090	4,965	13,375	18,340
1985	3,066	2,190	5,256	13,519	18,340
1990	3,128	2,106	5,234	15,219	20,453
1995	2,920	1,555	4,475	16,484	20,959
2000	2,708	1,384	4,092	17,793	21,885

Source: Budget of the United States 2002, http://www.whitehouse.gov/omb/budget/fy2002/hist.pdf.

TABLE 1.2 Top 10 Largest Private U.S. Employers

Company	Number of Employees
McDonald's	1.5 million
Wal-Mart	1.4 million
General Motors	362,000
United Parcel Service	359,000
Ford Motor Company	346,000
IBM	320,000
General Electric	313,000
Kroger	275,000
J.C. Penney	250,000

Source: "Ten Largest U.S. Employers' Hiring Plans for 2003," *America's Intelligence Wire,* January 23, 2003, http://galenet.galegroup.com.

continuum of administrative experience and technical skills ranging from small to vast. This book is for those individuals who desire to learn more about the possibilities and challenges of public service, whether or not they have had any previous experience in administration or background in a technical field.

For nonprofit employees and those considering nonprofit employment, the fact that public organizations and nonprofit organizations share a common purpose of serving the public is an important rationale for studying public administration. Both nonprofit and public organizations provide services free of charge to the community or on a reduced fee basis. Business's primary purpose is the pursuit of profits, which requires charging a price for the goods and services produced. While private organizations may indeed pursue other objectives besides profit-making, ultimately these tend to be less central to the firm's long-term existence; if a firm fails to be profitable in the long run, it will eventually go out of business. Moreover, public and nonprofit organizations pursue such community-oriented values as equity, representativeness, and openness. For many public and nonprofit organizations, these values are just as important as profit-making is to a private organization.

As the previous discussion shows, understanding public administration can be beneficial to people in all walks of life, not just those who wish to pursue it as a career. To help further our understanding of public administration, we need to be able to define it, a task we undertake in the section that follows.

Defining Public Administration

As a field of academic study, public administration has existed for over one hundred years. In all that time, however, defining public administration has proved to be very difficult indeed. Dwight Waldo, one of public administration's most renowned scholars, for instance, observes, "No single, agreed, and authoritative definition of Public Administration is possible."[8] Although public administration has been difficult to define, it has not been for lack of effort on the part of students and practitioners. Among the many attempts at definition, the following are broadly representative of public administration thought over the last one hundred years:

- Leonard D. White, author of the field's first textbook, writes: "Defined in broadest terms, public administration consists of all those operations having for their purpose the fulfillment or enforcement of public policy."[9]

- In their influential textbook from the 1940s, Simon, Thompson, and Smithburg observe: "By public administration is meant, in common usage, the activities of the executive branches of national, state, and local governments; independent boards and commissions set up by Congress and state legislatures; and certain other agencies of a specialized character. Specifically excluded are judicial and legislative agencies within the government and nongovernmental administration."[10]

Among more recent authors, the following represent significant attempts at defining public administration, although many more could be included.

- In David Rosenbloom's words: "Public administration is the use of managerial, political, and legal theories and processes to fulfill legislative, executive, and judicial governmental mandates for the provision of regulatory and service functions for the society as a whole or for some segments of it."[11]

- Grover Starling offers a succinct definition of public administration: "The process by which resources are marshaled and then used to cope with the problems facing a political community."[12]

- Graham and Hays provide a broader definition: "In ordinary usage, public administration is a generic expression for the entire bundle of activities that are involved in the establishment and implementation of public policies."[13]

Public policy Any decision-making done on behalf of or affecting the public, especially that which is done by government.

What, if anything, do these earlier definitions share? An important commonality is the concept that public administration and **public policy** are, in fact, interrelated. For instance, even in the relatively narrow definition by Simon, Thompson, and Smithburg, administrative agencies carry out all the activities of the executive branch of government. In other words, executive agencies implement the law, which is the embodiment of public policy. Whereas Simon, Thompson, and Smithburg restrict the term rather narrowly to the activities of the executive branch, the other authors quoted above recognize that important administrative functions are performed by the legislative and judicial branches as well. Thus, one view of public administration conceptualizes it as mainly the administrative functions and processes of the executive branch, which can be studied separately from policy-making. However, if we accept the idea that policy-making and administration are interconnected in practice, then we must broaden the definition to include the other branches of government as well, because the executive branch shares the policy-making function with the other two branches of government. Furthermore, as the scope of government continues to widen, the public sector is turning increasingly to the not-for-profit and for-profit sectors to deliver services once delivered solely by governmental entities. Therefore, any current definition of public administration must take this into account by also including nonprofits and business firms that work extensively with government.

To carry out the myriad operations and work processes of complex organizations requires skilled management and highly trained professionals. Therefore, any definition of public administration must take cognizance of its significant managerial dimension, as noted by several of the authors. Finally, all of the more recent definitions recognize the importance of the political process, political institutions, and political values to public administration. The political and policy-making aspects of public administration therefore need to be taken into account. Thus, based on the shared elements of the previous definitions, we can add our own definition to the list:

■ *Public administration consists of the managerial and political processes that occur in the executive, legislative, and judicial branches for the purposes of creating, implementing, and assessing public policy.*

Public Administration as a Field of Study

Early writers on public administration such as Woodrow Wilson and Frank Goodnow considered public administration a subdiscipline within political science.[14] It was centrally concerned with the executive branch, especially its political and administrative aspects. The exact origins of the field are in some dispute. Woodrow Wilson's seminal essay "The Study of Administration," published in 1887, is one possible origin. However, equally valid arguments can be made in favor of Goodnow's contributions in the 1890s and early 1900s, as well as Leonard D. White's first textbook in the field in 1926. What is abundantly clear, however, is that public administration has grown far beyond its initial boundaries of political science to embrace theories, concepts, and tools from all the social sciences. For example, a major subspecialization of the field is the study of individuals in organizations or groups; thus, public administration students interested in organizations must become familiar with research from areas such as sociology and psychology. Similarly, the importance of government's role in the economy requires that a student take courses in economics. As a result of these contributions from many different disciplines, some critics assert that public administration lacks the same disciplinary unity found in such fields as anthropology and geology. On the plus side, though, the public administration student obtains the benefits of a

President Woodrow
Wilson leading a
World War I
preparedness rally.
SOURCE: Library of Congress
Prints and Photographs Division

diversified education gained through the application of an interdisciplinary approach to the study of administration.

Professionalism and Public Service

Public administration's emergence as a separate discipline contributed to the creation of a profession of public administration. Furthermore, the increasing complexity of society, which started in the nineteenth century and continues unabated to the present day, has spurred the professionalization of the public sector. According to Frederick Mosher: "For better or worse—or better and worse—much of government is now in the hands of professionals (including scientists). The choice of these professionals, the determination of their skills and the content of their work are now principally determined not by the general government agencies, but by their own professional elites, professional organizations and the institutions and facilities of higher education."[15] Professional administration has important implications for many of the themes that will be discussed later in this text, particularly administrative power. For example, what is the proper role of the expert in the political process? Should laypersons be allowed to overrule a professional's decision that is based on sound scientific reasoning? These and similar questions arise as a result of the growing specialized knowledge of public administrators and their role in the policy process.

Administration versus Politics

An early, important attempt at reconciling public administration with the democratic political system came at the end of the nineteenth century. Among the first to be concerned with the question of public administration's accountability was a future U.S. president, Woodrow Wilson, whose essay "The Study of Administration" is generally recognized as the first major work of American public administration scholarship. One of Wilson's chief concerns in the essay was to establish the case for a science of administration that would assist government in achieving its policy objectives without undue interference from partisan politics. According to Wilson, "Administration lies outside the proper sphere of *politics*." In other words, administrative questions are not political questions. Although politics sets the tasks for administration, it should not be "suffered to manipulate its offices."[16] This approach came to be known as the **politics–administration dichotomy**, which served as one of the key doctrines of early public administration.

Politics–administration dichotomy The belief, popular in the early twentieth century, that government administration should be separated from politics and policy-making.

In making a clear-cut distinction between politics and administration, Wilson also sought to establish administration as a field of scientific study so that, as he put it, it would be "removed from the hurry and strife of politics." He believed that only through the application of principles, arrived at through rigorously systematic study, could government be run economically and efficiently like a business. This effort to arrive at a science of administration ultimately led to the founding of modern public administration.

While scholars continue to debate the exact influence of Wilson on his contemporaries, there is little doubt that his essay left an indelible mark on subsequent public administration thinking.[17] By the mid-twentieth century, however, it had become increasingly clear to Herbert Simon and others that the politics–administration dichotomy was not a practical theory of administration, nor was it even a very accurate description of how government actually operates.[18] However, the other major contribution of Wilson's essay—the notion that public administration can be run like business—has had a more lasting effect on administrative theory, as we discuss below.

How Is Public Administration Different from Business Administration?

During the 1990s, public administration scholars and practitioners hotly debated the merits of **government reinvention** (for more on reinventing government, see Chapter 4). The driving force behind this reform agenda was the belief that governments should take a more entrepreneurial, less bureaucratic approach to administration.[19] In 1993, President Bill Clinton ordered the federal government to adopt a new "business model," which he called the National Performance Review (NPR).[20] The NPR borrowed concepts and techniques from business administration, including "total quality management," "customer first," and "elimination and consolidation of repetitive functions." Reinvention

Government reinvention Efforts at the national and state levels to reform government during the 1980s and 1990s; proponents wanted to make government more efficient using business techniques and strategies. Also referred to as the "reinventing government" movement.

proponents believed, in the same way Wilson did, that the differences between private and public administration are relatively minor and therefore a business approach would improve the management of public organizations. However, some public management experts are unconvinced that business and public management are fundamentally alike. In fact, they are more inclined to argue, as Wallace Sayre did in 1953, that public and business management are fundamentally alike in all *unimportant* respects. In this section, we review the work of public management specialists who seek to answer the question of whether public management and private management are essentially the same.

On at least a general level, public service and private enterprise are similar: managers in both the private and public sectors are concerned with the three broad functions of management, according to Graham T. Allison.[21]

1. *Strategy*, which involves setting organizational objectives and priorities, as well as planning to achieve those objectives.

2. *Managing internal components*, which involves establishing organizational structures and procedures for coordinating actions, staffing, directing personnel and the personnel management system, as well as monitoring organizational performance.

3. *Managing external constituencies*, which involves interacting with different units and managers within the same organization, interacting with other organizations and individuals outside the same organization, and interacting with the press and the public at large.

Generally speaking, to be successful in either public or private organizations requires managerial competence in all three functions. While these functions

President Bill Clinton and Vice-president Al Gore, in front of federal regulations, at the press conference unveiling the National Performance Review, March 1993.

SOURCE: Cynthia Johnson/Time Life Pictures/Getty Images

are common across both sectors, significant differences exist between the private and public sectors in terms of the opportunities and constraints managers face in successfully performing these functions.

Another way of thinking about the differences between the public and private organizations is the approach taken by Barry N. Bozeman who examines the "publicness" of organizations along three important dimensions: *ownership*, *funding*, and *control*.[22] Government is "owned" by all the citizens in a democracy, whereas business firms are owned by entrepreneurs and shareholders.[23] In the case of public agencies, common ownership can lead to inefficiency, since citizens do not have a direct economic incentive to expend a great deal of effort monitoring agency performance.[24] By contrast, private owners have a great deal at stake in making sure that firms are run efficiently, since they benefit directly when companies increase their profits. Funding is another area where the public and private sectors differ. In order to achieve their objectives, governments are financed indirectly through taxes. However, a private firm's chief purpose is to make a profit by directly charging customers.[25] Private firms are therefore shaped by market forces, whereas public agencies are controlled by the political system rather than market system.[26] Because public agencies are controlled by political rather than economic forces, government's objectives are largely political in nature, and hence more diffuse than private firms'. Therefore, there is less clarity of purpose in the public sector.[27] Public organizations must consider other things besides the financial bottom line and to recognize that other values besides efficiency are important. For private firms, efficiency is the overriding consideration because of its significant impact on profitability. Of equal or greater importance to government, however, are values we usually associate with the political process, such as representativeness, responsiveness, fairness, consensus, compromise, and participation. These differences in purpose and objectives have a tremendous impact on how government and business perform the three common functions of management as discussed below.

Differences in Strategy and Planning

Since the entire community is affected by public policies, government—as part of its decision-making process—requires input from the diverse groups and individuals that make up the community. One public management expert refers to this as "complexity" and "permeability" in the external environment.[28] An example of this is the legal requirement that many local governments have to hold city council meetings that are open to the public. However, allowing access to the decision-making process by many different groups often serves to slow the process down. Furthermore, long-range planning becomes more cumbersome if a large number of groups become involved. Last, it is frequently the case that the groups and individuals that make up a community have conflicting views about the ultimate aims of public policy (e.g., taxpayers and service recipients, consumer groups and producer groups).[29] As a result, policies tend to be phrased in ambiguous terms in order to obtain the support of a wide range of groups.[30] This leads to a marked difference in strategic management styles between private firms and public agencies.[31] Policy ambiguity makes planning more difficult in the public sector because objectives tend to be more unclear.

Managing Internal Components

Managerial Discretion and Autonomy The political system tends to decentralize and diffuse political authority to prevent the concentration of power by a single group or institution in society. Thus, for example, neither the executive nor the legislative branch has control over the development and implementation of public policy. One scholar observes that in this system, "Power is up for grabs: it is vague, imprecise, hard to pin down, free to shift anytime and everywhere."[32] One consequence of this arrangement is that public managers serve several masters at the same time, and lines of authority are blurred on purpose.[33] In private firms, by contrast, authority is more top down and decision-making responsibility rests in large part with the chief executive officer. Allison quotes a former cabinet member, for instance, who says: "One of the first lessons I learned in moving from government to business is that in business you must be very careful when you tell someone who is working for you to do something because the probability is high that he or she will do it."[34] This means that business managers can typically respond more quickly to the opportunities and threats they face in their environment than can their public sector counterparts. In part because of the dispersal of authority, public administrators face greater constraints in budgeting, personnel decisions, and planning than business administrators do (another reason is that public sector rules and procedures are more inflexible).[35]

The Effect of Competing Values on Public Sector Performance Public administrators must attempt to strike a balance among many competing values. Because of the multiple, often conflicting goals of numerous constituents, "public agencies are pushed and pulled in many directions simultaneously. It is therefore especially important for public managers to be able to balance and reconcile conflicting objectives."[36] In private firms, however, performance is determined largely by the contribution an individual or division makes to the firm's profitability. The effect of competing values and objectives for public organizations is "policy ambiguity" and inherently unclear performance targets.[37] For example, public schools attempt to provide both equal *and* quality education for every child. However, the terms "equal" and "quality" are vague and create numerous difficulties when put into practice. What exactly does equal mean in an educational context? How do we define quality in the same context? Furthermore, there might be a fundamental tension between the goals so that fully achieving one might seriously jeopardize attaining the other. Ambiguities such as these abound in the public sector and make clear-cut performance measures difficult to design and implement. Consequently, success in achieving objectives is significantly harder to determine in the public sector than it is in business.

Differences in Personnel Systems The personnel system poses another major constraint for public administrators compared with private managers. In contrast to private firms, the public sector tightly restricts management's flexibility to make key workforce decisions. The bureaucracy imposes more formal procedures, has more inflexible rules, and is generally more risk averse as a result of the requirements of external oversight bodies and demands for accountability.[38] Furthermore, public policies designed to achieve specific social objectives, such as fairness and representativeness, can constrain hiring and other workforce decisions by managers. Many governments, for example, establish special provisions for hiring women and minorities. As important as these values are, hiring preferences limit the amount of discretion public managers can exercise in selecting employees. In addition, public employees are protected by rules that govern promotion and retention practices. Among other things, these rules establish due process procedures, which further circumscribe management's ability to direct personnel. Finally, limiting the power to promote or fire employees reduces the incentives and sanctions available to public managers to achieve organizational objectives.

Management Timeframe The time to accomplish objectives is another area where the private and public sectors diverge considerably. Public agencies are driven by the exigencies of the political cycle, which dictates that outcomes must be achieved within a relatively short period.[39] Typically, political executives strive for quick results from the bureaucracy because they seek reelection. This complicates the task of planning, which even under the best of circumstances is difficult for managers to do.[40] Public managers have a "short time-horizon imposed by the political cycle," and they often do not have the luxury to do long-term planning because they are too busy "putting out fires."[41]

Differences in Managing External Constituencies

Public administrators often operate in an open environment, one that is often described as being similar to a glass fishbowl. By contrast, business decisions, particularly routine ones, are typically made out of the public's view and beyond the average citizen's ability to influence the process.[42] In the case of the government, however, citizens and their elected representatives usually consider secrecy totally unacceptable except in matters involving national security. Since tax money is involved, citizens believe they have a right to know how "their money" is being spent. Public managers therefore must have the ability to withstand sometimes intense public scrutiny and the criticism that comes from the public and the news media. Public managers must also interact frequently with their counterparts from other levels of government, as well as representatives of interest groups, business, nonprofit organizations, and the community. This diversity of interaction is typically greater for public administrators than for private managers. As mentioned earlier, this contributes to the complexity and "open system" nature of public organizations, which imposes numerous and conflicting demands on public managers.

Bureaucratic Power and Accountability

Accountability
Responsibility to a higher authority for one's actions (e.g., workers are accountable to their supervisors for what they do on the job).

In any introductory discussion of public administration, it is necessary to address the issue of bureaucratic power and **accountability**. Government exercises considerable economic power through its consumption of a large part of society's financial and human resources for the production of public goods and services like streets and highways, police and fire protection, public health, schools, national defense, and so on. Altogether, government expenditures account for 32 percent of the gross domestic product (GDP).[43] The power of the bureaucracy, however, extends into the political sphere as well. Contrary to Wilson's famous dictum that politics and administration should be separate, in practice, administrators actually have a great deal to say regarding policy outcomes. As we shall see later, much of this policy-making influence is both inevitable and desirable. Furthermore, public agencies could not survive without this exercise of political power. Political scientist Norton E. Long noted that power is the lifeblood of administration.[44] This power rests largely on a public agency's command of three key resources: (1) expertise, (2) size and stability, and (3) administrative authority (i.e., the delegation of power).[45] In the following sections, we discuss these sources of public agency power. The power of bureaucracy to affect policy raises a very serious concern, one voiced by many, including renowned public administration scholar Frederick Mosher in the following passage:

> The accretion of specialization and of technological and social complexity seems to be an irreversible trend, one that leads to increasing dependence upon the protected, appointive public service, thrice removed from direct democracy. Herein lies the central and underlying problem . . . how can a public service so constituted be made to operate in a manner compatible with democracy? How can we be assured that a highly differentiated body of public employees will act in the interests of all the people, will be an instrument of all the people?[46]

Thus, due consideration must be given to the issue of political accountability of the bureaucracy.

Expertise

An important source of an agency's power is its control over certain kinds of specialized information that is critical to the policy-making process. The advantage of expert bureaucracies over generalist officials is made clear in the following passage:

> Nothing contributes more to bureaucratic power than the ability of career officials to mold the views of other participants in the policy process. Bureaucracies are highly organized information and advisory systems, and the data they analyze and transmit cannot help but influence the way in which elected officials perceive political issues and events.[47]

As the issues and problems confronting modern, technological society have become increasingly more complex, so too has the need for more specialized

Administrative discretion An administrator's freedom to act or decide on his or her own, which amounts to giving administrators policy-making powers.

Street-level bureaucrat Term coined by Michael Lipsky to refer to teachers, police office, welfare case workers, and any other frontline government workers with considerable administrative discretion.

and technical skills in the bureaucracy. This has led, in large part, to the increasing professionalization of the public service that we discussed earlier. During times like these, specialized information becomes a valuable—if not the most valuable—commodity in policy-making. For example, in the event of a flu pandemic, experts at the Centers for Disease Control (CDC) use their medical expertise to come up with the means to control the disease's spread and harmful effects.

The dependency of political officials on non-elected bureaucrats derives, in part, from the specialists' ability to increase their control over **administrative discretion**, which refers to the ability to choose from among alternatives in specific instances involving the implementation of policy.[48] Public service employees who exercise a great deal of administrative discretion and interact directly with citizens on a frequent basis are sometimes referred to **street-level bureaucrats** (see Vignette 1.2).[49] And, public agencies employing a sizable number of street-level bureaucrats in relation to their total workforce are called street-level bureaucracies.[50] Teachers, police officers, social service agency case workers, and workers in state motor vehicle bureaus are some examples of street-level bureaucrats.

Size and Stability

The size of the bureaucracy can be measured either in dollars (i.e., budgets) or in number of employees (see Chapter 2 for more on how government size can be measured). The federal budget accounts for $1.8 trillion in expenditures. The number of federal employees is similarly large, with roughly 2.2 million in 2005. Thus, its sheer size makes the federal bureaucracy a force to be reckoned with in American society. In addition, the bureaucracy is a bastion of stability compared to the political actors.[51] Much of this stability stems from civil service protections—more than 90 percent of the federal workforce falls under

VIGNETTE 1.2   Street-Level Bureaucratic Discretion

In delivering policy, street-level bureaucrats make decisions about people that affect their life chances. To designate or treat someone as a welfare recipient, a juvenile delinquent, or a high achiever affects the relationships of others to that person and also affects the person's self-evaluation. Thus begins (or continues) the social process that we infer accounts for so many self-fulfilling prophecies. The child judged to be a juvenile delinquent develops such a self-image and is grouped with other "delinquents," increasing the chances that

he or she will adopt the behavior thought to be incipient in the first place. Children thought by their teacher to be richly endowed in learning ability learn more than peers of equal intelligence who were not thought to be superior. Welfare recipients find or accept housing that is inferior to the housing of nonrecipients with equal disposable income.

SOURCE: Lipsky, Michael. p.13 in *Street-Level Bureaucracy: Dilemmas of the Individual in Public Services.* ©1980 Russell Sage Foundation, 112 East 64th street, New York, NY 10021. Reprinted with permission.

the merit system—which shields public employees from being fired on partisan grounds. This allows the bureaucracy to be a repository of expertise, institutional memory, and policy experience.[52] These attributes can be capitalized on by public agencies to influence policy decisions.[53]

Administrative Authority—Delegation of Power

Bureaucratic influence in policy-making is furthered by the wide latitude in power and responsibility given to public agencies by legislators. This delegation of authority by the legislature is necessary because lawmakers, practically speaking, must deal with a vast number of complex issues, which makes it virtually impossible to make direct decisions on all of them.[54] Therefore, laws include vague, sometimes ambiguous language, leaving to public agencies the task of interpretation as part of the process of implementing policies. Public agencies thus must translate the broad policy goals into specific, concrete objectives and programs. Through this process, the bureaucracy plays as central a part in policy-making as the executive, legislature, or judiciary. Dwight Waldo, one of public administration's most important scholars, has referred to this development as the administrative state.[55]

The growth of the administrative state has led to another source of bureaucratic power in the form of increased interactions between interest groups and bureaucrats. The traditional model of interest-group influence on government is known as "the iron triangle," in which agencies, interest groups, and congressional committees or subcommittees each form one side of a triangle. Each side reinforces the others as they all share a similar viewpoint on policy. We return to the idea of the iron triangle later in the book.

Another model of interest-group influence—issue networks—argues that the traditional model no longer serves as an accurate representation of interest group and agency interaction today. Instead, the contemporary policy process can be characterized as being more open as a result of interest groups having greater access than ever before.[56] The transformation from a rigid, closed process to a flexible, open one occurred largely because of the complexity of contemporary policy-making. In other words, as federal programs impact more and diverse segments of society, government relies more on external, nongovernmental entities to help deliver services.[57] We discuss both the iron triangle and issue network models in more detail in Chapter 6.

Public Administration and Accountability

As the scope of government continues to widen, the question "How do we ensure that bureaucrats remain accountable?" starts to takes on greater importance. Accountability entails responsibility for one's actions to some higher authority. In a democratic political system, public officials are ultimately accountable to the citizens. The path this accountability takes, however, is often indirect. For instance, a municipal parks department employee must answer to her supervisor, who in turn must answer to his division head, and so on up the organization's chain of command. At the very top, the parks commissioner is accountable to the mayor, who is elected by the voters. Thus, in a democracy, public administration accountability means that public officials must in the end answer to the will of the people. For elected officials, this means being held accountable for one's actions through the electoral process. Administrators, however, are appointed and not elected to their positions. How, then, can we guarantee their legitimate use of power?

Over time, a system of legal and organizational or professional constraints has evolved that serves to curtail the major abuses of administrative power. Later in the book, we examine the most important legal mechanisms that have emerged as a means to ensure administrative accountability in the political system. These legal arrangements, however, are generally considered inadequate to achieve complete accountability, so other types of constraints have developed over time. These organizational or professional constraints include greater emphasis on professional codes of conduct, standard operating procedures, organizational rules and regulations, and organizational culture. These nonstatutory constraints will also be discussed in various chapters.

Civil Society and Public Administration

Up until the last century, government in the United States had largely turned to voluntary associations and religious institutions to co-produce many public services (see Chapter 6 for more on co-production). Alexis de Tocqueville, the famous French observer of early American society and political institutions, wrote on Americans' propensity to form voluntary associations, which provided many community services in the early nineteenth century. (See Vignette 1.3.) In earlier times, families and schools were involved in educating children, neighborhoods and the police worked together to fight crime, and religious groups collaborated with government agencies to assist the poor, to a greater degree than is the case today. Recently, some scholars argue, there has been a sharp deterioration in what scholars refer to as "civil society." Civil society refers to the social institutions that bring people together on a voluntary basis due to shared concerns and values in pursuit of common objectives.[58] Political scientist Robert Putnam has extensively researched civil society in the United States and abroad. He finds that membership in voluntary associations has declined precipitously since 1965, a phenomenon for which he has coined the memorable phrase "bowling alone."[59] As a result of the erosion in civil society, societal resources for solving community problems have declined, he asserts.

It is by no means clear that there has been the decline in civil society that Putnam observes or that it is as severe as he suggests. This is a topic we discuss in detail later in the book. However, public administrators can still play a major role in strengthening the institutions of civil society, which would be a positive contribution whether or not Putnam's dismal assessment is correct.

VIGNETTE 1.3   Tocqueville on Civil Society in Nineteenth-Century America

The political associations that exist in the United States are only a single feature in the midst of the immense assemblage of associations in that country. Americans of all ages, all conditions, and all dispositions constantly form associations. They have not only commercial and manufacturing companies, in which all take part, but also associations of a thousand other kinds—religious, moral, serious, futile, extensive, or restricted, enormous, or diminutive. The Americans make associations to give entertainments, to found establishments for education, to build inns, to construct churches, to diffuse books, to send missionaries to the antipodes; and in this manner they found hospitals, prisons, and schools. If it be proposed to advance some truth, or to foster some feeling by the encouragement of a great example, they form a society. Wherever, at the head of some new undertaking, you see the government in France, or a man of rank in England, in the United States you will be sure to find an association . . . .

Thus the most democratic country on the face of the earth is that in which men have in our time carried to the highest perfection the art of pursuing in common the object of their common desires, and have applied this new science to the greatest number of purposes. Is this the result of accident? Or is there in reality any necessary connection between the principle of association and that of equality? . . . In aristocratic societies men do not need to combine in order to act, because they are strongly held together. . . . Amongst democratic nations, on the contrary, all the citizens are independent and feeble; they can do hardly anything by themselves, and none of them can oblige his fellow-men to lend him their assistance. They all, therefore, fall into a state of incapacity, if they do not learn voluntarily to help each other.

SOURCE: Alexis de Tocqueville, *Democracy in America*, Project Gutenberg EBook of *Democracy in America*, vol. 2, trans. Henry Reeve, http://www.gutenberg.org.

Helping to empower ordinary citizens can produce benefits for public administration as well as the community. Both administrators and communities profit when communities are stronger.[60]

Chapter Summary

U.S. public administration consists of the managerial and political processes that occur in the elective, legislative, and judicial branches for the purposes of creating, implementing, and assessing public policy. Public administration as a field of study dates back to the late nineteenth century and can be seen as a response to the growing need for professional administration in government at the time. Woodrow Wilson, an early theorist of public administration and the twenty-eighth president of the United States, articulated an administration—politics dichotomy in his seminal 1887 essay "The Study of Administration." The administration–politics dichotomy exerted a major influence over the discipline of public administration through the early twentieth century. Another important contribution of Wilson's article was the assertion that administration was a field of business. The notion that public administration and business administration are more similar than they are dissimilar has been challenged by contemporary public administration theorists such as Graham T. Allison. Allison and others assert that there are indeed significant differences between public and business administration. They note that the public and private sectors diverge on a number of important points, not least of which is that public organizations typically do not exist to make a profit, while a private organization must be profitable over the long run in order to stay in business.

The legitimate exercise of coercive power is another important distinction between public and private administration. "Street-level bureaucrats" wield considerable power over their fellow citizens, in large part through their exercise of administrative discretion. Furthermore, the bureaucracy as a social institution commands considerable economic and political power. However, as the scope of administrative influence has expanded, demands for accountability have likewise increased. In the United States, administrative accountability is fostered by a system of legal and organizational or professional mechanisms and arrangements. As the demands on government continue to grow, civil society's importance also increases, with government turning more and more to voluntary associations and nonprofit organizations to help "co-produce" public services. Public administration can encourage greater community organization contributions and, in so doing, strengthen its own ability to improve society's welfare and empower ordinary citizens.

■ Chapter Discussion Questions

1. What is the relevance of Wilson's essay "The Study of Administration," which was written in the late nineteenth century, to current issues in public administration?

2. Power is delegated to agencies by the legislature as a result of imprecise, general laws that require administrative interpretation. Some authors have suggested more precise legislation that carefully spells out what public agencies can and cannot do. Can you think of any advantages and disadvantages of this approach?

3. In 1993, President Bill Clinton, with a great deal of fanfare, introduced the National Performance Review. The centerpiece of the NPR was a plan for making federal agencies function more like businesses. What are the benefits to citizens of a more businesslike approach to public administration? What might be some disadvantages?

4. Government, at all levels, tries to improve the lives of ordinary citizens. Yet many Americans view government in a negative light. What can public administrators do to make Americans think more positively about government?

5. Civil society is the domain of families, religious institutions, and voluntary associations. It lies outside government. Why should government worry about the health of this sector? What can public administration contribute to civil society?

■ The Use of Brief Cases

Most chapters of this book will conclude with a brief case study based on one or more major themes from the chapter. For example, in the case for this chapter, we will focus primarily on the differences between managing in the private sector and managing in the public sector as encountered by a former CEO who was secretary of defense during one of the most turbulent eras in our national history, the 1960s. The questions at the end of each case are designed to get readers to think critically about some of the issues contained in the case. While most of the cases are based on actual events, a few are based on realistic situations rather than historical occurrences. Where a longer case from the fine Electronic Hallway Web site has been adapted for this text, the original case's author is duly noted. Chapter 7 foregoes the case study format in favor of organizational exercises, a pedagogical tool that invites readers to create their own case study.

BRIEF CASE   A BUSINESS "WHIZ KID" IN THE GOVERNMENT

Robert S. McNamara was, without doubt, one of the most talented and intellectually brilliant individuals ever to serve in the federal government. He received an MBA from Harvard in 1939 and, after working for a major accounting firm, returned to teach business there. During World War II, he was a captain in the U.S. Army Air Force (eventually attaining the rank of lieutenant colonel), in charge of conducting advanced statistical analysis to improve air force operations. His work led to increasing the efficiency and effectiveness of bomber missions.

After the war, McNamara went to work for the Ford Motor Company as one of ten "whiz kids," young former army officers who were invited to join the management team in order to help turn the company around after years of losses. He rapidly rose up the ranks, becoming president of the company in 1960, which marked the first time in its history that someone other than a Ford had headed the corporation.

When John F. Kennedy was elected president of the United States in 1960, he asked McNamara to join his cabinet. In fact, Kennedy gave him the choice of two high-profile cabinet posts: treasury or defense. McNamara, after some hesitation (he had only been president of Ford for five months), agreed to be the secretary of defense. As head of the Defense Department, he was responsible for a number of important reforms of the department and of defense policy in general.

McNamara served in the Kennedy administration and then in the Johnson administration until February 1968. His tenure coincided with one of the most tumultuous periods in U.S. history, and McNamara led the Defense Department through a series of crises, including the Bay of Pigs invasion (1961), the Cuban missile crisis (1962), and the Vietnam War (1964–1975). Throughout the period, the Cold War with the Soviet Union served as a constant backdrop for policy-making.

McNamara came to Kennedy's attention because of his success at instituting management changes at Ford. As secretary of defense, McNamara championed administrative reforms that placed a heavy emphasis on the most efficient solutions to management problems. For example, he supported innovative approaches such as systems analysis and program-planning-budgeting systems, or PPBS (discussed in Chapter 12), which increased the department's efficiency and effectiveness. In fact, one of the lessons that McNamara names in the documentary film based on his life, *Fog of War*, is "Maximize efficiency."[61]

McNamara proved to be a capable administrator, overseeing a period of unprecedented growth in defense spending as secretary. Nevertheless, by the time he left office, he had managed to alienate most of the generals and admirals with whom he worked, partly because McNamara stressed centralization in defense decision-making.[62] After all, it was this management style that helped him turn Ford around in the 1950s. McNamara also surrounded himself with policy intellectuals who were trained in state-of-the-art techniques and methods of statistical analysis. Before he made important defense decisions, he consulted with these civilian policy analysts and not the Joint Chiefs of Staff.

From the perspective of traditional business management principles, McNamara did all the right things: He instituted effective management reforms, and the Defense Department's budget grew. But on political grounds, his term in office must be viewed as a huge failure. In this there are important lessons to be learned regarding the differences between public and private administration.

Brief Case Questions

1. *Based on the brief case, in which of the three broad functions of management did McNamara encounter his greatest challenges as secretary of defense?*

2. *McNamara was responsible for some important innovations in the management of the Department of Defense. Indeed, some of the programmatic changes he helped put in place are still standard operating procedures in the department (e.g., program-planning-budgeting systems). However, the case suggests that his concern with maximizing efficiency might not have been universally shared by his colleagues and subordinates. What other values might compete with efficiency in the minds of Defense Department employees?*

3. *McNamara wanted to centralize authority in the Defense Department, similar to the successful approach he had taken at Ford. However, he met with tremendous resistance from high-level military officers. Why do you think the opposition to his management reforms was so intense?*

■ Key Terms

501 (c) 3 (page 6)
accountability (page 16)
administrative discretion (page 17)
civil society (page 4)
fiscal policy (page 5)
government reinvention (page 12)

monetary policy (page 5)
nonprofit organization (page 3)
politics–administration dichotomy (page 11)
public policy (page 8)
street-level bureaucrat (page 17)

■ On the Web

http://www.govtjob.net/
Comprehensive listing of government job opportunities.

http://www.local-government.net/
Local Government Association Web site.

http://www.statelocal.gov/
Comprehensive Web site of resources for state and local government employees.

http://www.infoctr.edu/fwl/
One-stop shopping point for federal government information on the World Wide Web.

http://www.fedworld.gov/
Fed World Government information portal; contains 30 million government Web pages.

http://www.aspanet.org/
Official Web site of the American Society for Public Administration, the professional association for public administrators.

http://www.pollingreport.com/
Comprehensive Web site containing national surveys updated on a weekly basis.

http://www.bowlingalone.com/
Official Web site for Robert Putnam's best-selling book; contains many useful links related to public administration.

http://www.naspaa.org/
National Association of Schools of Public Affairs and Administration; contains many helpful links for students.

CHAPTER 2

The Growth of Government and Administration

■ SETTING THE STAGE

Off-budget items Revenues and expenditures that are legally excluded from the federal budget; also include employees who are not officially counted as federal workers.

On-budget items Revenues and expenditures that are included in the calculations of the national deficit.

In his 1996 State of the Union address, President Bill Clinton declared that "the era of big government is over." This line won him approving applause from both the Republican and Democratic members of Congress who were in attendance. However, Clinton's optimism turned out to be premature, for just a few years into the administration of his successor, the *Wall Street Journal* noted a dramatic increase in the size of the federal government. The newspaper pointed out that from the time President George W. Bush took office in January 2001 to the time the article was published in September 2003, both the federal budget and workforce had expanded.[1]

For example, in the last year of Clinton's presidency, the "true size" of the national workforce, according to analyst Paul C. Light, was 11 million. By October 2002, the number was 12 million. This figure includes **off-budget** jobs created by contracts and grants—these jobs are outside the traditional civil service system. By contrast, the **on-budget** workforce consists of civil service employees, uniformed military personnel, and postal service employees. Altogether, off-budget jobs added another 8 million employees to the federal payroll. Light observes that "most of the 1.1 million new on- and off-budget jobs appear to reflect increased spending since the Bush administration entered office. Many of these jobs have been added at agencies involved in the war on terrorism, but many have been added at domestic agencies such as Health and Human Services."[2]

The size of government has been the focus of public attention and scholarly discussion for many years. Usually accompanying this has been concerns that the bureaucracy has gotten too bloated and government expenses too high. In this chapter, we will examine the question of the size of government and some of its implications for public administration.

■ CHAPTER PLAN

In the first chapter, we noted the important role public administration plays in the political and economic affairs of the country. In no small measure has this been due to the expansion of government at the federal, state, and local levels during the twentieth century;

25

which occurred under the aegis of both Republican and Democratic leadership. Furthermore, the growth of government has occurred despite Americans' supposed preference for smaller government as manifested in mechanisms such as tax and expenditure limitations.

The example at the start of the chapter raises several important questions regarding the size and scope of American government, such as how and why did government become so large? What role, if any, did bureaucrats play in this growth? Is increasing government size an inevitable product of modern times? What impact has this growth had on civil society? These and similar questions have occupied the attention of scholars through the years, and consequently much light has been shed on the topic. So we begin our discussion of the how's and why's of government expansion with an analysis in the first section of the major trends in public employment and expenditures since the end of World War II. The next section examines some of the major explanations that have been put forth for the growth of government. Once we have established the rationale for government intervention, we turn to an investigation of the causes for the growth of government. Part of the explanation lies with the economy. We discuss economic reasons for the growth of government in the third section. Politics provides another part of the answer. Thus, the fourth section deals with the political process as a contest between different groups in society to determine whose values become enacted as public policy. The expansion of government can be seen, therefore, as the political process responding to demands from different groups. The impact the increase in government has had on civil society is the topic we discuss in the final section.

Measuring the Size of Government

The size of government can be measured several different ways. As the chapter's introduction indicates, an often-used measure is the size of the public workforce. The chief advantage of this method is that the data are readily available and easy to understand. Government at all levels employed roughly 22 million people in 2000, as shown in Table 1.1 in Chapter 1. State and local governments employ the bulk of the public workforce, with almost 18 million employees, which is roughly 80 percent of the total. Of this figure, about half is accounted for by school districts. By contrast, the top ten largest private sector employers together employ a total of just over 5 million people.

Trends in Government Employment

The number of public employees is a simple way to gauge the size of government, but some severe limitations with this method diminish its usefulness. If we are primarily interested in the extent of government's influence over society, then using workforce size tells us only part of that story. For example, although there is currently a smaller ratio of federal workers to citizens than there was fifty years ago, the federal government spends more money than any other level of government, and its regulatory powers extend its influence well beyond workforce size.

While the amount of money that governments take in and spend continues to grow, government on-budget employment has remained fairly constant throughout the postwar era. Even including off-budget jobs, the size of the federal government was smaller in 2002 than it was at the end of the Cold War in 1990.[3] The real growth in the public workforce has occurred in the state and local government sectors since around 1950, a fact which points to another important aspect of government employment, namely that state and local governments are the most labor intensive because they provide services such as schools, police, fire fighting, streets and highways, and social services that employ millions. However, the federal government, with the exception of the armed forces and the post office, is far less involved in directly delivering services to citizens. Instead, it is more concerned with delivering checks to citizens and lower levels of government. Social Security, for example, is the single largest government program in the United States, distributing $430 billion in benefits annually. Because of Social Security and other income transfer programs, much of what the federal government does involves distributing cash, and not services, to people and organizations.

If counting employees has limitations as a true indicator of government size, what are better methods to determine size? Since control over society's economic resources is an important source of power, government expenditures serve as a more accurate indicator of government's power. Government expenditures consist of three basic types. First, governments purchase goods and services. The range of U.S. government purchases of goods and services runs the gamut from aircraft carriers to postal workers. State and local governments purchase everything from office buildings to the services of police officers. Second, governments transfer income; they take income from some people and give it to others. As noted, the federal government mainly transfers income to individuals, organizations, and other governments. State and local governments, however, also transfer income, although not nearly to the same extent as the federal government. Third, government pays the interest on the money it borrows to pay for services. The federal government's gross debt in fiscal year (FY) 2004 was $6.7 *trillion*. State and local governments also borrow, although there are more restrictions imposed on state and local government debt than on federal debt.

Trends in Government Expenditures

As shown in Table 2.1, total government spending, including the federal, state, and local governments, was $3.8 trillion in FY 2005. In contrast to government employment—where state and local governments together account for the largest share—the federal government accounts for more than two-thirds of total expenditures. The federal government, however, has not always outpaced state and local governments in spending money. Until the early 1940s, total state and local government expenditures actually surpassed federal expenditures.

Table 2.1 also shows the tremendous growth in government expenditures that occurred during the twentieth century. In FY 2005, total spending was over sixty times greater than it was in FY 1950. But this figure gives a distorted

TABLE 2.1 Summary of Government Expenditures (in billions of dollars)

| Year | Total Government | As % of GDP | Federal Government Outlays | | | | State and Local Outlays | |
			Total Outlays	On Budget	Off Budget	% of GDP	Total Outlays	% of GDP
1950	62.0	22.7	42.6	42.0	0.5	15.6	19.40	7.1
1955	97.6	24.7	68.4	64.5	4.0	17.3	29.20	7.4
1960	135.8	26.2	92.2	81.3	10.9	17.8	43.60	8.4
1965	181.9	26.5	118.2	101.7	16.5	17.2	63.70	9.3
1970	298.3	29.5	195.6	168.0	27.6	19.3	102.70	10.1
1975	499.8	32.0	332.3	270.8	61.6	21.3	167.50	10.7
1980	853.5	31.3	590.9	477.0	113.9	21.7	262.60	9.6
1985	1,347.4	32.5	946.4	769.4	176.9	22.9	401.00	9.7
1990	1,862.1	32.5	1,253.1	1,028.1	225.1	21.8	609.00	10.6
1995	2,318.3	31.6	1,515.9	1,227.2	288.7	20.7	802.50	11.0
2000	2,834.0	29.2	1,789.2	1,458.5	330.0	20.0	1,044.80	10.8
2005	3,872.4	31.6	2,472.2	2,070.0	402.2	20.3	1,400.20	11.4

Source: Total Government Expenditures 1948–2006, Historical Tables, Budget of the United States 2008, Tables 15.2 and 15.3, http://www.whitehouse.gov/omb/budget/fy2008/pdf/hist.pdf.

picture of the increase in government spending. Much of the increased spending can be attributed to increases in prices, population, and income since 1950. A more accurate description of government growth is gained by comparing government expenditures to the size of the economy, because it takes these factors into account.

Using this growth indicator, we see that government spending increased dramatically during the twentieth century, although not as dramatically as the figure mentioned earlier. By any measure, however, government just after the World War II was considerably smaller than today. Total government expenditures accounted for just over 22 percent of the **gross domestic product (GDP)** in 1950. By contrast, total government expenditures accounted for nearly 32 percent of GDP in 2005. Before World War II, state and local government spending exceeded federal spending. As a result of the war effort, however, federal spending soared during the 1940s, surpassing state and local government spending for the first time. Government spending has never returned to prewar levels, a fact which gives rise to the threshold effect theory of government growth (see the section on government growth and national defense below).[4]

Federal spending declined somewhat from wartime levels during the 1950s but rose again in the 1960s as a result of Great Society program spending and the Vietnam War. Between 1962 and 1982, federal expenditures as a percentage of GDP grew from about 18 percent to more than 23 percent. Throughout

Gross domestic product (GDP) The total value of all goods and services produced within a country during a specified period (most commonly, per year).

most of the 1980s and 1990s, however, federal spending remained relatively stable at around 22 percent of GDP. At the beginning of the twenty-first century, it went down slightly to 18 percent of GDP. Since 1972, state and local government spending has accounted for between 8 and 9 percent of GDP, or nearly half that accounted for by federal expenditures.

In addition to government expenditures as a proportion of the GDP, we can calculate real per capita spending, which is adjusted for inflation and population growth. Real per capita federal spending grew from $759 1948 to $4,300 in 2004.[5] Anyway one looks at it, government spending grew dramatically during the second half of the twentieth century. A large part of this growth can be attributed to the surge in mandatory spending occurring at the time. Mandatory spending items are ones whose annual budgets are predetermined by program enrollment and benefit formulas rather than the annual appropriation process. Examples of mandatory programs include Social Security, Medicaid, and most social welfare programs. Policymakers can alter mandatory spending totals only by changing the law governing how many people can receive benefits or modifying the benefit formula. Without significant changes to current benefits levels, total mandatory spending, according to the Congressional Budget Office, will almost double as a percent of the GDP by 2040, going from 5.4 percent to 15.6 percent.[6]

Trends in Government Regulation

One conclusion we can draw from Table 2.1 is that government spends a significant proportion of society's resources, and the level has remained fairly constant over the last thirty years. Government expenditures, however, tell only one part of the story regarding size of government. In addition to direct spending, regulations constitute a group of government activities that impose a cost on society far in excess of the expenditures government makes on those activities. The costs of issuing and enforcing regulations are exceeded by the costs to industry and individuals of complying with those regulations. Environmental laws that restrict automobile emissions, for example, raise the price of the vehicles the automobile companies make, although the trade-off for society is cleaner air. At the local level, zoning ordinances increase housing costs or the costs of doing business in a jurisdiction. Here the trade-off is more community control over land use decisions. Regulation is costly, but we must take into account its benefits in order to have a fair overall picture.

There are no accurate methods to calculate the exact costs of regulation, although according to a 1998 Office of Management and Budget (OMB) report, the total direct cost of regulation is in the range of $200 billion to $300 billion annually.[7] Table 2.2 lists major government regulatory programs whose elimination could result in a cost savings to society according to one economic study. Another OMB study, however, points out that the benefits of regulation slightly exceed the costs.[8]

TABLE 2.2 Regulations and Programs That Could Be Targeted for Elimination

Regulation/Act	Description	Welfare Loss
International Trade Restrictions	Various tariffs and quotas constrain international trade.	$3.5 billion annual welfare loss
Jones Act	Ships traveling between U.S. ports must be built in U.S. shipyards, owned by U.S. citizens, and operated by an American crew	$2.8 billion annual welfare loss
Milk Marketing Order	USDA price discrimination scheme raises the price of fluid milk and drives down the price of manufactured milk products.	$343–$608 million annual welfare loss
Davis-Bacon Act	Federally funded construction projects are required to pay laborers "prevailing wages."	$200 million, annual welfare loss
Corporate Average Fuel Economy Standards	Each auto manufacturer must meet federal average fuel economy standards.	$4 billion welfare loss from 1978 to 1989
Land Disposal Regulation	1995 rule prohibits the disposal of various untreated hazardous wastes.	$143 million annual expected cost. Benefits are not monetized
Off-Label Drug Use	Manufacturers cannot legally advertise a pharmaceutical product for any use that the FDA has not specifically approved.	Not available
Glass-Steagal Act	1933 act prohibits commercial banks from underwriting corporate securities.	Not available

Source: Robert Hahn, *Policy Watch: Government Analysis of the Benefits and Costs of Regulation,* (Journal of Economic Perspectives, Volume 12, Number 4, Fall 1998)

Explaining the Growth of Government

There is no lack of explanations for what has caused the growth of government over the last century. To simplify things, however, we discuss three of the major reasons for this growth (see Figure 2.1). The first reason asserts that the increasing size and influence of government is due in no small part to the transition from a simpler to a more complex economy. As economic conditions change, they produce social effects that require some form of government action. But what remains unclear is the type of government intervention to be employed or how much of it is needed.

The second reason attributes the increase in government to political factors. The political process allows interest groups to mobilize and exert pressure on legislators for benefits, which in turn leads to the creation of new programs and agencies. The rise of regulatory agencies to meet the needs of an increasingly complex and diverse society can be placed in this category. Changes and growth in population, the challenge of new technologies, and social upheavals have contributed to spur greater regulation of the sources of social problems. The third reason asserts that wars and national defense provide a major

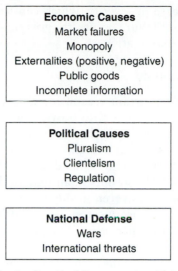

Figure 2.1   Major Reasons for the Growth of Government and Administration

impetus to government's increase. Modern conflicts require the mobilization of the entire economy, which only large government can achieve. Furthermore, since World War II, international tensions have ensured that considerable amounts are spent to maintain the United States' ability to defend itself against enemies.

The Mixed Economy and the Growth of Government

Mixed economy An economy in which the public sector plays a significant role and consumes a considerable proportion of the gross domestic product.

Previously, we have used the terms "private sector" and "public sector" to describe for-profit organizations and government respectively. Together they comprise what is called a **mixed economy**. In a modern economy, the government and the private sector form a partnership to assure the continued prosperity and well-being of the whole society. Each partner has its unique role to play. Nonetheless, it would be inaccurate to infer that there is a hard and fast line separating the public and private sectors. Increasingly, private companies depend on government contracts in fields such as housing, construction, aeronautics, civil engineering, healthcare, and computer technology just to name a few.[9] The free market is the best economic arrangement ever devised for the production and distribution of goods and services. When the free market is working well, consumers purchase all the products they want (at the price they want to pay) and producers sell all they can (at the prices that will make them a profit). Society's resources are efficiently used.

Market failure A class of economic occurrences (e.g., monopoly, externalities, etc.) in which private markets fail to perform efficiently; entails social costs that can be corrected through collective action, usually by the government.

Nonetheless, there are many times when markets fail to behave efficiently. **Market failure** can take several forms: (1) monopoly, (2) externalities, (3) public goods, and (4) incomplete information. Each one is discussed briefly below. As economies become more complex, market failures can increase in severity, which can lead to great social harm. Therefore, when market failure occurs, the government often intervenes in the economy to correct the situation.

Monopoly

One important reason for corrective action by government is a situation where only one firm provides a good or service, which allows it to charge a high price due to the lack of competition. The firm receives a windfall profit as a result, but overall, social well-being declines. The high price discourages consumers, who demand less of the product and therefore less of it is produced. This results in an underutilization of resources and lowering of total income. However, in the case of a *natural monopoly*, it is more efficient to have one producer serve an entire market. Natural monopolies occur in industries such as utilities (e.g., gas, electricity, water, and sewers), where it is less expensive to have one company provide the service, since it has already installed the lines and hook-ups, than to allow a competing company to install additional lines. Typically, government regulates natural monopolies, establishing the price they can charge for their services so that consumers do not pay monopolistic prices.

Externalities

Externalities represent another important type of market failure. These are economic activities that impose costs on third parties. For example, when a factory pollutes a river, a town downstream experiences the harmful effects. The owners of the factory do not take into account this social cost when they are pricing their product; instead, the people downstream end up bearing part of the costs. Government's role is to bring the production of the good more in line with its total social costs. In the case of pollution and other negative externalities, this means a reduction in production.

Not all externalities, however, are bad. Some externalities confer benefits on third parties, such as a scientific product that improves public health (e.g., a flu vaccine). But the firm making the discovery does not take into account total social benefits (i.e., everyone else who does not get sick) when it produces the good. Again, government's role is to bring the production of the good more in line with total social benefits. In this case, government wants to increase production of the good with positive externalities.

Public Goods

Left to its own device, a free market does not supply enough public goods to meet society's demands. Public goods are "shared" goods in the sense that one person's consumption of the good does not prevent others from consuming it at the same time. This is true regardless of who pays for the good. Examples include national defense, clean air, and clean water. There is no incentive for the market to provide these goods, because a private firm cannot make a

Free-rider problem A situation arising in the case of public goods in which a citizen receives benefits without paying for them.

profit. Who would willingly pay for something if they knew they would receive its benefits regardless? This gives rise to the **free-rider problem**, which requires the power of government to resolve. Governments can force people to pay taxes in order to provide for public goods such as education, public safety, highways, and so on, because otherwise citizens will try to enjoy the benefits without paying for them.

Incomplete Information

Another reason for government intervention is that the market, when left alone, will supply too little information about certain goods and services. The market, for instance, tends to undersupply information about the safety of certain products or the risks associated with certain occupations. In addition, certain types of information can be thought of as public goods, because adding one more consumer does not diminish the quantity or quality of the information.[10] Perhaps the best-known examples of this type of information are the weather reports provided by the U.S. Weather Bureau. In the case of incomplete information, government either provides the missing information itself or requires the private sector to provide this information for consumers.

A lighthouse is a classic example of a pure public good.
SOURCE: Craig Tuttle/CORBIS

The Need for Government Action

As the economy becomes more complex, the need for government action also increases. Our evolution from a largely agricultural to a postindustrial economy has provided a major impetus for the expansion of government. For example, industrialization led to an increase in pollution, which prompted demands for more environmental regulations. As we describe below, the growth of business monopolies in the late nineteenth century gave rise to legislation designed to curb monopolistic excesses. New technologies create social and environmental problems where none existed previously, such as the need to clean up toxic waste sites or to regulate Internet pornography. Examples of economic changes spurring government intervention could easily fill the rest of this book. While economic changes may give rise to the *need* for government intervention, whether it becomes translated into actual government programs depends on the political process and how it deals with citizen demands. That is the topic we turn to in the following section.

Political Reasons for the Growth of Government

As we noted in Chapter 1, government possesses a virtual monopoly on the legitimate use of power and force in society. This power, however, is not necessarily neutral in its effects. For instance, the decision to build a dam may entail forcing some people to sell their property to the government. While an entire community may enjoy the benefits of the dam, some property owners may suffer from the loss of their property, despite receiving compensation from government. Recognition of the effects of government's power to confer benefits and impose costs has led to a political arrangement called **pluralism**, in which individuals mobilize into groups—such as farm organizations, trade associations, and labor unions—for the purpose of influencing government and the public. As the example of the dam shows, there are winners and losers in even the most basic government decision. In a pluralist society, groups compete in the political process in order to maximize gains and minimize losses from government actions.

Pluralism A political arrangement in which different sectors of society organize into groups in order to exert political influence.

In contrast to other societies throughout history, the political struggle in the United States is usually peaceful—the ballot box typically takes precedence over bullets (the Civil War is the lone exception to this). The creation of new government programs, or the expansion of existing ones, can thus be explained in part as a natural outcome of the democratic process and pluralism. Counteracting to some extent the tendency of the political process to lead to big government is the U.S. Constitution's inherent bias in favor of limited government. We must briefly examine this before we discuss the political reason for the growth of government.

The Constitutional Legacy

The ambivalence of the American political system toward strong government is embedded in our political institutions as expressed in our core political document, the U.S. Constitution. The chief impulse driving the founders in

Separation of powers The constitutional doctrine that power should be diffused throughout the government, keeping the executive, legislative, and judicial branches distinct so that power is not centralized in one branch.

Checks and balances The constitutional doctrine that each branch of government should act as a control on the power and ambition of the other branches.

Federalism A system of government in which the national and subnational governments share power. To be contrasted with unitary systems (all political power is concentrated at the center) and confederations (political power is completely decentralized, with the subnational governments holding the upper hand).

drafting the Constitution was their distrust of centralized government—an artifact of their struggle against the British monarch. Moreover, they feared tyranny of the majority as much as they feared tyranny by one ruler. Their fear of big government found initial expression in the Articles of Confederation, which provided the first framework for American government but were scrapped in favor of the Constitution in 1789.

The Constitution corrected the Articles' most glaring defects with respect to national government. The founders' distrust of centralized power continued to exert a strong influence over the new system, however. They created a government that sought to prevent the excessive concentration of power by fragmenting and dispersing it. Their fear of centralization gave rise to several of the most important ideas in the Constitution. The **separation of powers** provides for the diffusion of authority among the executive, legislative, and judicial branches. By dividing governmental power three ways, the framers sought to avoid placing too much power in any one branch of government. **Checks and balances** refers to the ability of each branch to limit the power of the others. In effect, this means, that no one branch can dominate all the others. The Constitution also establishes a power-sharing arrangement among the national and state governments known as **federalism**, which is further discussed in Chapter 5.

The founders believed that political mechanisms would be the primary means to resolve social conflicts in the new United States. Thus, there is no mention of administration anywhere in the Constitution, although certain parts of the Constitution do anticipate the creation of government agencies. For example, Article 1, section 8, discusses the establishment of post offices and Article 2, section 2, states that the president "may require the opinion, in writing, of the principal officer in each of the Executive departments . . . "

The only founder who took an interest in administration was Alexander Hamilton, who supported a strong national government, largely to promote business interests.[11] Hamilton was the first to articulate a position whose influence continues to the present.[12] He believed a vigorous, effective national government requires a strong chief executive and capable administration. It is fair to say, however, that Hamilton's was the minority view. More influential, by far, were the views of Thomas Jefferson and James Madison, who argued that strong and dynamic government invites tyranny of the type the United States had gained freedom from. Their ideal of government, therefore, is generally hostile to large, professional administration.[13]

Thus, from the outset, there were considerable institutional and philosophical barriers to expansive government and strong administration. However, social and economic conditions soon gave rise to political demands that led to the expansion in the size and scope of administration.

Functional Departments and Client Agencies

From the beginning of the republic until the Civil War, the federal government was small and, with the exception of the Post Office, did not provide services directly to the citizens. This began to change as new departments were added

Clientelism The creation of departments and programs in order to serve the needs of specific interest groups or segments of society.

in the latter half of the nineteenth century, a development that signaled a major shift in the scope and activities of government. This growth of government occurred as the result of the increasing representation of interest groups in Washington, a phenomenon that political scientist James Q. Wilson refers to as **clientelism**. This is the process of creating departments and programs in order to serve the needs of specific groups, for example, farmers, tradesmen, and workers. The federal government was not alone in doing this; Wilson says that clientelism also flourished in state governments during the late nineteenth century.[14] Interest groups continue to shape administration, and in the process have received their share of criticism.

Initially, however, a small administration was all that was needed to conduct the national government's activities. In 1789, the year the Constitution was ratified, the core functions of the new American republic were performed by just five departments. The State Department managed the United States' foreign relations; the War Department (later the Department of Defense) protected the country from its external enemies; the Attorney General (who later became the head of the Department of Justice) provided legal counsel to the government; the Treasury Department managed the country's fiscal affairs; the Postal Services Department maintained the national mail system. Except for the Postal Department, the heads of four of these original departments still comprise the "inner cabinet," which is generally recognized as the president's closest advisers; the heads of the departments formed after 1789 are sometimes referred to as the "outer cabinet." For the most part, this was essentially the governmental structure that guided the United States through the first one hundred years of its existence.

In keeping with the Jeffersonian ideal of small and nonprofessional government, the early federal departments were a far cry from today's large, professional bureaucracies. These early executive departments were tiny in comparison to their current counterparts. For instance, the first State Department consisted of only eight clerks, twenty-five agents, and a single messenger in addition to Secretary of State Thomas Jefferson. The current State Department, in contrast, employs more than 25,000 employees.[15] In addition, early administrators were highly unrepresentative of American society. The elites' fear of the masses led them to restrict government employment to the top tier of society. (We discuss the development of the federal workforce in considerable detail in Chapter 14.)

The Impact of National Expansion on Administration

Spoils system The type of government personnel system introduced by President Andrew Jackson in which elected officials reward supporters by appointing them to public offices and positions.

The nation's westward expansion, which began with Lewis and Clark's 1804 expedition, contributed to shaping the federal administration, as did the later efforts to curtail the influence of social elites by President Andrew Jackson (1829–1837). Jackson's role in democratizing the national workforce and creating the **spoils system** is elaborated on in Chapter 14. Jackson's administration is also important because he pushed for an expansion of executive power as the expression of the will of the people.

President Andrew
Jackson as an evil
puppet-master
pulling the strings
of political office-
seekers.
SOURCE: The Granger
Collection

The push westward and the need for coherent national economic development policies led to the creation of the Department of the Interior in 1849. As the economy became more complex and industrial after the calamitous Civil War (1861–1865), the national government responded by creating new agencies and expanding its regulatory activity. The Civil War destroyed the economic system of the South, which was based on slavery, and unleashed the full industrial potential of the North. The rise of the North's industrial base brought with it the growth of cities, which in turn gave rise to new social problems (e.g., public health, safety, and sanitation) that could only be remedied through government action.

Growth in the Industrial Era

Client agencies The agencies that exist principally to serve the needs of certain interest groups ("clients").

The social conditions of late nineteenth-century America gave rise to powerful, specialized economic interests in the form of trade associations and labor unions. These interest groups provided the impetus for the development of a new type of bureaucratic organization—**client agencies**.[16] In contrast to the earlier federal departments that were specialized according to functional area—for example, military affairs, foreign relations, and so on—clientele departments were established in order to respond to the needs of specific groups of people with a common set of economic concerns.[17] The first group to be sufficiently well organized and powerful enough to push for its own department was the farmers. The Department of Agriculture (DoA) was created in 1862, when most Americans still made their living off the land. The DoA, however, did not attain full cabinet status until 1889. From the beginning, it provided direct services to citizens—a major hallmark of client agencies. Other examples of client agencies established during this time include the Department of Commerce and Labor (1903) and the Department of Labor, which split off from Commerce in 1913.

James Q. Wilson claims that clientelism reached its high-water mark during the administration of Franklin D. Roosevelt (1932–1945). Roosevelt's New Deal oversaw the heavy subsidization of different sectors of society and "the continued growth of specialized promotional agencies." The rise of client government is significant because, according to Wilson, it "makes it relatively easy for the delegation of public power to private groups to go unchallenged." Further, he asserts, the agencies and programs become self-perpetuating, "because a single interest group to which the program matters greatly is highly motivated and well-situated to ward off the criticisms of other groups that have a broad but weak interest in the policy."[18] We elaborate further on the influence of interest groups on administration in Chapter 6.

Regulation and the Growth of Administration

The second noteworthy development in the expansion of governmental authority also occurred as a result of the political response to the tremendous economic and social changes occurring in American society in the late nineteenth and twentieth centuries.[19] These led to successive waves of regulatory reform that gave enhanced power to administrative agencies. The first reform wave occurred between 1887 and 1890, during the era of the "trusts," when greedy businesspeople used monopolistic practices to drive out competitors and gain control of markets. Trust activity in oil, steel, railroads, and other important segments of the U.S. economy directly affected the livelihoods of many Americans. This unchecked economic power spurred the birth of **populism**, a grassroots political movement that appealed largely to farmers, small business owners, and other groups who felt at the mercy of the monopolies. Populist-inspired legislation made a permanent impact on the U.S. bureaucracy with the creation of the Interstate Commerce Commission (ICC) in 1887 and the Sherman Act (1890), which gave the Justice Department new enforcement powers to break up monopolies.

The second wave of regulatory reform, between 1906 and 1915, marked a continuance of the earlier efforts to rein in corporate power.[20] Congress passed laws regulating food and drugs and protecting American consumers from unsafe and impure products. It also passed legislation to regulate banking activities and created the Federal Trade Commission (FTC) as an independent regulatory body enforcing consumer protection and antitrust laws.

The economic devastation wrought by the Great Depression led to the next wave of regulatory reform, during the 1930s. Cosmetics, utilities, securities, and airlines all came under federal oversight during this period. The social upheaval of the 1960s and 1970s spurred the next wave of reform, which brought the environment, workplace safety, and civil rights under federal

Populism A grassroots political movement during the late nineteenth and early twentieth centuries supporting the rights and power of the people in the struggle against the social and economic elite.

A group of artists working for the federal government during the Great Depression.

SOURCE: New York Times Co./ Getty Images

protection. Since then, with some notable exceptions including people with disabilities and healthcare, the congressional mood has been generally antiregulation. This has led to successful attempts to lessen the regulatory burden on business and other social entities.

Each of the above periods of reform, according to James Q. Wilson, was characterized by forceful, progressive political leadership that overcame the normal institutional obstacles to successfully enact far-reaching regulatory legislation. The upshot of these developments was to increase administrative power in size and scope.

National Defense and the Growth of Administration

Threshold effect The theory that certain national disturbances (e.g., wars) cause a permanent jump in government expenditures.

Government spending literally explodes as a result of war and wartime activities. Since World War II, even during peacetime, the demands of maintaining an international military force to defend against external enemies has required ever greater spending on the part of the U.S. government. Although government activities grew in the late nineteenth and early twentieth centuries, this growth is dwarfed by the immensity of the U.S. response to global conflicts. Between 1920 and 1945, total federal expenditures increased more than tenfold, and much of this was the result of military spending for World War II (1940–1945). Although spending declined shortly after the war, it still exceeded prewar levels, a phenomenon referred to as the **threshold effect**. Economists theorize that the war effort caused taxpayers to drop their usual reluctance to higher levels of taxes and spending. After the need for war financing had passed, public tolerance of these high levels continued: "since the aftermath of war is typically accompanied by social upheaval and change, the revenue windfall coincides with a change in preferences and political powers which raise the effectively desired level" of public spending.[21]

Unlike previous postwar periods, the United States could not reduce spending on defense-related agencies and programs after World War II because of the Cold War (1945–1989). Thus, military spending has become a key component of the national economy, providing jobs for millions of Americans and a measure of prosperity for hundreds of communities. The collapse of the Soviet Union led some to believe that military spending could be decreased, but September 11, 2001, and the war on terrorism quickly put an end to the possibility.

Public Choice Theory

Public choice theory The theory that bureaucrats, voters, and politicians are concerned primarily with advancing their own economic self-interests through the administrative and political processes.

A critical view of the growth of administration comes from **public choice theory**.[22] Public choice theorists place a large part of the blame for big government on the voters themselves. Voters tend to underestimate the costs of government programs and to favor smaller government and cutting spending, except when it comes to their own favorite programs. Senior citizens, for example, support increasing Social Security benefits; families with children in public schools support additional educational funding; farmers want more agricultural subsidies, and so on. Citizens fail to recognize, however, that expenditures on these programs impose costs on the rest of society, or they think that someone else will pay the costs for them—for example, the government—while failing to recognize that we *are* the government.[23]

Legislators, meanwhile, encourage these delusions by using less visible taxes or nontax revenues to finance more and more government spending. Increasing a highly visible tax like the income tax will usually provoke outrage in taxpayers, so legislators prefer using less visible taxes—for example, selective sales taxes like the tobacco or gasoline taxes—or borrowing money to pay for popular programs. These are means of increasing revenues that tend to be less obvious and painful to the average taxpayer. In this way, legislators attempt to maintain the illusion that government benefits and services are "costless."

There is another side to the revenues debate, however. Voters may likewise underestimate the benefits they receive from government expenditures.[24] Whereas the benefits of private purchases are readily apparent to citizens, the benefits of government expenditures are less obvious. Individuals easily recognize the value of private goods, such as automobiles and television sets, because they have to pay for their consumption. They do not have to pay each time they use a public good such as driving on a highway, receiving police or fire assistance, or hiking in a state park. Thus citizens take for granted many of the services government provides because they do not have to pay for them directly.

Civil Society and the Growth of Government

The growth of government has had major consequences for civil society. This should not be surprising, given the close interdependence between government and civil society.[25] Regarding the effect of the increasing size and scope of government on civil society, there are two conflicting views: (1) as the scope of government activities increases, civil society also grows in strength, and (2) as the scope of government increases, civil society experiences a decline. Political scientist Theda Skocpol, a proponent of the view that civil society is aided by the growth of government, asserts "the enduring importance of the U.S. federal government in promoting a vibrant civil society."[26] Skocpol draws on recent historical evidence to advance the notion that big government fosters civil society. She notes that the U.S. postal system created a network of communication that spurred the growth of voluntary associations in the nineteenth century. She then traces the growth of government from the Civil War era through the twentieth century and argues that "the voluntary associations did not wither away. On the contrary, many established ones added new local and state units, recruited more individual members, and branched into new activities."[27] Skocpol thus believes that civil society has developed a mutually beneficial relationship with big government.

The view that civil society and big government exist in a kind of symbiotic relationship is disputed, however, by others who assert that as government grows, it weakens civil society. The position that civil society is harmed by big, national government is articulated by William B. Schambra, who contends that national community, while a laudable ideal, has shown itself to be a failure in actual political practice. Thus, the Great Society programs' "vast, impersonal institutions" could not provide the community and self-governance essential for human happiness. Instead, he believes, participatory democracy as it has always been practiced in the U.S., that is, "through dutiful citizenship within traditional local institutions like the church, neighborhood, and voluntary association," is still the preferred route to community revitalization. Furthermore, he writes scornfully of major national nonprofits like the PTA and the Red Cross because they are quick to take "orders" from their Washington headquarters and gladly accept federal money. The answer, he contends, is a return to "faith-based, grass-roots organizations," which he says are "civil society's trauma specialists—the true experts on civic renewal."[28]

Who is right on the question of whether big government helps or hinders civil society? Suffice it to say that the cause-and-effect relationship between government and civil society is still not completely known, and it is therefore worth further study by future researchers.

Chapter Summary

The last century witnessed the dramatic growth of American government and administration. The major reasons for this growth are the nation's economic and political concerns, including national defense. Economic factors that contribute to the expansion of government stem from market failures, which take four forms: (1) monopoly, (2) externalities, (3) public goods, and (4) incomplete information. Political reasons for bigger government include the democratic process, pluralism, the development of client agencies, national expansion, increased regulatory activity, and the impact of war and defense needs.

The growth of government and administration has been counteracted somewhat by the underlying framework of the U.S. political system. The Constitution provides the basic structures and the legal basis for the institutional constraints that arose in response to the growth of administrative power. Although there is no mention of administration anywhere in the Constitution, the founders' concern with the centralization of power led to the constitutional provisions limiting power and diffusing authority throughout the entire political system.

In the United States' first one hundred years, the national administration remained small and the scope of its activities limited. In the nineteenth century, national expansion, industrialization, and urbanization, however, helped to spur the growth of governmental activities and administration. This gave rise to the theory of clientelism. Client agencies were formed to promote the material welfare of interest groups such as farmers, tradespeople, and laborers. This same period also saw the rise of regulatory activity by government. The scope of regulation grew tremendously over the twentieth century and now includes the environment, communications, energy policy, civil rights, and many other sectors of the economy and society.

The last century also witnessed the birth of total war, which requires the fusion of the private economy with government power to wage. The entirety of society's resources must be brought to bear against an enemy, a task that only a strong, centralized government can carry out. The execution of such an effort requires administration that reaches into every sector of the community.

The growth of government has also had significant effects on civil society. Some scholars assert that the increasing scope of government has helped civil society, but others argue that increased government leads to a decline of civil society.

■ Chapter Discussion Questions

1. What do the trends examined at the start of the chapter suggest about the future size of government in the United States?

2. Explain how the founders' fears of too much centralized power affect our views of public administration today.

3. One reason for the growth in regulations is the public's mistaken perception that they are relatively "costless." Who actually pays the costs of regulations? Identify certain types of regulation (for example, environmental protection, food safety) and be specific as to who bears the financial burden of these regulations.

4. A number of authors have noted a connection between democratic politics and pressures for larger government. Can an argument be made that the reverse might also be true—that it is just as likely that politics can lead to smaller government? How?

5. What are some problems with trying to measure the "true" size of government?

BRIEF CASE   LIBRARIANS VERSUS THE USA PATRIOT ACT

After the terrorist attacks on September 11, 2001, Congress quickly passed the USA Patriot Act (i.e., the Uniting and Strengthening America by Providing Appropriate Tools Required to Obstruct Terrorism Act of 2001). It did not take long, though, for some civil liberties activists and others to object to certain provisions of the law. In addition to the expected indignation of civil libertarians, the act met with hostility from a surprising source: librarians. Many librarians objected to two parts of the law in particular, sections 215 and 216, which expand federal authority to obtain quick access to an individual's private information, including business, medical, education, and library records. The law requires that libraries hand over to FBI agents any circulation records, Internet usage logs, and registration information that they keep. This information can be gathered for citizens and noncitizens alike, and the FBI does not need probable cause, that is, a valid warrant, to obtain this information; the agency need only show some connection between the patron and an ongoing terrorism inquiry.

Libraries across the country reacted with alarm to this provision of the law. In Pennsylvania, for example, librarians were encouraged to "throw away, purge or shred unnecessary records every day" in order to protect their patrons' privacy. An American Library Association official said, "If a record doesn't exist, it can't be found."[29] As of July 2003, three states and 133 localities have passed ordinances instructing public libraries not to comply with the federal government. The governments adopting such measures include liberal ones such as Cambridge, Massachusetts, and Berkeley, California, and moderate to conservative governments in Reading, Pennsylvania, and the state of Alaska. In Montana, a state that typically casts its votes for conservative Republicans, the state's library association adopted a resolution condemning sections 215 and 216 as "a present danger to the constitutional rights and privacy rights to library users."[30]

The Justice Department, however, contends that the law permits the FBI to invade the rights of private citizens. "We're not after the average American, we're just going after the bad guy," asserted a Department of Justice spokesperson.[31] Moreover, the attorney general countered that the librarians' reaction was exaggerated. At a press conference in August 2003, Attorney General John Ashcroft said that warrants authorizing searches of an individual's records were subject to more scrutiny by judges than those of regular criminal investigations. In addition, Ashcroft pointed out that the law requires the FBI to prepare a report for Congress twice a year detailing the use of its powers.[32] Nevertheless, the president of the American Library Association, Carla Hayden, observed: "Librarians can't be quiet about this issue because it's so fundamental to what we do. As librarians we are in a position of trust. People know they can come to us and ask for information, and we won't judge them."[33]

Brief Case Questions

1. *This case study deals with an issue that we will take up again in Chapter 3, namely the ethical obligation of administrators to execute laws they oppose. In this case, the librarians, while*

generally careful to avoid doing anything illegal, focused on activities that they thought would best protect their patrons' privacy. What are some other issues raised by this case?

2. *As the scope of government grows to counter threats and exploit opportunities in the twenty-first century, administrators will encounter more situations in which there will be trade-offs between the rights of citizens and the good of society. What should administrators' responsibilities be to their clients? To society?*

3. *What do you think the response of traditional public administration would be to the librarians' opposition to the USA Patriot Act?*

■ Key Terms

checks and balances (page 35)
client agencies (page 37)
clientelism (page 36)
federalism (page 35)
free-rider problem (page 33)
gross domestic product (GDP) (page 28)
mixed economy (page 31)
market failure (page 31)

off-budget items (page 25)
on-budget items (page 25)
pluralism (page 34)
populism (page 38)
public choice theory (page 40)
separation of powers (page 35)
spoils system (page 36)
threshold effect (page 39)

■ On the Web

http://www.house.gov/Constitution.html
Full text of the U.S. Constitution.

http://www.whitehouse.gov/
Official Website of the White House.

http://www.nyu.edu/wagner/news/truesize.pdf
This website contains a summary of Paul C. Light's work on the true size of government.

http://www.ala.org/ala/washoff/WOissues/civilliberties/
The civil liberties webpages of the American Library Association; contains a discussion of the ALA's position on the USA Patriot Act.

http://www.epic.org/privacy/terrorism/hr3162.html
The full text of the USA Patriot Act.

http://www.govexec.com/
Government's business news daily and the premier website for federal managers and executives; frequently examines issues relating to size and scope of government.

http://www.brillig.com/debt_clock/
The National Debt Clock keeps daily count of the size of the national debt; contains useful links to other sites with information on government spending.

http://www.census.gov/statab/www/
The Statistical Abstract of the United States, published by the Census Bureau; contains a historical statistics section.

CHAPTER 3

Ethics and Public Administration

We will never bring disgrace on this our City by an act of dishonesty or cowardice.
We will fight for the ideals and Sacred Things of the City both alone and with many.
We will revere and obey the City's laws, and will do our best to incite a like reverence and
respect in those above us who are prone to annul them or set them at naught.
We will strive increasingly to quicken the public's sense of civic duty.
Thus in all these ways we will transmit this City, not only not less, but greater and more
beautiful than it was transmitted to us.

All free males of Athens, once they reached the age of nineteen, took the above oath, which admitted them to citizenship in the city.[1] The Athenian Oath exemplifies the timeless ethical and civic ideals of ancient Greek society. Today, many public servants in America, including members of the military, take an oath to uphold the nation's laws and the Constitution; betraying the oath is considered an act of treason. For most public administrators, however, it is far more common to subscribe to a code of ethics, which for most professions and organizations establishes ethical standards and behavioral expectations for members.

Despite codes of ethics and oaths of office, wrongdoing still occurs among public officials. Moreover, as we have seen in recent years, ethics scandals involving a small number of politicians or administrators can tarnish the image of the entire public service, regardless of the vast majority of public officials' dedication and commitment to live up to the highest ethical ideals. Unfortunately, when members of government become caught up in scandals, the result is usually a highly public spectacle, which often engenders cynicism among the public. If there is a good side to these events, however, it is that they spur efforts at reform and provide valuable lessons to students of public administration ethics.

The example of Oliver North offers one such lesson in the eternal conflict between public ethics and private ethics, and the sometimes ambiguous nature of right and wrong in the shadowy world of national security. North, a Marine Corps lieutenant colonel, was convicted in federal court for lying to Congress and two other felony charges; the charges were later dropped because of technicalities. North was a National Security Agency aide who, at the request of CIA Director William Casey, created a clandestine operation in 1985 to channel military aid to the Contra rebels of Nicaragua, even though Congress had prohibited such activities. At the time, the U.S.-backed Contras were trying to overthrow the Sandinista government in Nicaragua. In order to help support the

Contras, the U.S. government was secretly selling arms to Iran, which was then at war with Iraq. North was ordered to testify before Congress in July 1987 regarding these illegal activities. During the nationally televised hearings, North deliberately lied to Congress and falsified the chronology of events in the Iran-Contra affair.

North's purposeful lying to Congress was a violation of every known ethical code as well as a violation of the oath of office he swore upon receiving his commission in the U.S. Marine Corps. North's chief defense was that he was only following the orders of his superiors, including President Ronald Reagan.[2] Furthermore, North never considered telling Congress the truth, according to comments he later made to a judge.[3] North believed that telling the truth about Iran-Contra was not in the best interest of national security. Then and now, many people consider his actions justified in the name of national security. They argue that affairs of national security should be kept out of the public limelight. Who and what are we to believe in this case? Was Oliver North the patriot he claims to be? Or, by attempting to deceive Congress, did he violate the public trust and in the process damage the very national interest he swore to uphold? This chapter will provide a context for understanding the role and importance of ethics in public administration so that students can appreciate dilemmas like the one above.

■ CHAPTER PLAN

The chapter begins by examining why ethics are important for public administration. This is followed by a definition of ethics and a brief discussion of several different philosophical approaches to the subject. The chapter next examines the role codes of ethics have in setting high standards for public servants, and the utility of laws that impose constraints on administrators' behavior. We then briefly discuss several important issues in administrative ethics: the difference between responsibility and accountability; external versus internal controls; ethical obligations of administrators; ethical decision-making; leadership and ethics; and values in decision-making. We also look at some recent developments in administrative ethics, and we examine whistle blowing and the moral responsibility of administrators to report administrative wrongdoing. Finally, we examine the theory of administrative evil, or the concept that modern organizations provide an environment in which immoral or unethical actions can sometimes take root and implicate ordinary employees in wrongdoing.

The Importance of Ethics

Ethics A system or theory of moral values.

This is the first question we must ask ourselves: why should administrators attach any importance to the study of **ethics**? To some, the subject seems indirectly related to the very concrete, practical concerns of public administration. After all, what can the study of moral values contribute to effective and efficient public management? Many public administrators, however, would strongly disagree with the viewpoint that ethics do not matter. Values, they assert, "inhabit every corner of government," and not only principles in the sense of political beliefs or policy preferences, but moral beliefs as well.[4]

Indeed, some might argue that ethics is central to democracy and public administration, and that it directly affects the everyday activities of public servants and the operations of public agencies.[5] Moreover, without careful attention to ethical matters, administrators would quickly lose the confidence of the citizens they serve. For this reason, we argue that accountability and ethical behavior comprise the core of the role of public administrator.[6]

Another rationale for the importance of ethics stems from public administration's status as a profession. An important element of professions, one which sets them apart from other occupations, is their codification of ethical standards.[7] Indeed, to be a professional, "the distinguishing characteristic or edge is not merely the possession of expertise, but also dedication to ethical practice."[8] Thus, membership in a professional community requires not merely technical competence but also a commitment to the highest ethical ideals. In the case of public administrators, this entails dedication to the public interest and to what John Rohr calls **regime values**, the core values of a people, which for Americans include personal liberty, property, and political equality.[9] These are the values embodied in the U.S. Constitution, which every public administrator is morally bound to uphold.

Regime values The core values of a people; for the American people, these include personal liberty, property, and political equality and are derived from the Constitution.

Defining Ethics

Ethics has been defined in many different ways, but each definition shares certain elements. For instance, all of the definitions imply that ethics is morality in action.[10] In addition, ethics involves "making systematic, reasoned judgments about right and wrong and, equally important, taking responsibility for them."[11] Ethics is a set of values that guide behavior.[12] Ethics constitutes a branch of philosophy that is concerned with right and wrong behavior and involves the search for moral standards using reason.[13] While many more definitions could be included, the ones mentioned above are generally representative of different scholars' views on administrative ethics.

Based on the common threads we identify above, we can derive our own working definition of ethics:

- *Ethics is the process of using reason, guided by moral standards or personal values, to make decisions regarding right- and wrong-doing in one's professional and personal life, and taking responsibility for those decisions.*

Philosophical Approaches to Ethics

In Western cultures, serious study of ethics dates back to the ancient Greek philosophers, particularly Plato (427–347 BCE) and Aristotle (384–322 BCE). In Eastern cultures, ethical behavior was a central concern in the thought of Confucius, who lived in China from 551 to 479 BCE. In this section, we will be chiefly concerned with two approaches to ethics that have had a profound and lasting impact on public administration: deontology and utilitarianism.

Deontology is the earliest of the philosophical approaches to ethics that we examine here. In Western society, the classic example of deontological thought can be found in Judeo-Christian moral teaching. However, this approach is not restricted to any one set of religious beliefs. Indeed, deontologists can be either theistic (believers in a deity) or atheistic (nonbelievers). Proponents of deontology, whether religious or nonreligious, believe that "objective, ultimate or absolute standards or criteria for assessing the morality (rightness or wrongness) of human actions" can be arrived at by reason.[14] A deontologist believes that the existence of absolute moral ideals means that an action is right or wrong independently of its practical results. Thus, public administrators who take a deontological position would oppose any action that violates their moral code, even though the action might produce a positive outcome or be required by law. These administrators believe that one should perform one's duties or fulfill one's moral obligations regardless of the practical consequences.

Rawlsianism, which is based on the work of the American philosopher John Rawls (1921–2002), is a modern example of the deontological approach. In *A Theory of Justice* (1971) and other influential works, Rawls wrote that social equity or social justice should be the overriding concern of all public policy. In Rawls's view, society's overall welfare depends entirely on how it treats its least well-off persons. Therefore, the welfare of society, taken as a whole, is enhanced if the poorest individual is materially improved, even if this reduces everyone else's well-being.

By contrast, **utilitarianism** holds that the results of one's actions are more important than one's intentions. According to the English philosopher Jeremy Bentham (1748–1832), "Ethics [is] directing men's actions to the greatest production of the greatest possible quantity of happiness on the part of those whose interest is in view," namely those of the whole of society.[15] Thus, actions that produce the greatest good for the greatest number of people comprise what utilitarians view as ethical behavior. According to utilitarianism, there are no absolute moral standards to guide administrators' actions; instead, each decision must be made strictly on a cost-benefit basis to determine the likely outcomes. The ones with the most positive results for the most people should be chosen over all others.

How might each of the above ethical approaches be applied in an administrative setting? A utilitarian administrator would regard clearing out and developing an inner-city neighborhood as morally justifiable, even though it would require uprooting families and businesses that have been there for generations. The utilitarian administrator would argue that the old slum would be replaced by new businesses and better housing for the remaining residents. A deontologist might oppose the decision to raze the neighborhood on the grounds that it is always wrong to displace families and businesses. Although the outcome might be better for the rest of the community, the ends do not justify the means. A Rawlsian would strongly object to the decision, since the low-income residents in the community would be made worse off by the action.

Deontology An approach to ethics which asserts that there is an absolute or ultimate standard for morals that can be arrived at through reason.

Rawlsianism An approach to ethics named for the philosopher John Rawls; the theory that the welfare of society is enhanced if the poorest individual is materially improved even if this reduces the well-being of everyone else.

Utilitarianism The philosophy which holds that the results of one's actions are more important than one's intentions.

Codes of Ethics and Ethics Laws

The importance of administrative ethics is also revealed by the numerous attempts to develop codes of ethics by professional groups and the passage of ethics laws at all levels of government. Professional communities establish codes of ethics to promote ethical conduct and ethical standards among members of the profession. Moreover, serving as a still greater constraint on administrators' behavior are the numerous laws addressing ethics currently on the books in the states and the federal government. These laws, designed to prevent wrongdoing on the part of public officials, require strict compliance, which is often not the case with professional codes of ethics. As one public manager said, "You are expected to obey the law, you are told what the law means, and if you do not follow the law you are performing an illegal act. Whether or not it is an ethical act is another question."[16]

Codes of Ethics

Professionals in business and government consider codes of ethics to be an important means to promote ethics in the workplace.[17] In 1924, the International City Managers Association adopted the first code of ethics designed specifically for public sector professionals. the professional organization of public administrators, the American Society for Public Administration (ASPA), adopted a formal code of ethics in 1984 and significantly revised it a decade later. The ASPA Code of Ethics is grounded in serving the public in five core areas: (1) public interest, (2) legal interest, (3) personal interest, (4) organizational interest, and (5) professional interest (see Vignette 3.1). Each interest area represents a fundamental value or set of values that should be recognized in administrative decision-making. ASPA's ethics code acknowledges that moral choices for public administrators often involve reconciling competing sets of values, such as accountability and efficiency, political responsiveness and professional responsibility. In addition, rather than merely being a list of "do nots," the code conveys a "far richer sense of ethical behavior as both avoiding wrongdoing and pursuing rightdoing."[18]

Research indicates that the ASPA code has had a positive impact overall on officials' behavior. Fully 90 percent of administrators who responded to a survey said the code "provides an appropriate set of standards."[19] The same study found that public managers either "often" or "occasionally" use the code in their ethical decision-making at work. Based on these findings, one can say that the ASPA code has been somewhat successful in helping to shape the ethical attitudes of public servants.

Successful codes of ethics, other research indicates, share three characteristics: (1) They provide guidelines for, at minimum, a modest level of ethical behavior; (2) they cover a wide range of different occupations within the same profession; and (3) they have provisions for effective compliance. While the ASPA code has the first two attributes, it lacks an enforcement mechanism; thus, for all practical purposes, it remains largely "a statement of ethical

VIGNETTE 3.1   ASPA Code of Ethics

The following is the Code of Ethics of the American Society for Public Administration (ASPA), the professional society serving public administrators.

I. Serve the Public Interest

Serve the public, beyond serving oneself. ASPA members are committed to:

1. Exercise discretionary authority to promote the public interest.
2. Oppose all forms of discrimination and harassment, and promote affirmative action.
3. Recognize and support the public's right to know the public's business.
4. Involve citizens in policy decision-making.
5. Exercise compassion, benevolence, fairness, and optimism.
6. Respond to the public in ways that are complete, clear, and easy to understand.
7. Assist citizens in their dealings with government.
8. Be prepared to make decisions that may not be popular.

II. Respect the Constitution and the Law

Respect, support, and study government constitutions and laws that define responsibilities of public agencies, employees, and all citizens. ASPA members are committed to:

1. Understand and apply legislation and regulations relevant to their professional role.
2. Work to improve and change laws and policies that are counterproductive or obsolete.
3. Eliminate unlawful discrimination.
4. Prevent all forms of mismanagement of public funds by establishing and maintaining strong fiscal and management controls, and by supporting audits and investigative activities.
5. Respect and protect privileged information.
6. Encourage and facilitate legitimate dissent activities in government and protect the whistle-blowing rights of public employees.

7. Promote constitutional principles of equality, fairness, representativeness, responsiveness, and due process in protecting citizens' rights.

III. Demonstrate Personal Integrity

Demonstrate the highest standards in all activities to inspire public confidence and trust in public service. ASPA members are committed to:

1. Maintain truthfulness and honesty and to not compromise them for advancement, honor, or personal gain.
2. Ensure that others receive credit for their work and contributions.
3. Zealously guard against conflict of interest or its appearance: e.g., nepotism, improper outside employment, misuse of public resources, or the acceptance of gifts.
4. Respect superiors, subordinates, colleagues, and the public.
5. Take responsibility for their own errors.
6. Conduct official acts without partisanship.

IV. Promote Ethical Organizations

Strengthen organizational capabilities to apply ethics, efficiency, and effectiveness in serving the public. ASPA members are committed to:

1. Enhance organizational capacity for open communication, creativity, and dedication.
2. Subordinate institutional loyalties to the public good.
3. Establish procedures that promote ethical behavior and hold individuals and organizations accountable for their conduct.
4. Provide organization members with an administrative means for dissent, assurance of due process, and safeguards against reprisal.
5. Promote merit principles that protect against arbitrary and capricious actions.
6. Promote organizational accountability through appropriate controls and procedures.

(continued on next page)

VIGNETTE 3.1   **ASPA Code of Ethics** *(continued)*

7. Encourage organizations to adopt, distribute, and periodically review a code of ethics as a living document.

V. Strive for Professional Excellence

Strengthen individual capabilities and encourage the professional development of others. ASPA members are committed to:

1. Provide support and encouragement to upgrade competence.

2. Accept as a personal duty the responsibility to keep up to date on emerging issues and potential problems.

3. Encourage others, throughout their careers, to participate in professional activities and associations.

4. Allocate time to meet with students and provide a bridge between classroom studies and the realities of public service.

---

behavior."[20] The ASPA code is helpful for establishing a standard for behavior, but it cannot make these guidelines compulsory.

Ethics Laws

While ethics codes serve an important purpose for professional organizations, governments have often found them to be of limited usefulness for ensuring the good behavior of their employees. There are several reasons for this.[21] One is the wide diversity of occupations and professions found in the public service. Another is the vague and general nature of the codes themselves. Professional codes of ethics also have a tendency to focus on preventing bad behavior rather than on promoting good behavior. Finally, ethics codes are unable to provide guidance in specific situations. As a result of these limitations, governments have often turned to enacting legislation as a means to promulgate ethical behavior on the part of both elected and non-elected public officials. Since the Watergate scandal of the early 1970s, a number of significant federal ethics laws have been passed, as shown in Table 3.1. We discuss these briefly below.

There is considerable evidence that "the media and public opinion" are chiefly responsible for putting ethics on the politicians' agenda and that "ethics policy is being developed in a reactive mode driven by legislative scandals."[22] Moreover, once the scandals fade from the headlines, public demands for ethics reform also tend to disappear. At the federal level, ethics legislation emerged from the period of heightened public attention surrounding the Watergate scandal and President Nixon's subsequent resignation. In response to these events, Congress passed the Ethics in Government Act of 1978, which created the Office of Government Ethics (OGE) within the Office of Personnel Management. In 1989, Congress reorganized the OGE as a separate agency within the executive branch. The OGE is responsible for setting ethics policy

TABLE 3.1 Major Post-Watergate Federal Government Ethics Initiatives

Ethics in Government Act (1978) established the Office of Government Ethics responsible for administering the executive branch's ethics program. The act provides for comprehensive public financial disclosure in all three branches of the federal government. It established an independent office of special prosecutor charged with investigating and prosecuting federal officials. In addition, the act imposed stronger restrictions on federal officials' post-government employment.

Inspector General Act (1978) established Offices of Inspector General throughout the executive branch and charged them with the detection and prevention of fraud, waste, and mismanagement in government programs.

Civil Service Reform Act (1978) established the Merit Systems Protection Board, an independent agency charged with monitoring executive-branch personnel practices and protecting the merit system's integrity. The act strengthened whistle blowers' rights and prohibited various improper personnel practices. It also increased and strengthened the Office of Special Counsel.

Federal Managers' Financial Integrity Act (1982) required agencies to establish stringent and effective internal auditing systems in order to reduce waste of federal government resources.

Office of Government Ethics Reauthorization Act (1988) removed the OGE from the Office of Personnel Management and established it as an independent executive-branch agency in order to ensure its independence and effectiveness in fulfilling its role.

Whistleblower Protection Act (1989) strengthened federal whistle-blower protection by establishing the Office of Special Counsel, an independent agency empowered to litigate before the Merit Systems Protection Board.

Ethics Reform Act (1989) significantly strengthened and extended the existing federal ethics infrastructure. It extended coverage of post-employment restrictions to include members of Congress and their staff. It prohibited the solicitation and acceptance of gifts by federal officials and employees from certain sources. It imposed restrictions on earned income and employment outside the federal government by senior officials. It also prohibited members of Congress and any federal employee from receiving honoraria, defined as a payment of money or anything of value for an appearance, speech, or article. The Supreme Court ruled this provision unconstitutional in 1995.

Executive Order 12674 (1989) established the "Principles of Ethical Conduct for Government Officers and Employees," which sets forth fourteen principles of ethical conduct for executive-branch employees, and directed the OGE to promulgate standards for ethical conduct. These rules of conduct for executive-branch employees became effective on February 3, 1993. They set forth specific guidelines in areas including gifts, personal finances, impartiality, employment seeking, abuse of position, and outside activities.

Executive Order 12834 (1993) signed by President Bill Clinton on his first day in office, required noncareer senior appointees to sign a pledge limiting their lobbying activities for five years after termination of federal government employment.

Hatch Act Reform Amendments (1993) resulted in the easing of some restrictions on federal civilian employees' political activities stemming from the original 1939 Hatch Act. These changes allowed federal employees greater participation in the political process, while at the same time it maintained their protection from political solicitations.

Whistleblower Protection Act Amendments (1994) strengthened the 1989 act's scope and protections by closing several loopholes created by the federal courts and administrative agencies that limited employee protections.

Office of Government Ethics Authorization Act (1996) Amended the Ethics in Government Act of 1978 to authorize the OGE director to accept gifts for OGE use, and it extended the authorization of appropriations for the OGE.

Notification and Federal Employee Anti-Discrimination and Retaliation Act (2002) requires agencies to pay retaliation and discrimination judgments in whistle-blower decisions out of their own funds. This creates a financial incentive to follow the law.

for the executive branch only; its reach does not extend to the judiciary or to Congress. The president appoints the head of the OGE, subject to the Senate's approval.

With the OGE, Congress designed a system that is decentralized: The head of each agency is largely responsible for implementing ethics policy in the agency. Each agency chief appoints a "designated agency ethics official" to manage the agency's compliance with federal ethics laws and to conduct regular ethics training within the agency. The OGE, however, does not enforce the laws and refers all possible legal violations to the Department of Justice for enforcement.

The scope of the OGE's activities is actually much narrower than the name suggests. The federal ethics agency primarily focuses on possible conflicts of financial interest in the executive branch. It relies heavily on the tracking and reporting of employees' personal financial information.[23] Some observers have pointed out that while personal finances are indeed important, other aspects of employee behavior deserve the same attention but are currently overlooked by the law. Thus, the OGE's preoccupation with financial matters runs the risk of creating minimal standards, which, some argue, results in employees' thinking that behaving ethically simply means avoiding illegal activities with respect to finances. This is known as the **low road approach** to public ethics, which we will elaborate on later in the chapter.

Low road approach A minimalist approach to ethics which holds that adherence to the law is sufficient for ethical behavior.

At the state government level, there is a great deal of diversity where governmental ethics legislation is concerned. The first wave of state government ethics reforms occurred during the 1970s, mostly as a reaction to Watergate, just as at the national level. Many states merely copied federal government legislation, emulating the language and principles of the Ethics in Government Act of 1978. Some states, however, passed even stronger laws than the federal government's and established ethics agencies with greater authority than their federal counterpart. Consequently, there is a great deal of variation in state statutes. Some are quite strict, while others are looser and have many loopholes. For example, every state has a governmental entity that oversees official ethics in the state. But these offices vary considerably in their authority and the scope of activities that they oversee. Some state ethics agencies are very weak, while others have been assigned adequate authority and personnel, as well as a large enough budget to perform their responsibilities effectively. Weak or strong, however, most state ethics agencies and laws follow the federal government's heavy focus on personal probity in financial matters to the near exclusion of everything else.[24]

Ethics in Public Organizations

As we point out throughout this book, public service is different from private employment. Do the differences between the public and private sectors also affect ethical behavior? One answer hinges on whether you believe absolute moral standards exist (see the discussion on deontology earlier). If you do, then standards of ethical behavior would apply everywhere, regardless of the type of organization you work for. However, as we discussed previously, there is currently no universally agreed-upon approach to ethics. Therefore, it is still relevant to ask: does a public sector ethics exist distinct from a private sector ethics? On a related note, Thompson argues that personal or private ethics is different from government or political ethics. He contends, "Private virtue is not necessarily public virtue."[25] Public ethics arises from the need to establish impersonal standards with the aim of making government officials more accountable to the citizens. This approach is a reflection of the unique and important role that public administrators play in American society.

Public servants face greater ethical demands because of their unique responsibilities, which include: (1) legal and moral obligations to the poor and dependent populations, (2) regulatory and policing powers, (3) the provision of basic services, and (4) the stewardship of national resources. In order to effectively discharge these functions, public administrators must wield considerable political and economic power. As a result, their ethical obligations are "different and higher" than their private sector counterparts.[26]

Responsibility and Accountability

Administrative accountability The assignment of organizational responsibility in a hierarchical or legal manner, which is objective in quality.

The nature of public service gives rise to a heightened emphasis on accountability and responsibility. The two concepts are often used interchangeably, but they are different enough conceptually to warrant a clear-cut distinction in this discussion. **Administrative accountability** assigns organizational responsibility in a hierarchical or legal manner and is objective in quality. **Responsibility**, by contrast, is more subjective in nature and is unrelated to an individual's formal role, status, or power within an organization. In a democracy, elected officials, who are answerable to the voters, hold public administrators legally accountable for their actions, and this accountability becomes greater as one goes up a public organization's chain of command. Administrators, however, may be held morally responsible for their personal actions, without regard to their place on the organization chart. Furthermore, responsibility for collective decisions must be shared (that is, "it percolates down throughout the entire administrative apparatus"), whereas, accountability can never be shared, because it involves the formal relationships between and within the branches of government.[27] Indeed, the bureaucracy as a whole is accountable to the elected representatives of the people and to the courts.

Responsibility Moral obligations that are unrelated to an individual's formal role, status, or power within an organization.

External versus Internal Controls

Since the 1940s, there has been a lively debate in public administration over whether organizational accountability was enough to ensure administrative compliance with ethical standards. The initial debate took place between two well-known scholars of government, Herman Finer and Carl Friedrich, and concerned whether internal or external controls were more effective in guaranteeing full democratic accountability of administrators. Finer took the position that effective accountability could only be achieved through strong external mechanisms, such as legislative oversight and judicial review, established by political officials.[28]

Friedrich took the opposite position, arguing that the detailed legislation necessary to produce this level of administrative responsibility would prove too burdensome for both administrator and legislator alike.[29] He contended instead that the administrator's own sense of morality and responsibility were better safeguards of administrative probity than reliance on external controls. Thus, he believed that internal controls assured full accountability.

Related to the debate over external versus internal controls is one over the relationship of bureaucratic values to regime, or democratic, values. Two broad sets of administrative values have historically dominated discussions of public administration ethics: bureaucratic ethos and democratic ethos. Each one exists in a state of constant tension with the other, and sometimes they are in direct conflict with each other.[30] **Bureaucratic ethos** is associated with five core concepts: (1) efficiency, (2) efficacy, (3) expertise, (4) loyalty, and (5) accountability. This set of values stems from public and business administration. Ethics, suggests the latter ethos, consists mainly of making administrators subordinate to and accountable to elected officials.

Technical rationality is the driving force behind the bureaucratic ethos, and utilitarianism provides the philosophical foundation for its core values.[31] While emphasizing economic and rational values has advantages, particularly organizationally, this belief system contributes to what Menzel refers to as the "morally mute manager," or public administrators who do not voice or act on their moral values in the workplace. Bureaucratic organizational culture's chief values are technical competence, practicability, objectivity, and impersonality. Not included, however, are morals, which are "deep seated values that guide right and wrong behavior and ways of life."[32] We will return to this question later in this chapter when we examine the theory of administrative evil.

Democratic ethos, by contrast, consists of political, rather than management, principles. These include the values we typically associate with democratic governance, including citizenship, public interest, participation, and social equity. Another way of thinking about this ethos is that it provides a moral foundation for public administrators. According to Bowman, another cornerstone of administrative ethics consists of three main values: honor, benevolence, and justice. Each one warrants brief mention here. Honor represents "the highest standards of responsibility, integrity, and principle." Benevolence instills in the administrator the desire to always seek the common good and to "promote the welfare of others." Justice refers to a sense of fairness and respect for the rights of others, especially with regard to each person's inherent worth and dignity.[33] Strict adherence to these three values on the part of public administrators would go a long way to curb wrongdoing and to promote ethical behavior.

The Ethical Obligations of Administrators

Of the many lasting contributions Dwight Waldo has made to the field of public administration, certainly one of the most valuable is his map of the ethical

---

Bureaucratic ethos The principle of making administrators subordinate to and accountable to elected officials; also consists of management values such as a belief in efficiency, hierarchy, etc.

Democratic ethos Consists of political and regime values; serves as the moral foundation of public ethics.

obligations of public administrators. According to Waldo, administrators have a special duty to live up to twelve ethical obligations, which includes obligation to the Constitution, to law, to country, to democracy, to organizational norms, to profession, to family and friends, to self, to middle-range collectivities (e.g., race, class, church), to the public interest, to humanity or the world, and finally, to religion or God.[34]

Obviously, this is a tall order for any man or woman to fill. Above all else, the point of Waldo's list is to make us aware of the complexities involved with acting ethically as a public servant. Moreover, he says his list is not intended to be in any order, as it is a reflection of the "untidiness of the ethical universe."[35] An awareness of this moral complexity can lead to paralysis unless we know how to proceed. This is where the importance of ethical decision-making comes in.

Ethical Decision-Making

A key element of sorting through the ethical dilemmas of administration is instruction in the processes of moral reasoning and ethical decision-making. This type of training is designed to address the critical issue of analyzing a professional or organizational situation from an ethical perspective as well as from a purely managerial viewpoint. Ethical or moral reasoning skills can be developed with the proper training. However, it requires an understanding of the manner in which people develop as ethical beings.

No theorist has made a larger contribution to the study of moral development than the psychologist Lawrence Kohlberg (1927–1987). **Kohlberg's model of moral development** is based on cognitive reasoning and consists of six stages. As shown in Figure 3.1, these stages are grouped into three levels (preconventional, conventional, and post-conventional) through which individuals must progress in sequence to develop as moral persons. Kohlberg thought, however, that most people do not evolve all the way to the final two stages.

In Stages 1 and 2, the preconventional level, people are self-centered and primarily concerned with avoiding punishment and receiving rewards. In Stages 3 and 4, the conventional level, people make ethical choices based on social norms, rules, and laws—in other words, by the conventions of the society they live in. In Stages 5 and 6, the post-conventional level, people make ethical choices based on abstract universal principles, which take precedence over the moral conventions of their particular societies.[36]

Kohlberg's model has been used in an organizational setting by researchers attempting to determine the level of moral development of administrators. Stewart and Sprinthall found that public administrators tend to be Stage 4 moral thinkers, which is the stage that emphasizes law and duty in making decisions. These authors observed: "Our respondents are taking John Rohr's low road versus the high road approach to public ethics. This means addressing ethical issues exclusively in terms of adherence to agency rules." Both workplace culture and public administration graduate education tend to reinforce this careful, rule-based approach to ethical behavior, according to the authors.

Kohlberg's model of moral development A six-stage theory of an individual's growth as a moral person; developed by the psychologist Lawrence Kohlberg.

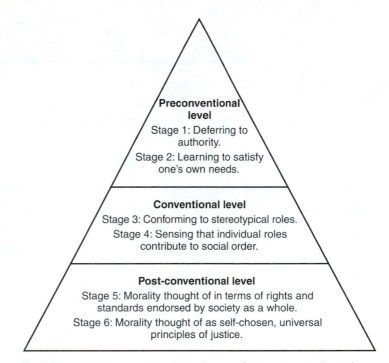

Figure 3.1   Kohlberg's Six Stages of Moral Development (Ethics of Justice/Rights)

High road approach An approach to administrative ethics emphasizing moral reasoning and ethical analysis.

Moreover, the "low road" in ethics impedes principled reasoning on the part of administrators. The **high road approach** to administrative ethics, on the other hand, emphasizes moral reasoning and ethical analysis. According to Stewart and Sprinthall, the best government would be one where administrators are skilled at recognizing ethical issues and are capable of moral reflection and ethical analysis. This requires that public administration programs include more opportunities to make students more conscious of their own personal values.[37]

Along with providing more opportunities for reflection on ethics in public administration education, Bowman and Berman recommend teaching four "pillars of ethics" as the foundation for thinking and acting in an ethical manner: (1) value awareness, (2) reasoning skills, (3) the role of law, and (4) organizational implementation.[38] First, administrators should be made aware that there is a near consensus about the values that form the basis of public service. These values include responsiveness, fairness, economy (efficiency), integrity, and competence. Second, public administrators should also be taught the tools necessary for **moral reasoning** (see Figure 3.2). Thus, ethics workshops, seminars, and classes should focus more on ethical decision-making and the skills necessary for making such decisions rather than on merely following the law and avoiding illegal behavior, or taking the "low road" to ethical behavior. Third, administrators should become thoroughly familiar with the ethics laws with which they must comply. Knowledge of laws alone, however, is insufficient

Moral reasoning The capacity to engage in ethical analysis and decision-making.

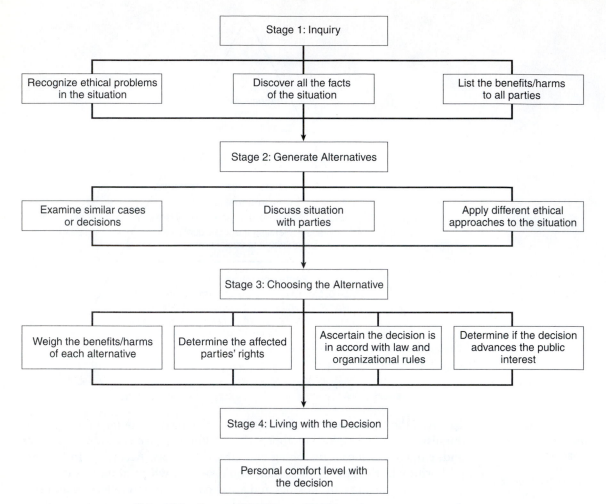

Figure 3.2   *Stages of Moral Reasoning*

to promote proper behavior on the part of officials. It is essential to create an organizational culture that promotes values from top to bottom. Training is therefore required for administrators to provide moral leadership in the workplace and to promote an ethical climate in public organizations. Finally, implementation strategies should be part of ethics training programs, because what looks good on paper might prove a dismal failure without careful attention paid to its execution.

Leadership and Ethics

One of the goals of ethics instruction is to promote in public managers the reasoning skills necessary for ethical leadership, in the hope that they can then transfer those skills to their subordinates. One advocate of ethics training asserts: "It becomes a responsibility of leadership to educate and train others toward the administrative and personal capacity for moral reasoning."[39] While the capacity to think ethically is useful for everyone in public service, it is particularly critical for those in management or leadership positions or those who aspire to these positions.

Public administrators should act as "moral beacons," Guy contends, "to serve as guideposts, lighting the path for people to follow as they encounter problems and seek solutions." She notes that public administrators frequently face no-win situations when they are called upon to make a choice. In most cases, they must choose between values that conflict: if they choose one value, the other must be sacrificed. Should the most efficient solution be chosen, the one that will save taxpayers the most money, or should the socially equitable alternative be picked, which will end up costing taxpayers more? Trade-offs must occur, and "It is imperative that norms guide trade-offs by promoting dominant values." For the values that should comprise the administrator's ethical core, Guy uses the acronym CHAPELFIRZ: *c*aring, *h*onesty, *a*ccountability, *p*romise keeping, pursuit of *e*xcellence, *l*oyalty, *f*airness, *i*ntegrity, *r*espect for others, and responsible citizenship. These are the central values of American society, which must be transmitted and strengthened through training and, particularly, through the culture of the public workplace. Administrators should play an important role in this process by sending "clear messages about what values are most important and what trade-offs among important values are justified."[40] As Bowman and Williams note: "It is difficult to overstate . . . the importance of management by example— i.e., the demonstration of desired conduct by department heads and elected officials."[41]

There is one major disadvantage, however, in putting too great an emphasis on management setting the moral tone for organizations. It fails to recognize the importance of promoting ethical behavior at all levels of the organization. While administrators should model ethical behavior for their subordinates, lower-level employees' actions should also be held to high ethical standards: "Everything still comes down to personal ethics" for the highest executive and the lowest employee alike.[42]

According to Rich, management typically imposes organizational codes of ethics on the rest of the organization, without first seeking meaningful input from lower-level employees. The problem with making ethics the exclusive domain of the top levels of the organization is that it produces a tendency to lower expectations for the moral responsibility of lower-level employees. For example, a study of Detroit garbage collectors found that overreliance on top management for ethical decision-making resulted in some collectors turning "a blind eye to criminal and immoral activities." According to the research, low-status workers, who were mostly concerned with economic survival, were unlikely to bring ethical matters to the attention of their supervisors. They preferred the safer strategy of "playing dumb."[43] This case study indicates some of the dangers inherent in a hierarchical approach to organization ethics.

Garbage collectors and other street-level bureaucrats frequently make ethical decisions.

SOURCE: Tony Savino/ The Image Works

Future Impact

Choices affecting the future of society occur frequently in public administration. Even "routine decisions" and actions taken by public agencies can have an impact on later generations. In some cases, these effects can be enormous. Nearly all instances of long-term public investment, environmental protection, historic preservation, endangered species protection, and public education, to name just a few, fall into this class of future-impact decisions.[44] How, then, are public administrators to incorporate ethical responsibilities in these types of decisions? What factors should be considered in this type of policy-making?

To understand the moral calculations these types of decisions involve, imagine that a city must decide whether to set aside acres of open space for a park or to allow the land to be developed commercially. If the city chooses the park over commercial development, people in the future will be able to enjoy the land in all its unspoiled natural beauty. Converting it into a park, however, means that present-day individuals will not be able to benefit commercially from its development, nor will the municipal government receive tax revenues from its commercial use. Do the city officials have an ethical obligation to consider the needs and preferences of future generations? Yes, according to H. George Frederickson. It is the moral duty of public officials, he believes, to "adopt and implement policies" that promote intergenerational fairness. He writes, "As public officials we hold some responsibility for social equity between generations; we must act as best we can based on what we know."[45] Acting on Frederickson's principles will lead our hypothetical municipal officials to consider not only the needs of the present-day city residents but also those of posterity as well.

Prudence

According to Dobel, prudence is a virtue that is necessary for political leadership. It can be argued with equal validity that it is important for non-elected public servants too. Prudence can be defined as self-command or self-mastery, without which a moral life would be impossible. This quality is also vital for ethical leadership.[46] Characteristics of prudent management include (1) avoiding ideological rigidity, (2) exercising foresight, (3) marshaling authority and resources to achieve aims, (4) acting with care and patience, but moving quickly as the opportunity arises, and (5) aligning the proper means and proper ends.

Recent Developments in Administrative Ethics

During the 1990s, government at all levels embraced the reinvention movement (discussed in Chapter 4) and new public management (NPM) theory (see Chapter 7). They did so because these management strategies offered the promise of more efficient and effective government. Several scholars, however, raise questions about the compatibility of these approaches with traditional ethics.[47] Gregory argues that the economic values underlying reinvention and NPM contradict certain core values: for example, the idea that public service constitutes a public trust. Business adheres to a different set of ethical standards than public service, and an action that would be lauded in the private sector might be condemned in the public sector.[48] Menzel contends that NPM advocates "are mostly silent about the place of ethics or morality in public management."[49] Ethics cannot easily be assigned dollar values and therefore does not fit into cost-effectiveness calculations.

The popular demand for government reform might arise more as a result of ethics lapses on the part of public officials rather than as a consequence of management failure or inefficiency. Indeed, as Zajac points out, "Ethics failure can be a much more potent corrosive upon public faith in government." He warns that by overemphasizing private management models, we too often ignore important ethical elements of public service. Character, integrity, justice, and dignity are just as important as technical "know-how" in determining the ultimate success of public sector endeavors.[50] In the next section, we examine attempts to encourage organization members to bring wrongdoing to the attention of people who can correct the abuses or punish the culprits.

Whistle Blowing

Time magazine usually gives its Person of the Year award to only one individual. In 2002, however, the magazine chose three women to share the honor. Even more surprising, instead of being well known, the women were ordinary people engaged in ordinary occupations. *Time* selected each one because "By risking everything to blow the whistle at WorldCom, Enron, and the FBI, Cynthia Cooper, Sherron Watkins, and Colleen Rowley reminded us what American courage and American values are all about."[51] Without a doubt, these were women of great personal courage, who risked their jobs and reputations by drawing public attention to corporate and governmental wrongdoing in an effort to fix it (see Vignette 3.2). But for every Cooper, Watkins, or Rowley, there are hundreds of other equally courageous people who act in obscurity and then pay a steep price for their actions, either in the form of pay cuts, demotion, or more severe punishment. Many whistle blowers lose their jobs as a result of their actions, as did two Los Alamos National Laboratory employees in January 2003 after they reported the misuse of laboratory credit cards and $2.7 million in missing computers along with other lab equipment. However, this story has a happy ending: the University of California rehired them with back pay to help with the investigation of the laboratory's practices.[52]

VIGNETTE 3.2   Portrait of an FBI Whistle Blower

FBI agent Colleen Rowley fits perfectly the profile of a government whistle blower described in this chapter. Rowley had served the Bureau for over twenty-one years when her bombshell memo outlining FBI intelligence lapses before and after September 11, 2001, made national headlines. Her detailed memo criticized the agency for ignoring her office's requests to investigate Zacarias Moussaoui, a French Moroccan man who wanted to learn to fly a 747 jet by taking lessons at a local flight school.

Rowley had wanted to be in the FBI ever since she was in the fifth grade. She sent away for a booklet about the FBI after watching a TV show. Although the pamphlet noted that women were not then employed as special agents, this did not deter Rowley. She made a decision to become an FBI agent, which she achieved after graduating from the University of Iowa's law school. At that time, there were very few female special agents in the Bureau. She began her career by investigating organized crime in New York City. By the time of the terrorist attacks, she had been at the FBI's field office in Minneapolis over ten years. In all that time, she never received any form of disciplinary action.

Whistle blowers tend to have very strong value systems. They also tend to deeply internalize their organization's core values. Rowley is no exception. She starts her memo, "I feel at this point that I have to put my concerns in writing concerning the important topic of the FBI's response to evidence of terrorist activity in the United States prior to Sept. 11. The issues are fundamentally ones of INTEGRITY and go to the heart of the FBI's law enforcement mission and mandate."

In the *Time* article honoring her as a Person of the Year, the author points out that Rowley "had higher expectations for the FBI than its top leaders. The bureau could be great, was her message, if only it put the goal of protecting Americans above the goal of protecting itself, if only agents were not rewarded for sitting still."

SOURCES: Keven Johnson, "Agent Fears for career after Criticizing Bosses," *USA Today,* May 28, 2002.

Amanda Ripfey and Maggie Sieger, "The Special Agent," *Time,* December 22, 2002.

Ann Curry, "Minneapolis FBI Agent Coleen Rowley's Career, Life, and Famous Memo," NBC News Transcripts, June 6, 2002.

The 2002 *Time* Persons of the Year included Colleen Rowley, FBI whistle blower about the Bureau's pre-9/11 lapses.

SOURCE: Gregory Heisler/ Time Inc./Time Life Pictures/ Getty Images

Whistle blowing Reporting incidents of waste, fraud, or abuse within an organization; often entails considerable personal cost through employment termination, demotion, or social exclusion.

Whistle blowing refers to the reporting of incidents of waste, fraud, or abuse within an organization by an employee to an entity, usually external, who is capable of taking proper corrective action.[53] Evidence indicates that whistle blowing is on the rise in both public and private organizations. There has been extensive research done on the subject, drawing largely from the disciplines of law, business and public administration. As a result of this work, we have a fairly detailed and accurate portrait of the "typical" whistle blower, in terms of personal and organizational characteristics.

Government whistle blowers possess several key attributes, according to a study by Miceli and Near. Compared to their non-whistle-blowing peers, government whistle blowers tend to

- Hold professional positions.
- Have more positive job responses.
- Work for organizations that are perceived to be responsive to complaints.
- Work in larger groups.
- Have been recognized for their job performance.
- Have more years of service.
- Consist largely of male employees; race, however, was not a factor in the decision to be a whistle blower.

The vast majority of the survey's respondents were males with longer service, and the authors suggest that "employees who feel relatively powerful or respected will be more likely to report perceived wrongdoing.[54] They contend that whistle blowing constitutes a form of "prosocial" behavior—or behavior designed to help others—that occurs in organizations. This conclusion was reinforced by a study that analyzed the results of a survey of 161 whistle blowers. Jos and Thompkins found that a majority believed in universal moral rules, were "intensely committed" to the organization's goals, and were willing to act on their personal beliefs despite strong pressures to stay quiet about the wrongdoing.[55] Clearly the majority of whistle blowers are not malcontents; if anything, they are among the most ethical and committed employees.

Despite the good intentions of those who become whistle blowers—they report on wrongdoing because they want to aid victims or because they think the organization is not living up to its stated values—these individuals often face severe personal retribution for their actions. Whistle blowers face organizational retaliation ranging from dismissal to on-the-job isolation. In the study of 161 whistle blowers, a majority of the respondents either lost their jobs, were harassed, were transferred, or had their salary and job responsibilities reduced.[56] The results of a survey conducted more than 10 years later by a whistle-blower advocacy group were nearly identical.[57] Almost half the respondents to the 2002 survey said they were dismissed after they reported a problem. Most of the others said they had been harassed or unfairly disciplined.

Louis Clark, executive director of the Government Accountability Project, an organization working on behalf of whistle blowers, contends that the personal costs of whistle blowing are too high for most employees: "Seventy percent of people who see something wrong don't do anything about it, because it's an incredibly stressful process. They don't want to be made into martyrs or commit career suicide."[58] Would-be whistle blowers all too clearly recognize the risks they face in "going public." The fact that so many are willing to accept the costs speaks highly of their moral fiber.

Civil Society and Administrative Ethics

Administrative ethics plays a major role in strengthening civil society. Chapter 6 discusses the importance of ethical values such as trust and honesty in fostering the types of reciprocal relationships that form the basis of social capital. Administrators' ethical behavior, particularly in their dealings with the public, contributes to the willingness of members of the community to form collaborative relationships with government and nonprofit agencies. Furthermore, ethical leadership traits and skills developed in ethical training are not only applicable in organizational settings but can be used on behalf of civil society as well. Thus the public's investment in inculcating moral reasoning in administrators can result in a dual payoff in terms of more ethical public organizations and a more robust civil society.

Administrative Evil: "I Was Only Following Orders"

Public administrators are generally reluctant to use words like "evil" when describing organizational wrongdoing. Evil is a word typically reserved for the likes of murderous tyrants such as Adolf Hitler, Joseph Stalin, or Saddam Hussein. Furthermore, the notion with its heavy religious overtones tends to make social scientists rather uncomfortable.[59] But there have been challenges to the public administration community's reticence on the subject. Adams and Balfour, for example, argue that **administrative evil**—harmful acts committed by public officials—is a problem that public administrators must forcefully confront.

Adams and Balfour believe that evil is inherent in the human condition. According to them, evil occurs when "humans knowingly and deliberately inflict pain and suffering on other human beings." They contend that administrative evil is particularly pernicious, since it is effectively "masked" or hidden from plain sight. It is so well hidden, in fact, that the task of unmasking it presents a great challenge to administrators. Further, public officials may commit heinous acts "without being aware that they are in fact doing anything at all wrong."[60] Examples of this include the thousands of anonymous bureaucrats who maintained the infrastructure of the concentration camps in Nazi Germany. Through their tireless, efficient work, they helped execute more than six million Jews and other "undesirables" during the Holocaust. Although they thought they were just doing their jobs, and in many cases

Administrative evil Harmful acts committed by public officials, who are often unaware that they are doing anything wrong.

Some have questioned the ethics of NASA in allowing the *Challenger* space shuttle launch despite information suggesting problems with the vehicle's O-rings.
SOURCE: NASA

doing it quite well, the end result was the destruction of men, women, and children. Adams and Balfour contend, however, that administrative evil cannot be applied exclusively to examples of obvious evil such as Hitler's Germany. They assert that the *Challenger* and *Columbia* space shuttle tragedies are contemporary examples, to which both public servants and the American people should pay close attention (see the case study on the *Columbia* shuttle at the end of the chapter).

The ultimate source of administrative evil, Balfour and Adams contend, is classical bureaucracy's overemphasis on technical rationality, which blinds public administrators to the "existence and importance of evil." We have heard echoes of this argument earlier in this chapter in the belief that technical rationality contributes to public managers' "moral muteness." The authors' proposed remedy to this situation includes a new public ethics which requires a fundamental reconstruction of the field of public administration. They argue, "Public administration should not be taught, practiced, or theorized about without considering the psychological, organizational, and societal dynamics that can lead public servants to confound the public interest with acts of dehumanization and destruction."[61]

■ Chapter Summary

Ethical behavior and standards are central to public administration and deserve serious study by administrators. This is true for both practical and professional reasons: by upholding the highest ethical standards, public servants retain the trust and confidence of the community, and to be a professional entails dedication to the values of one's field. Ethics, as we define it, is the process of using reason, guided by moral standards or core personal values, to make decisions regarding right- and wrong-doing in one's professional and personal life, and then taking the responsibility for those actions.

There are two major approaches to ethics, which have had a significant impact on public administration ethics. Deontology holds that absolute standards of right and wrong should guide human actions, regardless of the consequences of those actions. Utilitarianism holds that the results of one's actions should count more than the intentions that underlie the actions. According to a utilitarian, a morally correct course of action is one producing the greatest good for the greatest number of people.

Professional communities, such as public administrators, promote ethical behavior among their members through the creation and promulgation of codes of ethics. The code of ethics of the American Society for Public Administration (ASPA), the professional society serving public administrators, reflects the five core areas of interest to American public servants: (1) public interest, (2) legal interest, (3) personal interest, (4) organizational interest, and (5) professional interest. The ASPA code has helped shape the behavior of public administrators, but it is purely instructional in nature, since the society lacks the capacity to enforce the code.

Public servants are also held accountable for their actions by numerous ethics laws at the federal and state levels. Perhaps the most important of these statutes is the Ethics in Government Act (1978). The act created the Office of Government Ethics (OGE), which is responsible for overseeing executive-branch compliance with federal ethics regulations. The law emphasizes probity in the area of personal finances but overlooks other important aspects of employee behavior.

Two important values of administrative ethics are responsibility and accountability. Accountability involves a more legalistic and hierarchical approach, while responsibility involves the administrator's innate sense of right and wrong. The debate over accountability and responsibility deals with which of the two should be the most heavily relied on to ensure ethical behavior. Related to this debate is the allegiance of public servants to bureaucratic and democratic values, especially when they come into conflict, as they often do.

Ethics training is an important part of public administration and students acknowledge the significant contribution it makes to their overall preparation for public service. The goal of ethics training, and moral-reasoning development in particular, is to move public servants from the "low road" to the "high road" in their understanding and application of administrative ethics. Ethical leadership is crucial, since top administrators need to model good behavior for their subordinates and the public. However, ethics should not be viewed as the exclusive domain of mangers within organizations; lower-level employees must also behave in an ethical manner.

Whistle blowing should be encouraged in public organizations to the fullest extent possible. Governments are aware of the positive contributions whistle blowers make to their agencies and society in general and have written laws to make it easier for people to report wrongdoing. Nevertheless, many employees remain fearful of the repercussions of publicizing agency misdeeds, and only a few highly principled men and women actually come forth with their revelations.

Administrative evil consists of acts committed by public servants in the course of fulfilling their official duties, often without being aware they are doing anything wrong. Consequently, it is all the more insidious as it is masked. According to Adams and Balfour, administrative evil is the direct result of classical bureaucracy's overemphasis on technical rationality, which blinds people to the existence of evil in the world.

■ Chapter Discussion Questions

1. Read the ASPA Code of Ethics reprinted in this chapter. Which philosophical approach to ethics does it represent? Why?

2. Do *you* think public servants should be held to higher ethical standards than managers in the private sector? Why?

3. Many people think they have all the ethical and moral training they need before they start a public administration program. For many, ethics is

simply "doing good and avoiding evil." How might training in administrative ethics help you to become a better public manager?

4. How do organizations benefit from whistle blowing? How can exposing the organization's "dirty laundry" contribute to the organization?

5. According to Adams and Balfour, inflicting harm on another human being is an example of evil. Often, harm involves physical injury or even death, but not all acts of administrative evil entail bodily harm. What are some examples of administrative evil in a public agency setting that do not involve the infliction of physical harm?

BRIEF CASE   NASA'S CULTURE AND THE *COLUMBIA* SHUTTLE DISASTER

To anyone familiar with the 1986 space shuttle *Challenger* tragedy, the *New York Times* headline on February 4, 2003, must have seemed like the recurrence of an old nightmare. Written shortly after the space shuttle *Columbia* was destroyed on its return from space on January 16, 2003, the article reported that NASA had information as early as 1997 that there were problems with the spacecraft that could produce a catastrophe. Again, it seemed, the space agency had ignored warnings that something was wrong with the shuttle, and again, human lives may have been needlessly lost.

At issue was a report written by Gregory N. Katnik, a NASA engineer at Cape Canaveral, dated December 23, 1997. Katnik, observing that the *Columbia* had suffered damage to its ceramic tiles on a recent flight, wrote that the damage was "not normal."[62] He noted that hardened foam debris from the external fuel tank had harmed the tiles that protected the shuttle from the intense heat generated upon reentry into Earth's atmosphere. During other space flights, the vehicle sustained damage to the tiles, but the space agency decided that the harm caused by the foam debris did not warrant further investigation.

Other information surfaced in the months after the *Columbia*'s destruction. Email messages from NASA engineers discussed the possibility that damage to the shuttle's left wing from lift-off debris imperiled its reentry. A computer simulation that warned of impending disaster was dismissed by Boeing engineers. Little by little, like a jigsaw puzzle that is assembled painstakingly over time, a disturbing picture began to emerge of the space agency trying to run a "lackadaisical safety program on the cheap."[63]

NASA had come under intense scrutiny after the earlier *Challenger* tragedy. The space agency was criticized for ignoring engineers' concerns about faulty O-ring seals, which had led to the *Challenger*'s destruction and the deaths of its crew. Following the *Columbia* disaster, investigators focused their attention on management mistakes, primarily the question of whether warnings from below reached the agency's senior management. The board of investigators, headed by retired admiral Harold W. Gehman Jr., was not interested in fixing the blame on specific managers, or even on the agency itself. The executive director of the National Space Society, Brian Chase, said, "The blame does not lie just with NASA," a point also acknowledged by the board. Indeed, the White House and Congress cut back funding of the space shuttle program, micromanaged its operations, and "in general maintained an air of complacency."[64]

NASA managers argued that the organizational culture had changed as a result of the *Challenger* tragedy and the subsequent inquiry. That inquiry revealed, among other things, that a mechanical design expert, Roger Boisjoly, had warned NASA that the space shuttle was not ready for launch.[65] But his bosses overruled him and the launch went ahead as planned. Ron Dittemore, the shuttle program manager, however, said at a hearing of the investigative board that the agency fostered an environment in which open discussion and questioning were allowed. He told the investigators, "We want people in our system to challenge the assumptions."[66] In the wake of the *Columbia* disaster, it was learned that another whistle blower attempted to halt the launch. Don Nelson, a thirty-six-year veteran of the space agency, actually went to the White House with his warnings after they were ignored by the agency. Nelson sought a presidential order to suspend space shuttle flights in order to prevent "another catastrophic space-shuttle accident."[67] But the White House did not intervene.

There is strong evidence that NASA's organizational culture was unaltered by the earlier *Challenger* experience. An accident investigator for the United Space Alliance, the shuttle program's major contractor, said in a *New York Times* interview that NASA continues to have a "corporate culture of denial," which leads to cover-ups of safety problems rather than reporting them officially.[68] The investigator cited an August 2001 incident in which a highly toxic gas was accidentally released from a shuttle fuel tank. This release resulted in the evacuation of buildings, but NASA filed a "white paper" report, which did not require an official follow-up from the agency.

Other critics of NASA, both internal and external, note a "groupthink" mentality that creates an unreceptive environment to the warnings of whistle blowers. Engineers directly involved with the processes did not consider the foam a safety risk; therefore they all but ignored warnings from consultants and refused to pass their concerns along to superiors. An email message from one of these consultants is indicative of their level of frustration: "Any more activity today on the tile damage, or are people just relegated to crossing their fingers and hoping for the best?"[69]

Brief Case Questions

1. *What does the case study suggest are the reasons for the ethical lapses of NASA?*

2. *NASA exemplifies professional bureaucracy; however, as the case study shows, this has not prevented the agency from committing major blunders resulting in the loss of human life. What does NASA's experience suggest about the role of professionalization, technical expertise, and ethical values in professional organizations?*

3. *What does this chapter suggest can be done to prevent another Challenger or Columbia disaster from occurring?*

■ Key Terms

administrative accountability (page 54)
administrative evil (page 65)
bureaucratic ethos (page 55)
democratic ethos (page 55)
deontology (page 48)
ethics (page 46)
high road approach (page 57)
Kohlberg's model of moral development (page 56)

low road approach (page 53)
moral reasoning (page 57)
Rawlsianism (page 48)
regime values (page 47)
responsibility (page 54)
utilitarianism (page 48)
whistle blowing (page 63)

■ On the Web

http://www.usoge.gov/
U.S. Office of Government Ethics.

http://www.cogel.org/
Council on Government Ethics Laws.

http://www.citizen.org/congress/govt_reform/
ethics/index.cfm
Public Citizen government ethics page.

http://www.usafa.af.mil/jscope/
U.S. Military ethics website.

http://www.eppc.org/
The Ethics and Public Policy Center, a non-profit institution exploring the bond between the Western moral tradition and the public debate over domestic and foreign policy issues.

http://www.publicintegrity.org/
The Center for Public Integrity, a nonprofit, nonpartisan organization that conducts investigative research and reports on public policy issues in the United States and around the world.

http://www.iit.edu/departments/csep/Pub-licWWW/codes/
The Center for the Study of Ethics in the Professions, which maintains an online library of professional codes of ethics.

http://www.corporateethics.com./
The Council of Ethical Organizations, a non-profit, nonpartisan organization dedicated to promoting ethical and legal conduct in business, government, and the professions.

http://www.ethics.org/index.html
The Ethics Resource Center, which encourages strong ethical leadership worldwide by providing expertise and services through research, education, and partnerships.

CHAPTER 4

The Political Ecology of Public Administration

The Institutional Context of Public Policy

■ SETTING THE STAGE

One important consequence of September 11, 2001, at least in terms of public administration, has been to subject federal law enforcement activities to intense public scrutiny. As a result of these investigations, we know a great deal about the organizational problems plaguing federal law enforcement agencies before 9/11. According to the bipartisan National Commission on Terrorist Attacks upon the United States (9/11 Commission), the FBI was tracking suspicious flight training in Arizona while the CIA had an operative keeping an eye on two of the hijackers, but evidently dissension between the two agencies prevented their sharing this information.[1] Avoidable administrative problems such as this led a member of the commission, John Lehman, former secretary of the navy, to opine: "There's broad consensus that major changes are needed. This is not just a question of running faster, jumping higher. We need to ensure the fusion and sharing of all intelligence that could have helped us to avoid 9/11."

Congress appointed the 9/11 Commission in late 2002 and it finished its work in the summer 2004. The commission's responsibility was to investigate relevant government operations before the attacks and to recommend ways to better safeguard the country against terrorists in the future. In the process, it interviewed more than 1,000 witnesses, including President George W. Bush, and reviewed more than 2 million documents. The work of the 9/11 Commission is an example of the type of oversight that can be brought to bear on administrative agencies, especially in the wake of an event such as the terrorist attacks on September 11, 2001. One of the commission's main recommendations was to call for a "czar" in charge of national intelligence, which President Bush embraced in 2005 with his appointment of career diplomat John Negroponte to the post of director of national intelligence.

Members of the National Commission on Terrorist Attacks upon the United States (the 9/11 Commission) listen to testimony during the commission's final hearing in 2004.

SOURCE: Shaun Heasley/ Reuters/Corbis

■ CHAPTER PLAN

Public administration in the United States has been influenced by two separate strands of our national culture: democratic political values and management principles derived from the free enterprise system. American political values find their fullest expression in our electoral process and political institutions. In a democracy, the public's need to know is reflected in the activities of investigative committees like the 9/11 Commission, which serves as just one example of the tremendous influence political institutions have on the internal operations of public agencies. As will be seen in this chapter, American political institutions have had a profound impact on administrative activities at all levels of government. In the United States, this institutional setting consists principally of the three branches of government established by the Constitution: the executive, legislative, and judicial branches, as well as the staffs attached to each one. In this chapter, we discuss how each of these three branches influences public administration. We also address the limitations on each branch's ability to control the bureaucracy. Next, we look at recent federal government reform efforts, paying close attention to the National Performance Review (NPR), a federal reform initiative that was undertaken during the Clinton administration. The NPR experience encapsulates many of the tensions between administration and its political environment that are raised earlier in the chapter. We conclude the chapter by examining some of the effects of recent government reform efforts on civil society.

The Executive Branch and Administration

The bulk of the work performed by government occurs within the departments of the executive branch. At the federal level, the executive branch consists of the fifteen cabinet departments and their numerous offices and

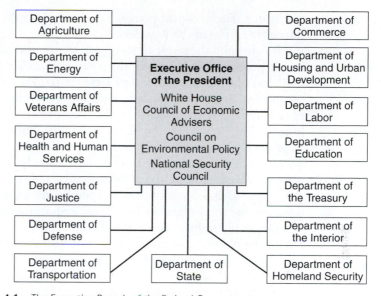

Figure 4.1   The Executive Branch of the Federal Government

SOURCE: Hanson, Russell L. *Intergovernmental Relations, in Politics in the American State: A Comparative Analysis,* 6th ed., Virginia Gray and Herbert Jacob, eds., 1995, p.43. Copright Russell © 1995 CQ Press, a division of Congressional Quarterly Inc.

bureaus (see Figure 4.1). At the state and local levels, the executive branch contains the departments and agencies that perform most of the vital services that citizens depend on, including highways and roads, law enforcement, and primary and secondary education. At the top of the federal executive branch sits the president; at the state level, the equivalent is the governor, and at the local level, the mayor. (All of these are elected offices; another type of chief executive at the local level is the city manager, who is not elected.)

The Organization of the Federal Government

The federal government's core unit, organizationally, is the bureau, which is sometimes known as an office, administration, or service. These in turn compose the larger federal entities known as agencies and departments. Congress has the responsibility for establishing departments and agencies, while the Constitution authorizes the president to reorganize the executive branch subject to congressional approval.

Executive, or cabinet-level, departments are perhaps the best-known components of the federal government. The largest department, in terms of budget and personnel, is the Department of Defense; the smallest is the Department of Education. Currently there are fifteen executive departments, with the most recent being the Department of Homeland Security, established in response to the war on terrorism. Together they employ approximately 1.8 million civilian employees, which account for 90 percent of the total executive branch workforce. The president exercises oversight over the departments through the Executive Office of the President.

It is beyond the scope of this book to discuss each and every department, and it probably would make for some tedious reading as well. However, a brief look at the Department of Defense (DoD) will give some sense of the complexity and variety of federal departments (see Figure 4.2). Defense, as noted above, is the largest of the departments in the federal executive branch. The DoD's mission is to provide the United States with the capacity to protect the country from foreign attacks and to deter any external threats. To accomplish its mission, DoD employs nearly 1.4 million uniformed personnel as well as more than 700,000 civilians, or a population roughly the size of San Diego. In 2006, DoD expenditures were $520 billion, or roughly one-fifth the total spending for the entire national government.

Originally known as the War Department, the Department of Defense is one of the oldest executive departments. From its establishment in 1789 until after World War II, however, the department managed only the U.S. Army; the U.S. Navy (including the Marine Corps) had its own cabinet-level department. When the military bureaucracy was completely reorganized in 1947 by the National Security Act, the army and navy were placed under the direction of the secretary of defense. The act also created the U.S. Air Force as a third branch of the armed forces. In addition to the three branches of the military, DoD houses fourteen other agencies that are responsible for functions as diverse as administering the ballistic missile program and managing the department's complex finances. In light of the tremendous variety of units within DoD, it is not uncommon for the different subunits to compete with each other for scarce resources. For example, early in George W. Bush's first term, Defense Secretary Donald Rumsfeld sought to close obsolete military bases while at the same time seeking additional funds for a missile defense program, thus setting off an internal struggle within the department over the allocation of the budget.

Another type of federal administrative agency is the independent regulatory commission or board. The independent commission is an outgrowth of the Progressive Era's desire to reduce the direct control of the executive branch over certain types of activities, typically involving economic regulation. These agencies differ from other executive departments in several major ways. First, they are small policy-making bodies with the authority to oversee areas such as telecommunications, international trade, nuclear energy, and labor relations (see Table 4.1). Second, they exist independently of the rest of the executive branch and therefore enjoy a degree of political and legal autonomy that is atypical for federal agencies. Third, their membership is bipartisan, which is another reflection of the Progressive wish to reduce the role of partisan politics in the area of administration. Finally, members of boards and commissions serve overlapping terms exceeding presidential terms, and they can be removed only on the basis of poor or corrupt performance in office. For all of these reasons, independent agencies are expected to reach their decisions in a nonpolitical, unbiased, and expert manner.

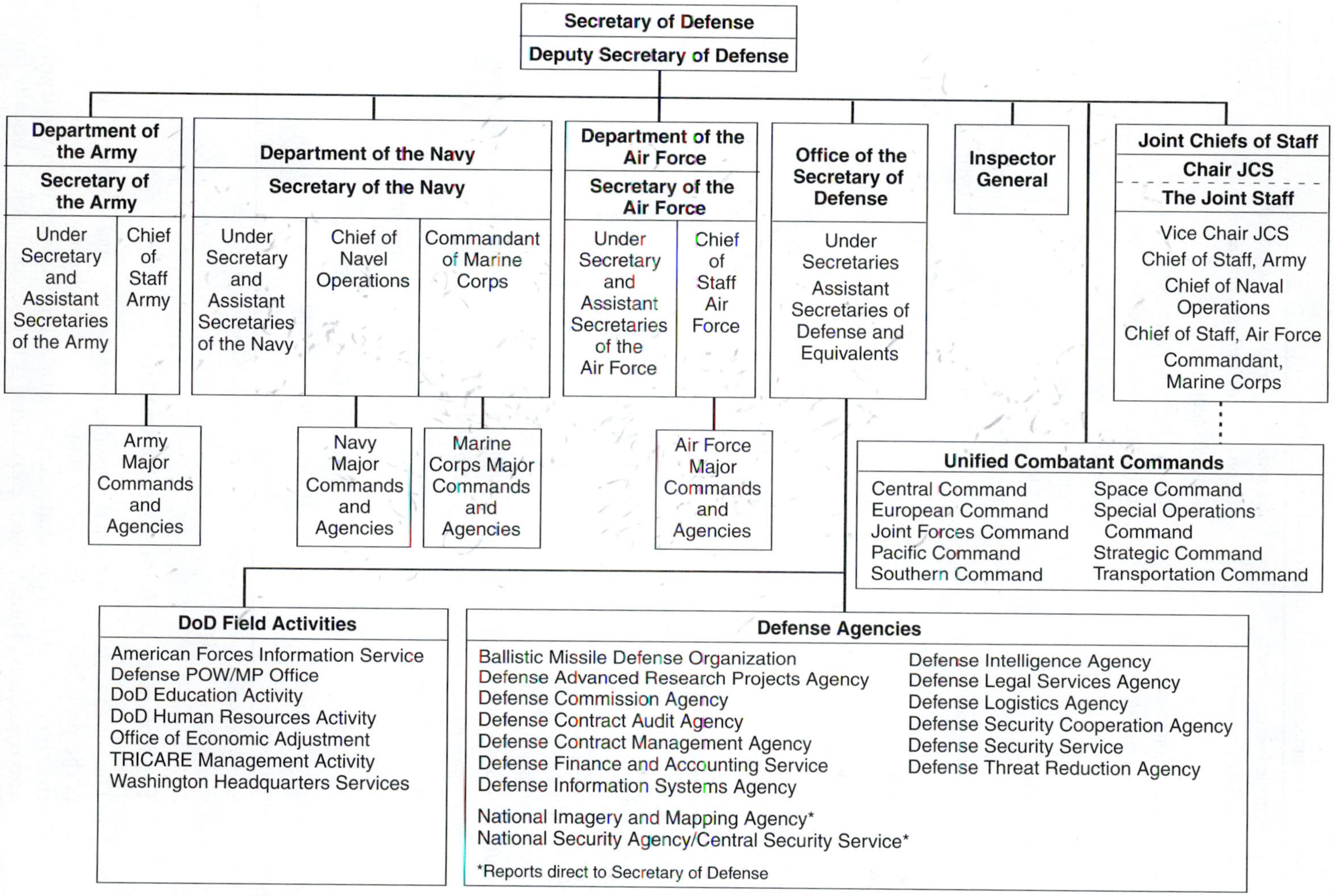

Department of Defense Organization Chart

Secretary of Defense
Deputy Secretary of Defense

Department of the Army

Secretary of the Army	
Under Secretary and Assistant Secretaries of the Army	Chief of Staff Army

Army Major Commands and Agencies

Department of the Navy

Secretary of the Navy		
Under Secretary and Assistant Secretaries of the Navy	Chief of Navel Operations	Commandant of Marine Corps

Navy Major Commands and Agencies

Marine Corps Major Commands and Agencies

Department of the Air Force

Secretary of the Air Force	
Under Secretary and Assistant Secretaries of the Air Force	Chief of Staff Air Force

Air Force Major Commands and Agencies

Office of the Secretary of Defense

Under Secretaries Assistant Secretaries of Defense and Equivalents

Inspector General

Joint Chiefs of Staff

Chair JCS
The Joint Staff

Vice Chair JCS
Chief of Staff, Army
Chief of Naval Operations
Chief of Staff, Air Force
Commandant, Marine Corps

Unified Combatant Commands

Central Command
European Command
Joint Forces Command
Pacific Command
Southern Command

Space Command
Special Operations Command
Strategic Command
Transportation Command

Defense Agencies

Ballistic Missile Defense Organization
Defense Advanced Research Projects Agency
Defense Commission Agency
Defense Contract Audit Agency
Defense Contract Management Agency
Defense Finance and Accounting Service
Defense Information Systems Agency

National Imagery and Mapping Agency*
National Security Agency/Central Security Service*

Defense Intelligence Agency
Defense Legal Services Agency
Defense Logistics Agency
Defense Security Cooperation Agency
Defense Security Service
Defense Threat Reduction Agency

*Reports direct to Secretary of Defense

DoD Field Activities

American Forces Information Service
Defense POW/MP Office
DoD Education Activity
DoD Human Resources Activity
Office of Economic Adjustment
TRICARE Management Activity
Washington Headquarters Services

Figure 4.2 Department of Defense Organization Chart

SOURCE: http://www.defenselink.mil/odam/omp/pubs/GuideBook/Pdf/DoD.PDF.

TABLE 4.1 Independent Commissions, Board, and Regulatory Agencies

Advisory Council on Historic Preservation	National Endowment for the Humanities
American Battle Monuments Commission	National Indian Gaming Commission
Central Intelligence Agency	National Mediation Board
Commodity Futures Trading Commission	National Railroad Passenger Corporation
Consumer Product Safety Commission	National Science Foundation
Corporation for National Service	National Transportation Commission
Environmental Protection Agency	Nuclear Regulatory Commission
Equal Employment Opportunity Commission	US Nuclear Waste Technical Review Board
Farm Credit Administration	Occupational Safety and Health Administration
Federal Communications Commission	Office of Federal Housing Enterprise Oversight
Federal Deposit Insurance Corporation	Office of Personnel Management
Federal Election Commission	Office of Special Counsel
Federal Emergency Management Agency	Overseas Private Investment Corporation
Federal Energy Regulatory Commission	Peace Corps
Federal Labor Relations Authority	Pension Benefit Guaranty Corporation
Federal Maritime Commission	Postal Rate Commission
Federal Reserve System	Railroad Retirement Board
Federal Retirement Thrift Investment Board	Securities and Exchange Commission
Federal Trade Commission	Selective Service System
General Services Administration	Small Business Administration
Institute of Museum and Library Services	Social Security Administration
International Broadcasting Bureau	Tennessee Valley Authority
Merit Systems Protection Board	Thrift Savings Plan
National Aeronautics and Space Administration	United States Agency for International Development
National Archives and Records Administration	United States Arms Control and Disarmament Agency
National Capital Planning Commission	United States International Trade Commission
National Commission on Libraries and Information Science	United States Office of Government Ethics
National Council on Disability	United States Postal Service
National Credit Union Administration	United States Trade and Development Agency
National Endowment for the Arts	Voice of America

Source: Adapted from *Official U.S. Executive Branch Websites,* a Library of Congress Resource. http://www.loc.gov/global/executive/fed.html

The President as Administrator in Chief

The bureaucracy, in a formal sense, answers to the chief executive, whether it is the president or governor or mayor. At all levels of government, however, the chief executive must share control of the bureaucracy with the legislature and the courts. Thus, while the executive is held accountable politically for the bureaucracy's performance, some important aspects of this performance are outside the executive's direct control. This fragmentation of authority is designed to keep the power of the executive in check. This division of authority often conflicts with a central tenet of public administration, which goes back to Alexander Hamilton: A strong, centralized executive is necessary for strong, effective management of government.

As the federal government grew rapidly during the 1930s, it became apparent that its effectiveness was hindered by the fragmentation and lack of coordination which characterized the system. Reformers of the American executive branch, such as the 1937 Brownlow Committee on Administrative Management, argued at the time that a strong executive could be a force to direct and coordinate the activities of administrators to better accomplish the worthy objectives of government. The presidency, as the Brownlow Committee pointed out, combines three important roles in one position: political leader or chief legislator, symbol of national power, and chief administrator. In his relations with administrative agencies, the president tends to rely most heavily on the first and last of these roles; indeed the roles of chief legislator and chief administrator are virtually indistinguishable. This is because the president's ability to exercise effective authority over the federal bureaucracy also allows him to deal effectively with Congress.[2] The roles of chief administrator and chief legislator are largely derived from powers authorized in the Constitution. For example, as the chief administrator, the president enforces the Constitution and laws passed by Congress; the president also appoints the key members of the bureaucracy. As the chief legislator, the president may use the veto to halt legislation and exert influence over Congress to pass legislation. Furthermore, the president can recall Congress into special session. The president can employ several tools to manage the bureaucracy. The experience of recent presidents, however, indicates that these tools alone do not automatically transform the bureaucracy into an effective instrument for executing the president's agenda.

Executive Appointment The most important direct means at the president's disposal to influence administration is the power to appoint and remove thousands of administrators, including hundreds at the top levels of the bureaucracy. Article II, section 2, of the Constitution gives the president the authority, subject to the approval of the Senate, to appoint ambassadors, Supreme Court justices, and department heads. The highest levels of the federal bureaucracy are included in the "Executive Schedule" pay list, which includes the cabinet secretaries, undersecretaries, assistant secretaries, agency and bureau chiefs, and other powerful presidential appointees. Altogether, the president appoints between 600 and 700 political executives. Moreover, the president's ability to remove political executives is nearly as absolute as his power to appoint, as a result of a 1926 Supreme Court decision, *Myers v. the United States*, which struck down a law requiring the Senate's consent for the removal of a postmaster.[3]

In addition to these top appointments, the president appoints between 1,600 and 1,700 mid-level officials who usually head the support staff for the higher-level appointments. There are, therefore, roughly between 2,200 and 2,400 political appointees—in addition to the civil service and nonpartisan employees who comprise the bulk of the federal workforce. In practice, however, the difference between civil service and political appointees is not always clear-cut, as Hugh Heclo observed: "Rather than picturing a single, clearly defined boundary line, one should think instead of an erratic smudge."[4] The Executive Schedule, for example, includes career bureaucrats; the president can exert influence over the civil service through his ability to reassign top-level career bureaucrats to different agencies.

Unfortunately, to the considerable woe of many presidents, the authority to appoint and remove bureaucrats does not always guarantee effective administration. One possible impediment to administrative effectiveness, for example, is the short time periods usually served by political appointees. Presidential appointees only remain in their position an average of two years, according to a National Academy of Public Administration report.[5] This short tenure may place the political executives at a relative disadvantage compared to career bureaucrats who spend considerably more time in the government. As a result of this shorter tenure, it is not uncommon for political executives to rely heavily on the institutional experience and specialized knowledge of the career bureaucrats in making and implementing policy. Thus career bureaucrats are likely to have more influence in more technical policy areas. It should be noted, however, that some political appointees can use their short time in office to make significant changes, confident in the knowledge that it will be their successors and not they who will have to undo any possible damage.

A second potential obstacle to political appointees exercising more control over the bureaucracy is their inability to choose their own staffs. The department head may want to appoint a subordinate with expertise or with managerial experience, but the president may want someone who is politically loyal in the position. President Ronald Reagan, for example, placed a heavy emphasis on appointing individuals to important policy positions who were loyal to his ideological principles.

The tension between good management and politics in making personnel decisions has received considerable scholarly attention. One 1990 study points to position cutting in agencies promoting organizational efficiency as evidence of recent administrations placing a higher priority on politics than on effective management.[6] For example, in the past, the Bureau of the Budget (BoB) cultivated an objective orientation to policy matters. However, as early as 1975, political scientist Hugh Heclo asserted that the Office of Management and Budget (OMB) had adopted a more partisan political approach. A study thirty years later noted that "the agency has benerally been viewed as more responsive to individual presidents' political interests".[7] Furthermore, some argue that politics has won out over management in the case of even lower-level appointments.[8] This can be attributed to the centralization of the appointment process in the White House, where partisan considerations override other concerns. This centralization is in contrast to an earlier time when cabinet secretaries exercised more control over the selection of their subordinates.[9]

Once a person has been appointed by the president and approved by the Senate, what factors determine his or her performance in office? Numerous variables shape an appointee's performance, including the external environment, the agency's mission, and the individual's personal relationship with the chief executive, to name just a few. Certainly, an important aspect of a political executive's effectiveness is his or her strategy or management style. James Q. Wilson says that strategy is a complex interaction of temperament and circumstances. He identifies four different types of strategies employed by agency leaders. "Advocates" are aggressive in pushing their agency's agenda with the president and Congress. "Decision makers" embrace "the role of leader, the person who probes for problems, gathers data, and acts decisively to solve problems." "Budget cutters" preside over the shrinkage of their agency's budgets. "Negotiators" seek to "reduce stress and uncertainty, enhance organizational health, and cope with a few critical problems" by negotiating with key constituencies in the environment.[10]

Reorganization Another significant power that the president has in controlling the bureaucracy is the authority to reorganize components of the executive branch. Since 1932, the Congress has delegated to the president broad restructuring powers, including creating new agencies and their subunits, and eliminating or merging existing ones, although Congress must review and approve any proposed **governmental reorganization**. The president, however, cannot create or abolish cabinet-level departments—the Congress retains this authority.

Governmental reorganization The restructuring of departments and agencies with the intent to streamline and improve administration.

Reorganization is often proposed by presidents as a way to improve the bureaucracy's efficiency. Far from being a neutral management tool, however, reorganizing the bureaucracy can have important political effects. For example, if an agency is transferred to a department that is hostile to its basic mission, the agency will find it difficult to achieve its objectives. Similar difficulties can also stem from an agency having reduced access to the department head as a consequence of diminished status in the department's organizational hierarchy resulting from reorganization. It is not surprising that in light of all the political implications, Congress requires that any plans to restructure executive agencies be approved by joint resolution of both houses.

Clearly, there are major impediments to large-scale reorganization of the executive branch if the experience of recent presidents is any indication. Since Herbert Hoover, most presidents have tried to use their reorganization authority to manage the bureaucracy more efficiently and make it a more effective instrument of presidential power. Only Harry S. Truman, however, was truly successful in getting Congress to approve a significant proportion of his reorganization requests.

Smaller-scale reorganizations or eliminations of individual agencies occur frequently.[11] However, efforts at broad reorganization of the bureaucracy typically fail, for a number of reasons. One stumbling block is that agencies and programs threatened with restructuring may obtain support from allies in Congress and clientele groups in order to prevent the changes. Congressional committees with jurisdiction over the threatened agency, and interest groups that receive benefits from the agency, may rally together to oppose any attempt to reduce the agency's influence and—by extension their own influence—in the policy process. This is an example of the **iron triangle**, which was briefly discussed in Chapter 1 and will be covered in some detail in Chapter 6. Other reasons for failure include reorganization plans that lack a specific focus and absence of political support stemming from the president's inability to persuasively articulate the benefits of reorganization.

In the final analysis, most presidents simply lack the political will and capital to challenge the entire bureaucracy. One recent exception to this was the creation of the Department of Homeland Security by President George W. Bush, which is discussed below. Reorganizations can make an impact if they significantly alter resource flows, affect organizational rewards such as promotions and salaries, and redefine agency tasks. Rarely, however, do these things happen.[12]

Iron triangle An important theory of interest groups' influence on government, suggesting that interest groups, legislative committees, and agencies work closely together in writing and implementing policies.

Budgeting and Other Administrative Tools An important institution for managing the bureaucracy is the Executive Office of the President (EOP), which was created in 1939 to strengthen the president's management capacity. The EOP owes its existence to the 1937 Brownlow Committee on Administrative Management, which, in its report to President Franklin D. Roosevelt, made the recommendation that "the president needs help." At the time of the report, Roosevelt was trying to run the entire federal government with a personal staff consisting of only a handful of personal secretaries and special assistants. Since then, the EOP has grown from around 600 employees in 1939 to over 1,600 today. It has become, in effect, a "counterbureaucracy," serving as an important means by which the president manages the large federal bureaucracy.[13] Among the key agencies in the EOP are the OMB, the National Security Council, the Council of Economic Advisers, the Office of Policy Development, and the Office of the White House.

Despite the EOP's growth both in size and organizational complexity, the number of career bureaucrats still dwarfs it, which makes executive control of the bureaucracy difficult. As one author points out, however, "The creation of an ever-larger EO has diminishing and eventually negative returns in terms of the ability to control the bureaucracy pursuant to presidential goals."[14] Indeed, what had been designed to help the president coordinate the activities of the executive branch has become itself difficult to control effectively because of its large size and specialized functions. One serious source for concern, for instance, is the White House staff's relations with cabinet members, which at times have been problematic. Department heads, for example, complain of the president's assistants undercutting their authority, having to go through the staff to see the president, or receiving conflicting messages on a policy issue from different members of the president's staff.

Executive budgeting represents another important means of exercising presidential control over the bureaucracy. The Budget and Accounting Act of 1921 gives the president the authority to prepare the annual budget for submission to Congress. In the process of preparing the budget, the OMB carefully reviews agency performance in order to make spending recommendations to the president based on its assessment of program effectiveness (see Chapter 13 for more about executive budgeting).

The Office of the White House and the OMB play the lead roles in helping the president direct the federal bureaucracy. The Office of the White House is another product of the Brownlow Committee, which recommended that the president's personal staff should consist of not more than nine persons—including six new personal secretaries added to the existing congressional liaison and two press officers. Today, the Office of the White House consists of hundreds of employees.

The OMB is an indispensable agency in the president's effort to control the federal bureaucracy. OMB's chief tasks, as noted earlier, are to review the proposed agency expenditures and assess agency performance in order to make spending recommendations to the president. OMB's largest components, therefore, are its budget and management divisions. Budget examiners scrutinize annual agency budget requests and in the process gain specialized knowledge of the agencies and their programs rivaling that of the agency's own personnel. This information about the agencies proves invaluable for managing the executive branch. The budgetary process itself serves as the chief means by which the president establishes the bureaucracy's policy agenda.

Limitations on the Executive's Influence

Perhaps the chief limitation on the president's influence over administrative agencies is that control of the bureaucracy is shared with Congress and the courts. Staffing the bureaucracy, for example, requires congressional approval. As pointed out earlier, the president's power to make appointments is broad but by no means absolute. The president's authority is held in check by the mandate that the Senate must confirm nearly 1,000 appointees to politically sensitive positions within the bureaucracy. In addition, while presidents have the authority to prepare budgets, approving them is still Congress's job. Other areas in which Congress and the president share control over the bureaucracy include agency reorganization, the personnel system, and agency spending. The judiciary also serves as a check on executive power. The courts, for example, can rule on the

Executive order The legally binding orders given by the president to federal agencies.

legality of executive orders. An **executive order** is a legally binding directive from the president to an agency or agencies in the executive branch. These orders do not require congressional approval but they have the same legal effect as a statute.

Even presidential authority to fire political executives is constrained. For instance, there may be political costs associated with firing certain political appointments. If nothing else, the negative media attention can create an embarrassing situation for the president. In one example, President Clinton's first surgeon general, Joycelyn Elders, was forced to resign after she stated that the spread of AIDS could be curbed by teaching children masturbation. Elders actually held onto office long after her actions created political problems for the president. Conservatives attacked Elders soon after she entered office, and she was viewed as a political liability by the news media. The president, however, was reluctant to fire such a high-profile African American in his administration; forcing her out might alienate an important segment of his supporters.

Several limitations on the president's ability to manage the executive branch relate to political appointees' personal characteristics and their performance in office. Recent presidents, as noted earlier, place more emphasis on loyalty and ideological compatibility in making their selections compared to earlier executives. Further, presidents must take a number of other nonmanagement-related considerations into account when choosing political appointees—including rewarding supporters and making appointments that are acceptable to Congress, interest groups, and different elements of their political party.

President Clinton, in his first term, made a highly visible effort to appoint individuals of diverse backgrounds to his administration, and to strike a

Joycelyn Elders (left), nominated by President Bill Clinton to take up the post of surgeon general, testifying at her Senate confirmation hearings in July 1993.

SOURCE: Kort Duce/AFP/ Getty Images

balance—at least in terms of the different factions within the Democratic Party—among the many competing interests. At the beginning of his first term, George W. Bush also made some highly symbolic appointments to his cabinet of minority men and women while at the same time appointing conservatives to key positions in order to shore up support among his party's influential right wing. These personal characteristics, however, do not guarantee effective administrators will be appointed or that the appointees will be able to supervise career bureaucrats.

Co-optation A situation in which presidential appointees promote an agency's position in conflict with the position of the president who appointed them.

Another obstacle to effective presidential oversight of the bureaucracy is the **co-optation** of political executives by their agencies. An appointee who is co-opted by the agency promotes the agency's positions—even those in conflict with the president. The psychological basis for co-optation is that appointees believe that the work they and their agencies perform is valuable to society. Furthermore, because appointees must rely on career administrators in order to achieve their objectives, they may be forced to take the agency's perspective on certain policy issues, in order to appease their subordinates. These positions, however, may not coincide with the president's.

At the state level, executive control over administration is even more fragmented than at the federal level. Not only must governors share influence over administrative agencies with state legislatures and courts, but they must also contend with numerous other elected officials in the executive branch. While the president and the vice president are the only elected officials in the federal executive branch, the states elect more than 450 officials to their executive branches in addition to the fifty governors.[15] The four most commonly elected statewide officials besides governor are lieutenant governor, attorney general, treasurer, and secretary of state. These positions are filled by presidential appointees at the federal level, with the exception of lieutenant governor, which is similar to vice president. Also compounding the governor's management difficulties are the multitude of independent boards and commissions that direct the operations of some agencies in most states.

As state governments took on more programmatic responsibilities, the need for improved administrative performance provided a stimulus for executive branch reorganization. The underlying premise of many of these reforms is that authority centralized in the hands of the governor would increase administrative accountability. Thus, the voters would hold the governor responsible for the bureaucracy's actions (or inaction) and vote accordingly in the next election. In order to effect this change, separately elected officials along with independent boards and commissions would be replaced by agency heads appointed by the governor and therefore directly accountable to him or her. Twenty-six states restructured their executive branch in this manner between 1965 and 1991.[16] Several studies indicate that executive reorganization has been successful in increasing bureaucratic accountability to the governor.[17]

The Legislature and Administration

The legislature's role is as fundamental and crucial as that of the executive's in overseeing the bureaucracy, although administration has been more closely identified with the executive branch. The Congress influences administrative actions through the following mechanisms: (1) enabling legislation, which includes establishing staffing levels, (2) budgetary actions, (3) oversight, and (4) appointee confirmation. All of these functions exist to a large extent at the state level as well.

It is through enabling legislation that the legislature establishes the organizational structure, the personnel policies, the procedural requirements, and the outside access guidelines for agencies, as well as authorizes positions for agencies. See Vignette 4.1 for an example of an authorizing statute that establishes the Defense Nuclear Safety Board, a federal regulatory agency overseeing the design and construction of defense nuclear facilities.

VIGNETTE 4.1 Enabling Legislation for the Defense Nuclear Safety Board

SEC. 311. ESTABLISHMENT. [42 USC 2286]

(a) ESTABLISHMENT. There is hereby established an independent establishment in the executive branch, to be known as the 'Defense Nuclear Facilities Safety Board' (hereafter in this chapter referred to as the 'Board').

SEC. 312. FUNCTIONS OF THE BOARD. [42 USC 2286a]

(a) IN GENERAL. The Board shall perform the following functions:

(1) REVIEW AND EVALUATION OF STANDARDS. The Board shall review and evaluate the content and implementation of the standards relating to the design, construction, operation, and decommissioning of defense nuclear facilities of the Department of Energy (including all applicable Department of Energy orders, regulations, and requirements) at each Department of Energy defense nuclear facility. The Board shall recommend to the Secretary of Energy those specific measures that should be adopted to ensure that public health and safety are adequately protected. The Board shall include in its recommendations necessary changes in the content and implementation of such

standards, as well as matters on which additional data or additional research is needed.

(2) INVESTIGATIONS.
(A) The Board shall investigate any event or practice at a Department of Energy defense nuclear facility which the Board determines has adversely affected, or may adversely affect, public health and safety.

(B) The purpose of any Board investigation under subparagraph (A) shall be:

(i) to determine whether the Secretary of Energy is adequately implementing the standards described in paragraph (1) of the Department of Energy (including all applicable Department of Energy orders, regulations, and requirements) at the facility;

(ii) to ascertain information concerning the circumstances of such event or practice and its implications for such standards;

(iii) to determine whether such event or practice is related to other events or practices at other Department of Energy defense nuclear facilities; and (iv) to provide to the Secretary of Energy such recommendations for changes in such standards or the implementation of

(continued on next page)

VIGNETTE 4.1   Enabling Legislation for the Defense Nuclear Safety Board *(continued)*

such standards (including Department of Energy orders, regulations, and requirements) and such recommendations relating to data or research needs as may be prudent or necessary.

(3) ANALYSIS OF DESIGN AND OPERATIONAL DATA. The Board shall have access to and may systematically analyze design and operational data, including safety analysis reports, from any Department of Energy defense nuclear facility.

(4) REVIEW OF FACILITY DESIGN AND CONSTRUCTION. The Board shall review the design of a new Department of Energy defense nuclear facility before construction of such facility begins and shall recommend to the Secretary, within a reasonable time, such modifications of the design as the Board considers necessary to ensure adequate protection of public health and safety. During the construction of any such facility, the Board shall periodically review and monitor the construction and shall submit to the Secretary, within a reasonable time, such recommendations relating to the construction of that facility as the Board considers necessary to ensure adequate

protection of public health and safety. An action of the Board, or a failure to act, under this paragraph may not delay or prevent the Secretary of Energy from carrying out the construction of such a facility.

(5) RECOMMENDATIONS. The Board shall make such recommendations to the Secretary of Energy with respect to Department of Energy defense nuclear facilities, including operations of such facilities, standards, and research needs, as the Board determines are necessary to ensure adequate protection of public health and safety. In making its recommendations the Board shall consider the technical and economic feasibility of implementing the recommended measures.

(b) EXCLUDED FUNCTIONS. The functions of the Board under this chapter do not include functions relating to the safety of atomic weapons. However, the Board shall have access to any information on atomic weapons that is within the Department of Energy and is necessary to carry out the functions of the Board.

SOURCE: Defense Nuclear Safety Board, Enabling Legislation (42 U.S. Code 2286), http://www.deprep.org/dnfsb/legislat.asp.

Oversight Powers

As pointed out earlier, Congress delegates broad authority to administrative agencies through its statutes. With this delegation, however, comes the need for legislative oversight of administrative actions. While the Constitution makes the president responsible for the faithful execution of the law, it holds Congress primarily responsible for ensuring that the president carries out this obligation. **Legislative oversight** thus serves an important function in achieving administrative accountability.

Legislative oversight The legal power that allows the legislature to monitor agencies in order to achieve accountability.

In its simplest terms, oversight refers to information-gathering on agency activities in order to ensure bureaucratic compliance with the law and with congressional preferences regarding the law. In practical terms, however, oversight could legitimately encompass most of the work that Congress performs, as the list below indicates. Students of Congress have identified the following seven purposes of oversight:[18]

1. Assure that the intent of Congress is being followed.

2. Uncover agency fraud, waste, and abuse.

3. Gather information on agency activities.

4. Assess agency performance.

5. Defend congressional prerogatives from presidential encroachment.

6. Provide a public forum for members of Congress.

7. Repeal unpopular agency decisions.

Oversight, therefore, embraces a wide range of Congressional activities—from helping constituents navigate their way through the bureaucracy to conducting exhaustive investigations of agencies covering every aspect of their operations. Casework, which involves helping constituents in their interactions with agencies, occupies a large proportion of Congressional staff members' time. Legislators view the heavy investment of staff time as a political necessity that pays dividends at election time. It is because of its potential for electoral benefits that legislators actively seek out casework from their constituents.[19] Moreover, casework can bring to light more systemic problems in agencies that require more thorough congressional committee investigation.

Oversight involving larger programmatic or policy issues is conducted by congressional committees assigned on the basis of whether an agency's spending activities or program implementation is being reviewed. The appropriations committees, for example, oversee the budgetary aspects of agencies, while the authorization committees oversee the implementation aspects. The authorization committees' tendency, however, is to focus principally on passing new laws. Therefore they make fewer resources available for overseeing the effectiveness of existing laws. The appropriations committees, moreover, have the power, staff, and expertise to conduct more thorough investigations. However, they are hindered by their voluminous workload, the time pressures of the budgetary process, and their primary focus on agency financial resources and budget changes from year to year.[20]

Oversight occurs most visibly in the public hearings process on Capitol Hill. Congressional committees conduct these hearings in which committee members can question administrators, lobbyists, and outside experts about agency operations and program effectiveness. Congress has the legal power to obtain testimony and other forms of relevant evidence from agencies as part of their agency investigations.

It would be incorrect to suggest that oversight is a formal process that occurs only in public hearings conducted by congressional committees or in casework on behalf of constituents. A great deal of oversight takes place during private interactions between members of Congress, their staffs, and administrators. These more informal contacts between Congress and the bureaucracy have the advantage of being "off the record," which allows both the administrator and member of Congress to avoid any unwelcome publicity. It also reduces Congress's reliance on costly and time-consuming formal reports and hearings.

Foreign leaders often appear before the U.S. Congress. Here former Italian Prime Minister Silvio Berlusconi addresses a joint session of Congress.
SOURCE: Mark Wilson/ Getty Images

Despite the institutional mechanisms in place for oversight and the constitutional requirement to oversee the executive branch's activities, many students of Congress would agree with the observation that "when oversight occurs, it is more likely to be unsystematic, sporadic, episodic, erratic, haphazard, ad hoc, and on crisis basis."[21] There are many reasons for this situation, including the bureaucracy's size, its wide range of activities, lack of congressional expertise, administrative resistance, and opposition from the president and interest groups.

It is clear from the previous discussion that while Congress takes its oversight duty seriously; there are some real obstacles to oversight being the chief legislative means to control the bureaucracy. Legislators tend to view oversight as a time-consuming and relatively thankless—although necessary—process that offers them fewer tangible rewards than passing new laws. However, the growth of bureaucracy has led to an increase in Congress's monitoring of administrative activities. This has been reflected in a marked increase in congressional monitoring activity indicators. Studies show that Congress holds more oversight hearings than before, congressional committees devote more time to oversight, and the number of staff members who are permanently assigned to committees and subcommittees has grown since 1961.[22]

Congress has also strengthened and enlarged its own administrative agencies, the Government Accountability Office (GAO, formerly the General Accounting Office), the Congressional Budget Office (CBO), and the Congressional Research Service, to help with its oversight activities. The GAO, in

Performance audit A type of evaluation assessing the effects of agency programs and not just the financial activities of agencies as in a financial audit.

particular, has expanded its oversight responsibilities over the last forty years. Since the 1960s, the GAO has broadened the scope of its activities to include a **performance audit** of agencies to assess the effects of agency programs. The GAO has also helped to strengthen the internal financial control systems of agencies in order to free itself of the burden of auditing agency transactions, which allows the GAO to focus more of its efforts on program evaluation.[23]

Legislative micromanagement The perceived tendency for legislators to "meddle" in the day-to-day operations of agencies.

Legislative oversight sometimes steps over the line and becomes **legislative micromanagement,** which refers to perceived excessive meddling by legislators in an agency's operations. Of course, not everyone believes that close legislative scrutiny of an agency constitutes meddling. Nonetheless, legislatures are criticized for engaging in this activity, especially the U.S. Congress. Congress micromanages, according to the political scientist, James Q. Wilson, in order to transform bureaucratic decisions into policy choices. In contrast to the past, however, when micromanaging occurred to exact benefits for certain groups, it is far more likely today to take "the form of devising elaborate, detailed rules." These rules are used to allocate jobs, contracts, projects and other benefits that were once distributed on an informal, case by case basis. The beneficiaries of these rules tend to be national interest groups.[24]

Legislative Veto

Legislative veto A procedure which allows the legislature to stop an executive action that it disagrees with; most courts have ruled this to be a violation of separation of powers.

Perhaps the most controversial means to influence the activities of the executive branch is the **legislative veto,** which gives the legislature the power to prevent an administrative action that it disagrees with. With the expansion of the modern presidency, Congress sought additional authority to serve as a more effective check on the powers of the executive branch. Congress, for example, enacted various forms of the legislative veto during the 1970s—such as the War Powers Resolution Act of 1973 and the Impoundment Control Act of 1974—mostly in response to actions taken by the Nixon Administration.

The Supreme Court in the *Immigration and Naturalization Service v. Chadha* decision (1983) invalidated one form of the legislative veto because it violated the Constitution's separation of powers clause. Section 244 (c) (2) of the Immigration and Naturalization Act allowed either chamber of the Congress, by resolution, to overturn an executive branch decision. The Court struck down this provision while leaving the remainder of the act intact. But it did not eliminate all forms of the legislative veto. After the Court's decision, Congress continued to pass other forms. But these usually require agencies to submit proposed actions to a period of review, usually thirty or sixty days, before they take can effect.

The device has simply proved too valuable for either the Congress or administrative agencies to relinquish completely, despite its problematic constitutional aspects. The legislative veto gives administrators flexibility while allowing Congress to raise objections to proposed executive branch decisions before they are implemented. Agencies usually attempt to eliminate those aspects that arouse the most congressional ire.

Limitations on the Legislature's Control

Agencies are selective in their search for supporters in the legislature. Bureaucrats cultivate key committee members with the idea to win the legislators over to a positive viewpoint regarding the agency's work. In this manner, the agency hopes to persuade significant committee members to help promote the agency's position in Congress.[25] In reciprocity, agencies assist legislators by providing valuable services to their constituents. For example, these range from the Social Security Administration helping a legislator's elderly constituent obtain her retirement benefits to the Department of Defense helping a member of Congress retain a military base in her district.

Although Congress has several important bureaucratic controls available, it can never act unilaterally to influence the bureaucracy. Congressional authority is checked by the requirement to obtain presidential approval and the agreement of both houses before proposed actions can take effect.[26] The decentralization of authority in Congress also makes it difficult to control administration. Authority is diffused among many committees, subcommittees, and the leadership of both houses. For example, several committees and subcommittees typically oversee the operations of a single agency. This allows the agencies to often play one committee off the other.

In addition to these institutional obstacles, students of Congress contend that legislators show a marked indifference to the task of monitoring administrators. A common feeling among members is that they are lawmakers and not baby-sitters for the bureaucracy, as necessary as that might be on occasion. Legislators, too, find that reviewing the agencies can be an onerous task, especially if this entails tackling subject areas that are too technical or dull from a member's perspective.

The main reason for the legislators' disinterest, however, is that monitoring the bureaucracy is a distraction from their primary objective of reelection. Achieving greater name recognition helps an incumbent's chances for reelection more than overseeing the activities of agencies. The payoff from mastering administrative details is therefore low compared with getting one's name attached to a piece of legislation or by taking a highly publicized position on some issue.

The above discussion underscores a number of critical differences between administrative values and political values as embodied by legislators. As noted earlier, the politics–administration dichotomy represents a woefully inadequate view of how government operates today. Administration requires expertise in every area affected by government, from law to medicine and much more. Legislators are generalists who must of necessity defer to experts when designing public policies. They must also rely on these same and other specialists to implement the policies once they have been enacted into law.

Legislators face another predicament that leads them to delegate decision-making authority to administrators: they can neither foresee every future possible detail related to the implementation of policies, nor can they know in advance the conditions affecting that implementation. Further, politicians frequently take vague positions on controversial issues in order to avoid the loss of support from important constituents. All of this translates into laws that are written without clear guidelines or standards for administrators. Lawmakers must therefore rely on administrators to fill in the details of the policy. In recognition of this, Congress provides authority for agencies to make rules or regulations. When Congress passed the Clean Air Act, for example, it lacked the technical expertise to set the standards for levels of harmful chemicals in the air. The Environmental Protection Agency decided what those levels are. As a result of the elected officials' dependence on administrative expertise and Congress's delegation of wide discretion, bureaucrats, in effect, become policy-makers. This delegation of law-making to the executive branch is known as **rule-making**.

Rule-making The process by which agencies create regulations that have the force of law; through rule-making, legislative authority is delegated to agencies.

The basis of bureaucracy's rule-making powers is the Administrative Procedures Act of 1946 (APA). In this act, a rule is defined as "the whole or part of agency statement of general or particular applicability and future effect designed to implement, interpret or prescribe law or policy." It is important to point out that rules are the byproducts of legislation.[27] The APA promotes greater accountability in administrative agencies by regulating the actions of federal bureaucrats and providing more public access to the administrative process. For example, administrative rules are published in the **Federal Register** before they are implemented by agencies so that interested parties can make comments on rules affecting their interests. In addition, the APA stipulates that agency actions are subject to court oversight.

Federal Register The public record that contains notices of federal agency rules and presidential documents, published daily.

The Judiciary and Administration

In addition to the executive and the legislature, the courts are also heavily involved in influencing administrative activities. Judicial review of the actions of the executive branch goes back to *Marbury v. Madison* (1803). Beginning in the 1960s, however, the courts expanded the scope of their review to include the full range of agency decisions and activities, going so far in some cases as to question bureaucrats' judgments in the areas of their expertise. **Judicial activism**—as this expansion of the courts' scope is called—has been criticized as being undemocratic, a violation of the separation of powers, and leading to poor decisions that fail to have the desired effect on administration.[28] Nonetheless, the judiciary has not shown any indication of returning to the pre-1960s situation when the courts did not seriously challenge administrative decisions—nor would current American society accept a bureaucracy unchecked in its power over citizens.

Judicial activism The expansion of the courts' scope used to review the full range of agency decisions and activities.

The courts have been especially concerned with the effects of the bureaucracy on individuals' constitutional rights. During the New Deal, the judiciary tended to ignore the blurring of executive, legislative, and judicial functions that occurred in administrative agencies.[29] During the early years of the Cold War, however, when some federal workers lost their jobs due to spurious claims of disloyalty and communist association, the courts began scrutinizing bureaucratic decisions for violations of constitutional rights. The net result of this heightened concern on the part of the judiciary has been increased legal protections for citizens in their dealings with the bureaucracy—either as employees or recipients of government benefits. Before the courts strengthened individual rights, the constitutional doctrine of privilege usually applied. This doctrine essentially held that government employment and benefits were privileges that could be withheld from citizens on virtually any grounds. As a result of several court rulings, however, government agencies must now follow due process procedures before they take any action that may harm a person.

The judiciary's willingness to challenge bureaucratic decisions has led to an increase in the number of people bringing court cases against administrators, and in a few extreme cases, courts have actually taken control of an administrative agency. Courts have mandated a wide range of reforms in areas such as state prisons, public schools, and facilities for the mentally ill and the mentally retarded.[30]

Another significant development in judicial control of the bureaucracy since the 1960s has been the emergence of the private attorney general role. **Private attorneys general** are individuals and organizations that sue the government on behalf of the public interest—for example, in the interest of consumers, the environment, or minorities. Private attorneys general sue the government in order to require it to take some action or to prevent it from taking some action. Groups ranging from the American Civil Liberties Union to law students at a university have assumed the role of private attorneys general in past lawsuits. In one case, a federal court allowed law students at George Washington University to sue the ICC over raising freight rates, which would, they argued, increase the shipping costs of recyclable goods and thereby contribute to environmental pollution.[31]

As a result of court decisions, contemporary public administrators no longer enjoy absolute immunity and may be sued for damages. The doctrine of **sovereign immunity** is based on the premise that the state's interest supersedes any single individual's interest, even if an individual's constitutional rights are involved. This concept was eventually extended to include government employees. Thus, before the 1970s, courts gave public employees absolute immunity in carrying out their official duties. This meant that a person whose constitutional rights were violated by a public employee could not sue that employee. During the 1970s, however, the Supreme Court ruled that public administrators would be liable if they knew, or should have known, that they were violating an individual's constitutional rights. Today, government officials have limited, or qualified, immunity. Abolishing absolute immunity, the Court argued, would act as a deterrent against future administrative abuse.

Private attorneys general Individuals and organizations who sue the government on behalf of the public interest (e.g., in the interest of government benefits recipients, minorities, consumers).

Sovereign immunity The idea that the government and its representatives will not be held liable for damages occurring from their decisions.

The Eleventh Amendment to the Constitution protects state government officials from liability for damages in federal courts, although it does not protect local officials. State and local officials, however, can be held personally liable for damages in federal courts under the section 1983 provision of the Civil Rights Act of 1871, which allows damages if a person was denied a constitutional right.

Judicial influence on the bureaucracy has been significant. Its net result has been to impose additional constraints on public administrators. In their relations with administrative agencies, the courts have strengthened the constitutional rights of citizens. The Constitution, however, is subject to constant reinterpretation by the courts. What is true today may not be tomorrow in the realm of constitutional law. In light of this, is it reasonable to expect that public administrators should be constitutional law experts in addition to everything else they must master in order to perform their jobs well? Whether or not this is desirable, the increased importance of the judiciary requires administrators who are aware of the legal ramifications of their actions.

Reinventing Government

National Performance Review An initiative of the Clinton administration to reform the executive branch along the principles of reinventing government.

The reinvention of government movement originated at the state and local level in the 1980s and was brought to the federal government in the form of the **National Performance Review(NPR)** by President Bill Clinton in 1993. Although "reinventing government" is a term of recent coinage, some of its principles bear a resemblance to those of previous administrative reform efforts dating back to the Progressive movement. As a result of the NPR, "No movement associated with the administrative aspects of modern American government has had the visibility of reinventing government."[32] The reinventing government movement is just one of several modern attempts by presidents to tame the bureaucracy. In order to understand the importance of the NPR, we need to examine these earlier efforts at reforming administration.

The History of Administrative Reform

The historical forces that helped shape the NPR include the various commissions and committees that were the chief reform mechanisms of the federal bureaucracy during the twentieth century. The Brownlow Committee, named after its chair, Louis Brownlow, was the first attempt to significantly alter the structure of the executive branch using an explicitly managerial approach. The goal was making democracy work by giving the government "thoroughly modern tools of management."[33] Thus the NPR can trace its reform lineage back to the pioneering efforts of the Brownlow Committee.

Between the Brownlow Committee and the NPR, there were several notable attempts to improve and streamline the bureaucracy. The first and perhaps the most important of these was the Commission on Organization of the

Executive Branch, better known as the first Hoover Commission (1947–1949), for its chair, former President Herbert Hoover. The Hoover Commission was a response to the administrative growth resulting from World War II. President Harry S. Truman charged the commission with the task of developing recommendations that would enhance the president's ability to manage the executive branch. Like the Brownlow Committee, the Hoover Commission recommended the strengthening of the executive. Many of the commission's major recommendations were implemented as part of the Reorganization Act of 1949.

The great success of the first Hoover Commission led to a second Hoover Commission in 1953–1955. It sought to improve administrative efficiency and to eliminate federal functions and activities that were in competition with private firms. However, the second commission's recommendations received little support in Congress, and therefore none were enacted into law.

The next large-scale effort at restructuring the federal bureaucracy came during the Nixon administration. President Nixon sought to reorganize the executive after the unprecedented growth of the administration that resulted from President Johnson's Great Society programs. To that end, Nixon proposed transformation of the budget office into a more management-oriented agency, formation of a Domestic Policy Council, and creation of four superdepartments that would oversee the bulk of the president's domestic agenda. In the end, he only accomplished the reorganization of OMB and the establishment of the Domestic Policy Council. Any attempt to concentrate more authority in the Nixon White House was doomed to failure after the Watergate scandal in 1973.

The pattern in these four attempts to reorganize the bureaucracy was an effort to centralize more authority in the president. From Roosevelt to Nixon, the chief solution to the problem of more effective executive control was to be found in hierarchy and greater integration of the bureaucracy. The next effort, during the Reagan administration, was the President's Private Sector Survey on Cost Control, better known as the Grace Commission, for its chair, J. Peter Grace. The Grace Commission took a somewhat different approach but one that was still very conventional in its basic orientation and emphasis. The commission tried to apply private sector managerial practices to government operations. This approach borrowed a page from traditional public administration in its belief in the interchangeability of private and public administration. However, both the GAO and the Congressional Budget Office criticized the Grace Commission's findings, which weakened its credibility with Congress. Consequently, the Grace Commission achieved nothing of substance.

The National Performance Review

In 1992, David Osborne and Ted Gaebler's book *Reinventing Government: How the Entrepreneurial Spirit Is Transforming the Public Sector* heralded a new approach to government, one that was intended to sweep away lumbering bureaucracy.[34] The book is filled with stories that show public agencies at all levels of government successfully coping with declining revenues resulting from the tax revolt movement and the Reagan budget cuts. The main principles of reinventing government can be summarized as follows:[35]

- Steering rather than rowing, i.e., separating policy-making from service delivery.
- Empowering citizens, i.e., taking control out of the hands of the bureaucracy and giving it to communities.
- Substituting the market for bureaucracy, i.e., taking advantage of market forces to produce greater efficiency in service delivery.
- Mission-driven government, i.e., eliminating rules and red tape to free employees to pursue the agency's mission.
- Earning rather than spending, i.e., turning government employees into entrepreneurs instead of bureaucrats.
- Preventing rather than curing, i.e., avoiding problems before they arise.
- Replacing the hierarchy with participatory structures, i.e., decentralizing government to encourage participation, innovation, flexibility, and productivity.

President Clinton picked up on the promise of reinventing government first as governor of Arkansas and later as president. He launched the NPR initiative in March 1993, giving it a high profile by appointing Vice President Al Gore as its head. When the group's report was completed in 1994, President Clinton noted: "Here's the most important reason why this report is different from earlier ones on government reform. When Herbert Hoover finished the Hoover Commission, he went back to Stanford. When Peter Grace finished the Grace Commission, he went back to New York City. But when the Vice President finished his report he had to go back to his office—20 feet from mine—and go back to working to turn the recommendations into reality."[36]

The chief mission of the NPR was to completely overhaul the organization of the federal government. According to the NPR's mission statement the major goals were to

> reinvent the systems of government, redesign agencies and programs to make them more responsive to their customers, and streamline the government. The system reinvention work will result in a framework for the development and delivery of cost effective policies and programs by the federal government. The framework will clarify managers' accountability for achieving results, create a focus on clearly identifying and serving the customer, and provide managers the tools and incentives to focus on results.[37]

The root of the problem, according to the NPR, was that the federal bureaucracy was designed for an environment that no longer exists, and consequently

TABLE 4.2 Contradictory Recommendations of the Reinvention Movement

Recommendation	Conflicting Recommendation
Encourage competition both within government and with the private sector	Avoid duplication
Prefer using private firms to deliver services	Governmental profit-making; government should act like a private firm
Decentralize authority to workers	Rational decision-making, which relies on centralized authority
Encourage innovation and "entrepreneurial government" by rewarding workers	Pay only for results; there should be "real consequences for failures"

Source: Adapted from Daniel Williams, "Reinventing the proverbs of Government," table 1.

its operations were unnecessarily cumbersome and costly. President Clinton declared that the NPR would result in a savings of $108 billion by the end of the 1990s.[38]

Results of Reinventing Government

From the beginning, the NPR and reinventing government have been criticized on both theoretical and practical grounds. Critics charge that the NPR was fundamentally flawed because it failed to recognize the major differences between the private and public sectors, it unfairly criticized administrators, and it provided conflicting advice without offering clear guidance as to when to choose which alternative.[39] Several examples of this contradictory advice are shown in Table 4.2.

At the end of the day, what did the federal reinvention efforts actually accomplish? The NPR sought to deregulate and decentralize the government's operations. It sought to empower federal bureaucrats, often at the expense of congressional oversight. At the same time, however, it attempted to strengthen the president's capacity for leadership within the executive. The NPR's objectives can be broken down into first-order and second-order categories.[40] The first-order objectives included making the bureaucracy smaller, reducing administrative costs, and reorganizing the federal personnel, purchasing, and budgetary systems. The second-order objectives included decentralizing agency authority, empowering frontline employees, and transforming the bureaucratic culture into an entrepreneurial one. Writing at the end of the Clinton administration, one observer noted: "The downsizing and cost reduction objectives have been substantially achieved. The partnership initiative appears to have met with some success, but there is no evidence of any significant, systematic improvement in quality of service or culture."[41]

Even though the NPR is no longer, there are still reinvention efforts occurring at the state level. For one example, see Vignette 4.2.

VIGNETTE 4.2   Reinventing Alabama State Government

Reinventing government may have ceased in Washington, D.C., but in some states, at least, the movement is still alive and well. When Don Siegelman was elected governor of Alabama in 2000, he set about trying to transform Alabama from the "make me" state to the "catch me" state. The "make me" label refers to the fact that "Federal judges are making the state do so many different things that the federal courts might as well be recognized as a de facto branch of state government." Governor Siegelman hopes that his administration will usher in a new era in the state in which education, social services, and quality of life will be improved enough to entice businesses and affluent families to move to the state while retaining those it has already.

Siegelman's effort to reinvent Alabama state government is focusing on performance measurement, one of Gaebler and Osborne's reinvention strategies. Upon taking office, Siegelman implemented performance-based budgeting in the state. He hoped to boost the state's revenues, low relative to the rest of the nation, to the point where state government can begin to provide decent services. Taxes in the state are kept low for the two biggest industries, farming and

timber, while the rest of the state shoulders the bulk of the burden of paying for government. Siegelman is gambling on performance measures providing the hard evidence to persuade skeptical Alabama taxpayers that the state government is producing what it promised, so that they will support spending what it takes to improve the state.

The reinvention movement's chief opponent, other than the farming and timber interests, is the state senate. The senators are reluctant to change a system that has benefited them throughout the state's history, "A significant part of the way business has been done over the years involves the time-honored tradition of directing a little money from Montgomery back to the senator's home districts." In this example, as earlier, the shift in power that would result from reforming government mobilizes the enemies of change to try to prevent it from occurring. Despite this opposition, a majority of business and good government groups have come out in favor of the plan. It remains to be seen whether the state will continue to do things the nineteenth-century way or catch up to the twenty-first century.

SOURCE: From Johnathan Walters, "Raising Alabama," *Governing*, October 2000, 28.

Civil Society and Governmental Reform

Public administration must be a "key actor" in any attempt to reinvigorate civil society "because of the complexity of providing public services in contemporary society."[42] Given public administration's central role, efforts to reinvent government that substantially affect the bureaucracy will have important effects on civil society. While critics maintain that certain aspects of reinvention have a detrimental effect, reinvention proponents argue that the reforms will have an overall positive impact on civil society.

Empowering citizens and participatory government, for example, have the potential to strengthen civil society. Osborne and Gaebler contend that government should create opportunities and reduce obstacles for maximum citizen participation. Reinvention, in their opinion, can help create "community-owned government," which would pull "ownership out of the bureaucracy, into the community" where it belongs.[43] Empowerment requires that citizens become proactive and that the bureaucracy should stop treating them like dependent clients. Instead, they argue, public agencies should help citizens understand their problems and cooperate in solving them. In other words, there should be collaboration between service deliverers and service recipients based on the "human necessity to act rather than to be acted upon; to be citizen rather than client."[44] As examples of collaboration between public administrators and citizens, Osborne and Gaebler cite programs such as community policing and recycling initiatives as well as programs fostering citizen involvement in public schools and public housing.[45]

There are some who take a less optimistic view of reinvention's effect on civil society. For them, reinvention's emphasis on making the bureaucracy perform more like a business contains cause for concern. They take issue, for example, with the "customer first" principle as applied to the public sector. Rather than customers, these critics say that individuals should be viewed as citizen owners of public agencies, since "only when citizens are viewed as owners is the assumption made that they will try to fix the business rather than abandon it."[46] This position is grounded in the notion of "exit" as a means of keeping public organizations accountable to the people. In other words, giving people the option of exiting an underachieving public agency can provide an impetus for the agency to improve its service.[47]

However, treating people as customers who can simply walk away from an agency if the service displeases them is inferior compared to creating opportunities for citizens to use their voice instead: "Voice is the key mechanism for those who seek to claim ownership of public agencies. A reform of public administration based on enhancing voice rather than exit could build the citizen base of American democracy."[48] The larger issue, in the minds of other critics, is that using a business model, while promoting efficiency, actually undermines "democratic governance" and "democratic consensus."[49]

Reinventing government has provoked a healthy debate in public administration circles regarding its possible effects on civil society, as the above discussion shows. One important contribution to the discussion reconciles reinvention's management- and efficiency-oriented principles with ideas that would bolster civil society.[50] Denhardt and Denhardt offer the following suggestions for administrative reform, which they believe will also help strengthen civil society:

1. *Serve, rather than steer.* Instead of trying to direct society, public service agencies should be helping citizens "to articulate and meet their shared interests."

2. *The public interest is the aim, not the by-product.* Through the sharing of interests and responsibilities, public administrators and citizens must build a collaborative understanding of the public interest.

3. *Think strategically, act democratically.* The public interest can best be achieved through collaborative endeavors that join citizens and administrators together and move them in the desired direction.

4. *Serve citizens, not customers.* The public interest should not be thought of as an "aggregation of individual self-interests." Rather, the focus should be on the forging of trust relationships with the community.

5. *Accountability isn't simple.* Instead of merely a market orientation, administrators should also be accountable to laws, community values, and citizen concerns.

6. *Value citizenship and public service before entrepreneurship.* Serving the public should be the primary focus; running public agencies like a business should be secondary.

Clearly, any serious reform of public administration will entail either positive or negative effects on governance, which in turn will produce impacts on civil society. Reformers must be cognizant of these intended and unintended consequences.

■ Chapter Summary

Different mechanisms to control the bureaucracy have emerged within each branch of government. Some have constitutional origins, such as the requirement that the Senate approve presidential nominees. Many others have evolved as a result of each branch's efforts to rein in the administrative state. No single branch, however, has absolute control or exerts significantly greater influence over administration than the other branches. Indeed, limitations exist on each branch's ability to affect bureaucratic operations. The chief constraint—imposed by the Constitution—is that the president, Congress, and the judiciary share control of the bureaucracy. Entities external to the government, such as interest groups, also try to influence public policy through their dealings with the bureaucracy.

In the 1990s, the reinventing government movement attempted to make government operate more efficiently and to transform the bureaucracy into a more businesslike organization. In doing this, the advocates of reinvention were hearkening back to earlier efforts at reforming the civil service, such as those of Woodrow Wilson and the Progressives. Wilson's plea to take politics out of administration and to run government like a private business found an echo in the reinventing government movement more than a hundred years later. The results, now as then, have been decidedly mixed; some goals were achieved while others were not.

■ Chapter Discussion Questions

1. The Brownlow Committee was created in order to make recommendations for reforming the executive branch to better cope with the Great Depression. How might a new Brownlow-type committee view the president's major powers with respect to the bureaucracy in light of current threats and opportunities?

2. In your opinion, which branch of government has more influence over the bureaucracy? Why?

3. Some critics have complained that power over the bureaucracy is too diffuse. What are the pros and cons of centralization in the context of administration?

4. Some complaints have been raised about the legislature micromanaging the bureaucracy. Legislators argue that this scrutiny is a necessary consequence of increasing oversight and casework demand. Which side is right? Why?

5. Reformers often focus their efforts on making governments perform more efficiently. But scholars and others point out that government seeks to serve more varied ends than just efficiency. Can these two positions be reconciled? For example, can governments provide services more efficiently and more equitably at the same time? Explain.

BRIEF CASE   OVERSEEING THE BUREAUCRACY

The following case study is adapted from "The Committee Chair, The Assistant Secretary, and Bureau Chief" case study available on the Electronic Hallway (www.hallway.org). The original case study was written by Richard F. Elmore based on the transcripts of a congressional hearing.

The setting is a state legislative hearing. The Assistant Director is a political appointee of the governor responsible for the budget of the state's social service department. The Division Chief is a career bureaucrat in charge of a division within the department, whose responsibilities include managing the Youth Services Program. The Committee Chair is a critic of the administration from the opposite party who has chaired the committee with jurisdiction over the department for several years. The Ranking Minority Member is of the same political party as the Assistant Director.

Committee Chair: As you know, Mr. Assistant Director, I am concerned about your department's spending priorities. I am referring to recent attempts by the Administration to reduce funding for programs that help disadvantaged youth in our state. In particular, I want to make a matter of public record my alarm over possibly cutting the Youth Services Program. It is my understanding, Mr. Assistant Director, that your department is finalizing next fiscal year's budget submission, is that correct?

Assistant Director: Yes, Madame Chair, we're finalizing our department's budget requests for submission to the Governor. We're evaluating the budget requests from the various programs for their compliance with the Governor's policies. Once they have been evaluated, the Director submits them to the Office of Budgeting and Planning for its approval.

Committee Chair: Is it true that you are planning deep spending cuts in the Youth Services Program? You will recall that last year, your department acting under orders of the Governor wanted to reduce the funding for the program by 30 to 35 percent. I fought to keep the program's budget from being slashed by that amount, which I believe would be catastrophic for the youth of this state. Is your department contemplating a similar request this year?

Assistant Director: We are in the process of finalizing our budget figures. Therefore, I could not give you a definitive answer.

Committee Chair: Mr. [Division Chief], could you tell the committee what is the Youth Services budget request for next fiscal year?

Division Chief: Unfortunately, Madame Chair, that request is an internal matter. As the Assistant Director pointed out, we are still in the process of finalizing our requests. The figures are subject to change until the Governor signs off on them.

Committee Chair: I'm sure that you could give me those budget request figures but your unresponsiveness comes as no surprise. I am not surprised by the Administration's reluctance in this matter since it has failed to cooperate on numerous occasions with this committee.

Your department, in last year's budget, made the case for huge budget cuts in the Youth Services Program because—and I quote from the budget narrative—"the program can be safely cut because much of the need for these services has been met by other programs within the department. The Youth Services Program is superfluous because there are other programs that address the needs of our state's youth."

I ask you, Mr. Assistant Director, do *you* think this program is superfluous?

Assistant Director: There are some services that it provides that overlap with other divisions and programs in the department.

Committee Chair: Mr. [Division Director] could you tell the committee whether you agree with the Assistant Director that the Youth Services Program is largely superfluous? Could you tell us which programs provide the same or similar types of services?

Division Chief: I fully agree with the Assistant Director. I cannot tell you at this moment which programs it overlaps with.

Committee Chair: When this issue arose last year, you might recall, this committee sought testimony from outside experts. The consensus among the experts was that the program provides needed services which no other program within the department provides. I then requested in a letter to the Director that he provide examples of the areas where there was significant overlap with other programs. In response, he merely restated the Administration's position and failed to produce any examples.

Can you, here today, provide any examples of how the program is superfluous, Mr. Assistant Director?

Assistant Director: I am not prepared to answer that question now, Madame Chair. However, I do not think there have been any developments in the last year to modify the accuracy of that statement.

Committee Chair: Could you, Mr. [Division Chief], tell the committee whether you share the Assistant Director's assessment of your program?

Division Chief: We are concerned about eliminating instances of significant redundancy in service delivery within the Department, Madame Secretary.

Committee Chair: I will take your answer as agreeing with the Assistant Director's.

Division Chief: Yes.

Committee Chair: I want to make sure I have it straight then. Do you want to tell the committee, Mr. [Division Chief], why you are reluctant to stand up to the Administration's efforts to slash the program's budget, even though experts in your area all agree that it is providing services that no other program provides?

I reiterate my question. Mr. [Division Chief], why do you support the Administration's decision to cut Youth Services' budget even though there is considerable evidence indicating that the program is meeting the needs of the state's youth in ways that other programs do not?

Division Chief: The state faces some difficult budget choices, as I am sure you know Madam Chair. Other worthwhile programs are experiencing similar or even deeper budget cuts. It is a matter of department priorities. At some point, as the overall budgetary situation improves, we expect to revisit those priorities. I think that current resources can best be expended in areas without the overlap with other programs.

Committee Chair: It appears, as I said here under similar circumstances last year, that the administration is willing to balance the budget at the expense of disadvantaged youth. I do not think there is any evidence your department can produce to contradict the findings of the experts. All indications are that the Administration is not interested and never has been interested in a program that perhaps more than any other helps those people in the state who are most in need of assistance.

Ranking Minority Member: With all due respect, Madame Chair, we are wasting time in committee debating an issue over which we have no jurisdiction. Until a budget request has been formally submitted to the legislature by the governor, this committee cannot require a department to divulge its requests. I suggest we move to another topic.

Committee Chair: I grant you that the department does not have to answer my question. I want to make a larger point though, which is that I feel that the Administration has stubbornly refused to make public its reasons for opposing the Youth Services program despite numerous requests from this committee to do so. I feel compelled, therefore, to ask the committee to draft a letter to the Director requesting that a study be done evaluating the effectiveness of Youth Services. I would like the study to address the issue of service redundancy, in particular. I believe I can gain the support of the committee and of the full House for this proposal.

Brief Case Questions

1. *What type of legislative oversight does the case study exemplify? Do you think the legislature is guilty of micromanaging in this case? Why, or why not?*

2. *In your opinion, how well do the public officials handle themselves in the case? Explain.*

3. *As Bureau Chief, how would you handle the Committee Chair's request?*

■ Key Terms

co-optation (page 83)
executive order (page 82)
Federal Register (page 90)
governmental reorganization (page 80)
iron triangle (page 80)
judicial activism (page 91)
legislative oversight (page 86)

legislative micromanagement (page 88)
legislative veto (page 89)
National Performance Review (page 92)
performance audit (page 88)
private attorney general (page 91)
rule-making (page 90)
sovereign immunity (page 92)

■ On the Web

http://www.firstgov.gov/
The federal government's official web portal.

http://www.gpoaccess.gov/fr/index.html
Access to the Federal Register online.

http://www.defenselink.mil/
The Department of Defense's official website.

http://www.usdoj.gov/
The Department of Justice's official website.

http://thomas.loc.gov/
Legislative information on the Internet.

http://www.supremecourtus.gov/
Information on the Supreme Court, with links to recent Court opinions and historical decisions.

http://acts.poly.edu/cd/npr/np-realtoc.html
From Red Tape to Results: search documents relating to the National Performance Review.

http://www.gpoaccess.gov/gmanual/index.html
The online version of the U.S. Government Manual, contains comprehensive information on the agencies of the legislative, judicial, and executive branches as well as quasi-official agencies, international organizations in which the United States participates, and boards, commissions, and committees.

CHAPTER 5

Federalism and Public Administration

■ SETTING THE STAGE

In May 1996, at the height of the national debate over welfare reform, the *Wall Street Journal* published an article with the provocative first sentence "Does Washington matter?" The article went on to add: "As Congress and the White House dither, state governments and the free market have been tackling some of the issues Washington couldn't."[1] This assertion of the federal government's irrelevance stands in marked contrast to the situation some thirty years earlier when most observers would have agreed that it was the federal government that truly mattered, since state governments had largely ignored the social problems occurring in the urban areas within their borders.[2] Clearly, in the intervening generations a major change had occurred in the roles and relative importance of the federal government and state governments in shaping social welfare policy.

Indeed, at the time when Congress and the president were wrangling over which version of welfare reform would be enacted—the Congress's or the president's—no fewer than thirty-eight states had already taken the lead in overhauling their social service systems. State reforms included many elements which eventually found their way into the Personal Responsibility and Work Opportunity Reconciliation Act (PRWORA), which was finally passed by Congress and signed into law by President Clinton in July 1996, replacing the Aid to Families with Dependent Children (AFDC) program. These state efforts included time-limited benefits, welfare-to-work requirements, drug testing, and attempts to reduce the incidence of teenage pregnancies. Nonetheless, the states first had to obtain permission from Washington before they could make alterations to their own welfare programs. This permission was granted in the form of a waiver.[3] Many governors found the process of obtaining waivers from the federal government to be burdensome and demeaning. For example, Michigan governor John Engler likened it to begging Washington "on bended knee."[4] Massachusetts governor William F. Weld, in a *Wall Street Journal* editorial, complained, "For every change we wanted to make, we had to ask Washington's permission . . . and then put up with half a year of paper pushing and haggling. Ultimately, the Clinton administration refused to grant us one of the cornerstones of our plan, the two-year limit."[5]

Despite the difficult task of obtaining a waiver, many states were successfully implementing their reforms when Congress passed the PRWORA. Some states, moreover, wanted to go beyond making minor changes. In Wisconsin, for instance, Governor Tommy

President Bill Clinton signs the Personal Responsibility and Work Opportunity Reconciliation Act of 1996, ending sixty-one years of federal guaranteed aid to the poor.
SOURCE: Stephen Jaffe/Reuters/Landov

Thompson sought to completely eliminate welfare, not simply reform it. Thompson, whom President George W. Bush later appointed as his secretary of health and human services, proposed a radical plan called "Pay for Performance," which sought to replace welfare checks with paychecks.

In July 1996, just months before the general election, President Clinton, who was running for reelection, signed the welfare reform legislation he had twice previously vetoed. "Many of the worst elements I objected to are out of it, and many of the improvements I asked for are included," Clinton noted.[6] In signing the legislation, he said he was fulfilling a campaign pledge of ending "welfare as we know it," made when he first ran for president in 1992. The PRWORA was an important milestone in the evolution of federalism in the United States. It marked the culmination of over a decade of **devolution**, or the shifting of programmatic responsibilities in certain policy areas from the national government to the states, a process which began with the election of President Ronald Reagan in 1980.

Devolution The shifting of programmatic responsibilities in certain policy areas from the national government to the states.

■ CHAPTER PLAN

Intergovernmental relations The web of interrelationships among governments at all levels, which increasingly includes nonprofit and private organizations.

In this chapter, we discuss the importance of federalism and **intergovernmental relations** (IGR) for public administration. The federal system is the environment within which public administration occurs, while public policy occurs within the context of intergovernmental relations, a complex network of relationships involving every level of government, as well as not-for-profit groups and private firms. The welfare example shows the complicated nature of public programs. The private and nonprofit sectors are increasingly involved in the delivery of public services as well. This involvement of so many actors in the policy process is an important hallmark of the federal system and has important ramifications for public administration.

In order to grasp federalism's significance for public administration, we must understand its constitutional and legal framework. In this chapter, we discuss the main attributes of federalism as found in the U.S. Constitution. Judicial interpretations of the Constitution have also had a hand in shaping the federal system. Thus, we discuss some major Supreme Court decisions that have had a significant impact on federal–state relations.

An important dimension of federalism, particularly in the last century, is the system of intergovernmental grants-in-aid used to help finance everything from low-income housing programs to building airports and dams. We take this issue up in the section on fiscal federalism.

A comprehensive overview of federalism must also include some mention of interstate and intrastate relations. It is a serious mistake to conclude that federalism consists only of Washington's relations with state and local governments. Federalism also includes the cooperation and conflict between and within states that are of great importance for the political system.

In the next section, we examine the structure of governments other than the national. We discuss what administrators must do to perform their jobs effectively in an intergovernmental setting—one that is often marked by fragmentation of responsibility, extreme decentralization, and confusion over roles.

We conclude the chapter by examining the effects the federal system's development has had on civil society. The history of civil society in the United States has been influenced by the tension between the Federalist and Anti-Federalist perspectives, a conflict we discuss in the last section.

Defining Federalism and Intergovernmental Relations

Unitary system A governmental system with power centralized in a national government.

Federalism refers to a governmental system characterized by a sharing of powers between the national government and subnational governments. Under this system, government power is, in effect, decentralized. By contrast, a **unitary system** centralizes power in a national government. Besides the United States, other examples of federalist governments include Australia, Canada, Germany, and India. Examples of unitary governments include France and the United Kingdom. Under the U.S. Constitution, both the national government and the state governments exercise independent power over their own jurisdictions. In practice, this means that each level of government maintains its own separate laws and officials through which it directly governs its own citizens. State laws and federal laws, for example, govern a resident of North Dakota. This stands in marked contrast to the situation existing before the Constitution was ratified, when only the state governments had any direct political authority over Americans.

Federalism thus represents a political compromise between the centralization and decentralization of government power. James Madison wrote to George Washington, "I have sought a middle ground which may at once support a due supremacy of national authority, and not exclude [the states]."[7]

From the beginning, therefore, federalism was viewed as an arrangement to help achieve limited government.

The federal system uses the states to rein in the power of central government, and vice versa. As Alexander Hamilton observed in the Federalist No. 28, "Power being almost always the rival of power, the general government will at all times stand ready to check the usurpations of the state governments, and these will have the same disposition towards the general government."[8] The states and the federal government are considered supreme in their own sphere of power, although there is considerable overlap, as shown in Figure 5.1. It should be noted, however, that local governments are considered the "legal children" of the state.[9] We discuss local governments' legal status later in this chapter.

The federal system decentralizes political authority, and this inevitably affects public administration's operations at all levels of government. Administration accordingly occurs within a complex environment in which authority is shared among the different levels of government and in which decision-making is fragmented. Political scientist Morton Grodzins, in a classic example, uses the rural health officer, or "sanitarian," to prove this point:

> The sanitarian is appointed by the state under merit standards established by the federal government. His base salary comes jointly from state and federal funds, the county provides him with an office and office amenities and pays a portion of his expenses, and the largest city in the county also contributes to his salary and office by virtue of his appointment as a city plumbing inspector. It is impossible from moment to moment to tell under which governmental hat the sanitarian operates.[10]

He goes on to say that, although this is an extreme example, it nevertheless accurately shows the shared functions that characterize the full range of governmental activities in the United States. While some argue that government

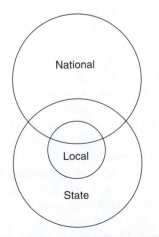

Figure 5.1   Current Configuration of Governmental Sphere of Power in the United States

Adapted from Russel L. Hanson, *Intergovernmental Relations*, in *Politics in the American State: A Comparative Analysis*, 6th ed., Virginia Gray and Herbert Jacob, eds., 1995, p. 43

decentralization fosters certain managerial values such as efficiency and better responsiveness to citizens/customers, this can come at the price of blurring and confusing the responsibilities and roles of the administrator.

According to Deil S. Wright, IGR represents the multiple and varied "connections, interactions, interdependencies, and influence" that take place between elected and appointed officials at all levels of government, and the actions and attitudes of human beings are at the core of IGR.[11] While our discussion of federalism has dealt with such abstractions as the relations between the national government and state governments, IGR reminds us that people and not abstract ideas solve policy problems at all levels of government. In this chapter we use the terms federalism and IGR interchangeably.

Benefits and Costs of Federalism

The federal system confers numerous benefits on the citizens of the United States. There are, nevertheless, several costs related to the system as well. In general, the chief benefits of federalism have to do with the political and administrative decentralization it promotes, while its chief costs are associated with the fragmentation of authority and lack of accountability.

Eight major advantages of federalism have been identified. First, government programs are more easily adapted to local needs in a federal system than in a unitary system. Second, a system of regional power centers helps keep the majority in check and prevents too much power from falling into the hands of any one group. Third, a federal system encourages the creation and diffusion of governmental innovations, with each government serving, in the words of Justice Louis Brandeis, as a "laboratory of democracy."[12] (See Vignette 5.1 for examples of how federalism encourages innovations in the states today.) Fourth, the existence of so many subnational governments relieves the administrative burden on the central government and contributes to making the system more efficient. Fifth, political conflict is localized, which makes it more manageable. Sixth, federalism provides more opportunities for participation in the political system, which in turn promotes a sense of self-reliance among the public. Seventh, in the arena of diplomatic and military affairs, a federal system enables subnational governments to project far greater strength by pulling together than if they act independently of each other. Finally, federalism promotes national economic development by removing impediments to free trade among subnational governments.

The blessings of federalism are not costless, however. In a federal system, subnational governments often fail to account for spillover effects or externalities that they produce. Pollution, for example, fails to honor political boundaries. The sheer number of governments also creates inevitable problems of coordination that can lead to numerous situations of administrative confusion. Federalism can also frustrate forces for change; what is one person's checks and balances is another one's delay and inaction. Another cost

VIGNETTE 5.1   Reinventing Government at the State and Local Levels

Louisville, Kentucky, believes in reinventing government from the bottom up. In 1992, Louisville created its City-Work program to transform its city bureaucracy into a responsive service delivery operation. Since then, the program has resulted in hundreds of large- and small-scale improvements in the work practices of employees. Reforms often originate within the departments and involve teams that cut across organizational and hierarchical lines. Examples of innovations include faster processing of abandoned properties, reorganization of the Law Department, and changing promotional requirements for the police. Other cities are taking a similar team approach to dealing with bureaucracy. These and other types of public sector reforms are transforming city halls across the country, according to reinvention advocates.

In West Virginia, the state, in collaboration with General Electric, created the Inspire program with the goal of finding new, collaborative ways for government employees and management to work together to solve problems. The program's operating philosophy is "Rank has nothing to do with good ideas." Thousands of state employees have gone through the training based on GE's quality principles of management, the objective of which is to empower bureaucrats to think up innovative ideas for delivering services. Dozens of other examples of similar efforts from other states could fill an entire book and have.[a]

Examples such as those above point to the continued viability of one of the chief benefits of federalism—the states and localities as laboratories of democracy. The 1990s was the reinvention decade for state and local governments. State and local calls to reinvent government have focused primarily on efforts to decentralize and flatten bureaucracy, create administration that is mission and customer driven, and create agencies that are competitive, performance based, and market oriented. However, some reinvention critics, such as management specialist Robert Behn, point out that despite all the reforms of the past decade, government at all levels still looks pretty much the same. According to Behn, "This is the flaw in the laboratory-of-democracy concept: Anything that works in one laboratory—be it a village, a city, a county or a state—must be adapted to work in every other laboratory. After all, the original innovation was invented to fit the specifics of the original setting; any replication must fit the specifics of the new setting."[b]

[a] See David Osborne and Ted Gaebler, *Reinventing Government: How the Entrepreneurial Spirit Is Transforming the Public Sector* (New York: Penguin Group, 1993); and Peter Plastrik and David Osborne, *Banishing Bureaucracy: The Five Strategies for Reinventing Government* (Reading, MA: Addison-Wesley, 1998).

[b] Robert Behn, "A Decade of Reinventing," *Governing*, October 1997, 40.

of American federalism is that it tends to put local priorities above regional or even national ones. The debate over military base closings for example, shows how difficult it is for Congress to put aside local needs in favor of national needs.

Another serious cost of federalism is the contribution it makes to the overall inequity in the political system. In the debate over welfare reform, for example, critics noted a great deal of variation among the states in terms of how well they treated their poor, with certain states providing lower levels of welfare benefits compared with others. The fragmentation of authority associated with decentralization contributes to the breakdown in administrative accountability. Citizens, for example, are confronted with a confusing number of governments and officials, which renders assigning responsibility for a decision or action all but impossible.

The Constitutional Framework

The Constitution's framers designed federalism as a pragmatic response to a real political problem—the failure of the Articles of Confederation. Federalism, however, was not the only constraint on the central political authority designed by the founders (see Figure 5.2). Under the Articles of Confederation (1781–1787), the states wielded more power than the national government. The government created under the Articles was nothing more than an alliance designed to address certain common problems, namely protection from foreign invaders. The Congress, for instance, could not raise armies or levy taxes without the permission of the states, and the states frequently withheld permission. Economic problems gave rise to violent uprisings such as Shays's Rebellion in Massachusetts (1786–1787). It was clear to many that the Articles, as the basis for a permanent government that could maintain civil order and promote external peace, were a failure.

The Federalists, therefore, supported a stronger central government at the expense of the states. They proposed a system in which "The powers delegated by the Constitution to the federal government are few and defined. Those which are to remain in state governments are numerous and indefinite."[13] This principle forms the foundation of section 8 of Article I in the Constitution, which delegates to the national government a number of clearly defined powers. Altogether there are fourteen **enumerated powers**, with the final one being the broadest: the authority "to make all laws which shall be necessary and proper" to carry out all the other powers of the U.S. government. This broad delegation of national authority has served as the basis for the expansion of the federal government since the early nineteenth century. This has been the focus of much judicial energy since the beginning of the republic, as we discuss in the next section.

Enumerated powers The fourteen governmental powers that are given to the national government by the U.S. Constitution. Also known as delegated powers. See reserved powers.

Although the Constitution identifies the national government's powers with great specificity, it is very general in granting authority to the state governments. According to the Tenth Amendment: "The powers not delegated to the United States by the Constitution, nor prohibited by it to the States, are reserved to the States respectively, or to the people." The Congress adopted

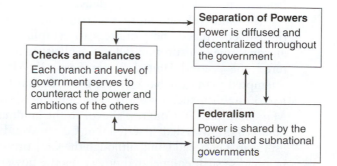

Figure 5.2   How the Constitution Checks Political Power

Reserved powers The powers inherent in the state governments according to the Tenth Amendment, in contrast to the enumerated or delegated powers of the federal government. See enumerated powers.

these **reserved powers** as part of the Bill of Rights in 1789. The Bill of Rights—the first ten amendments to the Constitution—was enacted to gain the support of the Anti-Federalists, who opposed the concentration of power in the national government proposed by the framers.

At the beginning of the republic, a "layer cake" version of federalism largely prevailed.[14] In a layer cake, each level is distinct from the others, so the idea was that each level of government would be distinct and independent of the others. The national government, for instance, would exercise supreme power in the sphere of foreign relations, while the state governments would have sole authority over domestic matters. Today, we have largely discarded the "layer cake" metaphor. In some respects, current federalism resembles more of a collage, in which governmental authority is dispersed and fragmented, while no functions "belong" exclusively to one level of government. Nonetheless, it is still the state and local governments that serve as the primary public service providers to citizens.[15] These governments operate public schools, public hospitals, public safety, sanitation, and public works to name a few vital services they are responsible for. However, they provide these services with some federal assistance or oversight, which is a far cry from the situation one hundred years ago.

The Courts and Federalism

Necessary and proper clause A provision of the U.S. Constitution (Article I, section 8, paragraph 18) authorizing Congress to pass all laws "necessary and proper" to fulfill its responsibilities.

Implied powers Those powers that are not stated in the Constitution but can be inferred from the enumerated powers.

Throughout federalism's evolution, as David H. Rosenbloom observes, "The central question has always concerned the extent of state sovereignty in the federal system. What, precisely, are the powers reserved to the states by the Tenth Amendment?"[16] The judiciary has struggled with this question over the last two centuries. From the beginning of the United States, the courts have played a significant role in shaping the federal system. One of the first major Supreme Court decisions involved clashing interpretations of the **necessary and proper clause** of the Constitution and what it meant for national power. Strict constructionists held that Congress could only exercise those powers that were spelled out in the Constitution, that is, the enumerated powers. Loose constructionists argued that Congress had **implied powers** that stemmed from the necessary and proper clause of the Constitution.

Alexander Hamilton, first secretary of the treasury and a loose constructionist, convinced the Congress to establish a system of national banks, although the Constitution did not explicitly permit this. When Congress chartered the second United States Bank in Maryland in 1811, Maryland attempted to tax the bank on the grounds that Congress had no legal authority to establish such an entity. The Supreme Court, under Chief Justice John Marshall, ruled in Congress's favor in the landmark case *McCulloch v. Maryland* (1819). Marshall asserted that Congress did indeed have the authority to establish a national bank, although the Constitution did not expressly approve it, because such enumerated powers as the power to tax and spend money, to borrow, and to support an army and navy implied that it also had the power to create such a bank. Furthermore, the Court asserted, the attempt by Maryland to levy a tax on the bank was a violation of the **supremacy clause**, in Article VI of the Constitution, which holds that the Constitution and all laws created under its authority are the supreme law of the land. In a famous quote from this decision, Marshall noted, "the power to tax involves the power to destroy."[17]

Supremacy clause The portion of the Constitution (Article VI, paragraph 2) which holds that the Constitution and all laws made under its authority are the supreme law of the land and take precedence over the states.

The *McCulloch* decision serves as one of the constitutional bases for expanding national power whenever necessary. It gives Congress the power to do what is "necessary and proper" in executing its functions. It also affirms the loose constructionist notion that the Constitution is a dynamic, not static, framework for dealing with our nation's problems. Again, in the words of Chief Justice Marshall, the Constitution is "intended to endure for ages to come, and consequently, to be adapted to the various crises of human affairs."[18]

Another area in which judicial decisions have helped shape the federal system is the interpretation of the **commerce clause**, in Article I, section 8, of the Constitution, which gives Congress the power to regulate interstate as well as foreign commerce. In *Gibbons v. Ogden* (1824), the Court said that commerce included the production, selling, and transport of goods as well as other types of commercial activity. It also ruled that Congress, in certain cases, could regulate commerce *within* a state as well as commerce crossing state borders. This broad interpretation of the commerce clause would later serve as a legal basis for the tremendous expansion of national regulatory powers in such diverse areas as industry, child labor, farming, labor unions, civil rights, and crime fighting. However, this broad expansion in national authority did not begin in earnest until the Great Depression of the 1930s and President Franklin D. Roosevelt's New Deal.

Commerce clause The section of the Constitution (Article I, section 8, clause 3) that states that Congress has the power to regulate interstate and foreign commerce.

Three recent cases involving the commerce clause warrant our attention because of their importance in shaping federalism's current environment. In *National League of Cities v. Usery* (1976), state and local governments maintained that the 1974 amendments to the Fair Labor Standards Act, which extended wage and hour protections to employees of state and local governments, were unconstitutional. The Court ruled that Congress exceeded its constitutional authority, under the commerce clause, because the amendments interfered with the states' ability to carry out their traditional governmental functions. This ruling marked the first time in forty years that the Supreme Court did not uphold Congress's use of the commerce clause to increase the national government's power to regulate an economic activity. It also represented a major victory for state power against encroachment from the national government. However, it was to remain an isolated example of the Court ruling in favor of states rights until the consolidation of the Court's conservative majority under Chief Justice William H. Rehnquist nearly twenty years later.

In *Garcia v. San Antonio Metropolitan Transit Authority* (1985), the Court essentially overruled its earlier *National League of Cities* decision. In the *Garcia* decision, the Court, by a narrow majority, ruled that application of the federal minimum wage and overtime requirements to a public mass-transit

The Supreme Court held in *Garcia v. San Antonio Metropolitan Transit Authority* that federal labor laws apply to municipal employees like the transit workers in this photo.

SOURCE: Peter Foley/Reuters/ Corbis

authority did not violate the Constitution. However, in a dissent that presaged the Court's future orientation with respect to federalism, Justice Sandra Day O'Connor wrote that "the states have legitimate interests which the national government is bound to respect even though its laws are supreme, and that if federalism so conceived and so carefully cultivated by the framers of the U.S. Constitution is to remain meaningful, the Court cannot abdicate its constitutional responsibility to oversee the Federal Government's compliance with its duty to respect the legitimate interests of the states."[19]

The question of Congress' ability to use the commerce clause to extend national power reached the Supreme Court again in the early 1990s. In *United States v. Lopez*, a San Antonio high school student, Alfonso Lopez, was charged with possessing a firearm on school premises in violation of the 1990 Gun-Free School Zones Act that prohibited carrying guns within 1,000 feet of a school. The Court in 1995 ruled the gun law unconstitutional in a 5–4 decision.[20] The Court found that Congress had overstepped its bounds in attempting to apply the commerce clause to a criminal activity that had no direct connection to commerce or any sort of economic enterprise.

Fiscal Federalism

State and local governments are responsible for delivering most of the public services in the United States. As a result, they require financial resources to support them in this crucial task. States and localities vary tremendously in

Fiscal capacity The financial ability of a community to sustain and support government programs through its system of own-source revenues.

Fiscal federalism The financial relations among different units of government at all levels.

their **fiscal capacity**—the ability to raise revenues from an economic base. Revenues come from many different sources. Revenues that governments raise within their own jurisdictions, own-source revenues, consist mainly of taxes, fees, and charges. Another important source of revenues is money from other levels of government, known as intergovernmental transfers. This aspect of the federal system, **fiscal federalism**, is examined more fully below. Although the discussion concentrates mainly on federal aid to states and localities, state aid to communities also is an important part of fiscal federalism.

Types of Grants

During the twentieth century, the system of intergovernmental transfers in the United States grew tremendously in size and complexity. Nowhere was this growth more pronounced than in the federal grant system. Early on, states received federal funds for such nation-building enterprises as constructing roads and schools.[21] The real growth, though, in federal aid to states began in the 1930s, when the Great Depression forced the national government to play a more active role in domestic policy. Grants grew slowly over the next two decades but entered a period of explosive growth during the 1960s and 1970s, as shown in Table 5.1. The peak year for intergovernmental transfers was 1978, when federal outlays accounted for 28 percent of state and local government total revenues, whereas they had amounted to just 5 percent in 1902.[22] By 2000, this figure had leveled off to 29 percent.

TABLE 5.1 Federal Grants-in-Aid to State and Local Governments, 1940 to 2002

Fiscal Year	In Millions of Dollars	In Billions of Constant (FY 1996) dollars	As Percentage of Federal Outlays	As Percentage of GDP
1940	872	10.8	9.2	0.9
1945	859	8.5	0.9	0.4
1950	2,253	15.6	5.3	0.8
1955	3,207	19.2	4.7	0.8
1960	7,019	36.4	7.6	1.4
1965	10,910	52.5	9.2	1.6
1970	24,065	94	12.3	2.4
1975	49,791	136.6	15.0	3.2
1980	91,385	169	15.5	3.3
1985	105,852	146.9	11.2	2.6
1990	135,325	157.6	10.8	2.4
1995	224,991	229.7	14.8	3.1
2000	248,659	262.5	15.9	2.9
2001	317,211	284.9	17	3.2
2002	351,550	312.2	17.5	3.4

Note: Values for Fiscal Years 2003–2008 are estimated by the U.S. Federal Government.

Source: Adapted from Summary Comparison of Total Outlays for Grants to State and Local Governments, Table 12.1, http://www.whitehouse.gov/omb/budget/fy2004/pdf/hist.pdf.

By 2003, as a result of economic recession, the states faced their worst fiscal situation since the early 1990s. In the past, the states could look to the federal government for assistance; however, the national government faced a massive budget deficit of its own, over $400 billion, because of tax cuts and costs associated with the war on terrorism and homeland security.[23] The president did include $10 billion in emergency Medicaid spending for the states in his $350 billion economic stimulus package, most of which was devoted to tax cuts, passed in May 2003.

Categorical grant A type of grant-in-aid with a narrowly defined purpose used to achieve very specific goals (e.g., building an airport, dam, or highway).

Block grant A type of grant-in-aid that can be used for a number of purposes within a functional area, which provides lower-level governments more discretion.

Federal grants to states and localities take different forms depending on the types of effects they are supposed to achieve. The two main classes of grants are **categorical grants** and **block grants**. Categorical grants are the most common and are used to achieve very specific goals set by Congress. Categorical grants number in the hundreds, and they represent the overwhelming percentage of total national grant funds. This type of grant, because of its narrowly defined purpose, substitutes Congress's discretion for that of state and local officials. As a result, it is the least favored by state and local governments.

The two types of categorical grants are project grants and formula grants. Project grants require potential recipients to make a grant application to a federal agency and to undergo a review process prior to receiving funding. In this process, federal administrators play a major part in determining who gets the money. In the case of formula grants, recipients who meet the grant's legislatively established criteria automatically receive federal funds.

By contrast, block grants provide state and local governments with considerably more discretion in using funds. With block grants, Congress targets a broad functional area—education, for example—and the recipient government then sets the spending priorities within that area. Block grants, because they give state and local officials more discretion, are a popular type of grant for elected officials who want to transfer power from the national government to the states. Block grants were an important part of the new federalism strategy of Presidents Nixon and Reagan. Under Nixon, two major block grant programs were created, Title I of the Comprehensive Employment and Training Act of 1973 (CETA) and the Housing and Community Development Act of 1974 (CDBG). CETA was a job training and employment program targeted to areas suffering from high rates of poverty and unemployment. CDBG was the consolidation of seven housing and community development categorical grants into one large block grant.

President Reagan's legacy in block grants came in the form of the Omnibus Budget Reconciliation Act of 1981 (OBRA). OBRA was part of Reagan's overall strategy of devolution—that is, turning over more responsibility for government programs to the states. He was successful in consolidating a large number of categorical grant programs into block grants and in giving the states chief responsibility for their administration. State officials were given more discretion to allocate funds and could shift some funds between categories.

A third type of grant—General Revenue Sharing (GRS)—went even further than block grants in giving state and local officials more autonomy in spending federal funds. GRS was passed in 1972 as the State and Local Fiscal Assistance Act. The program was immensely popular among state and local governments but, ironically, was ended during the Reagan administration, a victim of federal deficits. GRS was used mainly by the states to provide tax relief. States and communities could, as a result, maintain artificially low tax rates by substituting federal GRS funds to pay for their public services.

Reasons for the Grants-in-Aid Programs

As pointed out earlier, grants are used for a variety of purposes and consequently take a variety of forms. In general, these intergovernmental transfers are used to promote economic efficiency and promote greater equity within the federal system.

One major goal of grants is to correct inefficiencies in the allocation of society's resources. A major source of inefficiency involves spillover effects or externalities—in other words, activities whose costs or benefits extend beyond a jurisdiction's boundaries. As we observed earlier, this is a cost of federalism. Pollution from one state, for example, adversely affects environmental quality in a nearby state, thus imposing costs on the other state's residents. Left on its own, the source state might not address the problem, because it would only take account of the costs to its own residents and not those of affected communities outside the state. In this case, a federal grant might be used to lower the costs of reducing pollution, which would increase environmental quality in both states. In case of either positive or negative externalities, intergovernmental transfers are used to bring the externality more in line with society's preferences.

A second major goal of grants is to correct fiscal imbalances. In many states and communities, there is a mismatch between social needs and available resources. This is because different populations have different demands for governmental services, and social problems are not evenly distributed among jurisdictions. Resources are likewise not evenly divided among governmental units. As a result, residents in poorer jurisdictions might have to bear heavier tax burdens to receive the same level of services that residents in more affluent jurisdictions pay less in taxes for. Grants allow governments to target jurisdictions with the greatest needs but inadequate resources, providing additional funds to cover the shortfall. One example of this is in local public education. Fiscal disparities among school districts resulting from differences in property values have led states to increase their share of the financial burden for supporting local public schools. Vignette 5.2 discusses how the states are trying to deal with the fiscal demands imposed by the war on terrorism.

A third major reason for grants is related to the economic advantages of national government revenue sources compared with those of state and local governments. The national government collects the bulk of its revenues from personal and corporate income taxes, while state and local governments

VIGNETTE 5.2 The States and Homeland Security

Americans don't typically think of the state and local governments as being on the front lines when it comes to defending the United States, but in the new war against terrorism, they are. The first people to arrive at the World Trade Center and the Pentagon in response to the terrorist attacks on September 11, 2001, were local public safety and emergency medical personnel. Because of 9/11, states are now spending large sums of money on what was previously considered a national function, security from foreign attack. In February 2002, the nation's governors went to the White House to plead for help from the Bush administration to plug a $40 billion shortfall in revenues, resulting from recession, federal budget cuts, and the costs of responding to the 9/11 terrorist attacks.

California expected to spend $440 million on additional security measures to safeguard the state, and more than $200 million had been spent on overtime for the highway patrol guarding buildings, bridges, dams, reservoirs, and power plants. In addition, California had to pay for National Guard troops at bridges because Washington would only put them at airports. California Governor Gray Davis, a Democrat, argued that the costs of increasing the state's security should be a federal not state expense. "We were attacked, this was an act of war, and the costs we are incurring are to protect people from another act of war," the governor said.[a]

California was not the only state that expected to spend considerably more on security as a result of the terrorist attacks. Governor Mark Schweiker of Pennsylvania proposed spending $200 million for security and emergency response efforts.[b] As part of Pennsylvania's increased security efforts, the governor created a new Office of Homeland Security and appointed an FBI terrorism expert to head it. Other security-related initiatives included installation of computers in state police vehicles, increased security at the state Capitol, establishment of a terrorism threat assessment center, and creation of Community Emergency Response Teams.

[a] Zachary Colie, "State's Huge Terror Bill," *San Francisco Chronicle*, February 26, 2002, A1.

[b] John M. R. Bull, "Budget Fends Off Tax Increase," *Pittsburgh Post-Gazette*, February 6, 2002, A1.

depend chiefly on the sales tax and the property tax respectively. The income tax is much more responsive to economic conditions than are the state and local taxes. Because state and local governments provide most of the country's basic public services, as the population grows so does demand for these services. Federal grants can be used to supplement state and local spending on these needed services.

Another advantage of the national revenue system is its progressivity compared with state and local systems. Progressive taxes, such as the income tax, impose a greater tax burden on high-income taxpayers. Regressive taxes, such as the property tax and sales tax, impose a greater tax burden on low-income taxpayers. Consequently, federal grants, because they are financed mainly by the income tax, contribute to making the entire government finance system more equitable.

Finally, the grant system helps to diffuse innovative ideas and to encourage program experimentation among states. Grants can serve as incentives to promote more efficient and effective ways for governmental units to deliver services or address problems. States and communities may be hesitant in embracing new and untried programs if they have to bear most of the costs. However, this reluctance might be overcome if the national government contributes to the costs of programs. This aspect of grants helps to reinforce one of federalism's advantages, namely, the states as "laboratories of democracy."

Criticisms of the Grant System

Critics of the federal grant system assert that it promotes (1) greater centralization of authority in Washington, (2) more inefficiency in the aided programs, (3) lack of accountability, and (4) confusion over governmental responsibility. Furthermore, they argue that the system fails to achieve its stated goals. Joseph F. Zimmerman identifies sixteen specific complaints that have been leveled against grants.[24] In addition to the ones stated above, he includes the following: program dominance by national bureaucrats; reduced ability of state and local elected officials to oversee their own bureaucrats; state and local government budget distortions as nonfederal matching funds are spent for national and not state and local priorities; conflicting objectives of many grant programs and proliferation of rules and regulations.

Mandates and Other Federal Requirements

Mandates are requirements that a higher-level government imposes on a lower-level government, usually to perform some activity or provide a service. Most, if not all, mandates have a budgetary impact. These requirements prove particularly burdensome when they are unaccompanied by any financial assistance, as in the case of **unfunded mandates**. When this happens, the state or locality's taxpayers must bear the total costs of fulfilling the requirement. A 1996 study of federal mandates found that they cost state and local governments as much as $5 billion annually.[25] As a result of the proliferation of unfunded mandates in the 1980s, and the increasing hostility of state and local governments toward these requirements, Congress passed the Unfunded Mandate Reform Act of 1995. The purpose was to hamper the federal government's ability to pass legislation resulting in increased costs for state and local governments—costs that the federal government itself was unwilling to pay.

Federal mandate requirements take several different forms. A common type of obligation that often accompanies a federal grant is a **crosscutting mandate**. Crosscutting requirements apply across-the-board to most federal programs and grants. Some important examples of crosscutting mandates include making public transportation accessible to the disabled, mandatory clean water and air standards, and requiring jurisdictions to prohibit discrimination on the basis of race, sex, age, and other characteristics.

Federal requirements to states and localities can also take the form of **preemptions**. A preemption is a usurpation of state law based on the supremacy clause of the U.S. Constitution. Congress may add a preemption clause to a federal law that would supersede any existing state law in the same program area. Preemptions may be either total or partial. Total preemption gives the national government complete regulatory authority in a particular

Unfunded mandates A legislative or judicial requirement, usually but not always from a higher-level government to a lower-level government, to administer and pay for a government program.

Crosscutting mandate A legislative mandate that occurs across the board on all programs and grants.

Preemption A federal requirement that supersedes all state laws in a particular program area.

President George W. Bush shakes hands with Senator Ted Kennedy after signing the No Child Left Behind education bill during a ceremony at an Ohio high school in January 2002.

SOURCE: Reuters/Corbis

area, while partial preemption limits the national government's authority to establish minimum standards for state- and local-government administered programs. The number of preemptions has accelerated since the 1980s, with over one hundred created in that decade alone. According to a 2006 report published by the National Academy of Public Administration, between 1990 and 2004, Congress enacted 125 preemptions.[26]

Interstate and Intrastate Relations

Just as the U.S. Constitution establishes the legal framework for federal–state relations, it also lays the foundation for the relations between states. The Constitution, though, is notably silent on the relation of the states to their local governments. In effect, the Constitution acknowledges only the central government and the states as the seats of governmental authority in the American political system. According to the Constitution, state governments need only guarantee their residents a "republican" form of government. The courts, indeed, recognize localities as merely the "creatures of the state," according to **Dillon's Rule**, which asserts that local governments have only those powers granted them expressly by the state or ones that are necessary for carrying out those express powers (see the section on intrastate relations below). The rule was articulated in the nineteenth century by the American jurist John Forrest Dillon.

Dillon's Rule The principle that local governments have only those powers granted to them by the state government. Named after jurist John Forrest Dillon, who formulated the rule in the nineteenth century.

Constitutional Framework for Interstate Relations

Relations between states can be either cooperative or competitive. The Constitution encourages cooperation between the states in four separate formal clauses. We discuss each one briefly in the sections below.

Full Faith and Credit The full faith and credit clause in Article IV, section 1, of the Constitution requires that "Full faith and credit shall be given in each state to the public acts, records, and judicial proceedings of every other state." Simply put, states must honor each other's laws and court judgments. Residents of one state cannot evade their legal responsibilities simply by moving to another state—a Missouri resident, for example, cannot avoid paying back his debt by simply moving to Illinois. The court decisions of one state are also recognized as legitimate in all the others.

Where full faith and credit has been controversial recently is in the matter of same-sex marriages. In 2000, Vermont passed a law recognizing the legality of such marriages. Does this mean that every state must now accord a same-sex couple married in Vermont the same legal rights as any other married couple? It is likely that some state will challenge the legality of a same-sex marriage from another state as these unions become more common and as more states follow Vermont in granting same-sex marriages full legal status. In 1996, the U.S. Congress passed the Defense of Marriage Act, giving states the right to refuse to recognize same-sex marriages performed in other states. However, in 2003, the Supreme Court held in *Lawrence v. Texas* that same-sex couples had the same right to privacy as opposite-sex couples do. Also in 2003, the Massachusetts Supreme Judicial Court ruled that same-sex marriages were legal. However, the high courts in New York and Georgia ruled against same-sex marriages in 2006. As of this writing, the Supreme Court has not been asked to rule on the legality of same-sex marriages or on the constitutionality of the Defense of Marriage Act. Currently, thirty-seven states have laws banning same-sex marriages, and the U.S. Congress has considered passing a law banning such unions on the national level.

Extradition Article IV, section 2, of the Constitution gives states the power to order the return of someone who was charged with a crime and then fled to another state. For example, if a fugitive from New York is caught in Florida, the governor of New York must make a formal request to the governor of Florida for the fugitive's extradition back to New York. In most cases, the governor of the state the criminal fled to is only too happy to return him or her to the "home" state. However, what happens if a governor refuses the extradition request of another state? The Supreme Court in *Puerto Rico v. Branstad* (1987) decided that federal courts might require governors to extradite the fugitives of another state.[27] There is only one circumstance in which a state can legally deny the extradition request of another state, and that is when the fugitive can prove beyond doubt that, at the time the crime was committed, he or she was not in the state demanding extradition.

Privileges and Immunities Article IV, section 2, of the Constitution requires that "the citizens of each state shall be entitled to all privileges and immunities of citizens in the several states." This clause guarantees the right of every American to be treated the same way by every state with respect to being able to (1) travel freely across state borders, (2) engage in the same types of commercial activities as state residents, and (3) receive the same legal protections as state residents and pay the same taxes. States, however, may practice "reasonable" discrimination against nonresidents. Examples of this include higher out-of-state college tuitions, hunting and fishing license fees, and residency requirements for voting.

Interstate Compacts Article I, section 10, of the Constitution holds that, with the consent of Congress, states may enter into compacts, or treaties, with each other. Early on, these were used to negotiate boundary disputes that occurred between states. Interstate compacts are now used primarily to resolve issues involving two or more states in areas such as water resources, education, fishing, transportation, riverboat gambling, and pest management. Currently, there are 179 interstate compacts in existence. A well-known example of an interstate compact is the Port Authority of New York and New Jersey established in 1921 to operate transportation facilities in and around New York City.

In addition to the formal mechanism of the interstate compact, which under normal circumstances requires congressional approval, states may enter into informal arrangements with each other to find common solutions to a wide variety of problems. Often these associations between states arise to promote regional interests, particularly economic development. Examples include the Appalachian Regional Commission, the Western Governors' Policy Office, the Southern Growth Policies Board, and the Northeast Coalition of Governors.

Interstate Conflict

Despite constitutional provisions and informal arrangements, relations between the states do not always go smoothly. Indeed, there is much competition, particularly economic, among the states, which occasionally results in outright conflicts. The Constitution assigns the Supreme Court the task of refereeing legal conflicts between states. Boundary disputes between neighboring states often find their way to the Court. For example, it is not uncommon for disputes over water rights to pit states against each other. Montana and Idaho have threatened to sue Washington over its right to seed clouds over the Pacific Ocean, which deprives its neighbors further inland of rainwater. Controversies such as this are likely to increase in the water-poor West, if the scientific community's assessment of looming water shortages as a result of climate changes is correct.

Interstate conflicts also tend to be regional or sectional in nature—the rapidly growing sunbelt states of the South and Southwest versus the slow- or no-growth snowbelt states of the Northeast and Midwest, for example. These rivalries are driven chiefly by economic competition. The snowbelt has lost population and jobs to the sunbelt, and that population loss has translated into a transfer of political power: the congressional delegations of states such as California, Texas, and Florida have increased, while those of New York, Michigan, and Ohio have decreased. Interstate conflict also takes the form of disputes in Congress over national expenditures and economic development.

Another important sectional competition is between eastern and western states over such issues as land, water, and energy. A major source of friction in the West is federal government ownership of vast tracts of land. This tension over federal land management has erupted in recent decades into occasional civil disobedience, as in the sagebrush rebellion and the "Wise Use" movement (see the brief case study at the end of the chapter).

Intrastate Relations

As previously noted, Dillon's Rule asserts that local governments have no powers other than those delegated to them by their states, either by the state constitution or by statute. The power of the states in relation to their local governments is, as a consequence, nearly absolute and certainly has no equal in the American political system. Although the national government cannot abolish a state under any circumstance, states have the legal authority to terminate local government units, such as school districts or even towns. States, however, rarely use this power with respect to cities and towns, except when all the people have moved out. Whenever a conflict arises with regard to some local unit of government's scope of authority, the courts generally rule in favor of the state.

Home rule The granting of considerable decision-making powers to local governments by state legislatures or state constitutions.

Under Dillon's Rule, local governments can do only what the state allows them to do. Unless a city has a **home rule** provision in the state constitution (more on this below), it cannot take on any additional responsibilities or perform any new functions not previously agreed to by the state. The state legislature and governor thus have virtually complete control over the affairs of their localities.

An important area of intrastate relations involves financial matters. State law determines nearly every aspect of local government finance, from the types of revenues that may be collected to the amount of debt that localities can carry. States also have their own system of grants-in-aid, which they use to subsidize their local governments. However, since states are responsible for providing most governmental services, there is less direct financial aid to local governments. National political events have also played a major role in intrastate relations. Federal government devolution efforts and the states' tax and expenditure limitation movement, for example, have had a huge impact on state and local fiscal relations. (For more on tax and expenditure limitations, see Chapter 10.)

In the case of devolution, as states have taken on greater programmatic responsibility from the federal government, they have used their legal authority to force local governments to assume more of the costs for these services. Just

Fiscal note The part of proposed legislation that describes the fiscal impact of the legislation.

as federal unfunded mandates have provoked an outcry from the states, so too have state attempts to pass along their costs to local governments. As a result of local complaints, many state legislatures now require that **fiscal notes** be prepared whenever new programs are proposed, to gauge the fiscal impact on communities. A fiscal note is the part of proposed legislation that describes the fiscal impact of that legislation. In a few states, the legislature is required by law to reimburse local governments for the costs of new programs.

One unintended effect of tax and expenditure limitations in some states has been to centralize government financing at the state level and to reduce local government discretion in fiscal matters. California offers a good example of this. Since Proposition 13 was passed in 1978, California's local governments have experienced erosion in their fiscal capacity, although the citizens' demands for government services have not also declined. Localities are limited in their ability to raise taxes by the state's constitution; hence, they have had to resort to creative financing methods and, increasingly, state government aid to pay for these services.

But state authority over local governments is by no means unlimited. There are many informal limits on state power. First, states have to oversee a large number of governmental units—in some cases numbering in the thousands. With so many governmental units, however, state governments cannot control everything that local governments do. Second, local interests are represented in the state legislature, and local government officials continually lobby state government. These interactions afford abundant opportunities for local governments to provide input to and exert influence on state governments. Third, local governments can bypass states in the case of some federal grant programs. This gives communities a source of power outside state government control. Fourth, many states give the power of home rule to at least some of their cities and counties. This acts as a form of legal constraint on the power of states to interfere in the internal matters of some local governments.

Subnational Government Structure

A major hallmark of the American system is the huge number of governments. According to the Census Bureau, there are approximately 87,000 different subnational governments in the United States, including counties, municipalities, towns, school districts, and special districts, not including the fifty state governments.[28] This crazy-quilt pattern of governments spread across the land leads to the fragmentation of authority. Each type of subnational government in the federal system is discussed below.

State Governments

The state governments resemble the federal government institutionally to a striking degree. Every state government, for instance, consists of a legislature, executive, and judiciary. In addition, all states except Nebraska have bicameral legislatures composed of an upper house called the senate and a lower house usually called the house of representatives. In order for laws to pass in every state, they must gain the approval of both chambers of the legislature and the signature of the governor. In every case, the governor is elected by a vote of the people, as is the U.S. president. However, there is no electoral college at the state level, so a majority of the vote is all that is needed to win the governorship.

For much of the twentieth century, state legislatures were considered the backwater institutions of the American political system. In 1954, a committee of national experts declared that state legislatures were too ill equipped to serve as the public policy-making branch of state government.[29] Since the 1960s, however, state legislatures have become more professional, both in terms of the legislators themselves and the staff members who provide them with important support services.

Local Government

The largest part of government service delivery in the United States occurs at the local level. Local governments employ almost 18 million people and spend $910 billion on educating children, fighting crime, cleaning streets, picking up garbage, and many other services citizens often take for granted. Local government is the level of government closest to the people; most Americans have far greater contact with their local governments than with the state or national levels of government. The term "local government" technically refers to several different types of governmental units and not to a single type of entity. Subsumed under the label of local government are cities, towns, and counties, which most people view as examples of local governments. Special districts and school districts are also considered local governments.

One useful way of classifying local governments is according to the number of different tasks or functions they perform. A governmental unit that performs a variety of functions, such as operating hospitals and fighting crime, is called a **general-purpose local government**, while one that performs only one function, such as educate children, is called a **single-purpose local government**. Cities, towns, and counties are general-purpose units, and school districts and water districts are single-purpose units.

General-purpose local government A local government that performs a wide range of governmental functions.

Single-purpose local government A local government that performs a specific function (e.g., school district, water district, sewer district).

Counties

There are over 3,000 counties in the United States. Historically, counties served as the administrative arms of the state governments. However, due to the pressures of urbanization, county governments have grown beyond their traditional role as units of state government to become major actors in local policy-making in their own right. Counties are active in the areas of social services, transportation, healthcare, environmental protection, and other services that were traditionally provided by municipalities only.

Municipalities

Municipalities are cities; the two words are interchangeable. There are over 19,000 municipal governments in the U.S.[30] Historically, state legislatures have exercised nearly complete political control over their state's cities. Communities desiring the benefits of self-government, however, could petition the state legislature for a charter of **incorporation**. Early charters of incorporation were typically narrowly construed by the legislature and kept cities on a very short leash.

As a result of the early twentieth-century municipal reform movement, many state legislatures adopted general legislation for incorporation. These general laws had little regard for the unique factors often operating in communities. By contrast, special legislation dealt with communities on a case by case basis. Current laws in most states require that these factors, which include population and the total value of property in a community, be taken into account in classifying cities as either first- or second-class cities. First-class cities are significantly larger in population than second-class cities.

Cities are treated by the state legislature according to their classifications when laws are passed. This is in marked contrast to the earlier time when the legislature passed laws for specific cities. However, certain cities in a state—usually the largest—are still singled out for special treatment. As Zimmerman notes, "if the law stipulates 'the following charter shall apply to all cities with populations between 70,001 and 75,000,' it is reasonable to assume the charter will apply to only one city."[31] Such is the case, for example, with New York City's treatment in the New York State constitution. There is a wide range of variation in the governmental functions performed by cities—both from state to state and within state—with much of the variation related to city population.

Additionally, certain cities enjoy special privileges granted them by the state legislature in the form of home-rule legislation. Home rule offers four main benefits to cities and states. First, home rule removes or significantly reduces the state government's meddling in local government. Second, it gives the city the opportunity to choose its own governmental form and organization. Third, it reduces the time the legislature spends dealing with specific localities' problems and instead allows legislators to focus on state problems. Fourth, it encourages more citizen participation in local government by giving them more opportunities for input into local policy-making.

City governments are organized three different ways: the mayor–council plan, the council–manager plan, and the commission plan. Approximately half of all American cities use the mayor–council plan (see Figure 5.3), which tends to be popular in large cities (population over 250,000) and in small cities (population under 10,000). The council–manager plan (see Figure 5.4) is popular in cities of 10,000 to 250,000 people and is found mainly in newer suburban communities, particularly in the sunbelt.

Incorporation The state legislature's granting of a charter to create a municipality.

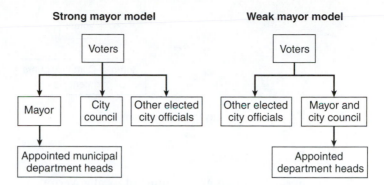

Figure 5.3 The Mayor–Council Form of Government

The commission plan (see Figure 5.5) is used in only a small number of cities; probably the best known is Portland, Oregon, which uses a variation of the commission plan.

Towns and Townships

Towns hold an almost sacred place in American society because of the lasting association between towns and direct democracy stemming from the New England town meetings of earlier times. The tradition of the town meeting, though, is dying off in New England, a victim of modern-day political pressures. Towns still survive, but they are officially recognized in only about half the states, mainly in the North and Midwest. In those states, townships are administrative arms of the county, performing many basic services such as road repair, minimal law enforcement, running elections, and tax administration. The functions that townships perform vary according to whether they are urban or rural. Urban townships, particularly in suburban areas, provide a wider range of services, including schools in some cases.

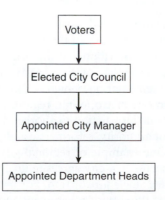

Figure 5.4 The Council–Manager Form of Government

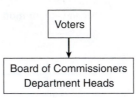

Figure 5.5   The City Commission Form of Government

Special Districts

Special districts are the units of local government most likely to be ignored by the general public, although both their numbers and importance are growing. More than half of the 87,000 local government units in the United States are special districts.[32] State law creates special districts with the purpose of performing some specific function, such as providing a water supply, sewer services, airports, housing, and pest control. Districts have the authority to raise revenues to pay for the services they provide. Taxes, user fees, and revenue bonds are the three most typical ways that districts use to produce revenues. One of the best-known special districts is the Port Authority of New York and New Jersey, whose activities include operating a commuter railroad, bridges and tunnels, and marine facilities. Before the September 11 terrorist attacks, the Port Authority also operated the World Trade Center.

Perhaps the most familiar type of special district, and certainly the most prevalent, is the school district. There are roughly 16,000 school districts in the United States, the vast majority of which are independent of any other local unit, and thus can raise their own revenues and make spending decisions subject only to state laws.[33] School districts are usually governed by school boards, which are typically composed of unpaid private citizens elected to their positions in nonpartisan elections.

Regional Government

As the preceding discussion makes clear, a distinguishing characteristic of subnational government in the United States is its size and diversity. On the positive side, this contributes to the beneficial aspects of federalism that were discussed earlier. However, on the negative side, the plethora of governments creates political fragmentation, which has problematic consequences for citizens. For example, in one metropolitan region, tax burdens and service levels can vary greatly from one jurisdiction to another. In order to overcome this extreme decentralization of authority, reformers usually advocate some form of regional government.

One example of regional government is city–county consolidation. In this arrangement, a city agrees to give up some of its power to the county in order to create a single jurisdiction. For instance, instead of two police departments—one serving the county government and the other serving the municipal government—there is one police department serving the consolidated entity. One of the major rationales for merging jurisdictions is to create economy of scale in the delivery of services. It is inefficient for a municipality to provide a service to residents when the same service can be provided at less cost by a larger government, in this case, the county. However, voters occasionally defeat efforts to consolidate city and county government. What proponents of consolidation view as inefficient, citizens of a municipality might view as positive, as in the case of varying tax burdens and service levels, which give taxpayers the ability to choose a city on the basis of a package of services and taxes that appeals to them.[34] Furthermore, attempts to merge city and county are sometimes opposed on the grounds that they can undermine the political influence of minorities.[35] It is not even certain that consolidated city–county government produces the expected savings in costs and taxes.

Civil Society and Federalism

The history of civil society in the United States has been influenced by the tension between the Federalist and Anti-Federalist points of view. Schambra asserts that the Federalists—James Madison and Alexander Hamilton, for example—did not want to leave individual rights up to the states, which were small and homogeneous at the time, because they feared tyranny of the majority, that is, the oppression of minorities by the majority. Thus, they endorsed the idea of a large republic. Anti-Federalists—such as Thomas Jefferson—believed that "public-spirited" citizens in "small, intense community" were the vital link in preserving the republic.[36] This conflict between two contrasting worldviews has played itself out through American history, according to Schambra.

In the twentieth century, Schambra obsserves, this old conflict took shape as a struggle between the forces favoring the idea of "national community" (i.e., Federalist) and the forces supporting local institutions (i.e., Anti-Federalist). In the first half of the twentieth century, the national community, or Federalist, faction held the upper hand. However, the latter half of the century witnessed the gradual domination of the group supporting local institutions and power. Beginning with the Progressives, Schambra states, the idea was that "old civil society's rambling, halting voluntaryism" was no match for the expansion of national power, supported by an "enlarged, rational view of governance."[37] This strengthening of national at the expense of local power reached its peak with the presidency of Lyndon B. Johnson (1964–1968), who proposed that the United States "must turn unity of interest into unity of purpose and unity of goals into unity in the Great Society."[38]

The national institution that was best suited to achieve the Federalist ideal was the presidency. However, during the late 1960s and the 1970s, as Schambra points out, the "Anti-Federalist, small republican impulses" began to reassert themselves. Furthermore, since Johnson, "Every president has placed at the center of his agenda the denunciation of centralized, bureaucratic government . . . and to reinvigorate states, small communities, and civil society's intermediate associations." For example, according to Schambra, Ronald Reagan called "for a return to the human scale . . . the scale of the local fraternal lodge, the church organization, the block club, the farm bureau."[39] George H. W. Bush (1988–1992) used the imagery of "a thousand points of light" to articulate his vision of civil society, by which he meant increasing reliance on voluntary community organizations. President Bill Clinton, a self-proclaimed "New Democrat," pledged to end big government and urged a return to what he called "organic networks." Social problems could be solved, he suggested, when "all of us are willing to join churches and other good citizens . . . who are saving kids, adopting schools, making streets safer."[40] The statements of these recent presidents reflects a strong belief that "only institutions closer to home—states, local communities, and churches—are held in high regard."[41]

There is an alternative point of view suggesting that a strong national government is not necessarily antithetical to strong community involvement. In other words, according to Theda Skocpol, "from the very beginning of the American nation, democratic governmental and political institutions encouraged the proliferation of voluntary groups linked to regional or national social movements."[42] Voluntary associations mimicked the federal organizational structure with written constitutions and shared power with lower levels or units.[43] Until the 1960s, the local membership looked up to their regional and national counterparts, and the structure provided "mobility ladders" for people in local communities to climb to national leadership positions.[44] These associations served as the training ground for millions to learn about the democratic process and how to run a group. However, beginning in the 1970s, there has been a transformation, according to Skocpol, from membership to advocacy, which has weakened the formerly strong connections between local and national associations. In advocacy groups, the focus is less on members and more on fund-raising to help their causes, which is more of a reflection on the costliness of national mass media campaigns.[45]

■ Chapter Summary

American public administration occurs within the unique context of a federalist political system. The hallmark of this political arrangement is the decentralization of authority, which is marked by the federal, state, and local levels of government sharing power and responsibility. Federalism is the result of a compromise struck by the Constitution's framers between the Federalist principle of centralized government and the Anti-Federalist principle of decentralized government. Throughout American history, the courts have played a significant role in shaping intergovernmental relations through their interpretation of the Constitution and laws passed by Congress.

Another significant aspect of American intergovernmental relations is fiscal federalism. This refers, in large part, to the complex system of grants-in-aid that exists. Throughout most of U.S. history, higher-level governments have provided lower-level governments with financial aid to help them accomplish worthwhile activities. In recent decades, however, higher-level governments have also imposed financial commitments on lower-level governments, which these entities have often found burdensome.

The Constitution provides the framework for interstate cooperation and also establishes the Supreme Court as the mechanism to resolve interstate conflict should it arise. States have also worked out other formal as well as informal arrangements to work with other states.

An overabundance of governmental structures is another unique characteristic of the American federal system, not to mention a multitude of different governments. This crazy-quilt pattern tends to fragment governmental authority and accountability, which often results in confusion for the ordinary citizen. Scholars continue to debate the effects of the evolution of federalism on civil society: Some argue that a strong national government does not result in weakening of community associations, while others believe that it does.

■ Chapter Discussion Questions

1. How is the decentralization of political authority both a cost and a benefit of the federal system?

2. Why has Congress's use of the commerce clause proven so controversial?

3. As the welfare example at the beginning of the chapter indicates, the role of the federal government and state governments in delivering programs can be quite complicated. Was this the founders' intention when they established a federal form of government?

4. Why is there nothing comparable to the Dillon Rule in the U.S. Constitution with respect to the federal government's power over the states? What are the implications for public administration?

5. How does each of the three city government structures discussed in this chapter seek to guarantee the accountability of the executive branch?

BRIEF CASE   THE WISE USE MOVEMENT

On July 4, 1995, a tense crowd gathered around Richard Carver and the two forest rangers who were trying to prevent him from bulldozing a road through a national forest in Nevada. Carver, a rancher and local official in Nye County, Nevada, was cheered on by supporters as he drove his bulldozer straight at one of the rangers. The ranger backed down and let the Constitution-waving Carver through. They had no choice. "All it would have taken was for them to draw a weapon," Carver said, "and 50 people with side-arms would have drilled him."[46]

A group studying development limits in Adirondack National Park in upstate New York and Vermont came under attack by people supporting development. They painted swastikas on office windows, issued death threats to environmentalists, threatened to burn down forest reserves, vandalized the Vermont conservation commissioner's car, and burned down several buildings in an attempt to prevent plans to limit development.[47]

These two incidents are part of an effort that has been occurring around the country with increasing frequency since the 1990s in opposition to environmentalism and the power of the federal government. People associated with the "Wise Use" movement carry out these militant actions. This movement consists of a loose coalition of property owners and industry groups that believe in absolute property rights and oppose any government regulations that restrict the use of property. One of the movement's founders, Ron Arnold, borrowed the name "Wise Use" from Gifford Pinchot, an early conservationist who advocated the wise use of natural resources. The current movement, though, interprets wise use very narrowly to mean the most profitable use, and thus supports the expansion of grazing, mining, oil and gas exploration, and logging on federal lands. Arnold, director of the Center for Defense of Free Enterprise, says that the movement's true aim is "to destroy environmentalism for once and for all."[48]

The Wise Use movement is an example of an enduring source of tension and friction in the federal system; that is, groups and individuals who believe that government's power, particularly the national government's, encroaches on their rights as citizens. Consequently, they engage in efforts to curb this power. Some of those efforts break the law. In this chapter, we largely talk about federalism as a matter between the different levels of government; but the Tenth Amendment to the Constitution says that the states *and* the people share the reserved powers. This can, of course, be interpreted in a number of ways. Wise Use proponents argue that federal laws prevent them from making full profitable use of their private property. Environmentalists argue that spillover effects from unrestricted uses create costs for the rest of society; hence, government regulations are necessary.

The anti-environmentalists assert that governmental considerations of harm ignore the rights of landowners, instead focusing exclusively on the harm to society or to the environment. They propose legislation that will require the government to pay property owners when environmental laws reduce its value for speculative purposes. Groups such as the Pennsylvania Landowners Association and People for the West argue that "takings" legislation is based on the Fifth Amendment, which says that the government must justly compensate the owners of private property that is taken for public use. This position, however, goes well beyond historical Supreme Court opinions on Fifth Amendment property rights.

Examples of recent Wise Use lobbying efforts in Congress include defeating a proposal to elevate the federal Environmental Protection Agency to cabinet-level status, attempting to roll back provisions of the Clean Water Act, Endangered Species Act, and Superfund site cleanup legislation, and delaying public land mining reforms and pesticide reduction legislation.

Brief Case Questions

1. *The case study points to the hostility engendered by some federal land-use policies, at least among a segment of the community. One argument is that this is a political problem, and therefore a political solution is appropriate. It can also be viewed as a management problem, though, specifically one involving intergovernment relations. Which of these two perspectives do you take and why?*

2. *Evaluate the Wise Use debate from the standpoint of the benefits versus costs discussion of federalism in this chapter.*

3. *Divide the class into federalists and antifederalists to discuss the idea that property owners have a "right to pollute" from a constitutional perspective. Include in the discussion the concepts of strict construction and loose construction of the Constitution.*

▥ Key Terms

block grant (page 114)
categorical grant (page 114)
commerce clause (page 111)
crosscutting mandate (page 117)
devolution (page 104)
Dillon's Rule (page 118)
enumerated powers (page 109)
fiscal capacity (page 113)
fiscal federalism (page 113)
fiscal note (page 122)
general-purpose local government (page 123)

home rule (page 121)
implied powers (page 110)
incorporation (page 124)
intergovernmental relations (page 104)
necessary and proper clause (page 110)
preemption (page 117)
reserved powers (page 110)
single-purpose local government (page 123)
supremacy clause (page 111)
unfunded mandates (page 117)
unitary system (page 105)

▥ On the Web

http://www.urban.org/ANF/
  Website that assesses the new federalism.

http://www.networkusa.org/fingerprint/page2/
fp-104–193-responsibility.html
  Examination of the 1996 Personal Responsibility and Work Opportunity Reconciliation Act.

http://www.federalismproject.org/
  The Federalism Project, published by the American Enterprise Institute for Public Policy Research.

http://memory.loc.gov/const/abt_const.html
  This site offers a review of the Constitution and its relevance to federalism.

http://www1.oecd.org/puma/malg/malglink.htm
  Links to intergovernmental-related websites.

http://www.csg.org/csg/default
  Home page of the Council of State Governments.

http://www.ncsl.org/
  Home page of the National Conference of State Legislators.

http://www.whitehouse.gov/omb/grants/
  Office of Management and Budget, Grant information.

http://www.governing.com/
  Online version of *Governing* magazine, the best publication dealing with state and local government and politics.

CHAPTER 6

Civil Society and Public Administration

■ SETTING THE STAGE

"Civil Society Rocks!" a *Pittsburgh Post-Gazette* editorial declared in 2003. According to the writer, gone are the days when the public viewed a nonprofit worker as "a dedicated dreamer who is content with a meager salary, works in a lax professional environment and maintains no job stability." Nonprofits have become professional big players on the community scene. In short, the writer opines, "these are not your grandmother's charities."[1] Indeed, one scholar declares local nonprofit groups are the "key to America's civic renewal."[2]

This civic rebirth is occurring as a result of countless community-building initiatives, large and small, throughout the country. Moreover, a new breed of public servant is helping to lead many of these efforts. In doing so they are capitalizing on a renewed spirit of civic engagement. As Paul Light observes, "It is a work force that comes to work in the morning motivated primarily by the chance to do something worthwhile, savoring the chance to make decisions on its own, take risks and try new things, and puts mission above all else."[3] While these groups and individuals often toil outside government, nonetheless, they time and again turn to government to help make their efforts successful. Such is the case with Philadelphia's Experience Corps, an organization that trains and coordinates senior citizen volunteers who work in the city's most disadvantaged public schools.[4] The seniors, many of whom live on fixed incomes, would not be able to volunteer as much of their time if they did not receive a small stipend from a federal program, AmeriCorps. (See case study at the end of this chapter.) Thus, while nonprofits and other voluntary groups are trying to improve the lives of their fellow citizens, "Public power is often a necessary ingredient in the building of community."[5]

■ CHAPTER PLAN

In this chapter, the importance of U.S. civil society and the role that public administrators can play to help revitalize communities are discussed. In recent years, civil society has become recognized as the foundation of democratic government. We defined civil society in Chapter 1 as "the social institutions that bring people together on a voluntary basis due to shared concerns and values in pursuit of common objectives." This definition is elaborated on in this chapter's first section. We also discuss the relationship between social capital and civil society in this context. Voluntary associations play a vital role in civil society, and thus we devote a section of the chapter to an analysis of the impact they have on administration. Social capital, which is a cornerstone of civil society, is correctly viewed as an asset. However, we also discuss some of the negative aspects of this resource. The recent surge of interest in civil society has been, in no small measure, due to concern that U.S. civil society has deteriorated since the 1960s. The chapter examines both sides of this controversy. Finally, we address several ways in which public administrators can facilitate civil society, enhance civic engagement, and help build social capital. We are particularly interested in the idea that public services can be co-produced in competent communities.

What Is Civil Society?

Civil society has been around ever since human beings began to live together as communities. The scholarly study of civil society, however, is relatively new, achieving considerable visibility in academic circles during the early 1990s; later in the decade, the mass media, politicians, and others also picked up on the idea. By the end of the 1990s, the concept of civil society had become popular with conservatives and liberals, a number of which viewed it as a solution for many of the country's serious social problems. One critic was even led to observe: "Civil society is increasingly touted as a newfound wonder drug for curing any number of problems, from fragmenting families to the decline of voter participation."[6] With such a diverse following, the term's original meaning became somewhat blurred. Indeed, before long, the idea of civil society became like "mom, baseball, and apple pie"; in other words, it came to stand for virtually anything positive and patriotic.

Civil society has a specific meaning, though, in academic discussion. It represents the part of society that exists outside the formal institutions of the government, commercial markets (i.e., industry and business organizations), and the legal system.[7] Thus, civil society consists of voluntary associations and, indeed, encompasses all forms of citizen participation in public matters. An enduring symbol of American civil society, for example, is the New England town meeting, where participants from every walk of life and representing every segment of the community gathered to discuss and vote on community issues. Other examples of civil society include the family, churches, and voluntary organizations like the PTA, Rotary, Knights of Columbus, and bowling leagues. Another important aspect of civil society is its influence on the moral character of a nation. As one observer puts it: "It is the sphere of society that is concerned with moral formation and with ends. Not simply administration or the maximizing of means."[8] Civil society is voluntary, participatory, inclusive, and character forming.

Social Capital and Civic Engagement

Social Capital A term that refers to the trust and relationships that bring and keep community members together, which enables them to achieve their common goals more effectively

Civic engagement The process by which citizens participate in civil society and democratic politics.

Civil society is the linchpin of democratic society, and **social capital** is the glue that holds civil society together. Social capital consists of the trust and relationships that bring and keep community members together, which enables them to achieve their common goals more effectively.[9] Unlike other forms of capital, such as financial and human capital, which are tangible in nature, social capital derives its principal value from the intangible personal networks we form with others and with our communities. Besides the idea of social capital as the glue holding society together, civic participation or **civic engagement** is a core value of civil society.[10] As one author noted: "Civic engagement implies meaningful connections among citizens and among citizens, issues, institutions, and the political system. . . . It implies active participation, with real opportunities to make a difference."[11] Without civic engagement, in other words, true democracy is virtually impossible. However, true civic participation without social capital is likewise impossible. Without adequate reserves of social capital, a community cannot utilize its other social resources (either human or financial) to the fullest extent.[12] Social capital thus serves to aid in the transformation of other forms of capital into the things that the whole community values, such as strong families and neighborhoods and a thriving local economy.[13] One study of schools, for instance, found that "social capital sets the context within which the human and financial capital of parents is converted into success in school by children."[14] It is for these reasons that students of public service should be aware of the importance of civil society and social capital.

Importance of Civil Society

According to civil society scholars, a crucial indicator of community strength is the strength of its social capital.[15] Further, as all levels of government struggle to cope with budget shortages and the lack of other major resources, the importance of social capital increases. Governments therefore find it is often in their best interest to encourage citizen self-governance and more active participation in civic matters. Civic engagement is not a new concept. It is an idea that Americans were quite familiar with in the early years of the republic. Based on his observations of civic life in nineteenth-century America, Alexis de Tocqueville wrote:

> Americans of all ages, all conditions, and all dispositions constantly form associations. They have not only commercial and manufacturing companies, in which all take part, but associations of a thousand other kinds, religious, moral, serious, futile, general or restricted, enormous or diminutive. The Americans make associations to give entertainments, to found seminaries, to build inns, to construct churches, to diffuse books, to send missionaries to the antipodes; in this manner they found hospitals, prisons, and schools. If it is proposed to inculcate some truth or to foster some feeling by the encouragement of a great example, they form a society. Wherever at the head of some new undertaking you see the government in France, or a man of rank in England, in the United States you will be sure to find an association. (Book 2, chap. 5)[16]

Alexis de Tocqueville, the nineteenth-century French observer of American civil society.

SOURCE: Roger-Viollet/Topham/The Image Works

Tocqueville recognized that without civic organizations, democracy itself would be endangered. Civil society as a necessary condition for democratic government is just as important today as it was in the nineteenth century. This point was brought home during the 1980s when Eastern European communist dictatorships were collapsing and new democratic societies were being born. In those countries, people were inspired by the idea of civil society as an alternative to the totalitarian government's control of both the economic and political systems.[17]

As Tocqueville observed, civil society helps to teach the core values and norms of democratic society. As mentioned earlier, scholars claim that among the most important functions of civil society is that it helps with the formation of a country's moral character and sense of purpose. Thus, some regard civil society's ultimate concern as determining the proper ends of American society. They look to civil society to give us answers to questions like "What is our purpose, what is the right way to act, and what is the common good?"[18]

Following Tocqueville's lead, recent scholars have probed the relationship between voluntary associations and democracy. Their findings strongly support the thesis that the stronger the civil society, the healthier the polity. Galston and Levine, for example, found that members of church groups, neighborhood associations, sports leagues, and similar groups are much more likely to vote and discuss politics. Being a part of a social network offers individuals increased opportunities to talk about politics and obtain information about candidates and issues, even when the groups are not politically partisan in nature. Given the importance of social capital to civil society, it should come as no surprise that research indicates a strong association between group membership and interpersonal trust.[19] Further, there is a connection between trust and confidence in the government. This relationship appears to be two-way; when we no longer trust each other, this negatively affects our attitudes toward politics and politicians, and when we lose faith in the political system, it also harms our ability to form trusting relationships with other people.[20]

Clearly, without a strong civil society and all that entails, our democracy would lose much of its vitality. However, as the foregoing indicates, the reverse is also true: without a vital democracy and government, civil society would lose its strength and wither. This is because government establishes the institutional and legal framework that allows civil society to take root and thrive.[21] As one philosopher of civil society recognizes, the state "both frames civil society and occupies space within it. It fixes the boundary conditions and basic rules of all associational activity (including political activity). It compels association members to think about a common good, beyond their own conceptions of the good life."[22]

Contrasting Views on Voluntary Associations

Factions A term used by James Madison to refer to voluntary associations formed to pursue their own interests often to the harm of the rest of society.

Tocqueville is largely responsible for the notion that voluntary associations are the foundation of democracy. By contrast, James Madison held a less charitable view of certain types of voluntary associations, namely, interest groups, which he called **factions**. Factions, for Madison, were "adverse to the rights of other citizens, or to the permanent and aggregate interests of the community." According to Madison, the "violence of factions" could only be controlled by (a) eliminating its causes or (b) controlling its negative effects. The first outcome could only be achieved by doing lasting injury to freedom, or by bringing about a situation in which all citizens naturally shared "the same opinions, the same passions, and the same interests."[23] Needless to say, the latter was impossible, short of a utopia. Thus, the only viable alternative was to control the destructive effects of factions. This could be done, Madison believed, by creating a system of government which would serve as a check and balance on factions, diffusing their negative effects.

The two views of voluntary associations—Madison's and Tocqueville's—need not be mutually exclusive. For example, Tocqueville points out that associations are not always beneficent, a viewpoint Madison shared. However, for the most part, Tocqueville believed that voluntary associations were a positive force in America, while Madison was skeptical and sought insurance in the form of constitutional protections.

Tocqueville's positive vision of civil society has had a profound impact on the way we think about voluntary associations. According to Elshtain, even in the current day, civic associations serve as "seedbeds of civic virtue" and are still the source of community competence, character, and citizenship.[24]

Because of its enduring nature, civil society draws its nourishment from many sources in American society and history. The ideas that shape American civil society come from many diverse traditions and social institutions, as shown in Vignette 6.1.

VIGNETTE 6.1   A Call to Civil Society: The Qualities of Good Citizenship

American democracy presupposes certain qualities of thought and character in the American people, at least in the founders' view. Unfortunately, according to some people, these characteristics are vanishing from society. Jean Bethke Elshtain, chair of the Council of Civil Society, in her essay "A Call to Civil Society," identifies twelve institutions and ideas that are important for good citizenship, but she implies there are more. The following is her list, along with a brief description of each:

1. *The family.* Ideas about self-governance begin with the family. Thus it is aptly called "the cradle of citizenship."
2. *The local community or neighborhood.* Next to the family, people's immediate experiences are shaped by their interaction with their neighborhoods and community. These should therefore be safe, stable environments in which people share a common life. True communities are rooted in "collective memory and shared values."
3. *Faith communities and religious institutions.* Religion is the "primary force . . . that transmits from one generation to another the moral understandings that are essential to liberal democratic institutions." It does this because it elevates our sights toward others and toward ultimate concerns, and away from self-centeredness.
4. *Voluntary civic organizations.* Tocqueville considered these the defining hallmark of American civil society. They promote pluralism and democracy by "limiting the homogenization of culture and the centralization of authority."

5. *Arts and arts institutions.* These contribute to civil society by affirming the important values of "good craftsmanship, sensitivity, creativity, and integrity of materials and expression." The arts, in a pluralistic society, serve as universal languages that raise human consciousness and activate the public imagination.
6. *Local government.* Local governments provide citizens with a forum for civic engagement and serve as "incubators of civic competence."
7. *Primary and secondary education.* Schools in a democracy act as the chief means to transmit core social values. Educators, for example, teach respect for adults and for other students, personal responsibility, and an appreciation of society's civic and moral ideas.
8. *Higher education.* Colleges and universities are one of the principal defenders of intellectual freedom in democratic society. They uphold the values of reason, scientific method, and objectivity of truth and knowledge.
9. *Business, labor, and economic institutions.* Because most work is inherently social, business and economic institutions are part of civil society. These institutions "are major custodians—and can themselves become major creators or destroyers—of social competence, ethical concern, and social trust."
10. *Media institutions.* Of all the sources of civil society's ideas, the media have been growing

(continued on next page)

VIGNETTE 6.1   **A Call to Civil Society: The Qualities of Good Citizenship**
(continued)

the fastest in size and influence. Most Americans, however, view the media as promoting negative values, especially among children and young people.

11. *Shared civic faith and common civic purpose*. As a country, the United States is dedicated to certain guiding principles, chief among them are constitutionalism, personal liberty, social equality, and republican self-governance. These values provide a sense of moral purpose to civil society.

12. *Public moral philosophy*. Americans are heir to the intellectual legacy of the classical Greek and Roman, Judeo-Christian, and Enlightenment traditions. This philosophical legacy serves as the cornerstone of the country's social health and political freedom.

All of these institutions and ideas, taken together, shape the qualities of the individual necessary for self-governance. In Elshtain's view, the values being the most strongly promoted by present-day society are ones that contribute to "a philosophy of expressive individualism, or belief in the sovereignty of the self." For civil society proponents, such a view is fundamentally flawed, however. They believe, as did the ancient Greeks, that humans must live in and participate fully in communities in order to experience actual self-realization.

Interest Groups, Administration, and Civil Society

Interest groups The organizations formed by individuals to advance their joint goals by influencing government.

Lobbyist A person working for an interest group or groups who attempts to influence the policy-making process.

While Tocqueville contemplated voluntary associations and observed public-spirited and cooperative groups, Madison saw self-interested and competitive factions. Both sides of voluntary associations still exist in contemporary American society. Today, just as in Madison's time, **interest groups** have a largely negative image, but they nonetheless play an important role in connecting citizens to government. Interest groups, as a result of government's far-reaching influence, seek to sway public agencies' decisions in ways that further their self-interest. The people who are employed by interest groups to influence government decision-making are called **lobbyists**. Lobbying refers to any attempt to influence either elected or non-elected policymakers.

The growth of administrative power has led to increased interactions between interest groups and public administrators, more so than in the past. As we saw in Chapter 2, nearly every federal department has a "clientele" actively seeking benefits from the government. Departments like Agriculture, Veterans Affairs, and Commerce are sometimes even referred to as "client agencies" because they focus so exclusively on a specific and narrow segment of society. Not only does the clientele benefit from the relationship, but also the agency. When the executive or Congress, for example, contemplates a decision that may harm an agency, the agency's client groups mobilize to exert political pressure to prevent the action from occurring. Farm organizations, for instance, fight against proposed cutbacks in subsidies for farm products administered by the Department of Agriculture. Similarly, veteran groups challenge reductions in their benefits. Thus, it is "essential to every agency's power position" to be attached by an "enduring tie" to an interest group."[25]

Tennessee Valley Authority (TVA) One of the first and certainly one of the most famous public corporations, created in the 1930s to bring electricity to the Tennessee Valley.

The influence of interest groups on government departments has long been a subject of scholarly study. A famous study from the 1940s examined the creation of the **Tennessee Valley Authority (TVA)**, and showed how the federal agency successfully cultivated a constituency.[26] The TVA and the region it was created to help evolved a relationship described as a "mutual dependence"— the agency provided numerous economic benefits, while the region gave the agency its complete political support.

Public agencies turn interest-group support into political power in several ways. Interest groups, for instance, can generate public support for an agency or take public stands on issues on an agency's behalf. Interest groups can act publicly in situations where the agency could not out of fear of political repercussions. Interest groups also help agencies resist budget cuts and other adverse actions planned by the legislature or executive. Generals and admirals must show deference to the commander in chief when he proposes a cut in their budget or seeks to reduce troop levels, but no such obligations restrict defense industries or service associations from expressing their disapproval of the proposed actions.[27] Interest groups can advance an agency's cause by engaging in an aggressive public relations campaign on its behalf. As the late Senator Barry Goldwater said, "The aircraft industry has probably done more to promote the Air Force than the Air Force has done itself."[28]

While client support certainly has advantages, agencies that depend too heavily on it may pay a steep price in the end. Special interests often ask for, and gain, an important voice in the agency's decision-making process. For example, the Department of Labor was established in 1913 to be the voice of the labor union movement in the cabinet. Over time, this meant that important

A Capitol Hill hallway crowded with lobbyists during discussion of tax reform legislation.
SOURCE: Terry Ashe/Time Life Pictures/Getty Images

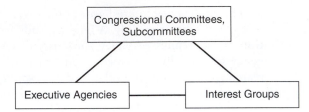

Figure 6.1 The Iron Triangle

agency decisions, such as the selection of key administrative officials, including assistant secretaries of labor, had to be run by key labor unions for their approval. An agency may become "captive" to its clientele when it is unable to move in any direction without its supporters' approval.[29]

As we have seen, the traditional view of interest-group influence on government is often referred to as the iron triangle (see Figure 6.1).[30] In the iron triangle, agencies, interest groups, and congressional committees or subcommittees each form a side of the triangle. Each side supports the other sides and shares a similar viewpoint on matters of mutual concern. The agency, for example, depends on the full political support of its clientele groups when it seeks more money to expand current programs or initiate new ones. Organized support is so critical to agencies that they will try to develop it if it does not already exist. The Department of Agriculture, for example, helped form the American Farm Bureau, the largest and most powerful agricultural interest group.[31] Successful agencies will also have the support of key committees and subcommittees in Congress. In this, the agencies are aided by the fact that committee membership is assigned on the basis of members' interest in a policy area or its importance to members' constituents. As a result, committee members are likely to be more supportive of agency goals and programs than other members of Congress are. In turn, committee members receive the benefit of the relevant interest group's electoral support in the form of campaign funds or mobilizing constituents as voters. For their part, the interest groups, via their support, gain access to the corridors of legislative power and the opportunity to influence policy. Vignette 6.2 gives an example of iron triangles at work in the sugar industry.

The AFL-CIO, the American Farm Bureau Federation, the Chamber of Commerce, and other interest groups that once dominated the policy process have suffered an erosion of their power due to the "advocacy explosion" that began in the 1960s. Numerous groups formed in support of civil rights, women's rights, and the public interest (e.g., Common Cause, Move-On, the Sierra Club).[32] As a result of these changes in the landscape of voluntary associations, the contemporary policy process has become more complex and fragmented, with a larger number of important actors than before. This has led to a questioning of the iron triangles model of interest-group influence. For example, political scientist Hugh Heclo was one of the first to challenge the traditional view's narrow focus on a powerful few while ignoring the many who increasingly wield considerable influence in the policy

VIGNETTE 6.2   Iron Triangles in the Sugar Industry

According to the Center for Responsive Politics, a nonpartisan research group that tracks money in politics and its effect on public policy, the sugar industry has long been the beneficiary of an iron triangle consisting of congressional agriculture committees, the farm lobby that also serves as a source of large campaign contributions, and the U.S. Department of Agriculture. Congress protects the interests of sugar farmers and agribusiness by authorizing loans and price-support programs that inflate sugar prices above the world rate. According to Center for Responsive Politics, "In early 1995, the world price for sugar was 16 cents a pound; in the United States it was 22.5 cents a pound." The center estimates that political campaign contributions from political action committees between 1979 and 1994 amounted to over $10 million. The ranking Republican on the House Agriculture Committee from 1982 to 1991 was later the secretary of agriculture during the administration of George H. W. Bush. Critics question whether the cozy relationship between the members of the sugar industry iron triangle serves the interests of the public at large.

SOURCE: Center for Responsive Politics, 2002.

process. According to Heclo, the growth of "unfamiliar policy issues" has led to the mobilization of "loose alliances" of "issue-activists," "issue-experts," and "issue-watchers" that come to "define public affairs by sharing information about them."[33]

The iron triangle is a rigid and closed system. But the **issue network** model (see Figure 6.2) is a fluid and open system in which "public policy issues tend

Issue networks A theory of interest group influence on government that states the policy-making process is marked by a high degree of openness and access by many different groups.

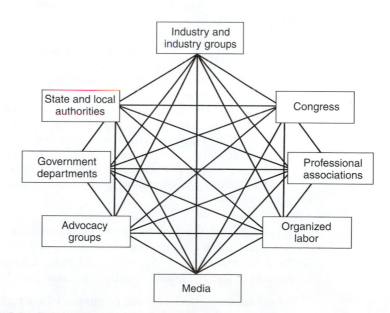

Figure 6.2   An Issue Network at the Federal Level

to be refined, evidence debated, and alternative options worked out—though rarely in any controlled, well-organized way."[34] The consequences of policy networks have been both positive and negative. On the plus side, Heclo points out, policy networks more accurately reflect some of the larger changes in society over the last fifty years (e.g., the decline in political party importance and the rise of experts), they can form more effective linkages between Congress and the executive, and their presence in the process can provide more political maneuvering room for political executives. On the negative side, issue networks help to undermine the legitimacy of the political process because they are insulated from the broader public, they further exacerbate the risk that political appointees will become captives of policy experts in the bureaucracy, and they lie outside the traditional accountability mechanisms of the legislature and the executive.[35]

Negative Aspects of Social Capital

Social capital, which was touted earlier as critical to the success of civil society, has a dark side. Some forms of social capital can contribute to destructive forces in the larger community. Relationships, trust, and informal networks can be used to the detriment of the social order just as easily as they can serve to further community interests. At the turn of the twentieth century, for instance, street gangs virtually ruled many lower-class neighborhoods in New York City. These gangs thrived in poor neighborhoods, which despite their poverty and crime were strong in some forms of social capital. According to historian Herbert Asbury, whose *Gangs of New York* was first published in 1927:

> As rapidly as the ranks of the gangs were depleted, either by death or by the occasional activity of the police, they were filled by the street boys and by recruits from the young men's social clubs which abounded throughout the East and West sides, bearing such names as the Twin Oaks, the Yankee Doodle Boys, the Go-Aheads, the Liberty Athletic Club, the Round Back Rangers, the Bowery Indians, the East Side Crashers, the East Side Dramatic and Pleasure Club, the Jolly Forty-eight, the Soup Greens and the Limburger Roarers. These organizations were patterned after, and in many instances, controlled and supported by, the political associations which had been formed in large numbers by the Tammany district leaders, who thereby strengthened their hold upon the voting masses.[36]

This colorful description of nineteenth-century New York City gang life points out that focusing exclusively on social capital's positive aspects can lead us to ignore some of its harmful, and indeed, criminal aspects. The more important of social capital's negative characteristics include the following:

1. *Exclusionary effects:* Strong group ties can act as obstacles to outsiders who want to participate in a community. Evidence for this historically

The Lower East Side of New York City, filled with gangs in the nineteenth century, provides an example of negative social capital.

SOURCE: Bettmann/Corbis

can be found in the domination of blue-collar occupations, or even entire industries, by certain ethnic groups in some American cities.

2. *Conformity-enhancing effects:* The other side of the close-knit community ideal is the intense pressure for social conformity that often accompanies such communities in real life. A well-known example of this is the small town in which the neighbors know everything about everyone else and are critical of any attempts to be different. For some, this situation is too socially confining, leading some independent-minded souls to flee to the anonymity of large cities.

3. *Strong social and economic class pressures:* Historically, tight-knit ethnic enclaves in cities tend to have considerable social capital. However, the social capital found therein creates pressures that make it difficult for a community member to move out of poverty. As the gang example points out, "The same kinds of ties that yield public goods also produce 'public bads': mafia families, prostitution rings, and youth gangs, to name a few."[37]

Clearly, the above examples show that not all manifestations of social capital should be encouraged. Public officials must be able to differentiate the positive forms of social capital from the negative forms and to encourage an increase and strengthening of the former while working to reduce the bad effects of the latter.

Is Civil Society Declining?

Bowling alone A term coined by the political scientist Robert Putnam to refer to the tendency of individuals in contemporary society to join fewer groups than earlier generations and to do more activities by themselves.

The political scientist Robert Putnam created something of a stir when he declared that civil society was on the decline in America. According to Putnam, "Evidence from a number of independent sources strongly suggests that America's stock of social capital has been shrinking for more than a quarter century."[38] He even coined a catchy phrase, **bowling alone**, to describe this phenomenon. "The most whimsical," he explained, "yet discomfiting bit of evidence of social disengagement in contemporary America that I have discovered is this: more Americans are bowling today than ever before, but bowling in organized leagues has plummeted in the last decade or so."[39] In addition, Putnam cites the decline in membership in organizations like the PTA, the League of Women Voters, the Red Cross, and labor unions since the 1960s as further evidence of this alarming trend. He also notes that Americans are spending less time socializing and less time in clubs and organizations than previously.[40] Putnam further contends that Americans' lack of political involvement is yet another indicator of lagging interest in civic matters. Finally, he says these trends are unaffected by rising education levels, which he finds baffling, because in the past, high levels of education have been closely associated with higher rates of civic participation. In the end, Putnam mentions many *possible* causes for the decline of civil society in America in recent decades (see Table 6.1).

After considering each of the possibilities for decline, Putnam concludes that generational effects and technological changes have contributed the most to the "bowling alone" phenomenon. He writes that there was a "long

TABLE 6.1 Eight Possible Reasons for the Decline of Civil Society

1. Busyness and time pressure—despite Americans feeling more pressed for time, time budget studies do not confirm this observation.

2. Periods of economic trouble—although the less affluent tend to be less engaged in civic matters, research indicates that the decline in civic engagement occurs at all income levels.

3. Personal mobility—current Americans show no marked tendency to move more frequently than earlier generations; therefore, this cannot be an explanation for lack of community involvement.

4. Movement to the suburbs—downtrends in civil society are "virtually identical everywhere," including cities, suburbs, towns, and rural areas.

5. Movement of women into the paid labor force—women in the workforce tend to be *more* involved in voluntary associations.

6. Breakdown of marriage and family ties—although the decline in marriage is a contributing factor in declining group membership and trust, there is a marked downturn in joining and trusting even among the happily married.

7. Social and political movements of the 1960s—less involvement in civic activities is reported across different races; disengagement among whites appears to have nothing to do with racial prejudice.

8. Expansion of the welfare state—international data show there is evidence that large government is positively correlated with social capital.

'civic' generation, born roughly between 1910 and 1940, a broad group of people substantially more engaged in community affairs and substantially more trusting than those younger than they."[41] But this generation is gradually dying off, and following generations show increasing disengagement from civic life. Putnam reserves his sharpest criticism, though, for television, which he considers the chief cause for the erosion of civil society. Television, according to Putnam, "privatizes leisure time" and inhibits social activities taking place outside the home.[42] He points to the growing body of research linking television viewing with negative effects on children, such as aggressive and antisocial behavior and declining academic achievement.

Not everyone agrees with Putnam's diagnosis of the problem, however. Skocpol, for instance, suggests that civic associations have been hurt by the shifting tastes and allegiances of middle-class citizens. It is the middle- and upper- classes who are the most active in civic affairs, so a decline in middle-class participation will have a dampening effect overall. By and large, research shows that the highly educated, professionals, and other members of the middle class have largely deserted local groups, like the Rotary Club and the Knights of Columbus, in favor of national organizations that can better represent their professional and business interests.[43] Whereas fifty years ago middle-class strivers viewed membership in the Lions Club as a means to get ahead, their contemporary counterparts are much more likely to view the local chapter of the American Bar Association as a more effective vehicle for self-advancement.

Perrow, on the other hand, asserts that "organizational society" has largely replaced civil society. According to this view, large organizations, like corporations and government bureaucracies, now provide their employees many of the benefits that were previously provided by churches, neighborhood associations, and public agencies (e.g., healthcare, education, recreation, and other services). Thus, civil society "has been replaced by one where your life chances and experiences are much more mediated by remote 'elites'—the heads of large employing organizations."[44]

Other scholars question some of Putnam's conclusions, such as civil society is declining. Some disagree with his view that civil society alone is sufficient to revitalize our democracy. Others take issue with his interpretation of major social trends. Some contend, for example, that Putnam overlooks some significant types of civic engagement. Rather than participating in groups like the League of Women Voters or the PTA, which have relatively low expectations for member participation, Americans are now joining organizations that require far greater personal involvement and commitment—for example, a church, synagogue, or neighborhood association.[45] As a consequence, although people may be more active civically, they are participating in fewer organizations than before. In the past, moreover, many people became members of voluntary associations like the YMCA for purely utilitarian reasons (e.g., to use the gym), which were completely unrelated to the organization's civic component. Increasingly, however, these individuals can now find commercial alternatives to satisfy their personal needs. So people get memberships in private health clubs or municipal recreation centers instead of the YMCA.[46]

Civil Society and the Role of Public Administration

Civil society is separate and distinct from the government, but it needs government's protection and support to thrive. Civil society and government, therefore, exist in a mutually beneficial relationship; both need each other to be healthy and strong. Meanwhile, public administration is "at the nexus of the state and civil society"—in other words, it serves as a connecting point between government and community. Thus, public administrators can be viewed as the intermediaries between citizens and government. However, this can result in role ambiguity: "Public servants, somehow, are neither fish nor fowl, and they are scorned by both the political representatives and the citizens they serve."[47]

Being at the nexus of government and civil society, though, need not always be a disadvantage. Indeed, public administration can use its central position to improve both government and civil society. Public servants are "naturals" for this role, since they already work at jobs that benefit the whole community. Many administrators would agree with the following observation from a Harvard student who worked in government: "It was motivating to get up every day and go to work and think that what I was doing was for the benefit of the common good, the everyman, or woman, as the case might be. . . . My friends who worked in the private sector didn't have that feeling or that experience or that reality. That was something lacking for them."[48] This perspective is by no means rare in public service, and many public administrators see their work as relating to community-building efforts.[49] City managers, for example, see themselves as community-builders and enablers of democracy.[50] Some scholars assert that public servants are helping citizens achieve self-governance.[51]

As of this writing, however, little research has been done examining the role of public administrators as catalysts for social capital creation. A study comparing the attitudes and behavior of public servants with other citizens allows us to reach some positive, albeit tentative, conclusions regarding the connection. The study found that government employees typically score higher than other citizens on the several indexes measuring, among other things, humanitarianism and **social altruism**. Based on the findings, the author concluded that public servants are slightly more trusting, more altruistic and helping, more tolerant, and more accepting of diversity than other citizens. Further, the study indicates, "As expected, public servants are more active in civic affairs than are other citizens. Apparently, public servants manifest more civic-minded norms and have a stronger proclivity to engage in civic-minded behaviors."[52] Public servants, in other words, are ideal candidates to play the role of civil society catalysts.

Social altruism A person's sense of connectedness and responsibility toward other people.

Competent community A community that makes the most of its social capital; competent communities can be found in less affluent areas as well as wealthy ones.

In light of public administration's significant influence on civil society, administrators can no longer content themselves with being merely competent professionals; they must also view their service within the larger context of **competent communities**. A competent community is one in which the diverse parts of a community (1) come together effectively to identify community problems and needs, (2) reach consensus over important goals and priorities, (3) decide on the actions necessary to achieve these goals, and (4) effectively implement the agreed-upon actions to reach its goals.[53] A competent community, in short, makes the most of its social capital. Community competence also requires a number of well-skilled and well-trained leaders to help in translating social capital into positive community outcomes. This is a role that public administrators increasingly are being called upon to play (see Vignette 6.3). In many communities, there is a willingness to engage in voluntary efforts to, for example, clean up neighborhoods, help fight crime, and combat drugs.

Often what is needed is competent leadership. Before the 1997 President's Summit on Community Service in Philadelphia, many thousands volunteered to take part in a massive cleanup of the city's dirtiest streets. However, hundreds of the volunteers had to be turned away, and at the end of the day a significant proportion of the work that needed to be done was unfinished and had to be completed by city employees. The chief cause for this failure, despite the best intentions, is that volunteers are inherently inefficient. Volunteers' enthusiasm and tirelessness cannot substitute for the skills, focus, or productivity of paid staff.[54] However, professionals working in tandem with community volunteers can make a tremendous difference. Public administrators in cooperation with community members can harness a potent social force for effecting change in many great and small ways.

According to Parr and Lampe, emphasizing social capital and civil society requires a new type of leader among public servants. In today's complex cultural environment, professional competency requires that administrators become effective at collaboration in addition to possessing the leadership and technical skills that contributed to success in the past. Collaboration and community-building means the ability to reach across different organizations, sectors, and cultures "to convene people from different backgrounds and help them toward results despite their divergent values."[55] Collaboration also means that being able to facilitate public meetings and encourage active participation from citizens is now as important as expertise in a policy area.

In their role as community-builders, public servants must adopt attitudes and behaviors that foster a spirit of active engagement with the community. Some authors suggest reframing the issue of civic engagement to include more than just encouraging the public to provide its input in community matters, as clearly important as this is.[56] Their contention is that community competence ought to be viewed as a tool of effective public management as well as a

Co-production A process in which government and citizens work together to carry out public programs.

means to promote civil society. The idea that ordinary citizens might have a role in the **co-production** of some public services has attracted a great deal of attention at the local level, as communities regularly face budget shortfalls and taxpayers resist tax increases.[57] Co-production offers the promise of reducing costs and empowering community members, who can be thought of as co-producers of some services instead of merely consumers. For example, neighborhood watch programs give local residents a greater sense of control over their own personal security and lessen the need for police patrols. Parents as Teachers is a national program that provides parents with educational resources, based on the philosophy that children's learning can occur at home as well as in school.

These and other examples show that citizen participation in public service delivery can help agencies achieve their program goals rather than hinder them. But, as Parr and Lampe observe, working effectively with citizens also requires that public servants recognize "people are not empowered by others." While public administrators can help create the conditions for citizen empowerment, they must recognize that citizens are in the end responsible for their own empowerment.[58] As former New Jersey Senator Bill Bradley states, "Public policy . . . can help facilitate the revitalization of democracy and civil society, but it cannot create civil society."[59] True citizen empowerment thus requires collaboration, which entails a willingness to allow people to take the initiative. Without a true spirit of collaboration and community involvement, the results may be disappointing to both administrators and citizens. As one observer commented about an experimental criminal justice program called Balancing Justice: "My main regret is that we lost track of the process. We didn't realize that the way we got people involved was as important as what they said in those discussions. We should've recognized the true value of Balancing Justice . . . that citizens and government were working together—and found ways of making a regular, permanent part of the way we make decisions and solved problems."[60]

Obstacles to Competent Communities

It is not an easy task, building competent communities (see Vignette 6.3). Despite the best intentions of administrators, it is by no means a foregone conclusion that citizens will respond to administration's overtures to collaborate as expected. Barriers to effective community building can come from both the administrative and citizen sides. On the one hand, obstacles to competent community stem from citizen attitudes and behavior, which include lack of interest in public affairs, the demands of work and family, and the distractions of modern life. On the other hand, certain aspects of administration can present hindrances to fostering community engagement. We focus on some of the more significant of these hurdles in the next section.

Administrators, for instance, might view the requirement to obtain citizen participation as cumbersome, time-consuming, and inefficient. For example,

VIGNETTE 6.3   Competent Communities and Administrators

Building community competence entails a high level of commitment to community. Commitment to one's community is enhanced when three things occurs. First, residents realize that what happens in the community and what it does has a large impact on their lives. Second, they feel that they play or can play a significant role in the community. Third, they observe that their participation results in positive outcomes. The following seven characteristics help develop the commitment of different groups to community:

1. *Self-other awareness.* This refers to the clearness with which each part of the community can identify its own interests and the awareness of how these interests relate to the other parts of the community. In essence, this requires that each segment have a clear and realistic view of the "degree of conflict or compatibility" of its own interests with those of different parts of the community. Public administrators can be helpful in this process of identification and awareness.

2. *Articulateness.* Related to the first characteristic is how well each community segment articulates its own position and its relationship to the positions of other parts. This is improved by building effective communication between parts. Administrators can assist in the dialogue among different segments by providing elementary training in communicative skills, including public speaking, how to run committee discussions, and helping groups devise clear position statements on community issues.

3. *Communication.* Reciprocity in communication is often missing in most community dialogue. "Meaningful communication requires that the sender of the message take the role of the recipient and respond covertly, i.e., incipiently to his own message in the way he anticipates that the other will respond." Administrators can assist community members in the development of this skill, which would contribute to the first item on this list.

4. *Containing and accommodating conflict.* As positions are identified and articulated, communication naturally increases, which often leads to more frequent conflicts between different parts of the community. Therefore it is necessary to develop procedures to accommodate these conflicts. Administrators can be trained in these practices and techniques, which they can use to assist community members, achieve some form of accommodation.

5. *Participation.* A necessary component of community competence is participation in civic matters. In order to instill this competence in others, the public servants should be active participants in the life of the community. There is an abundance of research indicating that they are.

6. *Managing relations with larger society.* "No man is an island" and neither is a community. Every community must therefore learn to adapt to its broader social context, that is, to seek out additional resources and reduce threats that come from the environment. This strategy entails learning to make full and effective use of its experts, and all other community members who possess technical skills relevant to community building. But communities should learn how to use experts without being controlled by them.

7. *Procedures for community decision-making.* Competent communities require effective communication and interactions among the different parts. Developing effective decision-making procedures can facilitate better communication. The role of the administrator is to make possible competent community by providing the "constant scrutiny and review of procedures" necessary to maintain the best possible communication and relations among the various segments of the community.

SOURCE: L. S. Cottrell, "The Competent Community," in *Further Explorations in Social Psychiatry,* ed. Berton H. Kaplan, Robert Neal Wilson, and Alexander Hamilton Leighton (New York: Basic Books, 1976).

public meetings can disrupt administrative routine, while obtaining citizen input often slows down the decision-making process, resulting in less efficient administration. Hence, some administrators view public engagement as something that needs to be "managed" in order to maintain agency stability and protect agency goals.[61]

Perhaps a more serious problem is that certain aspects of professional administration may unintentionally undermine civic competence. Ironically, certain elements of professionalization can have negative effects on the very communities that public service professionals are trying to help. Clearly, one of professionalization's strengths is the specialized skills and techniques that can be employed for solving complex social problems. However, ordinary citizens understand poorly, if at all, the "professional remedies" that are being utilized on their behalf. The professional, for his or her part, interprets this lack of comprehension as the "client doesn't understand what he needs."[62] This situation can lead to frustration on the part of the administrator and citizen. Further, ordinary citizens are often baffled by professional jargon, known sometimes as bureaucratese. Consequently, the community begins to lose confidence in its ability to even understand, much less address on its own, community problems. The end result of this process, in the worst case, is citizens who think the world "is understood only by professionals who know how it works, what I need, and how my need is met. I am the object rather than the actor. My life and our society are technical problems."[63] This, unfortunately, can lead to deterioration of social capital, as citizens grow increasingly disengaged from civic life, preferring instead to let professionals take care of them and their problems.

Of course, we are not arguing that professionalization is bad. Quite the contrary; it is necessary to deal with the problems of a culturally diverse, technological society. Rather, the main point is that administrators must be always aware of the potential for the public to misunderstand their actions and motivations. The discussion earlier about the need to view one's role in the context of building competent community is relevant here. One way to overcome some of the problematic aspects of professional administration is by learning skills of collaboration and community building.

Civil Society and the Future of Public Service

The future of public service is shaped in large part by the attitudes and beliefs of current public administrators as well as the attitudes and beliefs of those who will follow in their steps. Earlier in the chapter, we mentioned research that indicates current public servants generally express a strong sense of working for the greater good. Are future public administrators (i.e., current students) similarly predisposed? Paul C. Light identified several trends among recent public administration graduates which he thinks will characterize the new public service. The following trends will continue to have an impact on the capacity of future public servants to contribute to civil society.

1. *Greater diversity*. Increasingly, government service is no longer the chief occupational choice of public administration students. Fewer graduates of the top schools and programs in the country are making government their primary destination after graduation. On the plus side, however, public service is becoming more diverse in the areas of race and gender.

2. *Nonprofit jobs*. There is a great deal of interest in the nonprofit sector. Light's survey found that recent graduates were twice as likely to seek employment with nonprofit organizations than with government agencies. A majority of the graduates said that, although they believe government still represents the public interest, it was not as successful in helping people or in spending money wisely as is the nonprofit and private sectors.

3. *Sector switching*. There is an expectation of mobility across the public, private, and nonprofit sectors on the part of recent graduates. People in the new public service "believe that change is a natural, indeed, inevitable, part of one's career." As one graduate said, "Nothing is promised to us."[64] This leads to the belief that over time, one will be just as likely to be employed by a private or nonprofit organization as with a public agency.

4. *Sense of mission*. Among recent graduates, there is a continued deep commitment to making a difference in the world. Indicative of this attitude is one graduate's response: "I just felt being in the public service was better work, more honest work, helping people."[65] There is optimism to be found here. The future of public service appears to be in the hands of people who are just as dedicated to the greater good as are current public administrators.

Arguably, these trends portend both promise and peril for the future of public service. For example, a more racially and ethnically diverse public service is one that is able to more effectively communicate with different ethnic and racial communities and to recognize and respond to their needs. Such a public service transcends the normal cleavages of society to embrace the multiple economic, social, and ethnic communities that increasingly make up twenty-first-century America. In addition, a strong sense of mission is a necessary ingredient in the work of building competent community and encouraging civic engagement.

The trend toward more graduates seeking nonprofit jobs is a mixed blessing, however. On the one hand, it contributes to the greater diversity noted above, but on the other hand, it drains the public service of its most valuable resource—its human capital. Intersector mobility is another mixed blessing, in that it allows administrators to develop a good understanding of the private and nonprofit sectors, but it also means that competent, skilled individuals do not stay in the public service. It is still too early to tell whether the more positive trends will eventually come to predominate. However, all of the trends that Light identifies will have a significant impact on public administration and the impact of the public service on civil society.

■ Chapter Summary

Civil society is central to democratic government. Therefore, public administration inevitably plays a large role in assuring the vitality of civil society. This role is sometimes obscured by the other roles that administrators play in society, including those of expert and street-level bureaucrat. More recently, however, there has been an increasing awareness of the important role public servants can play in building competent community and with civic engagement. This is, moreover, a role that public administrators should be able to embrace, because public administrators show a predisposition to public service and working on behalf of the common good.

Recently, according to some scholars, American civil society has suffered some deterioration. Evidence for this includes a sharp decline in group membership and falling political participation, including lower voter turnouts. Others have challenged this contention, pointing out that these trends are ambiguous. Nevertheless, there is no disagreement over the need for a strong and vibrant civil society. If civil society suffers from erosion, public servants should be at the forefront of those who are attempting to shore it up. And when civil society appears vital and strong, public administrators should work to keep it that way. The future of public service is promising in this regard, as the sense of commitment to the public interest remains strong as ever. However, some areas deserve careful attention, particularly regarding the tendency for recent graduates of outstanding public administration programs to choose to work in nongovernmental jobs.

■ Chapter Discussion Questions

1. Why has the idea of civil society managed to appeal to both ends of the ideological spectrum—to liberals and conservatives? Do you think that both sides view the concept in the same way? Explain.

2. Some public administrators feel uncomfortable about a direct role for interest groups in administration. Should administration be insulated from the direct demands of external groups? Why or why not?

3. In what ways do interest groups benefit civil society? In what ways do they hurt it? Use specific examples in your answers.

4. Explain how the same aspects of social capital can have both positive and negative effects on communities. How can we reinforce the positive without at the same time encouraging the negative?

5. Based on the discussion in the chapter, can you think of specific ways that collaboration between public administrators and citizens can be fostered? What are some practical difficulties that might arise?

BRIEF CASE   HOW FEDERAL BUDGET CUTS AFFECT CIVIL SOCIETY

The following statement is from an opinion-page article that appeared in the *Boston Globe* on October 10, 2003: "Eighty-seven billion dollars is a lot to ask, even for the difficult task of building a democracy in a country that has never had one."

The authors of the piece, both members of AmeriCorps, then asked: "Two hundred million dollars? Not as impressive. Well, that's how much money AmeriCorps, the country's premier federally funded national service organization, asked for last year. They didn't get it."

AmeriCorps was founded in 1993 by President Bill Clinton as a network of over 2,000 nonprofit organizations and public agencies involved in public service activities ranging from cleaning up neighborhoods to homeland security and disaster relief. One of the programs funded by AmeriCorps is City Year, which has as its stated intention: "To improve the nation from within by doing community service in 15 sites across the country. City Year provides services ranging from domestic violence prevention to environmental protection, with the primary focus on teaching underprivileged children how to fight social injustice and 'build a beloved community', a term taken from a speech made by the Rev. Martin Luther King Jr."

The article goes on to note that the City Year program originated in Boston in 1988. During its existence, it has "revitalized more than 3,617 outdoor spaces, worked with more than 364 corporate partners, served more than 772,250 children, and completed more than 10.9 million total hours of service." The two young authors point out that, as City Year Corps members, they are required to put in fifty-hour work weeks while receiving a stipend that is the equivalent of about $3 per hour. As they say, "We are proof that the youth of today do care and are ready to make sacrifices for our country."

In their plea that funding for their program be restored, they end their article with the following poignant passage:

> As City Year Corps members, we constantly keep in mind the lives of children, who will be leading our country in the near future. We are planting seeds in the young so that when they grow they can be leaders and role models for the subsequent generation. Our funding has been cut, and while these cuts have been devastating, we are still striving for excellence and striving to make a difference. This is an important year for City Year and AmeriCorps as a whole. We must and will prove that national service is an important component to building a stronger, more ideal community.

Brief Case Questions

1. *In what other ways might cuts in public spending jeopardize social capital? Besides the examples given in the case study, what others can you think of?*

2. *Think of civic renewal efforts in your community. What role, if any, does government play in the success of these efforts? Does government provide other types of support besides financial assistance to these initiatives?*

3. *In the struggle over scarce resources, worthwhile groups and causes often must compete with each other. The groups that are most successful are not necessarily the most commendable, since arguably they all have a legitimate claim to merit. However, the ones that emerge with bigger budgets tend to be more persuasive in the budgetary process. Think of some ways the arguments made in this brief case might be strengthened, particularly in light of the points made in this chapter.*

▣ Key Terms

bowling alone (page 144)
civic engagement (page 134)
competent community (page 147)
co-production (page 148)
factions (page 136)
interest group (page 138)

issue network (page 141)
lobbyist (page 138)
social altruism (page 146)
social capital (page 134)
Tennessee Valley Authority (TVA) (page 139)

▣ On the Web

http://www.civnet.org/
 CIVNET is an online resource and service promoting civic education around the world.

http://www.iscv.org/
 The Institute for the Study of Civic Values is a Philadelphia-based organization promoting a renewed commitment to America's historic civic ideals.

http://www.civiced.org/
 The Center for Civic Education's mission is to promote an enlightened and responsible citizenry committed to democratic principles in the United States and abroad.

http://www.gwu.edu/~ccps/
 The Communitarian Network is a nonpartisan organization committed to shoring up the moral, social, and political environment.

http://www.movingideas.org/commonwealth/
 The Commonwealth site allows interested users to access the archives of *American Prospect* magazine articles from the past dealing with nonprofit issues and civil society.

http://www.ncl.org/
 The National Civic League, founded in 1894, is America's premier civic association.

http://www.arnova.org/
 The Association for Research on Nonprofit Organizations and Voluntary Action is an international organization dedicated to understanding the nonprofit sector, philanthropy, and volunteerism.

CHAPTER 7

Theories of Organization and Public Administration

■ SETTING THE STAGE

The modern world would be unimaginable without large organizations. We feel their impact in nearly every aspect of contemporary life. Among other things, organizations employ us, instruct us, protect us, entertain us, and heal us when we are sick. Almost everything we do requires the involvement of organizations. Today, even terrorist groups are organized along complex bureaucratic principles. Al Qaeda, for instance, has operations as complex and far-flung as a multinational corporation. According to the 9/11 Commission report, Osama Bin Laden's organization is "a hierarchical top-down group with defined positions, tasks, and salaries" and with offices in London, other European cities, the Balkans, Southeast Asia, and the Middle East. Structurally similar to any other large bureaucracy, Al Qaeda is organized into units specializing in intelligence, military affairs, finances, political matters, and even media and public relations.[1] Clearly, the capacity to inflict great damage, as well as to perform much good in the world, depends on the ability to organize effectively.

■ CHAPTER PLAN

In this chapter, we examine a number of different theories of organization, all of which have contributed to our current understanding of public administration. In general, organization theory assumes that all organizations, public or private, share certain basic characteristics (e.g., roles, coordination, structure, etc.); this is particularly true for early theories of organization. Some of the theories discussed in this chapter, however, deal exclusively with public organizations, although most do not. Table 7.1 presents a timeline showing some of the significant events and authors in the history of organization theory; many are discussed in this chapter and the next two chapters.

Even early classical organization theory, discussed in the first section of this chapter, contributes in an important way to contemporary public organizations. Early theorists tended to focus on the structural aspects of organizations and determining the

TABLE 7.1 Chronology of Selected Important Events in Modern Organization and Public Administration Theory

1903	Frederick W. Taylor publishes *Shop Management*.
1910	The term "scientific management" is used for the first time, by future Supreme Court Justice Louis D. Brandeis in his testimony before Interstate Commerce Commission. Brandeis argues that the railroads do not need a rate increase and that instead they should use scientific management techniques that would save them millions.
1911	Frederick W. Taylor publishes *The Principles of Scientific Management*.
1916	Henri Fayol publishes *General and Industrial Management* in France, the first work to offer a complete theory of management.
1922	Posthumous publication of Max Weber's description of the "ideal bureaucracy." In Weber, bureaucracy finds its first and in many ways most important theorist.
1924	Elton Mayo and associates begin Hawthorne studies at the Hawthorne Works of the Western Electric Company in Chicago. As a result of this groundbreaking eight-year research, a new approach to organization known as the human relations school arises.
1926	Mary Parker Follett anticipates participatory management techniques with her "power with" instead of "power over" approach.
1933	Elton Mayo publishes *The Human Problems of Industrial Civilization*, based on the Hawthorne studies; it is the first major work of the human relations school.
1937	Luther Gulick publishes "Notes on the Theory of Organization," which introduces the concept of POSDCORB as a means to understand the chief organizing responsibilities of the executive.
1938	Chester Barnard publishes *The Functions of the Executive*.
1939	*Management and the Worker*, by Roethlisberger and Dickson, associates of Mayo, is published; it is a major contribution to the human relations movement.
1943	Abraham Maslow publishes "A Theory of Human Motivation," which introduces the concept of the "needs hierarchy."
1946	Herbert Simon's "The Proverbs of Administration," a scathing critique of public administration principles, appears in *Public Administration Review*.
1947	Simon publishes *Administrative Behavior*, which argues that decision-making and administration are synonymous and calls for a true scientific approach to public administration to replace the inconsistent principles approach.
1951	Publication of Ludwig von Bertalanffy's "General Systems Theory: A New Approach to the Unity of Science," the intellectual forebear of the systems approach to organizations.
1956	William H. Whyte Jr.'s *The Organization Man* popularizes the concept of organization members as conforming to organizational norms and policies.
1957	Publication of Chris Argyris' *Personality and Organization*, which argues that modern organizations' needs are incompatible with the needs of mature adult members.
	Douglas M. McGregor introduces Theory X and Theory Y in his article "The Human Side of Enterprise."
	Anthony Downs's *An Economic Theory of Democracy* proposes that the economic model be applied to the political process, which serves as the intellectual basis for public choice theory.

TABLE 7.1 Continued

1959	Charles A. Lindblom's "The Science of 'Muddling Through' " introduces the theory of incremental-ism to organization theory.
	Frederick Herzberg, Bernard Mausner, and Barbara Snyderman's motivation-hygiene theory appears in *The Motivation to Work*.
1962	The power approach to organization theory is introduced by David Mechanic's "Sources of Power of Lower Participants in Complex Organizations."
1964	Aaron Wildavsky's *The Politics of the Budgetary Process* applies incrementalism to budgeting.
1967	James D. Thompson in *Organizations in Action* attempts to reconcile open and closed systems theory by asserting that organizations create functions to deal with the external environment.
	Anthony Downs's *Inside Bureaucracy* applies public choice theory to understanding how bureaucracy works.
1971	Graham T. Allison publishes *Essence of Decision*, a case study of the Cuban missile crisis, in which he disputes the claim that public policies are made by a single rational actor who is in control of government officials and organizations.
	H. George Frederickson becomes the chief spokesman of new public administration theory as a result of his article "Toward a New Public Administration," which argues for a public administration that will help improve society through a greater emphasis on equity.
1973	Publication of Vincent Ostrom's *The Intellectual Crisis in American Public Administration*, in which he views an overemphasis on bureaucracy and centralization as the causes for the intellectual crisis in public administration; he puts forth a public choice alternative.
1979	Rosabeth Moss Kanter in "Power Failure in Management Circuits" asserts that powerlessness creates more problems within organizations than power.
1981	Jeffrey Pfeffer publishes *Power in Organizations*, a leading work in the power and politics approach to organizations.
1992	David Osborne and Ted Gaebler's *Reinventing Government* provides a summary of new public management's ideas and reports on efforts at all levels of government to transform bureaucracy into what the authors call "entrepreneurial" government.
	David Farmer's *The Language of Public Administration* introduces a postmodern discourse approach to public administration.
1995	Charles J. Fox and Hugh T. Miller in *Postmodern Public Administration* assert that the task of public administration is to promote "authentic discourse" in society.

"one best way" for organizing. Humanist theories of organization are discussed in the next section. These authors studied human relations and other dimensions of organization missing from classical organization theory. The next several sections deal with more recent theories of organization, including open systems, public choice, new public administration, new public management, and postmodern public administration. The final section of the chapter deals with the relationship between civil society and organization theory.

Classical Organization Theory

Organization theory An area of study that seeks to explain and predict how organizations and their members behave.

Organizations are so deeply embedded in the modern world that we take them for granted most of the time: Most of us seldom stop to consider how organizations function. Given their importance, however, it is unsurprising that the study of organizations is a major field of scholarship. Furthermore, the multifaceted nature of modern organizational life overlaps several academic disciplines, including political science, psychology, business administration, sociology, and economics. In light of the topic's vast scope, students need something to help guide them in understanding the subject. **Organization theory** has developed over the last century as the overarching framework for studying organizations.

Organization A group of people who work together in order to achieve a common purpose.

What is an **organization**? To paraphrase one definition, an organization is a structured system of roles and functional relationships designed to carry out certain activities or policies.[2] We can add to this the idea of coordination, since coordination is required to direct activities toward a common purpose. Thus, gaining a complete understanding of organization entails studying the system of roles and functional relationships as well as the mechanisms to coordinate these to achieve organizational outcomes. Organizational theory helps to provide a map for this study.

Theory represents a body of thought designed to improve our comprehension of social reality by highlighting certain key elements and their interrelationships. Theory helps us make sense of the facts composing our reality by placing them into a coherent and integrated framework, which serves as a roadmap for our understanding of the world. As the nineteenth-century English scientist Thomas Huxley observed, "In scientific work, those who refuse to go beyond fact rarely get as far as fact." Without theory, what we know of the world would consist of a lot of facts but little understanding of the connections among them. Without theory, our ability to change the world and improve ourselves would be greatly diminished.

Early attempts to explain and understand organizations can be grouped together under the title of classical organization theory.[3] These early theories were also known by several other labels, including bureaucratic, hierarchical, scientific, mechanistic, and rational. Each underscores the nature of the core organizational values that the author of the theory subscribed to. For example, the sociologist Gareth Morgan notes the depiction of organizations as machines.[4] The use of adjectives like "mechanical" and "clockwork," which some of these early theorists used to describe an organization's operations, emphasizes the idea that efficiency was the chief goal. According to classical organization theory, maximizing output for the least input, or minimizing the input for any given level of output, becomes the chief hallmark of organizational success. Efficiency is achieved through the use of such tools as the division of labor and hierarchy. Another chief characteristic of the classical school is the belief that the most efficient methods of operation (i.e., the "one best way") can be identified in a systematic, rational manner and written down for future use. Organizations can thus be designed scientifically to produce optimal economic results. The two chief architects of classical organization theory discussed here are Max Weber and Frederick W. Taylor.

Ideal Bureaucracy

One of the most important theoretical advances of twentieth-century social science was the work of German social theorist Max Weber (1864–1920) explaining the increasing rationalization of modern society. As part of this work, Weber observed that bureaucracy was the most rational form of organization. He described the "ideal type" of bureaucracy, which does not refer to any actual bureaucracy. Instead, by means of this ideal type, Weber describes the pure form of a social phenomenon: in this case, how people can form optimal arrangements for the pursuit of particular tasks. He is primarily interested in identifying the key elements of rational organization rather than how organizations are actually structured or operate—and he does not intend to express a normative judgment by using the term "ideal."

Weber's study of bureaucracy must be viewed within the general context of the rest of his groundbreaking work on social structures and relationships. In examining the major institutions of modern society, Weber found that the legal–rational was the dominant mode of authority. The legal–rational is one of three types of authority, according to Weber, the others being traditional and charismatic. In his view, authority is merely socially legitimized power. Bureaucracy is the organizational expression of modern legal–rational authority. The legitimacy of this arrangement stems from rationally established rules, and owing obedience to an office and not to individuals occupying it. At the core of this system of authority is deference to an "impersonal order" rather than particular individuals. The chief objective of bureaucracy is to maximize control in a hierarchical manner.

By maximizing control in this manner, modern organization is able to achieve its goals efficiently and effectively. Rational or efficient administration is also uniform in its application, nonarbitrary in its procedures, and above all, impersonal. Bureaucracy's impersonal nature implies, at least in theory, impartial treatment of members and clients.

Characteristics of Ideal Bureaucracy Weber's ideal type consists of the following five major structural components:

Chain of command The structure in an organization that establishes the authority relationships among the different roles and functions.

1. *Systematic division of labor.* Tasks and functions are divided into separate areas, with a minimum of overlap between them. Each area is assigned "official duties" as well as the appropriate authority to successfully execute these duties.

2. *Hierarchy of offices based on the scalar principle.* Offices are arranged in a vertical **chain of command** in order to better coordinate and integrate the specialized tasks and functions of the different areas.

3. *Strict differentiation between organizational resources and those of members as private individuals.* This results in prohibiting the treatment of

offices as members' private property; in effect, this means that employees cannot sell or inherit offices.

4. *Administration based on written documents and file-keeping.* Documentation helps ensure that proper procedures are followed and a paper trail created, which enhances accountability.

5. *Bureaucratic operations are rule-governed.* Rules and regulations are designed to increase the predictability of certain activities and to ensure the impersonal treatment of individuals both inside and outside the organization.

In addition to the above principles, Weber identifies the five following key characteristics of bureaucratic employment:

1. Appointment and not election; services are specified according to legal contract.

2. Appointment is based on professional qualifications and technical expertise.

3. Income is derived from the position, which consists of a salary as well as pension and other benefits.

4. Bureaucrats move up through the hierarchy on the basis of merit and seniority.

5. Employees are subject to a system of internal discipline and control.

Negative Aspects of Bureaucracy Weber, in general, was highly ambivalent in his attitude toward bureaucracy. On one level, he recognized that this form of organization was the most rational and, therefore, the most efficient form of social arrangement for accomplishing complex tasks. Nonetheless, he also acknowledged that this efficiency could come at a heavy price in terms of the human personality. Bureaucracy can be oppressive to individual liberties to such an extent that Weber called it an "iron cage."[5] He refers to bureaucrats somewhat unflatteringly as "little cogs" in the machine.[6] He based this view on the notion that the impersonal rules of bureaucracy can dehumanize employees, turning them into robots. He argues further that, over time, the specialization that bureaucracy requires can cripple the personalities of workers.[7] For that reason, Weber seems to suggest, a trade-off is required between the repressive aspects of bureaucracy and the efficiency it produces.

Weber's understanding of the positive and negative aspects of organizations was truly profound. To the present day, no other thinker has produced a body of work rivaling Weber's in its influence on generations of organizational scholars.

Scientific Management

While Weber expressed concern over some of the dehumanizing aspects of bureaucracy, American engineer Frederick W. Taylor (1856–1915) had no such misgivings about **scientific management,** with its emphasis on efficiency

Scientific management A theory of administration that is notable for its emphasis on the most efficient method to perform a task ("one best way").

Charlie Chaplin caught in the gears of a factory machine. His film *Modern Times* presents a view of classical organization run amok.

SOURCE: Bettmann/Corbis

and the one best way to complete a task. Although he did not invent scientific management, Taylor was its best-known figure, and in *The Principles of Scientific Management* (1909), he codified its chief tenets. (See Vignette 7.1.) After several years in industry, Taylor spent the last years of his life trying to improve industrial relations. His reforms were based on creating cooperation in the workplace. By contrast, labor–management relations during the early twentieth century were often marked by bitter, often violent, confrontations. In his view, scientific management would replace class warfare with social harmony, since it offered a means for both workers and managers to improve their lot in life. Taylor believed that the gains in productivity brought about by his techniques should be shared equally between management and workers.

Despite Taylor's avowed concern for workers, his approach to management came under criticism for its simplistic view of human behavior. A tenet of scientific management was that employees were interchangeable, like the machines they operated. Thus, management's principal task was to make workers as efficient as possible, since greater productivity would lead to more money for the company. It was through this cause–effect relationship that Taylor hoped to win over workers to scientific management since increased company profits would be rewarded with higher pay for the employees.

Characteristics of Scientific Management Taylor made his case primarily to upper-level management, who he thought was chiefly responsible for the problem of organizational inefficiency. He argued that traditional managerial practices

VIGNETTE 7.1 Frederick W. Taylor: "Puritan Founder" of Scientific Management

Despite considerable tarnishing of his reputation over the years, Frederick W. Taylor (1856–1915) continues to exert a powerful influence over business and government organization. Indeed, the noted management author Peter Drucker said that Taylor and not Marx should be ranked with Freud and Darwin as the most revolutionary thinkers of modern time. What is not very well known, however, is the personal history of this influential figure in management theory.

By all accounts, Taylor was a man of severe rectitude and simple tastes. He dressed plainly, preferring "a plain sack business suit" to formal wear. He neither drank alcohol nor smoked tobacco. He even refused to drink coffee or tea or eat chocolate! By modern standards, he would be considered a "workaholic." Everything in his life centered on his work. In every way, he was the early twentieth-century embodiment of Puritanism, which is not surprising, since his father was a fourth-generation English Quaker and his mother was a sixth-generation English Puritan.

The principal influence on Taylor's life was his mother, Emily Winslow Taylor, whose ancestor, Kenelm Winslow, came to America aboard the *Mayflower* in 1629. It was Emily who inculcated in Frederick the character that shaped scientific management.

Her Puritan idealism burned strongly, as reflected in her views on child rearing, which she expressed as "work, drill, and discipline." Her household was, in her view, "a thing ruled regular," and her maxim was that "her boys grow up pure in mind and body." Like the early Puritans, she never set much store in using tact with people. Simple straightforwardness was her style, as it was Taylor's.

In 1874, instead of immediately going to Harvard after high school, Taylor, who seemed to be suffering the consequences of studying too hard, decided to take some time off to work as an apprentice machinist near his home in Philadelphia, Pennsylvania. He worked his way up through the ranks. In 1878, he went to work at the Midvale Steel works as a laborer, again working his way up, from laborer to foreman. His experiences in both jobs left an indelible impression on him. On the one hand, he concluded that all young people, especially the college bound, should spend a few years working in a factory. On the other hand, he had developed a deep dissatisfaction with the state of management and the attitude of workers that was to serve as the impetus for his theory of scientific management.

SOURCE: Adapted from Richard J. Stillman, "Latter-Day Puritan as Scientific Manager: Frederick W. Taylor," in *Creating the American State* (Tuscaloosa: University of Alabama Press, 1998), 98–120.

lacked a scientific basis; instead, managers relied mainly on rules of thumb. Workers were also part of the problem because they deliberately restricted output, a practice that he referred to as "soldiering" and "goldbricking." However, even with respect to that, management was largely at fault because it provided so little incentive for workers to produce more efficiently. Taylor believed managers had to implement the following principles of scientific management to get out of this predicament:

Time and motion study The method of observation used by scientific management to determine the "one best way" to complete a task.

1. Study the tasks of the enterprise in a scientific manner using **time and motion studies** to devise the one best way to accomplish tasks.

2. Select the best workers for each task, using the most stringent selection techniques available.

3. After they are hired, management must develop the workers' capacity for the job for the most efficient results.

4. Persuade workers that scientific management will best serve their interests, since the application of these principles would result in more money for them.

5. Draw a clear-cut distinction between the responsibilities of management ("brain workers") and those of labor ("hand workers"), with management shouldering the bulk of the responsibility for organizing work processes and ensuring that tasks are performed according to scientific principles.

Weber and Taylor shared a strong belief in rationality and hierarchy. Both men also thought that scientific knowledge was the basis for modern organization. In addition, they observed that in modern society, competence and merit should be the foundation for organization. In Taylor's view, the organization of the future would contain a higher ratio of "brain workers" to "hand workers."[8] In this regard, Taylor should be recognized as something of a prophet of the current computer age.

Administrative Management

Unlike Weber and Taylor, Luther Gulick (1892–1993) worked entirely in the public service, where his long and distinguished record earned him the epithet "Dean of Public Administration." Gulick in his long life made numerous contributions to the field of public administration, including his work as a member of the President's Committee on Administrative Management from 1935 to 1937. It was for this committee that he penned his famous essay "Notes on the Theory of Organization" (1937), which was first published in *Papers on the Science of Administration*.

The Principles of Administration Although Gulick worked mostly with government agencies, he viewed the problems of organization more broadly; in this respect, he is similar to both Weber and Taylor. His goal was to develop principles of administration that could be applied equally well to either public or private enterprises. Gulick, similar to Weber and Taylor, advocated using scientific methods to find those principles. To Gulick, science entailed using the most rigorous examination and categorization of facts, testing theories by means of experimentation, and a careful scrutiny of experimentation's results by other investigators.

In Gulick's view, all modern organizations face essentially the same problem: How do we achieve the coordination and control necessary to accomplish our objectives? An important part of the answer, he thought, was creating a strong chief executive. Gulick focuses primarily on the chief executive as the coordinating and controlling force necessary for organization.

The demands of organization require division of labor; this was an old idea even during Gulick's time. In 1776, the political economist Adam Smith noted that productivity gains result from specialization. The complex, technical nature of current society, however, requires far greater specialization than even Smith and his contemporaries dreamed of. Human beings are limited by time (our knowledge and skills are limited by our life spans) and by space (we cannot be in two places at once). Thus, division of labor is essential. Unfortunately, with increasing specialization, the potential for problems grows. As Gulick notes, "It is self-evident that the more the work is subdivided, the greater is the danger of confusion, and the greater is the need for overall supervision and coordination."[9] The degree of specialization, according to Gulick, was proportional to the complexity of the society. Modern society requires highly specialized governments.

Coordination and control are therefore matters of overriding concern to organization. Gulick favored a top-down approach, with a single directing authority (the executive) responsible for coordination and control. This was to be accomplished in four steps: (1) Define the tasks to be accomplished; (2) select an executive who will oversee the achievement of objectives; (3) divide the tasks and assign them to work units on the basis of the nature of the tasks and the existing technology; and (4) establish a network of communication and supervision between the executive and administration.

Under the executive, the chain of command consists of exactly one supervisor for each task, a principle that is referred to as unity of command. As Gulick observed: "A workman subject to orders from several superiors will be confused, inefficient, and irresponsible; a workman subject to orders from but one superior may be methodical, efficient, and responsible."[10] Moreover, effective **span of control** requires that there be limits on the number of subordinates each supervisor has, according to their ability and time constraints. Generally, managers can direct only a few persons at a time and remain effective. If the work process is routine and repetitive, however, the number of subordinates can be increased without jeopardizing work quality.

> **Span of control** The limited number of subordinates a manager can effectively supervise.

At the top of this control pyramid is the chief executive, who is responsible for ascertaining that all the activities are coordinated and integrated. In order to accomplish this task, the executive has to perform the following functions, summarized by public administration's most famous acronym, **POSDCORB:**

> **POSDCORB** The acronym coined by Luther Gulick as a way to draw attention to the essential management functions of the chief executive.

- Planning the general direction of policy. What must be done? Determining the methods for accomplishing these objectives once they are established.

- Organizing the structure to achieve the objectives. (See the discussion in Chapter 8.)

- Staffing, or overseeing the personnel system, which is responsible for hiring, training, and retaining competent workers.

- Directing or providing leadership. Having responsibility for making decisions, communicating them to subordinates, and overseeing their implementation.

- Coordinating the activities of the diverse units so tasks can be accomplished with a minimum degree of overlap.

- Reporting, or maintaining a system of records, research, and inspection for the purpose of internal and external information and accountability.

- Budgeting, or all of the functions associated with fiscal control of the organization, which includes accounting and fiscal planning.

Gulick clearly belongs in the classical theory school because of his top-down, centralized approach, as well as his belief that the "principles" of administration can be found by means of scientific study. Also, he believed that efficiency was the principal objective of organization. While he observed that "the common man is a better judge of his own needs" than experts, he qualified this by adding: "efficiency is one of the things that is good for him because it makes life richer and safer."[11] Thus, he had a paternalistic attitude toward the public—a perspective that was shared by many of his contemporaries.

Organizational Humanism

In contrast to classical theory, organizational humanism focused on the personal dimension rather than the purely structural and material aspects of organization. Above all else, classical theory was concerned with optimizing efficiency. Thus, it concentrated on the techniques, processes, and structures that would contribute the most to this goal. In line with this emphasis on efficiency, classical theory viewed employees as infinitely pliable; they could be persuaded to follow orders using monetary incentives alone. The organizational humanists, however, did not view employees as being swayed solely by material benefits; they recognized that the human personality is more complicated than that. Their research drew attention to the important role that interpersonal relations play in organizational life. Their humanism led them to challenge the notion of efficiency as the chief concern of organizations. The humanists made the employee the unit of analysis and changed the focus of research to include the thoughts and emotions of workers; they invented the premise that by understanding individual psychology better, they could improve productivity.

Mary Parker Follett

Mary Parker Follett (1868–1933) was one of the most innovative and advanced thinkers of her time, all the more so because she was a woman working in a male-dominated field and era. Her work on the local context of democracy and organization often went against the flow of mainstream social science thinking in her era. Follett's ideas on horizontal communication, pluralistic authority, and creative interaction set her apart from her contemporaries and foreshadowed some contemporary theories.[12] In some respects, she serves as a link between classical theory and humanism, which makes her one of the most important transitional figures in the field.

Follett was chiefly concerned with coordination in organization (this is similar to Gulick's focus and no doubt reflects the period in which they worked). However, she observed, in contrast to Gulick, that control and authority ought to flow from coordination and not the reverse. Further, she thought that control should be cumulative—that is, arising from below—and should be based more on the demands of the situation rather than on arbitrary personal demands and control, which was commonly the case in organizations at the time.[13] Situational demands should be determined by rational analysis, she thought. From this she developed the "law of the situation," in which the nature of the task determines the work orders, not the imposition of personal authority. This was designed to reduce the amount of coerciveness necessary to get things done in organizations.

The Law of the Situation

Follett viewed the role of the executive in a somewhat different light than Weber, Taylor, and Gulick. She believed that the executive is principally responsible for three functions: (1) coordination, (2) definition of purpose, and (3) anticipation. Coordination entails encouraging participation, training and educating, and unifying individual contributions among employees. Definition of purpose requires creating a sense of shared mission in the workforce. Anticipation requires that the executive develop a sense of the larger good and work to create situations to pursue this good within the organization.[14]

Follett's chief claim to being an organizational humanist rests on her support for some degree of worker participation in administration. Generally, she thought that employees should have input on matters in which they are qualified to have an opinion, but they should not be consulted on how to run the organization. Thus, file clerks giving advice on the best way to organize their work environment is acceptable, but their giving advice on organizational strategy is not. In some ways, her approach anticipates some of the key ideas regarding worker participation found in the more recent theory of total quality management.

Elton Mayo

The human relations school originated with Elton Mayo (1880–1944), who conducted studies of the Hawthorne Works of the Western Electric Company in Chicago for eight years, beginning in 1924. The research was designed to show the effect of factory conditions on worker output. In keeping with the scientific management popular at the time, the researchers from Harvard University wanted to show a positive cause-and-effect relationship between the quality of working conditions and worker productivity. For example, Mayo, in one of the experiments, wanted to see if increased lighting in the plant would lead to greater output. This was indeed the case. Surprisingly, however,

A present-day automobile factory. Today's factories rely more on technology than factories in Elton Mayo's time.

SOURCE: Jim West/The Image Works

when the researchers reduced the amount of lighting in the plant, it produced exactly the same result as increasing the lighting had.

This lack of relationship between environmental conditions and productivity led them to conclude that productivity was affected by something other than the external environment. This something, according to Mayo, was management's attention to the employees, which became known as the **Hawthorne effect**. Thus, factors beyond just material incentives play a decisive role in determining levels of productivity. This discovery marks a major break with a central tenet of classical theory. The results of the Hawthorne studies seemed to contradict the notion that workers could be motivated entirely by a system of material rewards, as believed by the classical theorists. The full implication of Mayo's findings was to show that nonmaterial incentives can have a significant impact on employee performance.

Hawthorne effect A finding of the Hawthorne research by Elton Mayo: that simply paying attention to workers made them more productive than physical changes in the factory; gave credence to the idea that informal workplace norms have an important effect on worker performance.

The Informal Organization

Another important finding of Mayo's was the role of interpersonal relations and group processes in improving overall efficiency. He noted that workers appeared to be more influenced by their social groups than by their physical conditions or even their supervisors. The informal dimensions of work—that is, the social aspects of the job—had been totally overlooked by the earlier researchers, but Mayo considered them the key determinants of increasing output and efficiency. The social group, and not management, effectively controlled productivity. Through informal norms and behavioral controls, the workers themselves decided the appropriate level of output from the unit.

Informal organization Aspects of organization, such as interpersonal relations, that exist alongside the formal structures and roles but do not show up on the organization chart.

Workers set production standards and enforced them, excluding from the group those who overproduced ("rate busters") or underproduced ("chiselers"). This **informal organization** existed alongside the formal one represented in the official organization chart, and it was created entirely by the workers, often without the knowledge of management.

While Mayo and his fellow researchers recognized the importance of social and psychological aspects of organization, their chief concern was still the best means to achieve efficiency. As a result of Mayo's research, however, the emphasis in organizational studies gradually shifted from the formal structures and processes of organization to developing a better understanding of employee psychology. Managers began to recognize that productivity can be affected by social forces within the organization, and that workers are not driven solely by economic motives. Mayo's work shows that employees are members of a smaller work group and of the larger organization, and they respond to management differently depending on the situation.

Other researchers challenged the Hawthorne studies many years after they initially appeared. Two of these studies examined Mayo's data and reevaluated his findings in light of more sophisticated statistical methods. Carey suggests that the Hawthorne studies erroneously deemphasized financial incentives and misinterpreted the findings on supervisory style. According to this research, increased worker output was the result of incentives alone. In addition, the supervisors were not as friendly as Mayo thought. All in all, Carey asserts that Mayo's Western Electric research was shoddy, filled with errors and distortions.[15] Franke and Kaul used statistical techniques in their examination of the Hawthorne research and found that most of the difference in productivity could be attributed to supervisory discipline and other factors, not the social conditions that Mayo claimed.[16]

Mayo's research methods and findings have been criticized and his conclusions attacked as reflecting personal bias, but Mayo's influence on organization theory remains undisputed. Prior to Mayo, the study of organization focused entirely on management and on formal structures and attributes. After Mayo, the social and informal dimensions of organization were included. Mayo might have been deficient as a researcher, but his emphasis on the human side has, without a doubt, contributed to a more comprehensive, hence realistic, approach to studying and thinking about organizations.

Chester Barnard

A theorist who combines elements of classical and humanist theory is Chester Barnard (1886–1961), whose famous book *The Functions of the Executive* (1938) is heavily indebted to the work of Mayo for its insights into the nature of employee behavior, but like classical theory, it emphasizes hierarchy and efficiency.[17] Barnard was a successful business executive with New Jersey Bell Telephone Company before he turned his hand to writing about administration. As a theorist, Barnard was chiefly concerned with bringing the informal aspects of organization under the control of formal management.

The Functions of the Executive

An organization, according to Barnard, is dependent on the voluntary contributions of employees, who, in exchange for their contributions, have their individual needs and motivations satisfied. It was the chief responsibility of the executive and managers, in his view, to maintain and coordinate this system of voluntary exchange. In light of this, he identified three key functions of the executive: (1) to obtain and maintain the cooperation of employees through the allocation of rewards, or "satisfactions," as he put it; (2) to maintain communication within the organization in support of this cooperation; and (3) to create a broad vision for the organization and to plan to achieve long-term objectives. The key to obtaining and maintaining employee cooperation, he believed, was employee motivation: "If the individual finds his motives being satisfied by what he does, he continues his cooperative effort; otherwise, he does not."[18] Thus, Barnard, while still emphasizing the central role of the executive (like Taylor and Gulick), borrows from the humanists, who assert that the informal aspects of organization are key to motivating employee behavior. Indeed, Barnard asserts that the nonformal elements are necessary to long-term organizational survival.

Barnard believed that cooperation could be achieved by management's ability to successfully moderate the influence of social forces within the organization. One way to do this, Barnard suggested, was for management to hire "compatible personnel." In other words, find people who will fit in with the organization's values and goals. Mere competence is not enough; employees should be selected based on matching their education, personal values, and other characteristics with those of the organization. If this is effectively done, the organization's informal norms will better reflect its formal values and objectives to a larger extent than if hiring was on the basis of technical skills only.

Zone of indifference The area defining an employee's level of comfort with an order: anything falling within this area will be followed; anything falling outside will not be followed.

Management also needs to be aware of the limits of cooperation. Barnard noted that every employee has a **zone of indifference**. Within this zone, management's orders will be followed "without hesitation."[19] However, directives falling outside the zone are more problematic. Only by increasing rewards and satisfactions will employees accept a wider range of orders, thereby expanding this zone. The larger the zone of indifference, Barnard thought, the smoother the administration.

Barnard's impact on public administration was not recognized immediately. Various aspects of his work, however, helped pave the way for Herbert Simon, whose work dominated early postwar thought in public administration. Barnard's contribution should be acknowledged in its own right, nonetheless, because of his union of classical theory with the insights of the humanistic approach to organizations.

Herbert Simon

Herbert Simon (1916–2001) has the unique distinction of being not only a leading light in public administration but a major figure in areas as diverse as information theory, psychology, and economics, for which he was awarded the Nobel Prize in 1978. Simon was among the first to study the decision-making process in organizations with real scientific rigor. Indeed, he believed that understanding decision-making lies at the very heart of effective management.

Early in his career, Simon made an indelible mark on the field of public administration with the 1946 publication of "The Proverbs of Administration." In this famous essay, Simon criticized the then dominant approach to public administration, which was exemplified by Gulick's principles of administration, on the grounds that it was unscientific. Simon asserted that these principles were contradictory and, therefore, they could not form the basis of a true science of administration, since it was uncertain when each one should be applied and under what set of circumstances. Simon challenged the following four principles in particular: (1) specialization, (2) unity of command, (3) narrow span of control, and (4) the bases of organization (for more on this, see Chapter 8).

Narrow span of control, for instance, requires more hierarchy, which contradicts the principle that in order to enhance control, organizations need fewer levels of hierarchy. In this and other examples, Simon observed, "Although the two principles of the pair will lead in exactly opposite recommendations, there is nothing in theory to indicate which is the proper one to apply."[20] Above all, Simon argued for a truly scientific administration, one that banished the "superficiality, oversimplification, lack of realism" which he saw as hindering the discipline's progress.[21] He also wanted the field to encompass more than just formal structures and the functions of authority. Although Simon sharply criticized important elements of traditional theory, he nevertheless agreed with the mainstream about efficiency and rationality. Simon believed along with the classical theorist that efficiency was the chief goal of an organization, and that organizations could achieve greater efficiency through the application of scientific methods.

Bounded Rationality

Simon fleshed out his theory of "scientific administration" in *Administrative Behavior* (1957). In this classic work, he was primarily interested in studying rational decision-making in organizations. He thought that the mainstream perspective on rationality was a very narrow and ultimately unrealistic description of human behavior. According to the mainstream viewpoint, decisionmakers have complete, accurate information about their environment and make their decisions on the basis of this information. They are able to prioritize their preferences according to a stable set of criteria and then make the best choice in any situation. Simon, by contrast, viewed rationality very differently from the way most orthodox theorists did. He recognized that individuals in organizations make more modest claims on rationality: They do not analyze every possible alternative, prefer simple cause-and-effect relationships to the more complex ones that mark the real world, and apply simple rules of thumb or "proverbs" in making decisions.[22]

Bounded rationality The concept developed by Herbert Simon that organizations are limited in their understanding and knowledge and therefore cannot make optimal decisions.

Satisfice A term originated by Herbert Simon for decisions that are less than optimal: they *satis*fy and suf*fice*.

Fact–value dichotomy Herbert Simon's concept that observations about the world can be divided into fact propositions (e.g., the earth is round) and value propositions (e.g., we ought to do something about poverty), and that a true science of administration can be based on only fact propositions.

For this reason, there is no perfect rationality, as traditional theorists implied. Instead, **bounded rationality** marks real-world decisions. Therefore, individuals and organizations can only **satisfice**, not maximize, and administrators have to accept that solutions to problems are inevitably less than ideal. Instead of attempting to ferret out all of the alternatives and attempting to understand a problem in all of its complexity, administrators should content themselves with what is possible given their narrow frames of reference.

Fact–Value Dichotomy

In his attempt to create a scientific administration, Simon proposed replacing the traditional politics–administration dichotomy with a **fact–value dichotomy**. The politics–administration dichotomy did not accurately reflect the reality of postwar public administration, although it might have been appropriate earlier on. Further, there was nothing inherently scientific about splitting administration from politics. A true science, Simon observed, divides statements about the world into value propositions and factual propositions. Value propositions consist of "ought to" or "should be" statements, such as "Government should spend more on the military," or "Government ought to provide more low-income housing." Statements like these cannot be proven true or false, since they are matters of personal belief regarding what government should or should not do. A factual proposition, on the other hand, consists of data from the world around us, such as "The freezing point of water is thirty-two degrees Fahrenheit," or "The Sun rises in the east and sets in the west." Fact propositions can be verified by means of observation.

Scientific administration, Simon contends, should be based entirely on factual propositions and not value propositions, because only factual propositions can be systematically investigated and subjected to rigorous scientific scrutiny. One implication of Simon's theory is "value-free" administration. But a completely value-free administration would be problematic, so Simon proposes that administrators internalize professional norms and ethical codes. Nevertheless, external controls are still necessary to ensure administrative accountability, because the norms guiding professional administrators are not the same as those guiding elected officials.

Criticisms of Simon's Theories

Simon's impressive body of work has had a significant impact on public administration since 1946, but he is not without his detractors.[23] The theory of bounded rationality, for instance, has been criticized because of its overly constrained view of decision-making. Thus, while the traditional view of rationality assumes maximization is possible, Simon contends that satisficing is the best we can hope for. Simon's fact–value dichotomy has been challenged on the grounds that his criterion of organizational efficiency in itself constitutes a value judgment, which contradicts his argument that value propositions should not be the basis for administration. Simon generally concurs with the mainstream theorists' emphasis on efficiency. In the public sector though, equity, representativeness, responsiveness, and other values are equally important, and they warrant the same consideration as efficiency in decision-making. Further, goals are inevitably the products of choices, and choices involve values. Thus, the means to achieve different objectives are also determined on the basis of different values. Simon's theory merely assumes these values without questioning their legitimacy. Despite these criticisms, Simon's contribution to our understanding of public organizations, and organizations in general, remains unsurpassed into the present day.

Open System Theory

Open system theory An approach to organization that includes the external environment as an important factor, as the recipient of output and provider of inputs.

Compared to classical organization theory, which views organizations as being essentially closed off from the environment and focusing consequently on internal structure, **open system theory** views the environment as the key factor for organizations. Open system theory originated in the physical sciences after World War II, drawing primarily on the living systems model of the biologist Ludwig Von Bertalanffy and the theory of cybernetics pioneered by the mathematician Norbert Weiner.[24] Organization theorists applied the living systems model to organizations, in the process shifting the field's emphasis from efficiency to survival. From the field of cybernetics, organization theorists derived the idea of organizations as self-regulating systems that use the information from their environment to maintain a steady state by adapting to the environment.

One of the earliest applications of open system theory to government organizations was found in the work of political scientist David Easton, who described the political process as a system with inputs and outputs.[25] The open system approach became an important force in organization theory through the research of Robert Katz and Daniel Kahn.[26] (See Figure 7.1.) They borrowed Bertalanffy's open system model and applied it to organizations in industry. Katz and Kahn used the example of a factory to depict an open system, with the raw materials and labor serving as inputs, the production activities representing the transformation of inputs, and the finished product corresponding to output.[27]

Contingency theory A theory of organization that asserts that success depends on the level of fit with the environment.

Contingency theory, building on open system theory, asserts that organizational success depends on an organization's ability to fit in with the environment. A "good fit" will assure the long-term survival of an organization, while

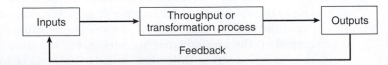

Figure 7.1 Open System Model

a "bad fit" will hasten its downfall. Contingency theory links environmental certainty and stability with internal structure.[28] In contrast to classical theory's "one best way," contingency theory does not hold up a particular model of organization as being any better than another, preferring instead an "it all depends" approach to organizing. Since organizational survival depends on environmental compatibility, it becomes imperative that management style and structure match the specific environment.

Public Choice Theory

Utilitarian An approach which asserts that people and organizations do something only if they expect material gain from it.

While Herbert Simon and others were in the process of discarding the traditional notion of organizational rationality as being too limited, another group of theorists sought to apply an alternative idea of rationality based on economic thinking to problems of administration. This economics-based approach came to be known as public choice theory, and it articulates a model of administration based on **utilitarian** logic. The basic premise of public choice theory is economic individualism: it assumes that individuals are materially self-interested. According to this theory, rationality means that people are concerned chiefly with advancing their own interests, generally by seeking the greatest possible benefits at the lowest possible cost to themselves. Although Simon's approach and public choice differ over their conception of human behavior, both are fundamentally rational models of decision-making. However, less charitable observers criticize the public choice concept because it "pursues individual interest, pleasure, and happiness without particular concern for community values and notions such as ethics, a 'greater good,' or the possibility of a public interest."[29]

Two public choice theorists whose work has had a large impact on public administration are Anthony Downs and Vincent Ostrom. Downs sought to explain the behavior of public agencies by using the economic individualism model and found that agencies have a tendency to emphasize the benefits they provide over the costs they incur to society.[30] For this reason, agencies view organizational growth as good, although from a social perspective, this might not be the case. Agencies also tend to view their services as being of universal benefit (i.e., "serving the public good") and not directed to a particular interest group. Thus, they are able to maintain the pretense that they are working on behalf of the general interest. Lastly, agencies believe that they are operating at or near total efficiency, and they highlight their achievements at every opportunity while they downplay their failures or else rationalize them away.

Unlike the private sector, Downs contends, government's tendency toward more expansion is unchecked by market controls. For instance, public agencies typically do not face competition or have to comply with consumer demands. Accordingly, as agencies are allowed to pursue their interests unchecked, they become bloated at the public's expense.

While Downs explained the mechanism for inefficient agency expansion, Ostrom pointed to a possible solution for the problem of public organization inefficiency.[31] He attempted to redirect public administration theory from an overemphasis on bureaucracy and centralization as the best means to organize. Efficiency, for Ostrom, requires a drastic restructuring of agencies based on his version of public choice, which consists of three parts. First, he borrows from economics the concept of rational self-interest.[32] Second, he argues that self-interested agencies are called upon to make decisions regarding the allocation of public goods, that is, goods that the market will either undersupply or not supply at all, such as national defense. Third, different kinds of decision-making arrangements produce different kinds of behavior in agencies that are seeking to maximize their own self-interest. In his view, any organizational arrangement will have its limitations. Thus, Ostrom concludes, "The optimum choice of organizational arrangements would be that which minimizes the costs associated with institutional weakness or institutional failure."[33]

Ostrom proposes an administrative model emphasizing decentralized arrangements involving many organizations delivering a diverse mix of services.[34] This is a far cry from traditional public administration, which viewed centralization as the best way to achieve efficiency and looked on decentralization as leading to all sorts of organizational sins. Ostrom contends, on the contrary, that decentralized administration is actually better at satisfying the demands of citizens. In effect, Ostrom advocates creating market-like conditions for public agencies. His theory has been used to support, for example, using private and nonprofit organizations to deliver public services.

Criticism of public choice theory has been made on three grounds. First, critics assert that the model represents a too limited and inaccurate view of human behavior on which to build a practical theory of organization.[35] Public choice theory reaches conclusions about organization that are based on untested assumptions regarding human motivation and which exclude other important human attributes, including emotions. Second, the public choice approach promotes social inequity, and the practical consequences of relying heavily on a market-like approach to public services raise many concerns. Low-income people who cannot afford to pay user fees might use certain government services less often. A reverse type of **redistribution** may occur, in fact, as low-income taxpayers help subsidize public services used mainly by higher-income people. A municipal golf course, for instance, might require users to pay a fee, which might unfairly exclude poor people, whose taxes also help pay for it. Further, the public choice notion that communities are markets, which consist of "bundles of services" in competition with other communities, encourages citizens to "vote with their feet." But not all citizens have the resources to leave one community and go to another one that might have a more desirable mix of public goods and services. Third, public choice theory has too cynical a view of human nature. The view of the administrator as being motivated entirely by self-interest and without concern for the public interest breeds "profound cynicism" about the motives of people in the public service. Public choice theory "sanctions a range of motives and practices that history—as well as most of the present-day public—regards as debased, if not unethical."[36]

Redistribution The transfer of income or wealth from one class of society to another, typically used to refer to a transfer from the rich to the poor.

In spite of these criticisms, public choice theory has had a major impact on public administration, in no small measure because the conservative political climate of recent decades provides an ideological perspective that is hospitable to it.

The New Public Administration

The new public administration was a response on the part of mostly younger scholars to the social and political turbulence that marked the 1960s. In line with the rebellious temper of the times, these dissenters challenged many of the fundamental doctrines of mainstream public administration theory. For example, the new public administration demanded that public servants be more aggressive in helping solve society's problems, contending that the knowledge and skills of administrators ought to be used proactively to improve human conditions.[37] Given this premise, they pushed for a break with what they perceived as the **value-neutral** approach of mainstream public administration (e.g., in the work of Herbert Simon). New public administration argued that while administration should be value based, or normative, it could still be scientific, since administrators would bring their technical expertise to bear on improving the lives of the disadvantaged in society.

Value neutral The notion that social science should not take moral positions but rather should stick solely with the facts.

The new public administration sought to make social justice the central concern for administrators and public agencies. In doing so, efficiency's importance was downplayed. As part of this new value-based approach, public servants would openly and aggressively advocate for society's downtrodden and the dispossessed. George Frederickson, one of the best-known new public administration figures, declared: "A public administration which fails to work for changes which try to redress the deprivation of minorities will likely be used to repress those minorities."[38]

A public administration engaged in righting social wrongs, however, is hard to reconcile with the traditional separation of politics and administration. Therefore, the new public administration simply did away with the notion that politics (or policy-making) and administration need be separate. Instead, it argued that administrators *should* take every opportunity to make policy. Far from being merely the instrument for executing laws, administration should be out front in setting the public's agenda and shaping its values.

This concern with social equity also included placing a higher value on employee and client participation in agency decision-making. In this respect, the new public administration directly challenged the hierarchical, bureaucratic structures long associated with traditional public administration. Some new public administration proponents even called for an end to all political and economic hierarchy and its replacement with more cooperative and noncompetitive arrangements.[39]

The new public administration has had a mixed record in terms of its long-term impact on public administration. It has been successful in identifying certain problems in mainstream theory and practice and issuing a call to correct those problems.[40] However, the new public administration failed "in theorizing and dealing with the inevitable reality of conflict." Ultimately, new public administration's chief contribution may have been to the development of alternative approaches to organizational change.[41] (For more on organizational change, see Chapters 8 and 9.)

The New Public Management

As pointed out in the first chapter, throughout U.S. history the notion of running government like a business has held considerable appeal among numerous theorists and practitioners. The new public management (NPM) approach is simply the most recent example of this effort to redesign the public sector to make it more like the private sector. NPM draws heavily from various organization theories, particularly public choice, and strives for a streamlined public administration that maximizes efficiency and productivity. This approach seeks to integrate market mechanisms into government to the fullest possible extent and encourages bureaucrats to view citizens as customers and consumers instead of clients.[42] NPM provides the theoretical rationale for the reinventing government movement (discussed in Chapter 4) and, to some extent, President George W. Bush's Management Agenda. The new public management theory shares with classical theory the idea that business practices introduced into government increase efficiency. Table 7.2 compares the two organizational approaches.

According to NPM, bureaucrats should be more like responsive entrepreneurs who try to fulfill the service demands of the citizen-customers. This marks a dramatic change in management style that contrasts with earlier approaches, including the classical model. Indeed, in the classical approach, the service recipient hardly warrants attention at all. NPM's emphasis is on competition and operating in much the same way as the private sector does. Thus, public agencies compete for the provision of goods and services internally and seek to streamline budgets by contracting out to private firms. For example, one of the initiatives in President Bush's Management Agenda focused on competitive sourcing: "To achieve efficient and effective competition between public and private sources,

TABLE 7.2 A Comparison of Classical Organization Theory and New Public Management

Classical Organization Theory	New Public Management
Centralization	Decentralization
Hierarchical structure	Less formal structure, horizontal control
Executive accountability	Performance-based accountability
Limited discretion	Increased autonomy
Scientific rationalism	Economic rationalism
Focus on efficiency and rationality	Focus on efficiency and rationality

TABLE 7.3 Public Administrator Motivations

Mainstream Public Administration	New Public Management
Public interest	Self-interest
Obligation	Utility
Equity	Efficiency
Agency loyalty	Supervisor or clientele loyalty
Project driven	Driven by monetary incentives

the Administration has committed itself to simplifying and improving the procedures for evaluating public and private sources, to better publicizing the activities subject to competition, and to ensuring senior level agency attention to the promotion of competition."[43]

As part of this emphasis on productivity and competition, public managers are performance driven in the sense that agency budgets and career advancement are tied to performance measures. An example of this is the stress placed on agency performance assessment in President Bush's 2003 federal budget. Another way to think about the differences between traditional public administration and the NPM is to compare both approaches on the basis of their view of administrator motivations (see Table 7.3).

Postmodern Public Administration

Postmodernism An approach to understanding politics and government that questions mainstream assumptions regarding organization, power, and capitalism.

Deconstruct The postmodern methodology of exposing the underlying assumptions that form the basis of political and economic institutions and social structures.

The last theory we examine, **postmodernism,** represents by far the most radical departure from the previous approaches to understanding organizations. Unlike the other theories discussed, postmodernism defies all attempts at a neat definition and categorization. This, moreover, is in keeping with postmodernism's central tenet: "The old terms that we used to rely on to establish reality no longer seem to work."[44] The purpose of postmodern thought, in general, is to **deconstruct** the modern world, that is, to critically examine meaning and rationality. In postmodern public administration, the main goal is to deconstruct major social and political institutions, namely bureaucracy and capitalism.[45] Two leading postmodern public administration theorists, Charles Fox and Hugh Miller, have identified a number of the essential differences between modern and postmodern public administration. These are outlined in Table 7.4. Where a traditional view of public administration focuses on integration and centralization, for example, postmodernism focuses on disintegration and decentralization. In general, postmodernism views society as being in a permanent state of flux.[46] As the last pair of differences in the table (Newton and Heisenberg) signifies, postmodernists believe that uncertainty underlies our understanding of how things really operate, as opposed to the comforting certainty of a Newtonian worldview.

TABLE 7.4 Differences between Modern and Postmodern Approaches to Public Administration

Modern	Postmodern
Integration	Disintegration
Centralization	Decentralization
Centripetal	Centrifugal
Totalization	Fragmentation
Melting pot	Salad
Impulse to unify	Hyperpluralism
Universalism	Relativism
Newton (certainty)	Heisenberg (uncertainty)

SOURCE: Adapted from Fox, Charles J. and Miller, Hugh T. (1996). *Post Modern Public Administration*. Thousand Oaks, CA: Sage. p.45.

What are the practical consequences of postmodernism for public administration? Postmodernists contend that hierarchical structures are stifling American democracy and that public administration theory must bear some of the responsibility for this situation. (In this regard, they are not too different from new public administration.) Postmodernists point out that organization is a social construction, a product of human thoughts and actions, and therefore inherently malleable.[47] Postmodernists argue that the manipulation of symbols characterizes current policy-making. They would replace this approach with one that promotes genuine, open dialogue. Therefore, it is public administration's task to empower citizens to participate in policy-making, and to make the means available for them to do so.

Postmodernists are also concerned with how language is used, since language is the chief means by which we understand and interpret our world (for more on the role of language in organizations, see Chapter 9). They believe that mainstream public administration, with its heavy emphasis on efficiency and hierarchy, is constrained by its language from embracing the changes necessary for adaptation to postmodern conditions.[48] Postmodernists assert that using language that promotes cooperation and social equity will help to create a mindset more conducive to a less bureaucratic, more person-centered public administration.

Critics of postmodernism point out that this approach is too theoretical to appeal to mainstream students and practitioners. Thus, while postmodernists have written a great deal about the problems of current public administration, they have produced little in the way of empirical studies to provide evidence supporting their theories. Further, their writings do not provide practical solutions to the problems of modern government and administration. It is one thing to say that public servants should empower citizens to become policymakers; it is quite another thing to bring about this empowerment using practical and voluntary means. For example, what if citizens do not want to participate? Should citizen involvement be required to ensure that "empowerment" occurs?

Civil Society and Organization Theory

Some of the organizational theories discussed above suggest that the issue of power that organizations exercise in the broader society is a perennial concern. Max Weber, for example, was very ambivalent about bureaucratic power. Although he marveled at modern organizations' capacity to increase efficiency and productivity, he foresaw bureaucracy's potential to dehumanize employees, turning them into mere cogs in a machine. Frederick W. Taylor believed that scientific management would usher in an era of industrial peace; but that managers would have the real power in organizations and workers none; hence, workers would lose power in the larger society as well.

Most early organization theory viewed centralization of authority as generally indispensable to organizations. Gulick thought that complex organizations require concentration of power to provide the necessary coordination and control; otherwise organizations would lose their internal coherence. Even the organizational humanists did not seriously challenge the traditional notion of hierarchy, although they pointed out that the informal aspects of organizations had more influence on organizational behavior than was previously thought. One exception to the prevailing view, however, was Mary Parker Follett, who believed that authority should flow from the demands of the situation rather than from personal power.

Other theorists were more interested in how actual decisions got made in organizations; they did not question the top-down authority of traditional bureaucracy. If anything, Barnard's writing suggests ways that the informal aspects of organizations can be used by executives to enhance their power. Further, Simon's fact–value dichotomy can be interpreted as justifying the inherent power relationships in organizations, because they fall within the domain of values, which are not valid grounds for organizational decision-making.

Public choice theory is openly critical of centralization and hierarchy in public organizations, developing a model of decentralized, nonhierarchical arrangements that can provide public services more efficiently. Similar in this viewpoint is new public management. Both public choice and new public management theories approach the study of public organizations from an economic viewpoint and emphasize market-like arrangements. In this new arrangement, power would be more diffuse throughout the system. Instead of a single locus of power at the top of an organizational pyramid, there would be multiple nodes of power spread throughout, similar to the federal system established by the U.S. Constitution. Public choice and NPM have been used to support calls for privatization, which some proponents contend would help to strengthen civil society by providing resources for voluntary associations such as nonprofit and religious organizations.

New public administration and postmodernism are decidedly antihierarchical in their orientation to public organizations and power. Both have radical roots: new public administration in the social and political tumult of the 1960s, and postmodernism in European social and political theories. New public administration emphasizes social equity over efficiency; it directly challenges traditional hierarchy. Postmodernists view hierarchy and the concentration of power in organizations as harmful to democracy and civil society.

Chapter Summary

Organization theory is the study of the internal and external elements of organizations, including organizational behavior as well as the interactions of organizations with the environment. Organizations are complex systems. They were viewed as closed systems by the classical theorists. Modern students of organizations, however, agree that they are best described as open systems. Classical theory was the first to explain organizations, emphasizing efficiency as the overriding value. The two foremost architects of classical theory are the German Max Weber and the American Frederick W. Taylor. Weber's major contribution is the theory of the "ideal bureaucracy," while Taylor is largely responsible for scientific management theory. Luther Gulick, another important early theorist, invented the acronym POSDCORB to represent the primary functions of the executive in organizations. The classical theorists were united in the belief that hierarchy and centralized power are the keys to effective organization.

In contrast to classical theory, the organizational humanists focused on the human side of organizations. This led them to challenge the idea that material incentives alone determine productivity. Major organizational humanists include Mary Parker Follett and Elton Mayo. Follett developed the "law of the situation," in which the task, not a person of authority, determines the work orders. Mayo's Hawthorne studies show that the informal and social dimensions of organizations have a large effect on productivity.

The latter half of the twentieth century witnessed a veritable explosion in organizational theory. Scholars examined how organizations actually make decisions and the factors that affect the decision-making process. The work of Herbert Simon is especially important for public administration. Early in his long, distinguished career he criticized Gulick's principles of administration approach, on grounds that it was not a true science of administration. For much of his career, Simon strove to achieve a science of administration through his research and writing.

Since the 1960s, several theoretical approaches have made their mark on the field of public administration. Public choice advanced a model of administration based on the idea of economic individualism and rationality. The new public administration approach emerged at the end of the tumultuous decade of the 1960s and shared many of that decade's beliefs regarding social equity and full democratic participation. New public management theory seeks to integrate market mechanisms into administration. Postmodern public administration's chief purpose is to deconstruct the assumptions that form the basis of mainstream organization theory.

◼ Chapter Discussion Questions

1. Despite considerable criticism, aspects of classical organization theory still exert an important influence on contemporary public administration. What are some examples?

2. Compare and contrast Gulick's administrative management theory with new public administration.

3. Some critics argue that the organizational humanists, despite their claims to emphasize the social and psychological aspects of organizations, are just as focused on efficiency as classical organization theory. Explain why this is and is not the case.

4. According to Herbert Simon, a true science of administration means an orientation toward facts rather than values. But can public administration ever be truly value free? Why or why not?

5. Explain how the principles of public choice theory embody a set of values regarding the role of government in society. Apply the same analysis to new public management.

◼ Organization Exercises

The preceding chapters of this text each concluded with a brief case study, and the organization exercises presented here provide an opportunity for you to conduct a case study of your own, based on your personal experiences within a particular organization. Through these exercises, you will gain a better understanding of the organizations you work for.

1. Think of an organization you have worked for (it can be one that you currently work for). Which of the theoretical approaches discussed in this chapter best exemplifies your organization? Give some examples to back up your answer.

2. Find out some basic information about the organization you identified in Exercise 1. What is its purpose? When was it created and why? Obtain or create an organizational chart. Write a brief history of your organization.

3. In-class exercise: Working as a class or in small groups, develop a typology of the organizations that students described in their answers to Exercises 1 and 2. Divide these organizations into public, private, and nonprofit. Size of organization is another important variable. Also include the organizations' purpose and mission (e.g., the Department of Human Services provides health and welfare services to low-income households in need).

■ Key Terms

bounded rationality (page 171)
chain of command (page 159)
contingency theory (page 172)
deconstruct (page 177)
fact–value dichotomy (page 171)
Hawthorne effect (page 167)
informal organization (page 168)
open system theory (page 172)
organization (page 158)
organization theory (page 158)

POSDCORB (page 164)
postmodernism (page 177)
redistribution (page 174)
satisfice (page 171)
scientific management (page 160)
span of control (page 164)
time and motion study (page 162)
utilitarian (page 173)
value neutral (page 175)
zone of indifference (page 169)

■ On the Web

http://www.aom.pace.edu/omt/
An organization and management theory
website.

http://cbae.nmsu.edu/~dboje/postmoderntheory.
html
An interesting and informative postmodern
organization theory site.

http://faculty.babson.edu/krollag/org_site/
encyclop/encyclo.html
An online encyclopedia of organization
theory; not all the links are working.

http://www.business.com/directory/management/
management_theory/
Management theories at Business.com
emphasize the private sector but are still very
relevant to public organizations.

CHAPTER 8

The Organizational Dimensions of Public Administration

■ SETTING THE STAGE

Shortly after the September 11, 2001, terrorist attacks, President George W. Bush announced that he would create an Office of Homeland Security (OHS) by executive order within the Office of the White House.[1] The director of the new OHS was the former governor of Pennsylvania, Tom Ridge, a longtime friend of the president. Ridge would have a cabinet rank and report directly to the president. The mission of the new office would be nothing less than "protecting Americans from every threat that terrorists might devise."[2] The job entailed, among other things, securing the nation's borders, guarding nuclear power plants, protecting public facilities, and combating the threat of bioterrorism. In order to do all of this, Director Ridge had to coordinate the activities of nearly four dozen agencies and offices. As Figure 8.1 shows, Ridge had his work cut out for him in attempting to maneuver around such a labyrinthine structure. Moreover, the OHS would not be a traditional cabinet department like Defense or Justice. The OHS, as originally constituted, even lacked the legal authority to make budgetary decisions. Instead, Ridge could only make spending recommendations to the Office of Management and Budget (OMB). Ultimately, budgetary power lay outside the agency.

From the start, members of Congress and others outside the federal government expressed profound disbelief that the new office and director could achieve their ambitious aims with the awkward organizational structure with which they were saddled. Many members of Congress and former federal officials argued that it was impossible for Ridge to effectively manage the OHS without control of the agencies' budgets. Early on, there were indications that relations between Ridge and the agencies under his command would sometimes be tense. Indeed, many of the law enforcement agencies remained "fiercely protective of their own power and independence." Some of the bureaucrats who, according to the organization chart, nominally reported to Ridge were openly dismissive of the new office's authority. "Let's face it," said a commissioner of the Immigration and Naturalization Service, "they are still getting organized, and they don't have anybody over there who are experts on immigration, customs, border enforcement. That's why they necessarily have to rely on us."[3]

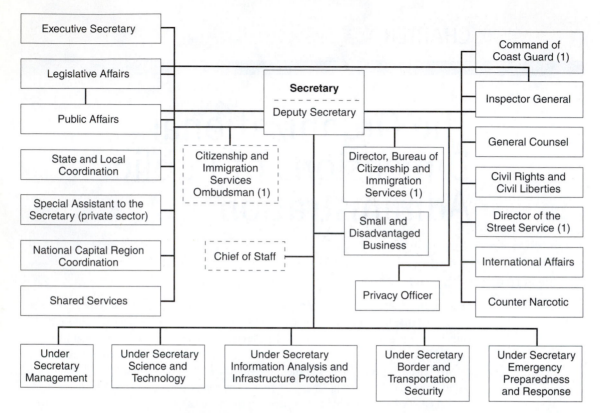

Figure 8.1   Department of Homeland Security

SOURCE: Department of Homeland Security, organization effective March, 2003.

In order to overcome these organizational weaknesses, Ridge had to rely on his close ties with the president. "Everyone knows that if you cross Tom Ridge, you cross the President of the United States," observed Connecticut Senator Christopher Shays, a Republican and strong supporter of Ridge.[4] However, there were limits to Ridge's ability to translate his friendship with President Bush into true organizational authority. As a result, some very real questions arose early on about the capacity for the OHS in its initial configuration to successfully coordinate the activities of so many different agencies and its ability to have a meaningful impact on the war on terrorism. Consequently, in November 2002, Congress created the new cabinet-level Department of Homeland Security (DHS). Integrating parts of eight other cabinet departments dealing with domestic defense, the reorganization constituted the most significant reshuffling of federal agencies since the Department of Defense was created in 1947.

■ CHAPTER PLAN

Structural issues, as the case above shows, are often key factors in an agency's success or failure. The OHS, for example, lacked the authority to effectively accomplish its mission and had to be reconstituted as a cabinet-level department. As we study public administration,

President George
W. Bush confers with
Tom Ridge, head of
the new Office of
Homeland Security,
in October 2001.

SOURCE: Eric Draper/White
House/Getty Images

organizational structure therefore warrants our close attention. In Chapter 7, we discussed some of the characteristics of bureaucratic organizations, including division of labor, coordination, and hierarchy. In this chapter, we continue our examination of the key aspects of organization, using as our framework the three-dimensional model of organizations. Examination of these dimensions allows us to probe more deeply the role of structure and the influence it has on the behavior of organization members.

Organizational influence is often closely intertwined with structure. Thus, we revisit the issue of organizational power, this time studying it from a slightly different perspective than in Chapter 1. In this chapter, we study how organizational roles and functions translate into the power that individuals and groups wield within organizations. Finally, we discuss how bureaucratic power and civil society are interconnected. Since bureaucracy exercises tremendous influence in society, it is important to understand who gains power within the bureaucracy and why.

Dimensions of Organizations

In this chapter, we discuss the formal design and structure of organizations and how they facilitate the accomplishment of tasks.[5] The importance of organizational structure and design, however, cannot be restricted solely to their role as instruments for pursuing goals. They also impact employees and clients of organizations in a profoundly personal way.[6] Employees' authority, discretion, responsibility, status, and opportunities for promotion are largely determined by their position in an organization's structure. Organizational roles also influence to a significant degree an employee's interpersonal

Formalization The level of standardization of jobs, employee behavior, and work processes in an organization.

Centralization The concentration of decision-making power and control within an organization.

Complexity The structural levels and diversity of occupational specializations within an organization.

Job standardization An arrangement that ensures standards along employment lines within organizations, which involves, among other things, preparing job descriptions.

relationships within the organization. For this reason, it is important to consider the effects of organizational design and structure on worker psychology and personality.

A useful framework for discussing organizational design and structure is the three-dimensional model of organization. According to this model, organizations have three dimensions: (1) formalization, (2) centralization, and (3) complexity.[7] **Formalization** refers to the extent to which jobs, employee behavior, and work processes are standardized throughout an organization. Standardization entails, to a large degree, the compatibility and interchangeability of organizational elements. **Centralization** measures the degree of concentration of decision-making power and control within an organization. **Complexity** involves the level of specialization, the diversity of occupations, and the geographic dispersion of units within the organization.

Formalization

The degree of formalization in an organization depends on several factors: job standardization, work process standardization, formal rules and regulations, and the level of professionalization. The first step in **job standardization** usually involves preparing job descriptions, which specify the exact tasks of the position along with the specific types of knowledge and skills necessary for its performance.[8] The intention is similar to that of machine parts standardization: making one part more or less interchangeable with another.[9] For instance, clerks in a state motor vehicle bureau can have exactly the same job description because each one, and there may be hundreds throughout a state, does essentially the same job as all the others—processing driver license applications. Job standardization fulfills a number of important organizational values. First, it makes organizations more predictable and stable; second, it reduces labor costs; and third, it minimizes the need for direct supervision of employees.[10] Further, built-in redundancy of function has advantages in some situations, as in the one described in Vignette 8.1.

VIGNETTE 8.1   The Two Horses: A Parable

Russian author Leo Tolstoy (1828–1910) tells the story of two horses that were carrying heavy loads. The first horse carried his load without trouble, but the second horse was lazy and dawdled. The owner began to transfer all of the second horse's load to the first one; when he finished, the second horse—thinking he had put one over on the owner—said boastfully to the first horse: "See what hard work will get you! The more you do, the more you suffer!" After a few more miles, they reached a tavern, where the man said: "Why should I feed two horses when I carry all on one? I'd better give the one all the food it wants and kill the other; at least I shall have the hide." And he did.

Another important task of formalization is standardizing work processes, or establishing **standard operating procedures**.[11] One way to think about standard operating procedures is to compare them with computers: the software is like the standard operating procedures, while the hardware is like the workers who actually carry out the instructions. Standard operating procedures spell out in detail the specific tasks and activities that must be done in typical job situations. Usually these practices and guidelines are found in a manual that, depending on the organization, might be quite extensive. For example, the manual for the Internal Revenue Service (IRS) is several volumes in length. The audit section alone fills one volume. The following is an example from the audit section, which gives a fairly good idea of the IRS guidelines' level of specificity:

1. The initial interview is the most important part of the examination process. The first few minutes should be spent making the taxpayer comfortable and explaining the examination process and appeal rights. This would also be a good time to ask the taxpayer if he/she has any questions. . . .

4. Remember, the taxpayer is being examined and not just the return. Therefore, develop all information to the fullest extent possible. If the appearance of the return and response to the initial questions lead the examiner to believe that indirect methods to determine income may be necessary, the factors in Chapter 500 should also be covered at this time.[12]

After reading this, it is hard to say whom we should feel sorrier for—the person being audited or the auditor who has to read through the 500 chapters of the manual! In the case of the IRS, and other organizations in which there is a high degree of formalization, the rules govern exactly what employees can do and what decisions should be made in nearly every imaginable situation.

Standardization does not refer only to work practices. Organizations often attempt to manage the personal characteristics of employees—including their appearance, behavior, and even personal beliefs—through official policies and regulations. In most organizations, people are expected to behave a certain way on and off the job. It would be unseemly, for example, for a priest, rabbi, or minister to be seen frequenting a casino. Indeed, all organizations demand a certain amount of obedience and conformity from their members. Certain types of organizations, particularly the military and police, require a high degree of personal conformity from their employees. Others, such as a theater company or university, typically require less conformity. The right of public organizations to control their employees' personal behavior was upheld by the 1986 Supreme Court decision in *Goldman v. Weinberger*.[13] In this decision, the Court decreed that the U.S. Air Force had the right to prohibit a serviceman from wearing a Yarmulke (a cap worn by an observant Jewish man), stating: "To accomplish its mission the military must foster instinctive obedience, unity, commitment, and *esprit de corps*," and in order to do this the individual must surrender his or her personal interests or desires on behalf of the larger interest of the service.[14]

Generally, organizations like the armed forces and the police require the greatest conformity because of the overriding need for internal control and predictability, particularly in dangerous or volatile situations. However, all organizations require a certain amount of role and group conformity in order to ensure organizational continuity. Indeed, this is the rationale for the socialization process in organizations, which inculcates the dominant values, behaviors, and social orientations to new organizational members.[15]

Job standardization, standard operating procedures, and personal conformity are all designed to contribute to greater organizational certainty and control. They serve to curtail individual discretion by making operations more predictable for both employees and clients. The disadvantages of too much standardization, however, include creating an inhospitable environment for risk-taking and innovation, along with the depersonalization of clients and employees. Clients often resent being treated "by the book" if it makes them feel as if part of their humanity has been taken away. Likewise, employees might feel alienated when there is too much job standardization. Conformity can have some negative effects as well. Groupthink, for example, occurs when there are strong pressures toward conformity in decision-making within a group or organization. Groupthink becomes harmful when individual group members feel intense pressure to agree with the majority viewpoint, without rational consideration of alternative courses of action.[16]

Professionalism The behavior, attitudes, and values stemming from training, socialization, and educational requirements that it takes to become a member of a profession.

The last aspect of formalization, **professionalism**, stems from two external sources: (1) the training, socialization, and educational requirements it takes to become a member of a profession, and (2) one's professional associations and peers.[17] As we recognized in Chapter 1, public organizations have become increasingly professionalized, which has had both advantages and disadvantages from an organizational standpoint. One benefit is that professional training and socialization generally occur externally, which means that fewer internal resources need to be devoted to these functions. Thus, organizations can reasonably expect that professionals already have been socialized into the norms and expectations surrounding the profession before they are even hired. One disadvantage, however, is that organizations have less control over an external socialization process compared to one that is done internally. Further, in situations where an organization's values conflict with a profession's values, professionals might be more loyal to the profession. After all, finding a new job tends to be easier than finding a new profession.

Complicating the situation is the inherent tension between government professionals and elected officials, which we discussed in the first chapter. The professional's power stems from his or her specialized knowledge or skills, while the politician is typically a generalist. Further, an effective politician is used to bargaining and compromise as part of problem-solving. A professional, however, uses a highly specialized approach that is grounded in principles of a profession and involves the application of highly technical standards to solve problems. Consequently, while a politician may be willing to back away from locating a homeless shelter in a particular neighborhood, a professional might view the decision as giving in to political pressure without consideration of the technical merits of the location.

Centralization

This dimension of organizational structure is concerned with whether decision-making authority is concentrated or diffused throughout the organization. Determining levels of centralization requires observing *who* is actually in control of key administrative functions such as budgeting, personnel, and procurement in organizations. The higher one goes up the hierarchy to find the actual decision-makers, the more centralized is the organization. Modern organization theory takes a somewhat mixed view of centralization. On the one hand, as noted in the last chapter, traditional theory equates centralization with efficiency. Thus, it is unsurprising that many public organizations tend to be moderately to highly centralized. On the other hand, decentralization is also an important organizational and political value in the United States.

The advantages of centralization are familiar from the previous chapter. Decentralization also has several advantages, according to some organization theorists.[18] These include increased organizational flexibility and capacity in decision-making, which contributes to a more efficient and effective organization. In addition, decentralization leads to more responsiveness to the consumer, which results in increased public satisfaction.[19] In general, of the two values, decentralization is viewed more positively in U.S. political culture.[20] The general belief is that decentralizing political authority (e.g., "power to the people") makes government more responsive to the citizens' will and serves as a bulwark against tyranny.

Complexity

The final organizational dimension —complexity— that encompasses the various mechanisms that organizations use to coordinate activities across specialization, up and down the hierarchy, and across spatially separated units. As noted earlier, specialization increases efficiency. However, a high degree of specialization, such as that which exists in modern organizations, can create problems for managers. Division of labor means that everyone in an organization becomes very good at what they do; however, if left entirely to their own devices, organizational ruin will quickly ensue. For example, in a post office, chaos would result if mail deliverers tried to perform their task without regard for the mail-sorting process. Imagine what would happen if mail carriers decided to deliver mail as it came in without bothering to follow route assignments. Further, in a complex society, organizations vary enormously in the number of different specializations they need to accomplish objectives.

Coordination The glue that holds an organization together; organizations require coordination to take full advantage of specialization and to accomplish crucial tasks.

Coordination is the glue that holds an organization together; organizations need coordination in order to take full advantage of specialization and to accomplish crucial tasks. But coordination needs differ tremendously across organizations. For example, a small rural school with few professionals (i.e., teachers, counselors, and administrators) will typically require less coordination than a large city hospital with a large number of professionals (i.e., doctors, nurses, other health care professionals, nonmedical professionals, and administrators).

The Pentagon, located in Arlington, Virginia, houses the Department of Defense. The building is almost an icon of hierarchical organization.

SOURCE: Hisham Ibrahim/ Getty Images

Departmentation The grouping of similar activities within an organization, key to coordination.

In Chapter 7, we discussed Gulick's examination of organizational coordination. Another aspect of his work in this area warrants our attention here. He viewed **departmentation**, or the grouping of similar activities, as being vital to the coordination of many diverse specializations in an organization.[21] Gulick identifies four types of departmentation: (1) unit purpose: for example, schools provide educational services to children, hospitals provide medical care to patients; (2) work process used by the unit: for example, an accounting unit does all the accounting for an organization; an engineering division performs the task of engineering; (3) persons or things the unit deals with: for example, the Department of Agriculture deals with farmers, a social service department serves people who require welfare assistance; and (4) geographic location the unit serves: for example, the Port Authority of New York and New Jersey serves the people who live in both states.

Purpose, work process, persons and things, and place are used to counteract the problems associated with coordinating across specialization. However, there exists a great deal of ambiguity as to precisely when each one should be used. Is it better to base a department on purpose or place, for instance? Under some conditions, the answer is straightforward (e.g., clientele agencies); in others, it is more difficult to determine. In some cases, a mixture seems appropriate (e.g., VA hospitals). Also, organizations differ considerably in how geographically spread out the units are. The State Department, for example, maintains an embassy in every foreign country that has diplomatic ties with the United States. Coordinating activities across all of these different embassies is a vast, complex undertaking. A neighborhood association, in contrast, would fall at the other end of the scale, because it has only one location.

To understand organizations, one must be thoroughly familiar with organizational structure and design, and one cannot properly design an organization without also taking into account issues of specialization and coordination. Yet structure and design are often considered less "sexy" than other topics, including leadership, decision-making, and behavior. No doubt this is due to the emphasis of traditional theory on the formal aspects of organization, which produced an inevitable backlash from later scholars. There is, however, another important reason to study organizational structure: it helps determine the physical and psychological environment in which people work. In the next section, we discuss different types of organizations and their effects on the people who work within them.

Types of Organizations by Dimension

We now have the conceptual tools needed to develop a typology of organizations based on the dimensions outlined above. Using this typology, organizations can be categorized along a continuum: at one end are traditional bureaucracies, marked by more formal structure and centralization; at the other end are organic organizations, characterized by less formal structure and decentralization (see Figure 8.2). We can use this scheme to make some basic observations about public organizations.

Classical Bureaucracy

Mechanistic organization The classical bureaucracy, where the emphasis is on machine-like efficiency.

Classical bureaucracy exemplifies **mechanistic organization**; that is, its chief objective is to enhance internal control by means of structures that emphasize predictability and accountability, just as in a machine.[22] Role specialization tends to be far reaching, and therefore we find a high degree of formalization throughout. Classical bureaucracy (Weber's ideal type) is the most hierarchical type of organization, with top-down authority. This type of organization is also referred to as a **tall hierarchy**: a structure in which authority and communication flow from the top down and there is close supervision of subordinates all along the chain of command (see Figure 8.3). For all of these reasons, classical bureaucracy ranks highest in terms of formal structure. On the scale of complexity, traditional organizations can be either very complex (e.g., the State Department) or quite simple (e.g., a local fast-food restaurant).

Tall hierarchy A classic bureaucratic structure in which authority and communication flow from the top down; involves close supervision of subordinates all along the chain of command.

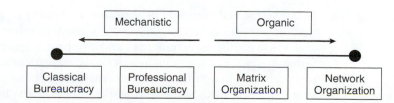

Figure 8.2   Formal Organization Structure Continuum

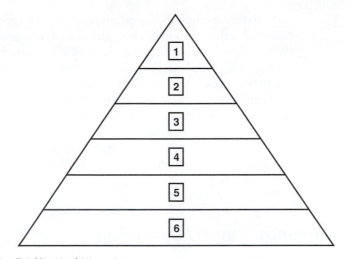

Figure 8.3   Tall (Classical) Hierarchy

A typical city police department provides an outstanding example of classical bureaucracy (see Figure 8.4). In terms of formalization, the police department demands unswerving personal conformity. From the beginning, the department instills its core values and beliefs into new recruits, in a manner similar to the military. The importance of control and hierarchy is established during training and reinforced throughout a police officer's career. The typical police department is a hierarchy consisting of clearly differentiated ranks and positions, which are defined with great specificity in the manual. The department's rules and regulations cover nearly every activity and aspect of the job, including personal appearance and behavior, both on and off duty.

The major criticisms of classical bureaucracy include slowness, unwieldiness, inflexibility, and inefficiency.[23] While these criticisms are sometimes valid, it must be noted that the emphasis on control, predictability, and accountability is absolutely vital for organizations such as the military and police, because they are called upon to employ violence to accomplish important social objectives. Notwithstanding the high degree of formalization in police departments, the potential for harm still exists, as the 2001 Cincinnati race riots indicate (see Vignette 8.2).

Professional Bureaucracy

Public sector and nonprofit organizations currently employ more professionals than at any earlier time. Consequently, the type of organization found more and more in the governmental and nonprofit spheres is the professional bureaucracy.[24] Examples include schools, universities, hospitals, and regulatory agencies. In a **professional bureaucracy**, members are trained in a profession (e.g., law, medicine, social work, or education) outside the organization and perform tasks that require a high degree of technical expertise. Top-down

Professional bureaucracy An organization that is dominated by professionals and different specializations; the top-down flow of authority is counteracted somewhat by the power of experts.

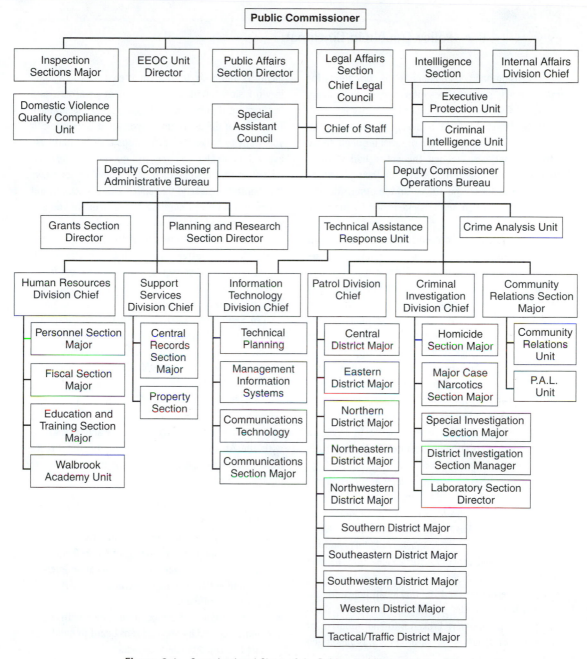

Figure 8.4   Organizational Chart of the Baltimore, Maryland, Police Department
SOURCE: Baltimore Police Department, http://www.baltimorepd.org.

VIGNETTE 8.2 Police Trouble in Cincinnati

Racial tension had been building in the community for many years over police interactions with black residents. The storm finally broke in the city in spring 2001. On March 14, 2001, a lawsuit filed accused the Cincinnati Ohio Police Division of racial profiling: thirty African Americans claimed the police had stopped them solely because of their skin color. Their grievances went back as far as the 1960s. On the other side, the police felt embattled and misunderstood by the black community.

The incident that proved to be the tipping point occurred on April 7, when an unarmed nineteen-year-old black man named Timothy Thomas was shot and killed by a white police officer in the predominately black Over-the-Rhine neighborhood. The youth was the fifteenth African American killed by Cincinnati's police since 1995. At a City Council meeting two days later, several hundred black residents showed up, many of them carrying signs bearing slogans such as "COP KILLERS" and chanting, "No justice, no peace." The protestors shouted down council members who tried to speak. The question on every protestor's mind was why an unarmed man without serious offenses in his record was shot down in an alley. Despite efforts to restore order, the meeting ended in chaos.

The riots began a few hours later as someone in a crowd of protestors hurled a brick through the window of District 1 Police Headquarters. Over the next three nights, Cincinnati was the scene of some of the worst urban turmoil since the Los Angeles riots following the acquittal of police officers in the Rodney Kings beating case in 1992. Hundreds were arrested, fires broke out, dozens were injured, and the Cincinnati police fought pitched battles in the streets with protestors. Businesses and homes were broken into and hundreds of thousands of dollars worth of property was vandalized or stolen.

The police responded to the criticism from the black community by virtually pulling out of many urban neighborhoods, leaving them at the mercy of gang members and drug dealers. Embittered police engaged in work slowdowns, and the number of arrests and traffic stops dropped dramatically during the summer. The leader of the police union wrote in a newsletter: "If you want to make 20 traffic stops a shift and chase every dope dealer you see, you go right ahead. Just remember that if something goes wrong, or you make the slightest mistake in that split second, it could result in having your worst nightmare come true for you and your family, and City Hall will sell you out." The violence continued unabated throughout the summer. Finally, Police Chief Tom Streicher formed a taskforce to halt the violence. Appalled by the violence that tore Cincinnati apart, community leaders and the police agreed to a truce to stop the bloodshed.

In September 2001, Stephen Roach, the police officer whose killing of Thomas sparked the April riots, was acquitted of the charge of negligent homicide. Although there was no street violence after the verdict, the African American community was, in the words of one of its leaders, "demoralized." In October, the federal Department of Justice, after an extensive investigation, issued a report on the Cincinnati police and its relations with the African American community. The Justice Department report made several recommendations to improve the police, including:

- Revise policies on the use of force, including use of guns and chemical irritants.
- Make changes in the internal operations of the police, including better tracking of bad behavior of police officers, improved communication internally, and better training of recruits and experienced officers.
- Increase interaction and communication with the community, and create a citizens board to handle cases of alleged police misconduct.

Cincinnati's police woes point to the inability of organizations acting alone to ensure proper control and accountability of their members, no matter how

(continued on next page)

authority tends to be minimized in this type of organization. Indeed, level of technical knowledge and formal position tend to determine one's authority within the professional organization. As a result, authority is based more on professional norms and standards rather than exclusively on organizational rank, which can pose control problems for the political leadership.[25] Professional bureaucracies can be either complex (a university) or simple (a small law firm).

Organic Organizations

Organic organization
An organization that is characterized by less formalization and concentration of authority than classical bureaucracy.

At the other end of the structure continuum are **organic organizations** (also known as adhocracies). Their structure tends to be less rigid than that of bureaucratic organizations (either classical or professional), and they are characterized by adaptation and flexibility rather than control.[26] In contrast to the classical, tall bureaucracy, organic organizations are flat, which allows them to adapt readily to changes in their environment (see Figure 8.5). They are also decentralized, which tends to increase their coordination needs. Consequently, authority is diffused more widely throughout the organization, at the same time; this authority is based more on technical competence than on formal rank. Roles and responsibilities are fluid and may change considerably over time. As a result of the flat hierarchy and decentralization, integration and coordination of activities become more difficult to achieve than in the other two types of organization.

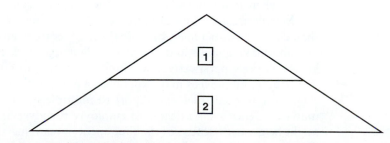

Figure 8.5   Flat (Organic) Hierarchy

Members of organic organizations often operate under more than one line of authority. Teams and task forces are thus the primary means of coordinating functions and tasks.[27] Take, for example, being employed as a finance specialist in an organic organization. For a project, you might be assigned to a team that includes specialists from other departments and is led by a project manager. In effect, you report to three bosses while on this project: your department head, the director of finance, and the project manager. The other specialists in the project team also come from different departments, including Real Estate Development and Legal Affairs, where they also report to their directors as well as to the project leader. When the project is completed, you no longer report to the project leader but you still report to your department head.

Matrix organization
The best-known type of organic organization, it employs a team-based structure instead of traditional hierarchy.

The most prevalent type of organic organization is the **matrix organization**, which has a structure very similar to that described in the last paragraph. This type of organization can be described as a loose arrangement where "the various specialists are joined in a common purpose . . . on a team that is supervised and coordinated by an individual with responsibility for achieving a defined set of project goals."[28] Matrix organizations use a program-based structure (i.e., flat hierarchy and dispersed authority) instead of the traditional department-based structure. As the previous paragraph's example shows, employees report to department heads, but they also work in teams under the direct supervision of a team manager or project leader, an arrangement that violates the traditional principle of unity of command ("one boss per employee").

One benefit of matrix organization is that coordination may be facilitated by breaking down the barriers existing between different departments and subunits in an organization. Another advantage is that communication and interaction might be increased among members of the organization as a result of teams, which might contribute to organizational learning (for more about this, see Chapter 9). Matrix organizations have their disadvantages too. Since there is no clearly defined hierarchy, mutual adjustment and teams are relied on for coordination. In practice, however, this overly fluid situation may cause conflicts. For example, tensions might arise between a department head and project manager regarding their differing expectations of employees. Such conflicts will have to be resolved at a higher level of the organization, which can lead to increased central authority. In addition, because of their flat structure, matrix organizations may be more costly to operate than other types of organizations. In order to be effective, they might require many managers and the duplication of effort that results when additional staff is needed to support project teams.

Matrix organizations are often viewed as being more "employee-friendly" than classic bureaucracies, because the flat hierarchy and team approach foster decision-making skills and create a challenging work environment. But from an employee's perspective, working in matrix organizations can be very demanding. Employees may experience a great deal of ambiguity and stress as they serve in dual roles and report to multiple bosses. Matrix organizations may experience a high degree of employee turnover as a result. Finally, costs might be greater because of the time spent in team meetings and in other coordinating activities in the organization.

Notwithstanding the theoretical appeal of matrix organizations, however, they tend to be extremely rare in the governmental and nonprofit worlds. The one notable exception to this is the federal space agency, NASA.[29] Many of NASA's impressive technological achievements are actually related to its matrix structure. The chief reason for the relative absence of organic organizations within the public sector may be due to their program-based structure. Thus, matrix organizations are "rapidly changing temporary systems" that deal with "specific problems-to-be-solved."[30] Governments and nonprofit agencies, however, tend to deal with permanent, intractable problems such as poverty, drug addiction, crime, and environmental pollution, where temporary systems are not as effective. Further, as a result of the turbulence and uncertainty typically found in the public and nonprofit environment, the political leadership often attempts to apply more control, centralization, and rules in order to ensure accountability; which makes it difficult to apply the organic approach.

Civil Society and Networks

Network organization A loose grouping of independent organizations coordinated by contracts rather than through formal hierarchy.

Governments and nonprofits are beginning to make use of **network organization**, a structure that is even more loosely connected than a matrix organization. For example, instead of directly providing services, governments are collaborating more and more with nonprofits, voluntary associations, and community organizations. Network structure refers to such a cluster of separate, independent organizations whose actions are coordinated by contracts and informal agreements rather than through formal authority.[31] Nonprofit community organizations are an example of network structures.[32] These community organizations deliver services that were previously provided by government as a result of federal transferal of program authority and responsibilities down to states and localities. Community organizations are especially concerned with addressing community needs in the areas of health and human services. The faith-based initiative of George W. Bush, discussed in a later chapter, is another example of the increasing use by government of network organization.

Network structures differ from traditional bureaucratic organizations in that "no one is in charge." Instead, network structures require extensive collaboration among the parties to accomplish objectives and goals. According to a recent study, network structures have three other defining characteristics. First, a common mission; usually the groups and organizations came together in the first place because working singly did not produce the hoped-for results. Second, members are interdependent; each one sees itself as part of a larger picture. Third, a unique structural arrangement results from the fact that all of the parties, which might include government, businesses, nonprofits, and community organizations, are equal partners. Thus, the emphasis is on coalition-building rather than hierarchical control. As a result of these characteristics, proponents of network structures view them as an innovative means to overcome traditional bureaucracy's inability to satisfactorily deal with complex, social problems.[33]

Network structures are subject to criticism, however. Concerns over this type of organizational arrangement relate primarily to accountability and responsiveness issues. For example, without formal lines of authority, where does accountability lie?[34] If all the parties are perceived as equal partners, who will be accountable when problems arise? Who will perform the necessary tasks of oversight? These are the types of questions that have been raised regarding network structures' accountability. Fredericksen and London argue that a lack of accountability creates a potential "shadow state," one "administered outside traditional democratic politics." Further, too much governmental interference into community organizations' administration could lead to their being less responsive to their constituents' needs.[35]

Power and Organizational Dimensions

"The lifeblood of administration is power," famously declared political scientist Norton Long. Indeed, administrative power is closely related to the three-dimensional model, because formalization, centralization, and complexity determine, to a large extent, the roles, structures, and relationships within an organization. Thus, these dimensions have a direct or indirect effect on organizational power. Power, while it is an inherent part of many types of social relationships, is usually context or relationship specific: a person is generally powerful (or powerless) with respect to other social actors in a specific situation.[36] Within an organization, positions and roles determine the contexts and relationships in which power gets played out.

Five important bases of organizational power are (1) legitimate power, (2) coercive power, (3) reward power, (4) referent power, and (5) expert power.[37] **Legitimate power** is related to the formalization dimension; this power source is dependent on official position or formal rank. In other words, authority is an attribute of the position rather than a person, according to Max Weber.[38] By dint of being atop the organizational hierarchy, one has a right to lead.[39] Power is delegated to mid-level administrators from their superiors as a means to accomplish organizational objectives. The social legitimacy of the exercise of power stems from the fact that it is done on behalf of the organization and not for purely personal reasons.

Coercive power refers to an administrator's ability to punish or discipline subordinates and is related to legitimate power. The fear of demotion or losing one's job can motivate subordinates to work harder and better. Truly effective administrators, however, typically do not need to resort to coercive measures in order to produce results. Further, managers who, on paper, appear to possess coercive power are not necessarily more effective than other managers. Although actual power and formal authority are typically equated in our minds, in fact, they might be quite different. For instance, the Constitution provides for the removal from office of cabinet members and other high-ranking noncareer civil service bureaucrats whose job performance displeases

Legitimate power
Power within an organization that is based on an individual's formal position in the organization.

President Richard Nixon, with his family, giving his farewell speech to White House staff at the end of the Watergate scandal, August 1974.

SOURCE: Mark Godfrey/The Image Works

the president. During the Watergate affair, President Nixon directed Attorney General Elliot Richardson to fire the special prosecutor, Archibald Cox. However, Richardson and his deputy, William Ruckelshaus, both resigned rather than comply with the president's order. The incident later became known as the Saturday Night Massacre because it occurred on Saturday, October 20, 1973.[40] Nixon ultimately resigned in August 1974. The point is that the president experienced heavy costs in exercising his coercive power, indicating that, in reality, there are limitations on what seems on paper to be a fairly broad authority to sack officials.

Competent administrators recognize that using persuasion to obtain voluntary compliance from subordinates often produces the best results. The presidents and other executives who wield the most influence over the bureaucracy are the ones who can win recalcitrant officials over to their positions.[41] The same principle applies equally well to public managers who must work within rules that place significant restrictions on their ability to discipline employees. Administrators in this situation might find it more to their advantage to follow the old saying, "You can catch more flies with honey than with vinegar." Persuasion can be enhanced by reward power to produce effective administration.

Reward power involves the ability to adjust behavior by means of promotions, raises, and other forms of material or psychological inducements. This base of power is related to the dimension of formalization. Control over incentives, for example, is closely tied to rank within organizations. In many public organizations, rules and regulations establish the framework that determines who receives pay raises and promotions, and under what conditions. For example, the principle of seniority, which is established by civil service laws, plays a significant role in the determination of raises and advancement in public bureaucracy. Professionalism, another aspect of formalization, creates a further set of incentives or disincentives. Administrators can use professional values, standards, and peer pressure to motivate professional employees. However, professionalism might interfere with the pursuit of some organizational objectives, as described earlier. Reward power can prove a very productive approach for mangers who seek to empower employees, on the theory that "Organizational power can grow, in part by being shared. By empowering others, a leader does not decrease his power; instead he may increase it—especially if the whole organization performs better."[42]

Referent power relates to the level of psychological identification we share with the people we work for and with. People we like or admire tend to exert considerable influence on our behavior; thus, we are more likely to follow their orders. Further, peers have a great deal of influence on members' behavior. People like to feel that they belong and are liked by their associates.[43] This source of power has more to do with the informal aspects of organization that we dealt with in Chapter 7.

Expert power comes from specialized knowledge or skills and professional training. Expert power both influences and is influenced by an organization's degree of formalization. As society becomes more complex and technical, organizations require larger numbers of experts to function effectively, which inevitably leads to greater internal specialization. As mentioned earlier, power is a function of organizational structure, namely the division of labor. According to Heffron, "When the overall tasks of the organization are divided into smaller parts, it is inevitable that some tasks will come to be more important than others. Those persons and those units that have the responsibility for performing the more critical tasks in the organization have a natural advantage in developing and exercising power in the organization." Heffron acknowledges that "individual skills and strategies can certainly affect the amount of power and the effectiveness with which it is used," but she goes on to point out that "power is first and foremost a structural phenomenon, and should be understood as such."[44]

Invariably, division of labor and scarcity of resources create dependencies within an organization, which make certain departments and employees more powerful, either because they are crucial for certain tasks or because they posses scarce resources.[45] Thus, an increasingly important part of a manager's job is to successfully negotiate and manipulate these dependent relationships in order to accomplish objectives. Reliance on others, however, can produce feelings of frustration within an organization. When administrators experience frustration, they might be more likely to use coercive power in order to make up for their inability to directly influence other organizational actors.

■ Chapter Summary

Design and structure are vital to comprehending organizational behavior. In addition, design and structure are closely interrelated with organizational power. In this chapter, we use the three-dimensional model of organization (formalization, centralization, complexity) to examine the key role that structures like departments and standardization play. Formalization, which includes standardization, conformity, and professionalization, is necessary to perform the multifarious tasks required of modern organizations. In public organizations, a relatively high degree of formalization is often necessary due to the nature of tasks (e.g., crime fighting, public education, defense, public health) and the external environment. Organizations can be categorized according to continuum of formalization ranging from mechanistic organizations at one end to organic organizations at the other. Classical bureaucracy is an example of mechanistic organization. A typical big-city police department is a good example of a mechanistic organization. The principal aim is to increase internal control using structures that promote predictability in operations and that strive for a high level of employee accountability. At the other end of the continuum are organic organizations; their structure tends to be fluid, stressing adaptation and flexibility rather than control. Organic organizations have flat hierarchy and are also decentralized. A good example of this type is the matrix organization, such as NASA.

Centralization is concerned with the concentration of authority in organizations. A top-down model of authority is mechanistic organization, while decentralized authority is exemplified by organic organization. The professional bureaucracy falls midway in the continuum from mechanistic to organic organization. Another type of structure, the network, increasingly common in government, is even more decentralized than organic organization. Proponents of either centralization or decentralization can be found in organization theory. Both sides claim that their position furthers organizational efficiency.

Complexity is the dimension dealing with the structures of coordination within organizations. Specialization is a fact of life for modern organizations, and therefore organizations need coordinating mechanisms and structures or else chaos will ensue. Departmentation is a major tool (along with standardization and conformity, which are covered in formalization) to coordinate organizational activities. The four bases of departmentation are (1) purpose, (2) work process, (3) persons or things, and (4) location.

Power is an intrinsic feature of organizational life. One source of power in organizations is legitimate power, which is derived from organizational position, role, or rank. Another is coercive power or the power to punish subordinates. Reward power refers to the ability to provide incentives to subordinates as a means to gain their compliance. Referent power stems from the identification with those in authority and the natural human desire to please those in positions of power. Expert power relates to the technical knowledge, skills, and expertise that a person possesses, or is thought to possess. Power is therefore a necessary byproduct of organization structure.

■ Chapter Discussion Questions

1. In this chapter, we observed that overspecialization might create problems. What about overcoordination? How might that bring about problems too?

2. Some critics suggest that public organizations suffer from too much formalization. Why might this be a problem for organizations?

3. Earlier we discussed the importance of centralization in the executive as a means to increase managerial control for accountability. What are some possible drawbacks that might result from centralization?

4. If you were designing an organization, which aspects of mechanistic and organic organizations would you choose to include and why?

5. Based on the discussion in this chapter, describe how you would expect organizational power to be allocated in a (1) classical bureaucracy, (2) professional bureaucracy, (3) organic organization, and (4) network organization.

 **BRIEF CASE** **CRISIS AT THE NEW YORK CITY DEPARTMENT OF JUVENILE JUSTICE**

Created in 1979, New York City's Department of Juvenile Justice (DJJ) faced its first major crisis in January 1983, just as Ellen Schall was appointed commissioner. Schall was asked to lead an agency beset by internal turmoil and attacked by critics from outside. The purpose of the DJJ was to keep youthful offenders in custody while they awaited sentencing, mainly for minor crimes such as vandalism and petty theft, and to provide them with social services before sentencing. A majority of these children (age seven to fifteen) were low-income blacks or Hispanics. As adults, they would not be held in jail for the same offenses. But since the parents or guardians were unwilling to take responsibility for them, instead of releasing them back onto the streets where they could get into more trouble, the city kept them at several nonsecure detention (NSD) facilities. More problematically, a significant number (one-third) had been arrested for violent crimes, and these serious offenders were held at a large detention facility, the Spofford Juvenile Center.

The DJJ was plagued by a number of organizational problems. The previous commissioner had recruited many employees who wanted to help troubled young people, but they felt they were being asked to assume the role of prison wardens, which they found repugnant. Schall's appointment helped to reinforce this perception, since her previous position had been deputy commissioner in the city's Department of Corrections. Furthermore, there was a division between the mostly white professionals working at the "downtown" administrative office and the mostly nonwhite unionized employees working at the "uptown" Spofford facility.

The DJJ could be characterized as highly complex organizationally because of the physical dispersal of its facilities, which made effective coordination from downtown headquarters especially difficult. Spofford, a 212-bed facility located in the South Bronx—one of the most impoverished parts of New York

City—had a particularly bad reputation. Violence, congestion, suicide attempts, and allegations of child abuse were commonplace. The NSD, on the other hand, was a loose network of group and foster homes scattered throughout the city. Many children simply walked away from these homes before their cases were even heard in court.

Arguably, too much decentralization was part of the problem. Upon her appointment, Schall observed: "Spofford was a place run by middle managers. They kept having a series of men executive directors. There was a group of women below that level who sort of ran it. But on some level, nobody ran it." The NSD, Schall also realized, was loosely run and suffered from poor coordination. As a result, lack of coordination and integration prevented the DJJ from effectively accomplishing its mission.

SOURCE: This brief case is adapted from a Harvard University Kennedy School of Government case study written by Pamela Varley. The entire case study, "Ellen Schall and the Department of Juvenile Justice," is available at the Electronic Hallway Network (http://www.Hallway.org).

Brief Case Questions

1. *What should be the first thing Schall does upon taking office?*

2. *What types of organizational problems did Schall face?*

3. *How would you respond to the problems if you had Schall's job?*

4. *How do the problems affect Schall's power as commissioner?*

For the DJJ's response to the crisis, see Vignette 8.3.

VIGNETTE 8.3   **The DJJ's Response to Crisis**

When she became commissioner of New York City's Department of Juvenile Justice (DJJ), Ellen Schall decided that she needed to address the structural issues immediately. Thus, the first three items on her agenda were (1) improving the situation at Spofford, (2) filling vacancies in top positions, and (3) addressing the split in the agency over mission.

An issue on the previous commissioner's agenda was replacing the Spofford facility with four smaller facilities, which would be less intimidating and permit more individualized treatment of the children. Schall decided that something had to be done with the Spofford Replacement Project. In the short term, she realized she needed to bring the facility under control and restore a sense of order.

Recognizing that she could not do this all by herself, Schall decided that quickly filling the vacancies in the hierarchy with capable and trustworthy individuals would be necessary before she could tackle any structural problems. She also realized the importance of establishing a common sense of mission that met with the approval of most of the organization members. She believed a strong signal should be sent regarding what direction the agency would move in, so in her first months in office, she spent a lot of time listening to the senior administrators, because they were the ones most familiar with the organization's operations and culture.

SOURCE: Adapted from "Ellen Schall and the Department of Juvenile Justice," *The Electric Hallway.* (www.hallway.org).

■ Key Terms

centralization (page 186)
complexity (page 186)
coordination (page 189)
departmentation (page 190)
formalization (page 186)
job standardization (page 186)
legitimate power (page 198)
matrix organization (page 196)

mechanistic organization (page 191)
network organization (page 197)
organic organization (page 195)
professional bureaucracy (page 192)
professionalism (page 188)
standard operating procedures (page 186)
tall hierarchy (page 191)

■ On the Web

http://www.whitehouse.gov/homeland/
Office of Homeland Security website.

http://www.defenselink.mil/
Department of Defense, a classic example of
a mechanistic organization.

http://www.nasa.gov/
National Aeronautics and Space Administration, an example of a matrix organization.

http://www.cs.tcd.ie/courses/ism/smis/topics/
org_ntwk/org_ntwk.htm
A module on the move to networked organizations, from Trinity College, Dublin, Ireland.

http://www.theipa.org/
The Institute of Public Administration,
a private, nonprofit organization concerned
with effective government.

http://www.tecn.rutgers.edu/itworkshop/Global
Proceedings of a workshop on global public
and private partnerships held at Rutgers
University in 2002.

http://www.cincinnati.com/race/
A website devoted to discussing racial issues
in Cincinnati, Ohio.

http://www.mapnp.org/library/guiding/influenc/
influenc.htm
The interpersonal power and influence
in organizations webpage of the Management Assistance Program (MAP) for
nonprofits.

CHAPTER 9

Motivation, Decision-Making, and Organizational Culture

■ SETTING THE STAGE

In October 1971, a New York City police officer named Frank Serpico shocked the country by publicly exposing city cops who were making millions of dollars in bribes from drug dealers, mobsters, and even small businesses.[1] Shortly thereafter, both a best-selling book and a hit movie came out with Al Pacino playing the incorruptible officer, Serpico. Serpico's allegations eventually led to the creation of the Knapp Commission, which was given the charge to investigate wrongdoing on the part of the New York City police. The new police commissioner, Patrick Murphy, used the commission's findings to press for major reforms of the Police Department, asserting that outsiders would seek to impose even more drastic changes unless the department cleaned itself up.

Unfortunately, the reforms Murphy instituted, while initially effective, did not prove long lasting in their efficacy. In the early 1990s, the city's police force became embroiled again in another major corruption and brutality scandal. Once more, the city's mayor appointed a special commission to investigate allegations of police corruption. Similar to the earlier Knapp Commission, the Mollen Commission made a number of recommendations relating to recruiting and training, which generally have been implemented. However, the city's powerful police union has successfully resisted stricter disciplinary measures and has totally ignored the commission's recommendation that the union take a more forceful approach to investigating further instances of corruption and brutality. The example of the New York City Police Department shows the importance of motivating employees to do the right thing even under the most stressful conditions; it also shows how certain organizational cultures can become resistant to organizational learning and change. These topics are the subject of this chapter.

■ CHAPTER PLAN

In this chapter, we continue our focus on the organizational aspects of public administration by examining how organizations motivate employees and make decisions, two processes that play a crucial role in an organization's ultimate success or failure.

Al Pacino in the movie role of Frank Serpico, who gained fame fighting corruption in the New York City Police Department.

SOURCE: Paramount Pictures/Getty Images

Organizations that are effective at motivating workers and ones that make consistently good decisions are generally better performers overall. Without motivated workers, very little would get done. The chapter also looks at the role of organizational culture in helping or hindering change. Change is a constant in contemporary society. All organizations must learn to adapt to environments that are in a state of constant flux. But this is particularly true for public organizations. Important components of effective adaptation include motivating workers, organizational decision-making, and organizational learning.

Perhaps the most important facet of organizations relating to change and adaptation, however, is organizational culture. As the New York City police example shows, effecting change in large bureaucracies can be difficult, and when it does occur, it usually takes considerable time. Furthermore, the changes might fail to produce lasting effects. Organizational culture can be well entrenched and closed off from the outside, making it very resistant to change, especially if the change is perceived as coming externally. Every organization possesses a unique culture that sets it apart from other organizations. In this chapter, we consider the importance of organizational culture in producing or resisting change. The chapter concludes with a discussion of organizational development and Total Quality Management, two important recent techniques for managing change in organizations.

Getting Work Done in Organizations: Motivation

What makes one employee devote all of his or her energy to a job while another employee avoids work? Without knowing all of the specifics, one can reasonably say that the first employee is highly motivated while the second one lacks motivation.

What Is Motivation?

Motivation A psychological state that stimulates and directs human behavior toward some goal that fulfills a need.

Motivation refers to a psychological state, specifically a drive or desire that stimulates and directs human behavior toward some goal that fulfills a personal need. Motivation is an important variable in individual performance, but several other variables also help explain performance. This is an important point to keep in mind as we discuss motivation in this chapter. In addition to motivation, an employee must have the ability to perform the task at hand. All of the motivation in the world will not turn a person who lacks ability in teaching into a good teacher. Another important factor contributing to or hindering performance is organizational structure. In the case of the public sector, the public budget and personnel system serve as constraints on management's ability to effect employee performance.[2] In contrast to the private sector, for example, use of financial incentives to motivate employees is much more limited.[3] Despite the aforementioned limitations, the importance of motivation should not be underestimated, since effective organizations are usually the ones that excel at motivating their employees.

Incentives and Motivators

Extrinsic rewards Organizational incentives to perform that are not related to position or employment.

Organizations can employ rules, extrinsic rewards, and intrinsic rewards as inducements for performance.[4] We dealt with rules in Chapter 8 (see the section on formalization). **Extrinsic rewards** consist of both material incentives to workers (e.g., pay and fringe benefits, health insurance, pension, use of company vehicles, day care for children, and health club memberships) and nonmonetary incentives (e.g., public praise from the boss, photo in the company newsletter, and other forms of recognition). Extrinsic rewards can be further divided into system rewards and individual rewards. System rewards, such as pay, bonuses, and fringe benefits, are provided as a means to attract and retain qualified people. These incentives can help build employee loyalty and assure a minimum level of worker satisfaction. For a university professor, a system reward is the awarding of tenure based on productivity in scholarship and teaching. Individual rewards, on the other hand, are given out on the basis of exemplary individual performance. Receiving a big promotion and pay raise or being named manager of the year would be an individual reward. Individual rewards are ego boosters; they satisfy the desire to be recognized as being superior from others in some way. Individual rewards can help improve organizational performance, but only if employees perceive a direct connection between the incentive and exceptional job performance. Further, individual rewards are effective to the extent that organization members believe they are fairly and equitably awarded.[5]

Intrinsic rewards are motivators that relate to the level of personal satisfaction and self-esteem experienced as a result of doing a job. When people use words like "interesting," "challenging," "worthwhile," "meaningful," and "creative" to describe their job, they are talking about the intrinsic rewards of the work. Not every organization member, however, responds the same way to this set of incentives. Work that is stimulating and challenging to one may be too difficult to another. A position of power and responsibility might motivate one person but not someone else. Another aspect of intrinsic rewards is the organization member's self-identification with the organization.[6] The more committed and dedicated one is to the goals of the organization, the more satisfaction one derives from one's job.

Public and nonprofit agencies use both types of motivators as inducements to employees. But the nature of public service may appeal more strongly to people who are motivated primarily by intrinsic rewards rather than extrinsic rewards. One study, for example, found that the public sector taps into an individual's higher-level needs, or makes more effective use of intrinsic motivators, than private companies.[7] In addition, public service deals with socially significant issues such as human welfare, justice, and the environment, which people find interesting and challenging.[8] Finally, research has found that public servants are motivated more by a sense of idealism or patriotic duty than are their private sector counterparts.[9]

Different Theoretical Approaches to Motivation

Early organization theorists showed little interest in the psychological aspects of motivation, instead placing an emphasis on rules and material incentives as the chief means for improving performance. The organizational humanists were the first to seriously investigate the role of human behavior in organizations, including a more sophisticated and multifaceted understanding of what drives organization members. As we have seen, Elton Mayo, Mary Parker Follett, Chester Barnard, and others thought that a better understanding of human emotions and desires could be useful to management. They also believed that productivity was shaped by certain intangible factors like group relations. Following the organizational humanists, other theorists began to study the psychological basis of motivation. In general, these motivation theorists subscribe to the needs-based model of motivation: when one need is fulfilled, humans move on to the next unfulfilled one (see Figure 9.1).

Intrinsic rewards The organizational incentives to perform relating to position or employment.

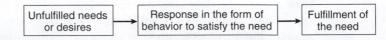

Figure 9.1 The Need Theory of Motivation in Organizations

Hierarchy of human needs A model developed by Abraham Maslow to explain how people are motivated by different levels of needs, from food to self-actualization.

The Hierarchy of Needs One of the first to devote considerable attention to psychological factors was Abraham Maslow, who was responsible for developing the **hierarchy of human needs** model.[10] According to Maslow, people are motivated by different levels of needs, which he arranged as a pyramid consisting of five levels, ascending from lowest to highest needs (see Figure 9.2). In theory, as one level of needs is satisfied, a person then moves up to the next level and attempts to satisfy those needs, and so on all the way to the top level. At the bottom level are the purely physiological needs such as food and shelter, which must be met merely to survive. The second level consists of safety and security needs, which encompass both freedom from physical harm and a secure personal environment. Social needs comprise the third level, which includes the need for love and affection as well as belongingness to a community. At the fourth level are self-esteem needs: feeling good about oneself and receiving the esteem of others. At the top of the pyramid Maslow places self-actualization, which he describes as realizing one's full human potential. As he says: "A musician must make music, an artist must paint, a poet must write . . . to be ultimately happy." According to Maslow, what we can be, we *must* be.[11]

It is important to recognize that after a need has been satisfied, it no longer serves to motivate. At that point, the next level of unsatisfied need becomes the principal motivator. From an organizational perspective, Maslow's hierarchy has several noteworthy implications. For example, before the prospect of increased responsibility can motivate a worker, his or her basic organizational needs, including adequate salary, good working conditions, job security, and recognition from management and peers must first be satisfied. In Maslow's view, management's goal with respect to motivation is to help employees develop psychologically and to achieve their highest level (see Vignette 9.1).

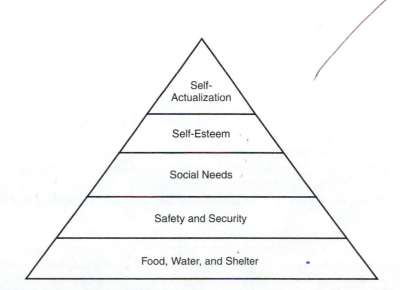

Figure 9.2 Maslow's Hierarchy of Needs

VIGNETTE 9.1   Abraham Maslow and the Hierarchy of Needs

Abraham Maslow, one of seven children, was born April 1, 1908, in Brooklyn, New York. His parents were uneducated Jewish immigrants from Russia. Maslow's childhood was lonely and unhappy. His parents wanted him to do well in their adopted country and pressured him to excel in school. After attending City College in New York, Maslow started law school but quit after three semesters and eventually ended up studying psychology in graduate school at the University of Wisconsin. While at Wisconsin, he worked with Professor Harry Harlow, an expert in primate development. Maslow's dissertation was entitled "The Role of Dominance in the Social and Sexual Behavior of Infra-human Primates," reflecting the influence of his mentor.

From 1937 to 1951, Maslow taught at Brooklyn College. There he came into contact with several people who would play an influential role in the development of his psychological theories: Ruth Benedict, Max Werthheimer, and Kurt Goldstein. These were individuals whom he admired on both personal and professional levels, to the extent that he studied them as exemplary human beings. In his future work, they would point the way toward fully realized human potential.

In Maslow's hierarchy of human needs, the pinnacle of this need pyramid is self-actualization. A person who ascends to this level of development has fulfilled each of the lower-level needs: physiological, safety, belongingness, and esteem. As a result, the person is able to perceive reality more clearly than non-self-actualized persons who are driven by their deficit needs, or "D-needs." It is important to note that in order to reach this highest state of being, all one's lower needs must be met at least to a large extent. Thus, self-actualization is relatively rare, because for many people, just meeting their D-needs is struggle enough. Maslow claimed that only 1 percent of the population could meet his criteria.

Self-actualizers perceive reality as it actually is; they are, in Maslow's words, "able to see concealed or confused realities more swiftly and more correctly." They can tell the real from the false in social situations.

Self-actualizers also are problem-centered; they focus on external problems rather than their own ego needs. According to Maslow, this is their most important characteristic. They have what Maslow calls acceptance of self and others, by which he means they have an easygoing attitude regarding others and prefer being themselves rather than something artificial. With this comes the quality of being spontaneous and creative. This creativity and spontaneity contribute to their resisting social pressures to conform. Despite their nonconformity, self-actualizers tend to be fairly conventional on the surface; they are simply natural and unself-conscious in their approach to social conventions and life in general. With self-actualizers, "what you see is what you get."

In contrast to the D-needs, being needs or values motivate self-actualizers. These values include truth, beauty, wholeness or unity, meaningfulness, justice, playfulness, simplicity, and self-sufficiency. When self-actualizers cannot fulfill these needs, they feel depressed, bored, and alienated. Maslow did not want to create an unattainable ideal of human perfection. He admitted that self-actualizers were not without fault or imperfection. Self-actualizers, in Maslow's view, "show many of the lesser human failings." These human flaws include anxiety and guilt, usually because they feel they are not living up to their own ideal of being all they can be. They can also be absent-minded, humorless, and overly compassionate. Perhaps most surprising is the self-actualizer's ability to appear coldhearted and ruthless if a situation calls for this. While this type of behavior might be unexpected, it is nonetheless reasonable if one considers that self-actualizers have a clearer perception of reality than the average person.

Peak experiences are moments that, according to Maslow, are spiritual, mystical, or religious in nature. We feel that we are part of something bigger or more meaningful than our individual selves. The metaphor is one of ascending a very tall mountain and surveying from this awe-inspiring vantage point the surrounding landscape. Such an experience transcends the ordinary

(continued on next page)

VIGNETTE 9.1   **Abraham Maslow and the Hierarchy of Needs** *(continued)*

and the mundane. While average people do have peak experiences, self-actualizers have more of them. Indeed, a hallmark of self-actualizers is their increased capacity to have peak experiences.

Maslow believed that although individuals bear the bulk of the responsibility for self-actualization, there is much that organizations can do to encourage the process. Organizations, in fact, would find it beneficial to provide numerous opportunities for employees for self-actualization. Self-actualized employees are more creative and harder working, and they make outstanding

leaders because they tend to attract dedicated followers or disciples. Maslow notes that Abraham Lincoln, Thomas Jefferson, Mahatma Gandhi, and Eleanor Roosevelt are examples of self-actualizers. Organizations can create favorable conditions for self-actualization by providing opportunities for employees to make decisions, take risks within reason, and develop a healthy self-sufficiency.

SOURCE: Maslow, Abraham H., *Encyclopedia Britannica 2007*. Encyclopedia Britannica online. www.britannica.com/eb/article-9051264. "motivation." *Encyclopedia Britannica 2007*. Encyclopedia Britannicaonline.www.britannica.com/eb/article-12712. The official Abraham Maslow website is located at www.maslow.com and is a useful online source for all things related to the man and his theories.

Mature Personality in Organizations Following Maslow's lead, other researchers began to take a more psychological approach to studying motivation in organizations. One of the most influential, Chris Argyris, asserts that the demands of traditional bureaucracy are often in direct conflict with human needs for full development and growth.[12] Argyris, like Maslow, thinks that psychologically mature individuals want to be independent, creative, and in control of their own destiny. He believes that bureaucracies, through structures like division of labor and hierarchy, treat their employees more like children than adults. This hinders workers' psychological growth, and as a result, they experience psychological disturbances, which can produce childlike behaviors. Argyris believes that managers can encourage subordinates to behave like adults by treating them as adults in the first place. Thus, his theory takes into account the needs of the employee's personality by giving more responsibility and encouraging more participation in decision-making, among other things. Assigning more responsibility, however, does not mean simply making employees do more. Argyris argues that most jobs have to be reconfigured to realize an employee's full potential, that jobs have to allow for more self-responsibility and more judgment. Encouraging greater participation gives workers increased confidence and decision-making skills, and it promotes more self-identification with the organization and its objectives.

Theory X and Theory Y Another theorist who recognized the psychological dimension of motivation is Douglas MacGregor. Since the publication of his book *The Human Side of Enterprise*, in 1960, MacGregor's work has had a significant influence on organizational theory and practice, in both the public and private sectors. In this book, MacGregor writes that managers can improve productivity by revising their assumptions regarding people's basic orientations toward work.[13] He calls the traditional approach to management **Theory X**. According to Theory X, people hate work and do all they can to avoid it. In addition, by nature, people lack ambition and shun responsibility, prefer to be led, and crave security above all else. Also in this

Theory X A view of human behavior which states that people hate work and do whatever is possible to avoid it.

view, employees put their personal needs before those of the organization and always oppose change when it directly affects them. MacGregor thinks that Theory X creates a self-fulfilling prophecy: when managers focus on workers' lower-level needs and ignore the higher-level needs that truly motivate, the result is that the workers behave according to the pathologies ascribed to them by Theory X.

By contrast, MacGregor proposes **Theory Y,** which he believes is based on a more complete and accurate view of human personality. Theory Y assumes that people are basically creative, and that work is a natural outlet for their creativity and effort. Further, individuals respond more positively to an achievement-oriented reward system than they do to threats and punishment. In addition, workers are self-directed and, given the proper incentives, will actually seek out more responsibility. Far from being passive and lazy, people actually want to be innovative and imaginative in their jobs, and thus they welcome opportunities to reach their full potential. In MacGregor's view, it is up to management to create an organization based on the premises of Theory Y rather than Theory X. However, this is not going to be an easy task, MacGregor recognized, since Theory X attitudes are deeply ingrained in society. Similar to Maslow, MacGregor believes that his humanistic approach would result not only in improvements in organizational productivity but in a better society overall.

Two-Factor Theory Frederick Herzberg used Maslow's hierarchy as the foundation for his own influential theory of human motivation. Herzberg wanted to learn what people wanted from their jobs, so in his research he asked workers which aspects of their jobs made them feel good and which aspects made them feel bad.[14] People's on-the-job attitudes, he found, could be summed up in terms of two factors:

1. **Hygienic factors** include working conditions, work rules, and pay. These are extrinsic to the work itself.
2. **Motivating factors** relate to the nature of the work itself and specifically to its level of challenge to the worker. Motivators are intrinsic to the work content and include opportunities for advancement and personal growth, as well as opportunities for recognition and increased responsibility.

The hygienic factors correspond to Maslow's lower-level needs. By focusing only on these factors, management merely prevents employee dissatisfaction at work (hence Herzberg also called them *dissatisfiers);* however, they do not challenge employees to achieve their full potential. On the other hand, motivating factors correspond to Maslow's higher-level needs, and as the name suggests, they motivate individuals' personal and professional development. Thus, organizations that concentrate exclusively on salary, security, working conditions, and other hygienic factors may avoid employee dissatisfaction, but organizations that try to satisfy motivating factors truly encourage their employees to reach their full potential.

Theory Y A view of human behavior which states that people are creative, and work is a natural outlet for their talents and efforts.

Hygienic factors The employee incentives that relate to working conditions, rules, and pay.

Motivating factors The employee incentives that relate to opportunities for organizational advancement and personal growth as well as recognition.

How Managers Apply Motivation Theories Each of the aforementioned theories produces a different impact on employees, although each one is rooted in the needs-based model of motivation introduced at the beginning of the chapter. For example, a manager using Maslow's approach would seek every opportunity to help employees to develop their personalities to the fullest extent possible. He or she would encourage employees to seek further training and education, to enhance their job skills and their "life" skills. Further, a Maslow-influenced manager would truly want to inspire people to strive for greater self-actualization both on and off the job. Managers who treat employees like adults would be following Argyris's advice, encouraging employees to take an active part in the decision-making process and take on greater administrative responsibility. An Argyris-type manager would make every effort to communicate in a manner that conveys to employees that they are being treated as mature adults who can be trusted with more responsibility. Theory Y managers would look for different opportunities to bring out the natural creativity and innovation within employees. A Theory Y manager recognizes that a certain level of risk must be tolerated in order to release people's creativity, which means rewarding new ideas that work while accepting occasional failures as the price of creativity. A manager who tries to make jobs more interesting and challenging for employees and who believes that they can reach their full potential would be influenced by Two-Factor theory.

It is apparent that these motivation theories seek the same general outcome—developing employees to their fullest potential—although they sometimes use different means to reach this end. Further, these theories all contend that intrinsic rewards matter more to employees than extrinsic rewards. These theories might be more successfully applied to middle- or upper-level management rather than jobs requiring a great deal of routinization, such as working on an assembly line. For more routine jobs or certain types of individuals (those more motivated by extrinsic rewards), the next two motivational theories—goal-setting and the behavioral approach—may be more effective.

Goal-Setting Implicit in every theory of motivation is the idea that individuals are rational and goal-directed. However, goal-setting theory goes beyond other theories in asserting that goals are the principal determinant of human behavior. Goals drive behavior because they set objective standards that individuals can measure their performance against. Standards are also associated with a system of rewards or incentives. If current performance is below a standard, workers' feel pressure to improve, because they would otherwise fail to achieve a desired outcome, such as more pay.

Goal-setting theory asserts that it is more effective for management to set specific job-related goals rather than trying to make work more fulfilling or challenging.[15] In one study on goal-setting and task performance, establishing specific goals was found to improve worker productivity 90 percent of the time. To be effective, the goals should present a challenge to workers; that is, they should require some effort to accomplish. However, goal-setting is only successful when the level of overall commitment workers feel toward the task and goal is high. In order to increase effectiveness, managers should provide subordinates with adequate feedback so that employees can measure their own progress toward the objective.[16]

What are some implications of goal-setting theory for public managers? The answer appears to depend on the complexity of the task. Most of the early research on goal-setting focused on relatively simple tasks that did not involve either learning new skills or developing long-term strategies for their successful completion. Recent studies indicate that more complex tasks appear to be affected less by establishing goals than are simple tasks.[17] Consequently, these studies suggest, as task complexity grows, goal-setting seems to have less of an impact on employee performance. The reason for this appears to be the difficulty in maintaining a high level of performance, which is required for completing a complex task compared with a simpler one. Thus, goal-setting might be an effective motivational strategy for jobs requiring low-level skills.

Behavioral Approach   The behavioral approach stems from classical conditioning theory and the work of B. F. Skinner. The most famous example of classical conditioning theory involves the early twentieth-century experiments by Russian scientist Ivan Pavlov, who found that he could make dogs salivate at the sound of a bell after repeated pairings of the bell with food. This work eventually led to reinforcement theory, which says that people engage in certain forms of behavior because this behavior has been rewarded in the past, or they avoid engaging in certain types of behavior because this behavior has been punished in the past. The behavioral approach extended and refined the fundamental ideas of reinforcement theory.

According to Skinner, the repeated association of some outcome with the desired behavior produces learning.[18] For example, workers who receive lavish praise from a supervisor every time they complete a project on schedule "learn" to associate finishing on schedule with strong praise, a positive outcome. Therefore, if they value their supervisor's praise, they will strive to finish every project on time. This is an example of positive reinforcement. Skinner thought that learning requires the application over time of either positive reinforcement or negative reinforcement. While **positive reinforcement** emphasizes material rewards, **negative reinforcement** involves the removal of negative consequences for certain actions.

Skinner believed that positive or negative reinforcement was more effective than punishment in altering a person's behavior. Punishment was ineffective for two reasons, according to Skinner. First, instead of learning the desired behavior, a person may only learn to avoid the punishment, which merely replaces an undesired behavior with another one. Second, punishment usually tends to make people feel angry and resentful toward the punisher. Thus, they might come to associate their negative feelings with management, which would be organizationally counterproductive.

For managers, the behavioral model seems to offer a possible solution to the problem of motivating certain types of workers. But this approach can be problematic for both practical and ethical reasons. Practically, the approach is flawed

Positive reinforcement   A motivational approach that emphasizes material rewards as the key to organizational learning.

Negative reinforcement   A motivational approach that emphasizes the removal of negative consequences as the spur to learning.

because the reinforcement or reward must be carefully tailored to the personality of each employee or else the desired learning will fail to occur. This makes it difficult to implement, because managers must become expert in each employee's individual psychology. Ethically, behavioral modification can be manipulative of human beings and therefore dehumanizing. Further, its effectiveness is reduced when employees become aware they are being manipulated in this fashion.[19]

Organizational Decision-Making

An important function of organizations is decision-making, an area that many researchers have devoted their careers to studying and understanding. In this chapter, we use Graham T. Allison's decision-making models as the framework for examining organizational decision-making. Allison's research identifies three different approaches to decision-making in public organizations: rational, organizational process, and governmental politics. The *rational model* posits a single authoritative decisionmaker and assumes decisions are made in a manner that is "orderly, intentional, purposeful, deliberate, consistent, responsible, accountable, explainable, and rational."[20]

In the *organizational process model*, in contrast to the rational model, many groups are involved, which necessitates a process of mutual accommodation and bargaining. The organizational process approach closely resembles the incremental model, in which administrators "muddle through." In the *governmental politics model*, decisions actually result from a process involving different contending forces within an organization. According to this model, there is no single authoritative decisionmaker or overarching rational process. The absence of a central decisionmaker creates numerous opportunities for different groups and actors to pursue their own individual objectives and agendas. They may find common ground with another's agenda, but more typically, their agendas are in conflict with each other. This situation produces "the pulling and hauling that is politics."[21]

The Rational Model

Allison's rational model is typically associated with traditional bureaucracies and with certain organizational processes, particularly the planning function (see the discussion of POSDCORB in Chapter 7). Simply put, the rational model consists of four elements: (1) identification of objectives and goals; (2) identification of alternative means of achieving those goals and objectives; (3) prediction and evaluation of outcomes resulting from each alternative; and (4) selection of the alternative that best achieves the desired objectives and goals. The rational model's core assumptions, however, were challenged in a famous article by Charles Lindblom, who disputes the idea that the decision-making process can ever be as comprehensive as the rational model avers.[22]

First, there is no clear-cut agreement over values. Lindblom observes: "The idea that values should be clarified, and in advance of the examination of alternative policies, is appealing. But what happens when we attempt it for complex social problems? The first difficulty is that on many critical values or objectives, citizens disagree, congressmen disagree, and public administrators disagree." Second, the model is problematic because social science theory is often weak at accurately attributing causes and predicting effects. For example, poverty may be viewed as being caused by a lack of education, which would necessitate a solution involving public education. Alternatively, however, poverty may be viewed as the result of broken or dysfunctional families, which would require a different type of intervention. Third, human intellectual capacity and available information are limited, which restricts the ability of the decisionmaker to be comprehensive.[23] For the aforementioned reasons, Lindblom believes that the rational model does not provide a realistic picture of the way public organizations actually make decisions. Nor, he believes, is the rational model an example of the process in which public organizations *should* make decisions.

The Incremental Model

Lindblom proposes the *incremental model* as an alternative to the rational model. Incrementalism, according to Lindblom, is the science of "muddling through." The incremental model resembles Allison's organizational process and governmental politics model described above. That is, many groups are involved in the decision-making process, and decisions emerge as a result of a process of bargaining and compromise rather than through rational and comprehensive analysis. Lindblom claims that "muddling through" more accurately reflects American political and social values such as interest-group pluralism and a preference for the free market. Thus, Lindblom expresses a preference for the incremental model's inclusive process in contrast to the rational model's attempt at comprehensive rationality.[24]

Mixed Scanning

A third model of decision-making, *mixed scanning*, incorporates elements of the rational model and the incremental model. Etzioni found the rational model too utopian due to its emphasis on comprehensiveness, while incrementalism was flawed because it overlooked opportunities for innovation. Thus, Etzioni recognizes along with Lindblom that real-life decisionmakers lack the resources and capabilities demanded by the rational model, but he also regards incrementalism as having a too-limited perspective, one that fails to account for social change. Further, he points out that the incremental model fails to recognize that incremental decisions occur within the context of fundamental decisions. He writes that these fundamental decisions guide and shape all subsequent decision-making: "For example, once the U.S. embraced the Truman Doctrine after World War II and decided to contain the U.S.S.R. . . . numerous incremental decisions were made in Greece, Turkey, and Iran. However, these were implemented and guided by the fundamental context-setting decision and cannot be understood without taking into account the basic decision."[25]

The mixed scanning approach offers a third way between rationalism and incrementalism. According to Etzioni, it combines "higher order, fundamental decision-making with lower-order incremental decision-making." Without the big picture provided by the fundamental decisions, incremental decisions lack meaningful context. Research has been done on major Supreme Court decisions applying the mixed scanning lens.[26] It was found that the model provided a good fit for the evidence, with groundbreaking Court rulings paving the way for more incremental decisions that altered basic relationships in society in areas such as race and education (*Brown v. Board of Education*) and criminal justice (*Miranda v. Arizona*).

Group Decision-Making

In the organizational process and governmental politics models, group or participatory decision-making is the hallmark of organizations. Moreover, recent management theories, such as total quality management (which we discuss later in this chapter), show a marked preference for participatory decision-making. In this section, we focus on two important questions regarding group decision-making: (1) What are the factors that contribute to more effective group decisions? (2) What are the major types of group decision-making techniques?

Group decision-making, while generally slower and less efficient than individual decision-making, is superior to it for several reasons. These include being able to draw on a broader base of knowledge and experience, the increased capacity to generate more and better ideas, and increased opportunities for more critical evaluation of alternatives.[27] Group decision-making appears to offer more advantages than individual decision-making, but which one is actually more effective in any situation depends on the following four "contingency factors":

1. *Group identity.* Members who are more comfortable with abstract thinking and who are younger tend to be better suited for group decision-making. Nonsocial, loner types do not make good group participants.

2. *Group composition.* Racial and gender diversity within the group contributes to more effective decision-making because it expands the range of information, life experiences, and skills that can be brought to bear on the issues facing the group.

3. *Group size.* The optimum size of a group is between five and twelve members. Medium-sized groups are more likely to produce higher-quality decisions and generate more ideas per member. In larger groups there is less participation, and in very small groups there is less knowledge and experience.

4. *Group process.* Consensual decisions tend to be superior in quality to those reached through other means, including leader choice and majority vote. The physical configuration of the group, including the seating arrangement and other factors affecting communication

among members, is another important influence on group decision-making. The research indicates that more open, democratic, and participatory group processes facilitate effective decision-making.[28]

Group Decision-Making Techniques Groups can be an effective means to decision-making for the reasons noted above. However, there are some problems associated with group dynamics that suggest the occasional need for corrective techniques and mechanisms. For example, assertive, extroverted individuals often exert a larger influence over groups than more introverted participants, who may have difficulty in getting their ideas heard. Furthermore, there exists the possibility of **groupthink**, a situation in which members become so strongly identified with the group that they isolate themselves from negative criticism and fail to rationally consider all alternatives (for more on groupthink, see Chapter 8). Another problem with groups is that they can lead to a situation known as the Abilene Paradox (see Vignette 9.2). Two group decision-making techniques that have proved to be effective in avoiding these and similar problems are the Delphi method and nominal group technique, discussed below.

The Delphi Method First developed by the Rand Corporation in the 1950s as a means to reduce or eliminate the problems resulting from decision-making in

Groupthink A situation in which members become so strongly identified with the group's identity that they isolate themselves from negative criticism and fail to consider all alternatives.

VIGNETTE 9.2 **The Abilene Paradox**

It is a hot summer's afternoon in Coleman, Texas. The temperature is hovering around 100 degrees as two couples sit on a house porch playing cards and sipping lemonade to try to stay cool. They have been playing list-lessly for some time, when one of them—thinking that the others would prefer to be elsewhere doing something else—suggests that they drive to Abilene to eat at a restaurant. They drive the 53 miles to Abilene in an old, unair-conditioned pick-up. When they get there, they find their first choice is closed, so they settle on a nearby fast food restaurant. The food is greasy and not very good. No one is in a good mood as they head back to Coleman. Upon arriving, they discover that no one really wanted to go. They all went along with the plan because everyone thought that everyone else wanted to go.

The above story is a famous scenario first proposed by management expert Jerry Harvey in 1974. He uses this story to show how easily groups can mistak-enly take actions that they believe are in their best interests but are really counter to the members' intentions. Quite simply, group members will go along with a bad idea because they are afraid of being left out of the group. Thus, this paradox is another example of how "groupthink" can get organizations in trouble. One anti-dote to "taking the trip to Abilene" is for organizations to encourage double-loop learning, an approach in which group members question past assumptions and, in the process, move away from ineffective practices. If group members can question the group's assumptions without fearing alienation, they will be able to help the group reach better decisions.

SOURCE: "Understanding the Abilene Paradox" originally published in *Association Management*, September 1, 1991 and found on Allof Business.com, www.allbusiness.com/management/255736=1.html?yahss=114-2974554-255736.

Delphi method A technique developed as a means to reduce or eliminate the problems resulting from member interaction in the group decision-making process; the participants do not meet with each other face to face.

groups, in the **Delphi method** participants do not communicate or even meet with each other face to face.[29] The first step of this method involves choosing a topic and identifying individuals who are experts in the topic. Next, a written questionnaire is developed and administered by mail to the experts, who respond in a manner designed to assure their anonymity. The results of the first round of questionnaires are then compiled and summarized, and feedback is provided to the group. The group comments on the feedback, and the responses are compiled and summarized and returned to the group for further review and comment. This process is repeated until no further agreement can be achieved. The technique has been shown to be successful in reducing or eliminating some of the biases associated with group decision-making (e.g., group conformity, and deference to those in authority); however, it is not without problems.[30] The process can be slow and cumbersome, experts can quit at any time during the process, questionnaires can be ambiguous, and anonymity can lead to superficial and frivolous responses on the part of participants.[31]

Nominal group technique A decision-making approach in which ideas are listed and then discussed only for clarification, followed by secret ballots to rank the ideas and eliminate weak ones until consensus is reached on the best decision.

Nominal Group Technique **Nominal group technique** (NGT) offers the advantages of participatory decision-making, albeit without many of its problems.[32] In contrast to the Delphi method, NGT participants meet face to face and are asked to individually write down solutions to a problem on a piece of paper. Next, the group's leader asks each member to present his or her ideas to the whole group. These are written on a blackboard or a flipchart until there are no more ideas left. No discussion is allowed until all the ideas have been listed. In the next step, the leader permits discussion of the ideas, but only for clarification purposes. No other types of statements are permitted, either positive or negative, regarding the listed ideas. Finally, a secret ballot is taken in order to rank the ideas; weak ones or duplicates are eliminated at this step. The last two steps are repeated until the group reaches a consensus regarding a solution.

Research on NGT indicates that it is a generally effective method for improving decisions while at the same time avoiding the problems of group decision-making. Some note, however, that NGT might inadvertently increase the group leader's or facilitator's power in the process, and because it is designed to avoid political influences on group decision-making, this assumes that politics is always undesirable.[33] Therefore, NGT seems to run counter to a major premise of the incremental model: that pluralism and politics are essential to public decision-making.

Organizational Culture

Organizational culture is to an organization what personality is to an individual. According to James Q. Wilson, it is "a persistent, patterned way of thinking about the central tasks of and human relationships within an organization."[34] An important but not very visible aspect of organizations, organizational culture usually operates subjectively, shaping nearly everything that happens within an

Organizational culture The unique character or "personality" of an organization, consisting of the core beliefs, attitudes, and values that influence employees' actions, often on a subconscious level.

organization through its influence on organization members' behavior. Although organizational culture consists of characteristics as subjective as values, norms, behaviors, and relationships, that does not mean its effects are any less powerful than the objective and formal attributes of organizations like rules and structures.

While an organization's culture may not be readily apparent to insiders, because they are used to it, it can have an immediate and dramatic impact on outsiders. Everyone who starts working for a new organization experiences, at least initially, some form of culture shock—similar to finding oneself in an unfamiliar, foreign country. Working for a new organization can be the same as learning to navigate around a strange land. It frequently requires learning a new set of norms, rules, and values—and sometimes even learning a new language, as familiar words take on new meanings in a different organizational context. It is no wonder then, that new organizational members can feel somewhat disoriented. This feeling gradually disappears as one becomes more and more integrated into the group. However, at the outset, the new person has a heightened awareness of organizational culture, an attribute of organizations that can sometimes be hard to define and identify.

James Q. Wilson holds that most organizations have multiple cultures. These subcultures exist because of the formalization and complexity of modern organizations, concepts we discussed in Chapter 8. Even though it operates mostly on an unconscious level, organizational culture nevertheless has tangible effects on employees. As Wilson points out, culture directly affects agency performance.[35] Organizational culture is usually a reflection

NASA's organizational culture was publicly criticized in the wake of the 2003 *Columbia* space shuttle tragedy.
SOURCE: NASA

of the nature of the work an agency performs. For instance, the culture within the CIA places a heavy emphasis on secrecy, since openness can jeopardize an agent's career and even life. Even more problematic are situations in which different organizations, each with its own unique culture and mode of communication, must coordinate activities to achieve a common objective. In such situations, there is often a high probability of miscommunication and failure to coordinate (see Vignette 9.3).

A society, whether large or small, has its own unique myths, legends, taboos, rites, language, symbols, and slogans that define that society and set it apart from others; these characteristics comprise the culture of that society. The same thing is true of an organization, which is like a mini-society in some

VIGNETTE 9.3   Miscommunication in the U.S. Intelligence Community

Following September 11, 2001, there was a great deal of criticism directed toward elements of the U.S. intelligence community, namely the CIA and the FBI, concerning whether the terrorist attacks could have been avoided. Early on, it was concluded that poor communication and miscommunication between the CIA and FBI probably impeded our ability to prevent the terrorists from striking.

Two examples show the extent to which communications between the CIA and the FBI failed. In January 2000, a group of al-Qaeda operatives met in Kuala Lampur, Malaysia, to plot the attack on the U.S.S. *Cole*, a naval vessel. Malaysian authorities caught the meeting on surveillance videotape and turned it over to the CIA. In summer 2001, the agency identified one of the attendees as Khalid al-Midhar, a Saudi who intelligence officials thought had entered the United States shortly after the meeting and left six months later. The CIA placed his name on a watch list and handed it over to the Immigration and Naturalization Service (INS), but by then al-Midhar had managed to slip back into the United States. Within the next few days, the CIA briefed the FBI on al-Midhar. FBI officials initiated a frantic manhunt for the suspected terrorist, but they never caught up with him. On September 11, authorities believe, he flew American Airlines flight 77 into the Pentagon. Al-Midhar bought his flight ticket under his own name, but American Airlines claims that no government authorities informed them that he was on a terrorism watch list.

In August 2001, the United States detained Zacarias Moussaoui, a man the French government knew was associated with Islamic extremists and who apparently wanted to learn how to fly jets but not how to land them. On August 16, 2001, Moussaoui was arrested for an immigration violation, just a day after the staff at the flight school where he was training told the FBI of their suspicions about him. Moussaoui has been associated with al-Qaeda networks overseas, from London to Malaysia. Agents in Minneapolis sought a national security warrant to search his computer files, but they were turned down by lawyers at FBI headquarters who said they didn't have sufficient evidence that he belonged to a terrorist group. The FBI did inform the CIA of Moussaoui's arrest, and the CIA ran checks on him while asking foreign intelligence services for information. But neither the FBI nor the CIA ever informed the counterterrorism group in the White House.

The above examples are just a couple of instances of "failure to connect the dots" that plagued the U.S. intelligence community prior to September 11. Subsequent reforms such as the formation of the Department of Homeland Security and the Patriot Act's passage were designed to rectify these problems and to prevent their recurrence in the future.

ways, as described by Trice and Beyer. Organizational myths and legends are the stories, sometimes apocryphal, that are passed down from one generation to the next. They glorify the exploits of the organization's founders and other exemplary members who personify the organization's virtues and values (see the case study at the end of this chapter). Group norms are another important aspect of organizational culture. These are the unwritten rules that channel member's behavior in areas such as interpersonal relations, interactions with clients, and even dress codes. Uniforms are often a potent symbol of organizational culture, as in the case of the military, police, and fire fighters. Taboos are similar to norms except they point out what is not permitted; they demarcate the boundaries of acceptable behavior. Rites serve a ceremonial or transitional purpose; for example, an annual awards dinner might honor retiring employees for their years of service.[36]

Bureaucratese The specialized, sometimes incomprehensible language of large organizations that is often satirized or ridiculed.

Every culture has its own common language or special use of language, which helps to establish clear boundaries with the outside and exclude nonmembers, while at the same time it strengthens bonds among the members. Group slogans, symbols, and logos are outward reflections of organizational culture; they convey the message "This is who we are" to members and outsiders alike.[37] The U.S. Marine Corps slogan s*emper fidelis* (Latin for "always faithful"), for example, conveys a strong sense of the Corps' mission and helps to distinguish it from other branches of the armed forces. However, the formal language of bureaucracy, sometimes called **bureaucratese**, is often the subject of satire or ridicule (see Vignette 9.4).

VIGNETTE 9.4   A Real-Life Example of Bureaucratese

United States Department of Commerce
The Assistant Secretary for Administration
Washington, D.C. 20230
Memorandum for Heads of All Operating Units

Subject: Gender-free Terminology

In my prior memorandum on this subject dated August 14, 1978, I recommended that the *1977 Dictionary of Occupational Titles* be the reference source for checking sex-specific job titles. I used as an example the terms *stevedore* and *longshoreman*, and stated in a footnote that since *longshoreman* did not appear in the Dictionary, stevedore should be used in its stead.

It has come to my attention that, contrary to the contention of the authors of the Dictionary, *stevedore* and *longshoreman* are not the same job.[a] Therefore, please advise your employees that the term *longshoreman* may be used when necessary to interpret the provisions of a statute. Otherwise, longshore worker is the preferred gender-free term.

It remains the policy of the Department of Commerce to replace gender-specific terms with nonsexist language whenever possible. Our intent is to use gender-free job titles where alternative titles exist, not to alter the substance of jobs. Although the *1977 Dictionary of Occupational Titles* appears to have erred with respect to this particular job, it shall remain the general reference for checking job titles.

[a] A stevedore is an employer who is responsible for the loading and unloading of ships. A longshoreman is an employee (of the stevedore) who actually loads and unloads ships. The International Longshore Association informs us that its female workers are called "longshoremen."

SOURCE: Trueblood, Carol and Fenn, Donna. (1982). *The Hazards of Walking.* Boston: Houghton-Mifflin Co.

Cultural Change in Public Organizations

Since culture is such a fundamental element of organizations, it is often necessary to change culture in order to bring about true organizational change. During President Ronald Reagan's term in office, for example, morale dropped in domestic-policy agencies such as the Occupational Health and Safety Administration because employees had to radically depart from their "get tough" enforcement attitude to adopt a more business-friendly approach favored by the administration. As Wilson suggests, accomplishing such a change can be difficult, because change occurs slowly, owing to the presence of multiple cultures within organizations.[38] Thus, fundamental, permanent change can take years to accomplish, as the story about the New York City police at the beginning of the chapter indicates.[39] Given the deeply ingrained nature of organizational culture, the challenge of change often can involve taking radical steps, such as the wholesale purge of current employees and their replacement with entirely new people who do not share the old organizational norms and values. However, such an endeavor is never to be taken lightly, and there is no guarantee that the new culture will prove any more effective than the old one.

Culture, especially in public organizations, can have important consequences not only for the organization in question but also for society as a whole. One case in point is the New York City police example from the beginning of the chapter. Another example is the CIA and FBI's intelligence lapses prior to September 11, 2001. During the 1990s, when the reinventing government movement was in its heyday, several studies showed that difficulty in changing agency culture was the chief impediment to reforming the federal government.[40] More recent studies, published after the National Performance Review (NPR), discussed in Chapter 4, confirm the earlier studies' findings. One study found that organizational culture either facilitated or hampered reinvention efforts depending on the role that leadership plays in promoting cultural change.[41] Another study analyzes an attempt to transform a state agency's organizational culture. This research found that the immediate reaction of employees to change was negative, and the old culture's foundations are the main barriers to change. In order to effect change, a vision and goals must be clearly communicated throughout the agency, and employees must perceive training as being necessary for change and not simply training for its own sake.[42]

Change is seldom welcomed enthusiastically by people in organizations. There are many reasons for this change-resistant attitude on the part of organization members. Change creates uncertainty, requires more work, and produces a change of routine for all involved. Thus, employees have to overcome their own personal struggles with change.[43] In light of this, strong leadership is required in order to effect permanent organizational change. Further, changing organizations requires considerable resources—both personal and material—to be successful, and there is no guarantee that change will achieve the desired outcomes. These are just some of the major issues that leadership must confront as they weigh the pros and cons of changing organizational culture. Organizational change can happen, but it takes hard work on the part of the leadership and the members to effect this change.

Organizational Development

Organizational development A top-down interventionist strategy designed to increase organizational effectiveness and health.

Managing organizational change, as we have seen, requires a considerable amount of intellectual and material capital to pull off successfully. In light of the great cost and the uncertain payoffs, few organizations will attempt to undertake serious change without first devising a systematic approach or strategy. One notable recent organizational change strategy is **organizational development** (OD). OD is, intellectually, an heir to both the human relations school and open systems theory. It is a top-down strategy designed to increase organizational effectiveness and health. OD is an organizational change model based on a diagnosis of an organization followed by an intervention stage.[44] Thus, an analyst must conduct a systematic organizational analysis in order to determine the relative strength of the forces that facilitate change and the forces that hinder change before he or she can develop an appropriate intervention strategy. Although the analyst or "change agent" is chiefly responsible for devising the change strategy, change is seldom successful unless organization members are also convinced of its necessity and become active participants in implementing the strategy.

OD analysis is useful because it reveals the elements of the organization resisting change and the elements supporting it. According to OD theory, people generally oppose change for the following reasons: (1) self-interest; (2) fear of the unknown; (3) mistrust of management's motives and intentions; (4) fear of failure; and (5) loss of status. The forces favoring change include (1) environmental factors, such as new laws and regulations; (2) socioeconomic, political, and technological changes; and (3) internal forces, like financial or political crisis, increased perceptions of the need for change, and increased knowledge about a problem. OD has become commonplace in the public and nonprofit sectors.[45] In general, public service's experience with OD has been largely positive. It has been credited with helping introduce a variety of participatory management strategies into organizations, including t-groups and team building.

Total quality management (TQM) An approach to administration that seeks the continuous improvement of processes based on the application of quantitative methods to organizational problems; other important goals include increasing customer satisfaction and empowering employees.

Total Quality Management

Another approach to organizational change that has had a significant impact in recent decades is **total quality management** (**TQM**), an approach that seeks the continuous improvement of work processes based on the application of mathematical and statistical methods to problems. TQM's chief objective is to increase customer satisfaction with the product or service. Another important objective is to help empower employees by increasing their role in management and the decision-making process. TQM proponents believe these two objectives are, in fact, interconnected, as empowered employees are also more productive and concerned with the overall quality of their work.

TQM began in the United States but had its largest initial impact in Japan. Before World War II, a Bell Labs scientist developed a management technique that he called "statistical process control." During the war, the U.S. government hired one of the scientist's students, W. Edwards Deming, to help retool American industry for the heightened industrial effort needed to win the war. After the war, Deming went to Japan to rebuild its shattered industrial base using the same quality control techniques he pioneered for the U.S. war effort. TQM, thanks in large part to the work of Deming and others, became the dominant management strategy in postwar Japan. Ironically, it had little impact in the United States until the 1970s, when foreign competition started to erode American industry's previously unchallenged economic dominance of the world. As a result of foreign economic pressures, American business leaders began to recognize the importance of quality in the production process and embraced TQM as a means to survive in an increasingly competitive environment.[46]

TQM breaks with the traditional management theory that managers should give directions and workers should follow orders (in other words, the scientific management recipe for success). By contrast, in TQM, workers are empowered to participate actively in managing the organization through the use of quality

W. Edwards Deming, shown here sipping tea in Japan, gained fame by helping postwar Japanese firms become globally competitive.
SOURCE: Catherine Karnow/ Corbis

circles and self-directed work teams. Through these techniques, workers are encouraged to contribute their ideas on improving work processes. The chief role of the leadership is to provide a long-term vision, which is most clearly articulated in the strategic planning process. This process requires shaping a vision of the desired future for the organization, gaining the commitment of stakeholders, and mapping out a strategy for achieving this state of affairs.[47]

A central belief of TQM is continuous process improvement, which shifts the focus away from outputs and toward work processes, as a means to achieve gains in productivity. By an ongoing emphasis on finding more effective ways of production, incremental gains are made in productivity. Moreover, the customer or client is the best judge of the quality of a good or service, not the expert, according to TQM. Thus, total quality is not achieved until every customer need is met. TQM incorporates statistical techniques as a means to measure results against standards. The goal is to reduce and eventually eliminate variance in the production of goods or delivery of services.

It is worth noting that TQM, with the exception of one key aspect, is still firmly in the tradition of classical management theory. The element that separates TQM from traditional theory is its emphasis on empowering workers by giving them input into the decision-making process. Traditional management theory, which minimizes the need for workers to think and make decisions, leaves decision-making to the managers and uses standard operating procedures and other constraints to limit employees' discretion. By contrast, TQM views workers as the source of ideas and suggestions to improve work processes and increase customer satisfaction. TQM's view of workers borrows heavily from the human relations approach and the work of theorists such as Follett, Maslow, MacGregor, Argyris, and Herzberg. The stress on employee empowerment, when taken to its logical conclusion, leads to flat hierarchies and team-based management, the hallmarks of organic organizations. Since workers are encouraged to contribute not only their muscles but also their minds to the job, TQM places great importance on training and retraining workers.

TQM and Public Organizations

Interest in TQM has grown steadily in the public sector, although it has made more inroads in the private sector as compared to government. The reinventing government movement played a big role in stimulating public sector interest in TQM, with its customer-service approach and emphasis on performance measures. A number of studies examine attempts to implement TQM by public agencies. In general, their findings are mixed. The GAO, in a 1992 report, found that federal agencies using TQM made gains in productivity, reduced costs, achieved customer satisfaction, and increased their timeliness.[48] A Texas administrator, however, declared that the political culture of government and the unlimited supply of customers create problems for transplanting TQM to state government, although he believed these problems were not insurmountable.[49] Another author found that TQM's implementation in the IRS resulted in monetary savings, fewer errors, and a reduction in taxpayer burden.[50] Less optimistic views on TQM can also be found in the recent literature. For example, one study discovered that four impediments hinder TQM's implementation in government: (1) defining the customer, (2) services vs. products, (3) focusing on inputs and processes, and (4) government culture.[51] Another article lists some negative consequences of TQM such as fears of middle-management, negative effects of downsizing on motivation, and often unfulfilled promises of empowerment. The article also points out that TQM's ideology can be "coercive," which is troubling to anyone concerned with democratic administration.[52]

■ Chapter Summary

In this chapter, we examined motivation, decision-making, and organizational culture: Each is critical to understanding how organizations work. Public managers should understand the basic principles of employee motivation if they want to get the most out of their workforce. Organizations employ three types of motivators to induce workers to be more productive: rules, extrinsic rewards, and intrinsic rewards. Rules are coercive, so modern managers tend to use extrinsic rewards and intrinsic rewards more. Beginning with the human relationists, several theorists have paid considerable attention to the problem of motivation. Maslow is responsible for the hierarchy of needs; Argyris thought that organizations should treat employees like adults; MacGregor challenged the traditional approach to management (Theory X) with his Theory Y; Herzberg proposed that motivating factors, as opposed to hygienic factors, actually provide the incentive to workers to be more productive.

Decision-making is an important function of organizations. Several models have been developed in order to better understand how organizations can make more effective decisions. Three decision-making models are the rational, organizational process, and governmental politics. The reality of current organizations is that more and more groups are involved in the decision-making process. Studies of group decision-making have found that it is generally superior to individual decision-making. Consequently, the use of different group decision-making techniques, including the Delphi method and nominal group technique, is on the rise.

Organizational culture consists of the core beliefs, attitudes, and values that influence employees' actions, often on a subconscious level. Typically, organizations have a dominant culture and several subcultures. While culture affects every aspect of organizational life, its role is particularly important when change is considered. Internal change is not possible without altering the old culture or replacing it with a new one. This means retraining workers or, in extreme cases, hiring new employees who are unaffected by the previous culture.

Two important strategies for managing change are organizational development and total quality management. OD uses a top-down, interventionist strategy to improve effectiveness, and TQM uses quantitative techniques and employee empowerment to improve the quality of the good or service produced.

■ Chapter Discussion Questions

1. Describe how motivating public organization and private organization personnel might be different? How might they be similar?

2. Compare OD and TQM to traditional public administration. How do they compare with regard to employee decision-making and responsibility?

3. Language and symbols are important for public organizations. What are some slogans, stories, or symbols that you associate with certain public or nonprofit organizations?

4. The chapter discusses some of the assumptions that the rational model makes regarding the decision-making process. What assumptions do the incremental and mixed-scanning models make regarding the decision-making process in organizations?

5. An important criterion for the successful use of TQM in organizations is identifying the customer. Who is the customer for a local police service? For the state budget office? For the CIA? Think of some other public agencies and try to identify their customers.

BRIEF CASE   U.S. ARMY VALUES AND HEROES

Certain organizations, the U.S. Army being one, are noted for their powerful and long-standing organizational cultures. An important aspect of the Army's dominant culture is its hierarchical and authority-based nature.[53] At its core is a set of fundamental values that guide the behavior of soldiers the entire time they serve. At enlistment, each person swears an oath, which reads:

> I do solemnly swear that I will support and defend the Constitution of the United States against all enemies, foreign and domestic; that I will bear true faith and allegiance to the same; and that I will obey the orders of the President of the United States and the orders of officers appointed over me, according to regulations and the Uniform Code of Military Justice. So help me God.

An official Army leadership manual says:

> When soldiers and DA [Department of Army] civilians take the oath, they enter an institution guided by Army values. . . . These values tell you what you need to be, every day, in every action you take. . . . They are the glue that binds together the members of a noble profession. Army values are nonnegotiable: they apply to everyone and in every situation throughout the Army.

The manual states that these values can be summarized in the form of the acronym LDRSHIP:

Loyalty
Duty
Respect
Selfless Service
Honor

Integrity

Personal Courage

The U.S. Army has a number of heroes and legends, stretching back to the American Revolution, that epitomize its core values. Their stories form the folklore of the organization. Some of the legendary figures, such as Joshua Chamberlain, Sergeant York, and Audie Murphy, also became heroes in the culture at large as the subjects of books and movies. However, a greater number of lesser-known men and women are accorded legendary status by the army by virtue of their exemplifying one or more of the organization's core values.

The story of Captain Viola B. McConnell, the only army nurse on duty in Korea as the war began in July 1950, provides an example of selfless devotion to duty. At the outbreak of the Korean War, she evacuated 700 American citizens from Korea to Japan in a ship designed to hold only twelve passengers. As a result of the rigors of the journey and the condition of the vessel, many people fell ill. Captain McConnell, working with a tiny medical team, was responsible for the care of these evacuees. After landing in Japan, she asked to return to Korea to continue serving her country. She was granted her request and tirelessly worked to care for the wounded until the war's end.

During the Vietnam War, the massacre at My Lai on March 16, 1968, was a stain on the U.S. Army; however, the actions of Warrant Officer Hugh C. Thompson serve as a moral counterpoint to the disgraceful behavior of other American soldiers. While flying a reconnaissance mission over the village of My Lai, Thompson and his two-man crew witnessed the slaying of an injured Vietnamese child by a U.S. soldier. Shortly afterward, Thompson saw soldiers rounding up villagers and marching them to a nearby ditch. He landed his helicopter and questioned an officer, who said that what happened on the ground wasn't Thompson's concern. Thompson resumed flying, but when it became apparent that the men were shooting the villagers, he landed again, this time placing his helicopter between the soldiers and villagers. Thompson ordered his gunner to fire on the soldiers if they came closer to the Vietnamese. He somehow managed to convince the villagers to board his aircraft and flew them to safety. His radio reports about the killings led to the cease-fire order that prevented more loss of civilian life.

SOURCE: *US Army Field Manual* (FM 22-100). https://atiam.train.army.mil/SoldierPortal/atia/adlsc/view/public/9502-1/fm/22-100/ch2.htm.

Brief Case Questions

1. *Which of the LDRSHIP values do McConnell's and Thompson's actions best exemplify?*

2. *In Thompson's case, he disregarded a fellow officer's order and interposed his helicopter between U.S. soldiers and Vietnamese villagers, thus violating the core values of duty and respect. Nevertheless, his actions are recognized today as heroic, and justifiably so. Can a person reconcile two or more core values when they are in conflict? What might such reconciliation look like in this situation?*

3. *How can an understanding of organizational culture provide guidance in such situations?*

■ Key Terms

bureaucratese (page 222)
delphi method (page 219)
extrinsic rewards (page 207)
groupthink (page 218)

hierarchy of human needs (page 209)
hygienic factors (page 212)
intrinsic rewards (page 208)
motivating factors (page 212)

motivation (page 207)
negative reinforcement (page 214)
nominal group technique (page 219)
organizational culture (page 220)
organizational development (page 224)

positive reinforcement (page 214)
Theory X (page 211)
Theory Y (page 212)
total quality management (TQM) (page 224)

■ On the Web

http://www.mapnp.org/library/grp_skll/grp_dec/grp_dec.htm

The group decision-making webpage of the Management Assistance Program for non-profits, a comprehensive resource.

http://www.amanet.org/

Website of the American Management Association, a leading provider of management education.

http://www.odinstitute.org/

The Organization Development Institute, a nonprofit association to promote the understanding of organization development.

http://www.hr.com/HRcom/index.cfm/74/

The OD and organization culture webpages of a site for human resource specialists.

http://www.excelgov.org/

Website of the Council for Excellence in Government, a nonprofit organization working to improve government's performance.

CHAPTER 10

Leadership in Public Administration

■ SETTING THE STAGE

In 1988, Jim Diers became the first director of Seattle's newly created Department of Neighborhoods (DON, originally named the Office of Neighborhoods). The DON's primary responsibility was to empower city neighborhoods and give them a voice in city hall. The department was charged with establishing thirteen district councils composed of representatives from neighborhood associations and local businesses. For those neighborhoods that did not have an organized council, the department would provide support in their efforts to organize. The DON also provided support for neighborhood planning, which was part of the city's comprehensive planning strategy. This was a significant challenge, as neighborhoods had a history of confrontation with city hall. Diers was himself a part of the NIMBY (not in my back yard) culture. He had been a community organizer trained in confrontational tactics prior to his appointment.[1] Indeed, the small DON staff faced numerous obstacles as they began supporting the needs of hundreds of Seattle's neighborhood organizations.

In spite of the challenges, the department flourished and today is an important part of city government. Diers played a key role in the success of the department by creating a collaborative vision and establishing close working relationships with neighborhoods. He developed several innovative strategies for working with neighborhoods, such as the Neighborhood Matching Grant program, which awards grants to neighborhood associations under the stipulation that the applicant match those grant dollars with labor (at $15 per hour), materials, or cash. The program has received widespread acclaim from both practitioners and scholars. Diers, who left his DON position several years ago, is still characterized as a "popular" and "charismatic" leader.

The above example demonstrates how important good leaders are to an organization. Diers led the DON through a critical time, using more than just good managerial skill. He created a vision, built trust, and was creative in developing departmental programs. He built a culture of service within the organization that valued relationships with neighborhoods. These abilities go beyond our common understanding of management and tell us something about what it means to lead.

This chapter was co-written with William "Scott" Kummeracher, who received his MPA from Saint Louis University.

In public administration, however, leadership maintains a curious position. It is often assumed that politicians lead and administrators follow. Early public administration theory, administrative law, and constitutional doctrine focused on limiting the discretion and reducing the autonomy of public bureaucrats. Administrators were thought to act like cogs in a machine that required "fine-tuning" in order to achieve the highest level of efficiency. Today, however, scholars understand the need for some form of leadership in the public and non-profit sectors. Whether as stewards of democratic values or as entrepreneurs for innovative agencies, public administrators are being called on to assume greater leadership responsibilities in more turbulent times. As society becomes more diverse and constituents demand more flexibility from agencies, approaches to leadership in public service organizations will need to weave together innovative ways to build institutional capacity, foster collaboration across communities, and enhance organizational performance.

■ CHAPTER PLAN

Leadership plays a significant role in determining the conduct and course of action within a given agency. Effective leaders can increase organizational efficiency, provide greater direction for employees, help members of an organization realize their potential, and improve organizational culture. Though most scholars agree that leadership matters, an overall understanding of the topic is far from complete. Leadership is a multifaceted concept that is difficult to generalize, considering the many differences among individual leaders. Adding to this complexity is the fact that leadership operates throughout the framework of an organization and across many contexts. Leaders are not confined to the top of administrative hierarchies. As we will see, mid-level and street-level bureaucrats can play an essential leadership role. At a time when government and nonprofits aim to "work better and cost less," understanding the many ways in which leadership works is a necessary tool for effective administration.

In this chapter, we navigate through the complexities of leadership in order to understand some of its primary characteristics and its relationship to public administration. First, the chapter provides an overview of leadership in a new era, followed by a discussion of the differences between leadership and management that examines the attributes and importance of each role. We then examine the levels of leadership, including executives, managers, and street-level bureaucrats, and the importance of their collaboration. With that groundwork in place, the chapter then provides a workable definition of leadership. Next, we look at several important theories about leadership traits and behaviors. The role of gender in leadership is explored, along with the influence of bias. Finally, we take a closer look at leadership in public service settings, the difficulties that administrative leaders face, and the current debates surrounding the proper approach to leadership in public administration.

Moving the Organization Forward: Leadership in a New Era

The convergence of several events at the start of the twenty-first century marked a defining moment for public service in the United States. For a number of decades prior, antigovernment attitudes, tax revolts, bureaucrat bashing, and even violent attacks such as the bombing of the federal building in

Oklahoma City haunted public administrators. Public servants were demeaned as wasteful and inefficient. Yet September 11, 2001, ushered in a renewed call for public service as Americans saw police officers and fire fighters rush to the aid of those in the World Trade Center towers and the Pentagon. Further, globalization, the war on terrorism, and other events have brought to the fore the need for a strong public service to cope with these changes. With mounting budget crises, overextended domestic and military personnel, and growing security threats on government facilities receiving greater attention, the difficult position that public administrators confront on a daily basis is more apparent now than ever.

Instability and uncertainty characterize the environment that administrators must confront on a daily basis. Public problems increasingly lack definitive answers and offer enduring consequences. These problems are fluid in nature and often context specific.[2] Combined with the problems typical of modern organizations, administrators are left in a difficult position. They must deal with the everyday pressures of efficiency, productivity, and accountability while dealing with conflicting messages from the external environment. Navigating through ambiguity and incorporating multiple perspectives are some of the key ingredients of leadership in this new administrative era, where the "public interest' is unclear. Leadership is needed in a number of areas in public service: (1) developing a clear vision for the organization, (2) working across multiple constituencies, (3) recognizing social and ethical values, (4) creating vibrant organizational networks, (5) enhancing organizational performance, and (6) maintaining democratic values.

Leadership occurs at various levels within an organization, from the top of administrative hierarchies on down. Executives and leaders must now cross various layers of American government to achieve far-reaching goals and facilitate a broad vision of the future. Relationships remain a key component of leadership, because they bring people together regardless of their organizational position or their place in the government structure.

Another important point about administrative leaders is that they move public policy forward by defining organizational goals and persuading others to accomplish them. This requires a measure of influence that is transmitted through authority, persuasion, and empowerment. Finally, leadership responsibilities are often linked with other responsibilities, such as management duties, and involve processes of change within the organization.

Leadership and Management

At first glance, leadership and management might seem indistinguishable. Both entail similar duties, such as coordination, direction, control, monitoring, and planning. Indeed, the leadership and management concepts are connected in many ways, and both terms are often used interchangeably. However, both concepts differ somewhat when applied to the public and private sectors. Students and practitioners of public administration are often left to their own devices when considering what characteristics fit under which conceptual umbrella. While the distinction between the two concepts is sometimes blurred, there are important differences that distinguish leadership from management.

Management Attributes

Management in public administration is primarily concerned with running the everyday operations of an organization. Early studies of management in the public sector focused on the routinization process. Management provides stability by routinizing tasks and procedures. Managers in both the public and private sectors used rules to establish familiar patterns of behavior and rationally structured organizations so that tasks could be completed efficiently. Their position within the organization was considered both technical and neutral. In essence, managers played a key role by making "the human machine run smoothly and on time."[3]

Later works on public management noted the influential role of human and political factors. This updated version of management addressed more than just systematic functions. Graham T. Allison, for instance, lists the modern management characteristics as

1. Establishing objectives and priorities
2. Devising operational plans
3. Organizing and staffing
4. Directing personnel and the personnel management system
5. Controlling performance
6. Dealing with external units
7. Dealing with independent organizations
8. Dealing with the press and public[4]

Although similar to Gulick's POSDCORB (see Chapter 7), this modern assessment of management incorporates the need for relationship skills and political competence. It further recognizes that managers operate under the direction set by leaders, devising strategies and solving problems along the way.

Leadership Attributes

Leadership plays a complementary role to management within an organization. It incorporates values, motivation, organizational culture, change, and vision into its conceptual framework. Leaders conduct the symphonic movements within the organization that outperforms the sum of its parts.[5] Public administration scholars have long recognized the difference between managing a system and leading it. Mary Parker Follett pointed out that leadership transcends managerial orders and requires a unified definition of purpose.[6] This conceptual distinction garnered more attention in the postwar era as scholars attempted to more clearly identify and distinguish the responsibilities of leaders and managers. Today, leadership is recognized as distinct because it

1. Instills certain values into an organization
2. Builds or upholds teamwork within the organization
3. Motivates or inspires followers
4. Provides a clearly defined vision or purpose for the organization
5. Keeps followers moving toward the vision established by the leader
6. Produces lasting change or innovation[7]

For a quick comparison of leadership and management that makes the distinction clearer, see Figure 10.1. Leaders provide an overall direction for the organization, helping subordinates avoid a singleminded sense of vision by keeping them focused on the big picture.[8] Managers implement this direction and arrange its structure in the most efficient and effective manner possible.[9] Leaders use a number of strategies to achieve an organizational purpose, from motivational techniques and power-sharing to the direct exercise of authority. These techniques often stray outside managerial boundaries, as managers often stick to familiar routines and avoid psychological methods such as inspiration and empowerment.[10] Relationships are key components of the leader–follower dynamic, involving shared expectations and reciprocal relations between leader and follower. Indeed, leaders have been found to be important to successful team building.[11] While managers may deal with employees as a function of their position, this relationship is often a one-way street.[12]

The Importance of Leadership and Management

It is important to note that most scholars now consider leadership and management equal partners in the organizational scheme. They are similar in many ways yet retain distinct qualities of their own. While management and leadership theories have taken separate paths, these concepts still remain vital to the

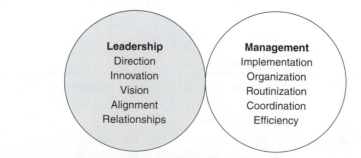

Figure 10.1 Characteristics of Leadership and Management

success of the organization as a whole. They are both primary pieces of the same system. Context also plays a key role in determining which functions receive the most emphasis. In times of reform, change, or crisis, leadership functions are most often required, while times of relative calm stress the efficiency and routinization functions of management. Executives, mid-level managers, and street-level bureaucrats weave in and out of these roles, using both concepts to help them achieve organizational goals.

Levels of Leadership: Executives, Managers, and Street-Level Bureaucrats

Within public service organizations, leadership is found on many levels and, in fact, is required throughout. There is an ebb and flow of leadership within the administrative setting, which varies according to the organizational level of those involved, the roles required by certain positions, and the nature of the external environment. Executives, managers, and street-level bureaucrats can all assume some form of leadership responsibility, yet it can vary given one's position within the organization. Leadership at the executive level is somewhat different from leadership at the other levels. For a quick overview, see Table 10.1. Each layer offers a different dimension of leadership and provides an overall robustness for leadership within the organization as a whole. Understanding how and why leadership is exercised at each level in the administrative system can help make these different dimensions of leadership more concrete.

Executive Leadership

The top level of leadership within an administrative system deals primarily with the executive position. Executives take on a number of leadership roles within their organization. They are primarily concerned with setting the direction for the organization, moving the organization through crises, or carrying out significant organizational change. This often involves strategic planning, coalition building, and other skills that are both political and technical in nature. Executive leaders must have a basic working knowledge of the

TABLE 10.1 Levels of Leadership in Public Sector Organizations

Organizational Level	Leadership Roles	Type of Influence	Environmental Pressures
Upper-Level (Executive)	Director, Innovator, Coalition Builder	Personal, Positional	Governing Bodies, Political Groups, Citizens
Mid-Level (Manager)	Teacher, Motivator	Personal, Positional	Resource Allocation
Ground-Level (Street-Level Bureaucrat)	Negotiator, Distributor, Allocator	Discretion, Knowledge of the Situation	Citizens, Political Groups, Governing Bodies

organization in order to maintain credibility and exert influence. Public sector leaders at the executive level must also be skilled at building collaboration with groups outside of the organization. Much of the public service leadership literature stresses the importance of these external constituencies and their interaction with executive leaders.[13] These roles are found at the state level as well, where executives split their time in leadership roles between external (political) duties and internal (administrative) responsibilities. Much the same is true for executives of nonprofits, too.

Leadership at the executive level requires a combination of practical, personal, and political skills. Although not all executives are leaders (some simply imitate managerial functions at a more authoritative level), they are the designated leaders of their organizations and are held accountable for them. They face the highest level of political pressure from the external environment. Those executives who exhibit no leadership qualities other than their status within an organization act only as "assigned leaders."[14] They make use of the authority that is derived from their position in order to achieve their objectives. "Personal" authority, however, derives from a leader's charisma, expertise, and relationships with peers. Executives who exhibit leadership qualities beyond their assigned status exercise influence through both **positional authority** (for example, allocating administrative resources) and **personal authority** (for example, held in high esteem by subordinates).

As the above shows, it is important not to confuse formal authority with leadership. Informal leadership qualities are also important. Consider that on a baseball team, the most influential person might be a trusted veteran ballplayer instead of the manager. Indeed, sometimes there are real advantages to being outside formal power structures within the organization: There is more flexibility and maneuverability, one can be closer to knowing what the employees really think, and one can concentrate on what one sees as the main issues instead of what the organization thinks are the issues.[15]

Positional authority The influence a person wields as a result of his or her role in an organization.

Personal authority The influence a person wields independent of his or her role in an organization.

Managers as Leaders

Mid-level leadership occurs among managers within the organization. Middle-managers may take on a number of leadership roles in addition to their strictly managerial functions. Managers act in a leadership capacity when they provide direction and motivation for those within their span of control. Although these leadership roles do not differ drastically from those of top-level executives, they are more limited in scope. Employees at this level exercise leadership by motivating subordinates and guiding them toward organizational goals. Similarly, mid-level managers lead by teaching. Leaders emphasize what areas of the organization require the most attention.[16] Through effective communication and guidance, mid-level managers convey a focus that other employees can use as a guiding mechanism for day-to-day operations.

Like executives, managers can wield both personal and positional authority. At the managerial level, however, there is a greater emphasis on formal controls. Managers are also well insulated from many external factors. Executives generally have to deal with the politics outside the organization, while street-level bureaucrats handle the needs of the general public. Still, managers who assume the leadership role must face a multitude of pressures. Managers cope with external pressures placed on them by resource allocation. If funds are withheld from the organization, managers who lead face a number of constraints in terms of personnel, equipment, and coverage. They can even lose their positions if their bureaus are reorganized or downsized. Internal pressures can also mount if managers must act as mediators when there is conflict between upper levels and ground levels within the organization.

Street-Level Leaders

At the ground level of the organization, street-level bureaucrats and lower-level administrators can exercise leadership roles. In Chapter 1, we discuss street-level bureaucrats, who are "public service workers who interact directly with citizens in the course of their jobs and who have substantial discretion in the execution of their work."[17] According to Vinzant and Crothers, street-level bureaucrats in the public sector assume leadership roles by "helping to draw norms and preferences from the community and . . . enact[ing] them within the boundaries of the law, departmental rules, and professional ethics." They also act as negotiators between the bureau as a service provider and the needs of the citizen. Part of this negotiation role involves developing a culture between the two that is acceptable.[18] Recall from the example at the beginning of the chapter that this was a key feature of administrative leadership in Seattle's Department of Neighborhoods. Lower-level administrators can also determine outcomes as a part of their leadership role, making them resource allocators who can impact the lives of those in the general public.

Street-level and lower-level bureaucrats exercise influence through discretionary authority and must deal with the external pressures that coincide with it. For administrators at this level, discretionary authority exists in the form of process and outcome. **Process discretion** is the latitude taken by an administrator when choosing the best problem-solving approach, while **outcome discretion** is the administrator's decision to choose a particular result among a set of possibilities.[19] A police officer may exercise process discretion when stopping drivers who are exceeding the speed limit, preferring to halt only cars that go in excess of 10 miles over the limit. The police officer uses outcome discretion when choosing between issuing a ticket or letting the driver go with a stern warning. External pressures often shape these discretionary acts. Pressures from the general public, particularly those using the agency's services, often prove to be sources of conflict and frustration.[20]

Process discretion The latitude taken by an administrator when choosing the best problem-solving approach.

Outcome discretion The administrator's decision to choose a particular result among a set of possibilities.

Importance of Collaboration

These dimensions of leadership must work together to provide a coherent system of operation within the organization. At lower levels, administrators use their discretion to lead their organization, while the upper-level executives and managers instill values and provide guidance. Those assuming leadership roles at all levels in the organization must communicate and coordinate their efforts to prevent critical gaps in the system. Bridging these gaps requires a unified effort on the part of all. Once again we note the importance of collaboration for leadership in the public sector. As recent breakdowns in intelligence operations in the CIA and the FBI have shown, getting all of the levels of leadership working together both in and across organizations is a difficult but vital task.

Leadership Defined

At this point, we should take a step back and go over some of the broad themes of leadership in public administration. First, leadership is a process that is intended to fulfill a purpose for the organization. It instills values, provides direction, and creates a vision that connects followers with the identity of the organization. Second, leaders operate in a shared power environment where diversity and ambiguity threaten to undermine common purposes. Getting groups to work together requires both formal authority and relational skills. Finally, public sector leadership requires collaboration on a number of different levels and across multiple constituencies. From these broad themes we can conclude the following:

- Leadership is the process of moving a group or organization toward a mutually defined goal.

Having laid out a basic definition of leadership, we can now turn to the different approaches that have been used to study this concept.

Leadership Theory

The study of leadership in the social sciences began in the 1930s. Since that time, it has grown to include thousands of research investigations, moving from the narrow scope of leadership traits to a diverse set of analytic frameworks. In this section, we will briefly discuss each of several major mainstream theoretical approaches to the study of leadership. We will begin by looking at leadership traits, then move on to leadership behaviors, contingency theory, path–goal theory, leader–member exchange theory, and transformational leadership theory. Each theory has a distinct set of characteristics and has made a significant contribution to leadership research. Much of today's studies take a multifaceted look at leadership, drawing off of the rich set of perspectives that are found in each approach.

Leadership Traits

Leadership traits The set of inherent qualities found in leaders, such as vitality, decisiveness, persuasiveness, responsibility, and intelligence.

One of the earliest approaches toward the social scientific study of leadership dealt with **leadership traits**. This approach aimed to identify the inherent qualities found in all leaders. Beginning in the early 1930s, researchers believed that leaders were born with certain traits that made them "great" men (never women during this time period). In this sense, these traits were the more modernized version of the divinity once ascribed to pharaohs and kings. Leaders were studied as individuals with special characteristic that helped them achieve great success. These traits were considered the defining element, regardless of context. Research on traits range from physical characteristics (such as height) to the more qualitative aspects of leader personalities. These early studies would provide insights into the number and depth of characteristics that are found in leadership today.

Many early public administration scholars had their say on what traits constituted a successful leader. Chester Barnard, for example, found five leader qualities to be most important: (1) vitality and endurance, (2) decisiveness, (3) persuasiveness, (4) responsibility, and (5) intellectual capacity.[21] Max Weber developed perhaps the most famous insight on leadership traits in his discussion of the charismatic leader. Charismatic leaders were defined specifically by their personality traits and mass appeal, emphasizing the characteristics that differentiate leaders and followers.

These early studies, however, failed to produce a comprehensive list of leadership traits that fit all situations. Even in the heyday of these early works on leadership traits, Mary Parker Follett recognized that the work situation had an important bearing on the effectiveness of the leader (see Chapter 7). Later studies on leadership traits took into consideration the various situations that leaders encountered. One famous early survey of the literature found that leader traits needed to match the situation in order for that leader to be effective.[22] The study also noted that leaders were the ones most capable at initiating and directing collective action in their organizations. This recognition began the move away from simple Trait identification and toward the understanding of how these traits operate in different environments.

Trait theory has its limitations. For example, there is a lack of consensus among researchers as to which traits directly constitute leadership ability, and there is considerable variation between researchers due to subjective determinations of traits. Still, trait theory has made a significant contribution to the field of leadership study. According to House and Aditya, the leadership traits approach has provided three key conclusions: and (1) Traits help delineate leaders from others; (2) certain traits are beneficial in certain situations; and (3) these traits tend to dominate in situations where leaders are open to their use and less so in others.[23] These contributions continue to inform leadership research today.

Leadership Behaviors

Another early approach to the study of leadership focused on leadership behaviors. While the traits approach looked at leader qualities, the behavioralist approach studied the actions taken by the leader. This type of study recognized that leadership was more than just a concentration of leader characteristics.

A number of prominent leadership investigations analyzed the way leaders related to others within the organization. Researchers found that **task-oriented behaviors** and **person-oriented behaviors** were two generalizable types of leadership behaviors.[24] Task-oriented behaviors are those actions taken by leaders that focus followers on specific goals, while person-oriented behaviors relate to the relationship between leaders and their followers.[25] Task-oriented leaders tend to exercise more direct control over subordinates. For example, a task-oriented executive might efficiently determine a plan on her or his own and then assign tasks and responsibilities to subordinates to implement it. A person-oriented leader, however, may suggest ways of accomplishing an objective but will influence or encourage employees to come up with their own solutions. This makes the employees feel more empowered and participative in decision-making. The study of leadership behaviors focuses on how these two generalized types work together and how they could be used to help produce the most effective type of leader for an organization.

Leadership behavior studies are an important part of leadership research because they moved away from the idea of inherent leadership characteristics and toward the notion of the leader–follower dynamic. For example, an early study by Kurt Lewin and associates looked at how three different leadership styles—democratic, autocratic, and laissez-faire—affected the way subordinates worked.[26] A democratic leadership style, one that emphasizes group achievement and incorporates other points of view, was found to produce the best results and follower satisfaction across most situations. This implies that leaders can be made as well as found, and this research marked the beginning of various leadership training techniques. The behavioralist approach also provides a benchmark for leadership evaluation. Leaders can reflect on their own efforts and make necessary changes. Because of its practicality and broad scope, this approach became a valuable tool for organizational development.

The leadership behavior approach, however, is not without some drawbacks. Like the traits approach, the behavioralist approach failed to produce a master list of universal leader behaviors.[27] Further, this style fails to account for the leadership environment and the situational factors that can alter the leader's relationship with followers.

Contingency Theory

An important step in understanding the role of the situation in the study of leadership came with the development of contingency theory. Although Mary Parker Follett and other organizational scholars had already emphasized that the organizational situation had an effect on leadership, contingency theory was a revitalized attempt at linking the two together. The **contingency theory** of leadership ties leader style directly to the situation. More specifically, the objective is to fit leaders with specific styles into situations that are "favorable" to

---

Task-oriented behaviors The actions that leaders take to get followers to reach certain goals.

Person-oriented behaviors Those actions that relate to the relationship between leaders and their followers.

Contingency theory The theory that effective leadership style is relative to the situation, and that creating the right environment can help build successful leadership within an organization.

them.[28] Contingency theory recognizes that an effective leadership style is relative to the situation, and that creating the right environment can help build successful leadership within an organization.

Contingency theory works by identifying leadership style and the situation the leader must confront. Fred E. Fiedler, the architect of the contingency model, developed a classification system to determine leadership style. This system is called the **Least Preferred Coworker** (LPC) score. To arrive at an LPC score, you first think of the person who was the most difficult you ever worked with.[29] Then you rank this person on a scale of 1 to 8 on a series of traits, such as those shown below:

Unfriendly	1 2 3 4 5 6 7 8	Friendly
Uncooperative	1 2 3 4 5 6 7 8	Cooperative
Hostile	1 2 3 4 5 6 7 8	Supportive
Guarded	1 2 3 4 5 6 7 8	Open

Leaders with a high LPC score have a relationship-motivated style, while leaders with a low score have a task-motivated style.

To identify the nature of the situation the leader faces, contingency theory looks at three types of variables. They are leader–member relations, task structure, and position power. The leader–member relations variable describes the amount of support the leader receives from followers. Of the three, this one is most under the leader's direct control. The others are determined by the organization. Task structure identifies the clarity and simplicity of the work to be done.[30] High levels of structure give the leader more control and leave less room for follower discretion. Position power measures the degree of clout that the leader wields in relation to subordinates.[31] Position power is the same thing as the legitimate authority discussed in Chapter 8. These factors are then combined to ascertain how well the situation corresponds to the leader's style. Contingency theory maintains that leaders with task-motivated styles do best when operating at the extremes (highly favorable or highly unfavorable), while those with relationship-motivated styles excel in more moderate conditions. Leadership styles that do not match the situation will likely produce failure.

There are some significant benefits in applying the contingency approach to the study of leadership. This theory broadens the scope of leadership study. Unlike the trait or behavioralist approaches described earlier, contingency theory looks at the characteristics of the situation and the leader. It demonstrates that there is more than one way to provide effective leadership. This approach provides reasons for leadership successes and failures that can be used by organizations to improve their own leadership capabilities.

Despite these positive contributions to leadership study, contingency theory has drawn some criticism. It implies that organizations should construct job situations in a way that will match them to available leadership styles.[32] This makes contingency theory particularly difficult to apply to public administration, because situations are already specified through agency rules and are difficult to change. Furthermore, leaders who are effective in terms of efficiency are not necessarily best suited for a public or nonprofit leadership position. Leaders in the public and nonprofit sectors must balance both equity and efficiency concerns.

Path–Goal Theory

Related to contingency theory, path–goal theory seeks to understand leader–follower relations and the work situation. Yet this theory emphasizes how a number of factors in the work environment impact goal accomplishments. As the name suggests, leaders create a path that followers use to cut through the complex environment to achieve organizational goals. Hence, path–goal theory places more emphasis on the followers and seeks to develop a better understanding of their role in the leadership dynamic. This theory holds that effective leadership is dependent on the nature of the complex work environment and requires an understanding of leaders, their subordinates, and the work itself.

Path–goal theory posits that leader behaviors can be effective only to the extent that they harmonize with subordinate characteristics and task characteristics. Subordinate characteristics consist of personal needs and preferences within the work setting, while task characteristics relate to how the work setting is laid out.[33] Path–goal theory builds on expectancy theory principles. Expectancy theory recognizes that systems of external motivators create expectations that can help leaders maximize followers self-interest in ways that move them toward organizational goals.[34] In turn, path–goal theory maintains that leader behavior should correspond to subordinates' needs and the work setting. In organizations that have highly routinized work environments, leadership styles that include supportive and considerate behaviors work best, because they fulfill the personal needs of subordinates.[35]

Thus, a supportive leader would be most effective in a high-volume service setting in which workers are feeling frustrated and stressed. In situations with an opposite set of factors, leadership styles with task-oriented behaviors are more suitable for fulfilling subordinate self interests. A more directive leadership style would be effective in situations where there is considerable ambiguity regarding tasks and rules and where subordinates tend to be inflexible in their task performance.

Path–goal theory has made a significant contribution to leadership study by providing a detailed look at the complex nature of the work environment. It shows how multiple dimensions work together in a larger system. Thus theory is particularly important because it provides insight into the impact that these factors have on subordinates. For example, research has shown that employees with high levels of job satisfaction produce a number of benefits for an organization, and that certain styles of leadership can help improve these levels.[36] Path–goal theory helps explain this relationship between leader behavior and employee satisfaction in the work environment and offers leadership prescriptions for improving them.

Looking at leadership from this perspective has some limits, however. Although empirical research lends some support to this theory, the results are far from conclusive. Some of the assumptions made by this theory restrict the scope of its application. It assumes, for example, that leaders and subordinates will behave rationally, yet we have already noted that many modern situations are highly uncertain and contain nonrational elements that would make this theory difficult to apply.[37]

Leader–Member Exchange Theory

Leader–member exchange (LMX) theory is another approach to the study of leadership that emphasizes relationships in the work environment. It provides a detailed look at the association between leaders and each of their followers. Although Chester Barnard had already recognized exchange systems between organization and employee (see Chapter 7), LMX theory was the first to investigate the leader–subordinate exchange relationship in great detail. Leaders are effective, according to this theory, when they create as many "high-quality" **dyadic relationships** (that is, individual leader–subordinate relationships) as possible.[38]

Dyadic relationships Leader–subordinate relationships that develop through a system of complex exchanges.

The dyadic relationship between each leader and subordinate is complex. This relationship develops through a system of exchanges between leader and subordinate. Leaders look at how subordinates react to their demands, while subordinates evaluate a leader's response. The measure of response by both leader and subordinate determines the dyadic relationship that is developed.[39] LMX theory has made a substantial contribution to leadership study. Because this theory looks at leadership from the perspective of both leader and subordinate, it has created an awareness of many previously unrecognized components. Research backs up the emphasis LMX theory places on these factors by showing that high-quality dyadic relationships have a positive net effect on the organization and many subordinate work characteristics.[40]

LMX theory has some weaknesses that constrain the use of this approach. This theory, for example, offers little guidance for leaders who seek to alter their behaviors in ways that build high-quality relationships. Indeed, LMX theory does not assert which leader behaviors actually facilitate high-quality relationships.[41]

Transformational Leadership

Transformational leadership theory focuses on the leader's ability to generate motivation and express a clear vision of the future. Gaining prominence in the 1980s and incorporating a renewed emphasis on Weber's notion of charisma, this approach looks at how leaders motivate followers in a way that is mutually transcendent. John F. Kennedy, Martin Luther King Jr., and Susan B. Anthony exemplify this type of leadership. Charismatic leaders are often transformational because they inspire followers to an unusually high level of commitment to a cause and to realize extraordinary accomplishments. They are

The Reverend Martin Luther King Jr., shown here at the March on Washington, August 28, 1964, is an example of a transformational leader who used his skills to build a more tolerant and peaceful society.

SOURCE: Topham/The Image Works

visionaries. This expanded view of leadership also shows how leaders and followers work together to construct value and belief systems.

To move followers toward their goals, transformational leaders go beyond transactional systems, which rely on external rewards to achieve results (see Table 10.2). Transformational leadership has been defined in many different

TABLE 10.2 Transactional Leaders versus Transformational Leaders

Leader Type	External Rewards and Incentives	Employee Motivation	
Transactional Leader	Uses rewards and other material incentives to get employees to perform and exert effort on organization's behalf	Uses self-interest and the desire to further it as main motivational factor	Views employees as instruments to serve organization
Transformational Leader	Downplays significance of material rewards and incentives; gets employees to transcend self-interest for the good of the organization	Inculcates in employees a sense of higher purpose or larger vision	Employees strive to fulfill themselves as persons (self-actualize) and in doing so serve the organization and society

Adapted from M. E. Doyle and M. K. Smith, "Classical Leadership," *The Encyclopedia of Informal Education,* 2001, http://www.infed.org/leadership/traditional_leadership.htm.

ways, but the core aspects of theory revolve around the emotional bond between leader and followers.[42] Leaders get their followers to transcend their own self-interest and work toward a greater purpose. This is not to say that transformational leadership does not recognize transactional motivators. Transformational leadership theory looks at how leaders and followers go beyond that system to achieve something greater.

Despite the mystical aura that sometimes surrounds transformational leaders, the concept still entails a power relationship, according to James Mac-Gregor Burns.[43] But in a typical power relationship, power is exercised solely to achieve the purposes of the powerful, whereas in transformational leadership, power fulfills the needs and interests of both the leaders and the followers. In effect, the goals, desires, values, needs, and other motivations of the followers become merged with those of the leader.

Transformational leadership incorporates a number of characteristics. Charisma, morality, ethical aspirations, and personal attention are key components of transformational leadership.[44] Themes from other approaches, such as vision creating, culture building, motivating, and inspiring, have also been incorporated in the transformational framework. Transformational leaders use these techniques and methods to foster change and achieve feats that exceed expectations. These leaders establish value systems by creating a cause or vision for which others in the group can aspire. By promoting the cause and inspiring followers, leaders cause these values to be internalized throughout the organization.[45]

The transformational approach furthers our understanding of leadership in a number of ways. It places an importance on the "process" undertaken by both the leader and follower. It is a wide-ranging approach that has provided a significant amount of research on the way leaders inspire followers to move beyond their own self-interest to internalize organizational goals. This theory attempts to explain the various characteristics that help leaders "transform" their followers in this way. By recognizing charisma and other emotionally laden qualities and behaviors, transformational leadership compels leaders to go beyond transactional leadership approaches.[46] Further, research has shown that transformational approaches are prevalent even in bureaucratic settings.[47] This approach has created an awareness of those factors that has often been overlooked by other leadership theories.

Despite these contributions to the study of leadership, there are some problematic aspects to this approach. There are no guarantees that transformational leaders will operate for the greater good. Indeed, history is filled with examples of leaders, such as Adolph Hitler and Osama bin Laden, who have inspired others to commit atrocities against humankind. By advocating charismatic, inspiring leaders who convince others to internalize their values and beliefs, organizations must be wary of misapplying this approach. Similarly, leaders who operate autonomously to instill their values throughout the organization can pose concerns because they overlook the moral positions of others.[48]

Osama bin Laden, head of Al Qaeda, a terrorist network, is an example of a transformational leader who used his skills for destructive purposes.
SOURCE: CBS/Landov

Gender and Leadership in Public Administration

In the twenty-first century, leadership in the field of public administration has become progressively more diverse. Gender roles are being redefined as women fill more and more key leadership positions. Women are taking on greater leadership responsibilities in government. Recent examples of women in prominent leadership positions include Speaker of the House Nancy Pelosi, Secretary of State Condoleezza Rice, and Senator Hillary Clinton. Though women have been leaders throughout history, it is only within the last few decades that gender issues in the workplace have gained prominence. The growing awareness of women's contributions to leadership in the public and nonprofit sectors is reflected in the increasing number of studies dealing with gender issues. Researchers have focused on the paradoxes that women face as leaders and the impact of gender differences on leadership style. In this section, we will take a closer look at a few of the gender issues confronting today's leaders in public service.

Women in leadership positions face difficult challenges beyond those of hiring practices and salary inequalities. Feminist theorists have pointed out how our current understanding of leadership is shaped by a historically male organizational culture that has not been conducive to women in positions of authority. Leadership concepts and definitions are embedded with underlying masculine connotations that grant privileged status to those values most often associated with male professionals.[49] In this context, it is not

Condoleezza Rice became the U.S. secretary of state in January 2005, the second woman to hold that office. Nancy Pelosi, Democratic Congresswoman from California, became the first female Speaker of the U.S. House of Representatives in January 2007.

SOURCE: (left) Rob Crandall/ The Image Works; (right) Kevin Dietsch/UPI/Landov

surprising that a male-oriented view of leadership dominates the current work environment. The culture of leadership that has developed as a result of this historic inequity systematically distorts how women are viewed as leaders. Feminine characteristics are foreign to this view of leadership. Women are often viewed in masculine terms, rather than judged on their own merit.

Influence of Gender Bias on Leadership

In her book *Gender Images in Public Administration*, Camilla Stivers examines the implications of gender bias for women in leadership positions. She notes that women in positions of authority are caught in a paradoxical situation where the avenue to success is severely restricted and qualitatively masculine. Women must walk a fine line between masculine and feminine roles. To suggest that a leader displays feminine qualities is to assert that the individual in question is also subordinate, weak, or indecisive. When women make use of their authority in ways congruent with their male counterparts, however, they are suddenly viewed as tyrants.[50] This no-win situation affects the roles that women play in the organization and the techniques they use to solve problems.

It is easy to see how the problem of gender bias carries over into everyday organizational practice. For example, an executive may suggest a certain solution to an organizational problem. The solution may be presented in a way that is open to other ideas and criticisms. If this approach is labeled "feminine" in its presentation and its presenter described in the same manner, an organization with a strong gender bias may summarily reject the solution. However, if this same solution is presented in a manner that is associated with masculine characteristics (assertive, decisive), its chances of success are significantly higher. Leadership is most often described by the latter qualities, making the expression of feminine characteristics inconsistent with the dominant male framework.

Gender bias is often built into the structure of the organization. Women may be funneled into leadership positions at institutions that exhibit qualities that are considered feminine. Gender balance is generally found in agencies with redistributive functions, for example, where salaries are lower and positions contain characteristics such as "nurturing" or "care-taking."[51] This process maintains a self-fulfilling prophecy as women who exhibit certain traits are placed accordingly. It becomes a type of segregation that constitutes a major barrier to gender equality in predominantly male institutions and at the upper levels of all organizations.[52]

While gender bias plays a significant role in legitimizing certain types of leadership styles and behaviors, many researchers maintain that there are some key differences in the way women and men lead. These differences must be qualified by noting that gender roles are socially constructed. It is always difficult to assess differences when "male" and "female" are determined both biologically and culturally. Still, whether rightly or wrongly, certain styles have been attributed to each gender.

In general, female forms of leadership are identified with democratic, open, and participatory leadership styles. Research indicates that women are often better communicators and are more involved in maintaining relationships in the workplace.[53] This is an important aspect of female leadership styles, because women must often exercise their authority through nontraditional channels in the organizational hierarchy in order to avoid negative stereotypes. Because of the constraints on legitimate leadership behavior, female leadership styles are often creative and adaptive, constructing and synthesizing multiple behaviors and styles to meet the situation at hand. At least one research study has shown that women exhibit leadership styles congruent with the transformational leadership outlined in the theory section of this chapter.[54]

It should be stressed that there are more similarities than differences between genders with regard to leadership style. These differences are often a consequence of the situation. Even in situations where leadership style is comparable between genders, there is an underlying gender bias involved. For example, women are often pressured to conform to the dominant cultural norms of the organization. When leadership styles do not reflect those norms, women exhibiting more "feminine" leadership styles are often viewed negatively.[55] The same does not hold true, however, for males.[56] In any case, the situation and the gender bias involved are often more determinate than any stereotypically gendered leadership behaviors.

The relationship between gender and leadership is a complex web of values, stereotypes, and socially constructed norms. Public agencies should be aware of the underlying bias that systematically limits female leadership. Women are restricted in the sense that they are pressured to meet the male-dominated norms of leadership and exhibit behaviors and styles that match those criteria. While women do exhibit leadership styles that are qualitatively different from those of men, it is often a matter of whether or not those behaviors fit the specific organizational context. Despite these constraints, women continue to excel in public leadership positions.

Leadership in the Public Context

Leadership in the government and nonprofit sectors presents a unique set of challenges. Leaders in government must meet typical demands for accountability to an increasingly diverse constituency by balancing efficiency and equity. These accountability issues make leadership in the public sector different from leadership in the private sector. In both the public and nonprofit sectors, leaders must set a course for the organization that strives to balance the traditional democratic values associated with the public interest and the demands for efficiency and productivity. In the field of public administration, scholars have debated where leadership fits along this spectrum. Some advocate entrepreneurial approaches, while others argue in favor of more bureaucratic notions of leadership in the public sector. In this section, we will cover some important points about the public context and look at the way they impact the leadership process.

Leadership and Accountability in the Public Sector

Differences between the public and private sectors translate into differences in leadership. While leaders in the private sector operate with high degrees of autonomy, public administrators must deal with formal controls that limit their ability to take risks and create dramatic change. As we have seen, bureaucratic mechanisms were established to maintain control and ensure the fiduciary responsibility of public officials to uphold the purposes designated by the state. Indeed, this emphasis on accountability provides an important check on administrative power and grants a measure of legitimacy to an unelected bureaucracy. Leaders in this environment must navigate through numerous demands on their organization and respond to an increasingly diverse set of interests.

Differences between Private and Public Leaders

As Chapter 1 points out, there are significant differences between the public and private sector, and these have direct implications for leadership. Private leaders operate in an entrepreneurial manner, often taking significant risks in bringing about innovation and change. Entrepreneurs frequently operate without regard for rules and without formal checks on authority. Within the organization, private sector leaders typically show progress toward performance goals and are given great latitude with respect to how these goals will be reached. Moreover, successful leadership in the private sector is measured in terms of profit and rarely receives the scrutiny of the public.

In the public sector, however, even the most entrepreneurial leaders must respect the rule of law and principles of fairness. Today's leaders are held accountable to a multitude of factions, each representing different interests. Understanding an organization's constituency is a primary responsibility for leaders in the public sector. Demands for accountability exist both internally, where executives expect their orders to be followed, and externally, where political pressures take the form of legislators, special interest groups, and others who demand that the organization show results and progress toward specified mandates. Leaders are highly visible and receive little margin for error. Even minor mistakes are a potential crisis, given the increasing attention to bureaucratic waste and unethical behavior.

Public Leadership and Accountability Mechanisms

A couple of major federal attempts to ensure bureaucratic compliance provide good examples of the multidimensional nature of accountability and the consequences it has for leadership in the public sector. In 1921, Congress established the General Accounting Office (GAO, now the Government Accountability Office) to audit agency accounts and evaluate their performance (we discuss this act in detail in Chapter 13). Leaders of public agencies must show fiscal competence and demonstrate program results. Legally, leaders are bound by a set of rules spelled out in the Administrative Procedures Act of 1946 (see Chapter 4). These rules inject a sense of fairness into the administrative environment and hold leaders accountable to standards of equity. Leaders must determine whether their actions fit within the requirements of proper scope of conduct that the Administrative Procedures Act specifies. Any failure to meet these requirements can have serious repercussions for both the leader and the organization.

Legal and legislative accountability offers two different and conflicting standards of accountability. Legislative accountability focuses on fiscal restraint and program efficiency. Given the standards set forth by the GAO, it is no wonder that cost-benefit approaches have been the norm for leadership action. Yet this measure of accountability conflicts with that presented by the Administrative Procedures Act. The demand for equity in administrative actions often requires inefficient procedures of inclusion and participation. This conflict between efficiency and equity poses problems as leaders negotiate standards of accountability to provide organizational direction. Recently, scholars have taken a closer look at how the emphasis, in one direction or another, translates into different leadership approaches.

Recent Approaches to Leadership

Another issue for leadership in the public context concerns the type of approach that leaders should take in an environment where administrators are expected to work for the public good. The need for leadership in public service is readily apparent, yet there is considerable disagreement about how one should lead on the public's behalf. All leadership approaches imply certain normative values that public administrators should strive to maintain. Most approaches fall somewhere along the continuum between market-based styles and those that advocate more traditional democratic values, such as conservatorship (see Figure 10.2). Each approach has important consequences for public servants as leaders of their organizations. Although these approaches differ in many ways, the ability of leadership to foster connections between government and civil society remains important for both.

Entrepreneurial Leadership

The classical version of public administration envisioned a bureaucracy that would simply implement the plans laid out by pieces of legislation, like a well-run machine. As a reaction to this view of administration, public administration scholars began examining the market-based approaches of the private sector as a method for improving administration in the public sector (we discuss many of these in Chapter 12). Osborne and Gaebler, for example, advanced a notion of the administrator as a **public entrepreneur** and conceptualized administration as "steering" rather than "rowing."[57]

Public entrepreneur An approach to public leadership emphasizing a market orientation similar to that found in private business.

This entrepreneurial approach has important implications for leadership in public administration. Drawing off of private sector notions, entrepreneurialism encourages a specific leadership style that is based on initiative, innovation, and organizational vision.[58] Leaders often fit into the mold described by charismatic and transformational leadership theories. They become change agents in the organization, instilling values of competition, self-interest, resource maximization, and customer satisfaction that contradict many classical public administration ideas.[59] The emphasis on entrepreneurial values is often reflected in privatizing and downsizing to achieve greater organizational efficiency. Proponents of this view argue that entrepreneurial leadership purges the organization of complacent tendencies and that it is a way of creating a streamlined, customer-oriented system that best fulfills public needs.

Conservatorship

As a reaction to the entrepreneurial approach, competing conceptualizations for administrative leadership developed. These approaches focused on traditional

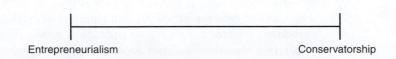

Entrepreneurialism   Conservatorship

Figure 10.2   Spectrum of Leadership Approaches in the Public Sector

democratic values, public service to citizens, and identifying and maintaining the public good. One noteworthy alternative to the entrepreneurial approach is the idea of the leader as a conservator of institutional values. The idea of **conservatorship** rests on preserving the values of the existing institution as a means of solidifying democratic governance. Leaders serve a guardian function by protecting these institutional values from erosion or corruption by internal and external forces. Part of this protection or preservation requires the deliberate attempt at not exercising the risk-taking behaviors found in the private sector.[60]

Critics point out various limitations to the conservator approach to leadership. If values are to be maintained, they must be used from time to time in a manner that does not always fit the "integrity" of the institution.[61] There is some empirical evidence that the threats to institutional values through the application of private sector approaches may be exaggerated. Further, there are concerns about the unresponsiveness to innovative solutions and the bureaucratic gradualism that this approach implies. If leaders are not to use their discretion, they are constrained from bringing about significant change, even when that change is an appropriate solution to a public problem.

The debate between entrepreneurialism and conservatorship shows the role that discretion plays in public leadership. Greater discretion gives leaders the flexibility needed to produce innovative solutions to public problems, while limited discretion ensures that leaders behave in a manner consistent with agency values. Other approaches to leadership in the public sector have looked at the ways in which administrators use their discretion to create connections with citizens and other parts of civil society. As we mentioned before in our discussion of the levels of leadership, street-level leadership provides another unique look at discretion and how lower-level administrators can use discretion to take a leadership role. This use of discretion, however, can only be called leadership if it coincides with mutual goals and values. Part of the leader–follower dynamic involves an effort to develop reciprocity and collaboration between administrators, civil society, and everyday citizens. These collaborative and democratic views of the role of public administrator can provide a framework for leadership.

Street-level leadership and other collaborative modes of administration are part of a process in which administrators abdicate some authority in favor of democracy. These approaches foster virtuous citizenship and political efficacy within the administrative context through the use of discretionary authority.[62] Leadership occurs when administrators build bonds with civil society that facilitate public input into problem-solving and reinforce democratic norms. It is the leader's responsibility to create opportunities for engaged citizenship and community empowerment, while continuing to generate positive improvements within the community. By building the collaborative process between citizen and government over the long term, these approaches develop a participatory process of empowered citizens.

Conservatorship A leadership style that emphasizes preserving the values of the existing institution as a means of solidifying democratic governance, and protecting institutional values from erosion or corruption by internal and external forces.

Chapter Summary

Leadership plays an important role in public service. Leaders must work to unify goals throughout the organization and create processes to further these goals. Throughout this chapter, a number of leadership aspects have been discussed. First, leadership is a distinct theoretical construct that coincides with other related concepts such as management. Leadership is also a dynamic process found throughout the organization, operating at multiple layers and including multiple actors. There are many different theories of leadership, from those that emphasize individual characteristics to those that focus on processes and situations. Several of the more important approaches include leadership traits, leadership behaviors, contingency theory, path–goal theory, leader–member exchange, and transformational leadership. Gender bias and leadership styles also play a role in legitimizing certain values and behaviors. Leaders in the public context must deal with multiple obligations and the paradoxes that they involve. Recent approaches to leadership in public administration concern private sector and public sector values such as conservatorship and entrepreneurial leadership.

Chapter Discussion Questions

1. How is leadership different across various levels of the organization? How is it similar?

2. What are the key challenges for today's leaders in the public sector? Why?

3. What are the differences between transactional and transformational approaches to leadership?

4. Identify the differences between leadership and management. Which difference is the most important? Why?

5. The public and private sectors are different in many ways. How does this affect leadership?

BRIEF CASE   LEADERSHIP IN TURBULENT TIMES

As we have seen, the volatility of today's environment makes questions of leadership vitally important to public organizations in the midst of major change. Nowhere is this more evident than in the area of national security. The leadership challenge presented to Tom Ridge was daunting if not overwhelming. As head of homeland security, Ridge was charged with coordinating multiple agencies across multiple levels and balancing the need to respond to daily threats with long-term efforts to make information sharing and collaboration the hallmarks of a new national security culture.

Following his years as a governor of Pennsylvania and member of Congress, and his distinguished service as a soldier in Vietnam, Ridge brought substantial leadership experience to his position, and some believed he was up to the task of leading the monumental effort. As Susan M. Collins, chair of the Senate Governmental Affairs Committee, stated at Ridge's confirmation hearing, his "background, temperament, and experience make him ideally qualified to be the first secretary of homeland security." His years in government suggested he would have the political skills needed to build external support. Ridge eventually relinquished his position as head of homeland security, and questions remain as to whether his different attributes and years of experience as a state executive translated into effective leadership of a federal department. Some question whether personal attributes and experience are ever enough.

For his part, as the first head of the department, Ridge had to set forth a clear direction for the nation's homeland defense. This task was more difficult than it might first appear. For a number of reasons, setting a direction for homeland security required a unified vision that synthesized a broad, and often conflicting, set of security perspectives. As we have already noted, the views of various intelligence and law enforcement agencies are often directly at odds with one another, making a unified vision difficult, if not impossible.

Another important responsibility for Secretary Ridge was his ability to balance horizontal and vertical leadership roles. Though he was responsible for domestic security, Ridge relied on a number of actors from different organizations. This required the ability to work horizontally with other groups in an effort to build networked coalitions and open up various silos of bureaucratic activity. Ridge also worked vertically to build his own organization's capacities that were initially quite underdeveloped. Leadership in this area required the proper alignment of resources and personnel that fit the direction set forth for national security issues. With an estimated 170,000 federal employees involved, this was a substantial challenge.

The challenges that Tom Ridge faced as the first secretary of homeland security show the many ways in which leadership affects policy in general and organizations in particular. Leaders play a significant role in the change process and carry great responsibilities for their organization's operation. With a system as vast as national security, leadership will certainly be needed beyond that of a few individuals located at the top of agency hierarchies. More collaborative forms of leadership between all groups will be necessary to handle the numerous issues involved.

Brief Case Questions

1. *If you had been on hand to advise Secretary Ridge regarding leadership, which theory of leadership discussed in this chapter would you have recommended to him for his monumental task of coordinating the federal government's homeland security efforts?*

2. *As explained in Chapter 8, Ridge originally directed the Office of Homeland Security, which was created by an executive order of the president shortly after September 11, 2001. Congress established the Department of Homeland Security in 2002. How would this change in structure affect Ridge's leadership and accountability?*

3. *Which element of Ridge's government experience—his governorship or his service in Congress—do you think would have most positively affected his ability to lead? Why?*

▪ Key Terms

conservatorship (page 253)
contingency theory (page 241)
dyadic relationships (page 244)
leadership traits (page 240)
Least Preferred Coworker (LPC) score (page 242)
outcome discretion (page 238)

person-oriented behaviors (page 241)
personal authority (page 237)
positional authority (page 237)
process discretion (page 238)
public entrepreneur (page 252)
task-oriented behaviors (page 241)

■ On the Web

http://www.ccl.org/
Website of the Center for Creative Leadership.

http://www.ksg.harvard.edu/leadership/
Harvard University's Center for Public Leadership, a site with many good links.

http://www.advocacy.org/
The Advocacy Institute works to make social justice leadership strategic, effective, and sustainable in pursuit of a just world.

http://govleaders.org/
This online resource is designed to help government managers cultivate a more effective and motivated public sector workforce.

http://www.academy.umd.edu/ila
The International Leadership Association promotes a deeper understanding of leadership knowledge and practices for the greater good of individuals and communities worldwide.

CHAPTER 11

The Policy Process

■ SETTING THE STAGE

On the morning of August 29, 2005, one of the strongest hurricanes ever recorded in American history made landfall in southeast Louisiana.[1] By the time the storm reached the Louisiana shores, it had been downgraded from a category 5 to category 3 storm. However, it was still sufficiently deadly to wreak havoc over an area of 100 square miles from its center. The storm surge caused immense damage along the coastlines of Louisiana, Mississippi, and Alabama, making Katrina one of the most devastating natural disasters in U.S. history. Perhaps the most lasting images associated with Katrina, however, were of the storm's path through the city of New Orleans and the aftermath of flooding there.

New Orleans, in the direct path of the storm, met with a disaster of epic proportions. The potential for destruction was so enormous because much of the city's metropolitan area is below sea level along Lake Pontchartrain, placing New Orleans at risk for severe flooding. On August 29, the nightmare scenario long feared by many in New Orleans occurred as the hurricane's storm surge breached the system of levees around the city in many places, putting approximately 80 percent of the city under water. Although New Orleans Mayor Ray Nagin had ordered a mandatory evacuation on August 28, thousands of residents remained behind as the storm battered the city. Many who took refuge in the Convention Center and the Superdome were stranded there for days in horrific conditions. Looting in parts of the city bore witness to a major breakdown in law and order.

While Katrina's catastrophic human and financial toll (more than 1,800 lives lost, almost as many declared missing, and approximately $75 billion in damage) assure its place in U.S. history as one of the deadliest storms, our primary interest with Katrina here has to do with what the disaster has to tell us about the policy process. Government responses to the storm at the federal, state, and local levels received severe criticism for the lack of planning and coordination that caused significant delays in providing needed assistance. Media coverage of the looting and suffering in New Orleans portrayed a breakdown in public policy.

Prior to Katrina, probably few Americans took more than a passing interest in the country's natural disaster policies and in the Federal Emergency Management Agency (FEMA). However, in the weeks and months after New Orleans was flooded, disaster

---

This chapter was co-written with George Reed, an associate professor in the School of Leadership and Education Sciences at the University of San Diego and former director of Command and Leadership Studies at the U.S. Army War College.

The aftermath of Hurricane Katrina (August 2005) revealed fatal flaws in the disaster policies of all levels of U.S. government.

SOURCE: Wesley Bocxe/The Image Works

policy at all levels of government was subject to intense scrutiny by politicians, the media, and the public. Hurricane Katrina provides a classic example of how a problem seizes the public's attention, temporarily forcing all other issues off the agenda. Public interest in an issue often reaches an intensity that then subsides as other problems assert themselves.

Public policy Any decision-making done on behalf of or affecting the public, especially that which is done by government.

To study the **public policy** process is to examine how government decides what to do and the impact those decisions have on the lives of citizens. It is the process by which problems come to the attention of government, agendas are developed, alternatives are established, and decisions are made, then implemented and evaluated. Students of public policy are driven by questions of why some problems capture the attention of policymakers and result in governmental action and others do not, and which government actions make a real impact on the lives of its citizens and why they have such an effect. Government officials are faced with an unlimited number of problems and limited resources in terms of time, money, and human capital. Yet regulations are established, laws do get passed, money is appropriated, and agencies are authorized.

▪ CHAPTER PLAN

The policy process can be a bewilderingly complex subject, with a multitude of participants both inside and outside government. In order to come to terms with this complexity, scholars have developed a number of theories and models of policy-making. Each highlights certain aspects of the process, diminishes others, and therefore contains both strengths and weaknesses. For practitioners of public policy, models and theories suggest possible means of influencing policy outputs and outcomes. It is important to note that there is no grand theory of the policy process that will completely explain or accurately predict governmental outcomes, but several fundamentals can be identified and explored for greater insights into how and why certain policies are proposed, decided upon, and implemented. In this chapter, we discuss several important theories of the policy process, beginning with a detailed examination of the policy cycle. We then explore some other helpful models, including incrementalism, policy streams and agendas, rational choice, and the advocacy coalition framework. The rest of the chapter discusses program implementation and evaluation, two important stages of the policy process.

Going Beyond the Institutional Approach

Students are often presented with a view of the policy process focusing on the government and its institutions. Most students have seen a basic flow chart describing how bills are introduced in the legislature, proceed to signature by the executive, and undergo the process of legislative review. This familiar depiction can be described as the institutional view of the policy-making process. This view of public policy is only partially accurate, however. Harold D. Lasswell defined the field as the "knowledge of and in the decision processes of the public and civil order."[2] His definition recognized that any attempt to draw a dividing line between government and nongovernment decision-making is difficult, since many public sector issues are heavily influenced by the private sector and vice versa.

Thus, any attempt to develop greater knowledge of the process must extend beyond a purely legalistic view of how laws are made or court decisions are reached. The institutional view of policy-making depicts the process as an organizational chart listing the various governmental institutions involved and their formal lines of communication. The policy process, however, also includes issues of power, conflict, influence, and perspective not included in the institutional approach. In this chapter, we go beyond the institutional model to examine the policy process through the different lenses provided by other frameworks.[3]

The Policy Cycle

The concept of policy as a cycle or series of stages is helpful as an introductory concept, since it represents an understandable, if not totally accurate, means of understanding the policy process. This model highlights the policy process as having a life cycle with different stages, and it recognizes that there are many participants involved, both inside and outside government agencies. The **policy cycle** consists of eight stages: (1) agenda setting, (2) problem definition, (3) alternative selection, (4) authoritative decision, (5) policy design, (6) program implementation, (7) program evaluation, and (8) termination or change (see Figure 11.1).

Agenda setting refers to the process by which problems first come to the attention of policymakers. Because society always faces myriad problems and

Policy cycle The concept of public policy as a cycle or series of stages.

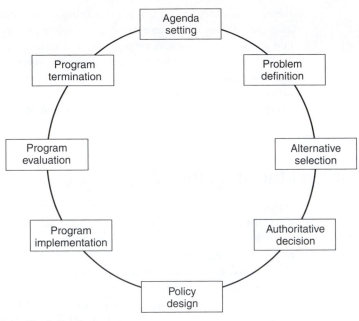

Figure 11.1   The Policy Cycle

issues, agenda setting involves a competition of ideas and a means of bringing those ideas to the attention of the public and those in positions of power. Mothers against Drunk Driving (MADD), for example, through effective use of the media, orchestrated a successful campaign to stiffen penalties on drunk drivers. Agenda setting is a means of setting the stage for subsequent action. By directing the public's attention to the emotional and economic costs of accidents involving drunk drivers, MADD helped to focus policymakers on this issue, and eventually legislation was passed to address the problem. Bill Clinton helped bring the issue of welfare reform to the forefront of national attention in his campaign for the presidency in 1992, although it had been a national priority for many years even before then. Republicans gained control of the House of Representatives in 1994 in part because they campaigned on a platform of welfare reform even more radical than the one Clinton advocated. Thus, reforming welfare was a well-established item on the national policy agenda by 1996.

Problem definition provides the framework within which interventions are considered and defined as potential solutions. Problem definition is a very important stage, since every definition carries with it a series of proposed solutions that lead directly to the stages of alternative selection and policy design. Problem definition is an inherently political process involving competition between interest groups that attempt to cast the problem in a way that leads to solutions they prefer. When problems are defined as organizational, restructuring is often the solution of choice. Communication problems can result in solutions involving education and advertising. Problems defined as involving leadership often result in the replacement of responsible administrators. In the case study at the end of this chapter, the problem of low numbers of army recruits was defined as a marketing issue, resulting in a predictable set of solutions. In the case of welfare reform, the problem was defined as dependency on government subsidies by many generations in the same family, and individuals who were dependent on society as a matter of personal choice, as opposed to hardship caused by illness or economic conditions. Defined in this way, any possible solution had to set strict limits on the amount of time one could spend on the welfare rolls. This provision was indeed an important part of the eventual legislation.

Alternative selection involves the means by which some solutions, and not others, are presented to policymakers for decision-making. Inherent in this concept is a rational decision-making model that includes the process of collecting information on the advantages and disadvantages of each alternative course of action, then selecting the best one. It involves a narrowing of alternatives to those that are feasible within existing constraints, including available resources and public will. Those who establish or control the listing of alternative courses of action hold real power, since they restrict the range of policies and programs that will result. For example, consider the possible responses of a city traffic engineer when residents complain to elected officials about an inordinate number of traffic accidents involving pedestrians at an intersection in their neighborhood. When presenting possible solutions, the engineer will look for alternatives that meet the demands of the citizens and the city council with an eye to cost effectiveness. The engineer might recommend to the council several courses of action, including more police drive-bys, speed-limit changes, or placement of a stop sign. The engineer probably would not suggest costly intersection redesign initiatives, such as building a pedestrian bridge or hiring full-time crossing guards. The community might later demand additional alternatives, but initially the council considers the list of alternatives provided by the engineer, who assumes an important role in the policy process because of professional expertise.

Authoritative decision-making recognizes that no public program or policy results without there being first an act of government. The legislature passes laws, authorizes spending for programs, and issues resolutions. The president issues executive orders and signs laws into effect, while administrative agencies promulgate regulations. The courts render opinions. Each is a means of publicly announcing the result of a decision by those invested with the authority to do so. Every authoritative decision represents the outcome of an inherently political process involving various interests and ideologies. Welfare reform was enacted as part of an election-year compromise reached by the Democratic president, Bill Clinton, and the Republican-controlled Congress. Neither side received exactly what it wanted from the 1996 welfare reform act, but both sides could legitimately claim victory and could use it as a campaign issue.

Policy design involves the stated intent of policymakers and its transla-
tion into plans for programs administered by government officials. It
involves the establishment of guidance to agencies that must achieve program goals and objectives that may or may not be stated in detail. It may
involve elements of intent, oversight, review, and revision. For example, in
response to highly publicized incidents of hate crimes and testimony by
civil-rights advocacy groups in the late 1980s, Congress passed Public Law
101–275, which was signed by President George H. W. Bush, directing the
attorney general to collect data about crimes that manifest prejudice based
on group characteristics. The law expressed the intent of Congress, including that the data should be used only for research or statistical purposes,
that the identity of victims of crime should be protected, and that nothing
in the law should create a cause of action based on discrimination due to
sexual orientation. In the case of welfare reform, the new Temporary Assistance for Needy Families (TANF) legislation meant that the states and not
the federal government would be responsible for designing new programs
to move people from the welfare rolls to jobs and increased personal
responsibility. Provided that they meet certain federal guidelines, states
now have greater discretion and flexibility in devising public assistance
strategies.

Program implementation recognizes that the actual outcomes of a program may not resemble what the decisionmakers originally intended. As the
number of participants involved in implementing a policy increases, so does
the likelihood that the program will not be implemented in the manner envisioned by the decisionmakers. This helps to explain why programs with otherwise good intentions sometimes fail when put into practice. In general,
states in implementing welfare reform have stressed both short-term job
strategies and long-term education and training programs. Most states realize that long-term strategies are needed to keep people off welfare by promoting job retention, increased earnings, and career development. Poverty
analysts are finding that because single mothers usually can get only low-
paying jobs, the government must still provide them with enough subsidies
for a decent living. (At the end of this chapter, we examine implementation
in more detail.)

Program evaluation is the means of determining what actually happens
after a policy has been implemented. It involves an assessment of program
processes and impacts, focusing on aspects that are observable or measurable.
It may involve the determination of whether the program is reaching its
intended targets, whether it is having the intended effect, whether administrators are meeting established standards of operation, or whether the program is
cost-effective. Key to the idea of program evaluation is that there should be
some assessment of the relative worth of a program. Program evaluation is
similar to the idea of the performance review or audit, discussed in Chapter 4.
Ideally, program evaluation should consider intended as well as unintended
consequences. (We discuss program evaluation in more detail at the end of this
chapter.)

Program termination addresses what happens to a program once the problem for which it was initiated has been solved. Programs and the organizations that administer them are extraordinarily resilient, especially within the government. They are far more likely to change their approach and goals to garner continued resources for operation than they are to actually terminate.

Models of the Policy Process

The policy cycle model is an elegant way of looking at the actions of government, but it is not without deficiencies. Other models have been developed to incorporate elements missing from the policy cycle model. These include policy streams, rational choice, and the advocacy coalition framework, each of which is discussed below. Several of the most notable problems with the policy cycle model surround the inference that the policy proceeds in an orderly progression from one stage to the next.[4] Reality rarely conforms to such a tidy and rational model. Multiple phases of the process occur simultaneously and out of order. Some rarely occur at all, as in the case of policy termination. Different players in the process have varying levels of power and access to information. Still, the cycle approach holds an influential spot in public policy circles, prompting a large amount of high-quality research. But other models highlight the contentious nature of competition for the attention of policymakers and the dynamic nature of policy change.

Incrementalism and Sweeping Change

Incrementalism The theory that public policy occurs in a series of small, incremental steps or changes and not all at once.

Incrementalism, which was discussed in Chapter 9 as a concept for explaining organizational decision-making, also has been used to explain the policy process, which often proceeds in small steps. Incrementalism reflects the limitations of humans in dealing with the complexity inherent in the policy process. Robert Dahl and Charles Lindblom introduced the concept of incrementalism as a means of comparing the gains and losses of closely related alternatives as a substitute for the rational calculation of all possible choices.[5]

Although incrementalism may serve to describe policy change most of the time, there are indeed periods of sweeping change.[6] The American democratic system is designed more to balance competing interests and to safeguard individual rights than it is to be efficient. It is therefore institutionally resistant to change, yet it also provides for mobilization of public opinion. Of the many issues facing elected officials, most do not engender widespread interest among the American public. Most issues are confined to groups of experts or advocates, and as long as the debate on a public issue is confined to interest groups, policy networks, or policy subsystems,

Policy subsystems
Groups of people with a common interest in an issue, including experts, advocates, and officials.

stability reigns supreme. **Policy subsystems** are groups of people with a common interest in an issue, including experts, advocates, and officials. Occasionally an issue will escape the confines of a policy subsystem and reach the national consciousness—and it is during these periods that widespread change takes place.

It is difficult to predict what will move an issue out of a policy subsystem, but it can involve pressures both internal and external to government. The role of the media is an important one in this process, as it focuses public attention on issues through investigative reporting and news coverage. For instance, during the 1980s, homelessness emerged from the poverty and housing policy subsystems to briefly capture the national interest, with the help of media attention, only to subside back to the relative obscurity of those subsystems by the early 1990s.

Policy Streams

The models discussed above emphasize the stable nature of the policy process over time. The policy cycle, iron triangles, and policy networks suggest a static policy process, and incrementalism suggests only small changes from one point to the next. Even the model accounting for sweeping change cannot tell us anything about what gives rise to these changes. To understand why events in the realm of public policy often appear to be random and unpredictable, we must turn to the model of policy streams.

Policy streams The theory that a complex combination of factors is responsible for the arrival of an issue on the policy agenda, and that attempts to pinpoint their origin are futile.

John Kingdon sought to understand why some issues come to the attention of decisionmakers while others do not.[7] His **policy streams** theory therefore focuses on the agenda setting and alternative selection stages of the policy cycle. He concluded that a complex combination of factors is responsible for the arrival of an issue on the policy agenda, and he advised that attempts to pinpoint their origin are futile. Using the metaphor of streams, Kingdon expanded on the garbage can model of change in organizations.[8] The **garbage can model**, or organized anarchy, reflects a fluid and somewhat random process as people, problems, and solutions flow together. (For more on the garbage can theory, see Vignette 11.1.) Kingdon asserts that there are three separate streams operating independently of each other, consisting of problems, policies, and politics. Problems are issues occupying the attention of people both inside and outside government. Policies refer to ideas and ready-made solutions held and promoted by specialists and policy entrepreneurs within policy communities. Policy community participants have their own agendas and seek to promote their desired solutions at every opportunity. The political stream represents public opinion, changes in political party dominance, and interest-group pressures.

Garbage can model The theory that the policy process is marked by fluidity and a certain degree of randomness as people, problems, and solutions flow together and apart.

At certain unpredictable times, the streams come together, often in response to a well-publicized focusing event or series of events, resulting in a window of opportunity for policy change. The focusing event might be a single

VIGNETTE 11.1 Garbage Cans and Public Policies

An influential approach to organizational decision-making that draws on bounded rationality is Cohen, March, and Olsen's "garbage can" model, or organized anarchies.[a] (Bounded rationality refers to the idea that in rational decision-making, humans have various limitations.) In this approach, decision-making is marked by fluidity, as people, opportunities, problems, and solutions flow together and apart at different times.[b] In contrast to the traditional model of decision-making, a degree of randomness characterizes the garbage can approach. Problems develop a life of their own, while "solutions no one originally intended or even expected may be generated, or no solutions at all. Some problems simply waste away."[c] As a consequence of bounded rationality, administrators participate in certain decisions on the basis of their needs, overall objectives, and time constraints. They have personal agendas they are trying to advance, which results in their putting forth ideas that are problems in search of a solution or solutions in search of a problem.[d] After a problem has been "solved," the participants presume a rational process existed all along. The difference with the traditional top-down approach could not be more striking.

[a] Michael D. Cohen, James C. March, and Johan P. Olsen, "A Garbage Can Model of Organizational Choice," *Administrative Science Quarterly* 17:1 (1972): 1–25.

[b] Michael Vasu, Debra Stewart, and G. David Garson, *Organizational Behavior and Public Management* (New York: Marcel Dekker, 1998), 42.

[c] Charles Perrow, *Complex Organizations: A Critical Essay* (Glenview, IL: Scott, Foresman, 1986), 135.

[d] Vasu, Stewart, and Garson, *Organizational Behavior and Public Management*, 42.

horrific event such as a plane crash, prompting calls for increased airline safety measures. Or a series of events such as the recurring depictions of widespread welfare fraud in the 1990s might bring public attention to the issue and contribute to calls for welfare reform. In any case, the window of opportunity for policy change remains open for only a limited amount of time. Attention eventually moves elsewhere. The problem may be solved, or realization of the complexity of the problem dawns and policymakers and the public begin to lose interest.

As an example of policy streams in action, consider the enactment of hate crime legislation mentioned earlier in the chapter. Anecdotal accounts of shocking crimes against minorities received media attention and served as focusing events. Watchdog agencies such as the Anti-defamation League and the Southern Poverty Law Center maintained lists of bias-motivated incidents and tirelessly advocated for a government response. Faced with the perception of a rising epidemic of hate crimes and a national mood that considered prejudice-motivated crimes unacceptable in a democratic and diverse society, Congress enacted the Hate Crimes Statistics Act of 1990. The act changed crime-reporting policy by mandating that the attorney general acquire and publish data on crimes motivated by prejudice. The FBI and Bureau of Justice Statistics both opposed the act, expressing doubts as to the degree to which the motivation of perpetrators could be discerned by police officers. But records of congressional testimony indicate that the initiative had widespread public support.

Hate crimes directed against minorities by groups such as the Ku Klux Klan received media attention and served as focusing events prompting legislation.
SOURCE: Michael Greenlar/ The Image Works

The policy streams theory recognizes the unpredictable nature of policy change, since it is not possible to predict the occurrence of focusing events. It is an approach best used retrospectively, when trying to explain a particular policy change.

Rational Choice

Rational choice The theory that individuals attempt to maximize their interests in the policy process.

Rational choice theory emphasizes organizational decision-making behavior as influenced by incentives and rules in an institutional setting. Decisionmakers are assumed to seek outcomes that are in their own self-interest. In other words, decisionmakers seek to maximize their personal interest—a concept examined in Chapter 7 in the discussion of public choice theory. Self-interest can be restated in rational choice terms as "utility." Utility refers to the extent to which the wants and needs of an individual are satisfied. Given a number of possible outcomes, a rational individual can be expected to choose a course of action that will produce the maximum gain. Such assumptions permit the computer modeling of decision-making under various incentives and rules, an application of rational choice known as **game theory**.

Game theory The application of rational choice theory to hypothetical situations using computer simulations.

The **Prisoner's Dilemma** (see Vignette 11.2) is a classic example of the application of game theory to a hypothetical situation.[9] The Prisoner's Dilemma is a simple game with only two decision points, limited information exchange between the participants, and outcomes that are precise. When there are multiple

Prisoner's Dilemma An example of the use of game theory in a simple decision-making situation.

VIGNETTE 11.2 The Prisoner's Dilemma

The Prisoner's Dilemma, an example of game theory, considers the possible courses of action available to two suspects who are arrested for committing a crime. In order to obtain a conviction, the police need to obtain the cooperation of one of the suspects. The suspects are held in separate cells and are not permitted to talk to each other. The police present both suspects with several options that depend on their level of cooperation. If neither suspect confesses, then both will be convicted of a minor offense with a one-month sentence. If both confess, they will both be sentenced to prison for a six-month sentence. If only one confesses, that prisoner will be released while the other will receive a nine-month sentence.

The options and payoffs can be depicted in several ways. For example, the following table depicts the various payoffs for the different courses of action.

Another way to depict the options is a decision tree. In the figure, the Payoff Decision Tree identifies

Table of Payoffs

	Confess	Don't Confess
Confess	-6, -6	0, -9
Don't Confess	-9, 0	-1, -1

the various courses of action at each stage of the game and their resulting payoffs. Number 1 in the figure indicates the first decision point. Decision points are also known as nodes. At the first node, the first prisoner has two choices, either confess or don't confess. Each branch of the tree represents an alternative choice. Number 2 indicates the second player's decision point. The second player is faced with the same two choices, confess or don't confess. The dotted line indicates that the second prisoner must make this decision without knowledge of the choice made by prisoner one. The payoffs for each course of action are depicted in parentheses at the end of the diagram.

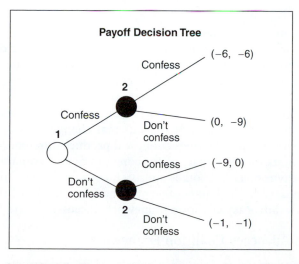

Payoff Decision Tree

Payoff Decision Tree

In the Prisoner's Dilemma, an example of game theory, prisoners have to make a decision: confess or stay silent.

SOURCE: Aaron Lambert-Pool/Getty

outcomes, varying amounts of information, and ambiguity of outcomes, the game can become quite complex and unwieldy.[10] Interestingly, some of the concepts from game theory can be applied to administrative or institutional settings.

A model by Elinor Ostrom applies elements of game theory to administration as it identifies a number of important structural elements present in organizational decision-making.[11] It recognizes that there are multiple levels in decision-making, each constrained by the decision of the level above it. For example, the provision of public services by government agencies is constrained by laws and regulations from the executive, legislative, and judicial branches of government that are themselves constrained by the Constitution. At each level, the actions of decisionmakers depend on resources available, attributes of the community, and rules in use. The decision outcomes are a function of the actors involved in decision-making, the situation at hand, and the patterns of interaction in place.

Institutional rational choice represents a sophisticated means of envisioning the policy process. It suggests that changes in any of the factors, such as rules or patterns of interaction, will produce different policy outcomes. It also accounts for the impact of the community and available resources on the policy environment. Another approach considering similar elements, but with an emphasis on the competitive and changing nature of the process, is provided by the advocacy coalition framework, discussed below.

The Advocacy Coalition Framework

Advocacy coalition framework (ACF) The theory that focuses on policy subsystems rather than official institutions of government and emphasizes the importance of core beliefs or values that drive coalitions to compete for influence in the policy process.

The **advocacy coalition framework (ACF)** focuses on policy subsystems rather than official institutions of government, and it emphasizes the importance of core beliefs or values that drive coalitions to compete for influence in the policy process.[12] (See Figure 11.2.) The key element in the ACF is the policy subsystem, where interested parties organize into a number of identifiable coalitions (usually one to four) composed of people inside and outside government who share a set of beliefs. Although coalition members may come and go, the coalitions themselves are relatively stable, because core beliefs are resistant to change over time. Think of the core beliefs that drive the various coalitions and actors in the abortion debate or the debate over gun control. These coalitions strategize against each other and make use of available resources to influence the decisions of lawmakers or authoritative decisionmakers.[13] Governmental authorities are the key decisionmakers, and their actions are shaped by rules, available resources, and appointments. The end results are policy outputs (laws, executive orders, and other government actions) that have impacts that serve to further influence the response of the competing coalitions.

The various participants in policy subsystems do not exist in isolation. They are impacted and constrained by a number of factors, including available resources, the degree of consensus needed for major policy change, and other variables that change over the short- and long-term. The ACF identifies variables that tend to change frequently due to external or system events. In this

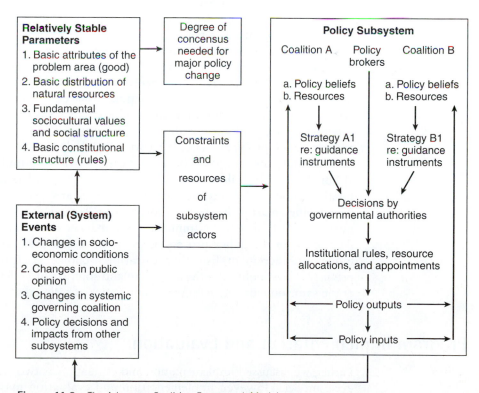

Figure 11.2 The Advocacy Coalition Framework Model

SOURCE: Sabatier, Paul. From *Theories of the Policy Process.* Reprinted by permission of Westview Press, a member of Perseus Books Group.

framework, "frequently" means over a ten-year period. These could include changes in the economy, swings in national mood or public opinion, or changes resulting from elections. Relatively stable system variables include constitutional rules, fundamental elements of the national character, and geopolitical forces. The ACF is particularly valuable in suggesting elements in policy change and the motivations behind coalitions. It reflects a systems view of the policy process. The ACF has been used to study educational reform in Michigan,[14] hazardous waste in the Netherlands,[15] public lands policy in the United States,[16] auto pollution control policy in California,[17] as well as other public policies around the world.

The Policy Paradox

Deborah Stone provides an elegant explanation of the policy process in her book *The Policy Paradox*. She asserts that academic disciplines such as political science and public administration strive to bring more rationality (i.e., scientific analysis) to the policy process. However, rational policy-making is impossible for public organizations. According to Stone, if viewed in relation to rational policy-making, "politics looks messy, foolish, erratic, and inexplicable." Indeed, rational analysis provides but an incomplete picture of policy, because, "The very categories of thought underlying rational analysis are themselves a kind of paradox, defined in political struggle."[18]

While policy itself is paradoxical, it can still be analyzed by breaking it down into three core elements: goals, problems, and solutions. Often the goals of policy are in conflict with each other (e.g., equity and efficiency). Furthermore, the goals themselves are open to multiple interpretations, which are themselves in conflict. Given this situation, Stone concludes that "the goals of policy are thus vague, contradictory, and protean." She defines problems as a "statement of a goal and the discrepancy between it and the status quo." To express policy problems, people resort to symbols (stories and other literary devices) and numbers. Both have the "capacity to have multiple meanings," although they also allow the problems to be better understood by everyone. Finally, policy solutions, according to Stone, are "ongoing strategies for structuring relationships and coordinating behavior to achieve collective purposes."[19] It should be immediately apparent to the reader that Stone's description of the policy process bears closer resemblance to the garbage can model and incrementalism than to rational choice. It clearly points to the primary role of politics in the definition and solution of policy problems while at the same time downplaying the significance of rational analysis.

Program Implementation and Evaluation

Earlier, we discussed implementation and evaluation as two stages in the policy cycle model. However, implementation and evaluation may be studied and understood apart from this model of the policy process. Each is discussed below.

Implementation

Implementation The stage of the policy process in which policies are carried out by public agencies; it recognizes that the actual outcomes of a program may not resemble what the decisionmakers originally intended.

Implementation is the stage of the policy process in which policies are carried out by public agencies, but the actual outcomes of a program may not resemble what the decisionmakers originally intended. Every policy results in at least three realities: policy in intention, policy in action, and policy in experience.[20] This notion recognizes that policy, as developed and intended by lawmakers, may markedly differ from the policy put into effect or implemented by agents of government, while the policy eventually experienced by the public may be something else entirely. Those who develop polices are usually not the ones who put them into effect. Pressman and Wildavsky addressed this phenomenon in a landmark work that analyzed why efforts to increase minority employment in Oakland California by a well-funded agency of the federal government, the Economic Development Administration, failed in the 1960s. The long title of the book is a particularly clever introduction to the contents: *Implementation: How Great Expectations in Washington Are Dashed in Oakland; or, why it's amazing that federal programs work at all, this being a saga of the Economic Development Administration as told by two sympathetic observes who seek to build morals on a foundation of ruined hopes.*

In the Oakland case, it initially appeared as though all the means for success were at hand. Plenty of funds were available, public and private entities were in agreement, agencies were staffed by dedicated and hard-working professionals, and there was a sense of urgency. The project was developed during a time of social unrest. Policymakers saw economic development leading to minority employment as a means of avoiding race riots. Despite the dedication of $23 million in federal funds in 1968, only $3 million were actually spent by 1969, and most of that went to a highway project that probably would have been built without the federal initiative.[21] But the program involved a myriad of players at the federal, state, local, and private levels. Each agency had its own agenda and definition of success, conflicting organizational goals, and preferences. As the authors conclude, "the multiplicity of participants and perspectives combined to produce a formidable obstacle course for the program. When a program depends on so many actors, there are numerous possibilities for disagreement and delay."[22]

The larger the number of participants involved, the greater the chance that a program will be distorted, changed, co-opted, or delayed. Pressman and Wildavsky also used probability theory to demonstrate that the ultimate success of public programs requires near-perfection in execution at each step in the process. Failure in any link in the chain of implementation practically guarantees failure for the program as a whole. Pressman and Wildavsky point out that even if a venture can be assured of a 90 percent likelihood of success at each step, it takes only seven steps to lower the probability of total program success to below 50 percent![23]

Given that public policies are hard to implement, what can administrators do to even the odds? Steven Kelman suggests several things that can be done to "have a fighting chance of success" in this endeavor. First, administrators must plan early. Second, they must be willing to deal with contingencies and other unforeseen problems. Third, planning requires group decision-making. Fourth, it helps to keep the program as simple as possible, since this reduces the need for a lot of coordination and control. Finally, successful implementation might require changing organizational culture.[24]

Pressman and Wildavsky's work was more than a call for simplicity in execution; it also sought a deeper understanding of the nature of policy. They observed that policy objectives are often vague, multiple, and contested, while our ability to understand is limited and the environment is constantly changing. They saw policy implementation as the process of constantly shifting relationships between resource constraints and objectives. Policy could not be viewed as an inclusive model or blueprint handed off to government workers to dutifully execute according to plan. According to Wildavsky: "If planning were judged by results, that is, by whether life followed the dictates of the plan, then planning has failed everywhere it has been tried. Nowhere are plans fulfilled. No one, it turns out, has the knowledge to predict sequences of actions and reactions across the realm of public policy, and no one has the power to compel obedience."[25] On the other hand, there is clearly a need for accountability in implementation, lest programs morph in ways outside of or in conflict with the intent of lawmakers. Programs are not fire and forget systems. They exist in an environment of democratic accountability wherein they must bear the continuous scrutiny of elected officials and the public at large.

Pressman and Wildavsky's research heralded an era of high-quality implementation studies that sought to gain insights into policy in action. Of particular interest was a means for determining whether programs could be deemed successes or failures. Programs are labeled as failures when they provide inconsistent service, not enough service, or the wrong service to the targeted population. Case studies like Pressman and Wildavsky's focused on a specific policy and provided context-rich insights into successes and failures of government programs. Some studies attempted to identify factors in general that contribute to successful program implementation. One study identified four variables that contribute to program success or failure: (1) quality and effectiveness of communication between decisionmakers and implementers; (2) sufficiency of resources such as staff, authority, equipment, and funds; (3) dispositions or attitudes of those implementing the policy; and (4) appropriate bureaucratic structure.[26]

Evaluation The means of determining what actually happens after policy approval; it involves an assessment of program processes and impacts, focusing on aspects that are observable or measurable.

Evaluation

The concept of implementation is closely associated with that of program **evaluation**, because it is through evaluation that interested parties obtain information about the reality of policy in action and policy in experience.[27] One definition of program evaluation is: "The use of social research procedures to systematically investigate the effectiveness of social intervention programs that is adapted to their political and organizational environments and designed to inform social action in ways that improve social conditions."[28] At the heart of evaluation is the concept that some relative worth or value can be attached to programs in order to judge their effectiveness and efficiency.

Evaluation is the means for answering the questions of what is happening to whom and at what cost. It provides a feedback loop to policymakers and implementers as they continually react to the public's demands for service. The means of doing so encompass a wide variety of methods of social science research, including survey research, program monitoring through management information systems, interviews and observation, experimentation, and cost-benefit or cost-efficiency analysis. (For more on management information systems, see Chapter 15).

Evaluation research gained prominence after the Great Society initiatives of the 1960s as questions arose over whether expensive and expansive programs were accomplishing their intended effects. Application of sophisticated social science research methods was heralded as a means to determine what works and what doesn't. Despite the rational basis of program evaluation, it takes place in a highly charged political environment that accounts for the contentious nature with which evaluation results are often received. It also helps explain why program administrators and policymakers often do not act on the best efforts and recommendations of evaluation researchers, an observation that causes no small amount of consternation among evaluators. Today, evaluation researchers are encouraged to conduct careful analysis of stakeholders (interested parties) and to determine the real purpose for an evaluation request before committing themselves to a project.[29] The objective for the evaluator is to provide information useful in developing future programs or modifying existing programs to better accomplish their intended purpose. In some cases this leads to recommendations that a program be expanded, curtailed, or cancelled—findings that will inevitably result in ardent challenge or support from those invested in the running of the program or its opponents. Evaluation reports rarely lack controversy.

While recognizing that no two evaluations are exactly alike, Rossi, Freeman, and Lipsey identify five common approaches to evaluation based on the types of organizational questions they address. First, needs assessments identify the scope and nature of problems in need of intervention. Second, program theory assessments make explicit how the program is supposed to attain its goals and then whether that approach is appropriate to the task. Third, process evaluations are oriented to the implementation phase of a program and are interested in how well the program is operating. Fourth, impact assessments are designed to determine the extent to which a program accomplished its intended outcome. Lastly, efficiency assessments are focused on the relationship of costs to program outcomes.[30] The environment of evaluation and the wide variety of tools available to the researcher suggest that the skilled evaluator is as much an artist and diplomat as scientist.

■ Chapter Summary

Various theories and models help us to understand the complexities of the policy process. The policy cycle depicts a process of eight discrete stages or steps: (1) agenda setting, (2) problem definition, (3) alternative selection, (4) authoritative decision-making, (5) policy design, (6) program implementation, (7) program evaluation, and (8) termination or change. Incrementalism views policy change as proceeding through a number of small steps or incremental adjustments over time. The policy streams model highlights the unpredictable nature of policy changes by focusing on the complexity of the mix of factors that lead to the emergence of an issue on the policy agenda. Rational choice models assert that the policy process can be treated like a mathematical problem; these models suggest that policy problems can be solved through the application of sophisticated methods like game theory. The policy paradox model, however, asserts that policy-making is anything but rational. Policy-making is a political art.

It should be clear that varying approaches are appropriate, given the lack of a grand theory and the desire to focus on a particular aspect of policy. The student interested in how policy changes over time might be well served by applying different facets of each theory.

The chapter also examines program implementation and evaluation. Implementation is a critical (perhaps the most critical) stage of the policy process and one that is still not well understood. It often poses seemingly insurmountable difficulties for administrators, who have to navigate a complex maze of players and their agendas. Finally, program evaluation is designed to get at the heart of the effectiveness and efficiency question for government programs. This often entails the use of quite sophisticated techniques and methods. Evaluation often occurs within a highly contentious setting as the fate of programs, or at least their reputations, might be at stake.

■ Chapter Discussion Questions

1. Why is it important to examine multiple theories and frameworks when explaining the policy process?

2. What are the advantages and disadvantages of viewing policy as a cycle or series of discrete stages?

3. What is the media's role in the policy process when issues escape policy subsystems?

4. According to Ostrom's framework, what constrains the actions of decisionmakers as they address public problems?

5. Why is there often such a difference between what policymakers intend when they authorize governmental programs and what happens at the local level when those programs are implemented?

BRIEF CASE   MARKETING THE ARMY TO GENERATION X

Despite force reductions resulting in the smallest U.S. Army since World War II, recruiters experienced increasing difficulty attracting qualified enlistees in the late 1990s. In fiscal year 1999, the army missed its recruiting goal by 8 percent, reflecting a shortfall of over 6,000 soldiers. A healthy economy, record low unemployment, and increased college enrollment from high school contributed to the problem. Increased enlistment bonuses and college tuition grants failed to attract sufficient recruits. In response, Congress approved $113 million to aid military recruiting, an increase from $85 million two years earlier.

In 2001, the army changed its long-standing recruiting motto from "Be All You Can Be" to "An Army of One." The new slogan replaced one of America's most recognized advertising campaigns, one that had been used for two decades. The new approach emphasized the U.S. Army as a collection of individual soldiers, each with a unique story. Slick television and print media commercials focused on the challenges and triumphs of specific named soldiers. The campaign was influenced in part by market research indicating that the young men and women of Generation X comprising the pool of eligible recruits were concerned about losing their individual identity.

In this example, we see that the problem of low enlistment was defined as a recruiting or marketing problem, a definition that at its outset held preset solutions, including increased spending on bonuses and advertisement. When financial inducements failed, emphasis switched to one of improving the army's image through advertising, but it remained essentially defined as a recruiting problem. Why wasn't the problem identified as one resulting from how recruits are treated once they enter the army? Such a problem definition would involve a completely different set of potential solutions, ones that would likely be associated with attitudes and practices within the organization. It is a definition that would require solutions that are potentially more difficult to implement and potentially threatening to some. The definition of the problem as a recruiting rather than an organizational issue therefore may have represented solutions preferred by the dominant group of policymakers.

Brief Case Questions

1. *What factors caused the army recruitment problem to reach the agenda of policymakers?*

2. *What possible alternative solutions are suggested if the problem is defined not as a recruiting problem but as an inability to keep trained personnel after they enlist? In what other ways could this problem be defined?*

3. *Who stood to gain by defining the problem as a marketing issue? Why?*

■ Key Terms

advocacy coalition framework (ACF) (page 268)
evaluation (page 272)
game theory (page 266)
garbage can model (page 264)
implementation (page 271)
incrementalism (page 263)

policy cycle (page 259)
policy streams (page 264)
policy subsystems (page 264)
Prisoner's Dilemma (page 266)
public policy (page 258)
rational choice (page 266)

■ On the Web

http://www.thisnation.com/public.html
    This website discusses the policy process
    with examples and research and study helps.

http://www.movingideas.org/, http://www.brook.
edu/, and http://www.ppionline.org/
    Moving Ideas, the Brookings Institution,
    and the Progressive Policy Institute present
    analysis of the policy process from a liberal
    perspective.

http://www.cato.org/, http://www.heritage.org/,
http://www.aei.org/
    The Cato Institute, Heritage Institute, and
    American Enterprise Institute's websites fea-
    ture policy analysis from a conservative
    angle.

http://www.rand.org/
    The website of the independent, nonprofit
    Rand Institute features many links to the
    organization's reports

CHAPTER 12

Privatization and Public Administration

▨ SETTING THE STAGE

The following two accounts reach dramatically different conclusions regarding privatization.

> "Maximus was one of the for-profit private companies the state of Wisconsin selected to operate the welfare program in Milwaukee County. The company appeared to operate as if it had complete latitude in how it spent taxpayers' money."
>
> The nonpartisan Wisconsin Legislative Audit Bureau reported in the summer of 2000 that Maximus violated its contract through questionable expenditures of more than $700,000, which included charging Wisconsin for questionable business expenses. The company also charged the state for various items including employee parties, hotels, meals for top executives and even thousands of dollars just for doughnuts. The company also spent $1.1 million of taxpayer money on advertising that appeared more likely to promote Maximus as a company than to have any role in informing, attracting or providing support to people with low incomes.[1]

> During Mayor Rudolph Giuliani's tenure, New York City pursued an aggressive program of privatization. During his administration, the city engaged in a number of high-profile privatizing efforts including selling city assets, using vouchers, and contracting out many city functions to private companies. According to one estimate, the city's one-time revenues from sales were at least $2.2 billion with an additional savings of more than a billion dollars a year resulting from the other privatization initiatives. The city used competition to improve the productivity of its workforce as well as to cut its expenses.[2]

The first example, on the Maximus corporation, is from the American Federation of State and County Municipal Employees (AFSCME), a public employees' union strongly opposed to turning government services over to private firms. The New York City example is from the Reason Public Policy Institute, a nonpartisan think tank that promotes the use of market forces by government. As these examples show, perhaps no other issue sparks as much difference of opinion within the public administration community as does

Privatization The transferring of functions and property from the government to private for-profit or nonprofit entities.

privatization. People with strong views can be found on both sides of the privatization debate. Some view privatization as a practical way to deal with problems of shrinking budgets and declining tax revenues; others view it as an attempt by ideologically motivated foes of government to cut the size of the public workforce and reduce government expenditures.

The strong emotions aroused by the topic are unsurprising, considering its enormous implications for public employees and public service delivery, not to mention its broader political ramifications. As with so much in public administration, attitudes on privatization are also intertwined with deeply held beliefs and values regarding the proper role of government in society. As one author asserts, "Whether a job belongs within or outside government . . . relates to personal values and views concerning the relationship between the individual and the state."[3]

◼ CHAPTER PLAN

In the first section of this chapter, we define privatization and briefly discuss different types and various rationales for privatization. We highlight several practical and theoretical problems that market-like service arrangements are designed to solve, and we discuss some of the chief economic and political arguments for privatization and the conditions and requirements for its optimal use by government. Next, we examine privatization trends and the experience of different levels of government with using private delivery of services. In the next section, we discuss four major problems associated with government's use of private companies to provide public services. The chapter concludes with an examination of civil society and privatization.

The Whats and Whys of Privatization

Although there is disagreement over the use of privatization, there is general consensus within public administration over what it means. Most would agree with one author that privatization is essentially "government's use of the private sector (both for profit and not for profit) to implement public programs."[4] Moreover, another author suggests that "privatization is the act of reducing the role of government, or increasing the role of the private sector, in an activity or in the ownership of assets."[5] Both authors imply that privatization results in a transfer of governmental authority to the private sector, or a transfer of assets from the public to the private sector (in this case, private refers to both for-profit and nonprofit organizations). This is done, according to theory, because the public sector is awash in rules, regulations, and red tape; whereas, in a market environment, there are fewer such restrictions. Consequently, privatization is supposed to result in cost savings, increased efficiency, and improved workforce productivity. Before we can discuss these claims, however, we must specify exactly what we mean by privatization, starting with the different arrangements that are covered by the term.

Types of Privatization

The four types of market-like arrangements most commonly used by government (here and abroad) are contracting out, load shedding, vouchers,

Public education is
one area where there
has been
considerable debate
over the pros and
cons of privatization.
SOURCE: Ellen B. Senisi/
The Image Works

Contracting out An
arrangement whereby
the government enters
into an agreement with
a private company to
provide a service for
citizens.

and asset selling. **Contracting out** refers to a legal relationship (a contract or other formal agreement) between government and a private organization, including nonprofits, for the purchase of goods or services (see Figure 12.1). It is the most common form of privatization arrangement in the United States.[6] For example, most of the equipment, supplies and facilities used by government are purchased or rented from private firms. The Department of

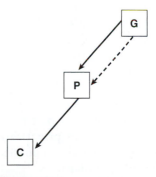

Contracting Out

Government authorizes (solid line) and pays
(dashed line) private business or nonprofit
organization to provide services for citizens

G = Government
P = Private business or nonprofit ogranization
C = Citizens

Figure 12.1   Contracting Out

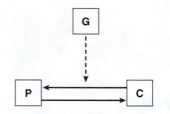

Loadshedding

Government relinquishes authority to provide services and allows citizens to make arrangements for services with private businesses directly

G = Government
P = Private business or nonprofit ogranization
C = Citizens

Figure 12.2   Load Shedding

Defense contracts out most of its annual budget; in fiscal year 2000, for instance, the department spent $102.1 billion on contracts with private companies.[7]

Governments at all levels contract out services. E. S. Savas identified no fewer than 180 city and county services that are contracted out, including airport operation, bridge management, cafeteria and restaurant operation, day care, environmental services, foster-home care, golf-course operation, housing inspection and code enforcement, insect and rodent control, jail and detention, library operation, museum management, nursing, opinion polling, park maintenance, risk management, school bus services, tax collection, utility billing, vehicle maintenance, water pollution abatement, and zoning.[8] Contracting out is an example of the increased blurring of the line that separates the private from the public sector.

Load shedding is more controversial than contracting out, and it is less frequently used. In load shedding, government completely discontinues a service (see Figure 12.2). For example, a municipal government may decide that it can no longer afford to run its public hospitals, so it closes them permanently, forcing citizens to rely on private hospitals. Load-shedding represents a serious attempt on government's part to reduce both its service responsibilities and expenses.[9] This form of privatization, however, has not been very popular, since officials fear the loss of political power attendant on shedding public services, especially popular ones.[10]

Vouchers are government coupons that allow recipients to purchase goods or services from private organizations at a lower than market price as a result of subsidies (see Figure 12.3). The use of vouchers is well established in certain government functions, including education, housing, job training, and health care for senior citizens. The federal government is probably the most frequent user of vouchers, although state and local governments have started employing this arrangement more often.

Load shedding A situation in which the government stops providing a service or good for the citizens, which forces citizens to turn to other providers if they want the good or service.

Vouchers Government coupons that allow citizens to purchase services from a private provider; the government agrees to pay the organization the amount of the coupon.

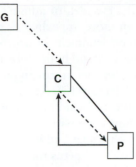

Government subsidizes (dashed line) citizens to
authorize (dashed line) and pay for (solid line)
services from private businesses (solid line)
G = Government
P = Private business or nonprofit ogranization
C = Citizens

Figure 12.3   Vouchers

Asset selling An
arrangement whereby
governments sell off
companies or other
assets that they own.

   In **asset selling**, governments sell off companies or other assets that they
own. Selling off government assets is relatively uncommon in the United
States. Other nations, however, make far greater use of this tool. The reasons
for this are both historical and cultural: in contrast to other countries, governments in the United States typically do not own companies, industrial facilities,
or other commercial assets to sell.

   The two most popular forms of privatization in the United States, contracting out and vouchers, are subject to significant government control of
public services while attempting to obtain efficiencies through market forces.
With privatization, the government continues to provide and pay for a service,
but a private firm instead of a public agency is responsible for delivery of the
service.

The Rationales for Privatization

Recently, the CEO of a private firm involved in taking over the operations of
an inner-city public school district claimed: "A business is business. Money is
money. . . . It's our job to try and figure out how to take more of the dollars
and redeploy them to instruction, to make sure these kids are getting a better
education."[11] The CEO's statement strongly implies that a large city's public
schools can be run like any other "business." The notion that "government
can be operated like a business" has been a constant refrain throughout the
history of American public administration.[12] In some respects, privatization is
simply another variation on this familiar theme of public administration.
However, recent advocates of privatization generally show a more sophisticated understanding of the differences between the private and public sectors
than do earlier writers.

Recently, the idea of administering government more like a business has become even more appealing as a result of economic and political pressures creating an environment in which the public sector must try to do more with less. Citizens demand both more and better-quality public services even as they resist paying for them through higher taxes (see, for example, the case study at the end of Chapter 13). At the same time, economic downturns and budget deficits result in dwindling revenues for government at all levels. Politicians must somehow cope with a public that is disillusioned with government taxing and spending policies and willing to show its displeasure at election time. This has provided the impetus for public officials' strong interest in privatization. A study found that elected officials' responses to a survey "suggested that reducing costs and improving service were the two most important factors in the decision to privatize services."[13]

While some politicians view privatization as a way to cut costs and improve services, others regard it as a possible solution to a number of other serious problems with government. These problems can be grouped into the following four broad categories:

1. Public sector inefficiency, in part, stemming from
2. too many rules and regulations dictating what public organizations can do, whom they can employ, how they budget, etc.;
3. too much political interference in public administration; and
4. financial losses stemming from public ownership (this is more common outside the United States).[14]

Why is the use of market forces viewed as a potential solution to such a wide-ranging set of economic and political problems, some of which may be inherent in the nature of public service (e.g., rules, regulations, and red tape)? Above we noted that the chief rationale for privatization is reducing costs and improving efficiency of public services. In addition to the economic rationale, however, many scholars observe a political reason for privatization. Indeed, some argue that the political aspects can be just as important as economic ones to decisionmakers. What follows is a discussion of the major economic and political rationales for privatization.

Economic Rationale Arguments in support of shifting public functions to private entities generally emphasize two separate but related causes for government's failures—the economic and political. Economic causes are the best known and typically the most persuasive to decisionmakers. The economic rationale is based largely on the work of economists and others who propose the use of market forces to improve public service delivery and cut government costs. Privatization expert E. S. Savas, for example, uses an economic argument when he says that the bulk of government activities no longer involve providing pure collective, or social, goods.[15] Pure collective goods are ones that no one can be prevented from using (e.g., national defense, air and water quality, public health, etc.) and, therefore, must be provided by government. He argues, however, that impure, or mixed, collective goods and services can be delivered more efficiently using private, market-like arrangements.

The economic rationale can be divided into three positions: (1) the private sector is economically superior to the public sector; (2) economic competition helps to bring down costs ("the competition prescription"); and (3) certain service functions are performed better by one sector over the other ("functional matching"). Supporters of the first position contend that government is inherently inefficient and wasteful. Thus, only private provision of services can keep costs down and improve productivity. Proponents of the first position generally seek to reduce the size of government and want to decrease government's role in society. Proponents of the second position argue that government often behaves like a monopoly, and that any monopoly, whether public or private, is economically wasteful and inefficient. The solution, in their view, is the introduction of competition in the form of market-like arrangements, with competition for market share and resources. The third position is based on the argument that "certain functions are most efficiently and effectively performed by the private sector, others by the nonprofit sector, and others by government." For example, public safety is a function best performed by government, nursing care is best performed by nonprofits, and general construction is best performed by private firms.[16] Accountability is the critical factor in assigning function to a particular sector. Functions such as public safety and criminal justice, where accountability concerns are foremost, should be performed by government and not by private organizations, according to this principle.

Political Rationale The chief political reason for privatizing stems from a desire to reduce the size of government agencies and programs; moreover, "Some proponents even contend that privatization is synonymous with reducing the size and *effects* of government."[17] As some argue, a government that is too large poses a threat to individual freedoms. Proponents defend this position by pointing out that the framers of the Constitution also worried about excessive governmental powers. Thus, the founders created a political system designed to keep the powers of government in check. According to the political rationale, current application of this principle requires cutting the size of the public sector and transferring more authority to the private sector.

When to Privatize

The previous discussion dealt with privatization on an abstract level. While helpful, economic and political arguments for privatization provide limited guidance to officials faced with the decision of whether to privatize or not. On a more practical level, governments need criteria that will help them determine when it is most appropriate to use private organizations. Governments also need guidelines regarding conditions that are most likely to produce successful results when privatizing. All too often, however, they lack even this basic knowledge. As one group of researchers observed, "Government officials often do not know which functions can best be performed by public or private organizations with the maximum degree of efficiency, effectiveness, or equity."[18] In recognition of this problem, some scholars have identified six situations that are most favorable to successful privatizing efforts:

1. When government can precisely specify the task in advance and the firm's performance can be accurately evaluated

2. When poorly performing private contractors can be easily replaced

3. When the ends (results) are more important than the means (procedures)

4. When the firm has considerable experience in the policy area (e.g., health care, social services, etc.) and substantial respect in the policy community

5. When government can intervene in the event of poor performance

6. When the firm provides other useful public services[19]

The above guidelines, which cover for-profit and nonprofit organizations, offer some fairly specific conditions and requirements that are necessary to obtain the best privatization results. The guidelines also suggest further activities government should undertake to ensure success. For instance, to satisfy the first condition, government must have the analytical capacity to judge the success of its privatization efforts.[20] This means that before using a private firm, government should have staff available (or be able to hire external analysts) that can accurately assess the performance of the private organization.

Further, the second and fifth guidelines suggest that government should retain at least some minimal in-house capacity to prevent service interruptions should a private company perform poorly or is otherwise unable to fulfill its obligations.[21] A municipal government, for example, could contract out for snow-removal services while at the same time maintaining its own fleet of snow-removal vehicles. While this could mean overlapping services, some scholars argue that this can actually help government to take advantage of competition and bring down costs as well as achieve other service improvements: "Forcing agencies to compete in the area of service delivery causes the agencies to change their business practices and operational values to become more efficient, or lose the business that is their reason for existence."[22] In effect, proponents assert that cost savings and productivity improvements can be best obtained when there is competition, regardless of whether the service providers are private or public. However, overlapping services go against the grain of traditional organization theory, which claims that service duplication only results in waste and inefficiency.

The authors of a recent study nonetheless conclude that "Some forms of duplication and overlap can lead to greater cost efficiencies. . . . Such redundancies introduce rivalries."[23] In addition, an overlapping services strategy reduces the likelihood that government will be forced to continue with a private service provider because no other providers are available. Practically speaking, however, many governments may find it difficult to justify to taxpayers the expense of maintaining overlapping services when one of the chief reasons to privatize in the first place was to bring down the costs of government.

Advantages of Nonprofits

The fourth and sixth guidelines suggest a major role for nonprofit organizations in delivering public services. This is particularly true in certain functional areas, such as social services, where nonprofits tend to have considerable experience and to command respect within the community. Nonprofit agencies like the United Way and Salvation Army, just to take two important examples, are part of the social capital in many communities and play an important role in strengthening civil society. Moreover, the last few decades have witnessed a veritable explosion in the number of nonprofit organizations, fueled in no small measure by an increase in government funding opportunities. Indeed, nonprofit service providers now receive more than half their funding from government.[24]

Increasingly, governments must choose between nonprofit or for-profit organizations when contracting out services. How does a government decide between a private firm and a nonprofit organization? The scholarly research indicates there are some areas where the nonprofit sector has clear advantages over the private sector in delivering particular services. For example, Osborne and Gaebler recommend using nonprofit agencies for tasks that

- generate little or no profits
- require compassion and commitment to people
- entail a comprehensive, holistic approach

The Salvation Army plays an important role in strengthening civil society in communities across the United States.

SOURCE: Joe Skipper/ Reuters/Landov

- require extensive trust on the part of the customers or clients.
- involve volunteer labor.
- necessitate hands-on, personal attention such as in day care, counseling, and services to the handicapped or ill.[25]

Cohen observes there are "two types of governmental functions that private organizations seem poorly suited to perform: (1) those that regulate or remove the freedom or free movement of individuals; and (2) activities that have no obvious customers with the resources to provide a profit to the organization that performs it." An example of the first type is the police, while an example of the second is homeless housing. In both cases, a nonprofit organization would be better suited to delivering the service than a private firm, according to Cohen. A nonprofit organization "provides the government with some of the advantages of privatization, but also provides the benefit of a staff that is mission driven and an organization that has a positive public image."[26] Nonetheless, increasing costs have driven governments to use private firms even in governmental functions that are better suited for nonprofits.

Recent Privatization Trends

Governments at all levels have used some form of privatization at one time or another during their history. The last few decades, however, have witnessed a huge explosion in these efforts, particularly at the federal level. The federal government spends an estimated $125 billion annually on the purchase of goods and services from private firms.[27] President George W. Bush has made privatizing federal functions one of the cornerstones of his attempts to streamline the federal bureaucracy. Early in his administration, President Bush asked federal agencies to review thousands of federal activities for possible off-loading to private firms. President Bush's efforts to privatize the federal government are a continuation of a long-standing trend, however. Even before he took office, the number of privately employed workers paid for by federal contracts exceeded by more than three times the total number of federal civilian employees.[28] In recent years, state and local governments have also moved aggressively to privatize services.

The Federal Government

Private companies have been employed by the federal government throughout the nation's history, but no formal policies were enacted until President Eisenhower issued an executive order in 1955, which required the federal government to purchase commercial goods and services in order to avoid competing with business firms. This policy was later amended by another executive document that identified certain government functions as being "inherently governmental in nature" (or "intimately related to the public interest") and therefore should not be contracted out. As previously noted, the reinvention movement endorsed privatization as a means to improve governmental performance. Consequently, as part of President Clinton's National Performance Review, the federal government during the 1990s took several steps to increase opportunities for privatizing government services.

The Office of Management and Budget (OMB) is responsible for administering the federal contracting system through its Office of Federal Procurement Policy. The size of the bureaucracy overseeing federal contracting is immense, requiring 67,000 employees in the "core procurement workforce."[29] As noted, George W. Bush sought to promote efforts to privatize the federal government soon after he took office. He asked the Office of Federal Procurement Policy to conduct a thorough review of current federal policies and practices. The administration's actions, however, alarmed thousands of federal employees who felt their jobs were threatened. Under the administration's plan, agencies would contract out 15 percent of all positions by 2004 and 20 percent per year after that. President Bush requested agencies in 2001, under the FAIR act, to identify positions that were commercial in nature in order that they might be contracted out. In all, the agencies identified some 850,000 positions. The Bush administration's original intention was to privatize at least half those jobs. As of this writing, there has not been an estimate of the number of federal jobs privatized as a result of this program.

In addition to contracting out, vouchers are another important tool of federal policy that involves using private service providers. Vouchers have been in use since the 1970s; however, the 1990s saw an upsurge in their use by the federal government. As previously noted, vouchers allow citizens to choose to receive their services from among several government-approved service providers. The government distributes vouchers to eligible citizens, who use them to pay for services from private companies, which are then reimbursed by the government for the amount of the vouchers. A voucher program can be empowering for citizens, since they use the vouchers to choose their own service providers and do not have to depend on the government to deliver the service.

Charitable choice The 1996 welfare reform legislation allows religious institutions to receive government funding for the provision of services.

Faith-based organization An entity whose principal mission is religious (i.e., church, temple, synagogue) but which provides social welfare services as part of its religious mission.

The two major federal government voucher programs are food stamps and Medicare. The federal budget allocates $22 billion a year to the food stamp program, which serves more than 21 million people each year. Since 1982, Medicare recipients may use a voucher that lets them choose a government-approved health maintenance organization. The federal government also uses "housing certificates" to help subsidize poor rent payers, and the Workforce Investment Act of 1998 established a voucher program to assist people who enroll in federal job-training programs.

Another important development involves the **charitable choice** provisions of the 1996 welfare reform act. Charitable choice enables churches and other **faith-based organizations** (FBOs) to receive federal funds to provide social welfare services to low-income people. Upon taking office, President George W. Bush announced his "faith-based initiative," headed by a prominent civil society scholar, John DiIulio. Religious organizations had received federal subsidies for social services in the past, but now federal law allows FBOs to provide these services without "secularizing," that is, without concealing their religious identities. The regulations that required "concealment" were originally designed to prevent religious groups from trying to convert or otherwise impose their religious practices on consumers in violation of the Constitution's ban on state-imposed religion.

Supporters of the legislation believed it was necessary because FBOs are better than traditional nonprofit groups or government agencies in delivering social services. Yet there is a lack of conclusive proof that FBOs are any more effective than other agencies in solving social problems. For example, a study of a church-based antismoking program found that while the program was more effective than a "self-help" approach in getting smokers to quit, there was no evidence that the program's religious aspect made any difference in the outcome. Research examining the relationship between recovering drug addicts and membership in a religious community also found no definite link between behavior and religious participation.[30] Despite the absence of data indicating that religious programs are any more effective than their nonreligious counterparts, it is clear that FBOs will continue to play a key role in social service delivery. Perhaps, over time, FBOs will substantiate the faith of their supporters and prove to be at least as effective as traditional social service agencies in helping poor and underserved communities.

Federal Employee Unions and Privatization

Since the 1980s, public employee unions have struggled with the federal government over the right to provide input in decisions involving the transfer of public jobs to the private sector. It is unsurprising that the unions and government should collide over this issue, since it is obviously something that both sides feel strongly about. Unions feel threatened by the loss of jobs due to contracting out, while the government views the decision as a management prerogative and as part of a strategy to streamline operations and reduce costs.

Federal policy encourages private contracting. The OMB requires that an agency contract out if a private firm can perform the same activities at less expense than the agency. Public employee unions accept this principle but assert that federal policy gives them the opportunity to have a say in the decision. They point to federal personnel rules that "encourage" participation by employees and their representative organizations in the contracting-out process. Further, the unions assert that the National Labor Relations Act requires that labor and management collectively bargain over the "impact and implementation of matters affecting employee working conditions."[31] The unions claim that since contracting out affects their workers' employment situation, the decision should therefore be subject to collective bargaining. Generally, however, the Federal Labor Relations Authority (FLRA) and the courts have favored management's side over the unions' on the question of privatization.

State Governments

State governments have embraced privatization as strongly as the federal government. States tend to rely heavily on contracting out, which accounts for over four-fifths of all state government efforts to privatize.[32] Figure 12.4 shows the number of state government services privatized by state. The areas of state governments most affected by privatization are education and transportation; health and social services are the functions least affected. Figure 12.5 shows the trend in state privatization during the 1990s. More than 86 percent of the respondents to a survey of state governments said they either increased or maintained their levels of privatization activity over this period. These same respondents expected this trend to continue, with over 85 percent saying that they would either expand or maintain current levels of privatization. The most common reasons given for increases in privatizing activity are cutting costs (40.9 percent) and lack of state personnel and expertise (32.5 percent).[33]

Local Governments

The same fiscal and political pressures spurring aggressive privatizing efforts at the federal and state levels are also at work at the local level, with much the same results. More than one-fourth of all city and county services are now delivered by nongovernment organizations.[34] Furthermore, local governments "are now expanding privatization into service areas that would not have been

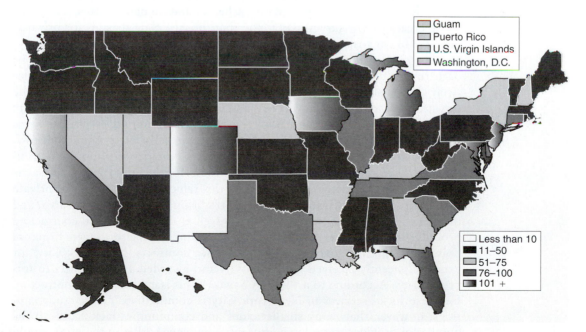

Figure 12.4   Number of Privatized State Functions by States

SOURCE: Council of State Governments Survey on Privatization in State Government, 1997.

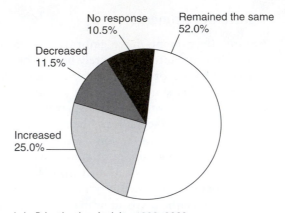

Figure 12.5   Trends in Privatization Activity, 1998–2002
A majority of agencies (77 percent) said they either increased or maintained the level of privatization in the past five years.

SOURCE: Keon S. Chi, Kelly A. Arnold, and Heather M. Perkins, "Privatization in State Government: Trends and Issues," *Spectrum: The Journal of State Government*, http://www.csg.org.

considered appropriate for privatization even a decade ago."[35] Virtually no local government service has been left untouched by this trend. Privatization does not affect all local public functions equally, though. Of all the municipal services privatized by the localities responding to a recent survey, most were in the public works, transportation, and government support areas, while a considerable number were in public safety, health and human services, and parks and recreation. The survey also found that the two chief reasons for privatizing were to cut costs and improve services.[36]

The most striking privatization trend at the local level, however, may be occurring in the area of social services, which until the 1990s had been relatively free of such efforts. Local governments are turning increasingly to the private sector in order to lower costs and improve services in the social welfare area, spurred on in large measure by welfare reform initiatives. Private firms have had to create a market in social services virtually from scratch. Historically, few for-profit organizations (as opposed to religious or nonprofit organizations) have received government contracts for social services. As Savas points out, several factors contributed to this reluctance on the part of private firms: For example, private firms had no tradition of working in the area, and they faced numerous barriers to entry, as well as a lack of formal contracting procedures. But times are changing, and a growing number of private firms are now competing for government social service contracts. New York City, for example, recently received 328 proposals and awarded 102 contracts to for-profit firms. According to a study by Savas, "This is evidence that contracting for these social services in New York City is competitive."[37] The study cautions, however, that many smaller cities and communities lack access to the number of providers found in a large city like New York and therefore would be unable to take advantage of competition's benefits.

Privatization Outcomes

As the earlier discussion shows, the use of privatization by government is not a new or temporary experiment. Indeed, government at all levels has had considerable experience contracting with private firms to deliver public services. This has spurred a great deal of analysis of the outcomes of such efforts. Summarizing some of the principal trends in privatizing in 2002, one study found that the primary reasons for privatization included cost savings, flexibility and less red tape, high-quality service, lack of government personnel or expertise, and speedy implementation.[38]

One of the principal reasons for privatization has been to cut government costs. Thus, it is unsurprising that cost reduction has been one of the principal benefits of privatization, according to the research. Further, local officials hope for improvements in services. One study examining privatization in sixty-six cities, for example, found significant cost savings in several service areas, ranging from nearly 21 percent in public works and transportation service to over 16 percent in government support functions. The same study also found substantial improvements in service delivery. Overall, the city officials were generally satisfied with their cities' efforts.[39]

Typically, improving governmental efficiency is one of the chief concerns of public officials when deciding whether to privatize. Scholarship on the connection between privatization and efficiency makes clear that competition is the key factor in cost savings, rather than simply whether a private firm or government provides the service. In other words, merely contracting out a service to a private provider does not guarantee that it will be done any more efficiently. Generally, the promise of greater efficiency helps spark local government's initial interest in privatization. As we saw in the case of social services, however, for many local governments, real efficiency gains turn out to be more difficult to achieve, since the absence of acceptable service providers within their jurisdiction curtails the possibility of competition. Thus, local governments, particularly nonurban ones, cannot take advantage of the cost savings that real competition offers. For example, although local governments in Oregon could cut costs by using private companies for public works projects, in rural areas it made more sense economically to use the public workforce instead.[40]

Not all government decisions to privatize can be explained solely on the basis of cutting costs or efficiency. An examination of municipal utilities privatization found that the municipalities wanted to "maintain existing relationships that are comfortable and do not threaten funding levels and established procedures."[41] Ironically, those were precisely the types of arrangement that the use of private providers was designed to replace. Another study found that over time, institutional factors (for example, the practices of other local governments) became more important than purely economic considerations in a locality's decision to privatize. In other words, cities are influenced by the privatization experiences of other cities. Further, the ability of any government to employ private providers also depends to a large degree on the existence of political obstacles such as public sector unions and other hostile groups.[42] Based on the evidence, privatization can offer tangible benefits to the governments that are in a position to take advantage of those benefits. However, not all governments are in such a position.

Problems with Privatization

Adverse selection In principal–agent theory, a situation in which the wrong firm is chosen to do something and therefore the desired outcome fails to occur.

As the Wisconsin example at the beginning of the chapter indicates, there are some problematic aspects of privatization. Some of these drawbacks arise out of the nature of the relationship between government and private firms in contracting out. Such a contracting arrangement has two inherent drawbacks. First, **adverse selection** might occur: The wrong firm might be chosen to perform a task. For example, a government might contract with a private firm that is unable to produce the desired outcomes. **Moral hazard** poses a second potential problem: Since a firm cannot be observed by the government at all times, the contractor may do less than the government wants or may fail to perform in the desired way.[43] It is difficult and expensive for government to always monitor the firm to make sure it is doing what it is supposed to. Finally, there may be **principal–agent conflict**. It is likely that the goals of the principal (government) and agent (private firm) will come into conflict in at least some cases and possibly more.[44] For example, government may want to make sure that a service is being delivered fairly and is available to everyone who is eligible, while the firm may be most concerned with its own profit margin. This may entail the firm's cutting services in certain high-cost areas or among high-cost populations to maintain profits.

Moral hazard A situation where a private provider fails to perform as desired because the government cannot monitor the organization at all times.

Principal–agent conflict The goals of the principal (government) and agent (private provider) are likely to conflict in at least some cases.

Accountability Problems

Public function test The determination of whether a power is traditionally reserved to the government.

Other criticisms of market-like arrangement revolve around public accountability issues. These have to do with the law's ambiguity regarding who is and who is not a public entity, and thus who ultimately bears the responsibility for actions taken in the public's name. Currently, according to Gilmour and Jensen, the courts "hold the government and its officials accountable legally for their behavior in order to protect the constitutional and statutory rights of citizens." Moreover, the courts tend to maintain a fairly clear-cut distinction between public and private actors, and consequently, "If private actors are not subject to the rules set for government action, delegating authority to private parties may allow the government to do through them what it cannot do itself." This situation provides numerous opportunities for possible abuse, either intentionally or unintentionally. For example, who is to blame if private prison guards harm inmates? Is it the government or the firm operating the prison? In order to get around this difficulty, the courts have relied on the **public function test**, which consists of determining whether the private actor exercised "power traditionally

Private prison facilities house thousands of inmates in the United States.

exclusively reserved to the State" or "exclusive prerogatives of the sovereign."[45] The courts have identified some examples of activities that typically involve the sovereign power, including education, fire and police protection, and tax collection.

Despite these court decisions, the matter of what is a purely public function is far from settled. The authors of a recent study suggest using the following four-step framework for recognizing whether an action is public:

1. Identify the actor. Is it private? If so, is it for-profit or not-for-profit?

2. Identify the function. Is the actor carrying out a core governmental function or exercising authority that involves the potential application of force or the deprivation of rights (for example, police or national defense)?

3. Identify the action. Does it constitute an action of the state (for example, making an arrest)?

4. Identify the safeguards. Does the action comply with legal requirements? If not, why not?

The purpose of these guidelines, the authors point out, is "for recognizing government transfers of authority" to private organizations as a means to ensure public accountability. There is no denying the importance of this attempt to clarify lines of accountability as government privatizes more and more services and the line between public and private becomes increasingly blurred.

Cost Savings Problems

Some critics maintain that cost savings attributed to privatization are either exaggerated or that costs are merely shifted to other groups in society. For example, one study found, "The largest savings may have been in personnel costs. . . . The private sector employees performed all general maintenance chores."[46] In effect, the cost savings resulted from shifting the burden of costs from the company to either their personnel or their clients. Another study examining privatizing social services finds that contracting to private organizations may actually lead to additional costs. These include the costs to develop program performance measures and evaluation tools, to develop and maintain agency capacity to monitor contracts and to ensure competition.[47] These costs, the study avers, are seldom included in the total costs of shifting to private production, which results in an overestimation of cost savings.

Other critics of privatization assert that private firms lower their costs in large part by relying heavily on part-time employees who do not receive healthcare benefits. In the end, critics charge, governments ultimately pay these "hidden" healthcare costs when the noninsured workers require medical care.[48]

Civil Society and Privatization

According to some analysts, the blurring of the distinction between the public and the private sectors has produced another unfortunate result: undermining civil society. One scholar argues that the mentality of "running government like a business means that public mangers increasingly regard the public as customers to be served rather than as citizens who govern themselves." As a result, there is a danger that this mindset might "degrade commitment to public service" reducing it to just another commodity to be marketed and sold to customers to the detriment of civil society.[49]

Critics also point to the danger of civic associations becoming "captured" by government. Government's relationship with nonprofit organizations has undergone a major transformation as a result of privatizing efforts in recent decades. In Chapter 8, we discuss these public–private partnerships as networks and note how their influence is rising. Networks receive a growing share of government funds and involve an increasing number of nongovernment organizations. There is a downside to this, however: As more nonprofits receive the bulk of their operating revenues from government, they might develop an unhealthy financial dependence on the public sector.[50] One consequence is that nonprofits, over time, begin to behave more and more like government agencies they serve. Savas refers to this as the "governmentalization" of nonprofits. Others have characterized it as a "fatal embrace" for nonprofits, which become "subject to coercive regulations" that "sap their initiative and thwart their efforts to find better ways to help the needy."[51]

Not everyone agrees that nonprofit organizations suffer as a result of an overdependence on government's resources. Some argue that nonprofits take the public's money and run: They take advantage of the government's dependence on them and its inability to effectively monitor them.[52] This issue is highlighted in an analysis of nonprofit organizations and social service delivery in New York City. According to the study, the nonprofit providers sometimes threatened to cancel their contracts and leave the government without a service provider. In addition, they began to behave like interest groups, forming coalitions to exert pressures on government in the contracting process. Government, in fact, preferred to deal with several providers working together, rather than having to deal with each one individually.[53] But this arrangement merely substituted a private monopoly for the old public one. In fact, the new arrangement, operating without competitive pressures, was no more efficient than before.[54] Based on the available research, it is unclear at the present time what all the long-term effects on civil society of privatization are.

Lastly, how does the shifting of public functions to the private sector affect the power of government agencies? Does it decrease administrative power, as might be expected, or actually increase it? At the beginning of this chapter, we said that privatization is one of the most controversial issues in modern public administration. Some view using private firms to perform public functions as an effective strategy to shrink the size of government. Naturally, agencies experiencing workforce reduction can be expected to lose at least some of their power and influence. Thus, market-like arrangements are often seen as a means to curtail the power of government bureaucracy. But the situation is more complicated than it appears on the surface.

Some observers argue that privatizing public functions does not automatically result in a diminution of government power. This is because the availability of government contracts stimulates the creation of private and nonprofit firms that lobby for more services for the populations they serve.[55] Further, as we noted in our prior discussion, governments may delegate authority to private entities to do things that the governments otherwise might not be allowed to do. Thus, while privatization might reduce the size of the public workforce, it may leave undiminished government's actual influence on society.

What other effects might privatization have on civil society? It depends on what role the citizen plays in the process. If transferring functions to the private sector means that citizens are treated more and more like customers and less and less as citizens, then public accountability is eroded.[56] If, however, citizens are treated as owners or stakeholders in the process, then shifting government functions to private providers may contribute to civil society in the end. Thus, as one scholar says, "Privatization efforts need to incorporate meaningful opportunities for citizen participation in order to validate the process as well as to provide a measure of dignity to those individuals who are especially affected by the service or regulation."[57]

■ Chapter Summary

Privatization can be defined as the use of private organizations to deliver public programs. This results in shrinkage in the size of government, as it no longer needs to employ as many workers. There are four types of privatization: contracting out, load shedding, vouchers, and asset selling. Although governments are shifting more and more services to the private sector, ultimate authority still rests with the public sector, since the funds to pay the companies come from the taxpayers.

The rationales given in support of privatization can be either economic or political, or some mixture of the two. While the rationales for privatization stem from economic and political theories, administrators look for practical guidelines to help them decide when to privatize. In recent decades, there has been considerable research into the optimal conditions for the use of private organizations. Issues include government oversight and the provider's experience and accountability.

All levels of government in the United States are consumers of private goods and services, a trend that has been on the rise. The federal government spends hundreds of billions of dollars annually on contracts with for-profit companies and nonprofit organizations, including churches and other faith-based institutions. Many state and local governments have sought to streamline operations and cut costs using privatization.

Market-like arrangements to provide public services are important tools of public policy and administration, and privatization will continue to be a popular policy option. However, it is not without some serious problems and concerns, such as selection of the wrong provider, a company's failure to perform as required, and principal–agent conflict.

■ Chapter Discussion Questions

1. Do you think that, as one author suggests, "Privatization is more a political than an economic act"? Explain why you agree or disagree.

2. In justifying the decision to privatize, which rationale would you use? Why?

3. Why would privatization require *more* public management rather than less?

4. Some scholars argue that bringing competition into the process of providing public services would lower the costs. How could public agencies be made more competitive without privatization?

5. As more government services are privatized, the lines separating public from private can become blurred. How can governments remain accountable to the public while more and more services are being delivered by nongovernment organizations?

BRIEF CASE   PRIVATIZING YOUTH SERVICES IN WASHINGTON, D.C.

Every year, hundreds of Washington, D.C., foster children and juveniles who are charged with crimes are put into group homes, psychiatric hospitals, and out-of-town residential treatment centers. The cost to D.C. taxpayers is roughly $69 million. Many of these facilities are privately run; the city contracts with for-profit companies to provide these services. These firms bill the city between $70 and $244 per day, per child. In return, the city receives poor care, little of the therapy promised, and under-maintained facilities, according to many observers. According to *Washington Post* reporters, "Rats, roaches, and rotting food are not uncommon. Outside drugs and guns are within easy reach."[58]

Perhaps the most egregious example of the failure of privatizing Youth Services is provided by Re-Direct Inc., which housed some of the District's worst juvenile offenders—children who were convicted of crimes including car theft, drug sales, armed robbery, and rape. The company was selected by the city because it promised to counsel teenagers and provide structure for their chaotic lives. The company had been in existence five years when it declared bankruptcy in 2003. During this period, when the company collected $3.1 million from the city, six juveniles in the Re-Direct system were murdered and a seventh committed murder. Other teenagers in Re-Direct's care committed robbery and assault—crimes for which they are serving prison sentences.

Re-Direct's owners charged the city between $100 and $170 per child, per day, for what they called a "holistic approach" to therapy and counseling. However, there is little evidence that they actually performed these services. According to a *Washington Post* article, "teenagers living in the company's group homes and apartments received little help and were allowed to roam free."[59]

The city's Youth Services must share at least part of the blame for Re-Direct's failure. The agency did little to oversee the company's performance. Meanwhile, in the company's homes, there was scant counseling and therapy, the children's meal cards never arrived some weeks, and children faced eviction from their apartments because the company was behind in the rent.

Privately operated Riverside Hospital has also been the focus of government and media investigations. The private D.C. facility consists of a 96-bed unit for children with profound emotional problems and a 54-bed residential treatment center offering counseling and other services. The chief accusations leveled against the hospital include Medicaid fraud, inadequate service, and keeping children for unneeded treatment. One former employee alleged that hospital personnel were offered commissions to recruit children to fill beds, a charge the hospital administration vigorously denied. According to a former associate administrator and human services director, "We were making money. That was always the priority: let's do whatever we can to ensure that the money comes in."[60]

Several times federal regulators threatened to revoke the hospital's Medicaid participation. Each time Riverside promised to correct the problems, and the hospital was allowed to stay open. Finally, the city audited the hospital's Medicaid bills and found that the hospital kept 148 children for 6,884 days of "unnecessary medical stays" from 1997 to 2001. The bill to the taxpayers for the unneeded services was more than $4.5 million. While many children were not benefiting from Riverside, the hospital's owners clearly were.

Brief Case Questions

1. *How does the Youth Services case study reinforce or confirm some of the research findings discussed in the chapter?*

2. *How might a defender of privatization respond to this case study? What reforms of the system need to be implemented in order to make it work?*

3. *During lean economic times, governments might be tempted to privatize services as a means to make money. However, government exists to provide needed services and not to make money. How can government resist the lure of profit-making that comes at the expense of citizens' well-being?*

Key Terms

adverse selection (page 292)

asset selling (page 281)

charitable choice (page 287)

contracting out (page 279)

faith-based organization (page 287)

load shedding (page 280)

moral hazard (page 292)

principal–agent theory (page 292)

privatization (page 278)

public function test (page 292)

vouchers (page 280)

On the Web

http://www.rppi.org

The pro-privatization Reason Public Policy Institute site provides information on market-like arrangements.

http://www.afscme.org/private/

The American Federation of State, County, and Municipal Employees site includes this page on privatization and takes a very strong antiprivatization position.

http://www.mackinac.org/pubs/mpr/

The Michigan Privatization report available at this site is published by the Mackinac Center for Public Policy, a nonprofit, nonpartisan organization with a pro-privatization slant.

http://www.manhattan-institute.org/

The free-enterprise-oriented Manhattan Institute website has many helpful links on privatization.

http://www.rand.org/

The Rand Corporation, a nonprofit, nonpartisan think tank, has published many reports on privatization that are available online.

http://www.epinet.org/

The Economic Policy Institute, a nonpartisan think tank with a liberal tilt, has many links and resources on privatization.

http://www.financeprojectinfo.org/management/privatization.asp

A comprehensive survey of online resources on welfare services, privatization, and outsourcing.

CHAPTER 13

Public Budgeting and Finance

■ SETTING THE STAGE

From October 1995 to January 1996, Americans watched with a mixture of anger and disgust as President Bill Clinton and the Republican-controlled Congress faced off over the budget. The seeds of the budget crisis were sown a year earlier when, spearheaded by Newt Gingrich (R-GA), the Republican Party gained control of the House of Representatives in the 1994 midterm elections. This marked the first time that Republicans had control of the lower chamber since 1952. When President Clinton submitted his budget to Congress that year, the Republicans declared it dead on arrival.

By the time September came around, the White House and Congress were locked in mortal combat over passage of the federal budget, which is due by law on October 1. As the hours and minutes moved closer to the deadline, President Clinton and the Republicans in Congress only hardened their positions. Clinton called the Republican plan to prevent a shutdown of the federal government "blackmail," and Gingrich threatened to risk the first default on the national debt to get a budget reflecting Republican spending priorities.[1]

As the days passed and still no budget deal was in sight, each side blamed the other for the stalemate. The Republicans released a plan that would require a balanced budget in seven years. President Clinton called this plan "a cynical assault on American values." He said the Republican plan attempted to wring savings out of Medicare and Medicaid. The Republicans countered that Clinton was making a "last desperate defense of big government, bloated budgets, and deficit spending."[2]

As a result of the budget impasse, "nonessential" parts of the federal government were shut down in November. National monuments, museums, and visitor centers at national parks were closed. During the shutdown, 800,000 federal workers, or 40 percent of the government's workforce, were temporarily laid off without pay.

To a large extent, it was federal employees who bore the brunt of the budget battle between the president and congressional Republicans. Congress and the president set aside their squabbling long enough to pass temporary spending measures, but these were merely stopgap efforts lasting only a few days at a time. On the major issues, Republican insistence on a seven-year plan to balance the budget and Clinton's resolve to preserve his

Newt Gingrich, Speaker of the U.S. House of Representatives, challenged President Bill Clinton over the 1995 federal budget.

SOURCE: Richard Ellis/AFP/ Getty Imgaes

spending priorities, there was little compromise. The government was partially shut down again in December, around Christmas time. In early January, after the longest federal government shutdown in history, Clinton gave in to the Republican demand for a seven-year balanced budget plan, and the Republicans conceded to Clinton's spending plan and increased taxes.

■ CHAPTER PLAN

Except in dramatic instances, such as the struggle between Congress and the White House just described, budgets are seldom the center of public attention. Yet the example underscores the importance of budgets and budgeting to both public administrators and ordinary citizens. In this chapter, we define budgeting and describe the different purposes of public budgeting. Next we explain the evolution of the budget process and discuss four major types of budget reforms: line-item budgeting, performance budgeting, the planning-programming budgeting system, and zero-based budgeting. The next section provides an overview of major revenue systems, followed by a discussion of the rational and incremental models of budgeting. The chapter concludes with a discussion of capital budgeting and debt management.

What Is Public Budgeting?

Public budgeting is the process by which scarce resources are allocated among competing activities and interests in society. These activities range from educating children and fighting crime to finding a cure for cancer. However, since human desires are unlimited while society's resources are not, setting priorities becomes an inevitable part of the process. Therefore in budgeting, there are winners and losers. The "winners" are the groups or individuals whose values and preferences prevail as reflected in larger program and project budgets; the "losers" receive smaller budgets for their programs and projects.

The Purposes of Public Budgeting

Public budgeting serves four distinct but related purposes. First, budgets reflect the policy preferences of elected policymakers at all levels of government. As one budget scholar noted, budgeting "lies at the heart of the political process."[3] Whether a municipality prefers education spending more than public safety spending, for example, can be determined by looking at the municipal budget. Similarly, a national consensus for increased defense spending versus domestic spending is reflected in the federal budget. To a large extent, the political values of American society influence governmental decisions on raising and spending money for public services and programs. Consequently, the size of government and its spending levels are often controversial political issues. In addition, there is a broad consensus that taxing and spending decisions should be made only with the approval of the public, and voters demand full accountability of how funds are spent by public officials.

Budgeting's second purpose is to serve as a means by which a government exercises control over the operations of its programs. It is a tool for increasing the efficiency and effectiveness of the delivery of public services. Budgeting sets goals and objectives, measures the progress toward achieving those goals, identifies weaknesses and poor performance, and controls and integrates the numerous activities that are carried out by the various units of government.[4]

Budgeting's third purpose, enhancing economic growth, is primarily a function of the federal government, although increasingly state and local governments make considerable investments to promote economic development. The federal government has had a significant role to play in the national economy since passage of the Employment Act of 1946. Federal policies are chiefly directed toward achieving full employment, maintaining low levels of inflation, and stimulating economic growth. In pursuing those objectives, the federal government uses a combination of fiscal policy and monetary policy. The budget is the chief mechanism to enact and implement fiscal policy, which uses taxes and spending to influence the economy. Monetary policy, which uses control of the money supply and interest rate, is the domain of the Federal Reserve Banking system. State and local governments attempt to use fiscal policy to encourage job growth and increase personal income, sales receipts, and property values.

Budgeting's fourth purpose is to serve as a mechanism for government accountability. Initially, public budgets, particularly at the local level, were designed to ensure fiscal accountability on the part of elected officials. Contemporary public budgeting still asks the question: Does government spend the taxpayers' money in a manner that meets the public's approval and in an honest fashion? However, an important function of budgets today is assessing program effectiveness as well as assuring accountability and expenditure control.

The Budget as a Plan of Action

Fiscal Year An accounting period covering twelve months; the fiscal year is designated by the calendar year in which it ends.

The budget is a plan of action that links specific tasks with the resources necessary to accomplish those tasks over a definite time period; typically one year, which is known as a **fiscal year**.[5] At its most basic, the budget is simply a document that reports and keeps track of government spending and income. However, contemporary budgets are often much more. Budgets as action plans typically evolve through four stages that comprise a cycle, which is discussed below.

Budgets may consist of one or several documents. At the federal level, the budget consists of several massive documents. At the local level, it is typical for city councils to approve the budgets submitted by their mayor as a single document. States' budgets vary between one and several documents, with the largest ones consisting of hundreds of documents. Most budgets that are submitted to legislatures contain the executive's budget message, which summarizes the government's priorities for the upcoming year and highlights revenue trends and economic conditions. The executive budget document contains the budget summary and sections on program and department details in addition to the budget message. These sections often include a narrative describing the functions of each program or department and a list of the **objects of expenditure**.

Objects of expenditure The numeric codes used by governments to classify expenditures by categories, such as personnel, supplies, and equipment.

The Budget Cycle

Budget cycle A process consisting of (1) preparation, (2) legislative review, (3) execution, and (4) audit and overlapping several years.

Budgeting occurs in cycles that can extend over a period of several years. The four phases of the **budget cycle** are

1. Preparation of the budget and its submission by the executive to the legislature.
2. Review of the budget by the legislature and approval.
3. Policy execution by the executive branch.
4. Audit by a specialized agency, typically separate from the executive branch.

Although U.S. governments vary in size, many governments retain the key elements of the above model, since they operate on the principle of the separation of powers between the executive branch and the legislative branch.[6] The budget cycle in a democratic government is thus an important mechanism for accountability and responsiveness, because it allows both executive and legislative input and assessment of the efficiency and effectiveness of programs.

Preparation and Submission by the Executive The chief executive begins the first phase of budgeting by distributing the guidelines to the agencies involved with budget document preparation. By following these guidelines, agency personnel develop program cost estimates and narrative justifications for submission to the department budget office. The department budget office and the director and his or her staff review and revise these budget requests, consolidating them for submission to the central budget office. The central budget office staff reviews the recommended department budgets for consistency with the chief executive's policy priorities and spending guidelines. Thus, the executive budget consists of the departmental budgets as revised and approved by the chief executive. The budget is then submitted to the legislature for its consideration and approval.

Legislative Consideration and Approval Submission of the executive budget document to the legislature initiates the second phase of the budget cycle. In order to expedite consideration of the budget, in many states and at the federal level, the budget is split into several parts for review by the appropriate legislative committees and subcommittees. At the federal level, the process results in twelve separate appropriations bills, which are reviewed by twelve different appropriations subcommittees. At the state level, however, there is considerable variation in the number of appropriations bills the legislature is required to approve. Many states have a single budget bill, while others have multiple budget bills, which can number to the hundreds.

Both houses of the legislature must approve the executive's budget. Typically the lower house (e.g., the House of Representatives at the national level and its equivalent at the state level) begins the process with subcommittee hearings in which agencies defend their budget requests. The public may be given an opportunity to provide input at this stage. After the lower house approves an appropriations bill, a similar process occurs in the upper house (e.g., the Senate at the national level and its equivalent at the state level). After the upper house's approval of the appropriations bill, both houses agree on a unified appropriations bill, which is returned to the chief executive to be signed into law.

Executive Implementation The fiscal year begins with the executive branch's implementation, or the execution phase, of the budget cycle. During this stage, the agencies spend their appropriations and perform the services required of them by law. In effect, the budget serves as executive policy, providing guidance for agency officials' decisions during the next twelve months.

Audit Stage The chief purposes of audit, the final phase of the budget cycle, is to ensure that public monies are spent in an appropriate, honest, and well-managed manner; that agency expenditures are made according to the provisions of the appropriations bill; and that no fraud, waste, or abuse occurs as programs are effectively carried out. An audit usually requires an external entity (i.e., outside the executive branch) to verify the statements and financial reports of public agencies.

The Government Accountability Office (GAO), an agency of the Congress, performs the audit function for the entire federal government. The comptroller general heads the GAO. State governments often require local governments to perform an annual audit that may be reviewed by the state. In contrast to the federal government, many states elect officials to audit the operations of government.

Evolution of Public Budgeting

The history of public budgeting in the United States is marked by several significant efforts at reform, which resulted in several types of budgets that pushed improvements in efficiency and effectiveness. The earliest types of budget reforms—executive budgeting and line-item budgeting—emphasized control aspects along with maintaining fiscal integrity and administrative accountability. With the growth of government during the first half of the twentieth century, however, these budget types were no longer considered sufficient for this purpose. Therefore other budget reforms were adopted to help public officials cope with the growing demands of managing government programs.

Early Budget Reforms

Executive budgeting The chief executive provides budgetary leadership.

Budgetary reform at the turn of the twentieth century took the shape of **executive budgeting**. Early budget reformers argued that the chief executive was the public official who could be held responsible for the administration of the entire government, and therefore only the executive could provide effective budgetary leadership. Another major impetus for change came from the Progressives, who viewed executive budgeting as an integral part of their agenda to strengthen the chief executive and make government more efficient. It was thought that executive budgeting would also increase honesty and efficiency in government. Shortly after the widespread adoption of executive budgeting, reformers began to push for line-item budgeting as a tool to improve the executive's fiscal stewardship.

Line-item budget A type of budgeting that reports the items to be purchased by a government (e.g., salaries, equipment, supplies) and the amount of money that will be spent on each item.

The focus of the **line-item budget** is on the inputs side, on labor, supplies, land, and other items that are purchased by government. Therefore public expenditures are classified according to categories such as salaries and wages, office supplies, professional services, travel, and equipment (see Table 13.1). Line-item budgets are supposed to keep agencies honest by drawing attention to what is acquired and spent, and as a management tool, its orientation is one of strict supervision and control of public spending. However, as V. O. Key pointed out in 1940, this approach leaves unanswered the fundamental question of governmental budgeting: "On what basis shall it be decided to allocate

TABLE 13.1 Line-Item Budget

Item	2003 Budget
Personal Services	
Salaries & Wages—Reg.	$100,000
Salaries & Wages—Temp.	$50,000
Retirement	$15,000
Insurance	$7,500
Other personal services	$10,000
Subtotal	$182,500
Operating Expenses	
Office Supplies	$5,000
Photocopying & Printing	$2,000
General Supplies	$500
Subtotal	$7,500
Capital Expenditures	
Computers	$20,000
Total	$210,000

X dollars to activity A instead of activity B?"[7] In other words, line-item budgets are excellent at showing *how public money is being spent but not why it is being spent in the first place.*

Performance Budgeting

The first Hoover Commission in 1949, recognizing the importance of Key's observation, recommended that the executive budget become more of a management tool for the federal government. The commission's report to President Harry Truman expressed the view that the budget should be "based upon functions, activities, and projects."[8] With **performance budgeting**, the emphasis shifts from inputs to government programs and functions, as well as to the tasks performed. Performance budgeting was implemented first in the armed services and was later extended to other federal departments and agencies.

Performance budgeting A type of budgeting that combines output and cost data from programs to show if they are being efficiently operated.

Performance budgets emphasize management by focusing on the efficient accomplishment of agency objectives, and they concentrate on the outputs of governmental activities (i.e., spending and personnel) instead of inputs (see Table 13.2). For example, in a municipal Streets and Highways Department budget, categories would consist of items such as number of street miles repaired, number of street miles replaced, and number of street signs replaced. The agency collects performance measures on those activities, which are then compared to the costs of performing those activities to determine efficiency in usage of financial resources. An example of this is determining the average

TABLE 13.2 Performance Budget

Planing New Trees

Number of new trees to plant: 200

Cost per new tree to plant: $50

Total annual cost: $10,000

Removing Dead Trees

Number of dead trees to remove: 50

Cost per dead tree to remove: $100

Total annual cost: $5,000

Total $15,000

Parks: Tree Maintenance

Summary: The parks department is responsible for maintaining the trees in the city's 10 public parks. Tree maintenance consists of planting new trees and removing dead trees. This year's appropriation request for tree maintenance is $15,000. Specific performance measure statistics follow:

Parks Department: Tree Maintenance Performance Measures

cost of repairing one mile of highway. Public officials can use this information to make better management decisions by comparing actual costs to planned costs and performance. Deviations from planned levels suggest problem areas that need to be corrected.

Thus, the important contribution of performance budgeting, from the perspective of government managers, is to improve agency efficiency by linking performance data with cost data. The resulting performance ratios can then be compared across agencies and within agencies over time to assess efficiency of operations.

Planning-Programming Budgeting Systems

Planning-programming budgeting system (PPBS) A type of budgeting that stresses the use of analytical techniques to improve policy-making; the budget format that comes closest to the rational budget decision-making model.

Secretary of Defense Robert S. McNamara introduced the **planning-programming budgeting system (PPBS)** to the federal government in 1961. In 1965, President Lyndon B. Johnson required every federal agency to use PPBS. The system has three basic steps. First, the goals and objectives of the unit are identified and prioritized; the same is done for the programs designed to achieve those goals. Second, a systems analysis capacity is developed that will relate the costs of achieving the goals as measured in outputs. Third, an information and reporting function is created to provide feedback to the system for planning and programming purposes.[9]

PPBS takes organizational missions or goals and breaks them down into specific objectives and subobjectives, and then groups similar activities into programs that relate to achieving those objectives and subobjectives (see Table 13.3). For example, the Department of Defense used a classification system called the program structure that grouped nearly one thousand

TABLE 13.3 Planning-Programming Budget

Protection of Persons and Property

Chief objective: To maintain high levels of personal and property security and to assure a safe and pleasant environment for people who live and work in the city.

Service Area—Police Protection:

To increase public and private safety through street patrol, criminal investigation, and preventive measures. $1,500,000

Service Area—Fire Protection:

To increase public and private safety through fire fighting and fire prevention. $1,000,000

Total $2,500,000

of these activities, known as program elements, together into nine major programs or missions as follows:

1. Strategic Retaliatory Forces
2. Continental Air and Missile Defense Forces
3. General Purpose Forces
4. Airlift and Sealift Forces
5. Reserve and National Guard Forces
6. Research and Development
7. General Support
8. Military Assistance
9. Civil Defense

The program structure grouped similar activities together from different branches of the armed services in order to facilitate analysis across agency lines.

Another key element of PPBS was its multiyear perspective. Secretary McNamara instituted five-year Defense Plans that projected costs and personnel needs based on the program structure. PPBS required agency analysts to do five-year budget projections and to show the future impact of current programs to aid in multiyear planning.

Despite the considerable effort to implement PPBS at the federal level, it was discontinued shortly after Richard Nixon assumed the presidency in 1969. Few people in Congress and the agencies mourned its demise. In general, there was a lack of understanding and commitment to this type of budgeting on the part of the departmental leadership. It required more specialized and technical skills than many agencies possessed. Furthermore, in certain types of programs (e.g., social services, national defense, public safety) there was considerable difficulty in establishing useful program measures. Although many state and local governments had jumped on the PPBS bandwagon after it was introduced in the federal government in the 1960s, few of these systems were still in place by the end of the decade. Although PPBS never really caught on, it did produce some lasting changes as more state and local governments began to make greater use of program information and quantitative analysis in the budgetary process.

Zero-Base Budgeting

Zero-based budgeting A type of budgeting in which a program's continued existence is not assumed, and all expenditures, not just new ones, must be justified every year; the goal is to eliminate unnecessary programs.

Jimmy Carter first used **zero-base budgeting (ZBB)** as governor of Georgia in 1973; after Carter was elected president in 1976, he applied the technique to the federal government. The main innovation was its systematic consideration of alternative levels of services with their associated costs. ZBB, as practiced by the Carter administration, consisted of three components. First, *decision units* were identified within the agency, which would generate the *decision packages*, or budget requests, including alternative means of accomplishing a goal. Second, three different funding levels were identified for each decision package: (1) the minimum level that provided services below current levels; (2) the current level that maintained services without either an increase or decrease in standards; (3) the improvement level that provided services beyond existing standards. Third, managers ranked the decision packages according to their importance.

Some federal government administrators observed that ZBB focused more attention on agency objectives, generated alternative spending and service levels, and encouraged the use of more quantitative data in budget requests, but overall, the federal government's experience with ZBB was largely negative.[10] Most public officials criticized the huge demands on their time and the mountains of paperwork that was required. For some programs, the identification of a minimal service level was a fruitless exercise because, as in the case of entitlement programs such as Medicare, annual expenditures are set by statute. Thus, changes in budget amounts can be achieved only by altering the enabling legislation. Furthermore, it was difficult to define goals and objectives both for the activities being budgeted and for the organization as a whole.[11]

ZBB was abandoned by Carter's successor, Ronald Reagan. And ZBB failed to make significant inroads among state and local governments despite considerable interest at first. Few state and local governments actually attempted anything as ambitious as the federal government did, although ZBB in modified form still survives in twenty states.[12]

Revenue Systems

Government expenditures are made to improve the lives of citizens. Before they can spend, however, governments must first raise money. They do this through various revenue sources, including taxes, fees, intergovernmental transfers, and borrowing. Most of government's general revenues are derived from taxes. Individual and corporate income taxes are the chief source of federal revenues. The most important tax at the state level is the general sales tax, which accounts for the majority of total revenues. The property tax is the most important tax for local governments, particularly school districts. Fees, or user charges, are becoming increasingly important, particularly at the local level, although in contrast to taxes, fees or charges are typically levied on the users of particular services (e.g., fees for driver's licenses, municipal recreation centers, and hunting licenses). As governments try to avoid raising taxes they increasingly turn to fees for services to replace the lost tax revenues.

Intergovernmental transfers are the funds that the federal government provides to state and local governments, and that state governments provide to their local governments, to help pay for public services. These transfers, or grants-in-aid, reached their peak in terms of dollar amounts in the late 1970s and have declined considerably since then but are still a major source of revenues for state and local governments.

Governments often incur debt to help finance their operations. State and local governments mainly use long-term borrowing to finance capital projects that extend over a period of several years (e.g., dams, highways, bridges, and buildings). They use short-term borrowing to cover deficits in their operating budgets for short periods of time. In contrast, the federal government borrows to finance both its day-to-day operating expenses and capital projects.

Taxes

Progressive tax A tax in which the ratio of tax to income increases as a taxpayer's income rises.

Regressive tax A tax in which the ratio of tax to income declines as a taxpayer's income rises.

Proportional tax A tax in which the ratio of tax to income stays the same as a taxpayer's income rises.

Several important criteria that must be considered when evaluating taxes are equity, yield, elasticity, ease of administration, and political accountability. Equity refers to the tax's fairness, that is, whether the tax burden is distributed according to the taxpayer's ability to pay. A **progressive tax** is one in which the tax burden increases as a person's income increases (i.e., a wealthy person pays more taxes than a middle-income person does). A **regressive tax** is one in which the tax burden decreases as a person's income increases (i.e., a wealthy person pays proportionately less in taxes than a middle-income person does). A **proportional tax** is one in which the burden stays the same regardless of income level.

Taxes can also be evaluated on the basis of their yield, or their efficiency in generating revenue. Efficiency is measured by subtracting the costs of administering the tax from the total revenues it produces. Taxes that are relatively inexpensive to administer have high yields, while taxes that are expensive to administer have low yields. The property tax is considered a low-yield tax, while income taxes are considered high-yield. Tax elasticity is related to yield. An elastic tax is very responsive to economic conditions. For example, when per capita income rises, an elastic tax's revenues will also rise. An inelastic tax is less responsive to economic conditions. The federal income tax is an elastic tax, while the property tax is inelastic.

Ease of administration refers to a number of factors related to tax collection and enforcement. A tax that is easy to understand, in which compliance is not difficult, and where evasion is difficult would rank high on this criterion.

Finally, the government should be held accountable by the public for the taxes it employs and how they are administered. Changes in taxes should be voted on directly by the people or by their representatives in the legislature. (See Table 13.4 for the major taxes used in the United States evaluated according to the above criteria.)

Individual and Corporate Income Tax The federal government and forty-three state governments employ some form of individual income tax, which accounts for 31 percent of total government revenues. The individual income tax offers several important advantages as a source of revenues. First, income is generally a good indicator of a person's ability to pay. Thus, using income as a tax base results in a fairer tax. As we mentioned above, the income tax is a progressive tax, which means that a higher-income person's tax burden is greater than someone with a lower income. This system is not perfect, however, since in some cases a person may have a relatively low current income but still possess considerable personal wealth (for example, owning an expensive house). But for the most part, income is closely associated with economic well-being. Second, tax liabilities take into account the personal circumstances of the individual taxpayer. For instance, two taxpayers may have the same income, but the one with the larger family will actually have a smaller tax burden under a progressive income tax system.

Third, its ability to combine all sources of income, including wages, interest, rent, profit, and royalties, results in a broader base, which avoids the

TABLE 13.4 Major Tax Systems Ranked According to Criteria

Criteria	Major Tax Systems
1. **Equity**	
High (progressive)	Personal and Corporate Income Taxes
Low (regressive)	Property Tax, Sales Tax
2. **Yield**	
High	Personal and Corporate Income Taxes
Moderate	Property Tax, Sales Tax
3. **Elasticity**	
Good	Personal and Corporate Income Taxes
Fair	Property Tax, Sales Tax
4. **Ease of Administration**	
Good	Personal and Corporate Income Taxes, Sales Tax
Poor	Property Tax
5. **Accountability**	
Good	Sales Tax
Fair	Personal and Corporate Income Tax
Poor	Property Tax

necessity of imposing unacceptably high tax rates in order to obtain a desired level of revenues. Fourth, the income tax ranks high on ease of administration due to the system of employer withholding, in which taxes are deducted from employees' paychecks and sent to the government. Fifth, at the federal level, the income tax is an important tool of economic policy. During periods of economic downturn, income tax rates can be lowered to stimulate aggregate demand and jump-start the economy. When the economy is experiencing high inflation, on the other hand, raising tax rates can slow economic growth and reduce inflationary pressures.

Some negative aspects of the income tax are: (1) it does not include non-wage income sources, such as in-kind services, which increase a person's net wealth; (2) tax revenues are extremely sensitive to changes in economic conditions—a recession results in a significant decline in revenues, which can lead to cutting public budgets; (3) the existence of numerous tax loopholes, often the result of special interest legislation, narrows the tax base and necessitates higher tax rates; and (4) part of the burden of administering the tax is shifted to the employers who must withhold taxes for the government and the individual taxpayers who are required to prepare an annual income statement to determine their total tax payment, which is due on April 15 every year. In addition, unindexed income tax systems are problematic due to bracket creep. This refers to a situation in which tax increases can occur without legislative action to raise tax rates. As a result of inflation, while a person's earnings rise, so do price levels, so that real income remains unchanged. When this occurs, the person is bumped into a higher tax bracket (i.e., tax rate) even though in real terms his or her income stays the same. While the federal government indexes income taxes, many states have not adopted indexing.

Corporate income taxes apply to the profits of corporations minus some deductions. Proponents of the corporate income tax argue that corporations receive special benefits from society and should therefore help pay the costs of government. Further, they assert, if corporate income goes untaxed this creates opportunities for tax avoidance, since taxpayers could reduce their income tax liability by allowing their income to accumulate within the corporation in the absence of a corporate earnings tax.[13] Opponents, however, believe that taxing corporation income results in a form of double taxation: first corporate income is taxed, and then individual income in the form of stock dividends.

Property Tax The property tax is a form of tax on wealth. The tax is levied on the value of an asset (land and buildings) rather than on current earnings like an income tax. Local governments rely heavily on this revenue source: 32 percent of total local revenues come from the property tax, and it is the chief source of revenues for school districts.[14] The property tax is generally considered regressive, and in many places, it has sparked significant opposition. General dissatisfaction with the property tax helped to launch **Proposition 13** in California and similar tax revolt movements elsewhere (this is discussed more fully below). Various localities were forced to diversify their tax base and to

Proposition 13 The California law passed in 1978 that restricted the property tax rate to 1 percent of market value, touching off a national tax revolt movement.

rely more heavily on other sources of revenue, including state aid. School districts are also relying to a greater extent on state aid and less on the property tax. The property tax is predominantly a local tax; it currently accounts for only 2 percent of the tax revenues for state governments.

Since the property tax is not based on a person's ability to pay, individuals on low or fixed incomes often find it difficult to pay their tax bills, especially if, unlike their income, the value of their property keeps increasing. In order to make the property tax less regressive, many states have passed **circuit breaker** laws to rovide property tax assistance in the case of low-income or senior citizen homeowners. Typically, a circuit breaker law imposes a limit on the amount of taxes owed, which is usually based on a percentage of income. If the tax paid by a homeowner exceeds this limit, the state refunds the taxpayer the amount of the difference. Circuit breakers help make the property tax less regressive because allowance is made for personal income in determining the tax burden.

Sales Tax The sales tax is the single largest source of state revenues. Forty-five states impose some type of a tax on sales receipts on purchased goods, and far less commonly on services. In addition, many states authorize local governments to impose their own sales taxes. As a result, sales taxes have become the second largest revenue producer for local governments after the property tax. Sales taxes are levied as a percentage (ranging between 3 and 7 percent) of the purchase price of goods, and are of two types: general (applied to a broad class of products) and selective (applied to particular products). An example of a general sales tax is the tax on general retail sales that many state revenue systems rely heavily on for a large proportion of their own-source revenues (i.e., from sources within the state). The tax on gasoline is an example of a selective sales tax. In addition, a **sumptuary tax** is a selective tax that is levied on certain items, such as alcohol and tobacco, to discourage their use.

The general sales tax is regressive because low-income persons spend a greater proportion of their disposable income on consumer goods than do high-income persons. Consequently, poor persons must bear a larger burden of the tax. To make the sales tax more equitable, most states exclude certain "necessities" from the base. All but one state (New Mexico), for example, exclude prescription drugs from the tax, while twenty-seven states exclude food purchases, and thirty-one states exclude utilities.[15]

Despite its regressivity, the sales tax retains its popularity among state and local governments because it (1) generates a large percentage (31 percent) of the states' own-source revenues; (2) is easy to administer, since the tax is collected by merchants at the retail level; (3) substitutes for user fees in some cases (for example, the gasoline tax is an indirect tax for road use); and (4) is easy to hide, since the tax is included in the final price of the good. Further, sales taxes tend to be less unpopular among taxpayers than property taxes and income taxes, since their perceived impact on the pocketbook is less than that of the other two taxes.

Circuit breaker A mechanism that reduces the regressivity of the property tax by exempting low-income elderly and other groups from some portion of their property taxes.

Sumptuary tax A selective sales tax imposed on certain items such as alcohol and tobacco, in part, to regulate undesirable consumption.

State governments could increase the fairness of their sales tax systems and increase the amount of revenues they collect by broadening the sales tax base to include personal and professional services. Equity would be increased because high-income individuals tend to be heavy users of such services. Currently half the states tax services such as auto repair, hair cutting and styling, dry cleaning, printing, and rentals. However, professionals such as doctors and lawyers are still untaxed. Attempts to tax professional services have proven unsuccessful, no doubt because of the opposition of powerful professional groups such as the American Bar Association and the American Medical Association.

Another area of controversy is the taxation of mail-order sales and Internet sales. In the case of mail-order sales, the states have been hindered in their efforts to tax this lucrative market because of Supreme Court interpretations of the interstate commerce clause that restrict the states' ability to tax interstate business transactions. Similarly, the Internet Tax Freedom Act of 1998, which has subsequently been extended, prohibited states from taxing the multibillion-dollar e-commerce market. This act imposes a moratorium on taxing sales that occur over the Internet. Many businesses support the moratorium, but state and local governments are generally opposed to it, because they forego several billion dollars a year in uncollected sales taxes on hundreds of billions of dollars in Internet sales. (See Vignette 13.1.)

User Fees

User fee A charge for a service (e.g., drivers license, hunting license, parks fees) that is levied by government.

Governments sometimes charge for certain services and privileges, similar to a private sector firm, with the price covering either all or part of the cost of providing the service or privilege. These charges are called **user fees,** and they have become an increasingly important method of government financing, particularly at the local level. User fees, however, are appropriate in only a limited number of cases. They can be used when only part of a community directly benefits from a service, rather than the service directly benefiting the whole community. For example, only people who participate in recreational fishing should pay the fees for a license allowing them to fish in a state's lakes and streams. Another instance when fees can be applied is when it is feasible to exclude some people from using the service. Thus toll booths and gates are a means of restricting the use of certain roads to only those who pay the toll.

User fees are viewed by public finance specialists as a fair method of obtaining revenues because frequent users, who benefit more, pay more for the service than do infrequent users. In addition, a user charge provides a reliable indicator of the actual level of demand for a particular service in a community, which leads to an efficient allocation of resources. A government can gauge how much to charge for an ice-skating rink or public pool by setting a price and seeing what happens with public demand. If it charges too much, demand will drop; if it charges too little, demand will exceed capacity.

VIGNETTE 13.1   Electronic Commerce and State Sales Taxes

The Internet has pluses and minuses for governments. On the one hand, the Internet can help governments keep in better touch with their constituents, and it is a source of quick information that helps officials do their jobs better. On the other hand, the increasing volume of commerce over the Internet represents a massive drain on state government revenues that adds up to billions of dollars a year.

Since the beginning of the World Wide Web, the Internet has been a rapidly growing source of retail sales. Merchandise sales on the Internet account for over $100 billion in revenues for retailers. Millions of Americans use the Internet to make online purchases every month. Most of these purchases are not taxed.

In 1998, Congress passed the Internet Tax Freedom Act, which imposed a three-year moratorium on state and local governments' ability to tax commerce on the Internet. The act was extended by Congress in 2001, and in 2004 President George W. Bush signed the Internet Tax Nondiscrimination Act, which again extended the moratorium on federal, state, and local taxes on e-commerce.

The online industry argues that taxing e-commerce hampers the Internet as an engine for economic growth. State and local government officials, however, contend that they are losing tax revenues that could be used to finance important government services, such as public safety and education. In addition, the absence of taxes on the Internet raises issues of fairness. Some consumers are at a disadvantage. A person with the means to buy a computer and Internet access can avoid taxes on a purchase that another person without those means must pay if buying the same good or service from a store.

Businesses that have not gone online also face a disadvantage. For example, a local store selling CDs is required to collect sales tax from customers who make purchases. But CD-sellers over the Internet have a competitive advantage in not having to collect the state sales tax. Therefore they can sell their products at a discount. However, online stores are required to collect sales taxes from consumers in states where the businesses have a physical presence, such as a store, business office, or warehouse. Therefore, retail stores such as Wal-Mart, Target, and Circuit City back efforts by state governments to formulate similar tax rules for all online retailers, which the chains see as a means to level the playing field.

There appears to be increasing consensus among business and government that some type of tax on economic transactions that occur over the Internet is inevitable. However, it is not known how these taxes will be collected. A major complication is that cyber businesses are not restricted by physical location. A business might be headquartered in California, have its server that processes its transactions in Iowa, and ship its products out of a warehouse in New Jersey. Its customers might be all over the world. The old ways of establishing tax liability no longer apply.

SOURCES: Bob Graham, "Should the Internet Be Taxed? Communities Hurt If Web Isn't Taxed," *Roll Call*, February 28, 1999; Matt Grayson, "Erosion of State Tax Bases," *Spectrum* (Fall 1998): 1–4; Michael Moynihan, "Taxing Web Wallets," *New York Times*, June 21, 1999, A15; Matt Richtel and Bob Tedeschi, "Online Sales Lose Steam," *New York Times*, June 17, 2007; Bob Tedeschi, "E-commerce Report: The Battle over Collecting Taxes for Online Sales Turns Acrimonious," *New York Times*, February 17, 2003.

User fees are not feasible when (1) nonpayers cannot be excluded from enjoying the benefits of a service; (2) the service intentionally benefits a low-income population and charges would discourage use; (3) the charges are too expensive to administer; and (4) the service maintains public order or safety (for example, police and fire).

Lotteries and Gambling

The most common form of legalized gambling activity in the United States is the lottery, a venerable tradition in America. The earliest lotteries were established in the 1600s and were common throughout the country until the late nineteenth century, when scandals led to their being banned by the states and the national government. Today thirty-seven states operate lotteries as revenue generators.

Lotteries offer several advantages to states. First, they are good revenue producers, bringing in between 3 and 4 percent of total state revenues. Second, lotteries are popular among residents, and because they are voluntary, they do not require periodic tax hikes. Third, they help to relieve the pressure on states to constantly increase taxes for costly services. Many states, for example, earmark lottery proceeds for education and other important functions.

These benefits, however, are offset by several disadvantages. One, lotteries are expensive to administer and consequently result in low revenue yields. The costs of administration include paying for advertising, security, high vendor commissions, and prizes that must be kept large enough to attract ticket buyers. Two, lottery proceeds can fluctuate from year to year, which makes it difficult for state governments to budget accurately, particularly in areas where lottery proceeds are earmarked. Three, buying lottery tickets accounts for a higher proportion of a low-income person's earnings, so the lottery is a regressive way for states to obtain revenues.[16]

Growing in importance as a means to generate revenues for the states is legalized casino gambling. At one time allowed only in Las Vegas and Atlantic City, casinos have spread to twenty-one states. Viewed by many states as a source of jobs, tourists, and taxes, casinos are nevertheless a mixed blessing for state governments and their citizens. Indeed, opponents of legalized casinos cite a number of moral and social ills that they argue counterbalance any short-term financial rewards. According to opponents, these social problems have economic costs as well, which has led some states to use a certain percentage of gambling revenues for programs to help people deal with gambling addiction and other related problems.

Further, lottery or casino gambling funds that are earmarked for specific public purposes, such as schools, may not be producing the revenue boon anticipated by their proponents. State legislatures, for example, that have earmarked lottery revenues for education have, in some cases, reduced funds for other education programs by equivalent amounts.[17] And in Florida, lottery earnings replace and do not supplement general-fund revenues to education.[18]

Tax Revolt Movement

With the passage of Proposition 13 in California in 1977, a grassroots tax revolt movement spread throughout the country. Taxpayer opposition to high taxes and big government fueled the movement. By the time the tax revolt movement began to lose momentum in the 1980s, eighteen states had passed statutory or constitutional limitations on state and local governments' ability to tax and spend, and more than half the states had reduced personal or corporate income taxes or the sales tax. Taxing and spending limitations are typically tied to growth in some economic indicator, such as per capita income or total value of all the private real estate property in a community. Although the movement had significantly weakened by the 1990s, its effects are still being felt by politicians, who are reluctant to raise taxes unless there is a compelling reason to do so.

Tax and expenditure limitations, according to some research, have not produced the intended impact of significantly reducing state spending.[19] In large part, states have avoided reductions in service levels by increasing their reliance on user fees and other revenue sources to replace the lost taxes, as in California's case, or by shifting the tax burden to other groups

Models of Budgeting

Models and theories help us to understand complex processes such as public budgeting by simplifying the process. Models identify the most important factors and highlight the major relationships between these factors. In this section, we discuss the rational and incrementalist models as applied to budgeting.

Rational Budgeting

Rational budgeting
An approach to budgeting that involves (1) selection of objectives, (2) identifying alternatives along with their costs, (3) comparison of alternatives on the basis of achieving the objectives, (4) choosing the best alternative.

In the **rational budgeting** model, budgetary decision-making proceeds according to a logical sequence of steps, as shown in Figure 13.1. The model assumes that the search for budget alternatives occurs within a context of complete and perfect information. Further, the decisionmaker can know all the relevant costs and anticipated benefits of each alternative. Finally, all of the factors that might affect an outcome are identified and quantified, so that analysis can occur within a cost-benefit framework. In short, the rational model makes nearly superhuman demands on decisionmakers. It also assumes that public budgeting occurs in an environment entirely free of politics; in other words, it assumes an environment in which management values always prevail. Despite these unrealistic assumptions, the rational decision-making model has influenced such budgeting reforms as PPBS and ZBB.

Incremental Budgeting

Incremental budgeting A model of budgetary decision-making that asserts the process is inherently political, that no single group dominates, budgetary changes are marginal and the result of mutual accommodation among diverse interests.

The **incremental budgeting** model was dominant during the period of national economic expansion and virtually uninterrupted government growth from the late 1940s until the late 1970s.[20] The basic premise underlying this model is summed up in the following:

> Budgeting is incremental, not comprehensive. The beginning of wisdom about an agency budget is that it is almost never actively reviewed as a whole every year in the sense of reconsidering the value of all existing programs as compared to all possible alternatives. Instead, it is based on last year's budget with special attention given to a narrow range of increases over decreases.[21]

Since decisionmakers do not face an unlimited menu of choices every year, incremental budgeting helps to expedite and order what might otherwise be an

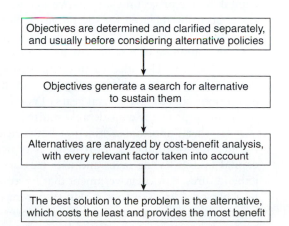

Figure 13.1   Rational Budgeting Model

SOURCE: The Rational Decision Making Model (Source: Robert T. Golembiewski and Jack Rabin, "PPBS: Theory, Structure, and Limitations," in *Public Budgeting and Finance*, 4th ed., eds. Robert T. Golembiewski and Jack Rabin (New York: Marcel Dekker, 1997).)

impossible task. Incremental budgeting takes the budget base as a given, thus leaving the agency to concentrate on (1) defending the base from cuts, (2) increasing the base by spending more on existing programs, and (3) expanding the base by adding new programs. Finally, the budgetary process is characterized by negotiation, which results in mutual accommodation, with nearly everyone eventually getting something and no single interest dominating all the others all the time.

Incremental budgeting has been attacked on both descriptive and normative grounds. One study, for example, examined Atomic Energy Commission appropriations and found significant variations in program budgets, although only incremental changes were noted for the total agency budget.[22] The study concludes that incrementalism misses significant policy changes by concentrating on the total budget while ignoring the key decisions made at the lower levels. On normative grounds, incrementalists have been criticized for being overly cautious, inherently conservative, and biased against innovative alternatives.[23] This is one of the reasons for the appeal of reforms like ZBB; they attempt to counter the incremental mindset by challenging the notion that there is an untouchable base that does not need to be justified annually.

Capital Budgeting and Debt

At the state and local levels, it is common for governments to divide their budgets into two separate parts, one for operating expenditures (day-to-day expenses of government), and one for capital investments (projects that are expected to have a long useful life). A dam that is built to last for several generations is a capital expenditure, as are airports, police stations, schools, and waste-water treatment plants. On the other hand, wages for personnel, office supply purchases, and purchases of periodicals are operating expenditures. Typically, to be classified as a capital item, a project must be above a certain expenditure threshold and should not need to be replaced for several years. But governments vary in which items are categorized as capital projects. For example, a small municipality might consider the purchase of a police car to be a capital expenditure, whereas a similar vehicle might be classified as an operating expenditure in New York City, with the durability of the car being the key factor. In the small town, the police car can be expected to give several years of good use; in New York City, its expected useful life is probably considerably shorter.

Another important distinction between capital and operating expenses is the method of financing. Borrowing is typically used to finance items on the capital budget, while taxes and user fees are mostly used to finance operating expenditures. A local government that borrows to build a new library is similar to a person who takes out a loan to purchase a new house. In both cases, the buyer incurs a debt that must be repaid over time. In the case of the local government, however, bonds are sold to investors who lend the money to build the facility; in return, the government undertakes the legal obligation to pay the investors the capital and interest out of the municipality's revenues every year.

Types of Debt

There are two types of government bonds: **general obligation bonds** and **nonguaranteed bonds**. The full revenue producing capacity of the borrowing government, including taxes and other revenues, backs general obligation (GO) bonds. In issuing these bonds, the government pledges to pay back the amount borrowed as well as interest by using every revenue-producing means at its disposal. Failure to make debt payments will cause a government to go into default. By contrast, nonguaranteed (NG) bonds do not have this means of financing, but are backed instead by the revenue-producing potential of the facility built by the proceeds of the debt. User charges are typically used to repay the loans. A municipal golf course, for instance, might be financed by revenue bonds that are paid off through the collection of fees from the users. In this way NG bonds have the advantage of making the people who benefit the most from a service also pay for it.

Government securities are given preferential treatment by tax laws. Investors in state and local government bonds do not have to pay federal and state income taxes on the interest on these bonds. This tax advantage is particularly attractive to high-income taxpayers. As a result of the special status of government bonds, state and local governments can sell these bonds at lower interest rates than private debt, which results in a considerable savings for these governments. However, during the early 1980s, many state and local governments abused this tax break, which led to an important change in the federal tax code in 1986. Congress, concerned about the loss of federal revenues, imposed tight restrictions on state and local governments' use of private

Municipal recreational facilities, such as the swimming pool shown here, are commonly financed using revenue debt.
SOURCE: Bob Daemmrich/ The Image Works

purpose bonds. As a result, the volume of private purpose bonds issued by state and local governments has declined considerably.

In most state and local governments that have separate capital and operating budgets, there is an effort to develop **capital investment plans** that project capital needs and costs several years into the future, with five years being the typical planning time period. These capital investment plans also serve as an important element in a government's asset management strategy. In many large cities, particularly older ones, deteriorating infrastructure is a major concern. Roads and bridges in an advanced state of disrepair are just two examples of decaying public works that make older cities less attractive places to live and work in. A key component of a state and local government's asset management plan is an inventory of existing infrastructure that assesses the current condition of facilities and has linkages with the capital budgeting process.

Capital investment plan A long-range plan used by governments to guide their capital investment policies; focuses on the expected infrastructure needs of a jurisdiction and includes costs estimates for projects in the plan.

Federal Capital Budgeting

Unlike every state government and many local governments, the federal government does not separate capital investments from operating expenditures in its budget. In contrast to the accepted financial practice at the state and local government levels, the federal government borrows funds to pay for its current activities. Also in contrast to the state governments, the federal government is not legally required to have a balanced budget. Thus, the federal budget has frequently run a deficit in recent years, as shown in Table 13.5. The accumulation of annual deficits increases the national debt, which is also shown in the table. Furthermore, much of the federal government's expenditures on capital items is concentrated in the area of defense and cannot be considered an investment in the same way that a dam or fire station would be. Defense systems become obsolete when they no longer fulfill their purpose of providing adequate protection from potential enemies. Thus the principle of useful life

TABLE 13.5 Federal Deficits and Debt, Selected Years, 1970–2005

Year	Deficit (in billions of dollars)	As Percentage of GDP	Debt (in billions of dollars)	As Percentage of GDP
1970	−3	−2.1	283	28.1
1975	−53	−3.4	395	25.4
1980	−74	−2.7	710	26.1
1985	−212	−4.9	1,500	36.5
1990	−221	−3.1	2,411	42.4
1995	−163	−2.8	3,603	49.2
2000	+236	−2.4	3,409	35.1
2005	−318	−2.6	4,592	37.4

Source: The Congressional Budget Office, The Economic and Budget Outlook, Fiscal Years 1998–2007, http://www.cbo/.

that applies to state and local government capital projects is not relevant in the case of defense expenditures.

The federal government also invests in capital projects that are designed to stimulate the economy. Every year, billion of dollars in federal grants flow to state and local governments, disguised as capital spending, but for the true purpose of providing economic assistance to those communities. A community might need a new highway less than the jobs and economic spillover that it produces.

In recent years, there have been a number of calls for capital budgeting at the federal level. Supporters of federal capital budgeting believe that it would make the federal government more efficient.[24] Capital budgeting can provide a more accurate picture of a government's financial health. From an accounting standpoint, purchase of a physical asset does not represent a "loss," since one asset (money) is exchanged for another (capital item). Only depreciation (the gradual wearing out) of the asset should be viewed as a loss and therefore counted toward the deficit. If only depreciation were included and not the total purchase amount, then the federal government's expenditures would actually be lower. However, the task of preparing a federal capital budget would be more complicated. At the federal level, there is no clear-cut distinction between investment and noninvestment spending. Thus, federal spending on education and job training could be considered capital spending in the sense that they are investments in human capital that help to lower future welfare and criminal justice costs. For instance, in the 1993 budget, the Clinton administration argued that welfare expenditures were human capital investments. But if we take such a broad view of capital spending, what would not be included in the capital budget?

Chapter Summary

Public budgeting is a process for determining who gets what in our society. Consequently, it lies at the heart of our political process. Public budgeting serves four distinct purposes: (1) It reflects the policy preferences of our representatives and other decisionmakers; (2) it is the means by which governments exercise control over the operations of public organizations; (3) it is a tool for managing economic growth, particularly at the national level; and (4) it acts as a mechanism for ensuring the accountability of our elected officials. The budget cycle consists of four phases which occur over a period of several years: preparation and submission; legislative review; executive branch execution; and audit. Efforts to improve the budgetary process have led to such historically significant reforms as executive budgeting, line-item budgeting, performance budgeting, the planning-programming budgeting system, and zero-based budgeting. Early budget procedures such as executive budgeting and line-item budgeting focused on centralization and control. Later budgeting systems aimed at bringing more data and systematic analysis into budgeting. However, not all of these reforms have proved successful; PPBS and ZBB were largely abandoned by the national government because of their considerable resource demands.

In order to improve citizens' lives, governments must obtain revenues and make expenditures. The chief sources of revenues in the United States are taxes, but user fees are becoming increasingly important at all governmental levels, while lotteries and legalized gambling are also becoming more significant. The chief types of taxes are property taxes, income taxes, and sales taxes. The important criteria that must considered when evaluating taxes include equity, yield, elasticity, ease of administration, and political accountability.

Models of budgetary decision-making help us to understand the complexity of the budgetary process. They also serve as guides for reformers in their efforts to improve the budgetary process. The rational model makes certain assumptions regarding budgetary decision-making that are difficult to fulfill in real-life situations. Nonetheless, it is implicitly the model for budget systems such as PPBS and ZBB. The incremental model provides a more accurate description of budgeting but has been attacked on grounds that it is too status-quo oriented. Capital budgeting is important because it draws our attention to the fact that much of government expenditures are investments and that citizens will be receiving benefits from public assets for many years in the future. Capital budgets are financed primarily by debt at the local and state levels, while federal capital expenditures come out of the general budget.

■ Chapter Discussion Questions

1. In reviewing the four purposes of public budgeting, it quickly becomes apparent that the potential exists for two or more purposes to come into conflict in any particular situation. What should an administrator do when encountering such a situation?

2. How does the budget cycle serve the objective of ensuring the public accountability of governmental actions?

3. What are some examples of efforts to increase the managerial effectiveness of budgeting? How might these attempts fare when they come up against the political aspects of public budgeting?

4. Progressive taxes such as the personal income tax are considered by policy analysts to be fairer than other types of taxes. However, polls consistently show that Americans dislike the income tax as much as the property tax and more than the sales tax (both regressive taxes). What aspects of the income tax might lead to this seeming disagreement between the experts and taxpayers?

5. Why are most states legally required to balance their budgets every year but the federal government is not? What are some negatives associated with deficit spending? What are the positive aspects of deficit spending?

BRIEF CASE   SCHWARZENEGGER'S BUDGET CRISIS

One of the first things that Arnold Schwarzenegger said publicly after he was elected California's governor in 2003 was: "I'm not going to cut dog food for blind people. It won't happen. I'm not going to take prosthetics from people that have disabilities and all that stuff."[25] Why did the former actor utter such things to the news media? California's worst budget crisis in years was the immediate cause for Schwarzenegger's remarks. Upon winning the governorship in a special recall election in November 2003, he inherited a budget gap of $38.2 billion for the fiscal years 2002–2003 and 2003–2004.[26]

California's budget crisis did not happen overnight. As a result of the late 1990s economic boom, California enjoyed several years of budget increases. In fact, Governor Gray Davis, the man Schwarzenegger replaced, presided over both record surpluses and record deficits during his term in office. While the state experienced the prosperity of the dot-com boom, California state revenues grew by 44 percent from 1997 to 2001. The state used this newfound money to fund new initiatives, particularly in education. California implemented a class size reduction program and, in general, spent dramatically more for public schools during this time. In addition, the state expanded healthcare coverage for uninsured children, made more college scholarships available, and gave raises to government employees. The governor and the legislature also cut the vehicle license fee by 67.5 percent.[27] However, when the economy turned south, the state's government revenue situation began to quickly deteriorate.

The causes for the rapid decline in California's budget fortunes are largely structural. On the one hand, the state relies heavily on the personal income tax, which falls and rises with the business cycle.[28] On the other hand, the programs the state spent heavily on during flush times locked it into future spending. "The state put into place wages and programs that committed the state to a certain level of spending that did not correspond to the reality of the situation," according to UCLA economist Christopher Thornberg.[29]

The governor, legislators, and voters must share equal blame. A poll issued in the summer of 2003, before the recall election, showed the voters' partial responsibility in the state's fiscal woes. Huge majorities of Californians were opposed to spending cuts in public schools (82 percent), health and human services (71 percent), higher education (69 percent), and transportation (61 percent). At the same time, the state's taxpayers opposed increasing taxes to pay for these programs. The poll indicated that the only solution that appealed to a majority of Californians was borrowing. Nevertheless, the poll's director noted that the people are "resentful about the choices they are being asked to make."[30]

The simple, unavoidable fact is that sacrifice is necessary, despite all the politicians' reluctance to admit this. A state budget expert says, "there are three ways out of the crisis: cutting spending, raising taxes or deferring some cuts through borrowing," all three will be necessary to solve the state's budget problems.[31] In recognition of this, Schwarzenegger declared a financial emergency shortly after he took office. He traveled around the state, holding campaign-like rallies, to garner support for the drastic measures necessary to bring the state's deficit under control. He criticized the state legislature, in particular the Democratic majority, accusing them of spending the state into a deep hole: "You are all supposed to keep within a budget to make ends meet. But for lawmakers there is a double standard. They go out and spend money they don't have."[32] He cut the car tax upon entering office, making good on a campaign pledge, which promptly increased the budget gap by an additional $4 billion. He then had to cut $150 million from mostly public health and welfare programs in order to make payments to local governments so that they could keep necessary facilities open and avoid laying off public safety employees.

Brief Case Questions

1. *If you were California's governor, would you borrow money to pay for current spending? Why or why not?*

2. *State polls show that Californians support spending on popular programs while wanting to keep taxes from growing. What can explain this apparent disconnection from reality?*

3. *How might the governor make a successful case for increasing taxes? In your answer, think of a package that might be palatable to the state legislature and the voters.*

■ Key Terms

budget cycle (page 302)
capital investment plan (page 320)
circuit breaker (page 312)
executive budgeting (page 304)
fiscal Year (page 302)
general obligation bonds (page 319)
incremental budgeting (page 317)
line-item budget (page 304)
nonguaranteed bonds (page 319)
object of expenditure (page 302)
performance budgeting (page 305)

planning-programming budgeting system (PPBS)
(page 306)
progressive tax (page 309)
proportional tax (page 309)
Proposition 13 (page 311)
rational budgeting (page 317)
regressive tax (page 309)
sumptuary tax (page 312)
user fee (page 314)
zero-based budgeting (page 308)

■ On the Web

http://www.rms.net/gloss_govt.htm
Glossary of U.S. budget terms.

http://www.whitehouse.gov/omb/budget/
The *entire* federal budget document can be found on this site.

http://www.cbpp.org/
The Center on Budget and Policy Priorities, a nonpartisan think tank conducting research and analysis on a range of government policies and programs, with an emphasis on those affecting low- and middle-income people.

http://www.gpoaccess.gov/usbudget/index.html
Government Printing Office's Budget Access website, an online portal for all federal budget documents.

http://www.kowaldesign.com/budget/
The Budget Explorer is an interactive site that introduces the user to important issues of the federal budget.

http://www.publicdebt.treas.gov/opd/opdpenny.htm
The federal debt to the penny, maintained by the U.S. Treasury.

http://www.budgetsim.org/nbs/
The national budget simulator gives you an idea of the trade-offs that policymakers need to make in creating federal budgets and dealing with deficits.

CHAPTER 14

Human Resource Administration in Public Organizations

▇ SETTING THE STAGE

Human resource administration (HRA) Of or relating to the management of personnel in an organization; the section of an organization that handles personnel and employee issues.

Human resource administration (HRA) is a vital function of public organizations; indeed, it is important for all organizations. If the public workforce is the heart of government, then it is the job of HRA to make sure that the heart is healthy by recruiting and retaining qualified workers. Despite its central role in public administration, HRA has come under considerable criticism from both scholars and managers. HRA's role has been criticized as outdated and inaccurate, while human resource offices are more often viewed as barriers to good management rather than as means to improve it.[1] At the same time, its task has been made more difficult as a result of several labor market trends. Since the 1980s, the public sector has struggled to maintain parity with the private sector in the recruitment and retention of skilled employees. The chief reasons for this failure appear to be the lower pay and status of governmental jobs compared with those in private business.[2] This inability to attract and keep good people could not occur at a worse time for governments, since the demand for a professional and highly skilled public workforce is on the rise.

Contemporary social and political demands place competing pressures on public human resource managers: they must be both efficient and responsive to social equity concerns; they must try to preserve the merit system's nonpartisanship while at the same time making it more accountable to the public; and they must simultaneously uphold professional values and be more responsive to the needs of political executives.[3] Clearly, the field of HRA offers many challenges, but there are also numerous opportunities to make a lasting difference on public management and public policy. These challenges and opportunities will occupy our attention in this chapter.

▇ CHAPTER PLAN

The chapter begins by defining human resource administration, outlining the multiple tasks it performs, and examining the differences between patronage and merit. Following that, we turn to a discussion of the evolution of HRA in the United States, focusing on the national government's human resource system. Since 1887, it has served as a model for state and local governments with respect to the personnel system. We then explore the public HRA process and the evolution of the position classification system. We next describe entering public service, the examination and selection processes, employee appraisals and pay, and removal from the civil service. The chapter also examines labor relations, collective bargaining, and equal opportunity policies and their effects on the public workforce.

What Is Human Resource Administration?

Human resource administration consists of the policies and the processes which determine the terms and conditions of employment of an organization's workforce. Every organization requires effective management of its human resources in order to achieve its objectives. Typical tasks assigned to HRA include human resources planning, recruitment, examination, selection, position classification, compensation policy, labor relations, productivity and quality management, human resources training and development, and performance appraisal.[4] While any organization, whether private or public, must perform these tasks, the most important quality distinguishing public from private HRA is the inherently political nature of the process in government. Indeed, this characteristic is the chief reason traditional merit systems have been designed to insulate public administration from political forces. Exploring this aspect of public HRA and its effects on the public workforce is one of the major purposes of this chapter.

Patronage and the Merit System

Merit The system in which employees are hired or promoted based on the quality of their work, education, and previous experience.

For over one hundred years, governmental employment in the United States has been guided by the principle of merit. The concept of **merit**, which will be explored in more detail later in this chapter, is a relatively recent import from Europe to the United States. Prussia, the forerunner of the modern state of Germany, had a career civil service system based on merit as far back as the mid-eighteenth century.[5] Other countries, such as France and Great Britain, followed Prussia's example, establishing civil service systems by the mid-nineteenth century. By contrast, the United States did not embrace the merit principle until the late nineteenth century, and then only after the assassination of President James A. Garfield, who was shot by a disgruntled job seeker, which compelled lawmakers to finally act on legislation that had been drafted many years before.

Patronage The system in which employees are hired or given promotions based on partisan affiliation.

The debate between merit and patronage relates to the vital question of public employment: "Who will get government jobs and on what basis?" **Patronage** refers to a personnel system in which hiring, promotion, firing, and other employment-related decisions are based principally on partisan political affiliation. Early in our history, civil servants were largely drawn from society's upper classes. President Andrew Jackson started a social revolution when he began the practice of appointing non-elite members of society to federal

The assassination of President James Garfield at the hands of a disgruntled office seeker in September 1881 led to the creation of the modern U.S. civil service in 1883.

SOURCE: Library of Congress Prints and Photographs Division

government service. Needless to say, over time the spoils system produced a government workforce that was inefficient, incompetent, and frequently corrupt. To correct this situation, reformers came up with a merit system, which was designed to replace patronage with neutral competence. This more business-like approach to public employment was intended to remove "politics" from the daily administration of public affairs.

Evolution of Public Human Resource Administration

The civil service, as it has evolved from the late nineteenth century to the present day, represents a compromise between the conflicting values of **neutral competence** and political responsiveness. Although most governments in the United States eventually adopted the ideology and methods of the reformers, they also retained some elements of pre-reform employment practices. It is therefore useful to review the history of the public employment system with this tension in mind. Some scholars have divided the history of public service in the United States into different eras or periods.[6] In this text, we follow their example and divide the evolution of the public service into eight distinct periods, each of which is described below.

Neutral competence
The idea that a government employee should be politically nonpartisan and possess the technical requirements and aptitude to perform a job.

The Era of Elites (1730–1829) During this period, the wealthy, well-educated landownerss and merchants, who were also white males, filled the top non-elective positions in government. George Washington, during his presidency, set the tone for this period by appointing men very much like himself—the cream of early American society. In general, these were men of high social standing and moral character who viewed public service as an important duty.

The Era of the Common Man (1830–1883) President Andrew Jackson established the system of patronage in Washington that flourished under subsequent presidents until the creation of the merit system.[7] Public service jobs were awarded to men with ties to the political party in power and who expressed political loyalty to the chief executive. At best, the spoils system resulted in poorly run government; at worst, it led to tragic consequences. In the Civil War, for example, a number of inexperienced men who received military commissions because of their political connections led men to their deaths in battle.[8]

The Era of Reform (1884–1906)   As every standard issue American government textbook says, President James A. Garfield's assassination in 1881 was the impetus for passage of the Pendleton Act (1883), which established a career civil service in the federal government. While President Garfield's death at the hands of a discontented job seeker certainly helped the reformers, efforts to dismantle patronage had been growing in intensity since the end of the Civil War, and some type of system-wide change probably would have occurred even without the tragedy.

The Pendleton Act sought to eliminate partisanship as the primary basis for hiring in the public service, replacing it instead with neutral competence as determined by entrance examinations. The act also created the Civil Service Commission, which consisted of three members appointed by the president and confirmed by the Senate. The commission did not have the exclusive authority to make agency appointments; it could only recommend the three best candidates for a federal position, a practice later referred to as the **rule of three**.[9]

Rule of three   The practice of recommending the three best candidates for a federal position.

The Era of Efficiency (1907–1932)   During this period, the Pendleton Act was extended to cover more and more of the federal workforce. The legislation originally stipulated that 10 percent of federal employees be included in the merit system. The act, however, gave future presidents the option to "blanket in" additional noncareer civil servants by way of executive order. Presidents used this authority to gradually expand coverage of the merit system to eventually include entire agencies.

The Era of Administrative Management (1933–1960)   This period coincided with several pivotal events in American history: the Great Depression, World War II, and the beginning of the Cold War. As a result of these events, unprecedented demands were placed on government, which could only be dealt with by strong, activist administration. Not only did government get bigger, but it also began to move away from its traditional emphasis on efficiency and neutral competence. In order to cope with the requirements of economic disaster and world war, government needed a workforce that was both effective and politically responsive. In order to cope with rapidly changing circumstances, the president assumed more responsibility for managing the federal government, and consequently the executive branch became more centralized (see Chapter 5). By the end of the period, the role of administrator was defined more broadly than the rather narrow technical role assigned to it previously.

The Era of Professionalism (1961–1977)   The government workforce at all levels became increasingly professionalized and specialized during this period. Although professionalization of public service began earlier as a means to overcome governmental corruption and inefficiency, the real upsurge occurred after World War II, as college graduates with specialized degrees went to work for governments in dire need of their technical qualifications and skills.[10] Writing at the end of the period, a public administration specialist observed: "For better or worse—and better and worse—much of government is now in the hands of professionals."[11]

The Era of Civil Service Reform (1978–1991) The milestone event of this period was the passage of the Civil Service Reform Act (CSRA) of 1978, which, next to the Pendleton Act, is the most significant piece of federal workforce legislation in U.S. history. The CSRA marked the culmination of nearly fifty years of on-again, off-again efforts to restructure and improve the federal civil service. The Civil Service Commission, created in 1883, was beginning to show its age and lose its effectiveness. As a candidate for president in 1976, Jimmy Carter recognized the political potential of the issue and campaigned on "fixing" the government's civil service system. After his election, he set about redesigning the federal personnel system to reconcile effective management with political responsiveness. The result of this effort was the CSRA. The CSRA produced several notable changes that are still in effect:

- Replaced the Civil Service Commission with the Office of Personnel Management (OPM) and established the bipartisan Merit Systems Protection Board (MSPB) to investigate alleged violations of federal human resource management laws.

- Created the Senior Executive Service (SES) to promote greater flexibility for top-level administrators and to provide financial incentives for good performance.

- Established the Federal Labor Relations Council (FLRC) to replace the Federal Labor Relations Authority (FLRA) as an oversight body for labor relations in the federal government and established a statutory framework for federal labor–management relations.

- Reformed several other aspects of the civil service system, making it easier to discharge nonperforming employees, instituted a new agency performance appraisal system, strengthened whistleblower protections, and established a merit pay system for mid-level administrators.

As Table 14.1 shows, federal senior executives are still primarily male: nearly 75 percent in 2000. However, women have made some gains, increasing their percentage of the senior executive service from approximately 11 percent in 1990 to slightly more than 25 percent in 2000, and minorities have increased from about 7 percent in 1990 to 14 percent in 2000. One problem for the near future is that the SES is becoming more retirement eligible; more than 40 percent are eligible for early retirement.

The Era of Reinvention and September 11 (1992–present) The Clinton administration's National Performance Review (discussed in Chapter 4) was

TABLE 14.1 Chief Characteristics of Senior Executive Service Members, 1990–2000

	1990	1992	1994	1996	1998	2000
Average Age	50.7	51.8	51.8	51.9	52.3	52.7
Average Length of Service	22.1	23.2	22.8	22.8	22.8	23.5
Retirement Eligible						
Regular	20.0%	22.0%	31.0%	24.3%	27.0%	27.6%
Early Out	34.0%	29.0%	36.0%	37.3%	39.2%	40.6%
Education						
Not College Graduate	5.0%	5.0%	5.0%	4.3%	4.4%	5.2%
College Graduate	29.0%	29.0%	26.0%	26.0%	26.4%	27.0%
Advanced Degree	66.0%	66.0%	69.0%	69.7%	69.0%	67.8%
Gender						
Male	88.8%	87.5%	83.5%	79.6%	77.6%	74.7%
Female	11.2%	12.5%	16.5%	20.4%	22.4%	25.3%
Minority	7.6%	8.0%	10.6%	11.7%	12.9%	14.4%
Occupation						
Scientist/Engineer	30.0%	29.0%	27.0%	24.4%	23.0%	22.3%
Other Professional	20.0%	24.0%	24.0%	25.5%	23.5%	23.3%
Administrative/Technical	50.0%	48.0%	49.0%	50.2%	53.5%	54.4%
Geographic Location						
DC Area	72.0%	72.0%	73.0%	73.5%	72.5%	72.6%
Other	28.0%	28.0%	27.0%	26.5%	27.5%	27.4%

Note: All data as of September 30 of selected year; percentages may not add to 100 due to rounding.

SOURCE: The Fact Book: Federal Civilian Workforce Statistics, 2001 ed., U.S. Office of Personnel Management, July 2001, 74.

another serious attempt at reforming the federal bureaucracy. After September 11, 2001, the energies of the federal government were directed chiefly toward national defense and homeland security concerns, which have diverted it from comprehensive reform of federal HRA. When Congress passed the law creating the Department of Homeland Security (DHS) in 2002, however, it gave the secretary the authority to waive civil service rules that apply to all other departments of the federal government. Supporters of the change assert that the sensitive and urgent nature of homeland security requires a more streamlined and flexible workforce than current civil service rules permit. One key aspect of the law makes DHS employees more accountable by giving managers more authority to discipline incompetent or inefficient workers. Opponents argue that the weakening of civil service regulations is an attempt to undermine federal job protections and ultimately reduce the size of the federal workforce.

Court Decisions Affecting Patronage

In addition to federal statutes, the Supreme Court has issued a series of decisions establishing constraints on the ability of elected officials to use patronage, especially at the state level, beginning with *Elrod v. Burns* (1976). Prior to this, the Court usually looked the other way in patronage cases, ignoring even its most blatant instances. But in *Elrod v. Burns*, the Court decided that the Democratic Sheriff of Cook County, Illinois, acted unconstitutionally when he dismissed non–civil service employees for purely political reasons. The Court ruled that political affiliation was not always relevant to every position that involved policy-making or confidentiality.[12]

In another important decision, the Supreme Court ruled in *Branti v. Finkel* (1980) that in some cases, political affiliation may be considered a requirement for certain types of government jobs.[13] However, the Court stipulated that the government had to prove that partisanship is essential to effective job performance and could not merely assert that the position is a policy-making one. Similarly, in *Rutan v. Republican Party of Illinois* (1990), the Court ruled that public employees' First Amendment rights are violated if they are denied a job or promotion or are transferred because of their political affiliation, unless the government can show that a vital government interest is served by an employees' partisan affiliation.[14]

One unintended consequence of the Court decisions has been a shift from public employment to contract awards to reward political supporters. Consequently, the courts have started to critically examine the role of political influence in obtaining governmental contracts. In *O'Hare Truck Service v. Northlake* (1996), the Court ruled in favor of the defendant, upholding the firm's contention that the city had violated its First Amendment rights when it stopped doing business with the company for political reasons.[15] The decision's upshot is that "patronage and First Amendment rights are generally not compatible. . . . The Court has served notice that the use of political influence to give advantage to prospective employees, to influence personal decisions within the employer-employee relationship, or to terminate government contractors will not be countenanced."[16] Thus, the courts have consistently upheld the fundamental tenets of the merit system.

Public Employees and Political Participation

The Hatch Act (1939), and subsequent revisions, delineate the rights of public employees with regard to partisan political activities. The Hatch Act served as a congressional response to the New Deal's unprecedented expansion of the federal workforce.[17] Its main provision states: "No officer or employee in the Executive Branch of the federal government, or any agency or department thereof, shall take part in political management or political campaigns."[18] The act covers most non-policy-making federal employees, including those not in the career civil service. The act was amended in 1940 and again in 1966; in each case, the amendments strengthened restrictions on the right of federal employees to participate in politics. In 1993, President Bill Clinton signed yet another amendment to the Hatch Act. This time, however, the law was changed to remove many of the restrictions on political participation. For example, the 1993 amendment permits federal employees to engage in most types of political activities, with the exceptions of running for political office, soliciting political campaign contributions, and engaging in political activity while on the job.

The Public Human Resource Administration Process

Human resource administration in government is complex, varying in its details from one level of government and one jurisdiction to another. To a large extent, however, the federal government has served as a model for state and local government, with significant reforms typically occurring at the national level first and then in due course filtering down to state and local governments. Most states carry out the basic human resource functions associated with civil service, including position classification, competitive examination, recruitment and selection, compensation, and removal. These elements are discussed below.

Position Classification

Position classification
A system of organizing an organization's jobs according to their duties and responsibilities, creating formal job descriptions, and establishing equitable pay.

Position classification refers to the organization of jobs according to their duties and responsibilities, creating formal job descriptions for the purpose of establishing formal authority and chains of command, and establishing equitable pay scales.[19] The position classification system, along with competitive examination, has long been one of the cornerstones of the civil service. This technique is an invention of the Progressive Era, and it reflects the goal of achieving efficiency in organizations. Thus, the goal of position classification is to describe and define each position in such level of detail that it becomes, according to several scholars, "not a person but a set of duties and responsibilities fully equivalent to an interchangeable machine part because that is exactly what it represents—a human interchangeable part."[20]

General Schedule (GS) The standard federal government pay scale and position classification system.

The national classification system consists of eighteen grades or levels of white-collar jobs organized into a basic pay structure, called the **General Schedule (GS)**.[21] Within each grade there is a range of ten pay levels based on years of service, and there are more than 450 job categories, called series. Grades GS-1 through GS-4 comprise lower-level clerical positions. Grades GS-5 through GS-11 encompass lower and middle management jobs. At the top of the career civil service pyramid are grades GS-12 through GS-18, the upper-level management positions; this also includes the SES, the highest-ranking nonpolitical appointments. Each increase in GS grade is generally associated with greater responsibility and authority, as well as more pay. Administrators at the top grades also play more of policy-making role. Table 14.2 provides a snapshot of the federal civil service from 1990 to 2000, including summary information and trends for GS grade, salary, and other significant characteristics.

Evolution of Personnel Classification Systems

Early government personnel systems were beset with many serious problems connected with patronage, including pay scales that were often more tied to personal and political connections than to actual job performance. Job classification was therefore intended in large measure to overcome these shortcomings. Position classification was first tried by the federal government on a limited basis as early as 1853.[22] The federal government, however, did not wholly embrace the concept until the Classification Act in 1923, which created the Personal Classification Board, formally establishing hierarchy and job standardization in the federal government.[23] At first, the act affected only a limited number of federal employees. Coverage was later extended to the entire

TABLE 14.2 Trends in Federal Service Employment, 1990–2000

	1990	1995	2000
Annual Base Salary	$32,026	$41,557	$51,618
DC area salaries	$39,834	$51,754	$64,969
Average GS Grade	8.7	9.3	9.5
DC area Grades	10.3	10.9	11.3
Pay System			
General Schedule	73%	75%	72%
Wage Systems	17%	14%	13%
Other	10%	11%	15%
Occupational Category			
White Collar	83%	85%	87%
Professional	21%	24%	24%
Administrative	24%	27%	31%
Blue Collar	17%	15%	13%
Supervisory Status			
Supervisors/Managers	12.4%	11.6%	11.1%
Permanent Appointments	89%	90%	91%
Full-time Permanent	87%	87%	88%
Work Schedule			
Full-time	93%	93%	94%
Part-time	4%	4%	3%
Intermittent	3%	3%	3%
Service			
Competitive	80%	80%	77%
Excepted and Senior Executive Service	20%	20%	23%

(Continued)

TABLE 14.2 Continued

Geographic Location			
U.S.	96%	97%	96%
DC area	14%	15%	16%
Average Age	42.3	44.3	46.3
Average Length of Service	13.4	15.5	17.1
Education			
Bachelors Degree or higher	35%	39%	41%
Veterans Preference	30%	26%	24%
Vietnam Era Veterans	17%	17%	14%
Retired Military	4.9%	4.2%	3.9%
Retired Officers	0.5%	0.5%	0.5%

Notes: All data as of September 30 of selected year. DC area comprises Washington, DC, Maryland, Virginia, and West Virginia metropolitan area.

Data shown for "Average Age" and "Average Length of Service" represent full-time permanent employees.

Data shown for "Retirement Eligible" represent full-time permanent employees under the Civil Service Retirement System (excluding hires since January 1984), and the Federal Employees Retirement System (since January 1984).

Data shown for "Annual Base Salary" represent the average for full-time permanent employees

SOURCE: The Fact Book: Federal Civilian Workforce Statistics, 2001 ED., U.S. Office of Personnel Management, July 2001, 10–11.

government, however. The original classification system was criticized by the first Hoover Commission as largely ineffective, which led to the passage of another Classification Act by Congress in 1949. The 1949 act essentially replaces the first one, introducing some important changes such as improving the federal government's pay system, transferring some human resource functions to agencies, and establishing a "supergrade" system at the top of the career civil service.

Problems with the Position Classification System

Observers of the current system have identified three major problems and suggested some modifications to improve its operation.[24] First, rigid job descriptions can become quickly outdated, as one writer notes: "Whereas rigid job descriptions and narrow classifications may once have been effective staffing tools, their relevance to the contemporary is, at best, debatable. Jobs involving rapid technological change quickly outgrow facile definitions and unreasonably constrain the efforts of knowledge workers. Moreover, restrictive classifications are widely perceived as deleterious to job satisfaction and motivation."[25]

Second, current classification practices give rise to such distortions as redesignating technical specialist positions into administrative positions in order to improve their grade levels. While the intention is good—it increases the organization's capacity to attract and retain professionals—this practice can ultimately lead to organizational confusion and meaningless job descriptions. Third, old job descriptions more accurately depict duties and responsibilities of easily standardized jobs, such as low-end clerical and technical positions, but are less accurate with regard to depicting the duties and responsibilities of professional and high-level administrative positions.

Although no single personnel classification reform can correct all of these problems, current efforts center on **broadbanding**, which has attracted considerable interest among scholars and public administrators. Basically, broadbanding collapses pay grades by reducing a myriad of job classifications into a smaller, more manageable number.[26] Proponents assert that it gives supervisors more flexibility in assigning and rewarding public employees on the basis of their performance. Workers also gain greater job flexibility, since they are no longer constrained by rigid job descriptions. Instead they can move around the organization more easily and take on new tasks and assignments that are better suited to their interests and skills.

Broadbanding A practice to collapse pay grades by reducing a large number of job classifications into a smaller, more manageable number.

Entering and Remaining in the Public Service

When a public agency identifies a staffing need, it first makes certain it has sufficient resources to support the new position. The agency then begins advertising the position to attract a pool of qualified applicants. The position is usually open to candidates from both inside and outside the organization. If the recruitment phase is successful, the agency will have enough qualified job seekers to make a good selection decision. The chief means that public agencies employ to select the most qualified applicant is the competitive examination process.

The Examination Process

Throughout the history of the American civil service, "merit has been equated with selection via competitive examination."[27] Government agencies use **competitive examinations** in order to select the best-qualified candidates for public employment. While often supplemented in the selection process with more specialized examinations, personal interviews, and other evaluative tools by the agencies, competitive examination remains the cornerstone of the governmental hiring process.

Competitive examination The system to determine merit in hiring new government employees.

Despite the close association of competitive testing with merit, the examination process has been nonetheless the target of considerable criticism over the years, particularly on grounds that it discriminates against racial minorities. Before 1974, the federal government administered the Federal Service Entrance Examination (FSEE), which was designed to be a single point of entry into the federal workforce; the FSEE replaced one hundred separate examinations. Minority job seekers, however, performed relatively poorly on the examination compared to their white counterparts. The Professional and Administrative Career Examination (PACE), developed to address these concerns, replaced the FSEE in 1974. But this examination also came under attack as biased in favor of white applicants. In 1981, the federal government agreed to drop the PACE as a requirement for entering the federal civil service. A new examination, Administrative Careers with America (ACWA), was developed in 1990.[28]

Problems with Civil Service Testing

Cultural bias A systematic form of discrimination against certain cultures, especially minorities.

Validation The criteria that determine the bias of an examination.

In its landmark 1971 decision in *Griggs v. Duke Power Company*, the U.S. Supreme Court ruled that continued use of a competitive test must be based on its job relatedness.[29] Since numerous factors are related to a candidate's ability to perform a job (motivation, working conditions, training, supervision, etc.), job performance can only be imperfectly tested by a written examination.[30] Another common criticism of civil service examinations is their alleged **cultural bias**. Critics contend that minority candidates are more likely than white candidates to receive lower scores on examinations for reasons that have nothing to do with the nature of the job. The process of **validation** can determine how biased an examination is in this regard. One type of test validity, content validity, measures whether the questions on the examination are directly related to the duties and responsibilities of the job being sought. For example, an examination for science teachers might ask questions related to the applicant's command of scientific concepts. Another type, criterion validity, measures the job relatedness of the examination by administering the test to current employees and correlating the results with supervisor's evaluations of the employees' job performance. Higher test scores are presumed to correlate strongly (i.e., to match up) with high performance ratings from supervisors.

Certification and Selection

The qualifying candidate, if he or she scores among the highest exam takers, is certified by the OPM, or the equivalent state or local agency, and included on a list that is then made available to the hiring agency. The agency may select one of the certified candidates, or if the original applicants are no longer interested in the position, the agency may ask the OPM to submit more names for its consideration.

One major exception to the principles of merit-based selection is the preferential treatment the civil service gives to military veterans. Since the Civil War, veterans have received special advantages in the government's hiring process. In 1944, near the end of World War II, Congress passed the Veterans Preference Act, under which bonus points are added to veterans' scores on civil service examinations. Moreover, disabled veterans with passing scores are placed at the top of the candidates list. As of 1999, the veterans' preference accounted for 24 percent of all federal employees (see Table 14.2). This is down slightly from 30 percent in 1990.

Employee Appraisal

Performance appraisal The process of systematically assessing employee productivity.

An employee's job performance is typically evaluated on a regular basis, usually annually, by his or her supervisor. **Performance appraisal**, the process of assessing employee productivity, is "viewed as a necessary evil," which generates a "considerable" amount of administrator and scholarly dissatisfaction.[31] Performance evaluations have serveral functions: employee development (ascertaining skill deficiencies and suggesting corrective measures); correcting poor performance; conveying management's notions of work quality to employees; determining whether pay is proportionate with duties; and documenting work history for disciplinary or promotion purposes.[32] Clearly, this procedure is important for the organization. Without it, it would not have an objective basis on which to determine employee productivity. Evaluating worker performance, however, is not without problems, which may include the following:

- The appraisal may more accurately reflect the rater's strengths and weaknesses than the employee's.

- The process can lack credibility: for example, if a supervisor gives the same rating to everyone.

- Measuring worker output is difficult in many public functions, particularly those that deliver services (e.g., police, welfare, human resource administration).

- Some performance appraisal functions may conflict with each other: employee development may conflict with documenting work history; using performance appraisal information for disciplinary purposes might send a mixed message.[33]

Pay for performance
Paying government employees according to the quality of their work rather than seniority.

Growing interest in **pay for performance**, which bases pay on quality of work rather than seniority, is stimulating more research into improving performance appraisal systems and in identifying successful examples of such systems. A 1996 case study, for example, describes an effective appraisal system operated by a municipal police department and identifies several factors that contributed to its success.[34] Employee appraisal, according to this research, could be improved by the following: significant user participation (both employee and supervisor) in the appraisal system's development; more thorough rater training; clear articulation of its rationale, goals, and objectives; and an employee rating format compatible with organizational culture and the objectives of the appraisal system. The ongoing efforts to improve public human resource management are likely to spur further improvements in performance appraisal techniques and systems.

Pay Comparability

While public employees often receive less compensation than their private counterparts, nonmonetary rewards of public service (e.g., contributing to the public good) offset these pay differences to some extent. Nevertheless, civil servants still need to pay the rent just like everyone else, so they are not unconcerned with wage and salary issues. Moreover, since the 1980s, the federal service pay gap has been growing, leading some observers to express concern over recruiting and retaining skilled workers, particularly in information technology services.[35] Pay comparability became official federal policy in 1962 with the passage of the Federal Salary Reform Act, which requires the president to submit to Congress an annual report comparing federal government and private business pay scales, and to make recommendations for salary adjustments based on this report.[36]

In 1990, Congress passed the Federal Employee Pay Comparability Act (FEPCA), which established the principle that public service pay should be comparable with the private sector for similar types of work. But a major loophole in the FEPCA proved a significant stumbling block for efforts to bring federal salaries more in line with those in the private sector. The FEPCA stipulates that, because of a national emergency or for economic reasons, the president can present an alternative plan to pay adjustments, subject to congressional override. This provision actually helped *increase* the private–public pay disparity from 3 percent in 1978 to 25 percent in 1990.[37]

The FEPCA also replaced the uniform national salary schedule with a system of locality pay, in an attempt to improve the federal government's efforts at recruiting and retaining qualified workers outside of Washington, D.C. Locality pay takes into account that different job markets exist in different geographical areas; therefore, the federal government, in some high cost-of-living cities, such as New York and San Francisco, must offer higher pay and benefit packages in order to attract and keep a high-quality workforce.

Confirming the FEPCA's suspicions, research found that recruitment and retention problems were indeed worse in New York, San Francisco, and Los Angeles (areas that initially received FEPCA pay increases) than in other cities.[38] But it also examined the other twenty-eight metropolitan areas that were eligible for FEPCA adjustments and found these localities did not differ significantly in their employee recruitment and retention patterns, which suggested that local pay adjustments had little effect. Thus, the jury is still out on the efficacy of locality pay to attract and keep a high-quality federal workforce, but clearly it is a step in the right direction for improving public employees' morale.

Removal from the Civil Service

The civil service system was designed in large measure to protect public employees from arbitrary dismissal or removal for partisan political reasons. But critics charge that the rules and procedures put in place for this purpose can also make it difficult for supervisors to remove poorly performing employees from their jobs. Termination of employment, of course, is a tool of last resort, which should only be used when all other means of disciplining employees, such as reprimand, suspension, demotion, and reassignment, have been tried and fail. A good administrator seldom prefers to dismiss an employee; usually he or she prefers to demote or reassign the worker if those options are available. The ultimate objective of the disciplinary process should be to improve job performance not to remove employees. To that end, standards of performance and disciplinary policy must be articulated in clear, understandable language and applied in a fair and judicious manner, or else punitive actions will fail to have their intended effect.

Public sector supervisors must build an especially strong case for removal, since due process requirements usually provide for appeals both inside and outside the agency, which generally take considerable time to work through. Federal employees, for instance, can choose to make a final appeal to the Merit Systems Protection Board, and many states have a similar type of ultimate appeals body for their employees. In the end, supervisors may choose to tolerate an ineffectual employee rather than spend the time and effort required to remove him or her, especially since the probability of success is uncertain.

Labor Relations in the Public Sector

The right of federal government employees to form and join unions dates from 1912 (the Lloyd-La Follette Act).[39] The highpoint of public unionism occurred in the 1960s and 1970s when both the number of unions and the percentage of the public workforce covered by collective bargaining agreements increased dramatically. Table 14.3 compares private sector and public sector labor union membership since 1983. As the table shows, while private sector unionization continues to decline, public sector unionization has remained constant. It is

TABLE 14.3 Trends in Public Sector and Private Sector Labor Unions, 1983–2000

Sector Total (1,000)	1983	1985	1990	1995	2000
Wage and Salary Workers					
Union Members	17,717.4	16,996.1	16,739.8	16,359.6	16,258.2
Covered by Unions	20,532.1	19,358.1	19,057.8	18,346.3	17,944.1
Public Sector Workers					
Union Members	5,737.2	5,743.1	6,485.0	6,927.4	7,110.5
Covered by Unions	7,112.2	6,920.6	7,691.4	7,986.6	7,975.6
Private Sector Workers					
Union Members	11,980.2	11,253.0	10,254.8	9,432.1	9,147.7
Covered by Unions	13,419.9	12,437.5	11,366.4	10,359.8	9,968.5
Percentage					
Wage and Salary Workers					
Union Members	20.1%	18.0%	16.1%	14.9%	13.5%
Covered by Unions	23.3%	20.5%	18.3%	16.7%	14.9%
Public Sector Workers					
Union Members	36.7%	35.7%	36.5%	37.7%	37.5%
Covered by Unions	45.5%	43.1%	43.3%	43.5%	42.0%
Private Sector Workers					
Union Members	16.5%	14.3%	11.9%	10.3%	9.0%
Covered by Unions	18.5%	15.9%	13.2%	11.3%	9.8%

SOURCE: U.S. Census Bureau, Statistical Abstract of the United States, 2001, Table 637.

Collective bargaining A legal arrangement whereby labor unions and management negotiate over the terms of employment.

Labor union A group formed by employees in an organization that is accorded special legal status to bargain with management over the terms of employment.

fair to say that today, a government worker is more likely to be a member of a labor union than is a private sector worker.

Collective bargaining is the heart of labor relations in both the private and public sectors. It is an arrangement in which a **labor union** and management agree to negotiate over the terms of employment in an organization. These terms of employment typically include pay and benefits, workers' complaints and grievances procedures, working conditions, and position classifications. As a result of collective bargaining, these and other human resource functions, once considered the exclusive domain of management, are governed by contracts.

Labor relations in the private and public sectors generally occur in four stages:

1. Organizing the workforce
2. Determining the bargaining unit (which employees are included) and the scope of bargaining (what terms of employment can be negotiated)
3. Negotiating a settlement or resolving an impasse, which may involve mediation, arbitration, or a strike or other type of work stoppage
4. Administration of the contract

Differences between Public and Private Labor Relations

Although labor relations in the private and public sectors generally follow these four stages, there are some marked differences between the two sectors in terms of collective bargaining arrangements. In the private sector, the following assumptions underlie the process:

■ Federal laws and directives assign labor and management co-equal legal status; neither side acting alone can alter the other side's basic rights in the bargaining relationship.

■ Market forces temper the demands of both sides; neither side will typically make demands that will make them uncompetitive in the market.

■ The labor–management relationship is essentially zero-sum: one side's gains are achieved by the other side's losses.

■ Strikes and lockouts are used to resolve negotiation impasses.[40]

In the public sector, however, a different set of assumptions operates:

■ Labor and management are not co-equal; according to law, management (i.e., government) dominates because it establishes the basic rules—laws, regulations, etc.—by which both sides must abide.

■ The market is not a constraint on either government or employees; neither side is concerned about competitiveness.

■ There is less of a zero-sum quality to labor relations; because taxpayers foot the bill, it is not necessarily the case that if one side gains the other side loses.

■ Alternative means to resolve breakdowns in negotiation exist because of the widespread legal prohibition on public employee strikes.[41]

Evolution of Federal Labor Relations

In the federal government, limited forms of unionization were permitted in certain agencies around the turn of the twentieth century. Until the passage of the Lloyd-La Follette Act (1912), however, no uniform policy gave federal employees the right to form and join unions.[42] The prohibition against federal strikes was accorded legal status with the passage of the Labor Management Relations Act of 1947, better known as the Taft-Hartley Act. Taft-Hartley was passed in response to the impressive gains made by unions during Franklin D. Roosevelt's presidency. Taft-Hartley's ban on striking was later tested during the administration of Ronald Reagan by the Professional Air Traffic Controllers Organization (PATCO) (discussed in Vignette 14.1).

VIGNETTE 14.1   A Tale of Two Federal Strikes

The two strikes described here trace the evolution of federal labor relations during a critical transitional period. The postal workers' strike occurred during the peak period for unionization efforts in government, while the air traffic controllers' strike occurred after this period ended. The differences in outcome could not be more striking. The postal workers' strike began on March 17, 1970, when New York City postal workers from Manhattan and the Bronx voted to go on strike. The next day, postal workers at other branches in New York City walked off their jobs, and within two days, more than 200,000 of the country's 750,000 postal workers were on strike.

The causes of the strike are not difficult to identify. One major reason for the strike was the abysmally low wage rates for postal workers, which started at $6,100 per year and increased to only $8,442 over a twenty-one-year period. This meant that in many expensive areas, postal workers had to supplement their incomes with second jobs, or go on welfare, as did 7 percent of New York City's carriers at the time of the strike. As a result of the low pay, workers suffered from poor morale, and the department experienced a high rate of employee turnover. Exacerbating the situation, the Post Office suffered from financial woes, which were the result of budget cutbacks during the 1960s. At the same time, demand for services grew throughout the decade, and facilities and equipment deteriorated due to age and the lack of replacement and repair. All of this led to increasing mail backlogs, which contributed to the stress experienced by the workers.

The strike halted mail service in 671 locations, including Detroit, Philadelphia, and other major cities. In an attempt to end the strike, President Nixon declared a national emergency and ordered out the National Guard, but the strike continued. Indeed, it quickly became apparent that union leaders had lost control of the situation to the more militant members. The striking workers were openly challenging the authority of the federal government, which issued criminal sanctions and court orders against the strike.

Strikes are prohibited by federal law. Workers who are found guilty of violating the no-strike prohibition face a fine or up to a year in prison. However, this threat ultimately proved ineffective. As one union head asserted of the workers, "They'll stay out until hell freezes over." The strike ended when the Nixon administration conceded to the union's chief demands, which included giving the union the right to negotiate wages and other financial matters with the government. This was in contrast to the previous practice of Congress setting pay rates as it does for all other federal service jobs. The government also agreed to a 14 percent pay hike for the postal workers. The other important consequence of the strike was the passage of the Postal Reorganization Act of 1970, which transformed the Post Office from an ordinary department to a government corporation.

(continued on next page)

The Professional Air Traffic Controllers Organization (PATCO) tried to achieve a similarly successful outcome for their strike, which began on August 3, 1981, when 13,000 controllers walked off their jobs. The union leadership hoped the federal government would capitulate to the their demands for higher wages, a shorter workweek, and increased retirement benefits, just as it had a decade earlier for the postal workers' union. However, times were different and the political situation did not favor the union: Ronald Reagan, the newly elected president, promised a tougher, more conservative approach to labor relations. Ironically, the union had been one of the few to support his successful run for the presidency.

PATCO was noted for its highly militant and confrontational approach to federal labor relations. The union was responsible for six serious disruptions of air travel from its creation in 1968 until the 1981 strike. Despite the controllers as a group having one of the highest salaries among federal employees—averaging $33,000 annually by the time of the strike—the union argued that the stressful nature of their job entitled them to a raise and a shorter workweek. For its part, the government was willing to negotiate. The FAA made a $40 million offer, which included a 10 percent pay hike for night shifts and shorter workweek. This offer, however, was not close enough to PATCO's original demands, and 95 percent of the membership voted against it.

The union had started preparing for a possible strike several years earlier. In 1977, it established the National Controller Subsistence Fund, which by 1981 had over $3 million. In addition to the union's annual dues income of $5.5 million, this meant that the union was in a strong position economically to weather a strike.

PATCO chose the busiest time of the year for the airline industry. Major airlines such as Eastern, American, and TWA would lose $30 million a day during the strike. The union hoped this economic pressure would force the federal government to accede to its demands. However, when the strike began on August 3, the FAA had a contingency plan on hand. Despite the union's dire predictions, the nation's air traffic system was not shut down and air safety was not seriously compromised during the strike. A mixture of supervisors and nonstriking controllers staffed airport towers. To reduce the risk of accidents, the FAA ordered airlines at major airports to reduce scheduled flights by 50 percent during peak hours. The union did succeed, however, at alienating the American public, whose lack of support for the strike allowed the government to take a strong stand against the striking controllers.

President Reagan lost no time in taking punitive action against the union. The day the strike began, he issued an ultimatum: return to work in forty-eight hours or be terminated. Soon the full weight of the legal system was brought to bear on the controllers' union. The government ordered PATCO leaders hauled off to jail for defying court injunctions against a strike. The Justice Department issued indictments against striking controllers. Federal courts fined the union $1 million a day and sequestered PATCO's strike fund to pay the fines. The FAA fired over 11,000 controllers, while 1,200 returned to airport towers under threat of termination.

The final blow came when the Federal Labor Relations Authority moved to decertify the union in October, under provisions of the Civil Service Reform Act of 1978. A federal appeals court later upheld decertification. By December, PATCO, a mere shell of its former self, filed for bankruptcy. The government had effectively put the union out of business permanently.

The differences between the 1970 and 1981 strikes could not be greater, particularly with regard to the outcome. In the case of the earlier strike, the union emerged stronger than before, with most of its demands met by the federal government. The 1981 strike, however, destroyed the controllers' union for all time. Ironically, going into the 1981 strike, PATCO was the stronger of the two unions, with a highly paid membership who enjoyed good working conditions and a sizable strike fund. The postal workers, on the other hand, were among the lowest-paid federal employees and toiled in many cases under difficult conditions. Politically, although both Nixon and Reagan were both conservative Republicans, Reagan took a harder stance against labor unions and viewed ending the strike as a defining event for his young presidency.

SOURCE: Pels, Rebecca. "The Pressures of PATCO: Strikes and Stress in the 1980s. *Essays in History:* Vol 37. http://etext.lib.virginia.edu/journals/EH/EH37/Pels.html and for an exhaustive discussion of the 1970 postal strike see www.nylcbr36.org/history.htm, which is the official website of the New York Letter Carriers Union that set in motion the chain of events that led to the national walkout by postal workers.

The Professional Air Traffic Controllers Organization went on strike in 1981 demanding more pay, better working conditions, and a shorter work week from the U.S. government.

SOURCE: Jim West/The Image Works

A pivotal event in federal labor relations was Executive Order 10988, issued by President John F. Kennedy in 1962. EO 10988, entitled "Employee-Management Cooperation in the Federal Service," gave federal employees the right to engage in collective bargaining, a right which private sector workers had had since 1935.[43] EO 10988, however, restricted collective bargaining to issues other than pay and benefits, which would still be determined by Congress. The order also established limited grievance arbitration procedures, which would be of a purely advisory nature and lacking in enforcement powers. Despite the limited nature of the rights guaranteed by EO 10988, President Kennedy's support for federal collective bargaining rights helped to spread collective bargaining to other levels of government. As a result, the 1960s and 1970s witnessed the peak of state and local public sector unionization, which saw public union membership climbing throughout the period.

President Jimmy Carter contributed to the framework of federal labor relations with his signing of the CSRA (see above) and creation of the Federal Labor Relations Authority (FLRA). The FLRA replaced the Federal Labor Relations Council, which had been established by President Richard Nixon. The FLRA was to serve as an independent and bipartisan body. Congress gave it rulemaking authority and the broad powers to address unfair labor practices in federal agencies. The prohibition on strikes and other work stoppages in federal agencies was continued by the CSRA. The FLRA's authority to prevent strikes, however, was tested by the air traffic controllers' strike in 1981. The FLRA took quick action by disbanding the union, which resulted in the layoffs of nearly eleven thousand employees (see Vignette 14.1).

State and Local Government Experience with Labor Relations

In contrast to the federal government, state and local governments do not operate under a common set of rules or institutions governing labor relations. Consequently, nonfederal labor relations do not form a single, uniform pattern; instead, there are numerous arrangements in place. For example, 47 percent of all local government employees and 34 percent of all state employees are unionized, which is a far greater percentage than in the private sector. Some states allow public employees a limited right to strike, although most states follow the federal practice of outlawing strikes. Not all state and local government functions are covered by collective bargaining contracts, even in the northeastern and the midwestern states, where public employee unions are strongest and more numerous. With the exception of Florida, state and local employee unions are less powerful or completely absent in the southern, southwestern and western mountain states.

Social Equity in the Public Workplace

Affirmative action A controversial attempt by the government to bring more minorities into the workforce.

There is probably no topic in public administration more controversial than **affirmative action** and the pursuit of social equity in the public workplace. Public administration, in this respect, reflects all the tensions and conflict over matters concerning race and gender that can be found in broader American society. For much of America's history, women, African Americans, and other minorities were treated as inferior to white males in nearly every respect. Only in the last century were women finally given the right to vote. In the case of African American males, even though the Fifteenth Amendment extended to them the right to vote in 1871, numerous obstacles were put in their way—particularly in southern states—until the 1960s. The civil rights and women's rights movements helped produce significant changes in American society, and their effects are felt in government employment as strongly as in other areas of society. Government, in fact, has made tremendous strides in equalizing employment opportunities in the last half-century.

The public sector, particularly the federal government, generally offers more employment opportunities to minorities and women today than does the private sector, as shown in Table 14.4. But this has not always been the case. In 1892, for example, there were just 2,393 African Americans employed by the federal government, mostly in low-paying, manual labor jobs.[44] Before the Civil War, the federal government employed no African Americans at all. Women fared hardly better, and both groups experienced significant job discrimination at the hands of the federal government well into the twentieth century. An important reason for increasing the numbers of minorities and women in government stems from a desire to make the public service more representative of society as a whole.

Representative bureaucracy A government workforce that reflects the people or the particular community that the government serves.

Representative bureaucracy refers to the idea that the demographic composition of the public workforce should reflect that of current American society. Samuel Krislov said that representative bureaucracy was important for a democracy because it helps to bind members of different social and ethnic groups to the government and its policies, which contributes to the government's overall efficiency and effectiveness.[45] Furthermore, greater representation in the bureaucracy assures that the represented groups' concerns and issues will be given due consideration by government, even if they are largely ignored by the other institutions of society. The composition of the federal workforce has remained stable in its race and gender makeup since 1988 (see Table 14.4).

Evolution of Equal Opportunity Policy

Equal opportunity (EO) programs are the chief means to promote equity in employment and are, therefore, central to the concept of representative bureaucracy. In recent decades, government at all levels has made considerable efforts to increase the number of minorities in public employment. According to one study of the 1972–1993 period: "There has been a steady increase in the government-wide employment of women and minorities overall and in higher-level positions."[46] The progress of women and minorities in government has been a

TABLE 14.4 Trends in Federal and Private Sector Employment of Minorities, 1988–2000

		Total		All Minorities			Black		Hispanic		Other Minorities
		Men	Women	Men	Women	Men	Women	Men	Women	Men	Women
1988	F	58.0%	42.0%	12.9%	14.2%	6.9%	10.1%	3.2%	2.0%	2.8%	2.1%
	P	55.0%	45.0%	11.8%	9.8%	5.2%	5.3%	5.0%	3.2%	1.6%	1.3%
1990	F	57.4%	42.6%	12.9%	14.6%	6.8%	10.3%	3.2%	2.1%	2.9%	2.2%
	P	54.7%	45.3%	11.9%	9.9%	5.1%	5.2%	5.2%	3.3%	1.6%	1.4%
1992	F	56.2%	43.8%	13.0%	15.2%	6.7%	10.5%	3.3%	2.3%	3.0%	2.4%
	P	54.6%	45.4%	12.5%	10.5%	5.2%	5.4%	5.4%	3.5%	1.9%	1.6%
1994	F	57.3%	42.7%	13.1%	15.0%	6.6%	10.4%	3.4%	2.3%	3.1%	2.3%
	P	54.4%	45.6%	12.7%	10.5%	5.2%	5.3%	5.5%	3.5%	2.0%	1.7%
1996	F	57.1%	42.9%	13.4%	15.3%	6.5%	10.5%	3.6%	2.4%	3.2%	2.5%
	P	53.7%	46.3%	13.6%	11.9%	5.1%	5.6%	6.2%	4.3%	2.2%	2.0%
1998	F	57.1%	42.9%	13.8%	15.7%	6.6%	10.5%	3.8%	2.6%	3.4%	2.6%
	P	53.7%	46.3%	14.0%	12.3%	5.2%	5.8%	6.5%	4.3%	2.3%	2.2%
2000	F	56.2%	43.8%	13.9%	16.4%	6.7%	10.9%	3.8%	2.7%	3.4%	2.8%
	P	53.5%	46.6%	14.4%	13.2%	5.2%	6.0%	6.8%	5.0%	2.4%	2.4%

Notes: F = Federal Civilian Workforce; covers full and part-time permanent employees in non-Postal Executive Branch agencies participating in Central Personnel Data File (CPDF).
P = Public Labor Force.

Percentages by gender may not add to 100 due to rounding.

SOURCE: *The Fact Book: Federal Civilian Workforce Statistics,* 2001 ed., U.S. Office of Personnel Management, July 2001, 40.

historical success story that, while far from complete, deserves much more public recognition than it generally receives.

Types of Social Equity Programs

H. George Frederickson divides social equity programs into two types: (1) those that enhance prospect opportunity, and (2) those that further means opportunity.[47] **Prospect opportunity** refers to when individuals, regardless of race or sex, can compete for the same position, with everyone enjoying roughly the same chances of success in attaining it. **Means opportunity** refers to when candidates of equal talent, skills, or qualifications, regardless of race or sex, can compete for the same position with roughly the same likelihood of success. The EO policies of the U.S. government are designed primarily to promote means opportunity in society. Perhaps the best example of EO policy at the national level is equal employment opportunity (EEO). The history of equal employment opportunity at the federal level begins in 1941 when President Franklin Roosevelt issued an executive order that banned discrimination on the basis of race, color, religion, or national origin from the wartime defense industry and the federal civil service.

The Evolution of Federal EEO Laws

Although federal EEO policy continued to evolve under Presidents Truman and Eisenhower, it was the civil rights movement of the early 1960s that pushed social equity concerns to the front of the national political agenda. President Kennedy dedicated his administration to furthering equal opportunity in employment, and his successor, Lyndon Johnson, continued this emphasis with the Civil Rights Act of 1964. The act prohibited discrimination based on race, color, religion, gender, or national origin. It also ensured equal employment opportunities for all federal employees regardless of race or gender. In 1965, President Johnson issued Executive Order 11246, which extended equal employment coverage to include all contractors and subcontractors receiving federal funds.

This order, in effect, created the policy of affirmative action by requiring employers to correct past discrimination practices through the use of special means to integrate their workforce. Affirmative action goes beyond equal opportunity by ordering employers to devise goals, timetables, and other methods to increase the hiring and promotion chances of minorities. But affirmative action stirred up a hornet's nest of controversy from the beginning. For example, in 1996 California voters passed Proposition 209 banning affirmative action programs by the state government. Other states have passed similar measures.[48]

The values of representative bureaucracy are sometimes at odds with the values of the merit system. Hiring and promotion based on diversity considerations may not necessarily correspond to the merit principle of the most qualified person gets the job. Supporters of affirmative action argue that it helps make government more responsive to the values, needs, and concerns of disadvantaged segments of American society, and provides important symbolic evidence of government's representativeness.

Prospect opportunity A type of social equity program in which people can compete for open positions and jobs regardless of minority status.

Means opportunity A type of social equity program in which candidates of equal talent and skills can compete for a position without minority status being a factor.

Congress created the Equal Employment Opportunity Commission (EEOC) to oversee private sector compliance with the 1965 Civil Rights Act and made the Civil Service Commission responsible for antidiscrimination policy for federal employees. The next major extension of employment opportunity law occurred in 1972 when Congress passed the Equal Employment Opportunity Act, which brought state and local governments under the federal guidelines and extended the EEOC's authority to include nonfederal public employment. The act also provided the legal authority for affirmative action and gave the Civil Service Commission new powers of enforcement.

The Carter administration's reform of the federal civil service led to the next significant expansion of equal employment opportunity policy. Congress decided in the CSRA that the federal bureaucracy should better reflect national diversity within its ranks. To that end, the CSRA required federal agencies to officially adopt affirmative action in order to increase the representation of women and minorities in middle- and high-level management positions.

Court Decisions Affecting Equal Employment Policy

Congress and the president were not the only actors shaping federal equal employment opportunity policy during this period. The courts handed down a number of important decisions that contributed significantly to the evolution of EEO policy. Perhaps the case with the greatest impact was *Griggs v. Duke Power Company* (1971), in which the Supreme Court declared that the Civil Rights Act prohibited the use of certain tests and other educational requirements by employers that did not directly relate to job performance. Originally, the decision applied only to private sector employees. However, in 1972, Congress extended coverage to include public employees as well.

Adverse impact
Previous employment practices and policies by a company bringing about discriminatory results.

At the heart of the *Griggs* ruling was the concept of **adverse impact**, which recognized that a pattern of employment practices and policies had brought about discriminatory results. According to *Griggs*, an employer's intent or motivation in using these tests and other selection devices was unimportant; what mattered most were the consequences of past hiring practices, particularly in terms of their impact on minority employment. The *Griggs* ruling led to the federal government's creation of the **four-fifths rule**, which established a numeric threshold for discrimination: if the selection rate for a particular group falls below 80 percent that of the rate of other groups, this constitutes, for enforcement purposes, statistical evidence of discrimination.

Four-fifths rule
Established a numeric threshold for discrimination: if the selection rate for a particular group is below 80 percent of the rate of other groups, this constitutes statistical evidence of discrimination.

The *Griggs* decision stood as the Court's final word on discrimination in selection practices for many years. In 1989, however, the Court reversed the *Griggs* decision by ruling that the burden of proof fell on the individuals alleging discrimination instead of on the employer. In the *Wards Cove Packing Co v. Atonio* ruling, the Court essentially rejected the earlier emphasis on employee selection rates as the primary evidence of discrimination.[49] As a result of *Wards Cove*, individuals bringing suit in EEO cases now had to show that specific employment practices caused the differences and that the adverse impact was intentional.

The Supreme Court made another important affirmative action ruling in 1989 with the *City of Richmond v. J.A. Croson Co.* decision. In *Croson*, the Court found that Richmond's minority set-aside program was unconstitutional because it was not justified by a compelling interest (i.e., the city failed to provide adequate evidence of racial discrimination) and the city's set-aside provisions were too broadly tailored to correct prior discrimination.[50] The *Croson* ruling meant that from now on, the Supreme Court would apply a strict set of criteria to judge the constitutionality of state and local governments' minority set-aside programs.

The response of Congress to these Court rulings weakening job discrimination protection laws was to pass the Civil Rights Act of 1991. The act specifically reverses the Court actions by making it easier for employees to win job discrimination cases. The strict standards set by the *Croson* decision, however, were not overturned by the act. As a consequence, state and local governments were held to stricter EEO criteria than federal government programs.

In *Adarand Constructor, Inc. v. Pena* (1995), the Supreme Court applied the **strict scrutiny test** to federal minority set-aside programs in order to determine whether affirmative action programs violated the Constitution's Due Process clause.[51] Although the Court stopped short of an outright prohibition of affirmative action, one analyst noted, "The ruling may have virtually the same effect because it creates extraordinarily tough standards that even state and local governments have been hard pressed to meet." Not surprisingly, the ruling has had a chilling effect on affirmative action programs at all levels of government. It sent the message to lower courts that federal affirmative action programs were on shaky legal grounds, which led the Clinton administration to suspend all federal set-aside programs beginning in 1996.[52]

Strict scrutiny test A court ruling that government affirmative action programs must fulfill three constitutional criteria: (1) there must be a compelling interest for the program, (2) the program must be designed narrowly enough to meet its specific goals, and (3) the law or policy must use the least restrictive means to achieve its objectives.

The Current State of Equal Opportunity Employment

Public organizations have made enormous strides in the past few decades in employing minorities and women, much more so than private organizations during the same period. While government should be proud of its record in promoting EEO, it is nonetheless still true that minorities are largely excluded from the middle and upper ranks of public management (see Table 14.5).[53] In addition, women in both the public and private sectors continue to earn less on average than men for similar work (see Table 14.6). The differences are particularly striking when pay rates of minority females are compared to those of white males (see Table 14.7).

Comparable Worth and the Glass Ceiling

Comparable worth programs are efforts to equalize the difference in pay or compensation levels between men and women who do different jobs that are of comparable value to an organization, or similar efforts on behalf of minority men who earn less than their white counterparts for performing similar

Comparable worth An attempt to equalize the difference in compensation levels between men and women who do different jobs that are of comparable value.

TABLE 14.5 Minority and Nonminority Workers by Occupation and Average Salary

Occupational Category	Total	Total Minority	Black	Hispanic	White, Non-Hispanic	Other Minority
White Collar	1,532,484	453,724	256,111	98,321	1,078,760	99,292
Avg Salary	$51,856	$45,171	$43,608	$45,278	$54,668	$49,102
Professional	420,482	91,756	36,571	18,484	328,726	36,701
Avg Salary	$66,381	$62,163	$59,999	$61,696	$67,559	$63,599
Administrative	547,862	141,913	83,008	34,192	405,949	24,713
Avg Salary	$60,825	$56,319	$56,971	$54,670	$62,401	$56,405
Technical	339,100	125,060	76,822	24,630	214,040	23,608
Avg Salary	$34,627	$32,918	$33,444	$33,050	$35,626	$31,690
Clerical	175,018	76,377	50,918	13,532	98,641	11,927
Avg Salary	$26,928	$26,555	$27,023	$25,656	$27,216	$25,504
Other	50,022	18,618	8,792	7,483	31,404	2,343
Avg Salary	$35,363	$34,974	$33,850	$37,531	$35,593	$31,000

Source: The Fact Book: Federal Civilian Workforce Statistics, 2001 ed., U.S. Office of Personnel Management, July 2001, 46.

jobs. Supporters of comparable worth note that jobs in traditionally "female" areas such as nursing and teaching typically earn less than jobs in traditionally "male" areas, although the men's jobs may actually require less formal education or training. For example, a mechanic might earn more than a schoolteacher or an administrative assistant. Although the Equal Pay Act of 1963

TABLE 14.6 Women and Men Workers by Occupation and Earnings

Major Occupation of Longest Job Held	All Workers				Full Time, Year Round			
	Women		Men		Women		Men	
	Number (1,000)	Median Earnings	Number (1,000)	Median Earnings	Number (1,000)	Median Earnings	Number (1,000)	Median Earnings
Total	70,387	$18,389	78,460	$30,104	40,404	$26,324	57,511	$36,476
Executive, Administrators, Managerial	9,404	$31,912	11,243	$51,274	7,302	$36,141	9,831	$55,261
Professional Specialty	11,858	$31,339	9,938	$50,366	7,061	$37,533	7,869	$54,616
White Collar Service Industries	28,635	$17,205	15,299	$30,442	16,274	$24,953	11,056	$37,107
Blue Collar Occupations	20,400	$11,522	41,309	$22,782	9,698	$17,959	28,143	$29,174

Notes: White Collar Services = Technical and related, support, sales, and administrative support.

Blue Collar Occupation = Precision production and craft, operators, assemblers, inspectors, transportation, handlers, service workers, farming, forestry, and fishing.

Source: U.S. Census Bureau, *Statistical Abstract of the United States*, 2001, Table 622.

TABLE 14.7 Trends in Employment and Earnings for U.S. Workers, 1985–2000

	Number of Workers (1,000)				Median Weekly Earnings			
	1985	1990	1995	2000	1985	1990	1995	2000
All Workers	77,002	85,804	89,282	99,917	$ 343	$ 412	$ 479	$ 576
Male	45,589	49,564	51,222	56,273	$ 406	$ 481	$ 538	$ 646
16–24	6,956	6,824	6,118	6,786	$ 240	$ 282	$ 303	$ 376
25+	38,632	42,740	45,104	49,487	$ 442	$ 512	$ 588	$ 700
Female	31,414	36,239	38,060	43,644	$ 277	$ 346	$ 406	$ 491
16–24	5,621	5,227	4,366	5,147	$ 210	$ 254	$ 275	$ 342
25+	5,793	31,012	33,695	38,497	$ 296	$ 369	$ 428	$ 515
White	66,481	72,811	74,874	82,475	$ 355	$ 424	$ 494	$ 591
Male	40,030	42,797	43,747	47,578	$ 417	$ 494	$ 566	$ 669
Female	26,452	30,014	31,127	34,897	$ 281	$ 353	$ 415	$ 500
Black	8,393	9,820	10,596	12,556	$ 277	$ 329	$ 383	$ 468
Male	4,367	4,983	5,279	5,989	$ 304	$ 361	$ 411	$ 503
Female	4,026	4,837	5,317	6,568	$ 252	$ 308	$ 355	$ 429
Hispanic Origin	NA	7,812	8,719	11,738	NA	$ 304	$ 329	$ 396
Male	NA	5,000	5,597	7,261	NA	$ 318	$ 350	$ 414
Female	NA	2,812	3,122	4,477	NA	$ 278	$ 305	$ 364

Notes: All workers includes workers of other races not listed separately.

Source: U.S. Census Bureau, *Statistical Abstract of the United States,* 2001, Table 621.

prohibits different pay rates for equal work or "substantially equal" work performed by men and women, the problem of wage discrimination between men and women persists to the present. In 2000, the Department of Labor found that women earned only 77 percent as much as men, only a slight improvement from the situation in 1963.[54] Moreover, the state of affairs regarding comparable pay has been significantly worse for African American and Hispanic women.[55]

Clearly, women and minorities face significant barriers to their advancement within public organizations. As pointed out previously, women and minorities have been recruited and hired in increasing numbers by government, but once within public agencies, many find their careers stalled at lower-level or middle-management positions. This pattern of failing to reach the top ranks of management is often referred to as hitting the **glass ceiling**. In one study that confirms the existence of ethnic and gender differences in the upper ranks of the federal civil service, the author found that white males continue to be the "gatekeepers" to the positions of power in the federal bureaucracy.[56] White managers effectively control access to career networks, while women and minorities continue to struggle to gain access.

Glass ceiling The concept that individuals (especially women and minorities) reach a certain level in an organization and are not able to rise above it.

Women are making increasing inroads into the executive positions of public organizations.

SOURCE: Journal-Courier/ Steve Warmowski/The Image Works

Fortunately, other research indicates that this situation might be gradually improving. In an exhaustive study of presidents and representative bureaucracy, two researchers examined OPM employment data from 1978 to 1996.[57] They found that the representation of minority and white women in the career Senior Executive Service has increased steadily since 1979, with the highest rates of growth occurring during the Clinton administration. On the negative side, the number of minority men at this level did not increase as fast as for women. Under President George W. Bush, several women and minorities have been appointed to high-profile cabinet positions, including secretary of state (Colin Powell and Condoleezza Rice).

Governments at all levels remain strongly committed to social equity even though, as a scholar of affirmative action observed, the courts no longer support or mandate affirmative action programs as they once did.[58] This commitment reflects public organizations' recognition of the importance of a representative workforce. As a scholar of constitutional law observes, "In the abstract, public organizations are value systems requiring legitimacy for survival. Currently, it is hard to conceive of a public organization claiming legitimacy if it does not recognize the value of social equity in its employment practices."[59] As minority populations continue to grow in the United States, there is also greater need for governments to hire more minorities as well as more women. Moreover, public and private organizations should embrace workplace diversity voluntarily, as they come to recognize the value for the public workplace of hiring people from different social and economic backgrounds.

Chapter Summary

Human resource administration is a vital part of organizations, whether private or public. The larger and more complex the organization, the more important is the role played by HRA. The chief difference between public and private HRA is the inherently political nature of government work. For over one hundred years, merit has been the guiding principle of the civil service system. Earlier in our history, patronage was accepted as the means to fill government jobs. The debate between patronage and merit is over who is employed and on what basis they are hired. Public agencies staffed by patronage were frequently corrupt, inefficient, and incompetent. Merit held the promise of competent and efficient government.

The federal government serves as a model for public sector HRA at all levels. The most important elements of HRA include position classification, competitive examination, recruitment and selection, compensation, and removal. Position classification, one of the hallmarks of the civil service, uses job descriptions that set down in minute detail all of a position's duties and responsibilities.

The civil service was designed to insulate public employees from the vagaries of the political process. In general, it has been very successful at protecting public workers from arbitrary dismissal for partisan reasons. Nevertheless, the civil service has been criticized for also making it difficult for managers to remove problematic employees. As a result of the complicated and time-consuming procedures for dismissing employees, many federal managers prefer to tolerate bad employees rather than attempt to remove them.

As private sector unions decrease in importance, public sector unions have risen in importance. The highpoint of public sector unionism came in the 1960s and 1970s; since then the percentage of the unionized workforce in government has remained fairly constant, while it has steadily fallen in the private sector. Public employees cannot legally strike; therefore they have had to resort to alternative means for resolving collective bargaining deadlocks.

Equal employment opportunity is perhaps the most controversial subject related to HRA in government. While government in general is better than private business in offering more employment and advancement opportunities for minorities and women, we are still some distance from a truly representative bureaucracy. However, the public sector has made serious and in many ways successful attempts to increase the number of minorities within its workforce.

Chapter Discussion Questions

1. What are the reasons for the claim made by some critics that human resource administration is more of an impediment to good public management than a means of improving it?

2. What aspects of reinventing government had the unintended consequences of circumventing civil service requirements?

3. List the elements of the civil service system that have contributed to the federal government's recruitment and retention problems discussed in this chapter. How might these problems be corrected?

4. Why has reforming of the federal HRA system proven so difficult to accomplish, despite numerous attempts over the years?

5. What aspects of representative bureaucracy are considered controversial and why?

BRIEF CASE APPRAISING EMPLOYEES' PERFORMANCE IN THE PARKS DEPARTMENT

Ralph Simpson, head of the Planning Division of the Parks Department of the City of Springfield, California, has to determine who in his division should receive annual merit raises. The division heads are to submit the names of four people deserving of the merit raise to the department head. However, due to budget considerations, only three employees will receive the merit pay.

In Simpson's approach to employee performance assessment, he emphasized honest and timely feedback to employees. He met with every employee at mid-year to discuss each one's job performance. The purpose of these meetings was to give his employees a clear sense of the areas of their work that they needed to improve or continue. There was never any discussion of money at these meetings. Removing the issue of merit raises seemed to reduce employees' feelings of tension and anxiety. The division's employees were not used to this much personal attention paid to them by their boss. They were glad to finally have a boss who took an interest in their work. In the past, Simpson learned, the division's appraisal process was handled very differently. There had been no employee input into the process; instead, employees were required to sign already completed appraisal forms and return them immediately to the division head. A few days afterward, merit raises would be announced. The whole process was done in secrecy. Worker morale was always low after merit raises were announced.

Perhaps Simpson's biggest challenge was avoiding the post-award letdown among his staff. He wanted to use the merit raise process as a means to encourage more staff productivity. With this goal in mind, he set about narrowing his list of candidates for the merit raise. Ten employees made the first cut; still, he could submit only four to the director.

He decided to raise the merit-pay issue for discussion at the weekly staff meeting. Employees vented their frustrations about the perceived lack of fairness with the system. A three-hour discussion ensued, with everyone having an opportunity to express an opinion. At this point, Simpson asked the staff for their suggestions on making the system more fair. His chief concern was that the reward be linked to performance that contributed to achieving the goals of the division. After an hour of further discussion, someone suggested that the staff vote on some general merit criteria and select four individuals who would be the division's nominees. The other employees supported this idea, and the remainder of the meeting was devoted to coming up with the criteria and the voting process. The criteria for merit raises that received the most support were the following:

1. Ability to set and accomplish priorities which match division objectives of improving park quality
2. Quality of work

3. Amount of improvement during the year
4. Quantity of work (relative workload)
5. Relative pay for equal work

Furthermore, the staff believed that the decision to award merit pay should be based entirely on this year's work. Before the staff gave him its nominations, Simpson generated his own list of the most worthy individuals in the division. The next day he received the staff's vote and saw that their list agreed with his, although the order was different. According to the department's rules, the top four nominees could be considered for the three merit raises, and the person he favored ranked only fourth according to the staff. On his way to the meeting with the director, Simpson considered how he would use this information. At the meeting, the director began by saying that as a result of budget changes, only one employee from each division could receive merit pay.

SOURCE: Adapted from "The Division of Water Resources," available at the Electronic Hallway, http://www.hallway.org. The original case was prepared by Jon Brock, an associate professor at the Graduate School of Public Affairs, University of Washington.

Brief Case Questions

1. *Simpson's first choice is the staff's last choice. How might going with his first choice affect his ability to lead the division? How might it affect his ability to improve the division's productivity?*

2. *A large part of Simpson's challenge is that he is saddled with an appraisal system that the staff distrusts, but which is viewed as objective by the department. On the other hand, the staff's criteria are perceived as fair because the staff participated in their development. Can the two approaches be reconciled? Explain.*

3. *How would you describe Simpson's approach to human resource management?*

■ Key Terms

adverse impact (page 347)
affirmative action (page 344)
broadbanding (page 335)
collective bargaining (page 340)
comparable worth (page 348)
competitive examination (page 335)
cultural bias (page 336)
four-fifths rule (page 347)
glass ceiling (page 350)
General Schedule (GS) (page 332)
human resource administration (HRA) (page 325)
labor union (page 340)

merit (page 326)
means opportunity (page 346)
neutral competence (page 327)
patronage (page 326)
pay for performance (page 337)
performance appraisal (page 336)
position classification (page 332)
prospect opportunity (page 346)
representative bureaucracy (page 344)
rule of three (page 328)
strict scrutiny test (page 348)
validation (page 336)

■ On the Web

http://www.osc.gov/hatchact.htm
An Office of the Special Counsel's website outlining the Hatch Act.

http://www1.worldbank.org/publicsector/civilservice/patronage.htm
A World Bank site on the problems with government patronage.

http://www.opm.gov/oca/payrates/
The Office of Personnel Management's official federal government salary information.

http://www.usajobs.opm.gov/
The official portal for all federal government jobs.

http://www.affirmativeaction.org/
The American Association of Affirmative Action's website includes a wealth of information regarding affirmative action's legal history.

http://www.eeoc.gov
The homepage of the Equal Employment Opportunity Commission.

http://www.breaktheglassceiling.com/
According to their website, BreakTheGlass-Ceiling.com "is a resource used by individuals to empower themselves for upward mobility."

http://www.afscme.org/
The American Federation of State, County, and Municipal Employees is the largest U.S. public employee union; their site has extensive links and resources dealing with government labor issues.

CHAPTER 15

Managing Information Resources in Public Organizations

■ SETTING THE STAGE

Government is information. Its employees are nearly all information workers, its raw material is information inputs, its product is those inputs transformed into policies, which are simply an authoritative form of information.[1]

According to a 2002 *New York Times* article, "it is increasingly possible to amass Big Brother-like surveillance powers through Little Brother means. The basic components include everyday digital technologies like e-mail, online shopping and travel booking, A.T.M. systems, cell phone networks, electronic toll-collection systems and credit-card payment terminals."[2] The article says that the Pentagon's antiterrorism efforts only require integrating these different sources of data to create a vast system to monitor the activities of terrorists at home and abroad. This national surveillance system, initially called Total Information Awareness (TIA), was later renamed the Terrorist Information Awareness because of concerns that the old name sounded too sinister. Former Admiral John M. Poindexter was appointed to direct the TIA.[3] The TIA's 2003 fiscal year's budget was $137 million. Congress, however, did not appropriate money in the 2004 budget for the program. The project operated under the Defense Advanced Research Projects Agency (DARPA), which was the agency responsible for creating the Internet during the Cold War.

The system employed advanced information technologies that were spun off from the Internet. With specially designed software, intelligence analysts in federal agencies could use computer networks to link different data sources, including airport surveillance video, credit card transactions, airline reservations, and telephone calling records. The information gathered in this manner could then be fed into a computer program called Groove, which is designed to detect patterns of suspicious behavior. Additionally, the program takes advantage of Extended Markup Language (XML) to make information in many different databases compatible so that it can be easily shared by thousands of networked computers in the government.

The TIA raised red flags among civil libertarians, who disputed the government's right to conduct electronic searches because they violate the Constitution. Supporters of the program, however, argue that the unique threat posed by terrorism requires certain trade-offs between protecting individual civil liberties and guarding national security. An expert

Data mining A software application that looks for patterns in a database that can be used to predict future behavior.

on technological warfare, for example, said, "In an age of terror wars, we have to learn the middle path to craft the security we need without incurring too great a cost on our civil liberties."[4] Meanwhile, computer industry experts question the program's overall feasibility. The CEO of a firm specializing in **data mining** observed: "The project is not going to have near-term contributions to the war on terrorism. It's not clear this is an economically valuable way to fight terrorism."[5]

Information technology (IT) The development, installation, and implementation of systems to gather, process, manipulate, and store data; includes computers and telecommunications.

The above example points to the promises and perils of public information resources and information policy in the twenty-first century. It underscores the importance of information for much of what government does, including fighting the war on terrorism, but it also raises serious issues regarding how information is used. So much of government's normal activities involve gathering and analyzing information that government *is* information.[6] Government at all levels invests billions of dollars in **information technology (IT)** every year. Consequently, management of information resources is becoming an increasingly important task for public administrators, while the impact of IT on governments and society as a whole has received a great deal of scholarly attention.

■ **CHAPTER PLAN**

In this chapter, we consider some of the important roles IT and information resource management play in public organizations, and we look at some major trends. The term "information resources" encompasses a broad array of IT-related issues, including information systems, information policy, and e-government. The chapter first discusses some concepts relating to information and describes the different types of information systems found in public organizations. We then examine the impact of information resources on public organizations and public employees; as might be expected, technology has had a significant impact on public administration. We next focus on the virtual organization, followed by an examination of government experience with managing IT and information resources. The chapter then turns to government policy regarding information access and privacy before and after September 11, 2001. We also examine the possibilities for using computer networks to help civil society.

Concepts and Types of Information Systems

Data The distinct, separate observations about some phenomenon.

At the outset, it will be helpful to define some basic concepts and terms relating to information and information networks. Many people think they know what information and data mean, but some important distinctions can be made among these and other terms. For example, while it is common to use "data" and "information" interchangeably, they actually refer to different, but interrelated, aspects of the same idea. **Data** serve as the "building blocks" of **information**.[7] Thus, data can be thought of as discrete observations or elements of some phenomenon.[8] For instance, in calculating a baseball player's batting average, the number of base hits constitutes the data. Data that are processed and organized in a meaningful way become information. To continue with our baseball example, the batting average is

Information Data that has been organized into meaningful patterns and that can be used for decision-making.

simply the information obtained from the number of plate appearances and base hits. This provides us with meaningful information about a hitter's performance over the season. Information is thus simply data ordered into useful patterns. We use data and information every day to make all sorts of decisions.

Another word that is often confused with information and data is **knowledge**. Knowledge builds on information as "the cause-and-effect framework that supports a particular course of action." Knowledge consists of more than just information. When a 911 operator at a police station decides to dispatch a police car, that decision is based on more than just objective data (i.e., the call itself).[9] (See Vignette 15.1.) Because these three elements are interconnected, accurate and unbiased data are necessary in order to produce reliable information, which in turn can be transformed into knowledge (see Figure 15.1). Erroneous data result in misinformation, which prevents or thwarts the construction of knowledge ("garbage in, garbage out"). In the context of decision-making, this can result in taking the incorrect course of action in a situation. In the next section, we discuss systems that transform raw data into usable information for organizational decision-making. These information systems are typically automated (i.e., computer-based) but they need not be.

Knowledge A body of information organized in a systematic manner; a cause-and-effect framework that supports a particular course of action.

Police dispatchers are trained to dispatch police cars using different types of information.
SOURCE: Chris Ware/ The Image Works

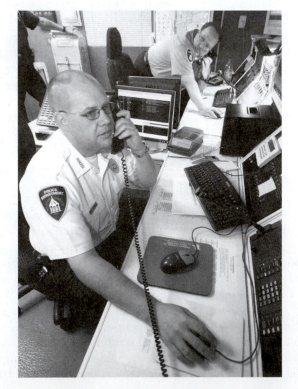

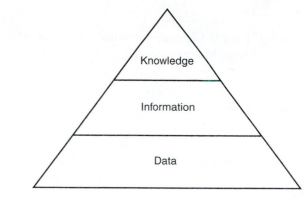

Figure 15.1   Data Information Pyramid

15.1   **"They Is Clowning Tough": 911 Operators as Organizational Knowledge Makers**

The following are examples of actual dialogue recorded between 911 police operators and callers in a midwestern city. In each case, the operator exercised a great amount of interpretive work to determine whether the call should result in dispatching a police car. Dispatching police officers entails the expenditure of organizational resources and means those resources cannot be allocated somewhere else where they could be more needed. Therefore, 911 operators are entrusted with the important task of making Knowledge based on often unreliable data or ambiguous information.

911: Emergency, 911.

Caller: This is (caller gives address), and there's been, a police officer been hit with a gunshot . . .

911: Huh . . . huh.

Caller: . . . and the police hasn't got here yet.

911: Hold on, let me see.

Caller: I can hardly hear you.

911: (Louder) Hold on, let me see.

911: (After an 8-second pause.) OK, was someone hurt, ma'am?

Caller: Yeah, a police officer just got shot . . . with the same guy.

911: And it happened just a few moments ago?

Caller: Yeah, when I first called you I didn't know he had gotten shot, but I happened to go back out again and he's been shot.

911: OK, Hon, I'll get someone out there.

Caller: OK.

911: Thanks, very much.

End of transmission.

In the example below, the operator does not dispatch a car.

911: Police Department.

Caller: Take care of this.

911: Mrs. Jones?

Caller: Yes, it is.

911: How are you?

Caller: I'm feeling a little better.

911: You're feeling better?

Caller: A little bit better.

911: Are you calling about the same thing, Mrs. Jones?

Caller: Oh, yes. Get somebody to stop them.

(continued on next page)

VIGNETTE 15.1 "They Is Clowning Tough": 911 Operators as Organizational Sense Makers *(continued)*

At this point, the transmission becomes quite garbled. This caller is mumbling. Finally, the operator interrupts.

911: Is it evil?

The caller continues mumbling, until the operator says:

911: Never ran into it in (this city).

Caller: Never.

911: Mrs. Jones, we'll take care of it.

Caller: God bless you, God bless you.

911: You're welcome.

End of Transmission.
In the next example, the operator dispatches a car after a great deal of interpretive work.

911: Emergency, 911.

Caller: Send the police to (gives address).

911: What's the matter?

Caller: I don't know but they're out there clowning.

911: What are they doing?

Caller: They is clowning tough.

911: Did you call already tonight?

Caller: No, I haven't . . . . I called earlier for a hit and run, yeah. But they is up there clowning for what I do not know. They got knives and pistols . . .

911: They got knives and . . .

Caller: I'm tired of this stuff, see because I've got to go to work.

911: Are they threatening each other?

Caller: Yes, they're out there trying to kill each other.

911: How many of them are there?

Caller: About four of them.

911: Black guys?

Caller: Yeah.

911: What do they look like?

Caller: I don't know I ain't looking at all them.

911: OK, we'll send somebody over.

Caller: OK, in an emergency please.

911: Yup.

End of transmission

SOURCE: Glisinan, James F. From "They is Clowning Tough: 911 and the Social Construction of Reality," *Criminology* 27(2), 329–344, 1989.

Information Systems

Transaction processing system (TPS) The most basic type of information system that can be used to create, store, and manipulate data.

The most basic type of mechanical information system (IS) is called a **transaction processing system** (**TPS**). It can create, store, and manipulate vast quantities of data. The chief purposes of TPS include assisting with organizational control functions (e.g., accounting, personnel, and payroll systems) and handling routine or "programmed" types of operations (records checking, tracking transactions, etc.). The emphasis in TPS is on accurately reporting and tracking data.

Management information system (MIS) A sophisticated type of information system used to assist management in decision-making.

A **management information system** (**MIS**) is a more sophisticated type of information system. Designed to assist in the management of organizations, it "makes some managerial decisions and provides managers at all levels of an organization with the information needed for making other decisions."[10] Five characteristics give a MIS its special qualities:

1. Depends heavily or entirely on computer technology
2. Is designed to support decision-making processes

3. Relies on a database

4. Consists of programs and applications that use the data from the database to simulate or model different conditions

5. Relies on telecommunications to provide fast access by managers to the data, programs, and models[11]

Decision support system (DSS) The most advanced type of information system that provides support for nonroutine or unstructured decision-making.

The most advanced type of information system is called a **decision support system (DSS)**. The DSS provides support for nonroutine or unstructured decision-making, activities that typically outstrip the ordinary capabilities of basic MIS. Typically, a DSS uses advanced statistical software, often specifically designed for it, in its decision-support functions. A government DSS may also consist of computer systems inside and outside the public sector (e.g., the TIA) that are interconnected to share information and computer programs. Similar to the way data, information, and knowledge form a pyramid, DSS depends on an MIS generating reliable and accurate information, while MIS requires an accurate, reliable TPS (see Figure 15.2).

Information Policy

Information policy Public policy regarding the use of, access to, and control of information by the government.

Information resources management (IRM) The administration of information policy and information assets by an organization.

In the context of public administration, **information policy** consists of "the laws, legislation, executive orders, and operating procedures associated with the control of and access to information" by government. It has also been defined more broadly as "those strategies that allow us to use information well and adapt government organizations and information systems to a rapidly changing environment."[12] An important element of effective public service information management and information policy is **information resources management (IRM)**. According to one author, "IRM governs information needs assessment, information uses and flows in the organization, and allocation of supporting resources such as information technologies and professional staff to meet information requirements. It encompasses information as a resource for the organization plus the media that collects, delivers, generates, processes, stores, and discards data and information."[13] As governments and

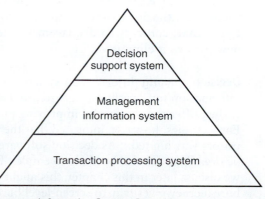

Figure 15.2   Management Information Systems Pyramid

nonprofits spend large amounts of money on IT, information policy and IRM become vital concerns, not just for information managers but for all other administrators as well. Information and its control are too important to leave only to computer programmers and other technology experts.

The Impact of Information Technology on Public Organizations

Several models have been put forth to explain the role of IT in organizations and to predict the long-term effects of technology on organizations.[14] One early model is based on the work of the Urban Information Systems (URBIS) group at the University of California, Irvine, which represents the best example of a specifically public sector orientation to computing resources.[15]

The URBIS Model

The URBIS model has been used to study the impact of IT on six important areas of public organizations: structure, employment, decision-making, quality of work life, management, and politics.

Organization Structure Computers can lead to either a flatter (less bureaucratic) or taller (more bureaucratic) hierarchy, depending on the needs and expectations of management regarding the technology. In general, top managers prefer more centralization of information rather than less; computers allow them to increase their span of control at the expense of middle managers. The likely outcome of this preference is taller hierarchy. Further research, however, shows that administrators are more likely to use additional staff to meet their computing needs, instead of dealing directly with the technology. This might contribute to flatter organizations as information becomes more widely dispersed throughout the organization.[16]

Employment At the dawn of the IT era, there was some concern that massive computerization would put many people out of work. Consequently, the URBIS researchers set out to test the accuracy of displacement theory, or the idea that computers could lead to unemployment. They found that, contrary to displacement theory, IT actually results in as many new jobs as it eliminates.[17]

Decision-making Information systems organize data to produce meaningful information for decisionmakers to use. Decision support systems, as discussed earlier, offer the promise of improving public organizations' decision-making. Early studies, however, indicated that the use of computer models by administrators was limited.[18] As decision software improves and declines in cost, public organizations will be likely to employ DSS with much greater frequency. As we discuss later in this chapter, this might prove a mixed blessing as street-level bureaucracy gives way to screen-level bureaucracy.

Quality of Work Life In contrast to much early speculation that computers would lead to worker unhappiness, the URBIS research suggests just the opposite: mastery of technology actually increases employees' sense of accomplishment. Instead of the alienating and "de-skilling" effects some observers predicted, IT was associated with a decrease in time pressure and an overall better working environment.[19]

Management The URBIS researchers found that there is no universal set of rules for the effective administration of information in public organizations. The public information manager exists in a competitive marketplace. IT units are often viewed as producers of a valuable organizational resource, with the rest of the organization as the consumers.

Politics Far from being a means to impose control by computer experts on public organizations, technology may actually increase the power of the status quo. Thus, control of computing resources may give more power to the already powerful. However, some studies challenge this finding, asserting that IT makes some units within the organization more powerful than they might otherwise have been.[20] Since the pioneering work of the URBIS group, there have been several attempts at applying their model to real public organizations, as well as research that examines other anticipated consequences of computers on organizations. We discuss a number of these below.

Control and Information Islands

No recent innovation has been more touted than IT as being able to transform public organizations' basic operations in far-reaching ways. As a consequence of the widespread use of IT, researchers are devoting a great deal of attention to technology's impact on management control of operations.

A belief shared by both information technology experts and public managers is that having more and better information allows greater control over projects. One study tested this assumption with surprising results. It found that quality of information had no impact whatever on project outcomes. The real importance of information, according to the authors, was to "maintain the appearance of accountability and a commitment to rationality. . . . In the minds of managers, information is often collected only to support the illusion of control."[21] Further, public managers collect information because they are legally required to do so and not necessarily because it helps them accomplish their tasks better. Thus, information alone is probably not enough to give administrators control over organizational outcomes.

Another study noted that, even as early as the 1960s, IT was recognized primarily as a tool for management control, particularly control of fiscal resources. This attitude grew during the 1970s, partly as a result of the urban fiscal crisis. The authors, using extensive survey data from city managers, found that automation of budgets "provided a moderate amount of managerial fiscal control which has not increased over time."[22] We should keep in

Computer technology has become an essential part of many public organizations.
SOURCE: Jeff Greenberg/ The Image Works

mind, however, that the study's data reflect an earlier period when computers were less powerful, slower, and not interconnected as they are today.

Inexpensive, fast computers with the capacity to gather, store, and manipulate large amounts of data have led to the existence of information islands within organizations. An **information island** is "a free-standing database, model, or analytic capability that is housed on its own CPU, has procedures separate from the organization's main databases, and serves a well-defined, usually very local purpose."[23] The proliferation of information islands throughout an organization can be a problem for several reasons. First, they create multiple, often conflicting sources of information within organizations, making centralized control of information more difficult. Second, they are costly for the organization because of unnecessary duplication of hardware and software. Third, they may "contaminate" datasets as individuals using nonstandard data practices contribute to organizational databases.

What might be viewed as a management-control problem may be quite the opposite when viewed from the employees' perspective, however. Employees value being able to control their own information environments, along with the flexibility to develop their own computer applications, which local control of IT can give them. Management should try to steer a middle path between local and central control: adopting a strategy that allows local users more flexibility but establishing organization-wide constraints to keep costs down and avoid some of the other negatives associated with information islands.[24]

Information islands
An information system that is stored on a separate computer, operates separately from the main databases, and serves a personal or unit purpose rather than organizational purpose.

Organizational Decision-making

Research suggests that IT might be fundamentally altering organizational dynamics in the public sector by reducing the authority of street-level bureaucrats and shifting their power to others within the organization. As the authors of one study assert: "Window clerks are being replaced by Web sites, and advanced information and expert systems are taking over the role of case managers and adjudicating officers." We may be witnessing the transformation of street-level bureaucracy into *screen-level* bureaucracy, these authors suggest. In more and more cases, routine decisions are being made by information systems instead of administrators. In addition, in many agencies web-cams and the Internet are replacing face-to-face interactions with citizens.[25]

Strategic Planning One important area of organizational decision-making that IT can help facilitate is strategic planning.[26] Administrators often use information systems to help rethink organization goals or missions as a result of changes in the environment or to take advantage of new opportunities as they arise.[27] A more important question is how many governments actually use IT's full potential? One study found that few governments actually use computers for strategic planning and far fewer use this tool effectively.[28] Another study suggests that for technology to be used successfully in strategic planning, government-wide information systems must be in place.[29] Furthermore, the authors add that while government officials generally agree about the need for an information system, this consensus soon breaks down over how it should be most effectively used.

Administrators and Information Technology In order to understand computing's impact on administration, we must consider the manner in which administrators use the technology and information. One study examined the usefulness of **computer-based information** (CBI) to public managers.[30] Based on a survey of public managers, the authors identify two different information user styles. The first style they call the **knowledge executive**, for whom IT is an important part of effective management. This user style emphasizes a hands-on approach to CBI: administrators perform their own computer searches, analyze data, and generate reports routinely as part of their decision-making process.

The second user style they call the **CBI consumer**, or an administrator who is an indirect user of technology. Consumers rely primarily on their staff to manipulate, analyze, and interpret information for them. In this style, the role of administrators is fundamentally unchanged by new technology. The study indicates that most public managers tend to view themselves as consumers rather than knowledge executives, perhaps because "very few managers have the time, expertise, and motivation to develop and sustain this level of personal competency and involvement with computing."[31]

Computer-based information Any information that is gathered, processed, manipulated, or stored by computers.

Knowledge executive Administrator who takes a hands-on approach to the use of computers.

CBI consumer Administrator who relies mainly on staff to work with technology and deals indirectly with technological issues.

Organizational Performance

Two important questions arise concerning IT and organizational performance. First, does the impact of IT vary according to whether an organization is public or private? Research suggests that differences between public and private organizations also translate into differences in their use of information systems. Second, do public agencies effectively use IT to share information? An important element of governmental effectiveness involves information-sharing among agencies. Effective information-sharing also has a positive impact on innovative administration. These two issues are discussed in more detail below.

Public versus Private Organizations' Use of IT Whether a public or private organization is using IT seems to have a deciding influence on organizational outcomes. Due to differences between public and private organizations, important differences exist in their use of information systems, which in turn have an impact on organizational performance.[32] According to one study, the following four technology-related characteristics appear to be unique to the public sector:

1. *Proprietary versus shared information.* Private information resources are typically considered to be proprietary: they are owned by the organization that gathered them. Government information, however, is more likely to be treated as a "public good," or as something to be shared as widely as possible with the community.

2. *Goals.* Public organizations' goals are typically multiple, intangible, and often conflicting. Thus, the information requirements of government are difficult to identify and are usually unstable.

3. *Bureaucracy and paperwork.* In response to complexity, governments institutionalize information resource management to provide for greater accountability, which in most cases requires centralization. This can contribute to the growth of red tape.

4. *Political influences.* Politics disrupts long-term planning. Public information systems, therefore, require mechanisms that provide continuity over time, including maintaining continuity of data sets and other information resources.

What effect do these four characteristics have on administrators? In a study conducted on a national sample of public and private organizations, the author found that public administrators experienced more checks on performance, including procedural delays and red tape, than did their private sector peers.[33] This stemmed from the need for increased accountability. Public managers were also forced to adapt industry-standard MIS procedures to fit their environment, in contrast to private managers, who implemented these procedures without modification. The impact of these adjustments is particularly pronounced in the area of information sharing.

Information Sharing The emergence of information networks makes it possible, at least in theory, to improve overall performance by allowing information sharing to occur among different agencies and even with the general public. The benefits of **interoperability** include more integrated government services, reduced paperwork, and greater responsiveness to citizens' needs. Yet before effective information sharing can happen, several key conditions must exist. These include a history of cooperation between agencies, a centralized funding source, the belief that data sharing is in each agency's interest, and exchange of transaction data (for example, census figures) rather than operational or strategic information.[34] The last condition is related to the idea that data exchanges are likely to be less threatening to organizational interests than sharing critical information. As we saw previously, however, the issue of information sharing among agencies has achieved even greater prominence following the terrorist attacks of September 11, 2001.

Technology for Innovative Administration Using IT to help make government "smarter, better, faster and cheaper" was given a ringing endorsement by the National Performance Review.[35] According to Vice President Al Gore: "Computers, and their interconnection through telecommunications, have made possible flatter organizations, wider spans of control and much faster information sharing." As Gore notes, "the information age allows the new federal manager to communicate effectively across very large organizations. And information technology also allows this to be done without sacrificing accountability."[36]

Others followed the vice president in proclaiming technology a powerful tool for reinventing government. To a large extent, the success of TQM and other new management techniques hinges on effective use of information resources: "If government is to reinvent itself through the pursuit of innovative management goals, such as increased quality of services in which quality is defined by the customer, then government must monitor itself, its services, and its customers' demands to know the degree to which quality is achieved, why it has or has not been achieved, and to insure that quality is maintained."[37] For instance, monitoring and evaluating performance do not need to be as complex and demanding if well-designed, effective information systems are in place.

IT's Effects on Public Employees

Since the 1970s, it has become commonplace for organizational scholars to point out the profound effects of technology on the workforce, although the exact nature of this impact is still the subject of intense debate. One example of this is the dispute over whether computers replace managers by more efficiently doing their tasks. Computers have been blamed for the elimination of millions of management jobs in the United States, according to some estimates.[38] Yet, an argument has been made that technology actually *increases* the number of managers in organizations.[39] In addition to the impact on managers, researchers

---

Interoperability The ability of different computer systems to share information with each other.

have explored IT's effects on nonmanagement public sector employees. The amount of scholarly interest in this area continues unabated.

Impact on Public Managers Writers on the impact of IT on middle management have predicted that machines will replace managers. According to this hypothesis, the middle manager's chief function is to facilitate information flows between the top and lower levels of the organization. But executives can now use computers to communicate directly with different parts of the organization—for example, by e-mail—instead of relying on middle managers to do this. The net result is to centralize decision-making and make organizations more hierarchical by removing layers of management from organizations.[40] This is also considered more efficient because computers, in contrast to managers, do not receive paychecks.

Another theory reaches exactly the opposite conclusion: rather than reducing the number of managers, IT actually increases demand for middle managers. According to this theory, the use of technology causes organizations to resemble a bulging pyramid rather than an hourglass.[41] Rather than serve merely as conduits of information from the lower to upper levels, middle managers actually play a vital function by synthesizing and organizing information for upper management. While the growth of computing threatens to swamp organizations with a flood of information, middle managers perform necessary data-processing and analyzing roles, which help bring this deluge under control. Thus, technology helps to decentralize decision-making authority and make organizations flatter.

Another theory—in effect, a compromise between the other two—predicts that technology's effect on middle management depends on how centralized decision-making is, particularly with regard to technological issues. The more top-down and hierarchical the decision-making, the greater the likelihood that IT will be used to replace middle managers. Decentralization produces the opposite effect, as managers use technology to enhance both their power and numbers. At this stage, more research is being done on the impact of computer technology on managers, so any conclusions are tentative at best.

Impact on Nonmanagement Employees Early work examining technology's effects on nonmanagement employees predicted negative consequences, particularly with respect to lower-level employees. Over time, however, there has been a shift in thinking. Studies such as those by URBIS did not support the predictions made by some that computers would lead to widespread unemployment. Indeed, their data support the opposite conclusion: computers actually generate more jobs.[42]

More recent research, however, paints a more mixed picture regarding technology's effect on street-level bureaucrats. IT has led to the elimination of many lower-level jobs, some researchers point out: "The hundreds of individual case managers have all vanished. Their pivotal role in the organization has been taken by systems and process designers."[43] Policy implementation takes on a new and different meaning as a result of the growing organizational emphasis on automated databases and information systems. Before, lower-level administrators had more discretion. More recently, however, their decision-making authority is being usurped by technology and programmers.[44]

Human Factors Influencing IT Adoption Since new technology has a tremendous impact on employees, they naturally experience a wide range of emotions regarding its introduction in the workplace. As a result, research on the spread of new technology in government tries to take into account employee perceptions and attitudes regarding computing and technology.[45] Some of the findings indicate that differences in employee experience can significantly impact IT adoption. For example, perceived personal advantage and previous computing experience were the two most important factors influencing employees' decisions to adopt new technology. Users who expected to receive direct personal benefits from the new technology were the ones who made the greatest effort to learn the technology. Furthermore, employees were more likely to embrace change if they had previously positive experiences with technology.

Other Personnel Issues An important aspect of technology is its impact on the workplace environment and other human resource concerns. Automation can affect **ergonomic** conditions; for example, it can produce uncomfortable workstations and equipment, as well as long periods of isolated and tedious work.[46] Employees complain of eyestrain, hand injuries, and other physical problems associated with heavy computer use, and more resources are being devoted to alleviate these conditions. If unaddressed, the total effects of poor ergonomic conditions can weaken workforce morale and possibly damage overall organizational effectiveness.

> **Ergonomic** Of, or related to, the design of workplace equipment, in order to maximize worker efficiency by reducing fatigue and discomfort.

Another important human resource issue is the need to continuously update employee skills to keep up with the rapid pace of technological change. This constant training can prove expensive to the organization and disruptive to employees, who must interrupt their normal tasks and routines for classes. Technology training also raises the issue of bridging the gap between reality and the formal job description in job classifications.[47] Take the example of an employee, hired without any formal computing background, who has to learn computing skills as part of his or her assignment in an agency. The formal job description, however, fails to include these new computer skills, although they have now become an important part of what the employee must do in carrying out the position's responsibilities. This failure to update job descriptions might lead to a failure to adequately compensate employees, which could make hiring and retaining qualified employees more difficult in the future.

Technology's Effects on Organizational Power

Technology has had major impacts on every facet of organizations, including on formal structure and power relationships. Early in the computer era (1960s and 1970s), scholars predicted that computers would increase the concentration of power in organizations. Then, at the beginning of the personal computer revolution (1980s), they predicted just the opposite, that computers would lead to more decentralized organizations and a wider diffusion of authority. Some authors contend that technology by itself is neutral with regard to organizational power, that its impact is completely a function of the organization's management style.[48] Because some administrators favor centralization, computers can lead to more centralized organizations.

There is not a simple cause–effect relationship between computers and centralization, however. Somewhat offsetting any centralizing tendencies is the preference of managers to use staff to deal with technology issues while they "manage."[49] (See the earlier discussion on user styles in the section on "Administrators and Information Technology.")

The Virtual Organization

Virtual state A term coined by Jane Fountain to refer to the linkages and interactions based on computers among governments and between government and other entities.

As IT has become a pervasive aspect of modern organizations, there has come into being the virtual organization, and even the **virtual state**. Table 15.1 compares key characteristics of virtual organizations with traditional organizations. As the table shows, there are several marked differences between the two types of organizations. Whereas earlier writers argued that technology merely reinforces traditional bureaucracy, more recent scholarship describes a more ambiguous situation. Thus, in virtual organizations, information resources and needs determine internal power relationships more than formal structure does. This manifests itself in the following ways: instead of hierarchical authority, teams engage in decision-making; informal and electronic communication replace top-down information flows; and documents are electronically stored and transmitted instead of as paper files. Virtual organization proponents assert that IT empowers employees by freeing them from a particular office or function and making them more organizationally versatile. The virtual organization, however, has not so much replaced classical bureaucracies as "grown up within them and 'sedimented' on top of them," producing a hybrid organizational called "hyperarchy."[50] Hyperarchy retains certain elements of bureaucracy while embracing aspects of the virtual organization.

System-level bureaucracy A public organization in which information technology and computer experts play a major role in policy-making.

One possible long-term impact of technology in public organizations is to create what some call **system-level bureaucracy**.[51] IT, in their view, has been transformed from being merely a support function in organizations to playing a decisive role in policy-making. The organizational role of technology has grown from providing data input and manipulation tools to include policy execution, control, and external communication functions. As previously noted, information system designers and IT experts are the key members of virtual organizations. Over time, as public organizations become transformed into virtual organizations, this will have important consequences for the way public services are delivered.

TABLE 15.1 Comparison of Characteristics of Bureaucratic and Virtual Organizations

Bureaucratic Organization	Virtual Organization
Strict division of labor, jurisdictional boundaries, strict boundaries between organizations	Flexible division of labor, organizational structure built on information systems; fluid boundaries both within and between organizations
Rigid hierarchy of offices and individuals	More "flat" hierarchy, fluid organizational roles, loosening of command and control systems, teams, networked organization
Most organizational information stored in the form of files and written documents with access limited to certain officials	Digital files stored on shared databases makes information available throughout organization; information detached from particular office empowers more employees
Impersonal rules and standard operating procedures	Rules are invisible and embedded in information systems and software applications; shift from overt supervisory control to covert control
Impersonal "street-level" bureaucrats are the organizational backbone	System designers and expert systems replace professional employees as organizational backbone
High level of human intervention with individual cases	No human intervention; interactions between human clients and computer systems only
Functions of IT are primarily data input, storing data; IT largely plays support role for administration	Functions of IT include execution, control, and external communication; IT plays decisive organizational role

SOURCE: Analysis adapted from: Jane Fountain, *Building the Virtual State: Information Technology and Institutional Change* (Washington, DC: Brookings Institution, 2001), 61; Nitin Nohria and James D. Berkley, "The Virtual Organization: Bureaucracy, Technology, and the Implosion of Control," in *The Post-Bureaucratic Organization: New Perspectives on Organizational Change*, ed. Charles Heckscher and Ann Donnellon (Thousand Oaks, CA: Sage, 1994), 109–128; James I. Cash Jr. et al., *Building the Information-Age Organization: Structure, Control, and Information Technologies* (Chicago: Irwin, 1994).

Managing Information Resources: Government's Experience

Government at all levels invests billions of dollars annually on computerization. During the 1990s, the federal government spent hundreds of billions of dollars on information technology and will spend more in the years to come.[52] Federal spending also stimulates billions of dollars of private investment in the area of technology innovation. The federal government, for example, funded the initial research and development behind the creation of the Internet, which has since spawned multibillion-dollar industries with significant global social and commercial impact. Table 15.2 presents a chronology of the key events in the history of the Internet, from its relatively humble origins as an experimental Defense Department project in the early 1960s to the World Wide Web of today.

After all this spending, Congress asked in the 1990s, "What has been the return on the government's gigantic investment in information resources?" The GAO's answer, unfortunately, was not as much as many had hoped. In a congressional report prepared by a special commission headed by former Senator William Cohen, it noted that "poor information management is, in fact, one of the biggest threats to the government treasury because it leaves

TABLE 15.2 Internet Timeline

1962–1969	The Internet is first conceived in the early 1960s. Under the leadership of the Department of Defense's Advanced Research Project Agency (ARPA), it grows into a small network (ARPANET) intended to promote the sharing of supercomputers among researchers in the United States.
1969	ARPANET connects first four universities in the United States: Stanford Research Institute, UCLA, UC Santa Barbara, and the University of Utah.
1970–1973	ARPANET is a success from the very beginning. Although originally designed to allow scientists to share data and access remote computers, e-mail quickly becomes the most popular application. ARPANET becomes a high-speed digital post office as people use it to collaborate on research projects and discuss various topics.
1971	ARPANET grows to twenty-three hosts connecting universities and government research centers around the country.
1973	ARPANET goes international with connections to London, England, and Norway.
1974	Telnet, the first commercial version of ARPANET, is created.
1974–1981	The general public gets a hint of how the Internet can be used in daily life as the commercial version of ARPANET goes online. ARPANET starts to move away from its military/research roots.
1975	Internet operations transferred to the Defense Communications Agency.
1981	ARPANET has 213 hosts. A new host is added approximately once every twenty days.
1982	The term "Internet" is used for the first time.
1982–1987	TCP/IP created, the common language of all Internet computers. For the first time, the loose collection of networks making up ARPANET is seen as an "internet," and the Internet as we know it today is born.
	The mid-1980s marks a boom in the personal computer and minicomputer industries. The combination of inexpensive desktop machines and powerful, network-ready servers allows many companies to join the Internet. Corporations begin to use the Internet to communicate with each other and with customers.
1984	The number of Internet hosts exceeds 1,000.
1985	Internet e-mail and newsgroups now part of life at many universities.
1986	Case Western Reserve University in Cleveland, Ohio, creates the first "Freenet" for the Society for Public Access Computing.
1987	The number of Internet hosts exceeds 10,000.
1988–1990	By 1988 the Internet is an essential tool for communications; however, it also begins to create concerns about privacy and security in the digital world. New terms such as "hacker" and "electronic break-in" are created.
	On November 1, 1988, a malicious program called the "Internet Worm" temporarily disables approximately 6,000 of the 60,000 Internet hosts.
1990	A happy victim of its own unplanned, unexpected success, ARPANET is decommissioned, leaving only the vast network of networks called the Internet. The number of hosts exceeds 300,000.
1991–1993	Corporations wishing to use the Internet face a serious problem: commercial network traffic is banned from the National Science Foundation's NSFNET, the backbone of the Internet. In 1991 the NSF lifts the restriction on commercial use, clearing the way for the age of electronic commerce.

TABLE 15.2 Continued

1991	The University of Minnesota releases "gopher," the first point-and-click way of navigating the files of the Internet. Tim Berners-Lee, working at CERN in Switzerland, posts the first computer code of the World Wide Web. The ability to combine words, pictures, and sounds on Web pages becomes a reality. Traffic on the NSF backbone network exceeds 1 trillion bytes per month.
1992	The first audio and video broadcasts take place over a portion of the Internet. More than 1 million hosts are part of the Internet.
1993	Mosaic, the first graphics-based Web browser, becomes available. Traffic on the Internet expands at a 341,634 percent annual growth rate.
1996	Approximately 40 million people are connected to the Internet. More than $1 billion per year changes hands at Internet shopping malls, and Internet related companies like Netscape are the darlings of high-tech investors.
	Users in almost 150 countries around the world are now connected to the Internet. The number of computer hosts approaches 10 million.
1997–present	The Internet is replaced by the World Wide Web in the minds of millions of users around the world.

Timeline adapted from http://www.pbs.org/internet/timeline/timeline-txt.html.

government programs susceptible to waste, fraud, and abuse." The report also said that the major obstacles standing in the way of effective usage appear to be organizational; they are related to staffing, leadership, and management issues.[53]

In response to the federal bureaucracy's failure to effectively implement IT programs, despite the outlay of billions of dollars, Congress passed several pieces of IT-related legislation, which include the following:

■ The Clinger-Cohen Act (1996), also known as the Information Technology Management Reform Act, which requires that agencies focus more on the results of IT investment, particularly with regard to efficiency, effectiveness, and productivity

■ The Paperwork Reduction Act (1995), which requires agencies to define their information needs and to develop strategies, systems, and capacities to meet those needs

■ The Government Performance and Results Act (1993), which requires federal agencies to prepare a strategic plan of all technology activities for annual submission to OMB and Congress

The Performance Institute, a private think tank, sought to measure the success of these federal efforts. While finding some positives, the Institute's report observed that overall, "Federal agencies continue to struggle with IT capital planning and performance measurement."[54] The associate Director for e-government at OMB, the report noted, admitted that federal agencies needed to focus more on "concrete and measurable" outcomes for their investments.[55] He also faulted program management and pointed to the failure of projects to be delivered on time and on budget. Clearly, the gap between reality and where we should be in the use of technology remains large. Despite the lack of consistent progress, however, the federal government can point to some successful IT initiatives, as shown in Vignette 15.2.

At the state and local government levels, an estimated $35 billion is spent annually on technology and related activities. States alone employ approximately 420,000 IT-related personnel.[56] Local governments are also heavily dependent on computers and computer experts. Local governments, it has been estimated, use around 450 computer applications to perform tasks ranging from automated transactions (payroll, utility billing, etc.) to word processing and spreadsheets.[57] While 85 percent of municipal governments have a website, most local governments have not yet progressed beyond the website stage in their use of IT. Further, "Many municipalities have not made a full commitment to developing a comprehensive strategic e-government plan to achieve a higher level of e-government."[58] However, there have been a number of state and local government successes in the area of IT; some of these are presented in Vignette 15.3.

Poor returns on their technology investment are a problem at the state and local government levels, just as at the federal level. Common criticisms of state and local government IT include overcomplexity, poor performance, and lack of interoperability.[59] For example, after spending $269 million for computers in the Los Angeles Police Department, an office of technology implementation had to be created to overcome serious failures in management and coordination that resulted in delays, systems failure, and cost overruns.[60]

Government at all levels has shown the willingness to invest heavily in technology and information resources. So far, however, the gains in productivity and efficiency have been less than expected. Governments hope that this is the inevitable result of the learning curve associated with dramatically new ways of conducting the government's business, and that over time technology will produce the returns on investment they counted on.

VIGNETTE 15.2   Successful Federal E-government Initiatives

A report by the Performance Institute recognized five federal agencies as being leaders in the effort to make government information and websites more accessible to the public. These five agencies provide the best examples at the federal level of the possibilities of e-government.

Department of Labor's E-authentication Program

The goal was to create a process that would protect personal information by "authenticating" users' identity during electronic transactions. The department devised a competition between two separate teams to devise the

(continued on next page)

VIGNETTE 15.2   Successful Federal *(continued)*

most effective and viable system of e-authentication. According to the report, "Creating an environment of spirited competition, the Department of Labor achieved a great level of commitment, ownership and dedication to this project, including quality, timeliness, and morale." The report also pointed to another major success factor for the Labor Department's e-government initiatives: strong buy-in and leadership from the agency's upper management.

The Navy's E-government Strategies to Redesign Operational Practices

The Department of the Navy established an eBusiness Operations Office to act as a catalyst for bringing e-government to the U.S. Navy. The office's main functions include serving as a clearinghouse of e-business and e-government innovations, conducting market research, and providing consultation services to the department. The eBusiness Operations Office has funded over thirty initiatives, including medical appointments on the Web, which was chosen to be implemented across the entire Department of Defense. The cost savings from this one initiative was $18 million. The Performance Institute attributes the office's success to the following factors: inventive leadership, advertising, functional area managers, and evaluation criteria.

Department of the Treasury, IRS EZ File

Partnering with a consortium of private companies, the Internal Revenue Service (IRS) offers online tax filing services to income tax payers. Sixty percent of the taxpayers receive the product free, while the other 40 percent pay for the services provided by the private partners. Under this arrangement, the IRS makes no investment in IT; rather the agency manages the project and hosts the webpage. The report noted that the initiative directly supports the IRS mission and promotes higher-quality services. Furthermore, the program has a significant return on investment because the IRS is not funding the IT that is delivering a high-quality service to its customers.

National Science Foundation's Fastlane and PRAMIS

The National Science Foundation (NSF) uses its online Fastlane system to process over 200,000 research proposals, peer reviews, and progress reports annually. The Proposal, Review, and Awards Management Integration System (PRAMIS) promises to build on the success of Fastlane. PRAMIS will improve internal NSF processing in the area of Merit Review and Award Management and Oversight. NSF's online system has achieved cost savings of over $700,000.

Small Business Administration's Anytime-Anyplace Access to Information

Two-thirds of the country's small businesses are connected to the Internet. The SBA's e-government initiative allows the agency's products and services to be delivered via the World Wide Web, saving the small business owner money and expanding the agency's outreach. The chief components of the SBA's effort to extend its services electronically include following

- The creation of a single Web portal for small businesses to provide full access to the entire range of services offered by SBA.
- Coordinating activities with nine federal regulatory and six state agencies in a Business Compliance One Stop Initiative. This would allow access to laws, regulations, compliance assistance tools, and online transactions from the Internet.
- Offering cross-agency, multifunctional, and inter-governmental services via the World Wide Web.

By these means, the SBA seeks to lower businesses' costs by streamlining requirements for complying with federal regulations, as well as making them easier to locate and understand.

SOURCE: "Creating a Performance-Based Electronic Government," Performance Institute, October 30, 2002, http://www.performanceweb.org/research/egovernmentreport.pdf.

VIGNETTE 15.3   State and Local E-government Success Stories

Most state and local governments have mastered some of the basics of e-government—if nothing else, they have created websites. However, relatively few have services that go beyond this and some other basic forms of e-government. For smaller and less-wealthy governments, the chief stumbling block to developing online services for constituents is lack of funds. Also, many elected officials are "behind the curve" technologically and view investments in new technology as too risky. Indeed, for some the early potential of the Internet has been largely unfulfilled. It would be foolish, however, to think that state and local governments have ended their experiments with electronic services or even that they could turn back. The era of e-government is here to stay. It will just take longer than the early overly optimistic forecasts. According to Darrell West, director of the Taubman Center for Public Policy at Brown University, "the reality is governments are making slow but steady progress. We are getting there."[a]

A number of state and local governments have made enormous strides with their e-government initiatives. In 2002, Tennessee state government received national recognition for its website. The Tennessee site offers many of the features considered the most important, including information availability, ease of use, access, privacy, and online services availability.[b]

A number of states are experimenting with personalized services on their websites. California allows users to create their own home page containing links, services, and information most useful to them. Every time users sign on to their "My California" home page, they see their information and links. Virginia offers a program called Live Help, which provides real-time assistance to users. Users who need help click on a button on the state's home page, which connects them to an actual person who can help them find the state-related information they are seeking. The following real-time exchange of text messages took place on Live Help.

Customer Service: Welcome to the Commonwealth of Virginia Online Help. How may I assist you today?

User: I want to know what the definition of a commonwealth is and why Virginia is a commonwealth rather than a state.

Customer Service: A definition is listed on the Secretary of the Commonwealth's Web site at http://www.commonwealth.state.va.us/common.htm. Would you like me to push your web browser to that web site?

User: Yes, thanks.

Customer Service: You are welcome. Thank you for visiting. Please contact us anytime.[c]

States and localities are also improving their electronic interface with the business community, referred to as G2B—government-to-business—in e-government parlance. As was the case with G2C—government-to-citizens—G2B suffers from lofty expectations, especially in the area of electronic procurement. E-procurement was supposed to be an important part of reinventing government at all levels, federal, state, and local; it was supposed to help streamline government and reduce costs. However, as the head of purchasing for the city of Nashville said, "It's a lot like teenage sex. No one's doing it as much or as well as they say they are. But eventually, they'll get the hang of it."[d]

As is the case with G2C, California is at the cutting edge of G2B innovation. The state operates an award-winning e-purchase system, CAL-Buy, which connects state government buyers with a database of products that they can purchase online. The system includes not only state agencies but also some cities, a school district, and a county. Eventually the system will encompass the whole state. Pennsylvania is using its Open for Business initiative to cut the costs of new businesses dealing with the state. The website allows businesses to submit all their registration information online and avoid the hassle of working with three

(continued on next page)

VIGNETTE 15.3   **S**tate and Local *(continued)*

different agencies, which the old system entailed. Maryland is helping small businesses in the state by providing them with online tools that will increase their productivity. The state in collaboration with the University of Maryland's business school offers state businesses access to business software applications for free or reduced prices for a year. The goal is to provide new small businesses with the same technological advantages available to larger companies.Progress in e-government appears to be incremental, with some states advancing faster than others. Over time, however,

successful innovations will diffuse to other states and the federal government. It is likely that states and localities will be among the future trendsetters in using technology to improve government services.

[a] Ellen Perlman, "The People Connection," *Governing*, September 2002, http://www.governing.com.

[b] Based on Brown University's Center for Public Policy annual ranking of state government websites; see http://www.InsidePolitics.org.

[c] Perlman, "The People Connection."

[d] Shane Harris, "Gettying Down to Business," *Governing*, September 2002, http://www.governing.com.

Government Information Policy Before and After 9/11

Two aspects of public information policy that have received a great deal of attention from citizens are (1) government use of personal information, and (2) public access to government information. Both were important and controversial concerns before September 11, 2001, and subsequent federal actions in response to terrorism have intensified the public debate over those issues. While some argue that certain aspects of the federal government's post-9/11 information policy represent a significant expansion of government power into the private affairs of individuals, supporters of the government's response assert that the war on terrorism requires a rethinking of the old balance between individual liberties and the public good.

Freedom of Information

Freedom of information Citizens' right of free access to government information.

Public access to government information, or **freedom of information**, is a cornerstone of information policy in the United States. The concept of freedom of information is subject to two different interpretations.[61] In everyday use, it refers to the citizens' right of free access to government information. The law, however, provides a somewhat more restrictive meaning to the term. According to statutes, it allows a reasonable level of citizen access to the *pre-existing* records maintained by the government. But the meaning of "reasonable" often changes according to whoever the current occupant of the White House is.

The chief law regulating public access to federal information is the Freedom of Information Act of 1966 (FOIA). The FOIA serves two distinct purposes that frequently conflict with each other.[62] On one side, the intention was to create a more open government by permitting more public access to information kept by the executive branch than previously had been the case. On the other side, the

FOIA sought to restrict access to records that could be disclosed without damaging personal privacy or divulging important operations of the government. Congress and the executive branch have struggled over interpretation of the FOIA. In general, Congress has supported efforts to liberalize the FOIA, while the executive branch has generally resisted those efforts and sought a narrower interpretation of the law. As a government information policy specialist pointed out, "the Executive Branch has continued to adapt the FOIA, to limit its scope and impact through economic strictures, procedural hurdles, and seeking special protection of certain kinds or classes of records, among other techniques."[63]

To complicate matters, individual agencies have considerable discretion in implementing the law, so "an agency must also explicitly decide what purposes its information access policy actually serves."[64] For instance, one agency might interpret the law narrowly and seek tighter controls over public access to information, while another might take a more open approach by allowing more public access to its records. However, both agencies are part of the same branch of government and are covered by the same law.

Privacy

In addition to access, another possible source of concern is the government's potential to invade privacy through its gathering of personal information. Louis D. Brandeis, a nineteenth-century Supreme Court justice, once famously referred to privacy as "the right to be let alone." This definition, however, is so broad and vague that, practically speaking, it offers policymakers little real guidance. When Brandeis wrote in 1890, government's activities were more limited, less intrusive, and based more on personal interaction than today. As government's scope and size expanded during the twentieth century, official records started replacing face-to-face interaction as the chief means of collecting information on individuals. "Decisions about us are based on impersonal organizational data banks" over which citizens have little direct control.[65] Legal scholar Alan Westin provided a definition that has served as the basis for current federal privacy legislation: privacy is "the claim of individuals, groups, or institutions to determine for themselves when, how and to what extent information about them is communicated to others."[66]

The Supreme Court has played a central role in shaping federal privacy policy. The Court addressed the question of individual privacy in four major decisions: *Griswold v. Connecticut* (1965), *Eisenstadt v. Baird* (1972), *Roe v. Wade* (1973), and *Whalen v. Roe* (1977).[67] In the first three decisions, the Court established the constitutional principle that "an independent right or zone of privacy exists."[68] In the *Whalen* decision, the Court ruled for the first time that a constitutionally recognized right of informational privacy exists.

With the Privacy Act of 1974, Congress attempted to quell the public's fear of government snooping into the private lives of citizens that had been aroused by the Watergate scandal. Its chief provisions include: prohibiting federal agencies from maintaining secret record systems; giving individuals the right of access to their own personal records; prohibiting data collected for one purpose to be used for a different purpose; and guaranteeing the reliability of personal records. The Court decisions and the 1974 Privacy Act were all designed to grant private citizens a means to control the information collected and maintained by the federal government regarding their personal lives.[69]

Privacy in the Information Age

The technological advances of recent decades have put to a serious test the law's protection of individual privacy. The speed and power of current IT make it easier to store and analyze vast amounts of personal data and to make this data available to more users in different agencies and to others within the government. The larger challenge to individual liberties, however, stems from the ability to integrate separate information systems to create one vast system containing the personal records of individuals, such as the system discussed in the TIA example at the beginning of the chapter.[70] In such a universal data system, personal data collected for one purpose could be used for an entirely different purpose. This worries many civil liberty activists, who see it as a possible violation of provisions of the Privacy Act. The three techniques that could enable the government to manipulate personal data in this manner are computer matching, front-end verification, and computer profiling. Each one is discussed below.

Computer matching refers to a process in which electronic information is shared among separate databases that are physically located in different agencies and maintained for different purposes. By using personal identifiers, such as a person's Social Security number, matches are obtained that permit the government to compare personal records stored in different databases. Matches, or "hits," are then checked again to verify that the records are indeed those of the same individual. Matching is used to check for persons who should *not* appear in two different databases, such as federal employees who earn above a certain salary and food stamp recipients.[71] It can also be used to check for persons who *should* appear in two systems but do not, such as men over the age of eighteen who are registered for the draft and men over eighteen with driver's licenses. Since 1977, numerous federal statutes have been passed that allow computer matching as a technique to prevent or identify waste, fraud, and abuse, particularly with regard to welfare recipients and others receiving federal benefits. Agencies' uses of computer matching include the following:

- AFDC recipients compared with Social Security Administration's earnings records
- Veterans benefits rolls matched with Supplemental Security Income rolls
- AFDC recipients matched with federal civilian and military payrolls
- State AFDC rolls compared with other state AFDC rolls[72]

Over time, the number of computer matches conducted by the federal government has involved billions of personal records.[73] State governments are also turning to computer matching to increase efficiency and to detect fraud, especially during times of fiscal stress. State governments have used computer matching to cross-check school bus driver applicants' driver's license data

---

Computer matching
A process in which electronic information is shared among separate databases that are physically located in different agencies and maintained for different purposes.

Front-end verification A computer application that checks the accuracy and completeness of personal information supplied by applicants for government benefits, employment, and services.

against police records, to check lottery winners' names against the list of delinquent taxpayers, and to go after "deadbeat dads" by checking data such as hunting and fishing license applications.[74]

Front-end verification checks the accuracy and completeness of personal information supplied by applicants for government benefits, employment, and services. Front-end verification differs from matching in several ways. For example, front-end verification

- Is done on an individual basis rather than for large groups of persons.
- Occurs before the applicant is granted eligibility or receives any benefits.
- Is proactive rather reactive: it is intended to prevent and deter fraud and abuse rather than detect and punish.
- Occurs online at the time of application.[75]

Front-end verification raises some troubling issues with regard to individual liberties. According to the Office of Technology Assessment, "The use of front-end verification is creating a de facto national database covering all Americans" through linkage of individual databases by means of telecommunications.[76] In front-end verification, personal information originally collected for one purpose (e.g., to obtain Social Security benefits) may be used in a process that might result in the denial of benefits or employment for an entirely different reason. Further, these information checks often occur without the full knowledge of the person being affected, which raises serious due process issues, including what protections individuals have if the information turns out to be false or out of date.

Computer profiling A computer application that allows several databases to be searched for personal information that matches a pattern of characteristics.

Computer profiling allows several databases to be searched for personal information that matches a pattern of characteristics, or a "profile." Agencies develop profiles based on personal characteristics of individuals who are likely to engage in certain types of behavior of interest to the agencies. For example, the FBI uses computer profiling to identify potential terrorists, the Drug Enforcement Agency (DEA) to identify possible drug dealers, and the IRS to identify people who may not pay their income taxes. Civil liberty concerns focus on whether people who are selected by computer profiling are treated differently from those not selected. In computer matching, databases are searched for specific individuals, but in profiling, specific types of people "are targeted for special investigation, not because a specific event or individual action warrants it, but because a computerized record fits a set of hypothetical conditions suggesting criminal conduct or civil violation."[77]

Government Information Policy After 9/11

The events of September 11, 2001, may have fundamentally altered the earlier delicate balance between individual privacy and national security. As a result of the war on terrorism, the government has approved the deployment of new surveillance technologies. In contrast to the pre-9/11 public attitude, "no longer is new technology necessarily viewed as a threat to individual

VIGNETTE 15.4   Key Patriot Act Provisions

- Authorization of "roving wiretaps," so that law enforcement officials can get court orders to wiretap any phone a suspected terrorist would use. The provision is needed, advocates say, because of the advent of cellular and disposable phones.
- The federal government is allowed to detain non-U.S. citizens suspected of terrorism for up to seven days without specific charges. The administration originally wanted to hold them indefinitely.
- Law enforcement officials are allowed greater subpoena power for e-mail records of terrorist suspects.

- The number of Border Patrol, Customs Service, and Immigration and Naturalization Service inspectors at the northern border of the United States is tripled, and $100 million provided to improve technology and equipment on the U.S. border with Canada.
- Measures against money laundering are expanded by requiring additional record keeping and reports for certain transactions and requiring identification of account holders.
- The statute of limitations is eliminated for prosecuting the most egregious terrorist acts, but the statute of limitation is maintained on most crimes at five to eight years.

privacy; rather, it is perceived as serving the common good and protecting freedom as reflected in legislative reactions such as the USA Patriot Act."[78] However, the public's view regarding privacy is not set in stone, and there is evidence suggesting a backing away from some of the more intrusive measures enacted soon after 9/11.

Following the terrorist attacks on September 11, Congress passed the Uniting and Strengthening America by Providing Appropriate Tools Required to Intercept and Obstruct Terrorism Act, better known as the USA Patriot Act. The law went into effect on October 26, 2001, just one month after the terrorist attacks. This statute gives law enforcement officials additional powers to fight terrorists, including greater access to personal e-mail and other electronic communications, the ability to track Internet sites visited by a person, increased use of secret searches, and the sharing of personal information among intelligence agencies. At the same time that the law increases the power of law enforcement authorities to conduct searches, it also loosens the judicial safeguards protecting privacy that were formerly in place (see Vignette 15.4). The act contains a sunset provision affecting many of the electronic surveillance provisions. In 2006, Congress renewed the Patriot Act with some minor alterations in the original provisions.

Civil Society and Information Resources

Jane Fountain in *Building the Virtual State* discusses the transformation of American government into what she calls a virtual state. The virtual state consists of public agencies and public and private networks that depend

E-government The use of technology to facilitate government administration, improve citizen access to government information and services, and encourage citizen participation in the government process.

on the Internet to provide linkages and expand organizational capacity.[79] She uses the term to describe all the computer-based interactions and exchanges between government and other entities, both profit and nonprofit. Her concept of the virtual state is closely related to the idea of e-government.

E-government is a concept which emerged in public administration literature during the 1990s. It stems from government's increasing adoption of e-business and e-commerce techniques and methods from the private sector. According to one study, "broadly defined, e-government includes the use of all information and communication technologies, from fax machines to wireless palm pilots, to facilitate the daily administration of government . . . that improves citizen access to government information, services and expertise to ensure citizen participation in, and satisfaction with the government process." Further, e-government "is a permanent commitment by government to improving the relationship between the private citizen and the public sector through enhanced, cost-effective and efficient delivery of services, information and knowledge."[80] IT and information resources therefore provide the infrastructure for e-governments to create the virtual state.

Governments are beginning to recognize and take advantage of the promise of technology. Not all governments, however, are moving at the same speed to adopt e-government principles. The size of the jurisdiction is an important factor in the degree to which IT is embraced. A survey conducted by the International City/County Management Association found that larger municipal governments are more likely to take a strategic and proactive approach to e-government.[81] However, even with the benefits to be gained, very few governments wholly accept the idea. Thus, the potential of IT to improve government services remains largely untapped. In addition, there exists considerable variation in the spread of e-government at the state level. The number of services provided by states online averages four; few states offer citizens more services over the Web.[82] Clearly, the idea of web-based government services will take some time to catch on—with good reason, we might add, since important privacy and security issues remain to be worked out.

The use of the Web to deliver services to citizens can produce cost savings and efficiency through reducing paperwork, cutting overhead costs, and decreasing data input errors. Furthermore, cost savings can be achieved through streamlining the procurement process, creating interagency partnerships, and sharing databases. Before governments can realize these efficiencies and savings, however, they must overcome several major challenges: the inability to handle high-volume and high-speed Internet; inadequate protection of personal privacy and information systems; need for new governance structures; and lack of cooperation between agencies. In the new world of e-government, some argue that effective administrators must be masters of the technological environment in their organizations, but at the same time they must remain astute public managers.[83] This requires more training, particularly in the area of IT and information resources.

Moreover, according to a number of observers, governments are broadening their use of technology to engage citizens as well as serve them better. "We're moving from e-government to e-democracy," as a law professor says in a 2004 *Governing* magazine article.[84] The techniques that are being used to involve citizens more in the governance process include government simulation games, online polls, and Internet chat rooms. All of these innovations can help improve the ability of public officials to accurately read and respond to public opinion. The technology's usefulness lies in its capacity to elicit more focused thoughts and comments from citizens, which can serve administrators better than sparsely attended public hearings that sometimes devolve into little more than shouting matches between rival factions.

Examples of the use of IT to help inform government decision-making increase every year. In Baltimore, when Mayor Martin O'Malley objected to the color of paint his predecessor had chosen for a new bridge, he held an online vote in which more than 5,000 people participated. His preferred color, green, lost. The governor of Maine used a budget simulation game on the Internet to obtain Maine residents' feedback on balancing the budget. The citizen-players could cut expenses or raise taxes to reduce the state's more than $1 billion deficit to zero. Their budget choices were sent to the governor along with an e-mail. The governor made mention of these messages in his annual state of the state message. The federal government has put rulemaking online at www.regulations.gov. This has excited the interest of scholars who see this as the first step toward interactive government. A Harvard professor sees e-rulemaking as the beginning of regulatory polling, or the use of online surveys to obtain public comments on proposed changes in federal regulations.[85]

The Digital Divide

E-government can conjure up a vision of a public sector version of Amazon.com, the successful online retailer. Citizens may be able to access a wide range of government services more conveniently and efficiently from their own homes and escape the hassle of dealing directly with bureaucracy. The downside of this, however, relates to the lack of access for many low-income Americans. Race and economic class restrict some individuals' access to the Web and other information resources, creating a gap known as the **digital divide**.[86] White households with incomes over $75,000 are far more likely to own a computer and have Internet access than are nonwhite households who make less than $75,000. This fundamental disparity between the "information haves" and "information have-nots" directly affects who receives services from e-government and who does not. As one scholar notes, "Recent research suggests that in a political environment where the citizen is increasingly viewed as a customer, the wealthy customer

Digital divide The gap between the less affluent and the affluent in terms of computer ownership and use as well as access to the Internet.

may receive better treatment as digital government architectures are designed and implemented."[87] Thus, governments need to address the gap in Internet access between high- and low-income households as part of their e-government initiatives.

The Virtual Town Hall

Facilitating citizen access to and participation in government has always been part of the appeal of computers to government, particularly at the local level. The ability of citizens to individually initiate direct contact with government can be enhanced by IT, according to e-government proponents. Yet this benefit of technology is sometimes overlooked by government, which tends to concentrate mainly on the service delivery aspects, leading one observer to say, "while automation can increase government effectiveness and efficiency, at times an intangible benefit to citizens, it is important that it also improve direct government-citizen relations, which is a very tangible benefit to citizens."[88]

If IT can provide opportunities for a more open and deliberative governance process, this may contribute to building civil society. The nexus of civil society and e-government has been explored by a number of authors.[89] Robert Putnam, for example, while skeptical of the grander claims of some supporters, concedes that IT represents the most important trend toward strengthening civic engagement.[90] According to political scientist Benjamin Barber, advances in IT reduce the opportunity costs of citizen participation.[91] In contrast, before the information revolution, citizen participation was constrained

One way to bridge the digital divide is by making computers accessible to children everywhere.

SOURCE: Jim West/ The Image Works

because of the costs incurred in taking time away from working, socializing with friends and family, or being engaged in leisure activities. As costs of participation fall, the level of civic engagement can be expected to rise, according to these authors.

If people have access to technology, some contend, they can make their voices heard in the halls of power. This might bring into being a virtual town hall, or the "electronic equivalent of the New England town meeting . . . the new means of constructing a public sphere that would help empower everyday citizens and public administrators and to strengthen our communities and democratic institutions."[92] The virtual town hall and e-government, some contend, can be valuable incubators of civil society in the future. Whether the potential of e-government and the Internet to strengthen civil society is fulfilled depends on the choices made today by public administrators and elected officials regarding issues of access and the role of information resources in governance.

Chapter Summary

It has been said that government is information. Indeed, much of what government does involves the collection, storage, analysis, and dissemination of information, which results in the expenditure of billions of dollars every year. Despite the common tendency to use words like information and data interchangeably, they stand for different concepts. Data are the building blocks of information. Information is the systematic arrangement of data into meaningful patterns. Knowledge is built on information that supports a course of action.

Information technology (IT) has had a profound impact on public organizations. Information resources have had the greatest effect in the areas of control, decision-making and policy-making, organizational performance, public employees, and power relationships. The chief impact of computing has been to automate operations and decision-making to some extent. Computers affect how jobs are done, worker safety, and nearly every other aspect of the current workplace.

Two important elements of public information policy are government's use of personal information and public access to government information. The federal government's response to 9/11 has focused renewed attention on both these aspects of information policy. Privacy has long been a contentious issue, one that has been exacerbated by the techniques and tools made available by the information age.

E-government is emerging as the consequence of the computerization of American society. In e-government, government agencies and other public entities increasingly depend on the Internet to deliver services in a manner more convenient to citizens. The virtual town hall taps into e-government to create an electronic public sphere, the current equivalent of the early New England town meeting.

■ Chapter Discussion Questions

1. How do differences between the public and private sectors influence how IT is used by each sector?

2. How has IT had an unexpected impact on public employees?

3. Despite spending enormous sums of money on IT, governments have not reaped the promised rewards of high tech. Why have governments received less than satisfactory returns on their technology investments?

4. What current tensions characterize the privacy policy of governments at all levels? How might we as a society reconcile the need to ensure national security with the need to protect personal privacy?

5. What are some of the promises and perils of the "virtual state" and the "virtual townhall"?

BRIEF CASE   STATE AND LOCAL GOVERNMENTS
AND ONLINE PRIVACY

Privacy is an issue at all levels of government. Indeed, state and local governments easily collect as much personal information as the federal government. As one writer points out, "Data privacy has become a hot button concern," and state government must find ways "to protect from unauthorized eyes the information it holds when that information is no longer kept in disparate files and no longer protected by lock, key and clerks."[93] Years ago, information was collected and stored manually, with government employees as the gatekeepers, who released information only to those who were entitled to it and who signed a form to identify themselves.

Times have changed, and easy access to personal records is now a cause for worry on the part of ordinary citizens. Today, people do not have to make a trip to city hall and rummage through dusty files to find out personal information about somebody. That information is just a keyboard click away. More and more governments have started to put personal data online for a variety of reasons: efficiency, openness, and access. From the citizens' perspective, however, not all of this transparency is good. There is a public consensus that government should not make sensitive personal information widely available. A Federal Trade Commission study, however, found that identity theft that results from public records is far less of a problem than it is from stolen credit cards or other private sources. Nevertheless, many Americans are more inclined to agree with B. J. Ostergren, a privacy activist from Hanover County, Virginia, who says that the dangers of making information available online are great as long as this information contains Social Security numbers, children's names, the maiden names of mothers, signatures, and loan and financial account numbers.[94]

Examples of Ostergren's worst fears are not difficult to find on state and local government websites. For instance, officials in Nassau County, New York, put on the county website the names and addresses of property owners as well as other confidential information so that property taxpayers could compare their property's assessed value to that of their neighbors, and in Mobile, Alabama, a court posted on the Web the names of people who were involuntarily placed in mental institutions.[95] A statewide police organization in Minnesota operated a database of confidential police files, in violation of state privacy laws.[96] In New Hampshire, a stalker was able to obtain a woman's work address and Social Security number from an Internet information broker; he used the information to locate the woman and killed her. The broker did nothing illegal, since he pieced this information together from public sources. In some cases, websites have been shut down by public demand. The New Hampshire supreme court ruled, as a result of the woman's murder, that Social Security numbers are confidential and cannot be posted on the Web. Mobile, however, still posts the names of its institutionalized citizens on the Web.

There is a general consensus in the public that government's information standards should be more strict than the private sector's. After all, people freely give out their personal information to companies to receive gifts or other benefits. When it comes to government though, Stuart McKee, a privacy expert and Washington state government official, says, "The standard is set exceptionally high. It's the Big Brother syndrome."[97] Private citizens, however, can also use the Internet to harass government employees. A computer engineer in the state of Washington maintains a website that lists police officers' addresses, home phone numbers, and Social Security numbers, all of which he lawfully obtained through voter registration, property, motor vehicle, and other official records. So far, the courts have been reluctant to prevent the dissemination of public information by private persons on the Web. The judge who ruled in the Washington case said that the website was "analytically indistinguishable from a newspaper."[98] This raises an important policy question. How is government's making personal information publicly available on the Web different from a private citizen doing the same thing?

Brief Case Questions

1. *Is there a double standard in the way governments use personal information versus the way private individuals and companies use the same information?*

2. *Should private persons or firms be allowed to post confidential personal information of other individuals (as some government websites do) on their websites? Why or why not?*

3. *What can governments do to reconcile their desire to open up government and increase citizen access to public information with the public's concerns about privacy?*

■ Key Terms

CBI consumer (page 365)
computer-based information (page 365)
computer matching (page 379)
computer profiling (page 380)
data (page 357)
data mining (page 357)
decision support system (DSS) (page 361)
digital divide (page 383)
e-government (page 382)
ergonomic (page 369)
freedom of information (page 377)
front-end verification (page 380)
information (page 357)

information islands (page 364)
information policy (page 361)
information resources management
    (IRM) (page 361)
information technology (IT) (page 357)
interoperability (page 367)
knowledge (page 358)
knowledge executive (page 365)
management information system (MIS) (page 360)
system-level bureaucracy (page 370)
transaction processing system
    (TPS) (page 360)
virtual state (page 370)

■ On the Web

http://www.gsa.gov/Portal/gsa/ep/
U.S. General Services Administration's electronic government and technology overview.

http://www.ostp.gov/
The Office of Science and Technology Policy advises the president on technology policy.

http://www.govtech.net/
Government Technology, one of the leading e-government websites.

http://www.firstgov.gov/Federal_Employees/
Electronic_Government.shtml
Federal employees' e-government and information technology webpage.

http://www.arpa.mil/
The Defense Advanced Research Projects Agency (DARPA) is the central research and development organization for the Department of Defense.

http://www.epic.org/
The website of the Electronic Privacy Information Center is a public interest research center based in Washington, D.C., whose primary focus is on safeguarding individual privacy in the information age.

http://www.whitehouse.gov/omb/egov/
The official website of the president's e-government initiatives.

http://www.govengine.com/
Comprehensive list of all e-government initiatives, including federal, state, and local governments.

Endnotes

CHAPTER 1

1. "Heroes amid the Horror," *New York Times*, September 15, 2001, 22.
2. http://en.wikipedia.org/wiki/Lightbulb_joke.
3. Brian J. Finegan, *The Federal Subsidy Beast: The Rise of a Supreme Power in a Once Great Democracy* (Sun Valley, ID: Alary Press, 2000); Randall Fitzgerald, *Porkbarrel: The Unexpurgated Grace Commission Story of Congressional Profligacy* (Washington, DC: Cato Institute, 1984); Leland H. Gregory, *Great Government Goofs* (New York: Dell, 1997).
4. Richard Stillman, *Preface to Public Administration* (New York: St. Martin's Press, 1996), 29.
5. John M. Pfiffner and Robert V. Presthus, *Public Administration*, 5th ed. (New York: Roland Press, 1967), 3.
6. Charles Goodsell, *The Case for Bureaucracy: A Public Administration Polemic*, 2nd ed. (Chatham, NJ: Chatham House, 1985), 83.
7. For a discussion of employment trends of graduates of public administration programs, see Paul Light, *The New Public Service* (Washington, DC: Brookings Institution Press, 1999).
8. Dwight Waldo, *The Enterprise of Public Administration: A Study of the Political Theory of American Public Administration* (New York: Macmillan, 1984), 58.
9. Leonard White, *Introduction to the Study of Public Administration* (New York: Macmillan, 1955), 3.
10. Herbert Simon, Donald Smithburg, and Victor Thompson, *Public Administration* (Brunswick, NJ: Transaction, 1991), 7.
11. David H. Rosenbloom, *Public Administration: Understanding Management, Politics, and Law in the Public Sector*, 2nd ed. (Syracuse, NY: Random House, 1986), 6.
12. Grover Starling, *Managing the Public Sector*, 5th ed. (New York: Harcourt Brace College Publishers, 1998), 10.
13. Cole Graham and Steven Hays, *Managing the Public Organization*, 2nd ed. (Washington, DC: Congressional Quarterly Press, 1993), 8.
14. Woodrow Wilson, "The Study of Administration," in *Classics of Public Administration*, 5th ed., ed. Jay Shafritz, Albert C. Hyde, and Sandra J. Parkes (Belmont, CA: Wadsworth, 1995), 22–34; Frank Goodnow, *Politics and Administration* (New York: Macmillan, 1900).
15. Fredrick Mosher, *Democracy and the Public Service* (New York: Oxford University Press, 1986), 183.
16. Wilson, "The Study of Administration."
17. Paul Van Riper observes that few public administration scholars at the time seemed to know about Wilson's essay and that Wilson's views were largely a reflection of the Progressive movement's deep-seated aversion to partisan politics—a point of view that had widespread currency among intellectuals and middle-class reformers long before Wilson's article was published. See Paul Van Riper, "The Politics–Administration Dichotomy: Concept or Reality?" in *Politics and Administration: Woodrow Wilson and American Public Administration*, ed. Jack Rabin and James S. Bowman (New York: Marcel Dekker, 1984), 203–217.
18. Criticism of the traditional politics–administration dichotomy on descriptive and normative grounds becomes widespread by the 1940s. See Paul Appleby, *Policy and Administration* (Tuscaloosa: University of Alabama Press, 1949).
19. The principal proponents of this perspective are David Osborne and Ted Gaebler. See especially their well-known *Reinventing Government: How the Entrepreneurial Spirit Is Transforming the Public Sector* (New York: Penguin Group, 1993). A less optimistic view is provided by Richard Box, "Running Government like a Business: Implications for Public Administration Theory and Practice," *American Review of Public Administration* 29:1 (1999): 19–43.
20. Studies that have examined the implementation of the NPR include Yuhua Qiao and Khai Thai, "Reinventing Government at the Federal Level: The Implementation and the Prospects," *Public Administration Quarterly* 29:1 (2002): 89–117; James R. Thompson, "The Clinton Reforms and the Administrative Ascendancy of Congress," *American Review of Public Administration* 31:3 (2001): 249–273; James R. Thompson, "Reinvention as Reform: Assessing the National Performance Review," *Public Administration Review* 60:6 (2000): 508–521; Robert T. Golembiewski, "As the NPR Twig Was Bent: Objectives, Strategic Gaps, and Speculations," *International Journal of Public Administration* 20:1 (1997): 139–172.
21. Graham T. Allison Jr., "Public and Private Management: Are They Fundamentally Alike in All Unimportant Respects?" in *Classics of Public*

Administration, ed. Jay Shafritz and Albert C. Hyde (Belmont, CA: Wadsworth, 1979), 72–91.

22. Barry Bozeman, *All Organizations Are Public: Comparing Public and Private Organizations* (San Francisco: Jossey-Bass, 1987).

23. George A. Boyne, "Public and Private Management: What's the Difference?" *Journal of Management Studies* 39:1 (2002): 97–123. Boyne asserts that the main conventional distinction between public and private organizations is their ownership, based on Rainey et al., 1976.

24. Boyne, "Public and Private Management," 99.

25. David Farnham and Sylvia Horton, "Managing Public and Private Organizations," in *Managing the New Public Service*, ed. D. Horton and S. Farnham (London: Macmillan, 1996). "It is success—or failure in the market which is ultimately the measure of effective private business management, nothing else" (31).

26. See, for example, Robert Dahl and Charles Lindblom, *Politics, Economics, and Welfare* (New Brunswick, NJ: Transaction, 2000).

27. Boyne, "Public and Private Management," 100.

28. Boyne, "Public and Private Management."

29. Boyne, "Public and Private Management."

30. John W. Kingdon, *Agendas, Alternatives, and Public Policies* (New York: HarperCollins, 1995), 159–162.

31. Paul C. Nutt and Robert W. Backoff, "Organizational Publicness and Its Implications for Strategic Management," *Journal of Public Administration Research and Theory* 3:2 (1993): 209–231.

32. Stillman, *Preface to Public Administration*, 38.

33. As Graham T. Allison points out, the goal of the system created by the Constitution was not to foster greater efficiency but to "create incentives to compete. . . . Thus, the general management functions concentrated in the CEO of a private business are, by constitutional design, spread in the public sector among a number of competing institutions and thus shared by a number of individuals whose ambitions are set against one another." From *Proceedings for the Public Management Research Conference*, November 19–20, 1979, in *Classics of Public Administration*, 2nd ed., ed. Shafritz and Hyde (Pacific Grove, CA: Brooks/Cole, 1987), 519.

34. Allison, *Proceedings for the Public Management Research Conference*, 523

35. Boyne, "Public and Private Management," 101.

36. Boyne, "Public and Private Management," 100.

37. Boyne, "Public and Private Management."

38. Boyne, "Public and Private Management."

39. Bozeman, *All Organizations Are Public.*

40. Graham, *Proceedings for the Public Management Research Conference*, 29.

41. Graham, *Proceedings for the Public Management Research Conference*. Also Boyne, "Public and Private Management," 100.

42. Peter S. Ring and James L. Perry, "Strategic Management in Public and Private Organizations: Implications of Distinctive Contexts and Constraints," *Academy of Management Review* 10:2 (1985): 277.

43. Total Government Expenditures 1947–2005, Historical Tables, Table 15.2, Budget of the United States, 2005, http://www.whitehouse.gov/omb/budget/fy2005/hist.pdf.

44. Norton E. Long, "Power and Administration," in *Classics of Public Administration*, ed. Shafritz and Hyde (1987), 203.

45. See Patricia W. Ingraham, *The Foundation of Merit: Public Service in American Democracy* (Baltimore: Johns Hopkins University Press, 1995), 3–7; Steven Kelman, *Making Public Policy: A Hopeful View of American Government* (New York: Basic Books, 1987), 31–37; F. Rourke, *Bureaucracy, Politics, and Public Policy*, 3rd ed. (Boston: Little, Brown, 1983).

46. Fredrick Mosher, *Democracy and the Public Service*, quoted in Ingraham, *The Foundation of Merit*, 51.

47. Rourke, *Bureaucracy, Politics, and Public Policy*, 21.

48. Rourke, *Bureaucracy, Politics, and Public Policy*, 36.

49. Michael Lipsky, *Street-Level Bureaucracy* (New York: Russell Sage Foundation, 1983).

50. Lipsky, *Street-Level Bureaucracy*, 3.

51. Ingraham, *The Foundation of Merit*, 4.

52. Ingraham, *The Foundation of Merit*.

53. Ingraham, *The Foundation of Merit*.

54. For example, see the discussion in Kelman, *Making Public Policy*, 89–90.

55. Dwight Waldo, *The Administrative State: A Study of the Political Theory of American Public Administration* (New York: Holmes and Meier, 1984).

56. Hugh Heclo, "Issue Networks and the Executive Establishment," in *The New American Political System*, ed. Anthony King (Washington, DC: American Enterprise Institute, 1978), 87–124.

57. Heclo, "Issue Networks and the Executive Establishment."

58. E. J. Dionne, "Introduction: Why Civil Society? Why Now?" in *Community Works: The Revival of Civil Society in America*, ed. E. J. Dionne, (Washington, DC: Brookings Institution Press, 1999), 3.

59. See Robert Putnam, "Tuning In, Tuning Out: The Strange Disappearance of Social Capital in America," *PS: Political Science and Politics* 28:4 (1995).

60. L. S. Cottrell, "The Competent Community," in *Further Explorations in Social Psychiatry*, ed. Berton H. Wilson, Robert N. Kaplan, and Alexander H. Leighton (New York: Basic Books, 1976).

61. "The Fog of War," directed by Errol Morris, won the Oscar for best documentary in 2003. Morris said he based the eleven lessons in the movie on statements that McNamara made in the twenty hours of interviews he gave for the movie and on McNamara's 2001 book *In Retrospect*.
62. Wilson, "The Study of Administration," 179.

CHAPTER 2

1. Tom Hamburger, "Despite Bush's Credo, Government Grows," *Wall Street Journal*, September 3, 2003.
2. Paul C. Light, "Fact Sheet on the New True Size of Government," Wagner School of Public Service, New York University, http://www.nyu.edu/wagner/news/truesize.pdf.
3. Paul C. Light, *The New Public Service* (Washington, DC: Brookings Institution Press), 1.
4. Richard Musgrave and Peggy Musgrave, *Public Finance in Theory and Practice* (New York: McGraw Hill, 1989), 127.
5. Thomas A. Garrett and Russell M. Rhine, "On the Size and Growth of Government," *Federal Reserve Bank of St. Louis Review* 88:1 (2006): 13–30.
6. Chris Edwards and Tad DeHaven, "War between the Generations: Federal Spending on the Elderly Set to Explode," Cato Institute, 2003, http://www.cato.org. Nonmandatory spending, or discretionary spending, refers to programs whose budgets must be decided on an annual basis by lawmakers. The largest discretionary spending item by far in the federal budget is defense. Other discretionary programs include roads and highways, environmental protection, law enforcement, and financial assistance to states and localities.
7. Office of Management and Budget, Report to Congress on the Cost and Benefits of Federal Regulation, 1998, 19.
8. Office of Management and Budget, Report to Congress on the Costs and Benefits of Federal Regulations, http://www.whitehouse.gov/omb/inforeg/chap2.html#table4.
9. Robert Lee, Ronald Johnson, and Philip Joyce, *Public Budgeting Systems*, 7th ed. (Sudbury, MA: Jones and Bartlett, 2004), 34.
10. Lee, Johnson, and Joyce, *Public Budgeting Systems*, 84.
11. James Pfiffner and Robert Presthus, *Public Administration*, 5th ed. (New York: Roland Press, 1967), 25.
12. Donald Kettl, "Reinventing Government? Appraising the National Performance Review," in *Classics of Public Administration*, 4th ed., ed. Jay Shafritz, Albert C. Hyde, and Sandra J. Parkes, 543–557 (New York: Harcourt Brace College Publishers, 1997).
13. Lynton Caldwell, "The Administrative Republic: The Contrasting Legacies of Hamilton and Jefferson," *Public Administration Quarterly* 13 (1990): 482.
14. James Q. Wilson, *Bureaucracy: What Government Agencies Do and Why They Do It* (New York: Basic Books, 1989), 79.
15. Richard Stillman II, *The American Bureaucracy: The Core of Modern Government* (Chicago: Nelson Hall, 1996), 47.
16. James Q. Wilson, "The Rise of the Bureaucratic State," *Public Interest* 41 (1975): 77–103.
17. Richard Schott, *The Bureaucratic State: The Evolution and Scope of the Administration Federal Bureaucracy* (New York: General Learning Press, 1972), 9.
18. Wilson, "The Rise of the Bureaucratic State."
19. Wilson, "The Rise of the Bureaucratic State."
20. Wilson, "The Rise of the Bureaucratic State."
21. Musgrave and Musgrave, *Public Finance in Theory and Practice*, 127.
22. Some important examples include James M. Buchanan, "Social Choice, Democracy, and Free Markets," *Economy* 62 (1954): 114–123; Anthony Downs, *An Economic Theory of Democracy* (New York: Harper and Row, 1957); James M. Buchanan, *Fiscal Theory and Political Economy* (Chapel Hill: University of North Carolina Press, 1960); William A. Niskanan, *Bureaucracy and Representative Government* (Chicago: Aldine-Atherton, 1971).
23. See Cheryl S. King and Camilla Stivers, *Government Is US: Public Administration in an Anti-Government Era* (Thousand Oaks, CA: Sage, 1998), for essays that deal with the topic of how governments can improve their interactions with citizens and help citizens take responsibility for their government.
24. Harvey S. Rosen, *Public Finance*, 5th ed. (New York: Irwin-McGraw Hill, 1999), 132–133.
25. See E. J. Dionne, "Introduction: Why Civil Society? Why Now?" in *Community Works: The Revival of Civil Society in America*, ed. E. J. Dionne (Washington, DC: Brookings Institution Press, 1998), 9; Dan Coats and Rick Santorum, "Civil Society and the Humble Role of Government," in Dionne, *Community Works*, pp. 101–106; Theda Skocpol, "Don't Blame Big Government: America's Voluntary Groups Thrive in a National Network," in Dionne, *Community Works*, 37–43.
26. Skocpol, "Don't Blame Big Government," 37.
27. Skocpol, "Don't Blame Big Government," 38–39.
28. William B. Schambra, "All Community Is Local: The Key to America's Civic Renewal," in Dionne, *Community Works*, 47–49.
29. A. Schlesinger, "Librarians Find Way around USA Patriot Act," Associated Press State and Local Wire, May 22, 2003.

30. Judith Kohler, J. "Librarians across the Country Chafe under USA Patriot Act Restrictions; Groups File Lawsuit," Associated Press, July 31, 2003.

31. Schlesinger, "Librarians Find Way."

32. Kohler, "Librarians across the Country Chafe."

33. Chryss Cada, "Librarians Are on the Front Lines against Easier Access to Records," *Boston Globe*, September 8, 2003, A3.

CHAPTER 3

1. The text for the Athenian Oath is available from many sources. The one used in this chapter can be found along with historical references at http://www.essentia.com/book/history/Athenian.htm.

2. In his autobiography, *Under Fire*, North claimed that "Reagan knew everything." Oliver North, *Under Fire: An American Story* (New York: HarperCollins, 1991).

3. Peter Leitner and Ronald Stupak, "Ethics, National Security and Bureaucratic Realities: North, Knight, and Designated Liars," *American Review of Public Administration* 27:1 (1997): 65.

4. George H. Fredericksen, *The Spirit of Public Administration* (San Francisco: Jossey-Bass, 1997), 160.

5. James Bowman and Russell Williams, "Ethics in Government: From a Winter of Despair to a Spring of Hope," *Public Administration Review* 57:6 (1997): 517–519.

6. James Fesler and Donald Kettl, *The Politics of the Administrative Process* (Chatham, NJ: Chatham House, 1996), 367.

7. Darrell Pugh, "The Origins of Ethical Frameworks in Public Administration," in *Ethical Frontiers in Public Management*, ed. James Bowman (San Francisco: Jossey-Bass, 1991), 9.

8. James Bowman, Evan Berman, and Jonathan P. West, "The Profession of Public Administration: An Ethics Edge in Introductory Textbooks," *Public Administration Review* 61:2 (2001): 194.

9. John Rohr, *To Run a Constitution: The Legitimacy of the Administrative State* (Lawrence: University Press of Kansas, 1986), 28.

10. Donald Menzel, "Rediscovering the Lost World of Public Service Ethics: Do We Need New Ethics for Public Administrators?" *Public Administration Review* 59:5 (1999): 444–447.

11. Carol Lewis and Bayard Catron, "Professional Standards and Ethics," in *Public Administration Handbook*, ed. J. Perry, 699–712 (San Francisco: Jossey-Bass, 1996), 708.

12. Donald Menzel, "The Morally Mute Manager: Fact or Fiction?" *Public Personnel Management* 24:4 (1999): 515–527.

13. Robert Denhardt and Joseph Grubbs, *Public Administration: An Action Orientation*, 4th ed. (Belmont, CA: Thompson Wadsworth, 2003), 124.

14. Patrick Sheeran, *Ethics in Public Administration: A Philosophical Approach* (Westport, CT: Praeger, 1993), 9.

15. Sheeran, *Ethics in Public Administration*, 51.

16. Harold Gortner, "How Public Managers View Their Environment: Balancing Organizational Demands, Political Realities, and Personal Values," in Bowman, *Ethical Frontiers in Public Management*, 59–60.

17. Robin (1989), cited in Bowman and Williams, "Ethics in Government," 520.

18. Montgomery Van Wart, "The Sources of Ethical Decision Making for Individuals in the Public Sector," *Public Administration Review* 56:6 (1996): 526–527.

19. Bowman and Williams, "Ethics in Government," 521.

20. Pugh, "The Origins of Ethical Frameworks in Public Administration," 28, 23.

21. Pugh, "The Origins of Ethical Frameworks in Public Administration," 18.

22. Marshall R. Goodman, Timothy J. Holp, and Karen Ludwig, "Understanding State Legislative Ethics Reform: The Importance of Political and Institutional Culture," in *Public Integrity Annual*, ed. J. Bowman, 51–57 (Lexington, KY: Council of State Governments, 1996).

23. See April Hejka-Ekins, *Ethics in Service Training: Handbook of Administrative Ethics* (New York: Dekker, 1994), 65–66; and Donald Maletz and Jerry Herbel, "Beyond Idealism: Democracy and Ethics Reform," *American Review of Public Administration* 30:1 (2000): 25–29.

24. Maletz and Herbel, "Beyond Idealism," 28–29.

25. Dennis F. Thompson, "Paradoxes of Government Ethics," *Public Administration Review* 52:3 (1992): 254–259.

26. Gary Zajac, "Reinventing Government and Reaffirming Ethics: Implications for Organizational Development in the Public Service," *Public Administration Quarterly* (Winter 1997): 394–395.

27. John Pfiffner and Robert Presthus, *Public Administration*, 5th ed. (New York: Roland, 1967), 539.

28. Lloyd Nigro and William Richardson, "Between Citizen and Administrator: Administrative Ethics and PAR," *Public Administration Review* (November/December 1990): 624.

29. Nigro and Richardson, "Between Citizen and Administrator."

30. Pugh, "The Origins of Ethical Frameworks in Public Administration," 26.

31. Menzel, "Rediscovering the Lost World of Public Service Ethics," 521.

32. Menzel, "The Morally Mute Manager" 523.

33. James Bowman, "Unearthing the Moral Foundations of Public Administration: Honor, Benevolence, and Justice," in Bowman, *Ethical Frontiers in Public Management*, 103, 104, 106.

34. Dwight Waldo, *The Enterprise of Public Administration: A Summary View* (New York: Holmes and Meier, 1980).
35. Waldo, *The Enterprise of Public Administration.*
36. Dianne Daeg De Mott, "Kohlberg's Theory of Moral Reasoning" (1998), http://www.findarticles.com.
37. Debra W. Stewart and Norman A. Sprinthall, "Strengthening Ethical Judgment in Public Administration," in Bowman, *Ethical Frontiers in Public Management*, 252, 255.
38. Bowman and Berman, "The Profession of Public Administration," 195–196.
39. Ralph Chandler, "Deontological Dimension of Administrative Ethics, Revisited," *Public Personnel Management* 28:4 (1999): 513.
40. Mary Guy, "Using High Reliability Management to Promote Ethical Decision Making," in Bowman, *Ethical Frontiers in Public Managemen*, 191, 194.
41. Bowman and Williams, "Ethics in Government," 519.
42. Bowman and Williams, "Ethics in Government," 524.
43. Wilbur C. Rich, "The Moral Choice of Garbage Collectors: Administrative Ethics from Below," *American Review of Public Administration* 26:2 (1996): 201–212.
44. George H. Fredericksen, "Can Public Officials Correctly Be Said to Have Obligations to Future Generations?" *Public Administration Review* 54:5 (1994): 461.
45. Fredericksen, "Can Public Officials Correctly Be Said to Have Obligations to Future Generations?" 463.
46. J. Patrick Dobel, "Political Prudence and the Ethics of Leadership," *Public Administration Review* 58:1 (1998): 74–81.
47. See Zajac, "Reinventing Government and Reaffirming Ethics." Also see Robert Gregory, "Social Capital Theory and Administrative Reform: Maintaining Ethical Probity in Public Service," *Public Administration Review* 59:1 (1999): 63–75; Menzel, "Rediscovering the Lost World of Public Service Ethics"; Menzel, "The Morally Mute Manager"; and James P. Pfiffner, "The Public Service Ethic in the New Public Personnel Systems," *Public Personnel Management* 28:4 (1999): 541–555.
48. Gregory, "Social Capital Theory and Administrative Reform," 64, 66.
49. Menzel, "The Morally Mute Manager," 520.
50. Zajac, "Reinventing Government and Reaffirming Ethics," 392, 399.
51. http://www.time.com/time/personoftheyear/2002/.
52. "Alamos Rehires Two Whistle Blowers, *New York Times*, January 18, 2003.
53. See Denhardt and Grubbs, *Public Administration*, 143; Marcia Miceli and Janet Near, "Individual and Situational Correlates of Whistle-Blowing," *Personnel Psychology* 41 (1988): 267–278.
54. Miceli and Near, "Individual and Situational Correlates of Whistle-Blowing," 278.
55. Philip H. Jos and Mark Thompkins, "In Praise of Difficult People: A Portrait of the Committed Whistleblower," *Public Administration Review* (1989): 552–561.
56. Jos and Thompkins, "In Praise of Difficult People," 558.
57. "Whistle-Blowers Being Punished, a Survey Shows," *New York Times*, September 3, 2002.
58. Julie Dunn, "Responsible Party: Helping Workers Who Spill the Beans," *New York Times*, January 19, 2003.
59. Menzel, "Rediscovering the Lost World of Public Service Ethics."
60. Guy Adams and Danny Balfour, *Unmasking Administrative Evil* (Thousand Oaks, CA: Sage, 1998), xix, xx.
61. Adams and Balfour, *Unmasking Administrative Evil*, 31, 72.
62. Martin Schramm, "A Whistle Was Blown—and No One Heard," Newsobserver.com.
63. Peter Spotts, "A Harsh Critique of NASA's Culture," *Christian Science Monitor*, August 27, 2003.
64. Spotts, "A Harsh Critique of NASA's Culture."
65. Martin E. Anderson, "Commentary: The Sad Tale of NASA's Space Shuttle Whistle Blowers," 2003, Government Accountability Project, http://www.whistleblower.org.
66. John Schwartz and Matthew L. Wald, "Space Agency Culture Comes under Scrutiny," *New York Times*, March 29, 2003.
67. Government Accountability Project.
68. Schwartz and Wald, "Space Agency Culture Comes under Scrutiny."
69. John Schwartz and Matthew L. Wald, "NASA's Curse? Groupthink Is 30 Years Old, and Still Going Strong," *New York Times*, March 9, 2003.

CHAPTER 4

1. See *The National Commission on Terrorist Attacks upon the United States*, 9/11 Commission Report (New York: Barnes and Noble, 2004).
2. William West, *Controlling the Bureaucracy* (Armonk, NY: M. E. Sharpe, 1995), 78.
3. *Myers v. United States*, 272 U.S. 52 (1926).
4. Hugh Heclo, *A Government of Strangers* (Washington, DC: Brookings Institution Press, 1977), 36.
5. Quoted in James Fesler and Donald Kettl, *The Politics of the Administrative Process* (Chatham, NJ: Chatham House, 1996), 99. A more recent analysis found virtually no change in the figure. See Stephen Barr, "When the Job Gets Old After 2 Years," *Washington Post*, June 2, 1994, A21.

6. Ronald Moe, "Traditional Organizational Principles and the Managerial Presidency: From Phoenix to Ashes," *Public Administration Review* 50 (1990): 129–140.

7. Hugh Helco, "OMB and the Presidency: The Problem of Neutral Competence," *Public Interest* 38 (1975): 80–98; Matthew V. Dickinson and Andrew Rudalevige, "Presidents, Responsiveness, and Competence: Revisiting the Golden Age at the Bureau of the Budget," *Political Science Quarterly* 119 (2005): 633–655.

8. James Pfiffner, "Nine Enemies and One Ingrate: Political Appointments during Presidential Transitions," in *The In-and-Outers*, ed. G. Calvin MacKenzie (Baltimore: John Hopkins University Press, 1987).

9. See Dean Mann and Jameson Doing, *The Assistant Secretaries* (Washington, DC: Brookings Institution Press, 1965).

10. James Q. Wilson, *Bureaucracy: What Government Agencies Do and Why They Do It?* (New York: Basic Books, 1989), 209, 212–215.

11. *The United States Government Manual*, Appendix B: Federal Executive Agencies Terminated, Transferred, or Changed in Name Subsequent to March 4, 1933, http://frwebgate.access.gpo.gov/cgi-bin/multidb.cgi.

12. Wilson, *Bureaucracy*, 265.

13. Louis Fisher, *The Politics of Shared Power* (Washington, DC: Congressional Quarterly Press, 1981), 141.

14. West, *Controlling the Bureaucracy*, 92.

15. Ann Bowman and Richard Keamey, *State and Local Government*, 5th ed. (Boston: Houghton Mifflin, 2002), 201.

16. James Conant, "Executive Branch Reorganization in the States (1965–1991)," in *The Book of the States, 1992–1993* (Lexington, KY: Council of the State Governments, 1993).

17. See Richard Elling, *Public Management in the States: A Comparative Study of Administrative Performance and Politics* (Westport, CT: Praeger, 1992). Also see F. Ted Hebert, Jeffrey L. Brudney, and Deil S. Wright, "Gubernatorial Influence and State Bureaucracy," *American Politics Quarterly* 11 (April 1983): 37–52.

18. Fesler and Kettl, *The Politics of the Administrative Process*, 321.

19. John Johannes, *To Serve the People: Congress and Constituency Service* (Lincoln: University of Nebraska Press, 1984), 63.

20. Fesler and Kettl, *The Politics of the Administrative Process*, 324.

21. Fesler and Kettl, *The Politics of the Administrative Process*, 321.

22. Congressional Research Service Index, (Washington, DC: Congressional Research Service, 1993); and Joel Aberbach, *Keeping a Watchful Eye: The Politics of Congressional Oversight* (Washington, DC: Brookings Institution Press, 1990), as quoted in West, *Controlling the Bureaucracy*, 140.

23. Fesler and Kettl, *The Politics of the Administrative Process*, 332.

24. Wilson, *Bureaucracy*, 241–242.

25. Fesler and Kettl, *The Politics of the Administrative Process*, 69.

26. Terry Moe, "An Assessment of the Positive Theory of 'Congressional Dominance,'" *Legislative Studies Quarterly* 12 (1987): 475–520.

27. Cornelius Kerwin, *Rulemaking: How Government Agencies Write Law and Make Policy* (Washington, DC: Congressional Quarterly Press, 1994), 3.

28. See David Rosenbloom and Rosemary O' Leary, *Public Administration and Law*, 2nd ed. (New York: Marcel Dekker, 1997); and Donald Horowitz, "The Courts as Guardians of the Public Interest," *Public Administration Review* 37 (1977): 148–154.

29. Rosenbloom and O'Leary, *Public Administration and Law*, 67.

30. William T. Gormley Jr., "Accountability Battles in State Administration," in *The Political Environment of Public Management*, ed. Peter Kobrak (New York: HarperCollins, 1993), 405.

31. Fesler and Kettl, *The Politics of the Administrative Process*, 357.

32. H. George Frederickson, "Comparing the Reinventing Government Movement with the New Public Administration," *Public Administration Review* 56:3 (1996): 263.

33. Frederickson, "Comparing the Reinventing Government Movement with the New Public Administration," 247.

34. David Osborne and Ted Gaebler, *Reinventing Government: How the Entrepreneurial Spirit Is Transforming the Public Sector* (New York: Penguin Group, 1993).

35. Frederickson, "Comparing the Reinventing Government Movement with the New Public Administration," 264.

36. Albert Gore Jr., *Creating a Government That Works Better and Costs Less*, September 1994 Status Report from *A Report of the National Performance Review* (Washington, DC: U.S. Government Printing Office, 1994), 8.

37. Mission statement of NPR Staff Handbook, quoted in John Kamensly, *A Brief History of Vice President Al Gore's National Partnership for Reinventing Government during the Administration of President Bill Clinton 1993–2001*, http://govinfo.library.unt.edu/npr/whoweare/historyofnpr.html.

38. James R. Thompson, "Reinvention as Reform: Assessing the National Performance Review," *Public Administration Review* 60:6 (2000): 511.

39. See Ronald Moe, "The 'Reinventing Government' Exercise: Misinterpreting the Problem, Misjudging the Consequences," *Public Administration Review* 54:2 (1994): 219–227. Also see Frederickson, "Comparing the Reinventing Government Movement with the New Public Administration," and Daniel W. Williams, "Reinventing the Proverbs of Government," *Public Administration Review* 60:6 (2000): 522–535.

40. Thompson, "Reinvention as Reform."

41. Thompson, "Reinvention as Reform," 510.

42. Richard Box, Gary Marshall, and Christine Reed, "New Public Management and Substantive Democracy," *Public Administration Review* 61:5 (2001): 611.

43. Osborne and Gaebler, *Reinventing Government*.

44. John L. McKnight, "Professionalized Services: Disabling Help for Communities and Citizens," in *The Essential Civil Society Reader*, ed. Don E. Eberly (Lanham, MD: Rowman and Littlefield, 2000), 187.

45. Osborne and Gaebler, *Reinventing Government*.

46. Hindy Lauer Schacter, "Reinventing Government or Reinventing Ourselves: Two Models for Improving Government Performance," *Public Administration Review* 55:6 (1993): 535.

47. Frank Thompson and Norma Riccucci, "Reinventing Government," *Annual Review of Political Science* 11 (1998): 248.

48. Thompson and Riccucci, "Reinventing Government."

49. See Frederickson, "Comparing the Reinventing Government Movement with the New Public Administration," and Box, Marshall, and Reed, "New Public Management and Substantive Democracy," 611.

50. Robert Denhardt and Janet Denhardt, "The New Public Service: Serving Rather than Steering," *Public Administration Review* 60:6 (2000): 549–559.

CHAPTER 5

1. Dana Milbank and Laurie McGinley, "While Washington Fiddles, Many States Devise Solutions to Problems of Welfare and Health Care," *Wall Street Journal*, May 31, 1996, A12.

2. See Roscoe Martin, *The Cities and the Federal System* (New York: Atherton Press, 1965), 45–47.

3. See Mark Rom, "Health and Welfare in the American States: Politics and Policies," in *Politics in the American States*, ed. Virginia Gray and Herbert Jacob, 399–437 (Washington, DC: Congressional Quarterly Press, 1996), 423.

4. Barbara Vobejda, "Most States Are Shaping Their Own Welfare Reform," *Washington Post*, February 3, 1996, 1.

5. William Weld, "Release Us from Federal Nonsense," *Wall Street Journal*, December 11, 1995, 12.

6. "The Welfare Bill: Text of President Clinton's Announcement on Welfare Legislation," *New York Times*, July 31, 1996, 24.

7. James Madison, *The Papers of James Madison*, ed. William Hutchinson, et al. (Chicago: University of Chicago Press, 1962).

8. James Madison, Alexander Hamilton, and John Jay, *The Federalist Papers*, ed. Charles S. Kesler, 1–495 (Middlesex, England: Penguin, 1961).

9. John Straayer, Robert Wrinkle, and J. L. Polinard, *State and Local Politics* (New York: St. Martin's Press, 1994), 30.

10. Morton Gordzins, "The American System," in *The American System: A New View of Government in the United States*, ed. Daniel Elazar (Chicago: Rand McNally, 1966).

11. Deil S. Wright, *Understanding Intergovernmental Relations* (Monterey, CA: Harcourt Brace, 1988).

12. *New State Ice Co. v. Liebmann*, 285 U.S. 262, 311 (1932).

13. Madison, Hamilton, and Jay, *The Federalist Papers*.

14. David Walker, *The Rebirth of Federalism* (New York: Chatham House, 2000), 24.

15. Walker, *The Rebirth of Federalism*, 25.

16. David Rosenbloom and Robert Kravchuk, *Public Administration: Understanding Management, Politics, and Law in the Public Sector*, 4th ed. (New York: McGraw-Hill, 1998), 123.

17. *McCulloch v. Maryland*, 17 U.S. 316 (1819).

18. *McCulloch v. Maryland*.

19. *Garcia v. San Antonio Metro. Transit Authority*, 469 U.S. 528 (1985).

20. *United States v. Lopez*, 514 U.S. 549 (1995).

21. Richard Aronson, and John Hilley, *Financing State and Local Government*, 4th ed. (Washington, DC: Brookings Institution Press, 1986), 48.

22. David C. Nice and Patricia Fredericksen, *The Politics of Intergovernmental Relations*, 2nd ed. (Chicago: Nelson-Hall, 1999), 52.

23. John Irons, *Half of 2004 Deficit Deterioration Due to Revenue-Reduction Legislation*, OMB-Watch Report, http://www.ombwatch.org/budget/pdf/cbo_percentages.pdf.

24. Joseph Zimmerman, *Contemporary American Federalism* (New York: Praeger, 1992), 119.

25. Marcia Ray and Timothy Conlon, "At What Price? Costs of Federal Mandates since the 1980s," *State and Local Government Review* 28 (1996): 7–16.

26. National Academy of Public Administration, *Beyond Preemption: Intergovernmental Partnerships to Enhance the New Economy*, http://www.napawash.org.

27. *Puerto Rico v. Branstad*, 483 U.S. 219 (1987).

28. U.S. Census Bureau, 2002 Census of Governments, vol. 1, no. 1, http://www.census.gov/prod/2003pubs/gc021x1.pdf.

29. Belle Zeller, *American State Legislature: Report of the Committee on American Legislatures of the American Political Science Association* (New York: Crowell, 1954).

30. U.S. Census Bureau.

31. Zimmerman, *Contemporary American Federalism*, 171.

32. U.S. Census Bureau.

33. David Berman, *State and Local Politics*, 9th ed. (Armonk, NY: M. E. Sharpe, 2000), 351.

34. Dennis Judd and Todd Swanstrom, *City Politics* (New York: Pearson Longman, 2004), 309.

35. Alan Greenblatt, "Anatomy of a Merger," *Governing* 16 (2002): 190–198.

36. William Schambra, "The Progressive Assault of Civic Community," in *The Essential Civil Society Reader*, ed. Don Eberly, 316–352 (Lanham, MD: Rowman and Littlefield, 2000), 319–320.

37. Schambra, "The Progressive Assault of Civic Community," 330.

38. Schambra, "The Progressive Assault of Civic Community," 333.

39. Schambra, "The Progressive Assault of Civic Community," 337–339.

40. Schambra, "The Progressive Assault of Civic Community," 340.

41. Schambra, "The Progressive Assault of Civic Community," 342.

42. Theda Skocpol, "Americans Became Civic," in *Civic Engagement in American Democracy*, ed. Theda Skocpol and Morris Fiorina (Washington, DC: Brookings Institution Press, 1999), 33.

43. Skocpol, "Americans Became Civic," 49.

44. Skocpol, "Americans Became Civic," 66.

45. Theda Skocpol, "Advocates without Members: The Recent Transformation of American Civic Life," in *Civic Engagement in American Democracy*, 491–498.

46. Peter Huck, "Environment: War on the Range," *Guardian*, November 22, 1995, T6.

47. B. Ruben, "Book Review: The War Against the Greens," *Environmental Action* 26:4 (1996).

48. B. Hanson, "Book Review: Going against the Green; Snapshots from the Front Lines of the Land-Use Confrontation; The War against the Greens: The Wise Use Movement, the New Right, and Anti-Environmental Violence by David Helvarg," *Los Angeles Times*, July 2, 1995, 7.

CHAPTER 6

1. Editorial, "Civil Society Rocks: Why Pittsburgh's Nonprofits Are Getting Stronger," *Pittsburgh Post-Gazette*, June 26, 2003.

2. William Schambra, "Local Groups Are the Key to America's Civic Renewal," *Brookings Review* 15:4 (1997), http://www.brookings.edu/press/review/fall97/schambra.htm.

3. Editorial, "Civil Society Rocks."

4. Jand Eisner, "American Rhythms: A Connected Community Built According to the Way We Live," Philly.com, 2003, http://www.philly.com.

5. Eisner, "American Rhythms." The quote is from Robert Putnam and Lewis M. Feldstein, *Better Together: Restoring the American Community* (New York: Simon and Schuster, 2003).

6. Jean B. Elshtain, "A Call to Civil Society," *Society* 36:5 (1999): 13.

7. Don Eberly, *The Essential Civil Society Reader* (Lanham, MD: Rowman and Littlefield, 2000).

8. Elshtain, "A Call to Civil Society," 3.

9. Robert Putnam, "Bowling Alone: America's Declining Social Capital," *Journal of Democracy* 6:1 (1995): 65–78.

10. Gene Brewer, "Building Social Capital: Civic Attitudes and Behavior of Public Servants," *Journal of Public Administration Research and Theory* 13:1 (2003): 5–26.

11. Martha McCoy and Patrick Scully, "Deliberative Dialogue to Expand Civic Engagement: What Kind of Talk Does Democracy Need?" *National Civic Review* 91:2 (2003): 117–135.

12. Jay Teachman, Kathleen Paasch, and Karen Carver, "Social Capital and the Generation of Human Capital," *Social Forces* 75:4 (1997): 1343–1359.

13. See Putnam, "Bowling Alone," and Tom Rice and Alexander Sumberg, "Civic Culture and Government Performance in the American States," *Publius* 27:1 (1997): 99–114.

14. Teachman, Paasch, and Carver, "Social Capital and the Generation of Human Capital."

15. E. J. Dionne, "Introduction: Why Civil Society? Why Now?" in *Community Works: The Revival of Civil Society in America*, ed. E. J. Dionne (Washington, DC: Brookings Institution Press, 1999); Don Eberly, *America's Promise* (Lanham, MD: Rowman and Littlefield, 1998); and Robert Putnam, *Bowling Alone: The Collapse and Revival of American Community* (New York: Simon and Schuster, 2000).

16. Alexis de Tocqueville, *Democracy in America*, full hypertext version on University of Virginia website, http://xroads.virginia.edu.

17. Alan Wolfe, "Is Civil Society Obsolete?" in Dionne, *Community Works*, 19.

18. Elshtain "A Call to Civil Society," 13.

19. William Galston and Peter Levine, "America's Civic Condition," in Dionne, *Community Works*, 30–36.

20. Galston and Levine, "America's Civic Condition."

21. Robert Post and Nancy Rosenblum, *Civil Society and Government* (Princeton, NJ: Princeton University Press, 2002), 11.

22. Michael Walzer, "The Idea of Civil Society," in Dionne, *Community Works*, 138.

23. James Madison, Alexander Hamilton, and John Jay, *The Federalist Papers*, ed. Charles R. Kesler (Middlesex, England: Penguin, 1961).
24. Elshtain, "A Call to Civil Society," 13–16.
25. Francis Rourke, *Bureaucracy, Politics, and Public Policy*, 3rd ed. (Boston: Little, Brown, 1983).
26. Philip Selznick, *TVA and the Grass Roots* (Berkeley: University of California Press, 1945).
27. Rourke, *Bureaucracy, Politics, and Public Policy*, 56–57.
28. Rourke, *Bureaucracy, Politics, and Public Policy*, 57.
29. Rourke, *Bureaucracy, Politics, and Public Policy*, 58.
30. Steven Kelman, *Making Public Policy* (New York: Basic Books, 1987), 238–239.
31. Rourke, *Bureaucracy, Politics, and Public Policy*, 54.
32. Theda Skocpol, "Americans Became Civic," in *Civic Engagement in American Democracy*, ed. Theda Skocpol and Morris Fiorina (Washington, DC: Brookings Institution Press, 1999), 472–474.
33. Hugh Heclo, "Issue Networks and the Executive Establishment," in *The New American Political System*, ed. Anthony King, 87–124 (Washington, DC: American Enterprise Institute, 1978).
34. Heclo, "Issue Networks and the Executive Establishment," 104.
35. Heclo, "Issue Networks and the Executive Establishment."
36. Herbert Asbury, *The Gangs of New York* (New York: Thunder Mouth Press, 1998), 249–250. Asbury's book was later made into a movie by noted director Martin Scorcese.
37. Alejandro Portes and Patricia Landolt, "The Downside of Social Capital," *American Prospect* 26 (May–June 1996): 18.
38. Robert Putnam, "Tuning In, Tuning Out: The Strange Disappearance of Social Capital in America," *PS: Political Science and Politics* 28:4 (1995): 666.
39. Putnam, "Bowling Alone: America's Declining Social Capital," 70.
40. Putnam, "Tuning In, Tuning Out," 675.
41. Putnam, "Tuning In, Tuning Out," 675.
42. Putnam, "Tuning In, Tuning Out," 678–679.
43. Theda Skocpol, "Unraveling from Above," *American Prospect* 25 (1996).
44. Charles Perrow, "Society at Risk in a Society of Organizations," in *Populations at Risk in America: Vulnerable Groups at the End of the Twentieth Century*, ed. George J. Demko and Michael C. Jackson, 19–35 (Boulder, CO: Westview Press, 1995), 21.
45. See Michael Schudson, "If Civic Life Didn't Die?" *American Prospect* 25 (1996): 17–20.
46. Schudson, "If Civic Life Didn't Die?"
47. Lisa Zanetti, "At the Nexus of State and Civil Society: The Transformative Practice of Public Administration," in *Government Is Us: Public Administration in an Anti-Government Era*, ed. Cheryl King and Camilla Stivers (Thousand Oaks, CA: Sage, 1998), 102–103.
48. See Paul C. Light, *The New Public Service* (Washington, DC: Brookings Institution Press, 1999), 67.
49. See Part 2 of King and Stivers, *Government Is Us*.
50. John Nalbandian, "Facilitating Community, Enabling Democracy: New Roles for Local Government Managers," *Public Administration Review* 95:1 (1999): 187.
51. Richard C. Box and Deborah Sagen, "Working with Citizens: Breaking down Barriers to Citizen Self-Governance," in King and Stivers, *Government Is Us*, 169.
52. Brewer, "Building Social Capital," 13–14, 19.
53. L. S. Cottrell, "The Competent Community," in *Further Explorations in Social Psychiatry*, ed. Berton H. Kaplan, Robert Neal Wilson, and Alexander Hamilton Leighton (New York: Basic Books, 1976), 45.
54. Jane Eisner, "No Paintbrushes, No Paint," in Dionne, *Community Works*, 75–80).
55. John Parr and David Lampe, "Empowering Citizens," in *Handbook of Public Administration*, ed. J. Perry (San Francisco: Jossey-Bass, 1996), 204.
56. See Mary Timmey, "Overcoming Administrative Barriers to Citizen Participation: Citizens as Partners, Not Adversaries," in King and Stivers, *Government Is Us*; Dolores Foley, "We Want Your Input: Dilemmas of Citizen Participation," in King and Stivers, *Government Is Us*; and Parr and Lampe, "Empowering Citizens."
57. See Jeffrey Brudney and Robert England, "Toward a Definition of the Co-Production Concept," *Public Administration Review* 43 (1983): 59–65; Roger B. Parks et al., "Consumers as Co-producers of Public Services: Some Economic and Institutional Considerations," *Policy Studies Journal* 9 (1981): 1001–1011.
58. Parr and Lampe, "Empowering Citizens," 202.
59. Bill Bradley, "America's Challenge: Revitalizing Our National Community," in Dionne, *Community Works*, 112.
60. Matt Leighninger, "Enlisting Citizens: Building Political Legitimacy," *National Civic Review* 91:2 (2003): 137–148.
61. Timmey, "Overcoming Administrative Barriers to Citizen Participation," 96–97.
62. John McKnight, "Professionalized Services: Disabling Help for Communities and Citizens," in *The Essential Civil Society Reader*, ed. D. Eberly (Lanham, MD: Rowman and Littlefield), 191.
63. McKnight, "Professionalized Services," 193.
64. Light, *The New Public Service*, 91.
65. Light, *The New Public Service*, 95.

CHAPTER 7

1. Thomas H. Kean et al., *The 9/11 Commission Report* (New York: W. W. Norton, 2003), 56.
2. James Pfiffner and Robert Presthus, *Public Administration*, 5th ed. (New York: Roland Press, 1967), 7.
3. See Jay Shafritz and Albert C. Hyde, *Classics of Public Administration* (New York: Harcourt Brace, 1997), 2.
4. Gareth Morgan, *Images of Organizations* (Newbury Park, CA: Sage, 1986).
5. Hans H. Gerth, and C. Wright Mills, *From Max Weber: Essays in Sociology* (New York: Oxford University Press, 1958), 50.
6. Quoted in David Rosenbloom, *Public Administration: Understanding Management, Politics, and Law in the Public Sector*, 2nd ed. (Syracuse, NY: Random House, 1986), 133.
7. Quoted in Brian Fry, *Mastering Public Administration: From Max Weber to Dwight Waldo* (Chatham, NJ: Chatham House, 1989), 33.
8. Fry, *Mastering Public Administration*, 60.
9. Luther Gulick, "Notes on the Theory of Organization," in *Classics of Public Administration*, 5th ed., ed. Shafritz, Hyde, and Parkes, 90–98) (Belmont, CA: Wadsworth, 2004).
10. Gulick, "Notes on Theory of Administration," 94.
11. Gulick, "Notes on Theory of Administration," 96.
12. Fry, *Mastering Public Administration*, 98–99.
13. Fry, *Mastering Public Administration*, 111.
14. Fry, *Mastering Public Administration*, 113.
15. Alex Carey, "The Hawthorne Studies: A Radical Criticism," *American Sociological Review* 32:3 (1967): 403–416.
16. Richard H. Franke and James D. Kaul, "The Hawthorne Experiments: First Statistical Interpretation," *American Sociological Review* 43:5 (1987): 623–643.
17. Chester Barnard, *The Functions of the Executive* (Cambridge, MA: Harvard University Press, 1938).
18. Barnard, *The Functions of the Executive*, 57.
19. Fry, *Mastering Public Administration*, 169.
20. Herbert Simon, *Administrative Behavior: A Study of Decision-Making Processes in Administrative Organizations* (New York: Free Press, 1957).
21. Herbert Simon, "The Proverbs of Administration," *Public Administration Review* 6:1 (1946): 53–67.
22. Simon, *Administrative Behavior*, quoted in Fry, *Mastering Public Administration*, 191.
23. Fry, *Mastering Public Administration*, 208–213.
24. Morgan, *Images of Organizations*, 44.
25. David Easton, *The Political System* (New York: Knopf, 1953).
26. Daniel Katz and Robert Kahn, *The Social Psychology of Organizations*, 2nd ed. (New York: Wiley, 1979).
27. Daniel Katz and Robert Kahn, "Organizations and the System Concept," in *Classics in Organization Theory*, 2nd ed., ed. Jay M. Shafritz and Steven Ott (Homewood, IL: Dorsey Press, 1987), 252.
28. Paul Lawrence and Jay Lorsch, "Differentiation and Interrelation in Complex Organizations," *Administration Science Quarterly* 12 (1967): 1–47.
29. H. George Frederickson, *The Spirit of Public Administration* (San Francisco: Jossey-Bass, 1997), 34.
30. Anthony Downs, *Inside Bureaucracy* (Boston: Little, Brown, 1967), 279.
31. Vincent Ostrom, *The Intellectual Crisis in Public Administration* (Tuscaloosa: University of Alabama Press, 1973).
32. Ostrom, *The Intellectual Crisis in Public Administration*, 50.
33. Ostrom, *The Intellectual Crisis in Public Administration*, 55.
34. Ostrom, *The Intellectual Crisis in Public Administration*, 70.
35. Robert Golembiewski, "A Critique of 'Democratic Administration' and Its Supporting Ideation," *American Political Science Review* 71 (1977): 1488–1507.
36. Frederickson, *The Spirit of Public Administration*, 36.
37. Frank Marini, ed., *Toward a New Public Administration: The Minnowbrook Perspective* (San Francisco: Chandler, 1971), 349.
38. H. George Frederickson, "Toward a New Public Administration," in Marini, *Toward a New Public Administration*, 211.
39. Frederick Thayer, *An End to Hierarchy! An End to Competition!* (New York: New Viewpoints, 1973).
40. Robert B. Denhardt, *Theories of Public Organization* (Fort Worth: Harcourt Brace College Publishers, 2000), 116.
41. O. C. McSwite, *Legitimacy in Public Administration* (Thousand Oaks, CA: Sage, 1997), 18.
42. Robert Behn, *Rethinking Democratic Accountability* (Washington, DC: Brookings Institution Press, 2001); and Richard C. Box, "Running Government More like a Business: Implications for Public Administration Theory and Practice," *American Review of Public Administration* 29:1 (1999): 19–43.
43. Executive Office of the President, Office of Management and Budget, "The President's Management Agenda," http://www.whitehouse.gov/omb/budget/fy2002/mgmt.pdf.
44. Denhardt, *Theories of Public Organization*, 176.
45. Ralph P. Hummel, *The Bureaucratic Experience: A Critique of Life in the Modern*, 4th ed. (New York: St. Martin's Press, 1994); D. Farmer, *The Language of Public Administration*

(Tuscaloosa: University of Alabama Press, 1995); and McSwite, *Legitimacy in Public Administration*.

46. Charles Fox and Hugh Miller, *Postmodern Public Administration: Towards Discourse* (Thousands Oaks, CA: Sage, 1995), 45–46.

47. Fox and Miller, *Postmodern Public Administration*, 8.

48. David Farmer, *The Language of Public Administration: Bureaucracy, Modernity, and Postmodernity* (Tuscaloosa: University of Alabama Press, 1995).

CHAPTER 8

1. Executive Order 13228, October 8, 2001.

2. Allison Mitchell, "Disputes Erupt on Ridge's Needs for His Job," *New York Times*, November 4, 2001, 7.

3. Joel Brinkley and Philip Shenon, "Ridge Meets Opposition from Agencies," *New York Times*, February 7, 2002, 16.

4. Brinkley and Shenon, "Ridge Meets Opposition from Agencies."

5. This section and the next one borrows heavily from Florence Heffron, *Organization Theory and Public Organizations* (Englewood Cliffs, NJ: Prentice Hall, 1989), chap. 1.

6. Cole Graham and Steven Hays, *Managing the Public Organization*, 2nd ed. (Washington, DC: Congressional Quarterly Press, 1993), 72–73, 81; and Michael L. Vasu, Debra Stewart, and G. David Garson, *Organizational Behavior and Public Management*, 3rd ed. (New York: Marcel Dekker, 1998), 123.

7. Heffron, *Organization Theory and Public Organizations*, 19.

8. Henry Mintzberg, *The Structuring of Organizations* (Englewood Cliffs, NJ: Prentice Hall, 1979), 3–9.

9. Even before Max Weber theorized on the advantages to organizations of specialization, Adam Smith in 1776 observed that division of labor permitted a task to be performed more quickly and expertly. Eventually, tasks could be made so specialized and repetitious that automation could occur.

10. Heffron, *Organization Theory and Public Organizations*, 20.

11. Mintzberg, *The Structuring of Organizations*, 3–9.

12. Heffron, *Organization Theory and Public Organizations*, 22.

13. *Goldman v. Weinberger*, 475 U.S. 503 (1986).

14. Heffron, *Organization Theory and Public Organizations*, 23.

15. Vasu, Stewart, and Garson, *Organizational Behavior and Public Management*, 128.

16. Irving Janis, *Victims of Groupthink* (New York: Houghton Mifflin, 1972).

17. See Heffron, *Organization Theory and Public Organizations*, 25–29. Professionalism is the dominant mode of formalizing employee behavior that exists outside the organization.

18. For example, Vincent Ostrom, *The Intellectual Crisis in Public Administration* (Tuscaloosa: University of Alabama Press, 1973); David Osborne and Ted Gaebler, *Reinventing Government: How the Entrepreneurial Spirit Is Transforming the Public Sector* (New York: Penguin Group, 1993).

19. See Osborne and Gaebler, *Reinventing Government*, 252–254.

20. Cheryl King and Camilla Stivers, *Government Is Us* (Thousand Oaks, CA: Sage, 1998).

21. Graham and Hays, *Managing the Public Organization*, 84–94.

22. Tom Burns and George Stalker, *Management of Innovation* (London: Tavistock, 1961), 119–125.

23. Graham and Hays, *Managing the Public Organization*, 74–75.

24. Heffron, *Organization Theory and Public Organizations*, 42–44.

25. Heffron, *Organization Theory and Public Organizations*, 10.

26. Burns and Stalker, *Management of Innovation*.

27. Graham and Hays, *Managing the Public Organization*, 90.

28. Graham and Hays, *Managing the Public Organization*.

29. Graham and Hays, *Managing the Public Organization*, 92.

30. Graham and Hays, *Managing the Public Organization*, 97.

31. Robin Keast, Myrna Mandell, Kerry Brown, and Geoffrey Woolcock, "Network Structures: Working Differently and Changing Expectations," *Public Administration Review* 64:3 (2004): 363–372.

32. Keith Provan, Mark Veazie, Lisa Staten, and Nicolette Teuffel-Stone, "The Use of Network Analysis to Strengthen Community Partnerships," *Public Administration Review* 65:5 (2005): 603–613.

33. Keast et al., "Network Structures," 364, 367–370.

34. Keast et al., "Network Structures," 363.

35. Patricia Fredericksen and Rosanne London, "Disconnect the Hollow State: The Pivotal Role of Organizational Capacity in Community-Based Development Organizations," *Public Administration Review* 60:3 (2000): 231.

36. Norton E. Long, "Power and Administration," in *Classics of Public Administration*, 2nd ed., ed. Jay Shafritz and Albert C. Hyde (Pacific Grove, CA: Brooks/Cole, 1987).

37. Graham and Hays, *Managing the Public Organization*, 161.

38. Robert Denhardt, *Theories of Public Organization* (Fort Worth: Harcourt Brace College, 2000), 226.

39. Graham and Hays, *Managing the Public Organization*, 161.

40. Carroll Kirkpatrick, "Nixon Forces Firing of Cox; Richardson, Ruckelshaus Quit," *Washington Post*, October 21, 1973, A01.

41. Richard Waterman, *Presidential Influence and the Administrative State* (Knoxville, TN: University of Tennessee Press, 1989).

42. Rosabeth Moss Kanter, "Power Failure in Management Circuits," *Harvard Business Review* 12 (1979).

43. Heffron, *Organization Theory and Public Organizations*, 194.

44. Heffron, *Organization Theory and Public Organizations*, x.

45. Heffron, *Organization Theory and Public Organizations*, 194.

CHAPTER 9

1. Frank Serpico maintains his own website, http://www.frankserpico.com/bio.html, which includes a biography and information regarding his testimony before the Knapp Commission.

2. Michael Vasu, Debra Stewart, and G. David Garson, *Organizational Behavior and Public Management*, 3rd ed. (New York: Marcel Dekker, 1998), 58.

3. James Q. Wilson, *Bureaucracy: What Government Agencies Do and Why Do It* (New York: Basic Books, 1989), 157.

4. Daniel Katz and Robert Kahn, *The Social Psychology of Organizations*, 2nd ed. (New York: Wilby, 1979).

5. Florence Heffron, *Organization Theory and Public Organizations* (Englewood Cliffs, NJ: Prentice Hall, 1989), 267.

6. Heffron, *Organization Theory and Public Organizations*.

7. Vasu, Stewart, and Garson, *Organizational Behavior and Public Management*, 81.

8. Hal Rainey, Robert Backoff, and Charles Levine, "Comparing Public and Private Organizations," *Public Administration Review* 36 (1979): 233–244.

9. H. George Frederickson, "The Public Service and the Patriotism of Benevolence," *Public Administration Review* 45 (1985): 547–553.

10. Abraham Maslow, "A Theory of Human Motivation," *Psychological Review* 50 (1943): 370–396, cited in *Classics of Public Administration*, ed. Jay Shafritz and Albert C. Hyde (Oak Park, IL: Moore, 1978), 123–130.

11. Maslow in Shafritz and Hyde, *Classics of Public Administration*, 129.

12. Chris Argyris, "Personality and Organization Theory Revisited," *Administration Science Quarterly* 18 (1978): 141–167.

13. Douglas MacGregor, *The Human Side of Enterprise* (New York: McGraw Hill, 1960).

14. Frederick Herzberg, Bernard Mausner, and Barbara Snyderman, *The Motivation to Work* (New York: Wiley, 1959).

15. See Gary Latham and James Baldes, "The 'Practical Significance' of Locke's Theory of Goal Setting," *Journal of Applied Psychology* 60:1 (1975): 122–124; and Mark E. Tubbs, "Goal Setting: A Meta-Analytical Examination of the Empirical Evidence," *Journal of Applied Psychology* 71:2 (1986): 474–483.

16. Edwin Locke, Karyll Shaw, Lisa Saari, and Gary Latham, "Goal Setting and Task Performance: 1969–1980," *Psychological Bulletin* 90 (1981): 125–152.

17. Robert Wood, Edwin Locke, and Anthony Mento, "Task Complexity as a Moderator of Goal Effects: A Meta-Analysis," *Journal of Applied Psychology* 72 (1987): 416–425.

18. B. F. Skinner, *Contingencies of Reinforcement* (New York: Appleton-Century-Crofts, 1961).

19. Heffron, *Organization Theory and Public Organizations*, 286.

20. Graham T. Allison, *The Essence of Decision: Explaining the Cuban Missile Crisis* (Boston: Little, Brown, 1971), 129.

21. Allison, *The Essence of Decision*, 144.

22. Charles Lindbloom, "The Science of Muddling Through," *Public Administration Review* 19 (1959): 79–88, cited in *Classics of Public Administration*, ed. Jay Shafritz and Albert C. Hyde (Belmont, CA: Thomson-Wadsworth, 2004), 177–187.

23. Lindbloom in Shafritz and Hyde, *Classics of Public Administration*, 179, 182.

24. Lindbloom in Shafritz and Hyde, *Classics of Public Administration*, 182–184.

25. Amitai Etzioni, "Mixed Scanning Revisited," *Public Administration Review* 46 (1986): 8–13.

26. Etzioni, "Mixed Scanning Revisited," 12.

27. Jon Katzenbach and Douglas Smith, *The Wisom of Teams: Creating the High Performance Organization* (Boston: Harvard University Press, 1993).

28. Vasu, Stewart, and Garson, *Organizational Behavior and Public Management*, 215–217.

29. Cole Graham and Steven Hays, *Managing the Public Organization*, 2nd ed. (Washington, DC: Congressional Quarterly Press, 1993), 40–41.

30. Vasu, Stewart, and Garson, *Organizational Behavior and Public Management*, 218.

31. Harold Sackman, *Delphi Critique: Expert Opinion, Forecasting, and Group Process* (Lexington, MA: D. C. Heath, 1975).

32. Bjorn Anderson and Tom Fagerhaug, "The Nominal Group Technique," *Quality Progress* 33 (2000): 144.

33. Vasu, Stewart, and Garson, *Organizational Behavior and Public Management*, 218.

34. Wilson, *Bureaucracy*, 91.

35. Wilson, *Bureaucracy*, 9.

36. Harrison Trice and Janice Beyer, *The Culture of Work Organizations* (Englewood Cliffs, NJ: Prentice Hall, 1993), 105–107, 33–34, 80.

37. Trice and Beyer, *The Culture of Work Organizations*, 90–100.

38. Wilson, *Bureaucracy*, 91–92.

39. Edgar Schein, *Organizational Culture and Leadership* (San Francisco: Jossey-Bass, 1985).

40. See, for example, Donald Kettl, "Reinventing Government? Appraising the National Performance Review," in *Classics of Public Administration*, 4th ed., ed. Jay Shafritz, Albert C. Hyde, and Sandra Parkes (New York: Harcourt Brace College Publishers, 1997), 543–557; James D. Carroll, "The Rhetoric of Reform and Political Reality in the National Performance Review," *Public Administration Review* 55 (1995): 302–312; and James D. Carroll and Dahlia Lynn, "The Future of Federal Reinvention: Congressional Perspectives," *Public Administration Review* 56 (1996): 299–304.

41. J. Thomas Hennessey Jr., "Reinventing Government: Does Leadership Make a Difference?" *Public Administration Review* 58 (1998): 522–532.

42. William Rago, "Struggles in Transformation: A Study in TQM, Leadership, and Organizational Culture in a Government Agency," *Public Administration Review* 56 (1996): 227–234.

43. Rago, "Struggles in Transformation."

44. Wendell French and Cecil Bell, *Organizational Development* (Englewood Cliffs, NJ: Prentice Hall, 1995).

45. See Vasu, Stewart, and Garson, *Organizational Behavior and Public Management*, 148. They point out that OD is used at all levels of government and that OD interventions have been largely successful.

46. Rudolph Ehrenberg and Ronald Stupak, "Total Quality Management: Its Relationship to Administrative Theory and Organizational Behavior in the Public Sector," *Public Administration Quarterly* 18 (Spring 1994): 75–24.

47. Ehrenberg and Stupak, "Total Quality Management."

48. General Accounting Office, "Quality in Management: Survey of Federal Organizations," 1992, GAO/GED-93–93R, Washington, DC: GAO.

49. William Rago, "Adapting Total Quality Management (TQM) to Government: Another Point of View," *Public Administration Review* 54 (1994): 61–64.

50. Bonnie Mani, "Old Wine in New Bottles Taste Better: A Case Study of TQM Implementation in the IRS," *Public Administration Review* 55 (1995): 147–158.

51. James Swiss, "Adapting Total Quality Management (TQM) to Government," *Public Administration Review* 52 (1992): 356–362.

52. Patrick Connor, "Total Quality Management: A Selective Commentary on Its Human Dimensions," *Public Administration Review* 57 (1997): 501–509.

53. Charles Beitz and John Hook, "The Culture of Military: A Participant-Observer Case Study of Cultural Diversity," *Public Administration and Management*, http://www.pamij.com/beitz.html.

CHAPTER 10

1. Carmen Sirianni and Lewis Friedland, "Civic Innovation in America: Community Empowerment, Public Policy, and the Movement for Civic Renewal (Berkeley: University of California Press, 2001).

2. Cheryl King, Kathryn Feltey, and Bridget Susel, "The Question of Participation: Toward Authentic Public Participation in Public Administration," *Public Administration Review* 58:4 (1998): 317–326.

3. Robert Behn, "What Right Do Public Managers Have to Lead?" *Public Administration Review* 58:3 (1998): 209–255.

4. Graham T. Allison, "Public and Private Management: Are They Fundamentally Alike in All Unimportant Respects?" in *Classics in Public Administration*, 4th ed., ed. Jay Shafritz and Albert C. Hyde (Fort Worth: Harcourt Brace College Publishers, 1997), 383–400.

5. Angelique Keene, "Complexity Theory: The Changing Role of Leadership," *Industrial and Commercial Training* 32:1 (2000): 15–18.

6. See Mary Follett, "The Giving of Orders," in Shafritz and Hyde, *Classics in Public Administration*, 53–60; Brian R. Fry, *Mastering Public Administration: From Max Weber to Dwight Waldo* (Chatham, NJ: Chatham House, 1997), 98–120.

7. See Behn, "What Right Do Public Managers Have to Lead?"; R. Wayne Boss, "Is the Leader Really Necessary? The Longitudinal Results of the Leader Absence in Team Building," *Public Administration Quarterly* 23:4 (2000): 471–486; Gerald T. Gabris, Robert T. Golembiewski, and Douglas M. Ihrke, "Leadership Credibility, Board Relations, and Administrative Innovation at the Local Government Level," *Journal of Public Administration Research and Theory* 11:1 (2001): 89–108; John P. Kotter, *A Force for Change: How Leadership Differs from Management* (New York: Free Press, 1990).

8. Kotter, *A Force for Change*.

9. Robert House and Ram Aditya, "The Social Scientific Study of Leadership: Quo Vadis?" *Journal of Management* 23:3 (1997): 247–260.

10. Behn, "What Right Do Public Managers Have to Lead?"

11. Boss, "Is the Leader Really Necessary?"

12. See House and Aditya, "The Social Scientific Study of Leadership"; Peter Northouse, *Leadership: Theory and Practice*, 2nd ed. (Thousand Oaks, CA: Sage, 2001).

13. Montgomery Van Wart, "Public-Sector Leadership Theory: An Assessment," *Public Administration Review* 63:2 (2003): 214–228.

14. Northouse, *Leadership*.

15. Ronald Heifetz, *Leadership without Easy Answers* (Cambridge, MA: Belknap Press, 1994), 180.

16. Peter Senge, *The Fifth Discipline: The Art and Practice of the Learning Organization* (New York: Currency Doubleday, 1990).

17. Michael Lipsky, *Street-Level Bureaucracy: Dilemmas of the Individual in Public Services* (New York: Russel Sage Foundation, 1980).

18. Janet Vinzant and Lane Crothers, "Street-Level Leadership: Rethinking the Role of Public Servants in Contemporary Governance," *American Review of Public Administration* 26:4 (1998): 456–476.

19. Vinzant and Crothers, "Street-Level Leadership."

20. Lipsky, *Street-Level Bureaucracy*.

21. Fry, *Mastering Public Administration*, 174.

22. Ralph Stogdill, "Personal Factors Associated with Leadership: A Survey of the Literature," *Journal of Psychology* 25 (1948): 35–71.

23. House and Aditya, "The Social Scientific Study of Leadership."

24. See House and Aditya, "The Social Scientific Study of Leadership"; also Arthur Jago, "Leadership: Perspectives in Theory and Practice," *Management Science* 28:3 (1982): 315–336.

25. Northouse, *Leadership*.

26. Kurt Lewin, Ronald Lippitt, and Ralph White, "Patterns of Aggressive Behavior in Experimentally Created Social Climates," *Journal of Social Psychology* 10 (1939): 271–299.

27. See House and Aditya, "The Social Scientific Study of Leadership"; and Northouse, *Leadership*.

28. See Fred E. Fiedler, "The Effects of Leadership Training and Experience: A Contingency Model Interpretation," *Administrative Science Quarterly* 17:4 (1972): 453–470; also Martin M. Chemers and Roya Ayman, *Leadership Theory and Research: Perspectives and Directions* (San Diego: Academic Press, 1993), a tribute to Fiedler's career of studying leadership.

29. Fiedler, "The Effects of Leadership Training and Experience."

30. Jago, "Leadership: Perspectives in Theory and Practice."

31. Northouse, *Leadership*.

32. See Jago, "Leadership: Perspectives in Theory and Practice," and Northouse, *Leadership*.

33. Northouse, *Leadership*.

34. Robert Isaac, Wilfred Zerbe, and Douglas Pitt, "Leadership and Motivation: The Effective Application of Expectancy Theory," *Journal of Managerial Issues* 13:2 (2001): 212–226.

35. Northouse, *Leadership*.

36. Soonhee Kim, "Participative Management and Job Satisfaction: Lessons for Management Leadership," *Public Administration Review* 62:2 (2002): 231–241.

37. House and Aditya, "The Social Scientific Study of Leadership."

38. George B. Graen and Mary Uhl-Bien, "Relationship-Based Approach to Leadership: Development of Leader–Member Exchange (LMX) Theory of Leadership over 25 Years: Applying a Multi-Level Multi-Domain Perspective," *Leadership Quarterly* 6:2 (1995): 219–247.

39. Robert Liden and John Maslyn, "Multidimensionality of Leader–Member Exchange: An Empirical Assessment through Scale Development," *Journal of Management* 24:1 (1998): 43–73.

40. See Graen and Uhl-Bien, "Relationship-Based Approach to Leadership"; and Terri Scandura and Chester Schriesheim "Leader–Member Exchange and Supervisor Career Mentoring as Complementary Constructs in Leadership Research," *Academy of Management Journal* 37:6 (1994): 1588–1602.

41. House and Aditya, "The Social Scientific Study of Leadership."

42. Bruce Avolio and Francis Yammarino, "Introduction to, and Overview of Transformational Leadership," in *Transformational and Charismatic Leadership: The Road Ahead*, ed. Avolio and Yammarino (Oxford: Elsevier Science, 2002): xvii–xxiii.

43. James M. Burns, *Leadership* (New York: Harper and Row, 1978).

44. Burns, *Leadership*.

45. Rivka Grundstein-Amado, "Bilateral Transformational Leadership: An Approach for Fostering Ethical Conduct in Public Service Organizations," *Administration and Society* 31:2 (1999): 274–260.

46. Benjamin Palmer, Melissa Walls, Zena Burgess, and Con Stough, "Emotional Intelligence and Effective Leadership," *Leadership and Organization Development Journal* 22:1 (2001): 5–10.

47. See Kevin Lowe, K. Galen Kroeck, and N. Sivasubramaniam, "Effectiveness Correlates of Transformational and Transactional Leadership: A Meta-Analytic Review of the Literature,"

Leadership Quarterly 7:3 (1996): 385–425. Also see Mansour Javidan and David Waldman, "Exploring Charismatic Leadership in the Public Sector: Measurement and Consequences," *Public Administration Review* 63:2 (2003): 229–242.

48. Grundstein-Amado, "Bilateral Transformational Leadership."

49. Camilla Stivers, *Gender Images in Public Administration: Legitimacy and the Administrative State*, 2nd ed. (Thousand Oaks, CA: Sage, 2002).

50. Stivers, *Gender Images in Public Administration.*

51. See Brinck Kerr, Will Miller, and Margaret Reid, "Sex-Based Occupational Segregation in U.S. State Bureaucracies, 1987–1997," *Public Administration Review* 62:4 (2002): 412–423; Katherine Naff, "Through the Glass Ceiling: Prospects for the Advancement of Women in the Federal Civil Service," *Public Administration Review* 54:6 (1994): 507–514; Meredith Ann Newman, "Gender and Lowi's Thesis: Implications for Career Advancement," *Public Administration Review* 54:3 (1994): 277–284.

52. Brinck, Miller, and Reid, "Sex-Based Occupational Segregation in U.S. State Bureaucracies."

53. Julie Indvik, "Women and Leadership," in Northouse, *Leadership.*

54. Alice Eagly and Mary Johannesen-Shmidt, "The Leadership Styles of Women and Men," *Journal of Social Issues* 57:4 (2001): 781–798.

55. See Nicole Stelter, "Gender Differences in Leadership: Current Social Issues and Future Organizational Implications," *Journal of Leadership and Organizational Studies* 8:4 (2002): 88–100; Stivers, *Gender Images in Public Administration.*

56. Indvik, "Women and Leadership."

57. David Osborne and Ted Gaebler, *Reinventing Government* (Reading, MA: Addison-Wesley, 1992).

58. Stanford Borins, "Loose Cannons and Rule Breakers, or Enterprising Leaders? Some Evidence about Innovative Public Managers," *Public Administration Review* 60:6 (2000): 498–507.

59. Turo Virtanen, "Changing Competencies of Public Managers: Tensions in Commitment," *International Journal of Public Sector Management* 13:4 (2000): 333–341.

60. Larry D. Terry, *Leadership of Public Bureaucracies: The Administrator as Conservator* (Thousand Oaks, CA: Sage, 1995).

61. Behn, "What Right to Public Managers Have to Lead?"

62. See Cheryl King and Camilla Stivers, eds., *Government Is Us: Public Administration in an Anti-Government Era* (Thousand Oaks, CA: Sage, 1998).

CHAPTER 11

1. The account of Hurricane Katrina is based on "Preparing for Emergencies" and "New Orleans" in the Encyclopedia Britannica Online, http://www.britannica.com; Matthew Cooper, "Dipping His Toe in Disaster," *Time*, September 4, 2005; Nancy Gibbs, "The Aftermath: The Nightmare after Katrina," *Time*, September 4, 2005; Nancy Gibbs, "Act Two," *Time*, September 25, 2005; Amanda Ripley, "How Did This Happen?" *Time*, September 4, 2005; Amanda Ripley, Karen Tumulty, Mark Thompson, and James Carney, "Four Places Where the System Broke Down," *Time*, September 11, 2005, http://www.time.com.

2. Harold D. Lasswell, *A Pre-View of Policy Studies* (New York: Elsevier, 1971). Lasswell is perhaps most famous for articulating the idea of a "policy science" in 1951 in his essay "The Policy Orientation," in *The Policy Sciences*, ed. Daniel Lerner and Harold Laswell, 3–15 (Stanford, CA: Stanford University Press).

3. For a detailed list of policy theories, see Paul Sabatier, ed., *Theories of the Policy Process* (Boulder, CO: Westview Press, 1999).

4. For an extensive critique of the policy cycle model, see Paul Sabatier and Hank Jenkins-Smith, eds., *Policy Change and Learning: An Advocacy Coalition Approach* (Boulder, CO: Westview Press, 1993).

5. See Robert Dahl and Charles Lindblom, *Politics, Economics, and Welfare* (Chicago: University of Chicago Press, 1952).

6. See James True, Bryan Jones, and Frank Baumgartner, "Punctuated-Equilibrium Theory," in *Theories of the Policy Process*, ed. Paul Sabatier (Boulder, CO: Westview Press, 1999).

7. John W. Kingdon, *Agendas, Alternatives, and Public Policies* (New York: HarperCollins, 1995).

8. For more on the garbage can model, see Michael Cohen, James March, and Johan Olsen, "A Garbage Can Model of Organizational Choice," *Administration Science Quarterly* 17:1 (1972): 1–25.

9. See Frank Zagare, *Game Theory: Concepts and Applications* (Newbury Park, CA: Sage, 1984), 52–63, for a detailed description of the Prisoner's Dilemma and other examples.

10. Nobel laureate Amartya Sen provides a critique of self-interest maximization in his book *On Ethics and Economics* (Malden, MA: Blackwell, 1987).

11. Elinor Ostrom, "An Assessment of the Institutional Analysis and Development Framework," in Sabatier, *Theories of the Policy Process.*

12. See Hank Jenkins-Smith and Paul Sabatier, "The Study of the Public Policy Process," in Sabatier and Jenkins-Smith, *Policy Change and Learning.*

Also see Paul Sabatier, "An Advocacy Coalition Framework of Policy Change and the Role of Policy-Oriented Learning Therein," *Policy Studies* 21 (Fall 1988): 129–168; and Paul Sabatier, "Toward Better Theories of the Policy Process," *PS: Political Science and Politics* 23 (June 1991): 147–156.

13. Christine Sanders, "The Hyde Amendment: A Case Study of the United States Congress 1990–2000," doctoral dissertation, Public Policy Studies, Saint Louis University, 2004.

14. Michael Mintron and Sandra Vergari, "Advocacy Coalitions, Policy Entrepreneurs, and Policy Change," *Policy Studies Journal* 24 (Fall 1996): 420–434.

15. Jan Eberg, "Waste Policy and Learning, Policy Dynamics of Waste Management, and Waste Incineration in the Netherlands and Bavaria," *Uitgeverij Eburon* (1997).

16. Charles Davis and Sandra Davis, "Analyzing Change in Public Lands Policy Making: From Subsystems to Advocacy Coalitions," *Policy Studies Journal* 17 (Fall 1988): 3–24.

17. Wyn Grant, *Autos, Smog, and Pollution Control* (Aldershot, UK: Edward Elgar, 1995).

18. Deborah Stone, *The Policy Paradox: The Art of Political Decision Making* (New York: W. W. Norton, 1997), 7.

19. Stone, *The Policy Paradox*, 138, 134, 259.

20. Yvonna Lincoln and Egon Guba, "Research, Evaluation, and Policy Analysis: Heuristics for Disciplined Inquiry," *Policy Studies Review* 5:3 (1986): 546–565.

21. Jeffrey Pressman and Aaron Wildavsky, *Implementation: How Great Expectations in Washington Are Dashed in Oakland* (Berkeley: University of California Press, 1984), xix.

22. Pressman and Wildavsky, *Implementation*, 102.

23. Pressman and Wildavsky, *Implementation*, 107.

24. Steven Kelman, *Making Public Policy: A Hopeful View of American Government* (New York: Basic Books, 1987), 162–164.

25. Aaron Wildavsky, *Speaking Truth to Power: The Art and Craft of Policy Analysis* (Boston: Little, Brown, 1979), 8.

26. George C. Edwards, *Implementing Public Policy* (Washington, DC: Congressional Quarterly Press, 1980), 10–11.

27. For additional information on implementation research, see M. Goggin, *Implementation Theory and Practice: Toward a Third Generation* (Glenview, IL: Foresman/Little, Brown, 1990).

28. Peter Rossi, Howard, Freeman, and Mark Lipsey, *Evaluation: A Systematic Approach* (Thousand Oaks, CA: Sage, 1999), 2.

29. Rossi, Freeman, and Lipsey, *Evaluation*, 37–77.

30. Rossi, Freeman, and Lipsey, *Evaluation*.

CHAPTER 12

1. American Federation of State and County Municipal Employees, http://www.afscme.org/workplace/sale12.htm.

2. Reason Public Policy Institute, http://www.rppi.org/giulianiprivatization.html.

3. Steven Cohen, "A Strategic Framework for Devolving Responsibility and Functions from Government to the Private Sector," *Public Administration Review* 61:4 (2001): 432–441.

4. Nicolas Henry, *Public Administration and Public Affairs*, 8th ed. (Upper Saddle River, NJ: Prentice Hall, 2001), 320.

5. E. S. Savas, *Privatization: The Key to Better Government* (Chatham, NJ: Chatham House, 1987), 3.

6. William Gormley, "Privatization Revisited," *Policy Studies Review* 13:3/4 (1994): 215–234.

7. "2000 Federal Procurement Report," Federal Procurement Data Center, U.S. General Services Administration, http://www.fpdc.gov/fpdc/FPR2000a.pdf.

8. Savas, *Privatization*, 73–74.

9. Gormley, "Privatization Revisited."

10. James Ward, "Privatization and Political Culture: Perspectives from Small Cities and Towns," *Public Administration Quarterly* 16:4 (1992): 498.

11. "Private Management Company Will Take Over St. Louis Public Schools in 'Turnaround' Plan," *St. Louis Post-Dispatch*, May 31, 2003, 7.

12. See Richard C. Box, "Running Government More like a Business: Implications for Public Administration Theory and Practice," *American Review of Public Administration* 29:1 (1999): 19–43, for a discussion of the author's view that there has been a "revival of the politics-administration dichotomy" as a result of a political culture that encourages the expansion of market-like practices into the public sector.

13. Jay Dilger, Randolph Moffett, and Linda Struyk, "Privatization of Municipal Services in America's Largest Cities," *Public Administration Review* 57:1 (1997): 223.

14. Cohen, "A Strategic Framework for Devolving Responsibility and Functions from Government to the Private Sector," 432.

15. Savas, *Privatization*.

16. Cohen, "A Strategic Framework for Devolving Responsibility and Functions from Government to the Private Sector," 433–434.

17. Robert Gilmour and Laura Jensen, "Reinventing Government Accountability: Public Functions, Privatization, and the Meaning of 'State Action,'" *Public Administration Review* 58:3 (1998): 247.

18. Fred Becker, Milan Dluhy, and John Topinka, "Choosing the Rowers: Are Private Managers of Public Housing More Successful than Public

Managers?" *American Review of Public Administration* 31:2 (2001): 181–200.

19. Gormley, "Privatization Revisited."

20. George Avery, "Outsourcing Public Health Laboratory Services: A Blue Print for Determining Whether to Privatize and How," *Public Administration Review* 60:4 (2000): 330–338.

21. Miranda Rowan and Allan Lerner, "Bureaucracy, Organizational Redundancy, and the Privatization of Public Services," *Public Administration Review* 55:2 (1995): 193–200.

22. Avery, "Outsourcing Public Health Laboratory Services," 331.

23. Rowan and Lerner, "Bureaucracy, Organizational Redundancy, and the Privatization of Public Services."

24. Arthur Brooks, "Is There a Dark Side to Government Support for Nonprofits?" *Public Administration Review* 60:3 (2000): 211–218. p.11.

25. David Osborne and Ted Gaebler, *Reinventing Government: How the Entrepreneurial Spirit Is Transforming the Public Sector* (New York: Penguin Group, 1993), 346.

26. Cohen, "A Strategic Framework for Devolving Responsibility and Functions from Government to the Private Sector," 435–436.

27. "Privatization of Federal Services," American Federal Government Employees Report, http://www.afge.org/Documents/01_privatization.pdf.

28. Paul Light, *The True Size of Government* (Washington, DC: Brookings Institution, 1999).

29. Light, *The True Size of Government*, 141.

30. Sheila Suess Kennedy, "Privatization and Prayer: The Challenges of Charitable Choice," *American Review of Public Administration* 33:1 (2003): 5–19.

31. Katherine. Naff, "Labor-Management Relations and Privatization: A Federal Perspective," *Public Administration Review* 51:1 (1991): 23–31. Further, federal laws do not provide for a union or employees to appeal a contracting-out decision outside of the agency.

32. Keon Chi, and Cindy Jasper, "Privatization Activities in State Governments," *Spectrum* 71:3 (1998): 8–15.

33. Council of State Governments, "Private Practices: A Review of Privatization in State Governments," 1998, 7–8.

34. Nicholas Henry, "Is Privatization Passé? The Case for Competition and the Emergence of Intersectoral Administration," *Public Administration Review* 62:3 (2002): 374–378.

35. Becker, Dluhy, and Topinka, "Choosing the Rowers, 181.

36. Dilger, Moffett, and Struyk, "Privatization of Municipal Services in America's Largest Cities," 22–23.

37. E. S. Savas, "Competition and Choice in New York City Social Services," *Public Administration Review* 62:1 (2002): 82–92.

38. Keon Chi, Kelley Arnold, and Heather Perkins, "Privatization in State Government: Trends and Issues," *Spectrum* 76 (2003): 12–21.

39. Dilger, Moffett, and Struyk, "Privatization of Municipal Services in America's Largest Cities," 23–24.

40. Brent Steel and Carolyn Long, "The Use of Agency Forces versus Contracting Out: Learning the Limitations of Privatization," *Public Administration Quarterly* 22:2 (1998): 229–251.

41. David Morgan, "Pitfalls of Privatization: Contracting without Competition," *American Review of Public Administration* 22:4 (1992): 251–261.

42. Richard Pouder, "Privatizing Services in Local Government: An Empirical Assessment of Efficiency and Institutional Explanations," *Public Administration Quarterly* 20:1 (1996): 103–126.

43. Cohen, "A Strategic Framework for Devolving Responsibility and Functions from Government to the Private Sector," 436–437.

44. Box, "Running Government More like a Business," 28.

45. Gilmour and Jensen, "Reinventing Government Accountability," 248, 250.

46. Becker, Dluhy, and Topinka, Choosing the Rowers," 188–189.

47. David Van Slyke, "The Mythology of Privatization for Contracting in Social Services," *Public Administration Review* 63:3 (2003): 296–315.

48. Dilger, Moffett, and Struyk, "Privatization of Municipal Services in America's Largest Cities," 24.

49. Box, "Running Government More like a Business," 22.

50. This is the central thesis of Steven Smith and Michael Lipsky, *Nonprofits for Hire: The Welfare State in the Age of Contracting* (Cambridge, MA: Harvard University Press, 1993).

51. Savas, "Competition and Choice in New York City Social Services," 90.

52. Jefferey van der Werff, "Privatization and Citizen Empowerment," *Journal of Public Administration Research and Theory* 8:2 (1998): 276–281.

53. Susan Bernstein, *Managing Contracted Services in the Nonprofit Economy* (Philadelphia: Temple University Press, 1991). She examined seventeen different social service agencies in New York City by interviewing their managers. Some of them describe the system as "crazy."

54. Morgan, "Pitfalls of Privatization," 257.

55. VanDerWerff, "Privatization and Citizen Empowerment," 278.

56. Box, "Running Government More like a Business," 22.

57. Van der Werff, "Privatization and Citizen Empowerment," 280.

58. Sewall Chan and Scott Higham, "Lax Oversight Unleashes Troubled Youths on City," *Washington Post*, July 13, 2003.

59. Sewall Chan and Scott Higham, "Firm's Lack of Control Has Deadly Consequences," *Washington Post*, July 14, 2003.

60. Scott Higham and Sewall Chan, "Poor Care, Abuses Alleged at Riverside," *Washington Post*, July 15, 2003.

CHAPTER 13

1. "Time Running Out for Budget Deal: Gingrich Threatens to Put U.S. in Default on Debts," September 22, 1995, CNN.com.

2. "President, GOP Blames Each Other for Budget Breakdown," October 7, 1995, CNN.com.

3. Aaron Wildavsky, *The Politics of the Budgetary Process* (Boston: Little, Brown, 1964), 5.

4. Robert Lee Jr. and Ronald Johnson, *Public Budgeting Systems*, 6th ed. (Gaithersburg, MD: Aspen, 1998), 3.

5. Lee and Johnson, *Public Budgeting Systems*, 191.

6. John Mikesell, *Fiscal Administration: Analysis and Applications for the Public Sector*, 4th ed. (Belmont, CA: Wadsworth, 1995), 42.

7. V. O. Key, "The Lack of a Budgetary Theory," in *Government Budgeting: Theory, Process, and Politics*, 2nd ed., ed. A. Hyde (Pacific Grove, CA: Brooks/Cole, 1992), 22.

8. Quoted in Lee and Johnson, *Public Budgeting Systems*, 96.

9. David Novick, "What Program Budgeting Is and Is Not," in Hyde, *Government Budgeting*.

10. Anne DeBeer, "The Attitudes, Opinions, and Practices of Federal Government Workers on the Zero Base Budgeting Process," *Government Accountants Journal* 29:1 (1980): 13–23.

11. Joseph Pilegge, "Budget Reforms," in *Public Budgeting and Finance*, 4th ed., ed. R. R. Golembiewski (New York: Marcel Dekker, 1997), 286.

12. Pilegge, "Budget Reforms."

13. Harvey Rosen, *Public Finance*, 4th ed. (Chicago: Richard C. Irwin, 1995), 401.

14. Ronald Fisher, *Public Finance*, 4th ed. (Chicago: Richard C. Irwin, 1996), 325.

15. Advisory Commission on Intergovernmental Relations, *Significant Features of Fiscal Federalism*, vol. 2, 1994, 96–97.

16. Charles Coltfelter and Philip Cook, "On the Economics of State Lotteries," *Journal of Economic Perspective* 2:4 (1990): 105–119.

17. Charles Spindler, "The Lottery and Education: Robbing Peter to Pay Paul?" *Public Budgeting and Finance* 15 (Fall 1995): 54–62.

18. Donald Miller and Patrocl Pierce, "Lotteries for Education: Windfall of Hoax?" *State and Local Government Review* 29 (Winter 1997): 34–42.

19. Tyson King-Meadows and David Lowery, "The Impact of the Tax Revolt Era State Fiscal Caps: A Research Update," *Public Budgeting and Finance* 16 (Spring 1997): 102–112.

20. Allen Schick, "Incremental Budgeting in a Decremental Age," in Hyde, *Government Budgeting*.

21. Wildavsky, *The Politics of the Budgetary Process*, 15.

22. Peter Natchez and Irvin Bupp, "Policy and Priority in the Budget Process," *American Political Science Review* 67:3 (1967): 951–963.

23. Thomas Lynch, *Public Budgeting in America*, 3rd ed. (Englewood Cliffs, NJ: Prentice Hall, 1990), 19.

24. U.S.General Accounting Office, *Budget Issues: Budgeting for Federal Capital* (Washington, DC: U.S. Government Printing Office, 1996).

25. Robert Salladay, "Governor's Tough Task: Finding the Waste to Cut: Budget Can Be Shrunk—But by $10 Billion?" *San Francisco Chronicle*, November 27, 2003.

26. "Just the Facts: California's State Budget," June 23, 2002, Public Policy Institute of California, http://www.pppic.org.

27. Jeffrey Rabin, "State Spent Its Way into Budget Crisis," *Los Angeles Times*, October 29, 2002.

28. "Just the Facts: California's State Budget."

29. Bruce Murray, "Sorting through the Blame Game in the California State Budget Crisis," December 18, 2003, http://www.facsnet.org/search/find.php3.

30. Press Release: Special California State Budget Survey: Californians Bitter, Partisan as Budget Crisis Drags, June 13, 2003, Public Policy Institute of California, http://www.pppic.org.

31. Murray, "Sorting through the Blame Game in the California State Budget Crisis."

32. "Schwarzenegger Pushes Budget Recovery Plan against Deadline to Put It Before Voters in March," December 5, 2003, California Taxpayers Association, http://www.caltax.org/taxletter.htm.

CHAPTER 14

1. Steven Hays, "The 'State of the Discipline' in Public Human Resource Administration," *Public Administration Quarterly* 20:3 (1996): 286.

2. Bernard Rosen, "Crisis in the U.S. Civil Service," *Public Administration Review* 46:3 (1986): 207–215; U.S. Merit Systems Protection Board, *Ten Years after the CSRA: A 10 Year Retrospective of the MSPB, 1978–1988* (Washington, DC: U.S. Government Printing Office, 1989); and U.S. Merit Systems Protection Board, *Why Are Employees Leaving the Federal Government? Results of an Exit Survey* (Washington, DC: U.S. Government Printing Office, 1990).

3. See Steven Hays and Richard Keamey, "Antici-pated Changes in Human Resource Management: Views from the Field," *Public Administration Review* 61:5 (2001): 586. They point out that public human resource managers must serve as "refer-ees" for the ideological battles that rage across the political landscape.

4. See Jay Shafritz, Norma Riccuccu, David Rosen-bloom, and Albert C. Hyde, *Personnel Manage-ment in Government: Politics and Process* (New York: Marcel Dekker, 1992).

5. Shafritz et al., *Personnel Management in Government*, 5.

6. See Frederick Mosher, *Democracy and the Public Service* (New York: Oxford University Press, 1982), chapter 3 for a discussion of the evolution of the national bureaucracy. Also see Patricia W. In-grahm, *The Foundation of Merit: Public Service in American Democracy* (Baltimore: Johns Hopkins University Press, 1995), especially chapters 2 and 3.

7. Despite the rhetoric, President Jackson largely continued the appointment practices of earlier presidents. While in office, he actually removed relatively few public servants. See Shafritz et al., *Personnel Management in Government*, 7.

8. See Ingraham, *The Foundation of Merit*, 22. She argues that the effectiveness of the Union Army during the first years of war was undermined by patronage.

9. This rule has been considerably modified and the number of considerations increased to as much as seven in order to ensure adequate numbers of mi-norities and females are considered.

10. Richard Stillman, *The American Bureaucracy: The Core of Modern Government*, 2nd ed. (Chicago: Nelson Hall, 1996), 161.

11. Mosher, *Democracy and the Public Service*, 142.

12. *Elrod v. Burns*, 427 U.S. 347 (1976).

13. *Branti v. Finkel, et al.*, 445 U.S. 507 (1980).

14. *Rutan v. Republican Party of Ill.*, 497 U.S. 62 (1990).

15. *O'Hare Truck Service v. Northlake*, 518 U.S. 712 (1996).

16. David Hamilton, "The Continuing Judicial As-sault on Patronage," *Public Administration Review* 59:1 (1999): 61.

17. See David Rosenbloom, *Building a Legislative-Centered Public Administration* (Tuscaloosa: Uni-versity of Alabama Press, 2000), 10. The author suggests that Congress was responding negatively to FDR's attempt to purge anti–New Deal incum-bent Democrats.

18. See James Fesler and Donald Kettl, *The Politics of the Administrative Process* (Chatham, NJ: Chatham House, 1996), 174.

19. Jay Shafritz, *The Facts on File Dictionary of Pub-lic Administration* (New York: Facts on File, 1985), 416.

20. Shafritz et al., *Personnel Management in Govern-ment*, 141. The authors call classification plans essentially a "time-and-motion" study for a gov-ernmental function.

21. See the U.S. Office of Personnel Management's Official Pay Chart, http://federaljobs.net/05base. htm, for up-to-date pay schedules.

22. Congress passed legislation in 1853 that provided for general examinations and a rudimentary clas-sification system for postal clerks. See, Ingraham, *Foundation of Merit*, 22.

23. See the OPM's website detailing the evolution of federal white collar pay, http://www.opm.gov/ strategiccomp/HTML/HISTORY1.asp#1900.

24. See Fesler and Kettl, *The Politics of the Adminis-trative Process*, 148; and Hays, "The 'State of the Discipline,'" 268.

25. Hays, "The 'State of the Discipline,'" 290.

26. See OPM's "Information Briefing on Broadband-ing," http://www.opm.gov/compconf/postconf01/ payband/Bechols.pdf.

27. Carolyn Ban and Patricia W. Ingraham, "Retaining Quality Federal Employees: Life after PACE," *Public Administration Review* 48 (1988): 708–718.

28. See Ingraham, *The Foundation of Merit*, 61.

29. *Griggs v. Duke Power Co.*, 401 U.S. 424, (1971).

30. These factors may exceed in importance the cog-nitive skills that are tested in objective examina-tions. See Shafritz et al., *Personnel Management in Government*, 187.

31. Gary Robert, "A Case Study in Performance Ap-praisal System Development: Lessons from a Mu-nicipal Police Department," *American Review of Public Administration* 26 (1996): 361.

32. Shafritz et al., *Personnel Management in Govern-ment*, 492

33. Shafritz et al., *Personnel Management in Govern-ment*, 493–495.

34. Robert, "A Case Study in Performance Appraisal System Development."

35. Starting wages in the federal IT workforce range from $23,000 to $35,000 per year, significantly be-low salaries paid to entry-level private sector IT pro-fessionals. See Patrick Thibodeau, "Feds Consider Upping Pay for IT Workers," *Computerworld*, April 24, 2000, 12.

36. Patricia W. Ingraham, "Of Pigs and Poke and Policy Diffusion: Another Look at Pay-for-Performance," *Public Administration Review* 53 (1993): 348.

37. Gregory Lewis and Samantha Durst, "Will Local-ity Pay Solve Recruitment and Retention Problems in the Federal Civil Service?" *Public Administra-tion Review* 54 (1995): 371.

38. Lewis and Durst, "Will Locality Pay Solve Re-cruitment and Retention Problems in the Federal Civil Service?"

39. Shafritz et al., *Personnel Management in Govern-ment*, 335. The Lloyd-La Follette Act permitted

federal labor unions but expressly prohibited the authorization of strikes or petitioning the Congress either individually or through their organization.

40. Shafritz et al., *Personnel Management in Government*, 322–328.
41. Shafritz et al., *Personnel Management in Government*, 327–328.
42. Shafritz et al., *Personnel Management in Government*, 335.
43. Mosher, *Democracy and the Public Service*. Excerpt from *Classics of Public Administration*, 4th ed., ed. Jay Shafritz and Albert C. Hyde (New York: Harcourt Brace, 1997), 420.
44. Shafritz et al., *Personnel Management in Government*, 209.
45. Samuel Krislov, "Representative Bureaucracy," in Shafritz and Hyde, *Classics of Public Administration*, 364–368.
46. Katherine Naff and John Crum, "The President and Representative Bureaucracy: Rhetoric and Reality," *Public Administration Review* 60 (2000): 100.
47. H. George Frederickson, "Public Administration and Social Equity," *Public Administration Review* 50 (1990): 230.
48. In 1998, Washington passed an anti–affirmative action measure. In 2000, Florida's governor, Jeb Bush, issued an executive order outlawing racial preferences in state college admissions.
49. *Wards Cove Packing Co. v. Atonio*, 490 U.S. 642 (1989).
50. *Richmond v. J.A. Croson Co.*, 488 U.C. 469 (1989).
51. *Adarand Constructors v. Pena*, 515 U.S. 200 (1995).
52. Norma Riccuci, "Cultural Diversity Programs to Prepare for Work Force 2000: What's Gone Wrong," *Public Personnel Management* 26:1 (1997): 30.
53. See, for example, Naff and Crum, "The President and Representative Bureaucracy," 100, for a listing of citations related to minorities' underrepresentation in management positions in government.
54. Department of Labor figure cited in Kenneth J. Meier and Vicky M. Wilkins, "Gender Differences in Agency Head Salaries: The Case of Public Education," *Public Administration Review* 62 (2002): 405.
55. U.S. Department of Labor, *Highlights of Women's Earnings in 1999*, Report 943 (Washington, DC: U.S. Government Printing Office, 2000).
56. See Dennis Daley, "Paths of Glory and the Glass Ceiling: Differing Patterns of Career Advancement among Women and Minority Federal Employees," *Public Administration Quarterly* 20 (1996): 144–160.
57. Naff and Crum, "The President and Representative Bureaucracy."
58. Riccuci, "Cultural Diversity Programs to Prepare for Work Force 2000," 31.
59. John Nalbandian, "The U.S. Supreme Court's 'Consensus' on Affirmative Action," *Public Administration Review* 49:1 (1989): 43.

CHAPTER 15

1. Harlan Cleveland, "Government Is Information (but Not Vice Versa)," *Public Administration Review* 46 (1986): 605–607.
2. John Markoff and John Schwartz, "Many Tools of Big Brother Are Now up and Running," *New York Times*, December 13, 2002.
3. Poindexter, the national security adviser for President Ronald Reagan, was convicted in 1990 for his role in the Iran-Contra affair. However, his conviction was overturned.
4. John Arquilla, an expert on unconventional warfare at the Naval Postgraduate School in Monterey, quoted in Markoff and Schwartz, "Many Tools of Big Brother Are Now up and Running."
5. Ryan Singel, "Total Info System Totally Touchy," Wired News, http://www.wired.com/news/politics/.
6. Cleveland, "Government Is Information."
7. John Stevens and Robert McGowan, "Managerial Strategies in Municipal Government Organizations," *Academy of Managment Journal* 26:3 (1983): 527–534.
8. The primary source for this discussion is Arnold J. Meltsner and Christopher Bellavita, *The Policy Organization* (Beverley Hills, CA: Sage, 1983).
9. Meltsner and Bellavita, *The Policy Organization*.
10. Niv Ahituv, Seev Neumann, and Norton H. Riley, *Principles of Information Systems Management*, 4th ed. (Dubuque, IA: Wm. C. Brown Communications, 1994), 137.
11. Ahituy et al., *Principles of Information Systems Management*, 138.
12. David Anderson and Sharon Daws, *Government Information Management: A Primer and Casebook* (Englewood Cliffs, NJ: Prentice Hall, 1991), 172, 13.
13. Sharon Caudle, "Managing Information Resources in State Government," *Public Administration Review* 50:5 (1990): 516.
14. See chapter 11 of Michael Vasu, Debra Stewart, and G. David Garson, *Organization Behavior and Public Management*, 3rd ed. (New York: Marcel Dekker, 1998), 311–346.
15. M. L. Vasu, D. W. Stewart, and G. D. Garson, "Public Management Information Systems: Theory and Prescription," *Public Administration Review* 46:6 (1986): 475–487.
16. Vasu et al., "Public Management Information Systems."

17. Vasu et al., "Public Management Information Systems."

18. Kenneth Kraemer and John King, "Computing and Public Organizations," *Public Administration Review* 46, special issue (1986): 488–496.

19. Kraemer and King, "Computing and Public Organizations," 490.

20. See, for example, G. David Garson, "Computers in Public Employee Relations," paper presented at the International Personnel Management Association, Alexandria, Va., 1987; and Garson, "Human Resource Management, Computers, and Organization Theory," paper presented at the American Political Science Association, 1987.

21. Sam E. Overman and Donna Loraine, "Information for Control: Another Management Proverb," *Public Administration Review* 54:2 (1994): 193–196.

22. Alana Northrop, Kenneth Kraemer, Debora Dunkle, and John King, "Payoffs from Computerization: Lessons over Time," *Public Administration Review* 50:4 (1990): 505–514.

23. Anderson and Daws, *Government Information Management*, 66.

24. Anderson and Daws, *Government Information Management*.

25. Mark Bovens and Stavros Zouridis, "From Street-Level to System-Level Bureaucracies: How Information and Communication Is Transforming Administrative Discretion and Constitutional Control," *Public Administration Review* 62:2 (2002): 177, 181.

26. See L. Douglas Smith, James Campbell, Ashok Subramania, David Bird, and Anthony Nelson, "Strategic Planning for Municipal Information Systems," *American Review of Public Administration* 31:2 (2001): 139–157; Stephen Bajaly, "Strategic Information Systems: Planning in the Public Sector," *American Review of Public Administration* 28:1 (1998): 73–85; Anderson and Daws, *Government Information Management*, 83; John W. Swain, Jay D. White, and Elice Hunnert, "Issues in Public Management Information Systems," *American Review of Public Administration* 25:3 (1995): 284–285.

27. Anderson and Daws, *Government Information Management*, 83.

28. See Bajjaly, "Strategic Information Systems"; Smith et al., "Strategic Planning for Municipal Information Systems."

29. Smith et al., "Strategic Planning for Municipal Information Systems," 154.

30. Kenneth Kraemer, James Danzinger, Debora Duke, and John King, "The Usefulness of Computer-Based Information to Public Managers," *MIS Quarterly* 17:2 (1993): 129–148.

31. Kraemer et al., "The Usefulness of Computer-Based Information to Public Managers," 143.

32. See Sharon Caudle, Wilpen Gorr, and Kathryn Newcomer, "Key Information Systems Management Issues for the Public Sector," *MIS Quarterly* 15:2 (1991): 172–173; Stuart Bretschneider, "Management Information Systems in Public and Private Organizations: An Empirical Test," *Public Administration Review* 50:5 (1990): 536–545.

33. Bretschneider, "Management Information Systems in Public and Private Organizations."

34. Bretschneider, "Management Information Systems in Public and Private Organizations," 213.

35. Mary Brown and Jeffrey Brundney, "Public Sector Information Technology Initiatives: Implications for Programs of Public Administration," *Administration and Society* 30:4 (1998): 421–442.

36. Albert Gore Jr., "The New Job of the Federal Executive," *Public Administration Review* 54:4 (1994): 318.

37. Rebecca Hendrick, "An Information Infrastructure for Innovative Management of Government," *Public Administration Review* 54:6 (1994): 545.

38. Alain Pinsonneault and Kenneth Kraemer, "The Impact of Information Technology on Middle Managers," *MIS Quarterly* 17:3 (1993): 271–276.

39. See Table 2 in Pinsonneault and Kraemer, "The Impact of Information Technology on Middle Managers," 276.

40. Pinsonneault and Kraemer, "The Impact of Information Technology on Middle Managers," 272–274.

41. Pinsonneault and Kraemer, "The Impact of Information Technology on Middle Managers," 275.

42. Vasu et al., *Organizational Behavior and Public Management*, 330.

43. Bovens and Zouridis, "From Street-Level to System-Level Bureaucracies," 80.

44. Jane Fountain, *Building the Virtual State* (Washington, DC: Brookings Institution, 2001), 61.

45. Zorica Nedovic-Budic and David Godschalk, "Human Factors in Adoption of Geographic Information System: A Local Government Case Study," *Public Administration Review* 56:5 (1996): 554–567.

46. Anderson and Daws, *Government Information Management*, 55.

47. Anderson and Daws, *Government Information Management*, 62–64.

48. See Kraemer and King, "Computing and Public Organizations."

49. Kraemer et al., "The Usefulness of Computer-Based Information to Public Managers."

50. Fountain, *Building the Virtual State*, 80.

51. Bovens and Zouridis, "From Street-Level to System-Level Bureaucracies," 180.

52. Brown and Brundney, "Public Sector Information Technology Initiatives," 422.

53. Cited by Brown and Brundney, "Public Sector Information Technology Initiatives," 429, 427.

54. "Creating a Performance-Based Electronic Government: Fiscal Year 2002 Progress," Performance Institute, 2002, http://www.performanceweb.org/research/egovernmentreport.pdf.

55. Amelia Gruber, "Report Praises Federal E-Gov Efforts, but Urges Agencies to Measure Results," GovExec.com, 2002.

56. Brown and Brundney, "Public Sector Information Technology Initiatives," 422–423.

57. Northrop et al., "Payoffs from Computerization."

58. M. Jae Moon, "The Evolution of E-Government among Municipalities: Rhetoric or Reality," *Public Administration Review* 62:4 (2002): 422–433.

59. Brown and Brundney, "Public Sector Information Technology Initiatives," 425.

60. Kavanaugh, 1997, cited in Brown and Brundney, "Public Sector Information Technology Initiatives," 425.

61. Anderson and Daws, *Government Information Management*, 114.

62. Jay Shafritz, *The Facts on File Dictionary of Public Administration* (New York: Facts on File, 1985).

63. Harold Relyea, "Access to Government Information in the Information Age," *Administration Review* 46:6 (1968): 636.

64. Anderson and Daws, *Government Information Management*, 114.

65. Anderson and Daws, *Government Information Management*, 117.

66. U.S. Congress, Office of Technology Assessment, *Federal Government Information Technology: Electronic Record Systems and Individual Privacy*, OTA-CIT-296 (Washington, DC: U.S. Government Printing Office, June 1986, 1986), 11.

67. *Griswold v. Connecticut*, 381 U.S. 479 (1965); *Eisenstadt v. Baird*, 405 U.S. 238 (1972); *Roe v. Wade*, 410 U.S. 113 (1973); *Whalen v. Roe*, 429 U.S. 589 (1977).

68. Priscilla Regan, "Privacy, Government Information, and Technology," *Public Administration Review* 46:6 (1986): 629–630.

69. Regan, "Privacy, Government Information, and Technology," 630.

70. Anderson and Daws, *Government Information Management*, 119.

71. U.S. Congress, Office of Technology Assessment, *Federal Government Information Technology*, 38.

72. U.S. Congress, Office of Technology Assessment, *Federal Government Information Technology*, 39.

73. Anderson and Daws, *Government Information Management*, 120.

74. Christopher Conte, "The Privacy Panic," *Governing* (December 2000): 21.

75. U.S. Congress Office of Technology Assessment, *Federal Government Information Technology*, 68.

76. U.S. Congress Office of Technology Assessment, *Federal Government Information Technology*.

77. Anderson and Daws, *Government Information Management*, 120.

78. Lisa Nelson, "Protecting the Common Good: Technology, Objectivity, and Privacy," *Public Administration Review* 62, special issue (2002): 69–73.

79. Fountain, *Building the Virtual State*, 4.

80. Moon, "The Evolution of E-Government among Municipalities," 425.

81. Moon, "The Evolution of E-Government among Municipalities," 431.

82. Jane Fountain, "The Virtual State: Transforming American Government," *National Civic Review* 90:3 (2001): 69–73.

83. Fountain, "The Virtual State," 249.

84. Christopher Swope, "E-Gov's New Gear," *Governing* 40 (March 2004).

85. Swope, "E-Gov's New Gear."

86. See Pippa Norris, *Digital Divide: Civic Engagement, Information Poverty, and the Internet Worldwide* (Cambridge: Cambridge University Press, 2001); Karen Mossberger, Caroline Tolbert, and Mary Stansbury, *Virtual Inequality: Beyond the Digital Divide* (Washington, DC: Georgetown University Press, 2003).

87. Mossberger et al., *Virtual Inequality*, 248.

88. Northrop et al., "Payoffs from Computerization," 511.

89. Benjamin Barber, *Strong Democracy: Participatory Politics for a New Age* (Berkeley: University of California Press, 1984); Robert Putnam, *Bowling Alone: The Collapse and Revival of American Community* (New York: Simon and Shuster, 2000).

90. Putnam, *Bowling Alone*, 166.

91. Barber, *Strong Democracy*.

92. Vincent Casaregola and Robert Cropf, "Virtual Town Halls: Using Computer Networks to Improve Public Discourse and Facilitate Service Delivery," 1998, http://www.gonzaga.edu/rr/v4n1/cropf.htm.

93. Ellen Perlman, "Trust Busters," *Governing* 23 (September 2003).

94. Alan Cooper, "Personal Data OK on the Web," *Richmond Times Dispatch*, October 21, 2003.

95. Perlman, "Trust Busters," 34.

96. P. Howe, "Police Database Shut Down," AP State and Local Wire, December 18, 2003.

97. Perlman, "Trust Busters," 39.

98. Adam Liptak, "A Website Causes Unease in Police," *New York Times*, July 12, 2003.

Glossary

Accountability Responsibility to a higher authority for one's actions (e.g., workers are accountable to their supervisors for what they do on the job).

Administrative accountability The assignment of organizational responsibility in a hierarchical or legal manner, which is objective in quality.

Administrative discretion An administrator's freedom to act or decide on his or her own, which amounts to giving administrators policy-making powers.

Administrative evil Harmful acts committed by public officials, who are often unaware that they are doing anything wrong.

Adverse impact Previous employment practices and policies by a company bringing about discriminatory results.

Adverse selection In principal–agent theory, a situation in which the wrong firm is chosen to do something and therefore the desired outcome fails to occur.

Advocacy coalition framework (ACF) The theory that focuses on policy subsystems rather than official institutions of government and emphasizes the importance of core beliefs or values that drive coalitions to compete for influence in the policy process.

Affirmative action A controversial attempt by the government to bring more minorities into the workforce.

Asset selling An arrangement whereby governments sell off companies or other assets that they own.

Block grant A type of grant-in-aid that can be used for a number of purposes within a functional area, which provides lower-level governments more discretion.

Bounded rationality The concept developed by Herbert Simon that organizations are limited in their understanding and knowledge and therefore cannot make optimal decisions.

Bowling alone A term coined by the political scientist Robert Putnam to refer to the tendency of individuals in contemporary society to join fewer groups than earlier generations and to do more activities by themselves.

Broadbanding A practice to collapse pay grades by reducing a large number of job classifications into a smaller, more manageable number.

Budget cycle A process consisting of (1) preparation, (2) legislative review, (3) execution, and (4) audit and overlapping several years.

Bureaucratese The specialized, sometimes incomprehensible language of large organizations that is often satirized or ridiculed.

Bureaucratic ethos The principle of making administrators subordinate to and accountable to elected officials; also consists of management values such as a belief in efficiency, hierarchy, etc.

Capital investment plan A long-range plan used by governments to guide their capital investment policies; focuses on the expected infrastructure needs of a jurisdiction and includes costs estimates for projects in the plan.

Categorical grant A type of grant-in-aid with a narrowly defined purpose used to achieve very specific goals (e.g., building an airport, dam, or highway).

CBI consumer Administrator who relies mainly on staff to work with technology and deals indirectly with technological issues.

Centralization The concentration of decision-making power and control within an organization.

Chain of command The structure in an organization that establishes the authority relationships among the different roles and functions.

Charitable choice The 1996 welfare reform legislation allows religious institutions to receive government funding for the provision of services.

Checks and balances The constitutional doctrine that each branch of government should act as a control on the power and ambition of the other branches.

Circuit breaker A mechanism that reduces the regressivity of the property tax by exempting low-income elderly and other groups from some portion of their property taxes.

Civic engagement The process by which citizens participate in civil society and democratic politics.

Civil society The domain of social life independent of government and private markets, consisting of voluntary and civic associations, necessary for the proper functioning of society.

Client agencies The agencies that exist principally to serve the needs of certain interest groups ("clients").

Clientelism The creation of departments and programs in order to serve the needs of specific interest groups or segments of society.

Collective bargaining A legal arrangement whereby labor unions and management negotiate over the terms of employment.

Commerce clause The section of the Constitution (Article I, section 8, clause 3) that states that Congress has the power to regulate interstate and foreign commerce.

Comparable worth An attempt to equalize the difference in compensation levels between men and women who do different jobs that are of comparable value.

Competent community A community that makes the most of its social capital; competent communities can be found in less affluent areas as well as wealthy ones.

Competitive examination The system to determine merit in hiring new government employees.

Complexity The structural levels and diversity of occupational specializations within an organization.

Computer matching A process in which electronic information is shared among separate databases that are physically located in different agencies and maintained for different purposes.

Computer profiling A computer application that allows several databases to be searched for personal information that matches a pattern of characteristics.

Computer-based information (CBI) Any information that is gathered, processed, manipulated, or stored by computers.

Conservatorship A leadership style that emphasizes preserving the values of the existing institution as a means of solidifying democratic governance, and protecting institutional values from erosion or corruption by internal and external forces.

Contingency theory A theory of organization that asserts that success depends on the level of fit with the environment.

Contingency theory The theory that effective leadership style is relative to the situation, and that creating the right environment can help build successful leadership within an organization.

Contracting out An arrangement whereby the government enters into an agreement with a private company to provide a service for citizens.

Co-optation A situation in which presidential appointees promote an agency's position in conflict with the position of the president who appointed them.

Coordination The glue that holds an organization together; organizations require coordination to take full advantage of specialization and to accomplish crucial tasks.

Co-production A process in which government and citizens work together to carry out public programs.

Crosscutting mandate A legislative mandate that occurs across the board on all programs and grants.

Cultural bias A systematic form of discrimination against certain cultures, especially minorities.

Data The distinct, separate observations about some phenomenon.

Data mining A software application that looks for patterns in a database that can be used to predict future behavior.

Decision support system (DSS) The most advanced type of information system that provides support for nonroutine or unstructured decision-making.

Deconstruct The postmodern methodology of exposing the underlying assumptions that form the basis of political and economic institutions and social structures.

Delphi method A technique developed as a means to reduce or eliminate the problems resulting from member interaction in the group decision-making process; the participants do not meet with each other face to face.

Democratic ethos Consists of political and regime values; serves as the moral foundation of public ethics.

Deontology An approach to ethics which asserts that there is an absolute or ultimate standard for morals that can be arrived at through reason.

Departmentation The grouping of similar activities within an organization, key to coordination.

Devolution The shifting of programmatic responsibilities in certain policy areas from the national government to the states.

Digital divide The gap between the less affluent and the affluent in terms of computer ownership and use as well as access to the Internet.

Dillon Rule The principle that local governments have only those powers granted to them by the state government. Named after jurist John Forrest Dillon, who formulated the rule in the nineteenth century.

Dyadic relationships Leader–subordinate relationships that develop through a system of complex exchanges.

E-government The use of technology to facilitate government administration, improve citizen access to government information and services, and encourage citizen participation in the government process.

Enumerated powers The fourteen governmental powers that are given to the national government by the U.S. Constitution. Also known as delegated powers. See reserved powers.

Ergonomic Of, or related to, the design of workplace equipment, in order to maximize worker efficiency by reducing fatigue and discomfort.

Ethics A system or theory of moral values.

Evaluation The means of determining what actually happens after policy approval; it involves an assessment of program processes and impacts, focusing on aspects that are observable or measurable.

Executive budgeting The chief executive provides budgetary leadership.

Executive order The legally binding orders given by the president to federal agencies.

Extrinsic rewards Organizational incentives to perform that are not related to position or employment.

Fact–value dichotomy Herbert Simon's concept that observations about the world can be divided into fact propositions (e.g., the earth is round) and value propositions (e.g., we ought to do something about poverty), and that a true science of administration can be based on only fact propositions.

Factions A term used by James Madison to refer to voluntary associations formed to pursue their own interests often to the harm of the rest of society.

*Faith-**based organization*** An entity whose principal mission is religious (i.e., church, temple, synagogue) but which provides social welfare services as part of its religious mission.

Federal Register The public record that contains notices of federal agency rules and presidential documents, published daily.

Federalism A system of government in which the national and subnational governments share power. To be contrasted with unitary systems (all political power is concentrated at the center) and confederations (political power is completely decentralized, with the subnational governments holding the upper hand).

Fiscal capacity The financial ability of a community to sustain and support government programs through its system of own-source revenues.

Fiscal federalism The financial relations among different units of government at all levels.

Fiscal note The part of proposed legislation that describes the fiscal impact of the legislation.

Fiscal policy Using the budget (i.e., government expenditures and revenues) to manage the economy; the counterpart to monetary policy.

Fiscal Year An accounting period covering twelve months; the fiscal year is designated by the calendar year in which it ends.

501 (c) 3 The provision of the federal income tax code giving nonprofit organizations special tax-exempt status. See nonprofit organizations.

Formalization The level of standardization of jobs, employee behavior, and work processes in an organization.

Four-fifths rule Established a numeric threshold for discrimination: If the selection rate for a particular group is below 80 percent of the rate of other groups, this constitutes statistical evidence of discrimination.

Freedom of information Citizens' right of free access to government information.

Free-rider problem A situation arising in the case of public goods in which a citizen receives benefits without paying for them.

Front-end verification A computer application that checks the accuracy and completeness of personal information supplied by applicants for government benefits, employment, and services.

Game theory The application of rational choice theory to hypothetical situations using computer simulations.

Garbage can model The theory that the policy process is marked by fluidity and a certain degree of randomness as people, problems, and solutions flow together and apart.

General obligation bonds Long-term debt that is guaranteed by the issuing government's entire revenue generating capacity.

General Schedule (GS) The standard federal government pay scale and position classification system.

General-purpose local government A local government that performs a wide range of governmental functions.

Glass ceiling The concept that individuals (especially women and minorities) reach a certain level in an organization and are not able to rise above it.

Government reinvention Efforts at the national and state levels to reform government during the 1980s and 1990s; proponents wanted to make government more efficient using business techniques and strategies. Also referred to as the "reinventing government" movement.

Governmental reorganization The restructuring of departments and agencies with the intent to streamline and improve administration.

Gross domestic product (GDP) The total value of all goods and services produced within a country during a specified period (most commonly, per year).

Groupthink A situation in which members become so strongly identified with the group's identity that they isolate themselves from negative criticism and fail to consider all alternatives.

Hawthorne effect A finding of the Hawthorne research by Elton Mayo: that simply paying attention to workers made them more productive than physical changes in the factory; gave credence to the idea that informal workplace norms have an important effect on worker performance.

Hierarchy of human needs A model developed by Abraham Maslow to explain how people are motivated by different levels of needs, from food to self-actualization.

High road approach An approach to administrative ethics emphasizing moral reasoning and ethical analysis.

Home rule The granting of considerable decision-making powers to local governments by state legislatures or state constitutions.

Human resource administration (HRA) Of or relating to the management of personnel in an organization; the section of an organization that handles personnel and employee issues.

Hygienic factors The employee incentives that relate to working conditions, rules, and pay.

Implementation The stage of the policy process in which policies are carried out by public agencies; it recognizes that the actual outcomes of a program may not resemble what the decisionmakers originally intended.

Implied powers Those powers that are not stated in the Constitution but can be inferred from the enumerated powers.

Incorporation The state legislature's granting of a charter to create a municipality.

Incremental budgeting A model of budgetary decision-making that asserts the process is inherently political, that no single group dominates, budgetary changes are marginal and the result of mutual accommodation among diverse interests.

Incrementalism The theory that public policy occurs in a series of small, incremental steps or changes and not all at once.

Informal organization Aspects of organization, such as interpersonal relations, that exist alongside the formal structures and roles but do not show up on the organization chart.

Information Data that has been organized into meaningful patterns and that can be used for decision-making.

Information islands An information system that is stored on a separate computer, operates separately from the main databases, and serves a personal or unit purpose rather than organizational purpose.

Information policy Public policy regarding the use of, access to, and control of information by the government.

Information resources management (IRM) The administration of information policy and information assets by an organization.

Information technology (IT) The development, installation, and implementation of systems to gather, process, manipulate, and store data; includes computers and telecommunications.

Interest groups The organizations formed by individuals to advance their joint goals by influencing government.

Intergovernmental relations The web of interrelationships among governments at all levels, which increasingly includes nonprofit and private organizations.

Interoperability The ability of different computer systems to share information with each other.

Intrinsic rewards The organizational incentives to perform relating to position or employment.

Iron triangle An important theory of interest groups' influence on government, suggesting that interest groups, legislative committees, and agencies work closely together in writing and implementing policies.

Issue networks A theory of interest group influence on government that states the policy-making process is marked by a high degree of openness and access by many different groups.

Job standardization An arrangement that ensures standards along employment lines within organizations, which involves, among other things, preparing job descriptions.

Judicial activism The expansion of the courts' scope used to review the full range of agency decisions and activities.

Knowledge A body of information organized in a systematic manner; a cause-and-effect framework that supports a particular course of action.

Knowledge executive Administrator who takes a hands-on approach to the use of computers.

Kohlberg's model of moral development A six-stage theory of an individual's growth as a moral person; developed by the psychologist Lawrence Kohlberg.

Labor union A group formed by employees in an organization that is accorded special legal status to bargain with management over the terms of employment.

Leadership traits The set of inherent qualities found in leaders, such as vitality, decisiveness, persuasiveness, responsibility, and intelligence.

Least Preferred Coworker (LPC) score To arrive at an LPC score, you think of the person who was the most difficult you ever worked with; then you rank this person on a scale of 1 to 8 on a series of characteristics such as unfriendly/friendly, hostile/supportive.

Legislative micromanagement The perceived tendency for legislators to "meddle" in the day-to-day operations of agencies.

Legislative oversight The legal power that allows the legislature to monitor agencies in order to achieve accountability.

Legislative veto A procedure which allows the legislature to stop an executive action that it disagrees with; most courts have ruled this to be a violation of separation of powers.

Legitimate power Power within an organization that is based on an individual's formal position in the organization.

Line-item budget A type of budgeting that reports the items to be purchased by a government (e.g., salaries, equipment, supplies) and the amount of money that will be spent on each item.

Load shedding A situation in which the government stops providing a service or good for the citizens, which forces citizens to turn to other providers if they want the good or service.

Lobbyist A person working for an interest group or groups who attempts to influence the policy-making process.

Low road approach A minimalist approach to ethics, which holds that adherence to the law is sufficient for ethical behavior.

Management information system (MIS) A sophisticated type of information system used to assist management in decision-making.

Market failure A class of economic occurrences (e.g., monopoly, externalities, etc.) in which private markets fail to perform efficiently; entails social costs that can be corrected through collective action, usually by the government.

Matrix organization The best-known type of organic organization, it employs a team-based structure instead of traditional hierarchy.

Means opportunity A type of social equity program in which candidates of equal talent and skills can compete for a position without minority status being a factor.

Mechanistic organization The classical bureaucracy, where the emphasis is on machine-like efficiency.

Merit The system in which employees are hired or promoted based on the quality of their work, education, and previous experience.

Mixed economy An economy in which the public sector plays a significant role and consumes a considerable proportion of the gross domestic product.

Monetary policy The federal government's management of the economy by the manipulation of the money supply, interest rates, and credit; the Federal Reserve banking system is responsible for directing monetary policy.

Moral hazard A situation where a private provider fails to perform as desired because the government cannot monitor the organization at all times.

Moral reasoning The capacity to engage in ethical analysis and decision-making.

Motivating factors The employee incentives that relate to opportunities for organizational advancement and personal growth as well as recognition.

Motivation A psychological state that stimulates and directs human behavior toward some goal that fulfills a need.

National Performance Review (NPR) An initiative of the Clinton administration to reform the executive branch along the principles of reinventing government.

Necessary and proper clause A provision of the U.S. Constitution (Article I, section 8, paragraph 18) authorizing Congress to pass all laws "necessary and proper" to fulfill its responsibilities.

Negative reinforcement A motivational approach that emphasizes the removal of negative consequences as the spur to learning.

Network organization A loose grouping of independent organizations coordinated by contracts rather than through formal hierarchy.

Neutral competence The idea that a government employee should be politically nonpartisan and possess the technical requirements and aptitude to perform a job.

Nominal group technique A decision-making approach in which ideas are listed and then discussed only for clarification, followed by secret ballots to rank the ideas and eliminate weak ones until consensus is reached on the best decision.

Nonguaranteed bonds Long-term debt in which the principal and interest are paid off using the revenues generated by the facility built with the funds from the bond.

Nonprofit organization An organization whose main purpose is to provide a service to the public, as opposed to making a profit; examples include the United Way, the Red Cross, and many hospitals and universities. See 501 (c) 3.

Objects of expenditure The numeric codes used by governments to classify expenditures by categories, such as personnel, supplies, and equipment.

Off-budget items Revenues and expenditures that are legally excluded from the federal budget; also include employees who are not officially counted as federal workers.

On-budget items Revenues and expenditures that are included in the calculations of the national deficit.

Open system theory An approach to organization that includes the external environment as an important factor, as the recipient of output and provider of inputs.

Organic organization An organization that is characterized by less formalization and concentration of authority than classical bureaucracy.

Organization A group of people who work together in order to achieve a common purpose.

Organization theory An area of study that seeks to explain and predict how organizations and their members behave.

Organizational culture The unique character or "personality" of an organization, consisting of the core beliefs, attitudes, and values that influence employees' actions, often on a subconscious level.

Organizational development A top-down interventionist strategy designed to increase organizational effectiveness and health.

Outcome discretion The administrator's decision to choose a particular result among a set of possibilities.

Patronage The system in which employees are hired or given promotions based on partisan affiliation.

Pay for performance Paying government employees according to the quality of their work rather than seniority.

Performance appraisal The process of systematically assessing employee productivity.

Performance audit A type of evaluation assessing the effects of agency programs and not just the financial activities of agencies as in a financial audit.

Performance budgeting A type of budgeting that combines output and cost data from programs to show if they are being efficiently operated.

Personal authority The influence a person wields independent of his or her role in an organization.

Person-oriented behaviors Those actions that relate to the relationship between leaders and their followers.

Planning-programming budgeting system (PPBS) A type of budgeting that stresses the use of analytical techniques to improve policy-making; the budget format that comes closest to the rational budget decision-making model.

Pluralism A political arrangement in which different sectors of society organize into groups in order to exert political influence.

Policy cycle The concept of public policy as a cycle or series of stages.

Policy streams The theory that a complex combination of factors is responsible for the arrival of an issue on the policy agenda, and that attempts to pinpoint their origin are futile.

Policy subsystems Groups of people with a common interest in an issue, including experts, advocates, and officials.

Politics –administration dichotomy The belief, popular in the early twentieth century, that government administration should be separated from politics and policy-making.

Populism A grassroots political movement during the late nineteenth and early twentieth centuries supporting the rights and power of the people in the struggle against the social and economic elite.

POSDCORB The acronym coined by Luther Gulick as a way to draw attention to the essential management functions of the chief executive.

Position classification A system of organizing an organization's jobs according to their duties and responsibilities, creating formal job descriptions, and establishing equitable pay.

Positional authority The influence a person wields as a result of his or her role in an organization.

Positive reinforcement A motivational approach that emphasizes material rewards as the key to organizational learning.

Postmodernism An approach to understanding politics and government that questions mainstream assumptions regarding organization, power, and capitalism.

Preemption A federal requirement that supersedes all state laws in a particular program area.

Principal –agent conflict The goals of the principal (government) and agent (private provider) are likely to conflict in at least some cases.

Prisoner's Dilemma An example of the use of game theory in a simple decision-making situation.

Private attorneys general Individuals and organizations who sue the government on behalf of the public interest (e.g., in the interest of government benefits recipients, minorities, consumers).

Privatization The transferring of functions and property from the government to private for-profit or nonprofit entities.

Process discretion The latitude taken by an administrator when choosing the best problem-solving approach.

Professional bureaucracy An organization that is dominated by professionals and different specializations; the top-down flow of authority is counteracted somewhat by the power of experts.

Professionalism The behavior, attitudes, and values stemming from training, socialization, and educational requirements that it takes to become a member of a profession.

Progressive tax A tax in which the ratio of tax to income increases as a taxpayer's income rises.

Proportional tax A tax in which the ratio of tax to income stays the same as a taxpayer's income rises.

Proposition 13 The California law passed in 1978 that restricted the property tax rate to 1 percent of market value, touching off a national tax revolt movement.

Prospect opportunity A type of social equity program in which people can compete for open positions and jobs regardless of minority status.

Public choice theory The theory that bureaucrats, voters, and politicians are concerned primarily with advancing their own economic self-interests through the administrative and political processes.

Public entrepreneur An approach to public leadership emphasizing a market orientation similar to that found in private business.

Public function test The determination of whether a power is traditionally reserved to the government.

Public policy Any decision-making done on behalf of or affecting the public, especially that which is done by government.

Public policy Any decision-making done on behalf of or affecting the public, especially that which is done by government.

Rational budgeting An approach to budgeting that involves (1) selection of objectives, (2) identifying alternatives along with their costs, (3) comparison of alternatives on the basis of achieving the objectives, (4) choosing the best alternative.

Rational choice The theory that individuals attempt to maximize their interests in the policy process.

Rawlsianism An approach to ethics named for the philosopher John Rawls; the theory that the welfare of society is enhanced if the poorest individual is materially improved even if this reduces the well-being of everyone else.

Redistribution The transfer of income or wealth from one class of society to another, typically used to refer to a transfer from the rich to the poor.

Regime values The core values of a people; for the American people, these include personal liberty, property, and political equality and are derived from the Constitution.

Regressive tax A tax in which the ratio of tax to income declines as a taxpayer's income rises.

Representative bureaucracy A government workforce that reflects the people or the particular community that the government serves.

Reserved powers The powers inherent in the state governments according to the Tenth Amendment, in contrast to the enumerated or delegated powers of the federal government. See enumerated powers.

Responsibility Moral obligations that are unrelated to an individual's formal role, status, or power within an organization.

Rule of three The practice of recommending the three best candidates for a federal position.

Rule-making The process by which agencies create regulations that have the force of law; through rule-making, legislative authority is delegated to agencies.

Satisfice A term originated by Herbert Simon for decisions that are less than optimal: they *satis*fy and *suffice*.

Scientific management A theory of administration that is notable for its emphasis on the most efficient method to perform a task ("one best way").

Separation of powers The constitutional doctrine that power should be diffused throughout the government, keeping the executive, legislative, and judicial branches distinct so that power is not centralized in one branch.

Single-purpose local government A local government that performs a specific function (e.g., school district, water district, sewer district).

Social altruism A person's sense of connectedness and responsibility towards other people.

Social Capital A term that refers to the trust and relationships that bring and keep community members together, which enables them to achieve their common goals more effectively.

Sovereign immunity The idea that the government and its representatives will not be held liable for damages occurring from their decisions.

Span of control The limited number of subordinates a manager can effectively supervise.

Spoils system The type of government personnel system introduced by President Andrew Jackson in which elected officials reward supporters by appointing them to public offices and positions.

Standard operating procedures The formal rules and regulations governing employee behavior.

Street -**level bureaucrat** Term coined by Michael Lipsky to refer to teachers, police office, welfare case workers, and any other frontline government workers with considerable administrative discretion.

Strict scrutiny test A court ruling that government affirmative action programs must fulfill three constitutional criteria: (1) There must be a compelling interest for the program, (2) the program must be designed narrowly enough to meet its specific goals, and (3) the law or policy must use the least restrictive means to achieve its objectives.

Sumptuary tax A selective sales tax imposed on certain items such as alcohol and tobacco, in part, to regulate undesirable consumption.

Supremacy clause The portion of the Constitution (Article VI, paragraph 2) which holds that the Constitution and all laws made under its authority are the supreme law of the land and take precedence over the states.

System-level bureaucracy A public organization in which information technology and computer experts play a major role in policy-making.

Tall hierarchy A classic bureaucratic structure in which authority and communication flow from the top down; involves close supervision of subordinates all along the chain of command.

Task-oriented behaviors The actions that leaders take to get followers to reach certain goals.

Tennessee Valley Authority (TVA) One of the first and certainly one of the most famous public corporations, created in the 1930s to bring electricity to the Tennessee Valley.

Theory X A view of human behavior which states that people hate work and do whatever is possible to avoid it.

Theory Y A view of human behavior which states that people are creative, and work is a natural outlet for their talents and efforts.

Threshold effect The theory that certain nation disturbances (e.g., wars) cause a permanent jump in government expenditures.

Time and motion study The method of observation used by scientific management to determine the "one best way" to complete a task.

Total quality management (TQM) An approach to administration that seeks the continuous improvement of processes based on the application of quantitative methods to organizational problems; other important goals include increasing customer satisfaction and empowering employees.

Transaction processing system (TPS) The most basic type of information system that can be used to create, store, and manipulate data.

Unfunded mandates A legislative or judicial requirement, usually but not always from a higher-level government to a lower-level government, to administer and pay for a government program.

Unitary system A governmental system with power centralized in a national government.

User fee A charge for a service (e.g., drivers license, hunting license, parks fees) that is levied by government.

Utilitarian An approach which asserts that people and organizations do something only if they expect material gain from it.

Utilitarianism The philosophy which holds that the results of one's actions are more important than one's intentions.

Validation The criteria that determine the bias of an examination.

Value neutral The notion that social science should not take moral positions but rather should stick solely with the facts.

Virtual state A term coined by Jane Fountain to refer to the linkages and interactions based on computers among governments and between government and other entities.

Vouchers Government coupons that allow citizens to purchase services from a private provider; the government agrees to pay the organization the amount of the coupon.

Whistle blowing Reporting incidents of waste, fraud, or abuse within an organization; often entails considerable personal cost through employment termination, demotion, or social exclusion.

Zero-based budgeting (ZBB) A type of budgeting in which a program's continued existence is not assumed, and all expenditures, not just new ones, must be justified every year; the goal is to eliminate unnecessary programs.

Zone of indifference The area defining an employee's level of comfort with an order: anything falling within this area will be followed; anything falling outside will not be followed.

Index